myPerspectives
ENGLISH LANGUAGE ARTS

Copyright © by Savvas Learning Company LLC. All Rights Reserved. Printed in the United States of America.

This program is protected by copyright, and permission should be obtained from the publisher prior to any prohibited reproduction, storage in a retrieval system, or transmission in any form or by any means, electronic, mechanical, photocopying, recording, or otherwise. For information regarding permissions, request forms, and the appropriate contacts within the Savvas Learning Company Rights Management group, please send your query to the address below.

Savvas Learning Company LLC, 15 East Midland Avenue, Paramus, NJ 07652

Attributions of third-party content appear on page R20 which constitutes an extension of this copyright page.

Common Core State Standards: © Copyright 2010. National Governors Association Center for Best Practices and Council of Chief State School Officers. All rights reserved.

Savvas® and **Savvas Learning Company®** are the exclusive registered trademarks of Savvas Learning Company LLC in the U.S. and other countries.

Savvas Learning Company publishes through its famous imprints **Prentice Hall®** and **Scott Foresman®** which are exclusive registered trademarks owned by Savvas Learning Company LLC in the U.S. and/or other countries.

Savvas Realize® is an exclusive registered trademark of Savvas Learning Company LLC in the U.S. and/or other countries.

Unless otherwise indicated herein, any third party trademarks that may appear in this work are the property of their respective owners, and any references to third party trademarks, logos, or other trade dress are for demonstrative or descriptive purposes only. Such references are not intended to imply any sponsorship, endorsement, authorization, or promotion of Savvas Learning Company products by the owners of such marks, or any relationship between the owner and Savvas Learning Company LLC or its authors, licensees, or distributors.

ISBN-13: 978-1-428-51645-8
ISBN-10: 1-428-51645-X
5 2024

myPerspectives
ENGLISH LANGUAGE ARTS

Experts' Perspectives	iv
Table of Contents	vi

Unit 1 — 2
CROSSING GENERATIONS
What can one generation learn from another?

Unit 2 — 106
LIVING AMONG THE STARS
Should we make a home in space?

Unit 3 — 206
TRANSFORMATIONS
Can people really change?

Unit 4 — 368
LEARNING FROM NATURE
What is the relationship between people and nature?

Unit 5 — 490
FACING ADVERSITY
How do we overcome life's challenges?

Glossaries in English and Spanish — R1
- Academic Vocabulary
- Concept Vocabulary
- Media Vocabulary

Indexes — R8
- Skills
- Authors and Titles

Acknowledgments and Credits

iii

EXPERTS' PERSPECTIVES

myPerspectives is informed by a team of respected experts whose experiences working with students and study of instructional best practices have positively impacted education.

"The teaching of English needs to focus on engaging a new generation of learners. How do we get them excited about reading and writing? How do we help them to envision themselves as readers and writers? And, how can we make the teaching of English more culturally, socially, and technologically relevant? Throughout the curriculum, we've created spaces that enhance youth voice and participation and that connect the teaching of literature and writing to technological transformations of the digital age."

Ernest Morrell, Ph.D., is the Associate Dean, College of Arts and Letters; Coyle Professor in Literacy Education; Director, Notre Dame Center for Literacy Education; and Director, NCTE James R. Squire Office for Policy Research at the University of Notre Dame. He was the Macy Professor of English Education and former Director of Teachers College's Institute for Urban and Minority Education (IUME), Columbia University. Ernest is an elected member of the National Academy of Education, a Fellow of the American Educational Research Association, and the Past-President of the National Council of Teachers of English (NCTE). Since its inception in 2015, Dr. Morrell has annually received recognition for being one of the top 100 university-based education scholars in the RHSU Edu-Scholar Public Influence Ranking. He is also the recipient of the ILA Adolescent Literacy Thought Leader Award, the Council of English Leadership Kent Williamson Exemplary Leadership Award, and the NCTE Distinguished Service Award. He is an award-winning published author of 15 books and more than 100 research articles and book chapters. In his spare time, he is an active gamer, coach of youth sports, and writer of fiction and poetry.

Elfrieda Hiebert, Ph.D., is President and CEO of TextProject, a nonprofit that provides resources to support higher reading levels. Dr. Hiebert has had an extensive career in the field of literacy, language, and culture, first as a teacher's aide and teacher in California's San Joaquin Valley and, subsequently, as a teacher educator and researcher. Her research addresses how fluency, vocabulary, and knowledge can be fostered through appropriate texts. Dr. Hiebert has worked with the *myPerspectives* team to develop approaches to teaching vocabulary, tackling complex texts, and assessing students' work.

"The signature of complex text is challenging vocabulary. In the systems of vocabulary, it's important to provide ways to show how concepts can be made more transparent to students. We provide lessons and activities that develop a strong vocabulary and concept foundation—a foundation that permits students to comprehend increasingly more complex text."

Kelly Gallagher, M.Ed., is a literacy education author and consultant, specializing in the teaching of English Language Arts for grades 4–12. Informed by a 35-year teaching career, Kelly has developed and shares an ever-evolving body of work that helps teachers engage and empower even the most reluctant readers and writers. Kelly is the former president of the Secondary Reading Group for the International Literacy Association and the author of several professional development books, including *Readicide* and *Write Like This*, and two books co-written with Penny Kittle, *180 Days* and *Four Essential Studies*.

" The *myPerspectives* classroom is dynamic. The teacher inspires, models, instructs, facilitates, and advises students as they evolve and grow. When teachers guide students through meaningful learning tasks and then pass them ownership of their own learning, students become engaged and work harder. This is how we make a difference in student achievement—by putting students at the center of their learning and giving them the opportunities to choose, explore, collaborate, and work independently."

" It's critical to give students the opportunity to read a wide range of highly engaging texts and to immerse themselves in exploring powerful ideas and how these ideas are expressed. In *myPerspectives*, we focus on building up students' awareness of how academic language works, which is especially important for English language learners."

Jim Cummins, Ph.D., is a Professor Emeritus in the Department of Curriculum, Teaching, and Learning at the University of Toronto. His research focuses on literacy development in multilingual school contexts. He has worked closely with educators in identifying instructional practices to increase students' literacy engagement and overall academic achievement. Dr. Cummins has influenced the development of *myPerspectives* in English Language Learner and English Language Development support.

Monica Yoo, Ph.D., is an associate professor of language and literacy in the Department of Teaching and Learning at the University of Colorado, Colorado Springs. She formerly coordinated the department's Secondary Education Program and was a university supervisor of student teachers at the secondary level. She previously taught high school English Language Arts and has worked extensively with middle school teachers and students. Her research centers on students' and teachers' approaches to language, literacy, and comprehension; disciplinary literacy; and equitable practices for teaching and learning.

" It is important to provide students with opportunities for decision-making, allowing them to be active participants in their own education. When it comes to projects and assignments that demonstrate students' learning and comprehension, students should be able to showcase their strengths and talents in ways that are personally meaningful and relevant."

UNIT 1 Crossing Generations

UNIT INTRODUCTION

VIDEO
Cyber-Seniors 2

MENTOR TEXT: PERSONAL NARRATIVE MODEL
Grandfather's Garden 6

WHOLE-CLASS LEARNING

SHORT STORY
Don't Just Sit There Like a Punk
Matt de la Peña 15

FEATURE ARTICLE
The Case of the Disappearing Words
Alice Andre-Clark 29

PERFORMANCE TASK
Write a Personal Narrative 42

WRITER'S HANDBOOK
Personal Narrative 44

PEER-GROUP LEARNING

MEMOIR
from Mom & Me & Mom
Maya Angelou
.... 59

COMPARE

MEDIA: TELEVISION INTERVIEW
Learning to Love My Mother
Maya Angelou with Michael Maher
.... 69

MEDIA: IMAGE GALLERY
Mother-Daughter Drawings
Mica and Myla Hendricks
.... 75

POETRY COLLECTION 1
Ode to My Papi
Guadalupe García McCall

Mother to Son
Langston Hughes

To James
Frank Horne
.... 86

PERFORMANCE TASK
Present a Personal Narrative 96

vi

ESSENTIAL QUESTION | What can one generation learn from another?

INDEPENDENT LEARNING
These selections are available online only.

POETRY COLLECTION 2	OPINION PIECE	REALISTIC FICTION	REALISTIC FICTION
Lineage Margaret Walker **Family** Grace Paley	**"Gotcha Day" Isn't a Cause for Celebration** Sophie Johnson	**Water Names** Lan Samantha Chang	**An Hour With Abuelo** Judith Ortiz Cofer

SHARE YOUR INDEPENDENT LEARNING
Share • Learn • Reflect 101

REFLECT AND RESPOND

Reflect on Your Unit Goals
Reflect on the Texts 102

Develop Your Perspective:
Unit Projects 103

PERFORMANCE-BASED ASSESSMENT

Personal Narrative 104

UNIT 2 Living Among the Stars

UNIT INTRODUCTION

VIDEO
6 NASA Technologies to Get Humans to Mars.................... 106

MENTOR TEXT: ARGUMENT MODEL
Humans Are Not Meant to Live in Space.......................... 110

WHOLE-CLASS LEARNING

MEDIA: IMAGE GALLERY
Space Settlement Art
National Space Society 117

SCIENCE FICTION
Dark They Were, and Golden-Eyed
Ray Bradbury 127

MEDIA: RADIO PLAY — COMPARE
Dark They Were, and Golden-Eyed
Ray Bradbury and Michael McDonough 147

PERFORMANCE TASK
Write an Argument: Editorial 152

WRITER'S HANDBOOK
Argument: Editorial 154

PEER-GROUP LEARNING

SCIENCE FEATURE
Japan to Start Research on the Moon and Mars for Humans
Tomoyuki Suzuki 169

ARGUMENT
Why We Should Continue to Explore Space
Sheri Buckner 179

ARGUMENT — COMPARE
Why We Should Save Earth Before Colonizing Mars
Bruce Dorminey 187

PERFORMANCE TASK
Conduct a Debate........................ 196

viii

ESSENTIAL QUESTION | Should we make a home in space?

INDEPENDENT LEARNING — These selections are available online only.

SCIENCE FEATURE
Beyawned Earth: Pillownauts and the Downside of Space Travel
Jennifer Mason

MAGAZINE ARTICLE
Danger! This Mission to Mars Could Bore You to Death!
Maggie Koerth

SHORT STORY
Time Capsule Found on the Dead Planet
Margaret Atwood

MEDIA: COMIC STRIPS
Space Comics
Various cartoonists

SHARE YOUR INDEPENDENT LEARNING
Share • Learn • Reflect 201

REFLECT AND RESPOND

Reflect on Your Unit Goals
Reflect on the Texts 202

Develop Your Perspective:
Unit Projects 203

PERFORMANCE-BASED ASSESSMENT

Argument 204

UNIT 3 Transformations

UNIT INTRODUCTION

VIDEO
How Do You Overcome a Fear of Spiders? 206

MENTOR TEXT: SHORT STORY MODEL
The Golden Windows 210

WHOLE-CLASS LEARNING

DRAMA
A Christmas Carol: Scrooge and Marley, Acts I and II
based on the novella by Charles Dickens
.... 221

NOVELLA EXCERPT | COMPARE
from A Christmas Carol
Charles Dickens

▶ **MEDIA CONNECTION**
from Scrooge
.... 285

PERFORMANCE TASK
Write a Short Story 296

WRITER'S HANDBOOK
Short Story 298

PEER-GROUP LEARNING

SHORT STORY
Thank You, M'am
Langston Hughes
.... 313

SCIENCE JOURNALISM
Learning Rewires the Brain
Alison Pearce Stevens
.... 325

POETRY COLLECTION
Trying to Name What Doesn't Change
Naomi Shihab Nye

I Myself
Ángel González

Do not trust the eraser
Rosamond S. King
.... 340

HUMAN INTEREST STORY | MEDIA: VIDEO
Makeup Artist Mimi Choi's Mesmerizing Art-Inspired Beauty Looks
Ryma Chikhoune

Mimi Choi Brings Fear to Life With Her Makeup Artistry
True Calling Media
.... 351

PERFORMANCE TASK
Deliver a Dramatic Adaptation 358

x

ESSENTIAL QUESTION | Can people really change?

INDEPENDENT LEARNING — These selections are available online only.

REFLECTIVE ESSAY	HISTORICAL NARRATIVE	SHORT STORY	FABLE
Little Things Are Big *Jesús Colón*	The Story of Victor d'Aveyron, the Wild Child *Eloise Montalban*	A Retrieved Reformation *O. Henry*	The Old Man and His Grandson *Jacob and Wilhelm Grimm*

SHARE YOUR INDEPENDENT LEARNING
Share • Learn • Reflect 363

REFLECT AND RESPOND

Reflect on Your Unit Goals
Reflect on the Texts 364

Develop Your Perspective:
Unit Projects 365

PERFORMANCE-BASED ASSESSMENT

Short Story 366

UNIT 4 Learning From Nature

UNIT INTRODUCTION

VIDEO
Protecting the Land of the Spirit Bear 368

MENTOR TEXT: RESEARCH-BASED ESSAY MODEL
Wildlife Rehabbers Are Here to Help 372

WHOLE-CLASS LEARNING

FEATURE ARTICLE	DESCRIPTIVE ESSAY	CREATION STORY	CREATION STORY **COMPARE**
The Bee Highway: Making a Place for Bees in the City *Kathryn Hulick* 381	*from* Silent Spring *Rachel Carson* 397	How Grandmother Spider Stole the Sun *Michael J. Caduto and Joseph Bruchac* 410	Coyote Steals the Sun and Moon *Richard Erdoes and Alfonso Ortiz* 412

PERFORMANCE TASK
Write a Research Paper 422

WRITER'S HANDBOOK
Research Paper 424

PEER-GROUP LEARNING

LYRIC POETRY	MEDIA: SPOKEN-WORD POETRY **COMPARE**	SCIENCE FEATURE	MAGICAL REALISM
Our Purpose in Poetry: Or, Earthrise *Amanda Gorman* 441	Earthrise *Amanda Gorman* 449	Creature Comforts: Three Biology-Based Tips for Builders *Mary Beth Cox* 457	He—y, Come on Ou—t! *Shinichi Hoshi, translated by Stanleigh Jones* 471

PERFORMANCE TASK
Give and Follow Instructions 480

xii

ESSENTIAL QUESTION | What is the relationship between people and nature?

INDEPENDENT LEARNING
These selections are available online only.

ADVENTURE STORY

from My Side of the Mountain
Jean Craighead George

FEATURE ARTICLE

How the Teens of St. Pete Youth Farm Fight Food Insecurity, One Harvest at a Time
Gabrielle Calise

SCIENCE ARTICLE

Rice University Researchers Are Turning Dead Spiders Into "Necrobots"
Ariana Garcia

LYRIC POETRY

Turtle Watchers
Linda Hogan

Jaguar
Francisco X. Alarcón

The Sparrow
Paul Laurence Dunbar

SHARE YOUR INDEPENDENT LEARNING
Share • Learn • Reflect 485

REFLECT AND RESPOND

Reflect on Your Unit Goals
Reflect on the Texts 486

Develop Your Perspective:
Unit Projects 487

PERFORMANCE-BASED ASSESSMENT

Research-Based Essay 488

UNIT 5 Facing Adversity

UNIT INTRODUCTION

VIDEO
This 15-Year-Old Beat a Rare Disease to Become a Competitive Cyclist 490

MENTOR TEXT: INFORMATIONAL ESSAY MODEL
Against the Odds 494

WHOLE-CLASS LEARNING

HISTORICAL NONFICTION
Black Sunday: The Storm That Gave Us the Dust Bowl
Erin Blakemore
503

COMPARE
HISTORICAL FICTION
from Survival in the Storm: The Dust Bowl Diary of Grace Edwards
Katelan Janke

▶ MEDIA CONNECTION
The Dust Bowl
511

INFORMATIONAL ARTICLE
A More Accessible World
Lisa Christensen
525

PERFORMANCE TASK
Write an Informational Essay 536

WRITER'S HANDBOOK
Informational Essay 538

PEER-GROUP LEARNING

SHORT STORY
The Circuit
Francisco Jiménez
553

COMPARE
INTERVIEW
How This Son of Migrant Farm Workers Became an Astronaut
José Hernández and Octavio Blanco
565

ORAL HISTORY
A Work in Progress
Aimee Mullins
579

LYRIC POETRY | VIGNETTE
Simile: Willow and Ginkgo
Eve Merriam

Four Skinny Trees from The House on Mango Street
Sandra Cisneros
594

PERFORMANCE TASK
Present an Informational Text 602

xiv

ESSENTIAL QUESTION | How do we overcome life's challenges?

INDEPENDENT LEARNING — These selections are available online only.

PERSONAL NARRATIVE
The Girl Who Fell From the Sky
Juliane Koepcke

PERSUASIVE SPEECH
Malala Yousafzai: Speech to United Nations Security Council
Malala Yousafzai

AUTOBIOGRAPHY
from The Story of My Life
Helen Keller

SHORT STORY
Rikki-tikki-tavi
Rudyard Kipling

SHARE YOUR INDEPENDENT LEARNING
Share • Learn • Reflect 607

REFLECT AND RESPOND

Reflect on Your Unit Goals
Reflect on the Texts 608

Develop Your Perspective:
Unit Projects 609

PERFORMANCE-BASED ASSESSMENT

Informational Essay 610

xv

Crossing Generations

▶ **WATCH THE ViDEO**

DISCUSS What are some examples of things that one generation can learn from another?

Write your response before sharing your ideas.

UNIT 1

INTRO

Essential Question
What can one generation learn from another?

PERSONAL NARRATIVE
Grandfather's Garden

MENTOR TEXT

WHOLE-CLASS LEARNING

Don't Just Sit There Like a Punk
Matt de la Peña

SHORT STORY

The Case of the Disappearing Words
Alice Andre-Clark

FEATURE ARTICLE

Write a Personal Narrative

WRITING: PERFORMANCE TASK

PEER-GROUP LEARNING

COMPARE

from Mom & Me & Mom
Maya Angelou

MEMOIR

Learning to Love My Mother
Maya Angelou with Michael Maher

MEDIA: TV INTERVIEW

Mother-Daughter Drawings
Mica and Myla Hendricks

MEDIA: IMAGE GALLERY

Ode to My Papi
Guadalupe García McCall

Mother to Son
Langston Hughes

To James
Frank Horne

POETRY COLLECTION 1

Present a Personal Narrative

SPEAKING AND LISTENING: PERFORMANCE TASK

INDEPENDENT LEARNING

Lineage
Margaret Walker

Family
Grace Paley

POETRY COLLECTION 2

"Gotcha Day" Isn't a Cause for Celebration
Sophie Johnson

OPINION PIECE

Water Names
Lan Samantha Chang

REALISTIC FICTION

An Hour With Abuelo
Judith Ortiz Cofer

REALISTIC FICTION

SHARE • LEARN • REFLECT

SHARE INDEPENDENT LEARNING

REFLECT AND RESPOND
GOALS • TEXTS • UNIT PROJECTS

PERFORMANCE-BASED ASSESSMENT
Personal Narrative
You will write a personal narrative that explores the Essential Question for the unit.

3

UNIT 1 INTRODUCTION

Unit Goals

Throughout this unit you will deepen your perspective about different generations by reading, writing, speaking, listening, and presenting. These goals will help you succeed on the Unit Performance-Based Assessment

SET GOALS Use a scale of 1 to 5 to rate how well you meet these goals right now. You will revisit your ratings later when you reflect on your growth during this unit.

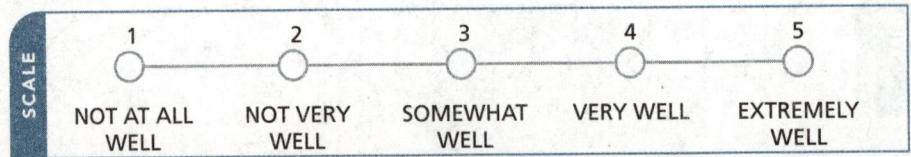

SCALE: 1 NOT AT ALL WELL — 2 NOT VERY WELL — 3 SOMEWHAT WELL — 4 VERY WELL — 5 EXTREMELY WELL

ESSENTIAL QUESTION	Unit Introduction	Unit Reflection
I can read selections that express various points of view about different generations and develop my own perspective.	1 2 3 4 5	1 2 3 4 5
READING	**Unit Introduction**	**Unit Reflection**
I can understand and use academic vocabulary words related to personal narratives.	1 2 3 4 5	1 2 3 4 5
I can recognize elements of different genres, especially realistic fiction, informational texts, and poetry.	1 2 3 4 5	1 2 3 4 5
I can read a selection of my choice independently and make connections to other texts.	1 2 3 4 5	1 2 3 4 5
WRITING	**Unit Introduction**	**Unit Reflection**
I can write a focused, well-organized personal narrative.	1 2 3 4 5	1 2 3 4 5
I can complete Timed Writing tasks with confidence.	1 2 3 4 5	1 2 3 4 5
SPEAKING AND LISTENING	**Unit Introduction**	**Unit Reflection**
I can prepare and present a personal narrative.	1 2 3 4 5	1 2 3 4 5
MY GOALS	**Unit Introduction**	**Unit Reflection**

STANDARDS

Language
- Use common, grade-appropriate Greek or Latin affixes and roots as clues to the meaning of a word.
- Acquire and use accurately grade-appropriate general academic and domain-specific words and phrases; gather vocabulary knowledge when considering a word or phrase important to comprehension or expression.

4 UNIT 1 • CROSSING GENERATIONS

Essential Question: What can one generation learn from another?

Academic Vocabulary: Personal Narrative

Academic terms can help you read, write, and discuss with precision. Many of these words have roots, or key parts, that come from Latin and Greek.

PRACTICE Academic terms are used routinely in classrooms. Build your knowledge of these words by completing the chart.

1. **Review** each word, its root, and the mentor sentences.
2. **Determine** the meaning and usage of each word using the mentor sentences and a dictionary, if needed.
3. **List** at least two related words for each academic term. Then, challenge yourself to write a sentence that contains two of the academic terms.

WORD	MENTOR SENTENCES	PREDICT MEANING	RELATED WORDS
dialogue GREEK ROOT: -logue- "word"	1. The television show was known for its well-written *dialogue* between characters. 2. The confusion between Dina and Janet started a *dialogue* that cleared the air.		monologue; catalogue
consequence LATIN ROOT: -sequ- "follow"	1. A *consequence* of oversleeping is being late for school. 2. Earning an A on my math test was a positive *consequence* of studying all week.		
perspective LATIN ROOT: -spec- "look"	1. The examples from around the world gave the article a global *perspective*. 2. The personal essay was written from the author's *perspective*.		
notable LATIN ROOT: -not- "mark"	1. Every *notable* person in the city was invited to the mayor's fund-raising gala. 2. It had been a long, boring week, and nothing particularly *notable* had happened.		
contradict LATIN ROOT: -dict- "speak"	1. The facts of the case remain unclear because the witnesses' statements *contradict* each other. 2. The new test results *contradict* what we once thought to be true about the product.		

UNIT 1 INTRODUCTION

MENTOR TEXT

PERSONAL NARRATIVE MODEL

READ As you read, look at the way the writer vividly describes her grandfather and their relationship.

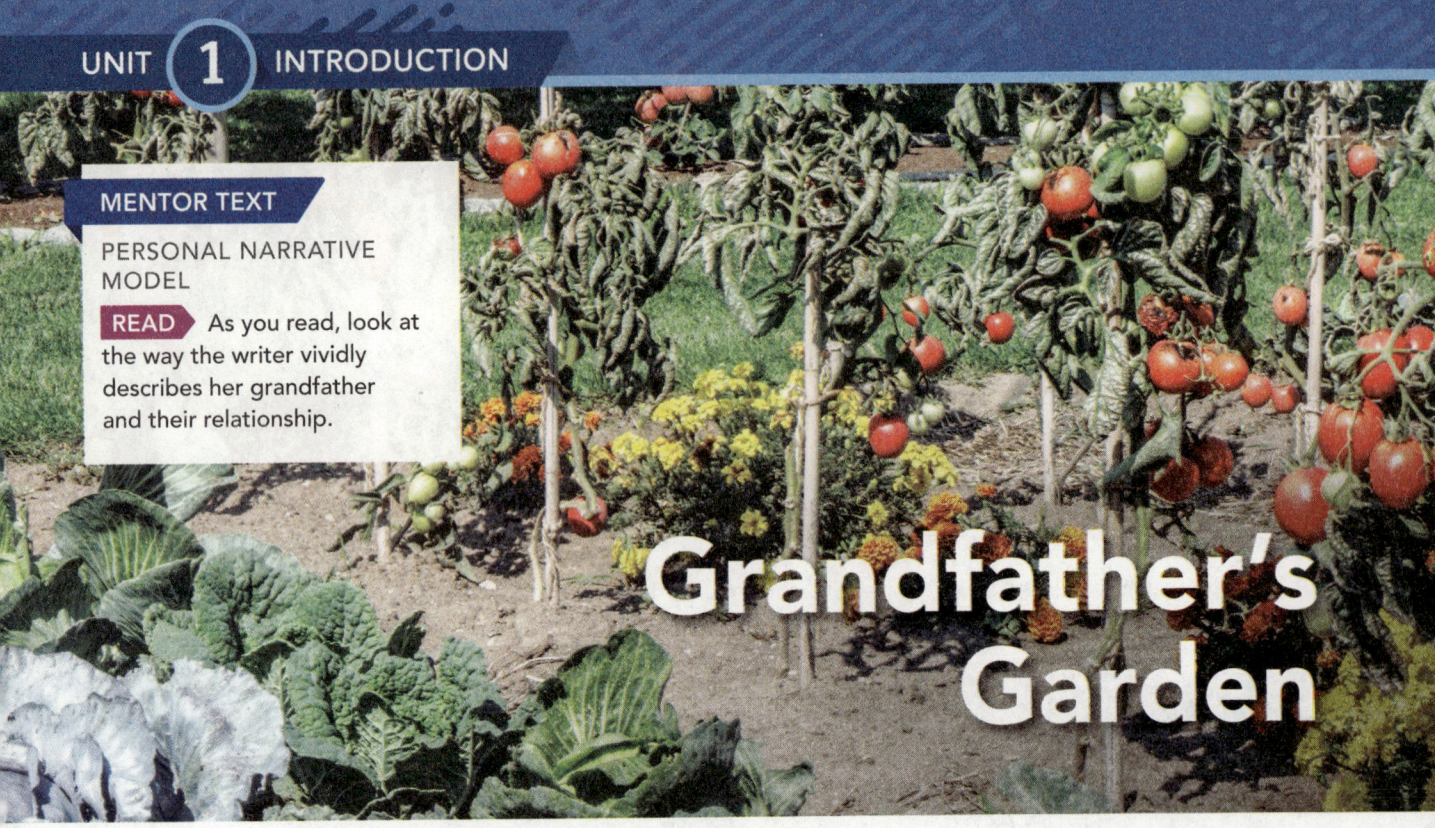

Grandfather's Garden

1 When I was very young, my grandfather suffered a stroke. As a result, the left side of his face drooped, he lost range of motion in his left arm, and he walked with a limp. The stroke had also affected his speech. His voice was low and scratchy, and his words were sometimes garbled and difficult to understand. To my young mind, he was a little frightening, and because I was shy, I tended to avoid him.

2 It took years for me to understand that these "scary" qualities were beyond his control. As I got older, my discomfort eased, but I didn't know how to connect with him. He didn't speak much, and he spent most of his time outside tending his garden. During visits to my grandparents' house, I spent most of my time inside talking and cooking with my grandmother.

3 My grandfather's fruit and vegetable garden encompassed a large portion of my grandparents' sizable backyard. Because of his physical limitations, the work he did there was slow and labored, but he did almost all of it himself. He took great pride in the quality and quantity of his produce, and he had good reason to be proud: The garden was both beautiful and plentiful. I longed to explore it but never had. I felt like that would be intruding, and I wasn't sure he would want me in his special space.

4 When I was twelve years old, I spent an entire week at my grandparents' house. On the day I arrived, my grandmother and I brewed a pitcher of iced tea and brought it out to the backyard. As usual, my grandfather was toiling in his sea of greenery. It was a warm day, and my grandmother called him over to rest in the shade and have a cool drink. He shuffled slowly towards us and

Essential Question: What can one generation learn from another?

plopped down into the patio chair next to mine. With a shaky hand he reached over and held out a plump red strawberry to me. Then he leaned in a bit closer to speak.

5   "You like strawberries?" he asked in his gravelly voice. I nodded timidly but didn't look at him. "Go ahead and eat it," he encouraged.

6   I took the shiny berry from his hand, slid it into my mouth, and bit down. It was perfectly ripe, sweet, and juicy. I looked my grandfather in the face and smiled, still timid. He chuckled, and one corner of his droopy mouth turned up. He was smiling too.

7   "Want another?" he tempted. I nodded that I did, more confidently now.

8   After a few minutes, he stood up—with a little effort—and started shuffling back into the garden. Then he stopped, turned around, and gestured for me to join him. I followed him through his wonderland of vegetation to the strawberry patch at the far end. There, the two of us munched until every one of those delicious strawberries was gone. Neither of us said much; nonetheless, I recognized that we were sharing a very special moment. I felt like I was finally connecting with my grandfather.

9   We spent the remainder of the afternoon in the garden. In fact, I spent every afternoon that week in the glory of the garden with my grandfather. He told me the names of all his plants and, with effort, showed me how to care for each one. He taught me the best types of soil to use for various species of fruits and vegetables, and he explained which ones grow well as companions planted beside each other in the bed. He noticed that I was interested, and he wanted to impart his knowledge. In that single week, my grandfather spoke more to me than he ever had before. He shared his lifelong passion for gardening and, without knowing it, inspired mine.

WORD WALL: CROSSING GENERATIONS

Vocabulary A Word Wall is a collection of words related to a topic.

As you read the selections in this unit, identify interesting words related to different generations, and add them to your Word Wall. For example, you might begin by adding basic words from the Mentor Text, such as *connect*, as well as more complex terms, such as *pride* and *inspired*. Continue to add words as you complete this unit.

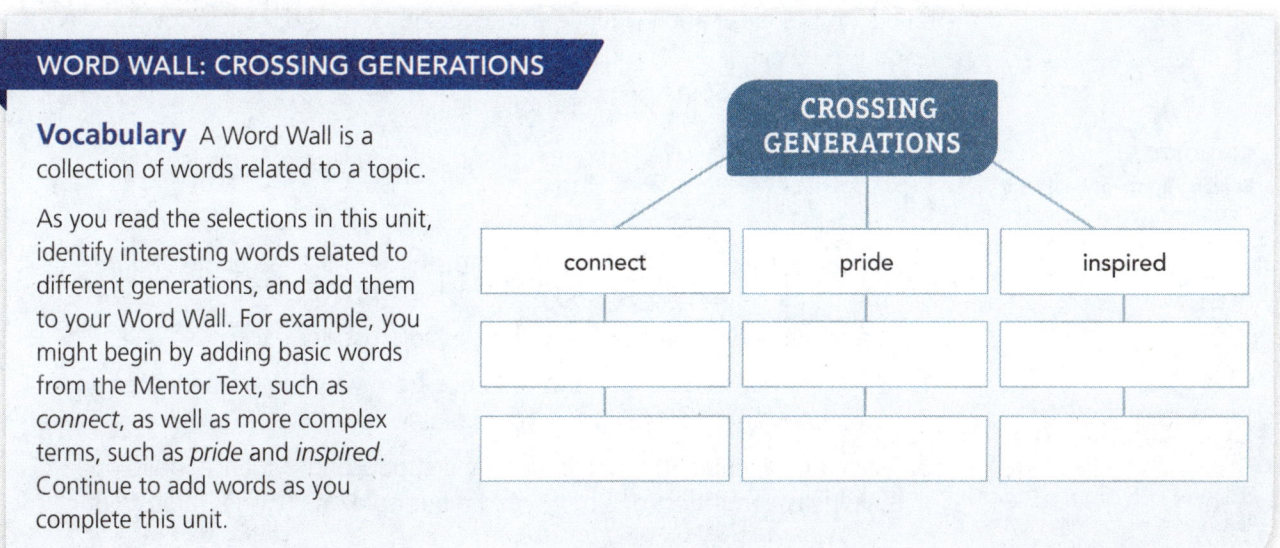

Grandfather's Garden 7

UNIT 1 INTRODUCTION

Summary

A **summary** is a brief, complete overview of a text that maintains the meaning and logical order of the original work. It should be objective and should not include your personal opinions.

WRITE Write a summary of "Grandfather's Garden."

_____
_____
_____
_____
_____
_____
_____
_____
_____
_____
_____

Icebreaker

Conduct a Class Discussion

Discussions allow you to learn from others. When discussing a topic in class, reflect on the ideas and evidence your peers present. Adjust your own responses as needed. Consider this statement: **Senior citizens can learn a lot from younger people.**

Mark your position on the statement, and consider the reasons for your opinion.

◯ Strongly Agree   ◯ Agree   ◯ Disagree   ◯ Strongly Disagree

Use these tips as you participate in the class discussion:

1. As you share your opinion, give evidence from your own experiences and background reading to support your ideas.

2. As your classmates share their ideas and supporting evidence, build on their ideas and reflect on your own. If your opinion changes, adjust your response and explain why.

STANDARDS

Reading Informational Text
Provide an objective summary of the text.

Writing
Write routinely over extended time frames and shorter time frames for a range of discipline-specific tasks, purposes, and audiences.

Speaking and Listening
Engage effectively in a range of collaborative discussions with diverse partners on grade 7 topics, texts, and issues, building on others' ideas and expressing their own clearly.

8 UNIT 1 • CROSSING GENERATIONS

Essential Question: What can one generation learn from another?

QuickWrite

Consider class discussions, the video, and the Mentor Text as you think about the Essential Question.

Essential Question

What can one generation learn from another?

At the end of the unit, you will respond to the Essential Question again and see how your perspective has deepened or changed.

WRITE Record your first thoughts here.

EVIDENCE LOG

What can one generation learn from another?

As you read the selections in this unit, use a chart like the one shown to record your ideas and list details from the texts that support them. Taking notes as you go will help you clarify your thinking, gather relevant information, and be ready to respond to the Essential Question.

TITLE	MY IDEAS / OBSERVATIONS	TEXT EVIDENCE / INFORMATION

Unit Introduction 9

WHOLE-CLASS LEARNING

Essential Question

What can one generation learn from another?

The famous Indian leader Mahatma Gandhi said, "Learn as if you were to live forever." You are always learning, from peers as well as from teachers, parents, and relatives. You will work with your whole class to explore ways in which generations can learn from each other.

Whole-Class Learning Strategies

Throughout your life, in school, in your community, and in your career, you will continue to learn and work in large-group environments.

Review these strategies and the actions you can take to practice them as you work with your whole class. Add ideas of your own to each category. Get ready to use these strategies during Whole-Class Learning.

STRATEGY	MY ACTION PLAN
Listen actively	• Put away personal items to avoid becoming distracted. • Try to hear the speaker's full message before planning your own response. •
Demonstrate respect	• Show up on time and make sure you are prepared for class. • Avoid side conversations while in class. •
Show interest	• Be aware of your body language. For example, sit up in your chair. • Respond when the teacher asks for feedback. •
Interact and share ideas	• If you're confused, other people probably are, too. Ask a question to help your whole class. • Build on the ideas of others by adding details or making a connection. •

Contents

SHORT STORY

Don't Just Sit There Like a Punk
Matt de la Peña

A boy learns a life lesson on the basketball court.

FEATURE ARTICLE

The Case of the Disappearing Words
Alice Andre-Clark

Is the language we speak always something one generation can pass on to the next?

PERFORMANCE TASK

WRITING PROMPT • WRITER'S HANDBOOK

Write a Personal Narrative

The Whole-Class readings illustrate the influence of one generation on another. After reading, you will write a personal narrative about an event in which you influenced someone from a different generation, or they influenced you.

LEARN ABOUT GENRE: FICTION

DON'T JUST SIT THERE LIKE A PUNK

Reading Short Stories

A **short story** is a brief work of fiction. **Realistic short stories** are products of writers' imaginations but seem true to real life.

The selection you are about to read is a short story.

SHORT STORY

Author's Purpose
- to entertain readers while providing an insight about life or human nature

Characteristics
- settings that provide a backdrop for the action
- characters whose personal qualities influence the story's action and resolution
- conflicts that are resolved by the end of the story
- dialogue that sounds true to life
- themes that express general truths or observations about life or human nature

Structure
- a plot, or a series of related events, that could happen in real life

Take a Minute!

LIST Create four short story titles, two that are realistic and two that are obviously not realistic. Write them here.

Share your titles with a partner and have them decide which stories are probably realistic and which are not. Discuss each other's choices.

STANDARDS
Reading Literature
Determine a theme or central idea of a text and analyze its development over the course of the text.

12 UNIT 1 • CROSSING GENERATIONS

Essential Question: What can one generation learn from another?

Theme

A **theme** is an insight about life that is revealed in a literary work, such as a short story. A theme is *not* an explanation of what happens in the narrative. Read these examples.

EXAMPLE	IS IT A THEME?
This story is about a runner who misses out on a chance to play in the state championship.	No, it's not a theme. It's an explanation of what happens in the story.
Sometimes a loss brings an unexpected sense of freedom.	Yes, it's a theme, an insight about life revealed through the story.

In most literary works, themes are not directly stated by authors. Readers determine theme by analyzing different elements that the author develops over the course of the text. Here are some elements that may offer clues to a short story's theme.

- **Characters:** their traits, actions, and attitudes
- **Conflict:** a problem that challenges the characters
- **Outcome:** what characters learn or how they change as a result of the conflict

Note that readers of the same story may arrive at different themes, or they may state the same basic theme using different words. As long as themes are supported by story details, they are valid.

PRACTICE Think of a story that you have read. Write a paragraph briefly describing what happens in it. Then state its theme.

Paragraph:

Theme:

Learn About Genre 13

PREPARE TO READ

Don't Just Sit There Like a Punk

About the Author

Matt de la Peña was born in California. He loves basketball and attended college on a basketball scholarship. He has published several novels and children's books, often taking inspiration from his Mexican American heritage and urban life. In 2016, his book *Last Stop on Market Street* won the Newbery Medal. He teaches literature at San Diego State University.

STANDARDS
Reading Literature
- Cite several pieces of textual evidence to support analysis of what the text says explicitly as well as inferences drawn from the text.
- By the end of the year, read and comprehend literature, including stories, dramas, and poems.

Concept Vocabulary

Predict The words listed here appear in the story. Judging from these words, explain what kinds of characters and events you think this story will be about.

WORDS	MY EXPECTATIONS
stunned (STUHND) *adj.* astonished; completely surprised	
paralysis (puh RAL uh sihs) *n.* loss of the ability to move	
doubt (DOWT) *n.* uncertainty	
unexplainable (uhn ihk SPLAY nuh buhl) *adj.* impossible to make clear or describe	
instinct (IHN stihngkt) *n.* inborn ability; natural impulse	
intense (ihn TENS) *adj.* highly focused; showing extreme concentration	

Reading Strategy: Make Inferences

An **inference** is an educated guess about information that is not stated directly in a story. To make an inference, connect specific text details with what you know about life. Doing so can deepen your understanding of the narrative. Here is an inference you might make as you read this short story.

Story Passage:

Dante strides over and points a finger in your face. "What, are you deaf, kid? I said leave!"

No words form in your brain.

No thoughts.

Possible Inference: Dante seems really angry. His words and actions are rude. The narrator freezes, suggesting that he is stunned by Dante's behavior.

PRACTICE As you read the story, make inferences and write them in the open space next to the text. Mark the story details that led to each inference.

14 UNIT 1 • CROSSING GENERATIONS

SHORT STORY

Don't Just Sit There Like a Punk

Matt de la Peña

BACKGROUND
In the summer before he enters the ninth grade, a young basketball player starts going to a different gym. He wants to learn from older, highly skilled players and improve his game. He does not, however, receive a warm welcome. The experience challenges him in many ways.

1   It won't be until week four that you finally get into a meaningful game.

2   By this time you'll know most of the guys by nickname. And you'll know how they play. At some point your focus will have shifted from wanting to play, to breaking down their various skill sets. There's one guy in particular you'll study.

3   Dante.

4   He's six four and thin. In his early thirties maybe. He's the only guy in the gym who's never said a word to you. He walks right by you like you don't even exist. But he can seriously play. Not only does he knock down almost every jumper he takes, he hardly ever grazes the rim. He has this sweet little fadeaway in the post, and whenever someone tries to challenge him on the break, they get mashed on, posterized[1], and the guys on the sideline fall all over each other, laughing and stomping and pointing.

5   After burying one particular game winner from the wing, two guys draped all over him, he'll turn to you suddenly and bark, "Hey, kid, why you still coming here?"

6   You pause your dribble, **stunned**. "Who me?"

---
1. **posterized** *v.* slang term for a move in basketball in which an offensive player dunks a ball over a defending player in a way that is spectacular enough be reproduced on a printed poster.

READ TO UNLOCK MEANING

1. First read the text for comprehension and enjoyment. Use the **Reading Strategy** and **Comprehension Check** questions to support your first read.
2. Go back and respond to the Close-Read note.
3. Identify other details in the text you find interesting. Ask your own questions and draw your own conclusions.

stunned (STUHND) *adj.* astonished; completely surprised

Don't Just Sit There Like a Punk   15

7 "Nobody thinks you're good enough to play here, comprende? Why don't you go on back to the barrio, esé."

8 Your whole body will freeze up from the shock of his words.

9 Everyone in the entire gym inching closer, waiting to see what happens next.

10 Dante strides over and points a finger in your face. "What, are you deaf, kid? I said leave!"

11 No words form in your brain.

12 No thoughts.

13 Dante spins to the rest of the guys. "Someone get this scrub out my face before I do something stupid."

14 A couple regulars will lead you toward the bleachers, but your legs aren't quite working yet. You're confused almost to the point of **paralysis**. Because what did you do wrong? Why does he hate you? Your heart thump-thump-thumping inside your chest. **Doubt** setting in. Maybe he's right. Maybe you really *are* a scrub. Maybe you *shouldn't* be allowed to show up like this every day, uninvited.

15 Maybe the whole summer has been one big mistake.

16 You grab your stuff off the bleachers and start toward the door, but for some **unexplainable** reason you stop. You turn around. You glare across the court at Dante, mumbling, "I just wanna play."

17 "What?" Dante shouts back. He picks up a ball and fires it at you, narrowly missing. "Speak up if you got something to say!"

18 "I wanna play," you repeat, louder this time.

19 "What?"

20 "I wanna play!"

21 A few of the guys start toward you again, wanting to get you out of the gym before you get hurt, but Dante puts a stop to that. "Get away from him! This is between me and the kid!"

22 The whole gym silent aside from your heartbeat.

23 Your short, nervous breaths measuring the time.

24 "Check it out," Dante suddenly announces. "The kid's got my spot this game." Then he turns back to you. "After you get smoked, you walk out them doors and never come back, you hear?"

25 You stand there studying him for a few extra beats, searching for his angle, trying to decide if it's some kind of trick, if you're still in danger. Before your ruling is in, though, you find yourself being shoved out onto the court.

26 "You got Dollar Bill," someone is telling you.

27 It takes a minute to realize what's happening.

28 They're letting you play.

29 And if you mess up, it's over.

30 As fast as your heart was beating when Dante got in your face, it slows back down once the ball is in play. Because this is the one

---

paralysis (puh RAL uh sihs) *n.* loss of the ability to move

doubt (DOWT) *n.* uncertainty

unexplainable (uhn ihk SPLAY nuh buhl) *adj.* impossible to make clear or describe

MAKE INFERENCES
What's happening in paragraph 21? Why might Dante be acting this way?

MAKE INFERENCES
In paragraph 30, what makes the narrator's heartbeat return to normal?

16 UNIT 1 • CROSSING GENERATIONS

place in the entire world where you're truly alive. Where your brain shuts off and every move is made on **instinct**.

instinct (IHN stihngkt) *n.* inborn ability; natural impulse

31   It only takes two trips up and down before you shake off the cobwebs and slip into the flow. First time the ball gets swung to you out on the wing, you skip past your defender and spin into the lane for a little ten-foot bank shot off the glass.

32   A few guys on the sideline oohing and aahing.

33   A few plays later you bury an open twenty-footer, nothing but net, Dante style.

34   You rip Dollar Bill near half court and race down the floor for a little finger roll over the rim. And as you retreat back down for defense after that one, you can hear the gym erupting.

35   Now you're buried deep inside the folds of the game.

36   The outside world slinks off and hides, and all you know are the choreographed movements around you. The dance. The beautiful symphony of squeaking sneaks and grunts and the thud of body meeting body. Each man's heavy breath and his eyes like a portal to his mind.

37   You bury two more deep jumpers, followed by a game-winning scoop shot in the lane, which results in the other team's big man tripping over his own feet and falling on his face.

38   The guys on your squad mob you near midcourt.

39   "That's right, young buck," they say.

40   "That's how you let fools know," they say.

41   A few go on about how they've been meaning to pick you up all summer, they just never got a chance, blah, blah, blah.

42   But just as you're starting to feel yourself, Dante will be back in your grill. "What, you make a couple jumpers, and now you supposed to be somebody?"

43   "No, I just—"

44   "Get off my court, kid."

45   "But—"

46   He'll grab you by the arm and fling you toward the bleachers, barking to everyone else, "Yo, I got my spot back! Check ball!"

47   You'll consider putting up a fight here, but don't.

48   Trust me.

49   What matters is you'll have proven you can play. What matters is every head who saw what you just did will see you differently

COMPREHENSION CHECK

How do the men react to how the narrator played? How does Dante react?

Don't Just Sit There Like a Punk   17

CLOSE READ

ANNOTATE In paragraphs 51–55, mark the dialogue between Rob and Slim.

QUESTION What does this conversation reveal about the two men's personalities?

intense (ihn TENS) *adj.* highly focused; showing extreme concentration

COMPREHENSION CHECK
Does the narrator's father support the narrator in playing basketball? Explain.

---

now. As proof, not thirty seconds later a guy who goes by the name of Slim will wander over and say, "Yo, young buck, I got next. Wanna run with me?"

50   "For sure."

51   Rob will overhear this exchange and bark, "Yo, Slim, I thought you already had five. Who you dropping?"

52   "You."

53   *"Me?"*

54   "You just seen this boy's skills, right? I gotta get me a point guard."

55   "But you said I was down, Slim. Don't play your boy like that...."

56   In the middle of this debate, a stray jumper will roll out of bounds toward you, and Dante will give chase. He'll grab the rock and kneel down, not five feet from you, to tie his shoe. "Hey, kid," he'll say in a quiet voice.

57   "Yeah?"

58   He'll look up at you, mid-double knot. "You wanna get in games, you don't just sit there like a punk, right? You stand up and challenge the baddest dude in the gym. Someone like me. Then you do your thing. Understand?"

59   His **intense** eyes will be like knives inside your chest. "Yes, sir."

60   He'll stand up and nod, then jog back onto the court, shouting, "Yo, check ball! Let's go!"

61   You'll think this is the beginning of some meaningful mentorship, but it won't be. In fact, Dante won't say another word to you the rest of the summer. Not even when you ask him a direct question. But over time you'll begin to see the power of his silence. And surprisingly, it will remind you of your old man's silence.

62   A few months into your ninth-grade season, you'll actually spot Dante in the stands at one of your games. He'll be alone, eating popcorn, watching. You'll be the starting point guard on the varsity squad—which is pretty legit for a freshman. And you'll be having your best game of the young season. You'll wave as you jog past him at halftime, but he won't wave back. He'll continue eating his popcorn. After the game you'll climb the packed bleachers looking for him, but he'll already be gone.

63   Your old man will be there, though.

64   And on the drive back to your apartment that night you'll realize something important. Your old man is always there. And he always has been. And so what if he doesn't say anything about how many points you just scored. How many assists. So what if he turns on his radio news show instead of breaking down the big win.

65   Maybe words aren't what's important.

66   Maybe words would just steal away your freedom to think for yourself. ❧

BUILD INSIGHT

First Thoughts

Choose one of the following questions to answer.
- What do you think of the narrator's use of "you" in the story? Whom do you think the narrator is addressing, and why? Do you like this storytelling technique? Explain.
- As you read the story, did you think Dante would become a mentor to the narrator? How did you feel when you read that he didn't? Explain.

Summary

Write a short objective summary of what happens in the story to confirm your comprehension. Include only the main characters, ideas, and events. Do not express your opinions about them.

Analysis

1. **(a)** What does the narrator do in response to his frustrating situation with Dante at the beginning of the story? **(b) Analyze** Would you describe the narrator's actions as brave? Use details from the story to support your answer.

2. **(a)** What advice does Dante give the narrator in paragraph 58?
   (b) Interpret What does this action reveal about Dante's character?

3. **Make Inferences** In paragraph 62, the narrator reveals that Dante shows up at one of his games. Why might Dante have done that? Why does Dante leave without talking to the narrator?

4. **(a)** How would you describe the narrator's way of speaking? **(b) Evaluate** Do you think the narrator's distinct style of speaking enhances or detracts from the narrative? Explain.

Exploring the Essential Question

What can one generation learn from another?

5. **Assess** The selection's last four paragraphs concern the narrator's father, or "old man." What has the son come to realize about his father? Record your ideas in your Evidence Log.

STANDARDS
Reading Literature
- Cite several pieces of textual evidence to support analysis of what the text says explicitly as well as inferences drawn from the text.
- Provide an objective summary of the text.

ANALYZE AND INTERPRET

DON'T JUST SIT THERE LIKE A PUNK

Close Read

1. The model passage and annotation show how one reader analyzed paragraph 36. Find another detail in the passage to annotate. Then, write your own question and conclusion.

CLOSE-READ MODEL

The outside world slinks off and hides, and *all you know are the choreographed movements around you. The dance.* The beautiful symphony of squeaking sneaks and grunts and the thud of body meeting body. Each man's heavy breath and his eyes like a portal to his mind.

ANNOTATE: This story contains lots of informal language and basketball terms. Here, however, the word choice changes.

QUESTION: What is the effect of this shift in word choice?

CONCLUDE: The shift in word choice helps readers understand ways in which basketball is an art.

MY QUESTION:

MY CONCLUSION:

2. For more practice, answer the Close-Read note in the selection.

3. Choose a section of the story you found especially meaningful. Mark important details. Then jot down questions and write your conclusions in the open space next to the text.

Inquiry and Research

Research and Extend Choose one of the following questions, and conduct short research on the internet to find an answer. Then, share what you learned with a partner.

- When and where was basketball first played, and who developed the game?
- What are the most important rules of modern basketball?

STANDARDS

Reading Literature
Determine a theme or central idea of a text and analyze its development over the course of the text.

Writing
Conduct short research projects to answer a question.

20 UNIT 1 • CROSSING GENERATIONS

Essential Question: What can one generation learn from another?

Theme

A **theme** is an insight about life conveyed through a literary work. To interpret a story's theme, you analyze story elements and how they develop over the course of the narrative.

STORY ELEMENT	DETAILS TO ANALYZE
Characters	What is important to each main character? What do characters' thoughts, actions, and words reveal about them?
Conflict	What problems do the characters face? What actions, positive or negative, do they take to address the problems?
Outcomes	How is the conflict resolved? What do the characters learn? How do the characters change as a result?

PRACTICE Complete the activities and answer the questions.

1. **Support** Consider this possible theme from the story: *Positive lessons can be learned from a difficult person.* Find and mark two details in the text that support this theme.

2. **Analyze** Reread paragraphs 29–34. Which possible theme listed in the chart do the details in the passage suggest? Mark and then explain your choice.

MARK THE MOST SUITABLE THEME	EXPLAIN YOUR CHOICE
When a person freely expresses their talent, they feel great joy.	
Anyone who wants applause and recognition must work hard first.	
Some people are destined to be stars, and they just have to wait for their moment.	

3. **(a)** Reread paragraphs 61–66. What comparison does the narrator draw between his father and Dante? **(b) Analyze** What has the narrator learned from those two men? **(c) Interpret** What theme can you formulate from those details?

Don't Just Sit There Like a Punk 21

STUDY LANGUAGE AND CRAFT

DON'T JUST SIT THERE LIKE A PUNK

Concept Vocabulary

Why These Words? These vocabulary words are related to thoughts and feelings that people often experience when facing new or difficult situations.

| stunned | paralysis | doubt |
| unexplainable | instinct | intense |

WORD WALL

Note words in the text that are related to the idea of crossing generations. Add them to your Word Wall.

PRACTICE Answer the questions.

1. How do the vocabulary words help you understand the concept of facing a challenging situation?

2. Use each word in a sentence. Provide context clues that hint at the meaning of the word.

3. Think of another related word that would fit well in this grouping. Explain your choice.

Word Study

Latin Suffix: -able The vocabulary word *unexplainable* contains the prefix *un-*, which means "not." It also contains the suffix *-able*, which means "capable of," "can be," or "able to." This suffix has two different spellings: *-able* and *-ible*.

PRACTICE Complete the following items.

1. Determine the meaning of the word *unexplainable*. Use your knowledge of the prefix *un-* and the suffix *-able* to write a definition.

2. Use your knowledge of the suffix *-able* to determine the meanings of these words: *questionable, disposable, allowable*. Write your definitions and then verify them by checking in a dictionary.

STANDARDS

Language
• Demonstrate command of the conventions of standard English capitalization, punctuation, and spelling when writing.
• Determine or clarify the meaning of unknown and multiple-meaning words and phrases based on grade 7 reading and content, choosing flexibly from a range of strategies.
• Use common, grade-appropriate Greek or Latin affixes and roots as clues to the meaning of a word.

Essential Question: What can one generation learn from another?

Nouns and Pronouns

A **common noun** names a person, a place, a thing, or an idea and is not capitalized. A **proper noun** names a *specific* person, place, thing, or idea and *is* capitalized. A **possessive noun** shows ownership using an apostrophe. Read these examples from "Don't Just Sit There Like a Punk."

COMMON NOUNS	PROPER NOUNS	POSSESSIVE NOUNS
basketball, sneaker, rim, nickname, cobweb	Dante, Dollar Bill, Slim, Rob	Each man's heavy breath This boy's skills

A **personal pronoun** takes the place of a noun, several nouns, or another pronoun referred to earlier in the text. A **possessive pronoun** shows ownership but does *not* use an apostrophe.

PERSONAL PRONOUNS	I, me, we, us, you, he, him, she, her, it, they, them
POSSESSIVE PRONOUNS	my, mine, our, ours, your, yours, his, her, hers, its, their, theirs

READ Read the following sentence. Mark the nouns and classify each one as common or proper. Finally, identify the possessive noun.

   The author's name is Matt de la Peña, and California is his birthplace.

WRITE / EDIT

1. Edit each sentence. Replace the underlined noun or noun phrase with the appropriate pronoun.

   (a) When Dante spoke, <u>Dante</u> got everyone's attention.

   (b) The narrator of the story felt fear, but he did not let <u>the narrator's</u> fear control him.

   (c) The other players watched, and <u>the other players</u> were amazed at the younger man's ability.

2. Write a paragraph about playing basketball. Include at least one type of each noun and one type of each pronoun. Be sure to check your capitalization and punctuation.

Don't Just Sit There Like a Punk 23

SHARE IDEAS

DON'T JUST SIT THERE LIKE A PUNK

TIP: In dialogue, punctuation marks usually come before a closing quotation mark: "I have an idea," said the coach. "Let's try a new strategy."

Writing

One narrative technique that authors often use is **dialogue,** which provides the exact words that characters speak in a story. The words the characters use and how they say them can reveal a lot about their personalities and their relationships.

Quotation marks (" ") are used to set off the spoken words.

Assignment

Reread paragraph 64 of the story. Imagine that the narrator and his father break their silence and have a conversation. Write a **dialogue** showing what they say. Think about these questions as you develop the event and the characters' experiences:

- What do the characters talk about?
- How do the characters' words reflect their personalities and experiences?
- What aspects of the father-son relationship become more clear through dialogue?

Remember to use quotation marks correctly.

Use New Words
Refer to your Word Wall to use new vocabulary you have learned. Also, try to include one or more of these vocabulary words in your writing: *stunned, paralysis, doubt, unexplainable, instinct, intense.*

Reflect on Your Writing

PRACTICE Think about the choices you made as you wrote. Also, consider what you learned by writing. Share your experiences by responding to these questions.

1. Was it challenging or easy to write in the voice of each character? Explain.

2. Which lines of dialogue do you think reveal the most about the characters and their experiences?

3. **Why These Words?** The words you choose make a difference in your writing. Which words did you specifically choose to make the dialogue interesting and expressive?

STANDARDS
Writing
• Write narratives to develop real or imagined experiences or events using effective technique, relevant descriptive details, and well-structured event sequences.
• Use narrative techniques, such as dialogue, pacing, and description, to develop experiences, events, and/or characters.

Speaking and Listening
• Use appropriate eye contact, adequate volume, and clear pronunciation.
• Adapt speech to a variety of contexts and tasks.

24 UNIT 1 • CROSSING GENERATIONS

Essential Question: What can one generation learn from another?

Speaking and Listening

In a **dramatic reading,** the speaker reads a text aloud, clearly pronouncing the words. Tone of voice and gestures help convey what is happening in the story and how the characters feel.

Assignment

Choose one of the passages listed here. Then, develop and deliver a dramatic reading that gives a distinct voice to each character and expresses the emotion of the moment.

- ◯ paragraphs 15–20
- ◯ paragraphs 35–40
- ◯ paragraphs 56–61

Plan Your Dramatic Reading Use the following ideas as you plan your performance.

- Decide where to pause and where to speak more quietly or loudly.
- Mark words that you wish to emphasize.
- Practice any phrases that are tricky to pronounce.
- Consider using gestures for emphasis.

Practice Your Delivery Adapt your speech to suit the context of the passage you chose. Experiment with volume and tone of voice to convey an emotion that a character is feeling, such as anger or joy.

Evaluate Presentations

Use a guide like the one shown to evaluate your own dramatic reading as well as those of your classmates.

PRESENTATION EVALUATION GUIDE

Rate each statement on a scale of 1 (not demonstrated) to 4 (fully demonstrated).

Statement	1	2	3	4
The speaker used adequate volume and clear pronunciation.	◯	◯	◯	◯
The speaker adapted their speech to express the emotion of the scene effectively.	◯	◯	◯	◯
The speaker's delivery showed confidence.	◯	◯	◯	◯

EVIDENCE LOG

Before moving on to a new selection, go to your Evidence Log and record any additional thoughts or observations you may have about "Don't Just Sit There Like a Punk."

Don't Just Sit There Like a Punk

LEARN ABOUT GENRE: NONFICTION

THE CASE OF THE DISAPPEARING WORDS

The selection you are about to read is a feature article.

Reading Feature Articles

A **feature article** is a longer work of journalism that reports information in an in-depth way.

FEATURE ARTICLES

Author's Purpose
- to present information about newsworthy events, issues, or people and explain why they are important and relevant
- to bring readers' attention to a subject in a powerful way

Characteristics
- a title that engages readers' interest
- one or more clear central ideas
- a variety of textual evidence, including quotations, facts, statistics, examples, and anecdotes
- diction, or word choice, that clarifies a complex subject

Structure
- often starts with a "lead," or an engaging first paragraph or section
- may use a variety of organizational patterns that show time order as well as causes or effects

Take a Minute!

FIND IT Think of a subject you enjoy, such as sports or music. Do a quick Internet search to find a feature article related to that subject. Jot down the title and publication.

STANDARDS

Reading Informational Text
- Cite several pieces of textual evidence to support analysis of what the text says explicitly.
- Determine two or more central ideas in a text and analyze their development over the course of the text.

26 UNIT 1 • CROSSING GENERATIONS

Essential Question: What can one generation learn from another?

Central Idea and Supporting Evidence

In a feature article, the author expresses at least one **central idea**—a thesis or main point—in a way that informs and entertains readers. The author weaves together several different kinds of **supporting evidence** to bring the topic to life and to develop the thesis. Readers analyze this explicit textual evidence to determine the author's central ideas.

TIP: A central idea is not a topic. A topic is what an article is about. A central idea is what it means.

EXAMPLE

TYPES OF EVIDENCE	EXAMPLES
facts: statements that can be proved true	In disc golf, players throw Frisbee-like discs into baskets.
statistics: numerical data gained from research	As of 2016, an estimated 12 million people have played disc golf in the United States.
examples: specific instances of a general idea	Disc golf courses will soon be everywhere. For example, Texas currently has 652 courses and more on the way.
anecdotes: brief stories that illustrate a point	I played disc golf on opening day in El Paso. I'm not a great athlete, so it was challenging but still fun.

Central Idea: Disc golf is one of the most exciting new games to come along in years.

> **PRACTICE** Read the paragraph. Cite each type of supporting evidence the author uses and write its letter on the line. (Two letters will not be used.) Then, determine the central idea of the paragraph.
>
> **(a)** Have you ever learned a new language? **(b)** I met my neighbor yesterday, and I was glad I had studied Spanish in school so that I could greet him. **(c)** Spanish is the official language of many countries, including Mexico, Cuba, El Salvador, and Spain. **(d)** There are 486 million native Spanish speakers worldwide. **(e)** That makes it the second-most spoken native language on the planet. **(f)** If you're thinking about studying a new language, consider learning Spanish.
>
> 1. Fact: _____
>
> 2. Statistic: _____
>
> 3. Example: _____
>
> 4. Anecdote: _____
>
> 5. Analyze the evidence the author gives and write a central idea for the paragraph. _____

Learn About Genre **27**

PREPARE TO READ

The Case of the Disappearing Words

About the Author
Alice Andre-Clark was born in Rochester, New York, and now lives in New Jersey. She studied Social Welfare at Harvard Kennedy School and Public Policy at Harvard University Graduate School of Arts and Sciences.

Concept Vocabulary

Preview Listed below are the basic forms of some words that appear in the article.

- Mark any of the words that you have heard or used in conversation or writing.
- Review forms of these words as you read the text that follows.

fluent (FLOO uhnt) *adj.* able to speak or write with ease
Are you fluent in Farsi?

linguist (LIHN gwihst) *n.* person who studies how languages work
My aunt is a linguist who specializes in Chinese dialects.

term (TUHRM) *n.* word or expression that has a specific meaning
The term "catch you later" is an idiom.

lecture (LEHK chuhr) *v.* talk in a critical way that seems unfair
Dad will lecture us on the importance of walking the dog.

record (rih KAWRD) *v.* capture something digitally, such as video or sounds
May I record your speech?

pronounce (pruh NOWNS) *v.* speak words correctly
How do you pronounce this word?

Reading Strategy: Make Predictions

Predictions are guesses you make about the information and ideas a text will include. Informational texts often have structural features that add to or organize the content. Before you read, scan the text for these features. Use the information they provide to make predictions about the article as a whole. Then, see if your predictions are right as you read on.

- **titles and subtitles:** indicate the topic and may suggest a central idea
- **headings:** indicate the ideas that appear in major sections of the text
- **images:** illustrate important ideas or information
- **captions:** suggest how images connect to ideas

> **PRACTICE** Before you read, scan the text features in the article, and use your observations to write three predictions. Then, read on to see if your predictions were accurate.

STANDARDS
Reading Informational Text
Analyze the structure an author uses to organize a text, including how the major sections contribute to the whole.
Language
Gather vocabulary knowledge when considering a word or phrase important to comprehension or expression.

FEATURE ARTICLE

The Case of the Disappearing Words

Saving the World's Endangered Languages

Alice Andre-Clark

BACKGROUND

You already know about endangered animals and plants, living things that are at risk of disappearing from Earth. Alice Andre-Clark believes that many languages are also endangered. But are languages living things? Decide for yourself as you read.

1   During World War II, American Navajo speakers worked with the United States military to create a secret code in their language that the Germans couldn't crack. Now Navajo children are unlikely to grow up speaking the language **fluently**. The Taa language of southern Africa is one of the most complex in the world, combining five distinct clicks of the tongue with other sounds to produce between 80 and 120 different consonants. Today, this unique language has only a few thousand speakers

---

READ TO UNLOCK MEANING

1. First read the text for comprehension and enjoyment. Use the **Reading Strategy** and **Comprehension Check** questions to support your first read.
2. Go back and respond to the Close Read note.
3. Identify other details in the text you find interesting. Ask and answer your own questions.

fluently (FLOO uhnt lee) *adv.* easily and smoothly

Breton is a Celtic language spoken in the Brittany region of France, where parents were once forbidden from giving children Breton names.

linguists (LIHN gwihsts) n. people who study how languages work

MAKE PREDICTIONS
Mark the word *Why* in the heading. What type of text structure might this word signal?

left. Earth is home to around 7,000 languages, but **linguists** are rushing to catalog them because around half are expected to disappear by 2100.

Why They Disappear

2   Languages tend to become endangered when a dominant culture swallows up a smaller culture. Sometimes younger generations stop learning a language because parents want children to fit in and get jobs in the majority culture. Sometimes societies force minorities to give up language and traditions. Many Native American children of the late nineteenth and early twentieth centuries were required to attend boarding schools where educators forbade them from speaking their native

languages. In China today, the government limits the time teachers may speak the language Uighur. Many Uighur language speakers feel their culture may be at risk.

Categories of Danger

3   The United Nations regularly releases lists of endangered languages, placing each in one of five categories. A "vulnerable" language is one that many children speak at home, but few speak outside of their homes. Zuni, spoken by 9,000 of New Mexico's Pueblo peoples, is vulnerable. A "definitely endangered" language is one that older generations speak, but children no longer learn in the home. Dakota, a language of the Great Plains with 675 speakers, is definitely endangered.

4   A "severely endangered" language is one that parents may understand but don't speak much. Grandparents are the primary speakers. Oklahoma's Chickasaw, with 600 speakers, mostly age 50 or older, is one example. A "critically endangered" language is one that few people younger than grandparents speak, and grandparents don't speak it often. New York's and Canada's Onondaga, with about 50 speakers, is critically endangered. An "extinct" language has no living native speakers—the last native speaker of Alaska's Eyak language died in 2008.

Why Save Them?

5   You could ask the same question of an endangered species of animal. Why should we save it? The answer is that having a variety of species benefits our environment. In the same way that different species create biodiversity, languages contribute to cultural diversity. Learning about and protecting endangered languages benefits our understanding of other cultures. A language's vocabulary paints a fascinating picture of a society's way of life. We know a little more about India's Gta' speakers when we learn that they have words like *nosor* (noh SAWR), meaning "to free someone from a tiger," *bno* (buh NOH), "a ladder made from a single bamboo tree," and *gotae* (goh TA), "to bring something from a hard-to-reach place with a long stick."

6   Languages can show how a society looks at the world and what it values. In Apache culture, a sense of place is so important that storytellers use descriptive names for land features, such as "White Rocks Lie Above in a Compact Cluster." Facing setbacks with laughter is important in the Jewish tradition, so it may not be surprising that the Jewish language Yiddish has words to describe two kinds of fools. A *schlemiel* is the kind who spills soup on other people, and the unlucky *schlimazel* is the one on whom soup always gets spilled.

CLOSE READ

ANNOTATE In paragraph 5, mark words from another language and their definitions.

QUESTION Why does the author call attention to these particular words and definitions?

COMPREHENSION CHECK

What is the difference between a "vulnerable language" and a "definitely endangered language"?

term (TUHRM) *n.* word or expression that has a specific meaning

lecture (LEHK chuhr) *v.* talk in a critical way that seems unfair

7   A language may contain hidden knowledge that the rest of the world has not yet discovered. The **term** for eelgrass in Mexico's Seri language alerted scientists that eelgrass, unlike most sea grasses, is a nutritious food. The Seri word *moosni hant cooit* (mohs nee ahnt koh eet), meaning "green turtle that descends," revealed something no one else knew—that green turtles hibernate, or overwinter, on the sea floor.

8   A language may describe something in a way that is funny, sharp, or beautifully poetic. In Welsh, it rains not cats and dogs, but old wives and walking sticks. If a Basque speaker tells you, "Don't take the beans out of your lap," you're being asked not to get on your high horse and **lecture** (which would probably be hard to do with a lap full of beans). The elegant Seri term for a car muffler means "into which the breathing descends."

9   Sometimes a language provides the exact right way to describe something that always needed a great word. The Cherokee word *ukvhisdi* (oh kuh huhs dee) is what you say to a cute baby

Garifuna is the last living remnant of languages once spoken by native peoples in the Caribbean islands. Now it's spoken mainly in Belize, Honduras, and Guatemala.

or kitten. If your neighbor pops in every day, you might be dealing with what the Ojibway call *mawadishiweshkiwin*, the habit of making visits too often. The Cheyenne capture a hilariously embarrassing moment with *mémestátamao'ó*, to laugh so hard you fart.

How to Save a Language

10   Linguists at projects like the Endangered Language Alliance are working to learn from speakers of disappearing languages, **recording** them singing songs, telling stories, **pronouncing** common words like the names of the colors, and explaining vocabulary that is important in their culture, such as the words that describe traditional arts or native plants.

11   Yet many speakers of endangered languages aren't content just to preserve scraps of their native languages in a digital museum. They hope that new generations will learn them, and that they will again become living languages. Different cultures have come up with different ways of bringing their languages back to life. Cherokee speakers can use an app that lets them text in their native alphabet. Yiddish speakers can enjoy weekly radio shows. In Wales, a community of writers is producing new science fiction (they had to come up with a Welsh word for "alien"), and young people in Chile are performing Huilliche-language hip-hop songs.

12   If an endangered language is going to make a real comeback, it'll probably get its start in schools. From 1896 to 1986, public schools in Hawaii did not teach the Hawaiian language. Then educators began opening "language nests," preschools where kids speak nothing but Hawaiian. Now there are elementary schools where kids not only take most classes in Hawaiian, but also learn about native traditions like gardening with Hawaiian plants and extending hospitality. Students can keep learning in Hawaiian into college and beyond—the University of Hawaii offers a Ph.D. in the Hawaiian language.

Me'phaa is a language of Guerrero, Mexico, where Spanish dominates.

recording (rih KAWR dihng) *v.* storing sounds in a form, such as a digital file, so that they can be heard again in the future

pronouncing (pruh NOWN sihng) *v.* speaking words correctly

The Case of the Disappearing Words

The Language That Came Back to Life

13 Can a language with zero native speakers come back to life? At least one did. In 1881, a Jewish newspaper editor and linguist named Eliezer Ben-Yehuda immigrated to Jerusalem. Ben-Yehuda imagined the founding of a Jewish nation, and he thought that nation needed a language of its own. Back then, people learned Hebrew mostly just to read religious texts, but it was no one's native language. He and his wife decided to raise their family to speak nothing but Hebrew.

14 Ben-Yehuda realized that the 3,000-year-old language needed two kinds of help. First, it had to have young speakers. He persuaded teachers and rabbis to hold all their classes in Hebrew. Second, Hebrew needed lots of new words. He wrote a dictionary that added new words to this ancient language for modern things like dolls, omelets, ice cream, and bicycles. Hebrew grew from 8,000 words to 50,000. Today it is one of the official languages of Israel, with over 4 million speakers.

COMPREHENSION CHECK
What are some ways people are trying to save endangered languages?

Gurung is a Tibeto-Burman language from the Himalayas in Nepal.

BUILD INSIGHT

First Thoughts

Select one of the following questions to answer.

- What do you find most interesting or important about this article? Why?
- What new idea about language and culture has this article revealed to you?

Summary

Write a short summary of the article to confirm your comprehension. Remember to include only the central ideas and to keep your summary objective and free of personal opinions.

Analysis

1. **Analyze Cause and Effect** According to the author, what are the main reasons languages are disappearing?

2. **(a) Analyze** According to the author, how does a culture's language show what life is like for the people who speak it? Explain.
   (b) Support Cite two examples from the article that support your response.

3. **(a) Draw Conclusions** Based on the article, what can you conclude is an important element of any effort to save an endangered language? Explain your answer, citing textual evidence. **(b) Connect** Why do you think this element is so important?

Exploring the Essential Question

What can one generation learn from another?

4. What have you learned about crossing generations by reading "The Case of the Disappearing Words"? For example, should people be responsible for passing down knowledge of language and culture to younger generations? Why or why not? Record your ideas in your Evidence Log.

STANDARDS
Reading Informational Text
- Cite several pieces of textual evidence to support analysis of what the text says explicitly as well as inferences drawn from the text.
- Provide an objective summary of the text.

The Case of the Disappearing Words 35

ANALYZE AND INTERPRET

THE CASE OF THE DISAPPEARING WORDS

Close Read

1. The model passage and annotation show how one reader analyzed paragraph 11. Find another detail in the passage to annotate. Then, write your own question and conclusion.

CLOSE-READ MODEL

Yet many speakers of endangered languages aren't content just to **preserve scraps of their native languages in a digital museum.** They hope that new generations will learn them, and that they will again become living languages. Different cultures have come up with different ways of **bringing their languages back to life.**

ANNOTATE: There is an interesting contrast between these phrases.

QUESTION: Why does the author emphasize this contrast?

CONCLUDE: The contrast highlights the difference between preserving bits of a dying language and keeping languages alive.

MY QUESTION:

MY CONCLUSION:

2. For more practice, answer the Close-Read question in the selection.

3. Choose a section of the feature article you found especially meaningful. Mark important details. Then, jot down questions and write your conclusions in the open space next to the text.

Inquiry and Research

Research and Extend Choose a culture or an organization named in the article and write a question about it. Conduct brief research to answer your question. Then, extend your learning by generating two additional questions you could use to guide further investigation. Use both print and digital sources to gather relevant information. For internet research, use effective search terms, such as the name of the culture or organization you chose.

STANDARDS

Reading Informational Text
• Cite several pieces of textual evidence to support analysis of what the text says explicitly as well as inferences drawn from the text.
• Determine two or more central ideas in a text and analyze their development over the course of the text.

Writing
• Conduct short research projects to answer a question, drawing on several sources and generating additional related, focused questions for further research and investigation.
• Gather relevant information from multiple print and digital sources, using search terms effectively.

36 UNIT 1 • CROSSING GENERATIONS

Essential Question: What can one generation learn from another?

Multiple Central Ideas

Feature articles present information in ways that keep readers interested and build **multiple central ideas**, or more than one main point. The writer uses **supporting evidence**—such as facts, statistics, examples, and anecdotes—to develop each central idea over the course of the text. Readers analyze this evidence to determine the article's central ideas.

> **TIP:** Each section or paragraph of an article develops a central idea that contributes to the central idea of the text as a whole.

A typical informational text follows this structure:
- an introduction that states the central idea of the text as a whole
- body paragraphs that develop multiple central ideas with evidence
- a conclusion that reinforces the text's central idea and presents an insight

PRACTICE Complete the activity and answer the questions.

1. **Analyze** Reread paragraph 1. Use the chart to cite the different types of evidence used to support the central idea of the paragraph.

CENTRAL IDEA: The diversity of languages people currently speak is declining very quickly.		
TYPE OF EVIDENCE	**EXAMPLE FROM PARAGRAPH**	**HOW IT SUPPORTS CENTRAL IDEA**
FACT		
STATISTIC		
EXAMPLE		
ANECDOTE		

2. (a) **Analyze** Reread paragraphs 13–14. What central idea is developed in these paragraphs? (b) **Support** What evidence supports it?

3. **Interpret** Determine the central idea of the article as a whole.

4. **Analyze** Explore how the text's structure develops the central idea of the article as a whole: (a) Which paragraphs make up the introduction? (b) Where does the author provide evidence to develop the article's central idea? (c) How do the headings help to develop the article's overall central idea? (d) With what memorable point does the writer conclude?

The Case of the Disappearing Words

STUDY LANGUAGE AND CRAFT

THE CASE OF THE DISAPPEARING WORDS

Concept Vocabulary

Why These Words? All of the vocabulary words relate to language as an idea. For example, *linguists* study language and may listen to a *recording* of native speakers.

| fluently | linguists | term |
| lecture | recording | pronouncing |

WORD WALL

Note words in the text that are related to the idea of crossing generations. Add them to your Word Wall.

PRACTICE Answer the question and complete the activity.

1. How might your knowledge of these vocabulary words help you discuss languages more precisely?

2. Use one vocabulary word to complete each sentence.

   (a) The reporter is _____ his interview for a broadcast tomorrow.

   (b) It takes practice to speak a foreign language _____.

   (c) Before her trip to Spain, Amy practiced _____ words in Spanish.

   (d) People are more likely to take your advice if you don't _____ them.

   (e) *Scarlet* is a more specific _____ for the color red.

   (f) Some _____ study how children learn language.

Word Study

Latin Root Word: *lingua* The Latin root word *lingua* means "language" or "tongue." The vocabulary word *linguists* is built on this root word.

PRACTICE Complete the following items.

1. Explain how the root word *lingua* provides a clue to the meaning of the word *linguist*.

2. The prefix *bi-* means "two." Given this information, explain what you think *bilingual* means. Use a dictionary to verify your definition.

3. Write a sentence that correctly uses the word *linguists*.

STANDARDS

Reading Informational Text
Determine an author's point of view or purpose in a text and analyze how the author distinguishes his or her position from that of others.

Language
Use common, grade-appropriate Greek or Latin affixes and roots as clues to the meaning of a word.

Essential Question: What can one generation learn from another?

Author's Purpose

Every author has a unique reason for writing, which makes their work distinct from that of other writers. This **author's purpose** is revealed through the writer's choices about language, text sections and features, and overall organization.

- **Diction:** An author's choice of words suggests their purpose. The use of formal, scientific words, for example, suggests a purpose of educating or informing readers.

- **Syntax:** Varied sentence structures can help authors achieve different purposes. Short, breezy sentences, for example, may create a humorous effect.

- **Text Sections / Features:** A text's title and subtitle may offer clues to an author's purpose. The same is true for the ways in which information is organized. Are headings or images used? If so, what purposes do they help to fulfill?

TIP: An author may have multiple purposes for writing, even within a single text. To target specific audiences who have different needs and interests, an author may write to persuade, inform, entertain, describe, recount, instruct, reflect, or a combination of these purposes.

PRACTICE Answer the questions and complete the activity.

1. **Draw Conclusions** What do the text's title and subtitle suggest about the author's purpose for writing? Explain your thinking.

2. **(a)** What text features and overall organization are present in the text?
   (b) Analyze What effect has the author achieved by making these organizational choices?

3. **Analyze** Complete the chart to analyze the author's use of diction and syntax in a few sections of the text. The first row has been done for you.

SECTION	DICTION / SYNTAX	EFFECT
Paragraph 3	use of formal words, definitions, and data / complex, declarative sentences	It seems as if the author is teaching readers in this section.
Paragraph 8		

4. **Draw Conclusions** Review your responses to items 1–3. Based on your responses, what is the author's purpose for writing?

The Case of the Disappearing Words **39**

SHARE IDEAS

THE CASE OF THE DISAPPEARING WORDS

TIP: Be sure to paraphrase the information you find. When you **paraphrase**, you restate in your own words something that has been written by someone else. When you **summarize** a text, you briefly describe its main points.

STANDARDS
Writing
Gather relevant information from multiple print and digital sources, using search terms effectively; assess the credibility and accuracy of each source; and quote or paraphrase the data and conclusions of others.

Speaking and Listening
Present claims and findings, emphasizing salient points in a focused, coherent manner with pertinent descriptions, facts, details, and examples; use appropriate eye contact, adequate volume, and clear pronunciation.

Language
Consult general and specialized reference materials, both print and digital, to find the pronunciation of a word or determine or clarify its precise meaning or its part of speech.

Writing

A **travel guide** is a type of writing that provides visitors with information to better appreciate a place. It may offer suggestions for sites to visit as well as explanations of an area's culture and language.

Assignment

Write a **travel guide entry** about a place in the world that is experiencing threats to its language. Gather relevant information from multiple print and digital sources, such as an encyclopedia and a web article. Paraphrase your findings by answering the following questions in your own words:

- Who speaks the language?
- Why is the language threatened?
- Are any efforts being made to save it? If so, what are they?

Finally, choose two words or phrases from the language that have particularly interesting meanings to include in your entry.

Use New Words
Refer to your Word Wall to use new vocabulary you have learned. Also, try to include one or more of these vocabulary words in your writing: *fluently, linguists, term, lecture, recording, pronouncing.*

Reflect on Your Writing

PRACTICE Think about the choices you made as you wrote. Also, consider what you learned by writing. Share your experiences by responding to these questions.

1. What was your favorite part of this activity—researching or writing about what you learned? Explain.

2. What was the most interesting thing you learned from your research? Why?

3. **Why These Words?** The words you choose make a difference in your writing. Which words did you specifically choose to strengthen your description of an endangered language? Why?

40 UNIT 1 • CROSSING GENERATIONS

Essential Question: What can one generation learn from another?

Speaking and Listening

An **oral presentation** is a speech that provides an audience with useful information about a topic.

Assignment

Choose an endangered language from the article. Research words from that language and select three that interest you. Then, deliver an **oral presentation** of your findings. Present basic information about the language—emphasizing important points with details and descriptions—and explain the example words you selected.

- Consult specialized reference materials, such as online translators, to find the pronunciations of your chosen words and to determine their precise meanings and parts of speech.
- You may have come across English words in your research that you don't know or aren't sure how to pronounce. Use a general dictionary to find their pronunciations and to clarify their precise meanings and parts of speech.
- To communicate well with the audience and keep them engaged, speak loudly and clearly and make eye contact periodically during your presentation.

Evaluate Presentations

Use a guide like the one shown to evaluate your own presentation as well as those of your classmates.

PRESENTATION EVALUATION GUIDE

Rate each statement on a scale of 1 (not demonstrated) to 4 (fully demonstrated).

Statement	1	2	3	4
The speaker presented their findings with key points about the chosen language.	○	○	○	○
The speaker presented three example words and their pronunciations, meanings, and parts of speech.	○	○	○	○
The speaker spoke clearly, used appropriate volume, and made eye contact with the audience.	○	○	○	○

USE NEW WORDS
Academic Vocabulary

Use the unit's academic vocabulary words as you discuss the presentations.

- dialogue
- consequence
- perspective
- notable
- contradict

EVIDENCE LOG

Before moving on to a new selection, go to your Evidence Log and record any additional thoughts or observations you may have about "The Case of the Disappearing Words."

PERFORMANCE TASK

Write a Personal Narrative

A **personal narrative** is a true story about a meaningful event in which the writer communicates a message about their life.

Assignment

Write a **personal narrative** that answers this question:

What experience helped you see how people of different generations can influence one another?

Include details about a conflict you faced and the reasons the experience was important. Use the elements of personal narratives in your writing.

Use Academic Vocabulary

Try to use the unit's academic vocabulary words in your narrative: *dialogue, consequence, perspective, notable, contradict.*

WRITING CENTER

Visit the Writing Center to watch video tutorials and view annotated student models and rubrics.

ELEMENTS OF PERSONAL NARRATIVES

Purpose: to share a real-life story that is meaningful to you

Characteristics

- first-person point of view, with you as the narrator
- a clear focus on a specific experience
- a conflict, or problem, related to the experience
- characters and settings that are real people and places
- reflection on the deeper meaning of the experience
- narrative techniques, such as dialogue, pacing, and description
- standard English conventions

Structure

- a well-organized structure that includes
  - an engaging beginning
  - a chronological sequence of events
  - a strong ending, or conclusion

STANDARDS
Writing
• Write narratives to develop real or imagined experiences or events using effective technique, relevant descriptive details, and well-structured event sequences.

• Use narrative techniques, such as dialogue, pacing, and description, to develop experiences, events, and/or characters.

• Provide a conclusion that follows from and reflects on the narrated experiences or events.

• Produce clear and coherent writing in which the development, organization, and style are appropriate to task, purpose, and audience.

42 UNIT 1 • CROSSING GENERATIONS

Essential Question: What can one generation learn from another?

Take a Closer Look at the Assignment

1. What is the assignment asking me to do (in my own words)?

2. Is a specific **audience** mentioned in the assignment?
   - ○ Yes   If "yes," who is my main audience?
   - ○ No   If "no," who do I think my audience is or should be?

   > **AUDIENCE**
   >
   > Your **audience** is your reader.
   > - Choose an experience that will engage readers' curiosity.
   > - Describe people or places with which your audience may not be familiar.

3. Is my **purpose** for writing specified in the assignment?
   - ○ Yes   If "yes," what is the purpose?
   - ○ No   If "no," why am I writing this narrative (not just because it's an assignment)?

   > **PURPOSE**
   >
   > A specific **purpose**, or reason, for writing leads to a more focused narrative.
   > **Vague Purpose:** *I'll write about fishing.*
   > **Specific Purpose:** *I'll write about the day my aunt taught me to fish.*

Write Your Personal Narrative

Review the assignment and your notes, and then begin writing your narrative. Keep these tips in mind:

- You are the person telling the story. Choose words and details that reflect your own experiences.
- Use descriptive details and sensory language to help readers picture the setting, people, and events in your narrative.
- Consider creating passages of dialogue, letting some plot events and character development take place in the course of conversation.
- Be sure to include an insight or reflection about your experience in your conclusion.

Writer's Handbook If you need help as you plan, draft, revise, and edit, refer to the Writer's Handbook pages that follow.

Performance Task: Write a Personal Narrative 43

WRITER'S HANDBOOK | **PERSONAL NARRATIVE**

Planning and Prewriting

Before you draft, discover the narrative you want to tell. Complete the activities to get started.

Discover Your Topic: Freewrite!

Topics for a personal narrative come mainly from your memories. These experiences establish an engaging context and point of view, with you as the narrator. Write freely for three minutes without stopping. Try one of these strategies to begin.

- Imagine a photo album of your life. Choose one image and write about it.
- List places you associate with strong feelings. Freewrite about one.
- Recall conversations that mattered to you. Freewrite about one.

> **Using the Writer's Handbook**
>
> In this handbook you'll find strategies to support every stage of the writing process—from planning to publishing. As you write, check in with yourself:
> - What's going well?
> - What isn't going well?
>
> Then, use the handbook items that will best help you craft a strong narrative.

WRITE What experience helped you see how people of different generations can influence one another?

_____
_____
_____
_____
_____
_____
_____
_____
_____
_____
_____
_____
_____
_____

STANDARDS

Writing • Write narratives to develop real or imagined experiences or events using effective technique, relevant descriptive details, and well-structured event sequences. • Engage and orient the reader by establishing a context and point of view and introducing a narrator and/or characters; organize an event sequence that unfolds naturally and logically.

Structure Your Narrative: Make a Plan

A **Choose a Focus** Review your planning notes and pull out the strongest idea. Describe it here in a few words.

_____
_____

B **Write Your Message** Write one sentence that explains what you learned from this experience. Also, list strong descriptive details you want to make sure to include.

_____
_____
_____

> **MESSAGE**
>
> Your **message,** or central idea, is the insight you want your narrative to convey. Hint at this message early in your narrative to help explain its personal value.

C **Plan a Structure** Plan how you will describe the **sequence of events** so that readers understand who was involved, what happened, and where and when events occurred. In addition, think about pacing, or the speed at which events unfold.

Who was involved?

_____
_____

What happened?

_____
_____
_____

Where and when did events happen?

_____
_____

How did the experience end?

_____
_____
_____

> **SEQUENCE OF EVENTS**
>
> The **sequence,** or order, of events in a narrative should flow in a logical way that readers can follow.
>
> - Begin by establishing the setting and the people who were involved in the experience.
> - Describe how a conflict or problem arose and what people did as a result.
> - Use chronological order, narrating events in the order in which they occurred.
> - Show how the conflict ended.
> - Include a section of reflection in which you discuss the deeper meaning of the experience.

WRITER'S HANDBOOK

Writer's Handbook: Personal Narrative

Writer's Handbook | Personal Narrative

Drafting

Apply the planning work you've done and write a first draft. Consider how you will develop your characters to bring them to life for readers.

Read Like a Writer

Mark details in this passage from the Mentor Text that give you a vivid sense of the grandfather and his garden. One observation has been done for you.

MENTOR TEXT

from **Grandfather's Garden**

My grandfather's fruit and vegetable garden encompassed a large portion of my grandparents' sizable backyard. ==Because of his physical limitations, the work he did there was slow and labored,== but he did almost all of it himself. He took great pride in the quality and quantity of his produce, and he had good reason to be proud: the garden was both beautiful and plentiful. I longed to explore it but never had. I felt like that would be intruding, and I wasn't sure he would want me in his special space.

> These details help describe the grandfather's physical appearance.

> Mark specific details that help you envision the setting.

WRITE Follow the Mentor Text example by using vivid details to portray someone who plays an important role in your narrative.

_____
_____
_____
_____
_____
_____
_____
_____

DEVELOP IDEAS

As you draft the rest of your narrative, make your writing vivid and precise.

- **Conflict** Make sure you clearly show the conflict and why it was important.
- **Characters** Show how people look and act.
- **Setting** Use specific details to help readers picture places in your narrative.
- **Development** Create a clear sequence of events.

STANDARDS
Writing • Write narratives to develop real or imagined experiences or events using effective technique, relevant descriptive details, and well-structured event sequences. **Language** • Demonstrate command of the conventions of standard English grammar and usage when writing or speaking.

46 UNIT 1 • CROSSING GENERATIONS

Coherence and Craft

A **coherent** piece of writing "holds together" and conveys a unified whole. Use these strategies to create coherence in your narrative.

- Write a beginning that gives a clear sense of what your narrative is about and who is involved.
- Use vivid details and precise verbs to show what people do and say.
- Use correct **pronoun-antecedent agreement** so that readers always know to whom you are referring.

> **PRONOUN-ANTECEDENT AGREEMENT**
>
> A **pronoun** is a word you can use in place of a noun or another pronoun. The **antecedent** is the word or words the pronoun replaces. A personal pronoun must agree with its antecedent in person, number, and gender.

PERSONAL PRONOUNS

	Always Singular	Singular or Plural	Always Plural
First Person	I, me, my, mine		we, us, our, ours
Second Person		you, your, yours	
Third Person	it, its, she, her, hers, he, him, his	they, them, their, theirs	

In these examples, notice that each underlined pronoun agrees with its highlighted antecedent in person, number, and gender:

- *I reminded* Grandma Sofia *to bring the car keys with* her.
- My parents *were concerned. I heard* them *talking.*

In this example, the underlined pronoun is vague. The antecedent of *they* is not stated; it is implied in an unclear, generalized way.

- *I think of Hank as a nice guy, but* they *tell me he can be a bully.*

WRITE Write a scene from your narrative. Use clear and correct pronoun-antecedent agreement.

_____
_____
_____
_____
_____
_____
_____

> **AGREEMENT IN NUMBER**
>
> **RULE:** When two singular antecedents are joined by "and," treat them as a plural pronoun.
>
> **EXAMPLE:**
> *Ann and Emma* finished *their* work.
>
> **RULE:** When two singular antecedents are joined by "or" or "nor," treat them as a singular pronoun.
>
> **EXAMPLE:**
> Neither *Ann nor Emma* finished *her* work.

Writer's Handbook: Personal Narrative

WRITER'S HANDBOOK | PERSONAL NARRATIVE

Revising

Now that you have a first draft, revise it to be sure it describes events and conveys meaning as vividly as possible.

Read Like a Writer

Review the revisions made to the Mentor Text. In particular, notice how the writer replaced vague, dull language with precise wording and descriptive and sensory details to make the narrative more exact and engaging. Then, complete the activities in the white boxes.

MENTOR TEXT

from Grandfather's Garden

When I was twelve years old, I spent an entire week at my grandparents' house. On the day I arrived, my grandmother and I brewed a pitcher of iced tea and brought it out to the backyard. As usual, my grandfather was toiling in his sea of greenery. It was a warm day, and my grandmother called him over to rest in the shade and have a cool drink. He ~~came over~~ *shuffled slowly towards us* and plopped down into the patio chair next to mine. With a shaky hand he reached over and held out a plump red strawberry to me. Then he leaned in a bit closer to speak.

~~In his gravelly voice, he asked if I like strawberries.~~ *"You like strawberries?" he asked in his gravelly voice.* I nodded timidly but didn't look at him. ~~Then he told me to eat it.~~ *"Go ahead and eat it," he encouraged.*

~~I took the berry and ate it.~~ *I took the shiny berry from his hand, slid it into my mouth, and bit down. It was perfectly ripe, sweet, and juicy.* I looked my grandfather in the face and smiled, still timid. He chuckled, and one corner of his droopy mouth turned up. He was smiling too.

"Want another?" he tempted. I nodded that I ~~did.~~ *did, more confidently now.*

> Mark words that describe what the characters experienced with their five senses.

> Why do you think the writer made a different word choice?

> The use of dialogue helps to develop grandfather's character and improves the pacing of the scene.

> Why do you think the writer replaced this sentence?

> The addition of a precise phrase captures how the writer's feelings are changing.

STANDARDS

Writing • Use a variety of transition words, phrases, and clauses to convey sequence and signal shifts from one time frame or setting to another.
• Use precise words and phrases, relevant descriptive details, and sensory language to capture the action and convey experiences and events.
Language Choose language that expresses ideas precisely and concisely, recognizing and eliminating wordiness and redundancy.

48 UNIT 1 • CROSSING GENERATIONS

Take a Closer Look at Your Draft

Use the Revision Checklist for Personal Narrative to evaluate and strengthen your narrative.

REVISION CHECKLIST FOR PERSONAL NARRATIVE

EVALUATE	TAKE ACTION
Clarity	
☐ Is the message of my narrative clear?	If the point of your narrative isn't clear, **revise** your conclusion. **Add** information that follows from and reflects on your experience and **explain** what it taught you.
☐ Will readers who do not know me understand my narrative?	Imagine that you do not know anything about your own story. **Add** information that is missing. For example, instead of writing *Leah attached the fishing line*, write *My cousin Leah attached the fishing line*.
Development	
☐ Is my narrative complete?	**Add** another scene or **clarify** reactions so that your readers fully understand your experience and your message.
☐ Have I used a variety of techniques to show what happened?	If your narrative seems dull or repetitive, introduce variety. **Add** descriptive details, **replace** explanations with dialogue, and **delete** unimportant details that slow down the pacing of the storytelling.
Organization	
☐ Does the event sequence make sense?	**Picture** each event in your mind to make sure it unfolds naturally and logically. If not, **number** the events in your draft, **reorganize** details, and then remove the numbering.
☐ Have I used transitions effectively	Be sure to **include** a variety of transitions to convey the sequence of events. If you haven't, **insert** them to signal shifts from one time frame or setting to another.
Style	
☐ Have I used dialogue and description effectively?	**Replace** lengthy explanations with dialogue. **Add** descriptive details to develop events and characters' experiences fully. **Include** sensory language to bring scenes to life.
☐ Does my narrative ramble or lose focus?	**Remove** unnecessary scenes or ideas that distract from your message. **Replace** vague language and wordy passages with precise, concise choices.

WRITER'S HANDBOOK — PERSONAL NARRATIVE

Editing

Don't let errors weaken the power of your narrative. Reread your draft and fix mistakes to create a finished work.

Read Like a Writer

Look at how the writer of the Mentor Text edited an early draft. Then, follow the directions in the white boxes.

MENTOR TEXT

from **Grandfather's Garden**

After a few minutes, he ~~He~~ stood up—with a little effort—and started shuffling back into the garden. Then he stopped, turned around, and gestured for me to join him. I followed him through his wonderland of vegetation to the strawberry patch at the far end. There, the two of us munched until every one of those delicious strawberries was gone. Neither of us said much; nonetheless, I recognized that we were sharing a very special moment. I felt like I was finally connecting with my Grandfather.

We spent the remainder of the afternoon in the garden. In fact, I spent every afternoon that week in the glory of the garden with my grandfather. He told me the Names of all his plants and, with effort, showed us how to care for each one. He taught me the best types of soil to use for various species of fruits and vegetables…

- The writer added a transitional phrase to show the passage of time.
- Correct two capitalization errors.
- Fix the incorrect pronoun-antecedent agreement.

Focus on Sentences

Pronoun-Antecedent Agreement Using pronouns in place of some nouns makes your storytelling sound more natural and your sentences less repetitive. Keep in mind that a personal pronoun must agree with its antecedent in person, number, and gender. For example:

Incorrect Person: *Drivers* know *you* have to obey speed limits.

Correct Person: *Drivers* know *they* have to obey speed limits.

> **PRACTICE** Fix errors in pronoun-antecedent agreement in these sentences. Then, check your own draft for correctness.
>
> 1. Mom hesitated but agreed to drive us in your car.
> 2. She chose songs to sing based on whether it inspired her.
> 3. Mom loved singing at the top of your lungs.

EDITING TIPS
- Mark the antecedent and consider its person, number, and gender.
- Mark any pronoun that goes with the antecedent and make sure the person, number, and gender match.

50 UNIT 1 • CROSSING GENERATIONS

Focus on Capitalization and Punctuation

Capitalization: Proper Nouns A common noun names a person, a place, a thing, or an idea and does not have to be capitalized. A proper noun names a specific person, place, thing, or idea and must be capitalized.

EXAMPLES:

I knew that Grandmother was not just another grandmother. Her car was a Chevy Impala.

Drive east of the Rocky Mountains. Then, hike the rocky path.

Punctuation: Dialogue Follow these rules to punctuate dialogue correctly:

- Place every word spoken aloud inside quotation marks.
  EXAMPLE: "Mac," I said, "you're not making sense."

- Set a new paragraph for each new speaker.
  EXAMPLE: "I know I'm right," she replied.

    "No, you're not," Mike insisted. "This is crazy."

- If the dialogue requires punctuation, place it inside the quotation mark.
  EXAMPLE: "This is exciting!" Elle exclaimed.

- Use a comma to separate dialogue from narration.
  EXAMPLE: I asked the group, "What do we do now?"

EDITING TIP
Read your narrative aloud to catch errors and check that dialogue sounds natural.

PRACTICE Correct capitalization and punctuation errors in the sentences. Then, review your own draft for correctness.

1. Dad, grandma's Red Convertible is important to her I said

2. Will you teach me to grow tomatoes I asked. I'd be happy to he replied

3. We drove to austin, Texas, to see her old Apartment Building.

Publishing and Presenting

Integrate Media

Share your personal narrative with the class. Choose one of these options.

OPTION 1 Create a **slideshow** based on your narrative. You can use existing photos or make illustrations to scan and upload.

OPTION 2 Record yourself reading aloud your personal narrative to share as part of a class **podcast**. Consider adding music and sound effects to enhance your recording.

STANDARDS
Writing
Use technology, including the Internet, to produce and publish writing.

Language
• Demonstrate command of the conventions of standard English grammar and usage when writing or speaking.

• Demonstrate command of the conventions of standard English capitalization, punctuation, and spelling when writing.

Writer's Handbook: Personal Narrative

PEER-GROUP LEARNING

Essential Question

What can one generation learn from another?

What people value can change from one generation to the next, but there are always some common threads despite these differences. You can gain new insight and knowledge when you understand the values and challenges facing other generations. You will work in a group to continue your exploration of the relationship between generations.

Peer-Group Learning Strategies

Throughout your life, in school, in your community, and in your career, you will continue to learn and work with others.

Look at these strategies and the actions you can take to practice them as you work in small groups. Add ideas of your own for each category. Use these strategies during Peer-Group Learning.

STRATEGY	MY ACTION PLAN
Prepare	• Complete your assignments so that you are prepared for group work. • Take notes on your reading so that you can share ideas with others in your group. •
Participate fully	• Make eye contact to signal that you are paying attention. • Use text evidence when making a point. •
Support others	• Build off ideas from others in your group. • Ask others who have not yet spoken to do so. •
Clarify	• Paraphrase the ideas of others to be sure your understanding is correct. • Ask follow-up questions. •

Contents

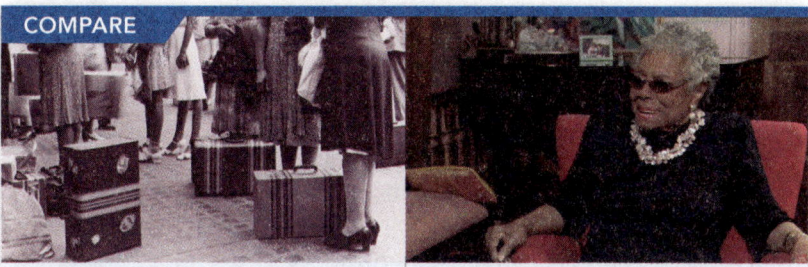

COMPARE

MEMOIR

from Mom & Me & Mom
Maya Angelou

Can forgiveness and love overcome disappointment and sadness?

MEDIA: TELEVISION INTERVIEW

Learning to Love My Mother
Maya Angelou with Michael Maher

Maya Angelou talks about her complicated relationship with her mother.

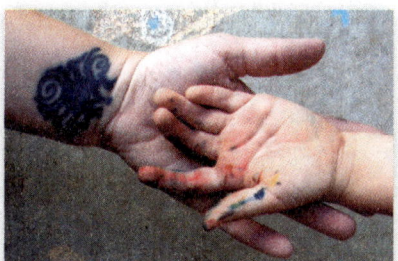

MEDIA: IMAGE GALLERY

Mother-Daughter Drawings
Mica and Myla Hendricks

What happens when an artist collaborates with her four-year-old child?

POETRY COLLECTION 1

Ode to My Papi
Guadalupe García McCall

Mother to Son
Langston Hughes

To James
Frank Horne

The bonds between generations are stronger than the difficulties of life.

PERFORMANCE TASK

SPEAKING AND LISTENING

Present a Personal Narrative

The Peer-Group readings explore the insights that people of different generations share with each other. After reading, your group will present autobiographical anecdotes about learning from people of different generations.

Peer-Group Learning 53

PEER-GROUP LEARNING

Working as a Group

1. Discuss the Topic

With your group, discuss the following question:

What kinds of ideas and experiences can young people and adults share?

As you take turns speaking, work to create an open and meaningful exchange of ideas. Listen to one another carefully. Share thoughtful examples that illustrate your ideas. After all group members have shared, discuss the similarities and differences among your responses.

2. List Your Rules

As a group, decide on the rules that you will follow as you work together. Two samples are provided. Add two more of your own. You may add or revise rules as you work through the selections and activities together.

- Everyone should participate in group discussions.
- People should not interrupt.
- _____
- _____

3. Apply the Rules

Practice working as a group, following your rules to ensure a friendly discussion. Share what you've discovered about the types of things young people and adults might have in common. Make sure each person in the group contributes. Take notes and be prepared to share with the class one thing that you heard from another group member.

4. Create a Communication Plan

Decide how you want to communicate with one another. For example, you might use online collaboration tools, email, or instant messaging.

Our group's plan: _____

STANDARDS

Speaking and Listening • Engage effectively in a range of collaborative discussions with diverse partners on grade 7 topics, texts, and issues, building on others' ideas and expressing their own clearly. • Come to discussions prepared, having read or researched material under study; explicitly draw on that preparation by referring to evidence on the topic, text, or issue to probe and reflect on ideas under discussion. • Follow rules for collegial discussions, track progress toward specific goals and deadlines.

Essential Question: What can one generation learn from another?

Making a Schedule

First, find out the due dates for the peer-group activities. Then, preview the texts and activities with your group and make a schedule for completing the tasks.

SELECTION	ACTIVITIES	DUE DATE
• from Mom & Me & Mom • Learning to Love My Mother		
Mother-Daughter Drawings		
• Ode to My Papi • Mother to Son • To James		

Using Textual Evidence

When you respond to your reading, use textual evidence to support your ideas. Draw on knowledge you've gained from the material to analyze the texts and to support, question, or build on the author's ideas. Apply these tips to choose the right evidence for any purpose.

Understand the Question: Different kinds of questions call for different kinds of evidence. For example, if you are *analyzing*, you are looking for specific details. If you are *interpreting*, you are looking for specific details that connect to build a larger meaning.

Notice Key Details: Notice details that stand out and make you feel strongly about a character or an idea. These details are probably important and may become textual evidence to support your position or interpretation.

Evaluate Your Choices: The evidence you use should clearly relate to the question you are answering. For example, if a question asks about a character's actions, choose evidence that shows the events, thoughts, or feelings that led them to behave in a certain way. Other details may be interesting but are not relevant.

Use strong and effective textual evidence to support your responses as you read, discuss, and write about the selections.

Peer-Group Learning 55

COMPARE ACROSS GENRES

NONFICTION and MEDIA
A **memoir** is a type of literary nonfiction in which an author shares memories of his or her life. A **television interview** is a structured conversation between two or more people that is aired on a television show.

MEMOIR

Author's Purpose
- to relate true experiences and express insights about them

Characteristics
- based on memories and true events
- uses narrative techniques, such as dialogue and description
- uses first-person point of view
- presents characters who are real people
- takes place in a certain setting, or time and place
- focuses on a specific time in or aspect of the writer's life

Structure
- often, relates events in chronological order
- may be organized in chapters or sections

TELEVISION INTERVIEW

Purpose
- to share a noteworthy person's experiences, knowledge, and insights

Characteristics
- one-on-one conversation, or dialogue, between an interviewer and interviewee, or subject
- sense of immediacy and authority because the interviewee has unique information or knowledge
- may include nonverbal media, such as images

Structure
- question-and-answer format
- often, includes an introduction or background segment

Essential Question: What can one generation learn from another?

Dialogue and Description

 Even though memoirs are a type of nonfiction, they often include storytelling techniques, such as **dialogue** and **description**, that make them seem like fiction. These techniques help reveal the interactions between people, events, and ideas in the text and bring them to life.

TECHNIQUE	EXAMPLE	PURPOSES
Dialogue: words people or characters in a narrative speak aloud; their conversations, set off by quotation marks	"What do you want from me, Marty?" I asked. "Nothin'," Marty muttered. "But I always treated you like a son."	• shows what characters are like and how they interact • moves the plot forward • makes a text more vivid
Description: language (usually adjectives and verbs) related to the senses (sight, hearing, taste, touch, smell) that show what people, places, and objects are like	The forest pool is a near-perfect circle of still green water troubled now and then by the splash of a fish.	• shows how the narrator or other people in a narrative perceive their environment • creates a specific mood, or emotional quality • gives necessary information

PRACTICE Work on your own to read the passage. Circle or mark instances of description. Underline or mark passages of dialogue. Then, analyze the interactions between individuals, events, and ideas by answering the questions. Discuss your responses with your group.

> Metal wheels screamed against iron rails as the train rounded the curve. I gasped and grabbed Alan's hand. "Too fast, too fast!" I cried, heart pounding.
> Alan glanced at me. "Hey," he said, squeezing my hand. "Stop being nuts. We're fine."
> None of the other passengers seemed nervous. I heard the gentle hum of voices and the occasional peal of laughter. No sobs of terror, no cries of anguish. "I just hate trains," I sighed.

1. What do the descriptions in paragraphs 1 and 3 tell you about the situation? Explain.

2. What aspects of the characters' personalities do you learn from the dialogue? Explain.

STANDARDS

Reading Informational Text
• Analyze the interactions between individuals, events, and ideas in a text.

• By the end of the year, read and comprehend literary nonfiction in the grades 6–8 text complexity band proficiently.

Compare Across Genres 57

PREPARE TO READ

from MOM & ME & MOM

LEARNING TO LOVE MY MOTHER

COMPARE: NONFICTION and MEDIA

In this lesson, you will read an excerpt from Maya Angelou's memoir **Mom & Me & Mom** and watch the interview **Learning to Love My Mother** with the author. You will then compare and contrast the memoir and the interview.

About the Author

Born Marguerite Johnson, **Maya Angelou** (1928–2014) struggled with racism, poverty, and ill treatment early in her life. Across her long career she was a dancer, an actress, a singer, a teacher, and a writer. Angelou became one of the best-known African American authors in the world, and she was an activist for women and for the African American community.

STANDARDS
Reading Informational Text
Determine two or more central ideas in a text and analyze their development over the course of the text.

Language
Determine or clarify the meaning of unknown and multiple-meaning words and phrases based on grade 7 reading and content, choosing flexibly from a range of strategies.

Concept Vocabulary

As you read the memoir, you will encounter these words. When you finish, work with your group to identify what these words have in common.

| supervision | charitable | philanthropist |

Base Words Base, or "inside," words along with context clues can help you determine the meanings of unknown words. Use this strategy to help unlock word meanings as you read the excerpt from the memoir.

EXAMPLE

Unfamiliar Word in Context: An *artisan* made the lovely bowl.

Base Word: *art*, or "something made with skill and imagination"

Conclusion: *Artisan* must mean some sort of artist.

PRACTICE As you read, mark base words that help you define unfamiliar words. Write a definition of each unfamiliar word in the open space next to the text.

Reading Strategy: Determine Central Ideas

When you **annotate**, or mark up, a text you personalize your own reading experience. As you read this memoir, mark details that are vivid, interesting, or important. Then, review your annotations to determine central ideas the author is sharing.

EXAMPLE

Annotations: I had become too frightened to accept the idea that I was going to meet my mother at last.

Notes: The author never met her mom before and she's afraid. Maybe one central idea is about handling difficult feelings.

PRACTICE As you read, mark details that stand out and take notes in the open space next to the text. Then, analyze your annotations to determine central ideas.

58 UNIT 1 • CROSSING GENERATIONS

MEMOIR

from Mom & Me & Mom
Maya Angelou

BACKGROUND
When Maya Angelou was three and her brother Bailey was five, her parents divorced and sent the children to live with their grandmother in Stamps, Arkansas. When Maya was thirteen, she and Bailey were sent back to San Francisco to live with their mother, Vivian Baxter.

Chapter 3

1 My grandmother made arrangements with two Pullman car[1] porters and a dining car waiter for tickets for herself, my brother, and me. She said she and I would go to California first and Bailey would follow a month later. She said she didn't want to leave me without adult **supervision**, because I was a thirteen-year-old girl. Bailey would be safe with Uncle Willie. Bailey thought he was looking after Uncle Willie, but the truth was, Uncle Willie was looking after him.

2 By the time the train reached California, I had become too frightened to accept the idea that I was going to meet my mother at last.

3 My grandmother took my hands. "Sister, there is nothing to be scared for. She is your mother, that's all. We are not surprising her. When she received my letter explaining how Junior was growing up, she invited us to come to California."

---
1. **Pullman car** *n.* type of railroad sleeping car built by the Pullman Company.

READ TO UNLOCK MEANING
1. First read the text for comprehension and enjoyment. Use the **Reading Strategy** and **Comprehension Check** questions to support your first read.
2. With your group, apply the vocabulary strategy to unlock word meanings.
3. Find other details in the text you find interesting. Ask your own questions and draw your own conclusions.

Mark base words or indicate another strategy you used that helped you determine meaning.

supervision (soo pehr VIH zhun) *n.*
MEANING:

4   Grandmother rocked me in her arms and hummed. I calmed down. When we descended the train steps, I looked for someone who could be my mother. When I heard my grandmother's voice call out, I followed the voice and I knew she had made a mistake, but the pretty little woman with red lips and high heels came running to my grandmother.

5   "Mother Annie! Mother Annie!"

6   Grandmother opened her arms and embraced the woman. When Momma's arms fell, the woman asked, "Where is my baby?"

7   She looked around and saw me. I wanted to sink into the ground. I wasn't pretty or even cute. That woman who looked like a movie star deserved a better-looking daughter than me. I knew it and was sure she would know it as soon as she saw me.

8   "Maya, Marguerite, my baby." Suddenly I was wrapped in her arms and in her perfume. She pushed away and looked at me. "Oh baby, you're beautiful and so tall. You look like your daddy and me. I'm so glad to see you."

9   She kissed me. I had not received one kiss in all the years in Arkansas. Often my grandmother would call me and show me off to her visitors. "This is my grandbaby." She would stroke me and smile. That was the closest I had come to being kissed. Now Vivian Baxter was kissing my cheeks and my lips and my hands. Since I didn't know what to do, I did nothing.

10   Her home, which was a boardinghouse,[2] was filled with heavy and very uncomfortable furniture. She showed me a room and said it was mine. I told her I wanted to sleep with Momma. Vivian said, "I suppose you slept with your grandmother in Stamps, but she will be going home soon and you need to get used to sleeping in your own room."

11   My grandmother stayed in California, watching me and everything that happened around me. And when she decided that everything was all right, she was happy. I was not. She began to talk about going home, and wondering aloud how her crippled son was getting along. I was afraid to let her leave me, but she said, "You are with your mother now and your brother will be coming soon. Trust me, but more than that trust the Lord. He will look after you."

12   Grandmother smiled when my mother played jazz and blues very loudly on her record player. Sometimes she would dance just because she felt like it, alone, by herself, in the middle of the floor. While Grandmother accepted behavior so different, I just couldn't get used to it.

13   My mother watched me without saying much for about two weeks. Then we had what was to become familiar as "a sit-down talk-to."

---

2. **boardinghouse** *n.* house where people rent one or more rooms for either short or long periods of time.

14   She said, "Maya, you disapprove of me because I am not like your grandmother. That's true. I am not. But I am your mother and I am working some part of my anatomy[3] off to pay for this roof over your head. When you go to school, the teacher will smile at you and you will smile back. Students you don't even know will smile and you will smile. But on the other hand, I am your mother. If you can force one smile on your face for strangers, do it for me. I promise you I will appreciate it."

15   She put her hand on my cheek and smiled. "Come on, baby, smile for Mother. Come on. Be **charitable**."

16   She made a funny face and against my will, I smiled. She kissed me on my lips and started to cry. "That's the first time I have seen you smile. It is a beautiful smile. Mother's beautiful daughter can smile."

17   I was not used to being called beautiful.

18   That day, I learned that I could be a giver simply by bringing a smile to another person. The ensuing[4] years have taught me that a kind word or a vote of support can be a charitable gift. I can move over and make another place for another to sit. I can turn my music up if it pleases, or down if it is annoying.

19   I may never be known as a **philanthropist**, but I certainly want to be known as charitable.

❋ ❋ ❋

20   I was beginning to appreciate her. I liked to hear her laugh because I noticed that she never laughed at anyone. After a few weeks it became clear that I was not using any title when I spoke to her. In fact, I rarely started conversations. Most often, I simply responded when I was spoken to.

21   She asked me into her room. She sat on her bed and didn't invite me to join her.

22   "Maya, I am your mother. Despite the fact that I left you for years, I am your mother. You know that, don't you?"

23   I said, "Yes, ma'am." I had been answering her briefly with a few words since my arrival in California.

24   "You don't have to say 'ma'am' to me. You're not in Arkansas."

25   "No, ma'am. I mean no."

26   "You don't want to call me 'Mother,' do you?"

27   I remained silent.

28   "You have to call me something. We can't go through life without you addressing me. What would you like to call me?"

---

3. **anatomy** (uh NAT uh mee) *n.* the structure of the body.
4. **ensuing** *adj.* following.

---

charitable (CHAYR ih tuh buhl) *adj.*

MEANING

philanthropist (fih LAN thruh pihst) *n.*

MEANING

COMPREHENSION CHECK

How does Maya feel around her mother, Vivian?

from Mom & Me & Mom   61

29 I had been thinking of that since I first saw her. I said, "Lady."
30 "What?"
31 "Lady."
32 "Why?"
33 "Because you are beautiful, and you don't look like a mother."
34 "Is Lady a person you like?"
35 I didn't answer.
36 "Is Lady a person you might learn to like?"
37 She waited as I thought about it.
38 I said, "Yes."
39 "Well, that's it. I am Lady, and still your mother."
40 "Yes, ma'am. I mean yes."
41 "At the right time I will introduce my new name."
42 She left me, turned up the player, and sang loudly with the music. The next day I realized she must have spoken to my grandmother.
43 Grandmother came into my bedroom. "Sister, she is your mother and she does care for you."
44 I said, "I'll wait until Bailey gets here. He will know what to do, and whether we should call her Lady."

Chapter 4

45 Mother, Grandmother, and I waited at the railway station. Bailey descended from the train and saw me first. The smile that took over his face made me forget all the discomfort I had felt since coming to California.

62 UNIT 1 • CROSSING GENERATIONS

46   His eyes found Grandmother and his smile changed to a grin, and he waved to her. Then he saw Mother and his response broke my heart. Suddenly he was a lost little boy who had been found at last. He saw his mother, his home, and then all his lonely birthdays were gone. His nights when scary things made noise under the bed were forgotten. He went to her as if hypnotized. She opened her arms and she clasped him into her embrace. I felt as if I had stopped breathing. My brother was gone, and he would never come back.

47   He had forgotten everything, but I remembered how we felt on the few occasions when she sent us toys. I poked the eyes out of each doll, and Bailey took huge rocks and smashed to bits the trucks or trains that came wrapped up in fancy paper.

48   Grandmother put her arm around me and we walked ahead of the others back to the car. She opened the door and sat in the backseat. She looked at me and patted the seat beside her. We left the front seat for the new lovers.

49   The plan was that Grandmother would return to Arkansas two days after Bailey arrived. Before Lady and Bailey Jr. reached the car I said to Grandmother, "I want to go back home with you, Momma."

50   She asked, "Why?"

51   I said, "I don't want to think of you on that train all alone. You will need me."

52   "When did you make that decision?" I didn't want to answer.

53   She said, "When you saw the reunion of your brother and his mother?" That she should have such understanding, being an old woman and country, too: I thought it was amazing. It was just as well that I had no answer, because Bailey and his mother had already reached the car.

54   Vivian said to Grandmother, "Mother Annie, I didn't look for you two. I knew you would go to the car." Bailey didn't turn to look at me. His eyes were glued to his mother's face. "One thing about you that cannot be denied, you are a true sensible woman."

55   Grandmother said, "Thank you, Vivian. Junior?"

56   She had to call twice to get his attention, "Junior, how was the train? Did somebody make food for your trip? How did you leave Willie?"

57   Suddenly he remembered there was someone else in the world. He grinned for Grandmother. "Yes, ma'am, but none of them can cook like you."

58   He turned to me and asked, "What's happening, My? Has California got your tongue? You haven't said a word since I got in the car."

59   I made my voice as cold as possible. I said, "You haven't given me a chance."

60   In a second he said, "What's the matter, My?"

61   I had hurt him and I was glad. I said, "I may go back to Stamps with Momma." I wanted to break his heart.

DETERMINE CENTRAL IDEAS
Reread paragraphs 49–53. Why does Maya want to go home with her grandmother? What evidence supports your answer?

COMPREHENSION CHECK
What do Bailey and Maya communicate to each other through their fingers?

62 "No, ma'am, you will not." My grandmother's voice was unusually hard.

63 My mother asked, "Why would you leave now? You said all you were waiting on was your brother. Well, here he is." She started the car and pulled out into traffic.

64 Bailey turned back to her. He added, "Yep, I'm in California."

65 Grandmother held my hand and patted it. I bit the inside of my mouth to keep from crying.

66 No one spoke until we reached our house. Bailey dropped his hand over the back of the front seat. When he wiggled his fingers, I grabbed them. He squeezed my fingers and let them go and drew his hand back to the front seat. The exchange did not escape Grandmother's notice, but she said nothing.

BUILD INSIGHT

First Thoughts

Do you think Maya will ever call Vivian "Mother"? Should Vivian expect her to do so? Explain your reasoning.

WORKING AS A GROUP
Discuss your responses to the Analysis and Discussion questions with your group.

Support your ideas with evidence from the text.

Analysis and Discussion

1. **Interpret** What does Maya learn when she smiles for her mother?

2. **Compare and Contrast** Why do you think Maya's reaction to seeing her mother again differs so much from her brother's reaction? Cite textual evidence to support your answer.

3. **Analyze** In paragraph 46, the author says, "My brother was gone, and he would never come back." What do you think she means by this statement?

4. **Get Ready for Close Reading** Choose a passage from the text that you find especially interesting or important. You'll discuss the passage with your group during Close-Read activities.

Exploring the Essential Question

What can one generation learn from another?

5. (a) What ideas about life has Maya learned from her mother?
   (b) What might Vivian have learned about life from Maya?

64 UNIT 1 • CROSSING GENERATIONS

ANALYZE AND INTERPRET

Close Read

from MOM & ME & MOM

PRACTICE Complete the following activities. Use text evidence to support your responses.

1. **Present and Discuss** Engage effectively in a collaborative discussion with your group by sharing passages from the memoir that you found especially interesting. Build on others' ideas and express your own clearly. For example, you might focus on the following passages:

    - **Paragraphs 20–44:** Discuss this scene and the reasons for Maya's confusion about what to call her mother.
    - **Paragraph 66:** Discuss what Bailey does and the responses of both Maya and her grandmother.

2. **Reflect on Your Learning** What new ideas or insights did you uncover during your second reading of the text?

STUDY LANGUAGE AND CRAFT

Concept Vocabulary

Why These Words? The vocabulary words are related.

| supervision | charitable | philanthropist |

1. With your group, determine what the words have in common. Write your ideas.

2. Add another word that fits the category: _____

3. Use each vocabulary word in an original sentence. Include context clues that hint at each word's meaning.

Word Study

Greek Root: -phil- The word *philanthropist* is built on the Greek roots *-phil-*, which means "love for," and *-anthrop-*, which means "human."

PRACTICE Use a print or digital dictionary to find the meanings of the words *audiophile, philosophy,* and *bibliophile*. Then, explain how the root *-phil-* gives clues to the meanings of all three words. Finally, write a sentence for each word, demonstrating its usage.

WORD WALL
Note words in the text that are related to the concept of crossing generations. Add them to your Word Wall.

STANDARDS

Reading Informational Text
Cite several pieces of textual evidence to support analysis of what the text says explicitly as well as inferences drawn from the text.

Speaking and Listening
Engage effectively in a range of collaborative discussions with diverse partners on grade 7 topics, texts, and issues, building on others' ideas and expressing their own clearly.

Language
Use common, grade-appropriate Greek or Latin affixes and roots as clues to the meaning of a word.

STUDY LANGUAGE AND CRAFT

from MOM & ME & MOM

Dialogue and Description

Readers of memoirs can gain insight into an author's experiences by analyzing the interactions between people, events, and ideas in a text. In *Mom & Me & Mom*, much of this information is revealed through **dialogue, description,** and **exposition**. Consider the examples.

TECHNIQUE	PASSAGE	PURPOSE
Dialogue: characters' spoken words; conversations	"Sister, there is nothing to be scared for. She is your mother, that's all."	• reveals characters' personalities and interactions • moves the plot forward • brings the text to life
Description: sensory language that creates word pictures in readers' minds	…the pretty little woman with red lips and high heels came running to my grandmother.	• shows how characters see people and places • adds to a specific mood
Exposition: explanations	My grandmother made arrangements with two Pullman car porters and a dining car waiter for tickets…	• gives basic information about situations • provides background

PRACTICE Work with your group to complete the activities.

1. **Analyze** Complete the chart. For each passage, identify the technique the author uses and cite details that show interactions between people, events, and ideas. Then, explain what those details reveal about the author's feelings and experiences.

PASSAGE	TECHNIQUE	DETAIL(S)	EXPLANATION
Paragraph 12			
Paragraphs 22–25			
Paragraph 48			

2. **(a) Summarize** In paragraph 11, summarize the information given in exposition. **(b) Connect** Why is this information important?

3. **(a) Distinguish** Cite details in paragraph 46 that show what happens when Bailey sees his family. **(b) Interpret** How does this description support the author's feeling that her brother "was gone"?

STANDARDS
Reading Informational Text
Analyze the interactions between individuals, events, and ideas in a text.

Language
• Demonstrate command of the conventions of standard English grammar and usage when writing or speaking.
• Explain the function of phrases and clauses in general and their function in specific sentences.

66 UNIT 1 • CROSSING GENERATIONS

Essential Question: What can one generation learn from another?

Independent and Dependent Clauses

A **clause** is a group of words that has both a subject and a verb. An **independent clause** has a subject and a verb, and it can stand by itself as a complete sentence. A **dependent,** or **subordinate, clause** has a subject and a verb, but it cannot stand alone as a sentence. When added to an independent clause, a dependent clause can provide detail, such as why, where, or when something happened.

TYPE OF CLAUSE	EXAMPLES
Independent Clause	• My grandmother took my hands • Grandmother rocked me in her arms and hummed • She asked me into her room • Mother, Grandmother, and I waited at the railway station
Dependent Clause	• Because I was a thirteen-year-old girl • Since I didn't know what to do • While Grandmother accepted behavior so different • When he wiggled his fingers

READ Work on your own to complete the activities. Then, discuss your answers with your group.

1. Identify each group of words as an independent clause or a dependent clause and explain your choice.

   a. I had not received one kiss in all the years in Arkansas

   b. That woman who looked like a movie star

   c. I was beginning to appreciate her

   d. Before Lady and Bailey Jr. reached the car

2. Reread paragraph 20 of *Mom & Me & Mom*. Mark and label one example of an independent clause and one example of a dependent clause. Then, explain the function of each clause.

WRITE / EDIT Write a brief paragraph that describes how Maya's interactions with her mother changed before Bailey's arrival. Include two independent clauses and two dependent clauses in your writing. Then, label these types of clauses in your finished paragraph.

EVIDENCE LOG

Before moving on to a new selection, go to your Evidence Log and record any additional thoughts or observations you may have about the excerpt from *Mom & Me & Mom*.

from *Mom & Me & Mom* 67

PREPARE TO VIEW

from MOM & ME & MOM

LEARNING TO LOVE MY MOTHER

COMPARE: NONFICTION and MEDIA

In the video **Learning to Love My Mother**, an interviewer asks Maya Angelou about some of the experiences she described in her memoir. Pay attention to similarities and differences in the ways the memoir and the interview tell the author's story.

About the Interviewer

Michael Maher has produced and filmed numerous videos, including many for *BBC News Magazine*. In most of his work—even when he is the interviewer—he is not very visible, and the focus of the video doesn't stray from the subject.

Media Vocabulary

These words describe characteristics of TV interviews. Use them as you analyze, discuss, and write about the selection.

interview subject: the person being interviewed	• The subject is someone with special knowledge, experience, or status. They have wisdom or insight to share with viewers.
set: location where a movie, play, or other production takes place	• Color and other visual elements create a mood that fits the personality of the subject. • The set may be a television studio or a more personal place, such as the subject's home.
tone: the emotional quality of the conversation between the interviewer and the subject	• The overall tone of an interview will reflect the topic and interviewer's purpose. • Word choice, vocal qualities, and facial expressions set the tone of an interview.

Viewing Strategy: Make Connections

When two selections explore the same topic, you can gain insight into each one by making connections between them. Each author focuses on different details to convey ideas in particular ways. To make connections between selections, consider the following elements:

- central ideas
- supporting evidence and details
- word choice, style, and tone
- genre

PRACTICE As you watch the interview, note details that also appeared in *Mom & Me & Mom*. Afterwards, use your notes to analyze how the same information was shared, but in different ways.

STANDARDS

Reading Informational Text
Analyze how two or more authors writing about the same topic shape their presentations of key information by emphasizing different evidence or advancing different interpretations of facts.

Language
Acquire and use accurately grade-appropriate general academic and domain-specific words and phrases; gather vocabulary knowledge when considering a word or phrase important to comprehension or expression.

68 UNIT 1 • CROSSING GENERATIONS

MEDIA: TELEVISION INTERVIEW

WATCH AND LISTEN ▶

Learning to Love My Mother
Maya Angelou with Michael Maher

BACKGROUND
When Maya Angelou was three years old, she and her brother were sent to live with their grandmother. Their mother, Vivian Baxter, was not ready to be tied down with a family. Ten years later, the two children returned to live with their mother. More than seventy years later, Angelou wrote about this transition in her memoir *Mom & Me & Mom*. In this interview, she tells Michael Maher some of the lessons she learned from her experiences

TAKE NOTES As you watch and listen, take notes to connect the TV interview to the excerpt from *Mom & Me & Mom*.

BUILD INSIGHT

LEARNING TO LOVE MY MOTHER

First Thoughts

Choose one of the following questions to discuss with your group.

- Angelou mentions several lessons she learned from her relationship with her mother. Which one do you find most powerful?
- What are some questions you would like to ask Angelou? What are some questions you have for her mother?

Summary

Write a short summary of the interview that presents the most important points Angelou made. Be objective; avoid giving your opinions. Consider sharing your summary with your group.

Analysis and Discussion

1. **(a) Distinguish** What qualities did Angelou see in her mother after she had lived with her for a while? **(b) Analyze** How did Angelou's recognition of these qualities affect her feelings for her mother? Explain.

2. **(a)** According to Angelou, what would Vivian Baxter have thought about the election of an African American president? **(b) Make Inferences** What does this detail suggest about Vivian Baxter's personality and the effect she had on her daughter?

3. **(a)** What one message does Angelou pray someone will hear in her book? **(b) Make Inferences** Why do you think this one message is so important to her?

Exploring the Essential Question

What can one generation learn from another?

4. In what way has Angelou been successful in navigating life lessons learned from her mother?

5. What does Angelou hope to teach other generations about life by participating in this interview and writing a book about her experiences? Note your ideas in your Evidence Log.

WORKING AS A GROUP

Discuss your responses to the Analysis and Discussion questions with your group.

- Note points of agreement and disagreement.
- Ask follow-up questions of peers, as needed, to clarify their ideas.

If necessary, revise your original answers to reflect what you learn from your discussion.

STANDARDS

Speaking and Listening
Analyze the main ideas and supporting details presented in diverse media and formats and explain how the ideas clarify a topic, text, or issue under study.

Language
Acquire and use accurately grade-appropriate general academic and domain-specific words and phrases.

70 UNIT 1 • CROSSING GENERATIONS

ANALYZE AND INTERPRET

Close Review

Watch the interview again. Take notes about important details that Angelou shares, and jot down a main idea that she expresses. Then, consider how this main idea clarifies Angelou's relationship with her mother. Write a question and your conclusion.

MY QUESTION:

MY CONCLUSION:

STUDY LANGUAGE AND CRAFT

Media Vocabulary

These words describe characteristics of TV interviews. Practice using them as you write and discuss your responses.

| interview subject | set | tone |

1. If you were conducting this interview, what location would you choose? Explain.

2. Identify one question you wished the interviewer had asked Angelou. Explain your thinking.

3. How would you describe the emotional quality of this interview? Explain, citing details from the video.

Learning to Love My Mother 71

TEST PRACTICE

MEMOIR

from MOM & ME & MOM

TV INTERVIEW

LEARNING TO LOVE MY MOTHER

COMPARE: NONFICTION and MEDIA
Multiple Choice

These questions are based on the excerpt from the memoir *Mom & Me & Mom* and the interview "Learning to Love My Mother." Choose the best answer to each question.

1. When the author travels by train to California, how does she feel?

   A She feels happy to be leaving Stamps, Arkansas.

   B She feels sad to leave her brother behind.

   C She feels excited to be meeting her mother at last.

   D She feels frightened to be meeting her mother at last.

2. Read paragraph 20 from the memoir and the transcript of a similar section in the interview. What do you learn from the interview that Angelou does *not* share in her memoir?

   Memoir

   I was beginning to appreciate her. I liked to hear her laugh because I noticed she never laughed at anyone. After a few weeks it became clear that I was not using any title when I spoke to her. In fact, I rarely started conversations. Most often, I simply responded when I was spoken to.

   Television Interview

   00:45: INTERVIEWER: . . . What allowed you to somewhat establish a relationship?

   00:56: ANGELOU: She loved me. And she told me. She said, "I really wasn't ready to be a parent." And I realized there are some people who are great parents to small people. My mother was just the opposite.

   A Her mother was eager for children.

   B Her mother had been unprepared for children.

   C Her mother did not laugh at anyone.

   D Her mother did not appreciate people.

3. In both the memoir and the interview, what important idea does Angelou share?

   A She learned to be kinder from the experience.

   B She wished that her childhood had been easier.

   C She hopes to forgive her mother someday.

   D She knew that her grandmother loved her mother.

STANDARDS

Reading Informational Text
Compare and contrast a text to an audio, video, or multimedia version of the text, analyzing each medium's portrayal of the subject.

Writing
• Write informative/explanatory texts to examine a topic and convey ideas, concepts, and information through the selection, organization, and analysis of relevant content.

• Apply grade 7 Reading standards to literary nonfiction.

72 UNIT 1 • CROSSING GENERATIONS

Essential Question: What can one generation learn from another?

Short Response

1. **(a) Describe** In the memoir, what overall impression does the author give of her mother's appearance and behavior? **(b) Synthesize** Cite at least one detail in the interview that adds to that portrayal. Explain.

2. **(a) Synthesize** What information do the photos and video included in the interview add to the viewers' understanding of Angelou's life?
(b) Speculate The young Angelou had difficulty understanding her mother. Do you think she would have understood her own adult self? Explain.

3. **Connect** In the TV interview, Angelou says that her mother loved her. Which details in the memoir suggest that love? Cite at least one statement and one action, and explain your choices.

Timed Writing

A **comparison-and-contrast essay** is a piece of writing in which you discuss the similarities and differences between two or more topics.

Assignment

Maya Angelou gave the interview "Learning to Love My Mother" to promote her memoir *Mom & Me & Mom*. Write a **comparison-and-contrast essay** in which you analyze both versions and explain which one provides a more vivid sense of Angelou's experience.

- How does each version portray Angelou?
- Which version helps you better understand Angelou and her family?
- Which version offers more detail, and why?

5-Minute Planner

1. Read the assignment carefully and completely.
2. Decide what you want to say—your central idea or thesis. Make sure to state it in your introduction, develop it in your body paragraphs, and restate it in your conclusion.
3. Decide which examples you'll use from the two versions.
4. Organize your ideas, making sure to note details you learn from the text that you don't learn from the video, and vice versa.

> **EVIDENCE LOG**
>
> Before moving on to a new selection, go to your Evidence Log and record any additional thoughts and observations you may have about *Mom & Me & Mom* and "Learning to Love My Mother."

Test Practice 73

PREPARE TO VIEW

Mother-Daughter Drawings

About the Author

Mica Angela Hendricks was born into a military family and traveled to many countries. As a child, she would carry a sketchbook everywhere she went. People who didn't know her well would simply call her "that girl who draws." Hendricks is now an illustrator and has collaborated with her four-year-old daughter, Myla, on the sketchbook "Share With Me."

Media Vocabulary

These words describe characteristics of drawings. Here, the drawings are presented with captions to create a multimedia text. Use these words as you analyze, discuss, and write about the selection.

composition: arrangement of elements in a work of visual art	• Artists consider color, line, shape, space, form, and texture when composing an image. • Composition may emphasize one part of an image over others.
light and shadow: elements that define and enhance parts of an image	• An artist's use of light and shadow can make a two-dimensional shape look three-dimensional—a circle becomes a sphere. • Varying degrees of light and shadow may create different moods.
proportion: sizes of objects in relation to each other or to the background	• Realistic proportions make objects seem true to life. • Exaggerated proportions make objects seem odd, imaginary, or dreamlike.

Viewing Strategy: Synthesize Information

When you **synthesize information**, you pull together ideas from different sources in order to develop your own perspective. You allow your thinking about a topic to grow and change. To synthesize as you read, follow these steps:

- Identify important points in a text.
- Consider connections, similarities, and differences among those points.
- Use these sentence starters to organize your thinking and express your new understanding:

At first I thought _____.

Then I learned _____.

Now I think _____.

PRACTICE As you study this gallery of visual art, synthesize your observations of the drawings and the caption text to create a new understanding. Jot down your ideas in the Take Notes sections.

STANDARDS
Language
Gather vocabulary knowledge when considering a word or phrase important to comprehension or expression.

Mother-Daughter Drawings
Mica and Myla Hendricks

BACKGROUND
Artist Mica Angela Hendricks had always tried to teach her four-year-old daughter Myla the importance of sharing. But it's easier to talk about sharing than to do it. Mica found that out when Myla noticed her mother drawing in a sketchbook and asked if she could draw in it too. Mica was afraid Myla would ruin her drawings but decided she had to set a good example by practicing what she preached, especially after Myla quoted her words back to her: "If you can't share, we might have to take it away."

IMAGE 1: Mica had just drawn a woman's face from an old photograph. She let Myla draw the woman's body and then used acrylic paint to add color, highlights, and texture to the entire piece.

TAKE NOTES

76 UNIT 1 • CROSSING GENERATIONS

IMAGE 2: Mica was impressed that her collaboration with her daughter turned out so well and wanted to try it again.

TAKE NOTES

IMAGE 3: Mica began filling her sketchbook with drawings of heads and letting Myla draw the bodies.

TAKE NOTES

Mother-Daughter Drawings 77

IMAGE 4: At first, Mica tried telling Myla what kinds of bodies to draw. She soon realized the drawings turned out better when Myla did what she wanted. "In most instances, kids' imaginations way outweigh a grown-up's," Mica says.

▸ TAKE NOTES

IMAGE 5: Working with her daughter taught Mica that giving up control is not just fun, but necessary. "Those things you hold so dear cannot change and grow and expand unless you loosen your grip on them a little," she says.

▸ TAKE NOTES

BUILD INSIGHT

First Thoughts

Choose one of the following questions to discuss.
- Would you recommend this selection to a friend? Why, or why not?
- Do you agree with Mica that "kids' imaginations way outweigh a grown-up's"? Explain.

Comprehension

1. **Reading Check** (a) Why did Mica let Myla draw in the sketchbook? (b) What did she think would happen? (c) What actually happened?

2. **Strategy: Synthesize Information** (a) Explain at least one way in which your understanding of the art changed when you synthesized your observations of the drawings with information from the captions. (b) How might the strategy of synthesizing help you in other school tasks, such as writing a research paper? Explain.

Analysis and Discussion

3. (a) **Contrast** What are some of the most striking differences between the parts of the drawings Mica drew and the parts that Myla drew? (b) **Modify** How might the drawings be different if Mica had not collaborated with her daughter? Explain.

4. In the caption for Image 5, Mica says, "Those things you hold so dear cannot change and grow and expand unless you loosen your grip on them a little." (a) **Interpret** What does she mean by that statement? (b) **Connect** In what ways do you think this idea comes through in the drawings? Explain.

5. **Take a Position** In the creation of art, which matters more: imagination or skill? Explain your thinking, using the drawings as evidence.

Exploring the Essential Question

What can one generation learn from another?

6. What have you learned about the ways different generations teach one another from reading and viewing this image gallery? Go to your Evidence Log and record your thoughts.

WORKING AS A GROUP

Discuss your responses to the Analysis and Discussion questions with your group.

- Ask your groupmates to elaborate on the ideas they share.
- Respond to questions and comments with relevant observations and by referring to evidence in the text.
- If the discussion goes off track, respond to the last comment someone made to bring the conversation back on topic.

STANDARDS

Speaking and Listening
- Come to discussions prepared, having read or researched material under study; explicitly draw on that preparation by referring to evidence on the topic, text, or issue to probe and reflect on ideas under discussion.
- Pose questions that elicit elaboration and respond to others' questions and comments with relevant observations and ideas that bring the discussion back on topic as needed.

ANALYZE AND INTERPRET

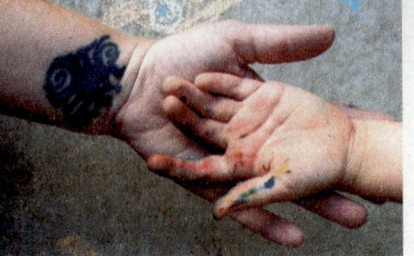

MOTHER-DAUGHTER DRAWINGS

Close Review

Review the text and images in "Mother-Daughter Drawings." As you review, take notes about important details and jot down your observations. Then, write a question and your conclusion. Share your notes with your group.

MY QUESTION:

MY CONCLUSION:

STUDY LANGUAGE AND CRAFT

Media Vocabulary

These words describe characteristics of visual art. Practice using them as you analyze the drawings and discuss the questions.

| composition | light and shadow | proportion |

1. Why do you think Image 1 is made up of four separate photographs? What is the effect of this choice?

2. What mood is suggested by Image 2? Which details or elements of the drawing create that mood?

3. In Image 5, how does the size of the head relate to other parts of the body? What is the effect? Explain.

STANDARDS

Writing
Write narratives to develop real or imagined experiences or events using effective technique, relevant descriptive details, and well-structured event sequences.

Speaking and Listening
- Define individual roles as needed.
- Include multimedia components and visual displays in presentations to clarify claims and findings and emphasize salient points.

80 UNIT 1 • CROSSING GENERATIONS

SHARE IDEAS

Speaking and Listening

A **multimedia presentation** provides information to an audience through a combination of words, images, video, and audio.

> **Assignment**
>
> Mica Hendricks learned a valuable lesson when she shared her sketchbook with her daughter. Develop a story that taught someone an unexpected but positive lesson. Choose one of the following options:
>
> ◯ Write a new narrative.
>
> ◯ Choose a story to retell.
>
> Then, deliver your story as a **multimedia presentation.**

Draft As a group, discuss possible story ideas and choose one that you agree on. Then, select one of the narrative options and begin drafting. Make sure every group member has an opportunity to make suggestions for the story. As you draft the presentation, be sure to use standard English grammar, usage, and conventions, just as you would for a written task.

Choose Media Include multimedia components and visual displays, such as videos, audio clips, or images, that will best enhance the presentation of your narrative. Discuss these questions as a group:

- Which elements of the story could you clarify if you used media?
- What types of media would best emphasize the most important points in your story?

Plan the Project Decide which piece of media will go with each section of the narrative. Arrange the media components in sequence. For each one, define individual roles by jotting down the name of the group member who will speak at that time. That person should write brief notes about their section of the presentation.

Revise and Rehearse Work with your group to revise, edit, and finalize your story. Then, rehearse your presentation to ensure that speakers are prepared and media pieces are integrated smoothly.

Present Share your multimedia narrative with the class. Be sure to use proper English grammar, usage, and conventions as you speak. Avoid slang and informal grammar, and speak clearly to engage your audience.

> **EVIDENCE LOG**
>
> Before moving on to a new selection, go to your Evidence Log and record any additional thoughts or observations you may have about "Mother-Daughter Drawings."

Mother-Daughter Drawings **81**

LEARN ABOUT GENRE: POETRY

POETRY COLLECTION 1

Reading Free-Verse Poetry

A **free-verse poem** breaks "free" from the standard patterns of rhyme or rhythm found in many other forms of poetry.

Each selection you are about to read is an example of free-verse poetry.

FREE-VERSE POETRY

Author's Purpose
- to use language in a unique way to convey powerful feelings or ideas

Characteristics
- does not follow the "rules" commonly associated with poetry
- may include rhyme or rhythm but not in a regular pattern
- has a speaker, or voice that "tells" the poem
- may use imagery and figurative language
- often breaks the rules of standard English

Structure
- has irregular line lengths; absence of formal patterns
- may use visual elements to reinforce or create meaning

STANDARDS
Reading Literature
- Analyze how a drama's or poem's form or structure contributes to its meaning.
- By the end of the year, read and comprehend literature, including stories, dramas, and poems.

Take a Minute!

FIND IT Work with a partner to find a free-verse poem online or in this program. Read it aloud. What unique, "free" elements do you notice in the poem?

82 UNIT 1 • CROSSING GENERATIONS

Essential Question: What can one generation learn from another?

Visual Elements in Poetry

The arrangement of words in a poem creates visual effects and gives the poem structure. In poetry, a **line** is a row of words, and a **stanza** is a group of lines, usually separated from other stanzas by space. The following visual elements make a poem look a certain way, which contributes to its meaning.

- line lengths, which may be long or short
- stanza lengths, which may be just one line or many lines
- spacing, including use of "white" (empty) space
- punctuation and capitalization, which may be unconventional
- italic, bold, and other text formatting

EXAMPLE

    The chair where you sat
    Is   empty.
    Your place at the table
    Is   bare.
5   Your sweet clear rich voice
    Is   silent.

    But my *heart* my *heart* my *heart* my *heart*
    sees … hears … remembers

TIP:
- Lines 2, 4, 6: White space emphasizes a sense of absence.
- Line 7: Italics emphasize a heartbeat-like rhythm.
- Line 8: Punctuation shows a struggle to find words.

PRACTICE Work on your own to complete the activity. Then, discuss your responses with your group.

1. Read the poem, and mark the following: **(a)** short lines; **(b)** unconventional punctuation and capitalization; **(c)** use of white space.

    Ana can
    NOT "Sit still!"
    Ana   r-u-n-s & hops(!)
    up
        steps
            r-u-n-s & hops(!)
        down
    steps!
    Ana, STOP! No never no ever for Ana
    is 3 & free & whe-e!-e-e! e-e!

2. Explain how one element you marked adds to the poem's meaning.

PREPARE TO READ

POETRY COLLECTION 1

Ode to My Papi • Mother to Son • To James

Concept Vocabulary

As you read Poetry Collection 1, you will encounter these words. After reading, work with your group to identify what these words have in common.

| transported | catapulted | lurched |

Context Clues The context of a word is the other words and phrases that appear close to it in the text. Clues in the context can help you figure out word meanings. There are various types of context clues that you might encounter as you read.

- **Restatement:** As they fought to get past the finish line, one runner *hurled* himself forward, throwing his body over the line.
- **Synonym:** At the beginning of the race, he *launched*, or propelled, himself over the start line.
- **Contrast:** The winners of the race *glided* across the finish line, while the remaining competitors stumbled behind them.

PRACTICE As you read these poems, study the context to determine the meanings of unfamiliar words. Mark your observations in the open space next to the text.

Reading Strategy: Create Mental Images

By **creating mental images** as you read, you can more easily understand difficult passages and deepen your understanding of the poems.

- Notice sensory language that refers to color, shape, texture, sound, and sensations.
- Focus on a word and consider the image that comes to mind.

EXAMPLE

Notice the words related to shape and texture in these lines from "Mother to Son." Use them to "see" this scene in your mind.

It's had tacks in it, / And splinters, / And boards torn up, / And places with no carpet on the floor— / Bare.

PRACTICE As you read these poems, deepen your understanding by marking sensory details and pausing to create mental images.

STANDARDS
Language
- Determine or clarify the meaning of unknown and multiple-meaning words and phrases based on grade 7 reading and content, choosing flexibly from a range of strategies.
- Use context as a clue to the meaning of a word or phrase.

84 UNIT 1 • CROSSING GENERATIONS

Essential Question: What can one generation learn from another?

About the Poems

Ode to My Papi

BACKGROUND

The writer Guadalupe García McCall was born in Mexico and emigrated to the United States with her family as a child. She wrote this poem in memory of her late father, el Señor Onésimo García (1940–2020).

Guadalupe García McCall is the author of numerous short stories, young adult novels, and children's poems. In 2012, she was awarded the prestigious Pura Belpré Medal for her novel *Under the Mesquite*. She currently serves as a Visiting Professor of Creative Writing at Antioch University in Los Angeles, California.

Mother to Son

BACKGROUND

Even after the abolition of slavery, life was very hard for most African Americans. Poetry, music, and the other arts were creative outlets that allowed them to express the hardships of their lives and to find inspiration.

Langston Hughes (1902–1967) was an African American writer known for jazz-inspired poems that portrayed African American life in America. His work was controversial. Some critics worried that it played into racial stereotypes. Others praised Hughes for reaching everyday people by using language and themes "familiar to anyone who had the ability simply to read."

To James

BACKGROUND

From 1914 through 1937, Harlem, a neighborhood in New York City, was the setting for an awakening of African American culture that came to be known as the Harlem Renaissance. During this period, African American writers such as Langston Hughes and Frank Horne searched for the truest way to express their experiences. Each developed a unique style that ultimately helped shape not just African American culture but also world culture.

Frank Horne (1899–1974) was an African American writer and activist. As a director at the U.S. Housing Authority, he fought to end segregated housing. As a poet, he fought discrimination with poems that conveyed dignity and pride.

Poetry Collection 1   **85**

FREE-VERSE POETRY

Ode to My Papi

Guadalupe Garcia McCall

READ TO UNLOCK MEANING

1. First read the text for comprehension and enjoyment. Use the **Reading Strategy** and **Comprehension Check** questions to support your first read.
2. With your group, apply the vocabulary strategy to unlock word meanings.
3. Find other details in the text you find interesting. Ask your own questions and draw your own conclusions.

In loving memory of my papi, el Señor Onésimo García (1940–2020)—

because you did so much to make us strong.

He could only give me one dollar
a week. On Fridays, when I'd serve him
dinner after work, he'd pull the single dollar bill
out of his worn wallet with weathered
5   hands—hands that had cut and transformed
mesquite, planks, shingles, tiles, and cement.

In cold, sleet, rain, and sun, my papi's
weathered hands framed offices, erected hotels,
covered roofs, threw cement, built homes,
and helped put up a dam named Amistad
in Fort Worth, Galveston, Eagle Pass, Del Rio, and
every other town along the Rio Grande and beyond.

That dollar, he knew, would buy me
a billion galaxies, countless stars, oceans,
a rain forest and miles and miles of desert—fictions,
dark and light, sweet and tart, all of them
affordable, within his means, pulled out
of the ten-cent bin at our local library.

Those books **transported** me. Since then,
I've traveled a long road, negotiated borders,
been recognized and awarded
gold medallions, plaques, and certificates
because those strong hands provided,
nurtured, made me feel loved, adored.

In giving me what little he could,
my papi gave me the universe.

Mark context clues or indicate another strategy you used that helped you determine meaning.

transported (trans PAWR tihd) *v.*

MEANING:

FREE-VERSE POETRY

Mother to Son

Langston Hughes

CREATE MENTAL IMAGES

Mark details in the poem that relate to the five senses. What do these details help you envision?

Well, son, I'll tell you:
Life for me ain't been no crystal stair.
It's had tacks in it,
And splinters,
5   And boards torn up,
And places with no carpet on the floor—
Bare.
But all the time
I'se been a-climbin' on,
10 And reachin' landin's,
And turnin' corners,
And sometimes goin' in the dark
Where there ain't been no light.
So boy, don't you turn back.
15 Don't you set down on the steps
'Cause you finds it's kinder hard.
Don't you fall now—
For I'se still goin', honey,
I'se still climbin',
20 And life for me ain't been no crystal stair.

FREE-VERSE POETRY

To James
Frank Horne

Do you remember
How you won
That last race . . . ?
How you flung your body
5   At the start . . .
How your spikes
Ripped the cinders[1]
In the stretch . . .
How you **catapulted**
10 Through the tape . . .
Do you remember . . . ?
Don't you think
I **lurched** with you
Out of those starting holes . . . ?
15 Don't you think
My sinews[2] tightened
At those first
Few strides . . .
And when you flew into the stretch

Mark context clues or indicate another strategy you used that helped you determine meaning.

catapulted (KA tuh puhl tihd) *v.*
MEANING:

lurched (LURCHT) *v.*
MEANING:

---
1. **cinders** *n.* ashes.
2. **sinews** *n.* strong tissues that connect muscle to bone.

20 Was not all my thrill
   Of a thousand races
   In your blood . . . ?
   At your final drive
   Through the finish line
25 Did not my shout
   Tell of the
   Triumphant ecstasy
   Of victory . . . ?
   Live
30 As I have taught you
   To run, Boy—
   It's a short dash
   Dig your starting holes
   Deep and firm
35 Lurch out of them
   Into the straightaway
   With all the power
   That is in you
   Look straight ahead
40 To the finish line
   Think only of the goal
   Run straight
   Run high
   Run hard
45 Save nothing
   And finish
   With an ecstatic burst
   That carries you
   Hurtling
50 Through the tape
   To victory. . . .

COMPREHENSION CHECK

The speakers in these poems reach across generational lines to convey messages. With which generation is each speaker connecting?

BUILD INSIGHT

First Thoughts

Which of the three poems most vividly reminds you of something you have experienced? Describe that experience.

Comprehension

1. **Reading Check** (a) In "Ode to My Papi," what does the speaker do with the dollar bill her father gives her every Friday? (b) In "Mother to Son," what lesson does the mother want her son to learn? (c) In "To James," what event does the speaker refer to at the beginning of the poem?

2. **Strategy: Create Mental Images** (a) Which moment or detail in each poem were you able to picture most clearly? Why? (b) In what ways did this strategy add to your reading experience?

Analysis and Discussion

3. **Make Inferences** In "Ode to My Papi," what can you infer about the father from the speaker's description of his "weathered hands"?

4. (a) **Analyze** In lines 8–13 and 18–20 of "Mother to Son," what personal qualities does the mother demonstrate? (b) **Draw Conclusions** Why do you think she uses herself as an example in her message to her son?

5. (a) **Analyze** Reread lines 12–18 in "To James." How does the speaker react to James's physical efforts? (b) **Make Inferences** What do these reactions suggest about the speaker's emotional connection to James? Explain.

6. **Get Ready for Close Reading** Choose a passage from the text that you find especially interesting or important. You'll discuss the passage with your group during Close-Read activities.

Exploring the Essential Question

What can one generation learn from another?

7. What have these poems revealed about the reasons people reach out to others of different generations? Go to your Evidence Log and record your thoughts.

WORKING AS A GROUP

Discuss your responses to the Analysis and Discussion questions with your group.

- If you notice the discussion going off track, respond to the last comment a group member made to bring the conversation back on topic.

If necessary, modify your original answers to reflect what you learn from your discussion.

STANDARDS

Speaking and Listening
- Respond to others' questions and comments with relevant observations and ideas that bring the discussion back on topic as needed.
- Acknowledge new information expressed by others and, when warranted, modify their own views.

Poetry Collection 1 91

ANALYZE AND INTERPRET

POETRY COLLECTION 1

Close Read

PRACTICE Complete the following activities. Use text evidence to support your responses.

1. **Present and Discuss** Discuss the following passages with your group.

   - **"Ode to My Papi," lines 19–24:** Discuss what has happened in the speaker's life since she was young.
   - **"Mother to Son," lines 2–13:** Discuss the nature of the life the speaker has lived.
   - **"To James," lines 29–51:** Discuss the attitude toward life the speaker hopes to have inspired in James.

2. **Reflect on Your Learning** What new ideas or insights did you uncover during your second reading of the text?

WORD WALL

Note words in the poems that are related to the idea of crossing generations. Add them to your Word Wall.

STUDY LANGUAGE AND CRAFT

Concept Vocabulary

Why These Words? The vocabulary words are related.

| transported | catapulted | lurched |

1. With your group, determine what the words have in common.

2. Add another word that fits the category: _____

3. Use each vocabulary word in an original sentence.

Word Study

Synonyms and Antonyms You can use the relationship between words, such as synonyms and antonyms, to better understand the words that poets use in their work.

PRACTICE Reread lines 12–14 from "To James." Use a thesaurus to choose two synonyms and two antonyms for *lurched*. Then, rewrite lines 12–14 twice. In the first version, replace *lurched* with one of the synonyms. In the second version, replace it with one of the antonyms. Share your new lines with your group and discuss how replacing a word changes the poem.

STANDARDS

Reading Literature
Analyze how a drama's or poem's form or structure contributes to its meaning.

Language
- Use knowledge of language and its conventions when writing, speaking, reading, or listening.
- Use the relationship between particular words to better understand each of the words.

92 UNIT 1 • CROSSING GENERATIONS

Essential Question: What can one generation learn from another?

Visual Elements in Poetry

Visual elements give a poem structure. They affect how a poem looks and how readers follow the flow of ideas. When you read free-verse poems, focus on how the following elements develop a structure that contributes to the poem's meaning.

VISUAL ELEMENTS IN POETRY	
Line Length	• Even line lengths make a poem look orderly. • Varied lengths make a poem look expressive.
White Space	• Empty space suggests pauses or adds meaning.
Punctuation	• Conventional punctuation may guide readers. • Unconventional or missing punctuation may leave the reading of a poem more open.
Capitalization	• Each line may start with a capital letter, which adds a sense of order. • Capitalization may stress certain words.

TIP: Poets choose punctuation for effect and to suggest meaning.
- An ellipsis (…) shows a pause, an ongoing thought, or a struggle to speak.
- A dash (—) emphasizes the words that follow or shows an urgent interruption.

PRACTICE Work on your own to answer the questions. Then, discuss your responses with your group.

1. **Analyze** In "Ode to My Papi," does the poet use conventional or unconventional punctuation? Why do you think she made that choice?

2. (a) **Distinguish** In "Mother to Son," how does line 7 differ from the other lines? (b) **Interpret** What is the effect? Explain.

3. **Analyze** In "Mother to Son," how does punctuation affect the way you read line 17? Explain.

4. (a) **Interpret** In "To James," what do the ellipses suggest about the questions the speaker is asking? (b) **Analyze** Why do you think the poem ends with an ellipsis? Explain.

5. (a) **Compare and Contrast** How is the use of capitalization in the three poems similar and different? (b) **Interpret** What is the effect of the use of capitalization in each poem?

Poetry Collection 1 93

STUDY LANGUAGE AND CRAFT

POETRY COLLECTION 1

Figurative Language: Metaphor

In poetry, **figurative language** conveys meaning in powerful ways. One type of figurative language is **metaphor**, which creates imaginative comparisons that show how the poem's speaker feels and perceives the world. When you read a poem, strive to determine the meanings of words and phrases that are used figuratively, such as metaphors. This will help you understand the ideas the poet wants to express.

DESCRIPTION	EXAMPLE
Metaphor: shows similarities between two seemingly unlike things; it presents one thing as though it is another	*Hope is a flame.*
Extended Metaphor: builds a comparison over several lines, a stanza, or an entire poem	*Hope is a flame / A spark in the darkness / Pale at first but then / Brighter, growing / Becoming bonfires of belief*

STANDARDS

Reading Literature
Determine the meaning of words and phrases as they are used in a text, including figurative and connotative meanings.

Writing
• Use precise words and phrases, relevant descriptive details, and sensory language to capture the action and convey experiences and events.
• With some guidance and support from peers and adults, develop and strengthen writing as needed by planning, revising, editing, rewriting, or trying a new approach.

Language
Demonstrate understanding of figurative language, word relationships, and nuances in word meanings.

PRACTICE Demonstrate understanding of figurative language by analyzing the extended metaphors in "Mother to Son" and "To James." Work on your own, and then discuss your responses with your group.

1. **(a)** In "Mother to Son," what metaphor does the speaker use to describe her life? **(b) Make Inferences** In lines 1–7, what do the descriptive details suggest about the type of life the mother has lived? Explain. **(c) Interpret** In lines 8–13, what do the mother's actions tell you about the ways in which she has responded to challenges? **(d) Connect** In line 14, how does the poem change? In what ways does the poet extend the metaphor in the rest of the poem?

2. **(a)** In "To James," what events does the speaker describe in lines 1–28? **(b) Analyze** What metaphor begins in line 29, and how does the rest of the poem develop that metaphor? **(c) Interpret** How does the speaker want James to live his life, and in what ways does the metaphor help to convey that message?

94 UNIT 1 • CROSSING GENERATIONS

SHARE IDEAS

Writing

A **free-verse poem** breaks "free" from the usual structures, rhymes, and rhythms of poetry to express feelings or ideas in a way that mimics natural speech.

> **Assignment**
>
> Write a **free-verse poem** in which the speaker shares a life lesson learned through personal experience. You will work individually to craft your poem. Then, you will revise and discuss it with your group.

TIP: Before you start to write, reread the poems in this collection, noting how each poet uses descriptive details and visual elements to create vivid images.

Plan Your Poem Identify the experience your poem will describe and the life lesson it will convey. Decide who the speaker will be and whom the speaker will address.

Develop Your Draft As you write your poem, explore your ideas from different angles. Consider these elements as you write:

- **Language:** Use precise words, relevant descriptive details, sensory language, or metaphor to convey experiences and events. Apply your knowledge of language and conventions to decide how you will group ideas into stanzas.

- **Structure:** Include visual elements to make your most important ideas stand out. Try varying line lengths, inserting extra space, using unconventional capitalization, and choosing punctuation for effect.

Seek Guidance From Peers Exchange the first draft of your poem with a group member. As you read your partner's poem, see if you can identify the speaker, the person being addressed, and the life lesson. Also, consider whether any visual elements are confusing or if there are places where the details could be more vivid. If so, give your partner some guidance and support to help strengthen the poem. For example, you might suggest rewriting a stanza or trying a new approach, such as adding sensory details or using a metaphor to appeal more strongly to your readers.

Share and Discuss Read the final version of your poem to your group. As you speak, follow the English conventions you used in your poem, even if they are unusual. As others speak, listen for the use of unconventional language, which poets often use to emphasize specific ideas.

After sharing, discuss your writing process with your group.
- What did you find most enjoyable and most challenging about writing a free-verse poem?
- Why did you choose the visual elements you used in your poem?
- Were you able to include a metaphor? Was it effective? What purpose did it help you achieve?

EVIDENCE LOG

Before moving on, go to your Evidence Log and record any additional thoughts or observations you may have about Poetry Collection 1.

PERFORMANCE TASK

SOURCES

- *from* Mom & Me & Mom
- Learning to Love My Mother
- Mother-Daughter Drawings
- Ode to My Papi
- Mother to Son
- To James

Present a Personal Narrative

Assignment

You have read selections about conflicts and connections between generations. Now, write an **autobiographical anecdote**, a brief true story, about a real experience or event in your life. Then, work with your group to present your personal narrative to the class. Use your anecdote to respond to the following question:

What new knowledge or skills have you learned from someone of a different generation?

Prepare and Plan

Analyze the Texts Each of the texts in this section presents insights into the lessons different generations can teach one another. With your group, identify the lesson each text conveys. Use this chart to summarize your ideas.

TITLE	LESSON TAUGHT / SUMMARY
from Mom & Me & Mom	
Learning to Love My Mother	
Mother-Daughter Drawings	
Ode to My Papi	
Mother to Son	
To James	

Plan Use your summaries to inspire your own anecdote. Jot down two or three ideas and discuss them with your group. Ask for guidance using these questions: *Which idea is the most interesting or powerful? Which most clearly answers the assignment question? Which is most appropriate for an audience of your peers?* Use your group's feedback as you develop your anecdote.

Apply Narrative Techniques Work on your own to write your anecdote. Develop a logical, well-structured event sequence to describe what happened in time order. Use relevant descriptive details to show what the situation was like, and use dialogue to express what people said and how they interacted.

Essential Question: What can one generation learn from another?

Rehearse and Present

Practice Your Presentations Work as a group to revise your anecdotes and to plan an effective sequence in which to present them.

- Have each group member read their anecdote aloud.
- Provide and accept constructive feedback.
  - When providing feedback, begin by saying what worked well. Then offer specific suggestions for elements that could be strengthened. Remember to speak respectfully when offering ideas for revision.
  - When accepting feedback, listen closely to your peers' suggestions. Then revise, edit, or rewrite to improve your work.
- Decide on the order in which group members will present. For example, you might want to start with a funny anecdote and end with an inspirational one.

Share Your Presentations As a group, deliver your anecdotes to the class. Then, invite discussion and questions from your audience.

TIP: Constructive feedback is concrete information someone can use to make improvements. Be specific and provide helpful suggestions rather than simply giving criticism or making vague statements.

Listen and Discuss

Listen to the Presentations As other groups present their anecdotes, listen carefully and jot down notes and questions. Use these tips:

- Take notes but don't write whole sentences. Instead, jot down key words that will jog your memory later.
- Notice details that affect you in a strong way.
- Write down questions you would like to ask the speakers after the presentation to learn more about their experiences.

Discuss and Reflect As a class, engage in a meaningful conversation about the anecdotes.

- Ask questions of the presenters to learn more detailed information about their experiences.
- Respond to others' questions and comments with relevant ideas from your anecdote and observations from the original experience itself.

Finally, explain how the ideas shared through this project help clarify the topic of crossing generations. What new insights have you gained about people of other age groups, about your interactions with older and younger people, and about yourself?

STANDARDS

Writing
- Write narratives to develop real or imagined experiences or events using effective technique, relevant descriptive details, and well-structured event sequences.
- With some guidance and support from peers and adults, develop and strengthen writing as needed by planning, revising, editing, rewriting, or trying a new approach, focusing on how well purpose and audience have been addressed.

Speaking and Listening
- Follow rules for collegial discussions.
- Pose questions that elicit elaboration and respond to others' questions and comments with relevant observations and ideas.

Performance Task: Present a Personal Narrative

INDEPENDENT LEARNING

Essential Question

What can one generation learn from another?

People of different generations may have unique ways of looking at the world. How can learning about different perspectives broaden your own views? In this section, you will choose a text about crossing generations to read independently. Get the most from this section by establishing a purpose for reading. Ask yourself, "What do I hope to gain from my independent reading?" Here are just a few purposes you might consider:

Read to Learn Think about the selections you have already read. What questions do you still have about the unit topic?

Read to Enjoy Read the descriptions of the texts. Which one seems most interesting and appealing to you?

Read to Form a Position Consider your thoughts and feelings about the Essential Question. Are you still undecided about some aspect of the topic?

Independent Learning Strategies

Throughout your life, in school, in your community, and in your career, you will need to rely on yourself to learn and work on your own. Use these strategies to keep your focus as you read independently for sustained periods of time. Add ideas of your own for each category.

STRATEGY	MY ACTION PLAN
Create a schedule	• Be aware of your deadlines. • Make a plan for each day's activities. •
Read with purpose	• Use a variety of reading strategies to deepen your understanding. • Think about the text and how it adds to your knowledge. •
Take notes	• Record key ideas and information. • Review your notes before sharing what you've learned. •

Contents

Choose one selection. Selections are available online only.

POETRY COLLECTION 2: LYRIC POETRY

Lineage
Margaret Walker

Family
Grace Paley

What do you inherit from your ancestors?

OPINION PIECE

"Gotcha Day" Isn't a Cause for Celebration
Sophie Johnson

Can you yearn for a past that you barely remember?

REALISTIC FICTION

Water Names
Lan Samantha Chang

An eerie tale that has been passed down for generations.

REALISTIC FICTION

An Hour With Abuelo
Judith Ortiz Cofer

A grandfather still has the ability to surprise his grandson.

SHARE YOUR INDEPENDENT LEARNING

SHARE • LEARN • REFLECT

Reflect on and evaluate the information you gained from your Independent Reading selection. Then, share what you learned with others.

Independent Learning 99

INDEPENDENT LEARNING

Close-Read Guide

Establish your purpose for reading. Then, read the selection through at least once. Use this page to record your close-read ideas.

A Close-Read Guide and Annotation Model are available online.

Selection Title: _____

Purpose for Reading: _____ Minutes Read: _____

Close Read the Text

Zoom in on sections you found interesting. **Annotate** what you notice. Ask yourself **questions** about the text. What can you **conclude**?

Analyze the Text

Think about the author's choices of literary elements, techniques, and structures. Select one and record your thoughts.

QuickWrite

Choose a paragraph from the text that grabbed your interest. Explain the power of this passage.

100 UNIT 1 • CROSSING GENERATIONS

Share Your Independent Learning

Essential Question

What can one generation learn from another?

When you read something independently, your understanding continues to grow as you share what you have learned with others.

Prepare to Share

WRITE One of the most important ways to respond to a text is to notice and describe your personal reactions. Think about the text you explored independently and the ways in which it connects to your own experiences.

- What similarities and differences do you see between the text and your own life? Describe your observations.
- How do you think this text connects to the Essential Question? Describe your ideas.

Learn From Your Classmates

DISCUSS Share your ideas about the text you explored on your own. As you talk with others, take notes about new information that seems important, and consider whether it changes your views about particular ideas.

Reflect

EXPLAIN Review your notes, and mark the most important insight you gained from these writing and discussion activities. Explain how this idea adds to your understanding of crossing generations.

STANDARDS
Speaking and Listening • Engage effectively in a range of collaborative discussions with diverse partners on grade 7 topics, texts, and issues, building on others' ideas and expressing their own clearly. • Acknowledge new information expressed by others and, when warranted, modify their own views.

UNIT 1 REFLECT AND RESPOND

In this unit, you encountered many different perspectives on crossing generations. Now, take some time to reflect on the selections you explored and to express your own ideas.

Reflect on Your Unit Goals

Review your Unit Goals chart from the beginning of the unit. Then, complete the activity and answer the question.

1. In the Unit Goals chart, rate how well you meet each goal now.
2. In which goals were you most and least successful?

Reflect on the Texts

Interview If you could interview one person from this unit, who would it be? Use the chart to list one person connected to each selection, whether an author or a character (real or fictional). Then, mark your top choice for an interview subject. Briefly explain the reason for your choice and write down one question you'd like to ask that person.

TITLE	AUTHOR/CHARACTER	REASON AND QUESTION
Don't Just Sit There Like a Punk		
The Case of the Disappearing Words		
• from Mom & Me & Mom • Learning to Love My Mother		
Mother-Daughter Drawings		
• Ode to My Papi • Mother to Son • To James		
Independent Learning Selection:		

102 UNIT 1 • CROSSING GENERATIONS

Essential Question: What can one generation learn from another?

Develop Your Perspective: Unit Projects

Choose one of the following Unit Project ideas.

SONG

Write a song about a person from a different generation whom you admire. Write lyrics that express what makes this person worthy of your admiration, using at least two of the Concept Vocabulary words you learned in this unit. If you are a musician, consider writing music to accompany your lyrics and then performing the song for your class. Alternatively, you might share the lyrics on your school's website.

VISUAL DISPLAY

Create a poster that focuses on a quotation from one of the unit selections. Around the quotation, add your own writing as well as photos, drawings, or pictures from magazines to emphasize your ideas. Together, all the components should convey a clear message about the value of crossing generations. Include at least two of the Concept Vocabulary words from the unit. Present your poster to the class, and then display it for others to see.

GROUP DISCUSSION

With a small group, **hold a collaborative discussion** about the following quotation:

> "Each generation has something different at which they are all looking."
> —Gertrude Stein

Work together to clarify Stein's meaning. Then, decide whether you agree or disagree with her. Support your viewpoint by explicitly drawing on evidence from the unit selections and from your own experiences. Ask questions of groupmates who hold the opposite view in order to probe and reflect on their ideas. Work to integrate at least two Academic Vocabulary words into the conversation.

USE NEW WORDS

Academic Vocabulary

Use the Academic Vocabulary from the unit as you plan, draft, and discuss your project:

- dialogue
- consequence
- perspective
- notable
- contradict

Concept Vocabulary

Review your Word Wall and write down any words you want to use in your project.

STANDARDS

Writing
Produce clear and coherent writing in which the development, organization, and style are appropriate to task, purpose, and audience.

Speaking and Listening
- Engage effectively in a range of collaborative discussions with diverse partners on grade 7 topics, texts, and issues.
- Include multimedia components and visual displays in presentations to clarify claims and findings and emphasize salient points.

PERFORMANCE-BASED ASSESSMENT

SOURCES

- Whole-Class Selections
- Peer-Group Selections
- Independent Learning Selection
- Your own experiences and observations

Personal Narrative

Assignment

In this unit, you read various perspectives about the ways in which people of different generations can learn from one another. You also practiced writing personal narratives. Now, apply what you have learned.

Write a **personal narrative** that reflects your new understanding of the Essential Question.

Essential Question
What can one generation learn from another?

Review and Evaluate Evidence

Review your Evidence Log and your QuickWrite from the beginning of the unit. Have your ideas changed?

⬤ Yes	⬤ No
Identify at least three pieces of evidence that changed your ideas about people of different generations.	Identify at least three pieces of evidence that reinforced your initial ideas.
1.	1.
2.	2.
3.	3.

State your ideas now:

How might you express your thinking about the ways in which we learn from people across generations in a personal narrative?

Essential Question: What can one generation learn from another?

Share Your Perspective

The **Personal Narrative Checklist** will help you stay on track.

PLAN ▶ Before you write, read the Personal Narrative Checklist and make sure you understand all the items.

DRAFT ▶ As you write, pause occasionally to make sure you're meeting the checklist requirements.

Use New Words Refer to your Word Wall to vary your word choice. Also, consider using one or more of the Academic Vocabulary terms you learned at the beginning of the unit: *dialogue, consequence, perspective, notable, contradict*

REVIEW AND EDIT ▶ After you have written a first draft, evaluate it against the checklist. Make any changes needed to strengthen the structure, message, and language of your writing. Then, reread your narrative and fix any errors you find.

EVIDENCE LOG
Make sure you have pulled in details from your Evidence Log to support your ideas.

PERSONAL NARRATIVE CHECKLIST

My personal narrative clearly contains...

- [ ] a beginning that engages readers by establishing the setting and situation and by introducing the people involved.
- [ ] a clear point of view with myself as the narrator.
- [ ] an organized event sequence that unfolds in a natural, logical order.
- [ ] a lesson I learned that I wish to convey to readers.
- [ ] dialogue, precise words, descriptive details, and sensory language that convey my experiences by painting a picture in readers' minds.
- [ ] varied transitions that show sequence and signal shifts between time frames and settings.
- [ ] a conclusion that follows from the information I shared by wrapping up the events and reflecting back on my experiences.
- [ ] correct use of standard English grammar and usage, including pronoun-antecedent agreement.
- [ ] no capitalization, punctuation, or spelling errors.

STANDARDS
Writing
• Write narratives to develop real or imagined experiences or events using effective technique, relevant descriptive details, and well-structured event sequences.

• Engage and orient the reader by establishing a context and point of view and introducing a narrator and/or characters; organize an event sequence that unfolds naturally and logically.

• Use precise words and phrases, relevant descriptive details, and sensory language to capture the action and convey experiences and events.

• Provide a conclusion that follows from and reflects on the narrated experiences or events.

Living Among the Stars

DISCUSS Why are people curious about our galaxy and what lies beyond?

Write your response here before sharing your ideas.

UNIT 2

INTRO

Essential Question
Should we make a home in space?

ARGUMENT
Humans Are Not Meant to Live in Space
MENTOR TEXT

WHOLE-CLASS LEARNING

Space Settlement Art
National Space Society
MEDIA: IMAGE GALLERY

COMPARE

Dark They Were, and Golden-Eyed
Ray Bradbury
SCIENCE FICTION

Dark They Were, and Golden-Eyed
Ray Bradbury and Michael McDonough
MEDIA: RADIO PLAY

Write an Argument: Editorial
WRITING: PERFORMANCE TASK

PEER-GROUP LEARNING

Japan to Start Research on the Moon and Mars for Humans
Tomoyuki Suzuki
SCIENCE FEATURE

COMPARE

Why We Should Continue to Explore Space
Sheri Buckner
ARGUMENT

Why We Should Save Earth Before Colonizing Mars
Bruce Dorminey
ARGUMENT

Conduct a Debate
SPEAKING AND LISTENING: PERFORMANCE TASK

INDEPENDENT LEARNING

Beyawned Earth: Pillownauts and the Downside of Space Travel
Jennifer Mason
SCIENCE FEATURE

Danger! This Mission to Mars Could Bore You to Death!
Maggie Koerth
MAGAZINE ARTICLE

Time Capsule Found on the Dead Planet
Margaret Atwood
SHORT STORY

Space Comics
Various cartoonists
MEDIA: COMIC STRIPS

SHARE • LEARN • REFLECT
SHARE INDEPENDENT LEARNING

REFLECT AND RESPOND
GOALS • TEXTS • UNIT PROJECTS

PERFORMANCE-BASED ASSESSMENT

Argument
You will write an argument in response to the Essential Question for the unit.

107

UNIT 2 INTRODUCTION

Unit Goals

Throughout this unit you will deepen your perspective about living in space by reading, writing, speaking, listening, and presenting. These goals will help you succeed on the Unit Performance-Based Assessment.

SET GOALS Use a scale of 1 to 5 to rate how well you meet these goals right now. You will revisit your ratings later, when you reflect on your growth during this unit.

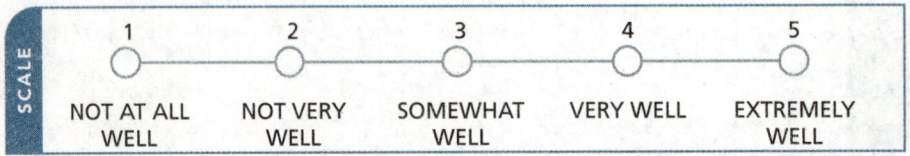

	Unit Introduction	Unit Reflection
ESSENTIAL QUESTION		
I can read selections that express different points of view about living in space and develop my own perspective.	1 2 3 4 5	1 2 3 4 5
READING		
I can understand and use academic vocabulary words related to argument.	1 2 3 4 5	1 2 3 4 5
I can recognize elements of different genres, especially arguments, informational texts, and science fiction.	1 2 3 4 5	1 2 3 4 5
I can read a selection of my choice independently and make connections to other texts.	1 2 3 4 5	1 2 3 4 5
WRITING		
I can write a focused, well-organized argumentative essay.	1 2 3 4 5	1 2 3 4 5
SPEAKING AND LISTENING		
I can prepare an argument for one side of an issue and participate in a debate.	1 2 3 4 5	1 2 3 4 5
MY GOALS		

STANDARDS
Language
- Use common, grade-appropriate Greek or Latin affixes and roots as clues to the meaning of a word.
- Acquire and use accurately grade-appropriate general academic and domain-specific words and phrases; gather vocabulary knowledge when considering a word or phrase important to comprehension or expression.

108 UNIT 2 • LIVING AMONG THE STARS

Essential Question: Should we make a home in space?

Academic Vocabulary: Argument

Academic terms can help you read, write, and discuss with precision. Many of these words have roots, or key parts, that come from Latin and Greek.

PRACTICE Academic terms are used routinely in classrooms. Build your knowledge of these words by completing the chart.

1. **Review** each word, its root, and the mentor sentences.
2. **Determine** the meaning and usage of each word using the mentor sentences and a dictionary, if needed.
3. **List** at least two related words for each academic term. Then, challenge yourself to write a sentence that contains two of the academic terms.

WORD	MENTOR SENTENCES	PREDICT MEANING	RELATED WORDS
justify LATIN ROOT: -jus- "law"; "right"	1. Raymond had to *justify* his position on a controversial subject during the debate. 2. Lucy decided to *justify* her lateness by saying she was stuck in traffic.	The right thing in a situation	justice; justification
dissent LATIN ROOT: -sent- "feel"	1. Robin expressed her *dissent* from the opinion of the majority of the people in the class. 2. The king used all of his power to quash political *dissent* within his country.	to experience something	experience, feel
certainty LATIN ROOT: -cert- "sure"	1. It was a *certainty* that everyone would want to play the popular new game. 2. The astronomers knew with *certainty* that the comet would return again.	to be certain about something	absolute, certainty
discredit LATIN ROOT: -cred- "believe"	1. The scientist had to *discredit* his partner's work because the correct procedure was not followed. 2. The lawyer used facts to *discredit* the testimony of the star witness.	to have faith in someone or something	faithful, faith
assumption LATIN ROOT: -sum- "take up"	1. The scientist made an *assumption* about life on Mars based on his experiments. 2. It is not wise to make an *assumption* if you do not have all the facts.	to fill a space	fill, assume

Unit Introduction

UNIT 2 INTRODUCTION

MENTOR TEXT

ARGUMENT MODEL

READ As you read, look at the way the writer advances the argument that the human body is designed to stay here on Earth.

Humans Are Not Meant to Live in Space

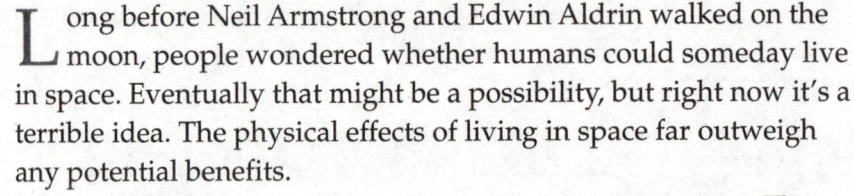

1 Long before Neil Armstrong and Edwin Aldrin walked on the moon, people wondered whether humans could someday live in space. Eventually that might be a possibility, but right now it's a terrible idea. The physical effects of living in space far outweigh any potential benefits.

2 Human bodies are made to exist in Earth's environment. They are not designed to live in microgravity. *Microgravity* refers to the near absence of gravity in space. Whenever the downward pull of gravity is removed, bones and muscles weaken because they are no longer being used to support the body. According to studies conducted on astronauts, bone loss accelerates from 3% per *year* on Earth to 1% per *month* in microgravity. Studies also suggest that over time microgravity alters the ability of bones to heal after fractures. Sure, exercising during space travel reduces these negative effects, but it's impossible for space travelers to work out enough to maintain full bone and muscle strength.

3 An astronaut's body can take up to three years to recover from a four-month period in space. What, then, might happen to a space traveler who spends far more time in space or journeys to another planet? The travel time from Earth to Mars is estimated at about nine months. Therefore, it could take up to seven years for a Mars traveler to recover from the trip alone. The surface gravity on Mars is about 38% of the gravity of Earth. Rather than bouncing back after landing on Mars, travelers would continue to experience the physical impacts of microgravity.

110 UNIT 2 • LIVING AMONG THE STARS

Essential Question: Should we make a home in space?

4   Microgravity also affects the body's fluids. In an environment of low or zero gravity, blood and spinal fluids do not properly circulate. This causes swelling of the face, eyes, and brain. It also causes weakening of the heart muscle and changes both in the inner ear and in blood pressure. All of these effects result in a lowered production of red blood cells, loss of balance, nausea, and premature aging. They also cause the loss of the body's ability to sense movement, action, and location.

5   All space travelers will eventually suffer the negative effects of microgravity, but that is not the only hazard they face. Exposure to radiation is ten times higher in space than it is on Earth. Lead insulation could provide protection for travelers, but it is too heavy for use in spacecraft. Because of this, humans are exposed to much higher—and therefore more dangerous—levels of radiation when they journey outside Earth's atmosphere. Radiation can damage the eyes, brain, and other sensitive tissues of the body—and this damage is permanent.

6   Some people argue that space travel to other planets is important for the future of the human race. Their ideas are compelling: We must be prepared to colonize other planets if Earth's population continues to increase. But space colonizers would have to deal with the life-threatening effects of microgravity and radiation. This isn't a reasonable solution to overpopulation on Earth.

7   Perhaps one day scientists will find a way to drastically reduce the negative physical effects of space travel. Until then, however, it doesn't make sense to send humans on long-term trips into space.

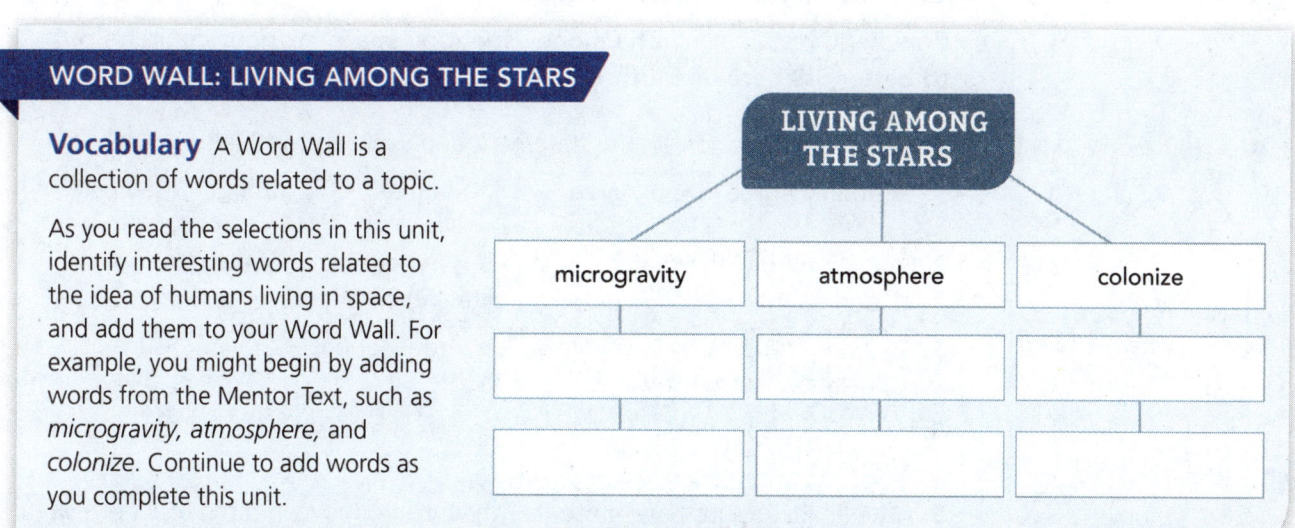

WORD WALL: LIVING AMONG THE STARS

Vocabulary A Word Wall is a collection of words related to a topic.

As you read the selections in this unit, identify interesting words related to the idea of humans living in space, and add them to your Word Wall. For example, you might begin by adding words from the Mentor Text, such as *microgravity*, *atmosphere*, and *colonize*. Continue to add words as you complete this unit.

LIVING AMONG THE STARS: microgravity, atmosphere, colonize

Humans Are Not Meant to Live in Space **111**

UNIT 2 INTRODUCTION

Summary

A **summary** is a brief, complete overview of a text that maintains the meaning and logical order of ideas in the original work. It should be objective and should not include your personal opinions.

WRITE Write a summary of "Humans Are Not Meant to Live in Space."

_____
_____
_____
_____
_____
_____
_____
_____
_____
_____
_____
_____

Icebreaker

Conduct a Four-Corner Debate

Consider this statement: **The money spent on space missions could be put to better use here on Earth.**

1. Record your position on the statement and explain your thinking.

   ◯ Strongly Agree ◯ Agree ◯ Disagree ◯ Strongly Disagree

2. Form a group with like-minded students in one corner of the classroom. Take turns sharing your ideas in a polite and collaborative way.

3. Ask your groupmates questions to learn more about their views, such as "What led you to take this position?"

4. Have a representative from your group give a brief summary of the group's position to the class.

5. After all the groups have presented their views, move into the four corners again. If you learned new information from another group that changed your position, you may switch corners, but be ready to explain why.

STANDARDS

Reading Informational Text
Provide an objective summary of the text.

Speaking and Listening
- Follow rules for collegial discussions.
- Pose questions that elicit elaboration.
- Acknowledge new information expressed by others and, when warranted, modify their own views.

Essential Question: Should we make a home in space?

QuickWrite

Consider class discussions, the video, and the Mentor Text as you think about the Essential Question.

Essential Question

Should we make a home in space?

At the end of the unit, you will respond to the Essential Question again and see if your perspective has deepened or changed.

WRITE Record your first thoughts here.

___

EVIDENCE LOG

Should we make a home in space?

As you read the selections in this unit, use a chart like the one shown to record your ideas and list details from the texts that support them. Taking notes as you go will help you clarify your thinking, gather relevant information, and be ready to respond to the Essential Question.

TITLE	MY IDEAS / OBSERVATIONS	TEXT EVIDENCE / INFORMATION

Unit Introduction 113

WHOLE-CLASS LEARNING

Essential Question

Should we make a home in space?

Some people gaze up at a starry sky and wonder at its beauty. Some people look up at the same sky and imagine who or what is up there. You will work with your whole class to explore different perspectives on living among the stars.

Whole-Class Learning Strategies

Throughout your life, in school, in your community, and in your career, you will continue to learn and work in large-group environments.

Review these strategies and the actions you can take to practice them as you work with your whole class. Add ideas of your own to each category. Get ready to use these strategies during Whole-Class Learning.

STRATEGY	MY ACTION PLAN
Listen actively	• Look at the person who is speaking and give them your full attention. • Jot down notes about important points the speaker makes, but keep your focus on listening. •
Demonstrate respect	• Keep an open mind about the ideas your classmates share. • Do not interrupt others when they are speaking. •
Make personal connections	• Recognize that literature explores human experience—the details may differ from your own life, but the emotions it expresses are universal. • Actively look for ways in which your personal experiences help you find meaning in a text. • Consider how your own experiences help you understand characters' actions and reactions. •

114 UNIT 2 • LIVING AMONG THE STARS

Contents

MEDIA: IMAGE GALLERY

Space Settlement Art
National Space Society

How do artists envision life in outer space?

COMPARE

SCIENCE FICTION

Dark They Were, and Golden-Eyed
Ray Bradbury

Something strange is happening to these settlers on Mars.

MEDIA: RADIO PLAY

Dark They Were, and Golden-Eyed
Ray Bradbury and Michael McDonough

Experience this Ray Bradbury story as a radio play.

PERFORMANCE TASK

WRITING PROMPT • WRITER'S HANDBOOK

Write an Argument: Editorial

The Whole-Class selections imagine the experience of living in space in ways that might surprise you. After viewing, reading, and listening, you will write an editorial in which you take a position on the importance of space exploration.

Whole-Class Learning **115**

PREPARE TO VIEW

Space Settlement Art

About the Organization

The **National Space Society**, a nonprofit organization based in Washington, D.C., supports the idea that humans should establish settlements in space. These colonies could provide homes and jobs for people and make use of natural resources found on other planets. The National Space Society publishes magazines and organizes conferences. It also sponsors art contests.

Media Vocabulary

These words describe characteristics of the art in the image gallery. Use them as you analyze, discuss, and write about the images.

realism: style of art that emphasizes natural-looking people, objects, and places	• Realism in art avoids exaggerations, such as heroes with superhuman strength. • Realistic art can be highly imaginative as long as it stays within true-to-life limits.
medium: material or technology an artist uses to create their work	• Mediums for visual art include paint, pen, pencil, charcoal, and torn paper. • Some contemporary artists use technical mediums, which include different types of software, such as Photoshop.
digital art: art that is created or enhanced using computers, software, or other digital tools	• Digital art may be entirely generated by a computer, or it may include other elements, such as scanned photos. • Digital artists must be skilled in both creating art and using technology.

Viewing Strategy: Make Inferences

An **inference** you make when viewing art is a well-reasoned guess based on explicit evidence given in the image, its title, and its caption. Sometimes, at first glance, certain aspects of a picture may seem unclear. By carefully examining elements of the art and how they work together, you can infer what is happening or what the artist wants to emphasize.

EXAMPLE Here is an inference you might make about Javier Arizabalo's *Imitating the Earth*.

Evidence: Two huge, sleek space vehicles float above Earth. No people are visible, but teams of scientists must have developed these complex vehicles for an important purpose. The title hints that the vehicles imitate planet Earth in some way.

Inference: These spaceships contain environments similar to those on Earth, so people can live and work in them.

PRACTICE As you explore this image gallery, make inferences based on evidence in the art, the titles, and the captions. Write your inferences in the Take Notes space on each page.

STANDARDS
Reading Literature
Cite several pieces of textual evidence to support analysis of what the text says explicitly as well as inferences drawn from the text.
Language
Gather vocabulary knowledge when considering a word or phrase important to comprehension or expression.

VIEW

MEDIA: IMAGE GALLERY

Space Settlement Art
The National Space Society

BACKGROUND
The National Space Society has sponsored art contests for which they invited students aged 13 through 25 to submit original art. The images had to depict realistic-looking space settlements far from Earth. This image gallery includes some of the artworks submitted for those contests.

IMAGE 1: Imitating the Earth
Javier Arizabalo

Small orbital cities prepare for a future outside the terrestrial atmosphere.

Medium/Tools Used: Electric Image, Photoshop

TAKE NOTES

IMAGE 2: After the Storm
Raymond Cassel

After a sandstorm, people begin to clean up the greenhouses on Mars.

Medium/Tools Used: LightWave, Poser, and Photoshop

TAKE NOTES

IMAGE 3: Skylight of the Universe
Alfred Twu

This is a commemoration of the Chinese Mid-Autumn Moon Festival and associated folktales.

Medium/Tools Used: Colored pencil and metallic gel pen

TAKE NOTES

IMAGE 4: Closest Approach
Jonathan Chapin

On an asteroid passing by Mars, a parent teaches his daughter about the "Red Planet."

Medium/Tools Used: Cinema 4D R10, with body paint for the astronauts, asteroid, and planet; Photoshop for the stars and lights

▸ TAKE NOTES

BUILD INSIGHT

First Thoughts

Choose one of the following items to answer:
- Would you want to live at any of the space settlements shown in the gallery? If so, which one and why? If not, why not?
- Do the images and the tools the artists used inspire you to learn how to create digital art? Explain.

Comprehension

1. **Viewing Check** (a) Which different locations are represented in the image gallery? (b) What types of activities are people involved in?

2. **Strategy: Make Inferences** (a) What types of background knowledge did the artists need in order to create these images? (b) **Support** What evidence from the art supports your answer?

Analysis

3. **Analyze** (a) What is realistic about the art in the image gallery? (b) What is imaginative about it?

4. **Compare and Contrast** Alfred Twu's *Skylight of the Universe* is the only artwork that is not digital. (a) How is it similar to the other images? (b) How is it different?

5. **Evaluate** Is it valuable to study artworks showing situations that don't yet exist? Why or why not?

Exploring the Essential Question

Should we make a home in space?

6. Do you find the images of space settlements comforting or alarming? What insights about making a home in space have you gained from viewing these images? Record your ideas in your Evidence Log.

STANDARDS
Reading Literature
Cite several pieces of textual evidence to support analysis of what the text says explicitly as well as inferences drawn from the text.

Space Settlement Art 121

ANALYZE AND INTERPRET

SPACE SETTLEMENT ART

Close Review

Review the image gallery and note interesting details. Record any new observations that seem important. Then, write a question and your conclusion.

MY QUESTION:

MY CONCLUSION:

STUDY LANGUAGE AND CRAFT

Media Vocabulary

These words describe characteristics of the visual art in the image gallery. Practice using them in your responses.

| realism | medium | digital art |

1. In your opinion, which artist used their chosen medium(s) most effectively? Explain your answer.

2. What skills are needed to create digital art?

3. Are the artworks in the image gallery examples of realism? Explain your answer.

STANDARDS

Writing
- Use precise words and phrases, relevant descriptive details, and sensory language to capture the action and convey experiences and events.
- Use technology, including the Internet, to produce and publish writing.

Language
Acquire and use accurately grade-appropriate general academic and domain-specific words and phrases.

122 UNIT 2 • LIVING AMONG THE STARS

SHARE IDEAS

Writing

A **story synopsis** describes the main characters, settings, and events in a fictional story. It is not a narrative itself—instead, it explains what happens in a narrative. A synopsis is shorter than a fully written story and includes only the most essential relevant details that convey the story's action, experiences, and events.

TIP: A synopsis does not include dialogue. It can, however, mention conversations characters have.

Assignment

Choose one image from the gallery and imagine a story that takes place. Write a **story synopsis** following these steps:

- Imagine characters who might live in the setting, a problem they might face, and the actions they might take to resolve it.
- Outline the story's beginning, middle, and end, making sure to include only the most essential details that convey the action, experiences, and events. Then write your draft using correct grammar and conventions.
- With your classmates, publish your synopses as a digital booklet arranged by image.

Use Academic Vocabulary
Challenge yourself to include one or more of these academic vocabulary words in your writing: *justify, dissent, certainty, discredit, assumption*.

Reflect on Your Writing

PRACTICE Think about the choices you made as you wrote. Also, consider what you learned by writing. Share your experiences by responding to these questions.

1. Did you find starting from an image helpful or limiting? Why?

2. Did you use only details that appear in the image, or did you add elements that were not in the art? Explain.

3. **Why These Words?** The words you choose make a difference in your writing. Which words did you specifically choose to bring your space story to life?

Space Settlement Art 123

COMPARE ACROSS GENRES

FICTION and DRAMA

Science fiction is a type of writing that brings elements of science and technology into a made-up story. A **radio-play adaptation** is an audio drama that is based on an existing story.

SCIENCE FICTION

Author's Purpose
- to tell a story that combines imagination and scientific fact

Characteristics
- settings that feature imaginary elements, such as other worlds and advanced technology
- often takes place in the future
- characters that may be human or non-human
- a narrator, or "voice" that tells the story
- conflicts, or problems, that are often caused by the setting
- a theme, or insight about life

Structure
- Exposition, or explanation, as well as dialogue and description convey the story's setting and plot.

RADIO-PLAY ADAPTATION

Author's Purpose
- to retell an original work of fiction as an audio drama

Characteristics
- often part of a radio show or podcast
- settings, characters, conflicts, events, language, theme, and plot based on those of the original story
- an announcer or a narrator
- background music
- sound effects

Structure
- Dialogue, or characters' spoken words, convey the story's setting and plot.

124 UNIT 2 • LIVING AMONG THE STARS

Essential Question: Should we make a home in space?

Setting and Figurative Language

The **setting** of a story is the time and place in which it occurs. Science fiction usually features invented settings, such as alien planets in the future. To make these settings clear and vivid, science-fiction writers often use **figurative language,** such as personification, metaphors, and similes. This is language that works imaginatively rather than literally.

- **Personification** presents non-human things as though they have human qualities: *The forest is lonely without the owls.*
- **Metaphors** imply a similarity between two unlike things by saying one thing *is* another: *The suns of yellow flowers blaze in the vase.*
- **Similes** use the words *like* or *as* to state a similarity between two unlike things: *The flowers are like blazing suns.*

TIP: In the examples, personification gives human feelings to the forest. The metaphor and the simile convey a similarity between suns and flowers.

PRACTICE Identify items 1–4 as *personification, metaphor,* or *simile*. Explain how you made your determinations. Then, answer question 5.

1. The mirror of the lake reflects the moons.

2. The storm won its argument with the Martian colony.

3. Gravity held on, unwilling to let the spaceship go.

4. The sea is like a sheet of silver covering the planet.

5. Given these examples, describe the purpose you think figurative language might serve in a science-fiction story.

STANDARDS

Reading Literature
Determine the meaning of words and phrases as they are used in a text, including figurative and connotative meanings.

Language
- Demonstrate understanding of figurative language, word relationships, and nuances in word meanings.
- Interpret figures of speech in context.

Compare Across Genres

PREPARE TO READ

DARK THEY WERE, AND GOLDEN-EYED (short story)

DARK THEY WERE, AND GOLDEN-EYED (radio play)

COMPARE: FICTION and DRAMA
In this lesson, you will read the short story **Dark They Were, and Golden-Eyed** and listen to a radio play performance of it. You will then compare the short story to the radio play.

About the Author

As a boy, **Ray Bradbury** (1920–2012) loved magicians, circuses, and science-fiction stories. He began writing at the age of 12 and went on to become one of the most celebrated writers of science fiction and fantasy. *The Martian Chronicles,* a collection of Bradbury's stories about Earth's colonization of Mars, was published in 1950 and is considered a classic today.

Concept Vocabulary

Predict The words listed here appear in the story. Judging from these words, explain what you think the setting of this story will be like.

WORDS	MY EXPECTATIONS
submerged (suhb MURJD) *adj.* completely covered with a liquid	
forlorn (fawr LAWRN) *adj.* abandoned or deserted	
canals (kuh NALZ) *n.* artificial waterways for transportation or watering land	
immense (ih MEHNS) *adj.* very large	
atmosphere (AT muh sfihr) *n.* gas surrounding a planet; air	
mosaic (moh ZAY ihk) *adj.* made of many small pieces of colored glass or stone	

Reading Strategy: Make Inferences

Inferences are educated guesses you make based on evidence in a text. Making inferences as you read will add to your understanding and enjoyment. To make inferences, notice clues in the story and think about what they suggest about characters or events.

EXAMPLE

Evidence: In paragraph 82, Mr. Bittering thinks, "Aren't you frightened? Aren't you afraid?"

Inference: No one else is upset. Mr. Bittering may be the only one who senses something is wrong.

PRACTICE As you read the story, write your inferences in the open space next to the text. Mark evidence that supports each one.

STANDARDS
Reading Literature
Cite several pieces of textual evidence to support analysis of what the text says explicitly as well as inferences drawn from the text.

Language
Gather vocabulary knowledge when considering a word or phrase important to comprehension or expression.

126 UNIT 2 • LIVING AMONG THE STARS

SCIENCE FICTION

Dark They Were, and Golden-Eyed

Ray Bradbury

BACKGROUND

The astronomer Carl Sagan once wrote, "Mars has become a kind of mythic arena onto which we have projected our earthly hopes and fears." People have always been fascinated by the possibility of alien life on Mars. In this story, author Ray Bradbury explores the aura of mystery that has always surrounded the Red Planet.

1   The rocket metal cooled in the meadow winds. Its lid gave a bulging *pop*. From its clock interior stepped a man, a woman, and three children. The other passengers whispered away across the Martian meadow, leaving the man alone among his family.

2   The man felt his hair flutter and the tissues of his body draw tight as if he were standing at the center of a vacuum. His wife, before him, seemed almost to whirl away in smoke. The children, small seeds, might at any instant be sown to all the Martian climes.

3   The children looked up at him, as people look to the sun to tell what time of their life it is. His face was cold.

4   "What's wrong?" asked his wife.

5   "Let's get back on the rocket."

6   "Go back to Earth?"

7   "Yes! Listen!"

8   The wind blew as if to flake away their identities. At any moment the Martian air might draw his soul from him, as marrow

READ TO UNLOCK MEANING

1. First read the text for comprehension and enjoyment. Use the **Reading Strategy** and **Comprehension Check** questions to support your first read.
2. Go back and respond to the Close-Read notes.
3. Identify other details in the text you find interesting. Ask your own questions and draw your own conclusions.

CLOSE READ

ANNOTATE In paragraph 2, mark the things that are being compared.

QUESTION What overall impression has Bradbury created with these comparisons?

Dark They Were, and Golden-Eyed **127**

submerged (suhb MURJD) *adj.* completely covered with a liquid

MAKE INFERENCES
After reading paragraph 13, jot down an inference you make and details from the story that support it.

comes from a white bone. He felt **submerged** in a chemical that could dissolve his intellect and burn away his past.

9 They looked at Martian hills that time had worn with a crushing pressure of years. They saw the old cities, lost in their meadows, lying like children's delicate bones among the blowing lakes of grass.

10 "Chin up, Harry," said his wife. "It's too late. We've come over sixty million miles."

11 The children with their yellow hair hollered at the deep dome of Martian sky. There was no answer but the racing hiss of wind through the stiff grass.

12 He picked up the luggage in his cold hands. "Here we go," he said—a man standing on the edge of a sea, ready to wade in and be drowned.

13 They walked into town.

14 Their name was Bittering. Harry and his wife Cora; Dan, Laura, and David. They built a small white cottage and ate good breakfasts there, but the fear was never gone. It lay with Mr. Bittering and Mrs. Bittering, a third unbidden partner at every midnight talk, at every dawn awakening.

15 "I feel like a salt crystal," he said, "in a mountain stream, being washed away. We don't belong here. We're Earth people. This is Mars. It was meant for Martians. For heaven's sake, Cora, let's buy tickets for home!"

16 But she only shook her head. "One day the atom bomb will fix Earth. Then we'll be safe here."

17 "Safe and insane!"

18 *Tick-tock, seven o'clock* sang the voice-clock; *time to get up*. And they did.

19 Something made him check everything each morning—warm hearth, potted blood-geraniums—precisely as if he expected something to be amiss. The morning paper was toast-warm from the 6 A.M. Earth rocket. He broke its seal and tilted it at his breakfast place. He forced himself to be convivial.[1]

20 "Colonial days all over again," he declared. "Why, in ten years there'll be a million Earthmen on Mars. Big cities, everything! They said we'd fail. Said the Martians would resent our invasion. But did we find any Martians? Not a living soul! Oh, we found their empty cities, but no one in them. Right?"

21 A river of wind submerged the house. When the windows ceased rattling Mr. Bittering swallowed and looked at the children.

22 "I don't know," said David. "Maybe there're Martians around we don't see. Sometimes nights I think I hear 'em. I hear the wind. The sand hits my window. I get scared. And I see those towns way up in

---

1. **convivial** (kuhn VIHV ee uhl) *adj.* sociable and friendly.

128 UNIT 2 • LIVING AMONG THE STARS

the mountains where the Martians lived a long time ago. And I think I see things moving around those towns, Papa. And I wonder if those Martians *mind* us living here. I wonder if they won't do something to us for coming here."

23 "Nonsense!" Mr. Bittering looked out the windows. "We're clean, decent people." He looked at his children. "All dead cities have some kind of ghosts in them. Memories, I mean." He stared at the hills. "You see a staircase and you wonder what Martians looked like climbing it. You see Martian paintings and you wonder what the painter was like. You make a little ghost in your mind, a memory. It's quite natural. Imagination." He stopped. "You haven't been prowling up in those ruins, have you?"

24 "No, Papa." David looked at his shoes.

25 "See that you stay away from them. Pass the jam."

26 "Just the same," said little David, "I bet something happens. "

27 Something happened that afternoon.

28 Laura stumbled through the settlement, crying. She dashed blindly onto the porch.

29 "Mother, Father—the war, Earth!" she sobbed. "A radio flash just came. Atom bombs hit New York! All the space rockets blown up. No more rockets to Mars, ever!"

30 "Oh, Harry!" The mother held onto her husband and daughter.

31 "Are you sure, Laura?" asked the father quietly.

32 Laura wept. "We're stranded on Mars, forever and ever!"

33 For a long time there was only the sound of the wind in the late afternoon.

34 Alone, thought Bittering. Only a thousand of us here. No way back. No way. No way. Sweat poured from his face and his hands and his body; he was drenched in the hotness of his fear. He wanted to strike Laura, cry, "No, you're lying! The rockets will come back!" Instead, he stroked Laura's head against him and said, "The rockets will get through someday."

35 "Father, what will we do?"

36 "Go about our business, of course. Raise crops and children. Wait. Keep things going until the war ends and the rockets come again."

37 The two boys stepped out onto the porch.

38 "Children," he said, sitting there, looking beyond them, "I've something to tell you."

39 "We know," they said.

40 In the following days, Bittering wandered often through the garden to stand alone in his fear. As long as the rockets had spun a silver web across space, he had been able to accept Mars. For he

CLOSE READ

ANNOTATE Mark details in the beginning of paragraph 34 that describe Bittering's inner thoughts.

QUESTION Why are these thoughts expressed in incomplete sentences with a lot of repetition, and what does this reveal about Bittering's emotional state?

COMPREHENSION CHECK

Why do the Bitterings think they are stuck on Mars forever?

CLOSE READ

ANNOTATE Mark examples of descriptive language in paragraph 41.

QUESTION How does this use of language build suspense?

had always told himself: Tomorrow, if I want, I can buy a ticket and go back to Earth.

41   But now: The web gone, the rockets lying in jigsaw heaps of molten girder and unsnaked wire. Earth people left to the strangeness of Mars, the cinnamon dusts and wine airs, to be baked like gingerbread shapes in Martian summers, put into harvested storage by Martian winters. What would happen to him, the others? This was the moment Mars had waited for. Now it would eat them.

42   He got down on his knees in the flower bed, a spade in his nervous hands. Work, he thought, work and forget.

43   He glanced up from the garden to the Martian mountains. He thought of the proud old Martian names that had once been on those peaks. Earthmen, dropping from the sky, had gazed upon hills, rivers, Martian seats left nameless in spite of names. Once Martians had built cities, named cities; climbed mountains, named mountains; sailed seas, named seas. Mountains melted, seas drained, cities tumbled. In spite of this, the Earthmen had felt a silent guilt at putting new names to these ancient hills and valleys.

44   Nevertheless, man lives by symbol and label. The names were given.

45   Mr. Bittering felt very alone in his garden under the Martian sun, anachronism[2] bent here, planting Earth flowers in a wild soil.

46   Think. Keep thinking. Different things. Keep your mind free of Earth, the atom war, the lost rockets.

47   He perspired. He glanced about. No one watching. He removed his tie. Pretty bold, he thought. First your coat off, now your tie. He hung it neatly on a peach tree he had imported as a sapling from Massachusetts.

48   He returned to his philosophy of names and mountains. The Earthmen had changed names. Now there were Hormel Valleys, Roosevelt Seas, Ford Hills, Vanderbilt Plateaus, Rockefeller Rivers,[3] on Mars. It wasn't right. The American settlers had shown wisdom, using old Indian prairie names: Wisconsin, Minnesota, Idaho, Ohio, Utah, Milwaukee, Waukegan, Osseo. The old names, the old meanings.

49   Staring at the mountains wildly, he thought: Are you up there? All the dead ones, you Martians? Well, here we are, alone, cut off! Come down, move us out! We're helpless!

50   The wind blew a shower of peach blossoms.

51   He put out his sun-browned hand and gave a small cry. He touched the blossoms and picked them up. He turned them, he touched them again and again. Then he shouted for his wife.

52   "Cora!"

---

2. **anachronism** (uh NA kruh nih zuhm) *n.* something that seems to belong to the past instead of the present.
3. **Hormel Valleys . . . Rockefeller Rivers** The colonists have named places on Mars after well-known families from mid-twentieth-century America.

53 She appeared at a window. He ran to her.

54 "Cora, these blossoms!"

55 She handled them.

56 "Do you see? They're different. They've changed! They're not peach blossoms any more!"

57 "Look all right to me," she said.

58 "They're not. They're wrong! I can't tell how. An extra petal, a leaf, something, the color, the smell!"

59 The children ran out in time to see their father hurrying about the garden, pulling up radishes, onions, and carrots from their beds.

60 "Cora, come look!"

61 They handled the onions, the radishes, the carrots among them.

62 "Do they look like carrots?"

63 "Yes . . . no." She hesitated. "I don't know."

64 "They're changed."

65 "Perhaps."

66 "You know they have! Onions but not onions, carrots but not carrots. Taste: the same but different. Smell: not like it used to be." He felt his heart pounding, and he was afraid. He dug his fingers into the earth. "Cora, what's happening? What is it? We've got to get away from this." He ran across the garden. Each tree felt his touch. "The roses. The roses. They're turning green!"

67 And they stood looking at the green roses.

68 And two days later Dan came running. "Come see the cow. I was milking her and I saw it. Come on!"

69 They stood in the shed and looked at their one cow.

COMPREHENSION CHECK

Why are the Bitterings suddenly alarmed?

Dark They Were, and Golden-Eyed **131**

70 It was growing a third horn.

71 And the lawn in front of their house very quietly and slowly was coloring itself like spring violets. Seed from Earth but growing up a soft purple.

72 "We must get away," said Bittering. "We'll eat this stuff and then we'll change—who knows to what? I can't let it happen. There's only one thing to do. Burn this food!"

73 "It's not poisoned."

74 "But it is. Subtly, very subtly. A little bit. A very little bit. We mustn't touch it."

75 He looked with dismay at their house. "Even the house. The wind's done something to it. The air's burned it. The fog at night. The boards, all warped out of shape. It's not an Earthman's house any more."

76 "Oh, your imagination!"

77 He put on his coat and tie. "I'm going into town. We've got to do something now. I'll be back."

78 "Wait, Harry!" his wife cried.

79 But he was gone.

80 In town, on the shadowy step of the grocery store, the men sat with their hands on their knees, conversing with great leisure and ease.

81 Mr. Bittering wanted to fire a pistol in the air.

82 What are you doing, you fools! he thought. Sitting here! You've heard the news—we're stranded on this planet. Well, move! Aren't you frightened? Aren't you afraid? What are you going to do?

83 "Hello, Harry," said everyone.

84 "Look," he said to them. "You did hear the news, the other day, didn't you?"

85 They nodded and laughed. "Sure. Sure, Harry."

86 "What are you going to do about it?"

87 "Do, Harry, do? What *can* we do?"

88 "Build a rocket, that's what!"

89 "A rocket, Harry? To go back to all that trouble? Oh, Harry!"

90 "But you *must* want to go back. Have you noticed the peach blossoms, the onions, the grass?"

91 "Why, yes, Harry, seems we did," said one of the men.

92 "Doesn't it scare you?"

93 "Can't recall that it did much, Harry."

94 "Idiots!"

95 "Now, Harry."

96 Bittering wanted to cry. "You've got to work with me. If we stay here, we'll all change. The air. Don't you smell it? Something in the air. A Martian virus, maybe; some seed, or a pollen. Listen to me!"

97 They stared at him.

CLOSE READ

ANNOTATE Mark details in paragraphs 83–95 that indicate disagreement between Bittering and the other men.

QUESTION Why might Bradbury have chosen to build conflict through the use of dialogue?

98 "Sam," he said to one of them.
99 "Yes, Harry?"
100 "Will you help me build a rocket?"
101 "Harry, I got a whole load of metal and some blueprints. You want to work in my metal shop on a rocket, you're welcome. I'll sell you that metal for five hundred dollars. You should be able to construct a right pretty rocket, if you work alone, in about thirty years."
102 Everyone laughed.
103 "Don't laugh."
104 Sam looked at him with quiet good humor.
105 "Sam," Bittering said. "Your eyes—"
106 "What about them, Harry?"
107 "Didn't they used to be gray?"
108 "Well now, I don't remember."
109 "They were, weren't they?"
110 "Why do you ask, Harry?"
111 "Because now they're kind of yellow-colored."
112 "Is that so, Harry?" Sam said, casually.
113 "And you're taller and thinner—"
114 "You might be right, Harry."
115 "Sam, you shouldn't have yellow eyes."
116 "Harry, what color eyes have *you* got?" Sam said.
117 "My eyes? They're blue, of course."
118 "Here you are, Harry." Sam handed him a pocket mirror. "Take a look at yourself."
119 Mr. Bittering hesitated, and then raised the mirror to his face.
120 There were little, very dim flecks of new gold captured in the blue of his eyes.
121 "Now look what you've done," said Sam a moment later. "You've broken my mirror."

122 Harry Bittering moved into the metal shop and began to build the rocket. Men stood in the open door and talked and joked without raising their voices. Once in a while they gave him a hand on lifting something. But mostly they just idled and watched him with their yellowing eyes.
123 "It's suppertime, Harry," they said.
124 His wife appeared with his supper in a wicker basket.
125 "I won't touch it," he said. "I'll eat only food from our Deepfreeze. Food that came from Earth. Nothing from our garden."
126 His wife stood watching him. "You can't build a rocket."
127 "I worked in a shop once, when I was twenty. I know metal. Once I get it started, the others will help," he said, not looking at her, laying out the blueprints.

COMPREHENSION CHECK

What does Bittering think about building a rocket? What do the other men think?

128 "Harry, Harry," she said, helplessly.

129 "We've got to get away, Cora. We've *got* to!"

130 The nights were full of wind that blew down the empty moonlit sea meadows past the little white chess cities lying for their twelve-thousandth year in the shallows. In the Earthmen's settlement, the Bittering house shook with a feeling of change.

131 Lying abed, Mr. Bittering felt his bones shifted, shaped, melted like gold. His wife, lying beside him, was dark from many sunny afternoons. Dark she was, and golden-eyed, burnt almost black by the sun, sleeping, and the children metallic in their beds, and the wind roaring **forlorn** and changing through the old peach trees, the violet grass, shaking out green rose petals.

132 The fear would not be stopped. It had his throat and heart. It dripped in a wetness of the arm and the temple and the trembling palm.

133 A green star rose in the east.

134 A strange word emerged from Mr. Bittering's lips.

135 "*Iorrt. Iorrt.*" He repeated it.

136 It was a Martian word. He knew no Martian.

137 In the middle of the night he arose and dialed a call through to Simpson, the archaeologist.

138 "Simpson, what does the word *Iorrt* mean?"

139 "Why that's the old Martian word for our planet Earth. Why?"

140 "No special reason."

141 The telephone slipped from his hand.

142 "Hello, hello, hello, hello," it kept saying while he sat gazing out at the green star. "Bittering? Harry, are you there?"

143 The days were full of metal sound. He laid the frame of the rocket with the reluctant help of three indifferent men. He grew very tired in an hour or so and had to sit down.

144 "The altitude," laughed a man.

145 "Are you *eating*, Harry?" asked another.

146 "I'm eating," he said, angrily.

147 "From your Deepfreeze?"

148 "Yes!"

149 "You're getting thinner, Harry."

150 "I'm not."

151 "And taller."

152 "Liar!"

153 His wife took him aside a few days later. "Harry, I've used up all the food in the Deepfreeze. There's nothing left. I'll have to make sandwiches using food grown on Mars."

154 He sat down heavily.

155 "You must eat," she said. "You're weak."

156 "Yes," he said.

forlorn (fawr LAWRN) *adj.* abandoned or deserted

CLOSE READ

ANNOTATE Mark the Martian word Mr. Bittering says in paragraph 135.

QUESTION Why does the author have Bittering speak Martian at this point in the story, and why is this event significant?

157 He took a sandwich, opened it, looked at it, and began to nibble at it.

158 "And take the rest of the day off," she said. "It's hot. The children want to swim in the **canals** and hike. Please come along."

159 "I can't waste time. This is a crisis!"

160 "Just for an hour," she urged. "A swim'll do you good."

161 He rose, sweating. "All right, all right. Leave me alone. I'll come."

162 "Good for you, Harry."

163 The sun was hot, the day quiet. There was only an **immense** staring burn upon the land. They moved along the canal, the father, the mother, the racing children in their swimsuits. They stopped and ate meat sandwiches. He saw their skin baking brown. And he saw the yellow eyes of his wife and his children, their eyes that were never yellow before. A few tremblings shook him, but were carried off in waves of pleasant heat as he lay in the sun. He was too tired to be afraid.

164 "Cora, how long have your eyes been yellow?"

165 She was bewildered. "Always, I guess."

166 "They didn't change from brown in the last three months?"

167 She bit her lips. "No. Why do you ask?"

canals (kuh NALZ) *n.* artificial waterways for transportation or watering land

immense (ih MEHNS) *adj.* very large

COMPREHENSION CHECK
Why hasn't Bittering been eating, and how is it affecting him?

Dark They Were, and Golden-Eyed **135**

168 "Never mind."

169 They sat there.

170 "The children's eyes," he said. "They're yellow, too."

171 "Sometimes growing children's eyes change color."

172 "Maybe *we're* children, too. At least to Mars. That's a thought." He laughed. "Think I'll swim."

173 They leaped into the canal water, and he let himself sink down and down to the bottom like a golden statue and lie there in green silence. All was water-quiet and deep, all was peace. He felt the steady, slow current drift him easily.

174 If I lie here long enough, he thought, the water will work and eat away my flesh until the bones show like coral. Just my skeleton left. And then the water can build on that skeleton—green things, deep water things, red things, yellow things. Change. Change. Slow, deep, silent change. And isn't that what it is up *there*?

175 He saw the sky submerged above him, the sun made Martian by **atmosphere** and time and space.

176 Up there, a big river, he thought, a Martian river; all of us lying deep in it, in our pebble houses, in our sunken boulder houses, like crayfish hidden, and the water washing away our old bodies and lengthening the bones and—

177 He let himself drift up through the soft light.

178 Dan sat on the edge of the canal, regarding his father seriously.

179 "*Utha*," he said.

180 "What?" asked his father.

181 The boy smiled. "You know. *Utha's* the Martian word for 'father.'"

182 "Where did you learn it?"

183 "I don't know. Around. *Utha!*"

184 "What do you want?"

185 The boy hesitated. "I—I want to change my name."

186 "Change it?"

187 "Yes."

188 His mother swam over. "What's wrong with Dan for a name?"

189 Dan fidgeted. "The other day you called Dan, Dan, Dan. I didn't even hear. I said to myself, That's not my name. I've a new name I want to use."

190 Mr. Bittering held to the side of the canal, his body cold and his heart pounding slowly. "What is this new name?"

191 "Linnl. Isn't that a good name? Can I use it? Can't I, please?"

192 Mr. Bittering put his hand to his head. He thought of the silly rocket, himself working alone, himself alone even among his family, so alone.

193 He heard his wife say, "Why not?"

194 He heard himself say, "Yes, you can use it."

atmosphere (AT muh sfihr) *n.* gas surrounding a planet; air

195 "Yaaa!" screamed the boy. "I'm Linnl, Linnl!"

196 Racing down the meadowlands, he danced and shouted.

197 Mr. Bittering looked at his wife. "Why did we do that?"

198 "I don't know," she said. "It just seemed like a good idea."

199 They walked into the hills. They strolled on old **mosaic** paths, beside still pumping fountains. The paths were covered with a thin film of cool water all summer long. You kept your bare feet cool all the day, splashing as in a creek, wading.

200 They came to a small deserted Martian villa with a good view of the valley. It was on top of a hill. Blue marble halls, large murals, a swimming pool. It was refreshing in this hot summertime. The Martians hadn't believed in large cities.

201 "How nice," said Mrs. Bittering, "if we could move up here to this villa for the summer."

202 "Come on," he said. "We're going back to town. There's work to be done on the rocket."

203 But as he worked that night, the thought of the cool blue marble villa entered his mind. As the hours passed, the rocket seemed less important.

204 In the flow of days and weeks, the rocket receded and dwindled. The old fever was gone. It frightened him to think he had let it slip this way. But somehow the heat, the air, the working conditions—

205 He heard the men murmuring on the porch of his metal shop.

206 "Everyone's going. You heard?"

207 "All going. That's right."

208 Bittering came out. "Going where?" He saw a couple of trucks, loaded with children and furniture, drive down the dusty street.

209 "Up to the villas," said the man.

210 "Yeah, Harry. I'm going. So is Sam. Aren't you Sam?"

211 "That's right, Harry. What about you?"

212 "I've got work to do here."

213 "Work! You can finish that rocket in the autumn, when it's cooler."

214 He took a breath. "I got the frame all set up."

215 "In the autumn is better." Their voices were lazy in the heat.

216 "Got to work," he said.

217 "Autumn," they reasoned. And they sounded so sensible, so right.

218 "Autumn would be best," he thought. "Plenty of time, then."

219 No! cried part of himself, deep down, put away, locked tight, suffocating. No! No!

220 "In the autumn," he said.

221 "Come on, Harry," they all said.

222 "Yes," he said, feeling his flesh melt in the hot liquid air. "Yes, in the autumn. I'll begin work again then."

mosaic (moh ZAY ihk) adj. made of many small pieces of colored glass or stone

CLOSE READ
ANNOTATE Mark the words or ideas that are repeated in paragraphs 212–222.

QUESTION What important change in Bittering does the repetition suggest?

COMPREHENSION CHECK
In paragraph 204, what is the "old fever" that is now "gone"?

Dark They Were, and Golden-Eyed **137**

223 "I got a villa near the Tirra Canal," said someone.
224 "You mean the Roosevelt Canal, don't you?"
225 "Tirra. The old Martian name."
226 "But on the map—"
227 "Forget the map. It's Tirra now. Now I found a place in the Pillan Mountains—"
228 "You mean the Rockefeller Range," said Bittering.
229 "I mean the Pillan Mountains," said Sam.
230 "Yes," said Bittering, buried in the hot, swarming air. "The Pillan Mountains."
231 Everyone worked at loading the truck in the hot, still afternoon of the next day.
232 Laura, Dan, and David carried packages. Or, as they preferred to be known, Ttil, Linnl, and Werr carried packages.
233 The furniture was abandoned in the little white cottage.
234 "It looked just fine in Boston," said the mother. "And here in the cottage. But up at the villa? No. We'll get it when we come back in the autumn."
235 Bittering himself was quiet.
236 "I've some ideas on furniture for the villa," he said after a time. "Big, lazy furniture."
237 "What about your encyclopedia? You're taking it along, surely?"
238 Mr. Bittering glanced away. "I'll come and get it next week."
239 They turned to their daughter. "What about your New York dresses?"
240 The bewildered girl stared. "Why, I don't want them any more."
241 They shut off the gas, the water, they locked the doors and walked away. Father peered into the truck.
242 "Gosh, we're not taking much," he said. "Considering all we brought to Mars, this is only a handful!"
243 He started the truck.
244 Looking at the small white cottage for a long moment, he was filled with a desire to rush to it, touch it, say good-bye to it, for he felt as if he were going away on a long journey, leaving something to which he could never quite return, never understand again.
245 Just then Sam and his family drove by in another truck.
246 "Hi, Bittering! Here we go!"
247 The truck swung down the ancient highway out of town. There were sixty others traveling in the same direction. The town filled with a silent, heavy dust from their passage. The canal waters lay blue in the sun, and a quiet wind moved in the strange trees.
248 "Good-bye, town!" said Mr. Bittering.
249 "Good-bye, good-bye," said the family, waving to it.
250 They did not look back again.

251   Summer burned the canals dry. Summer moved like flame upon the meadows. In the empty Earth settlement, the painted houses flaked and peeled. Rubber tires upon which children had swung in back yards hung suspended like stopped clock pendulums in the blazing air.

252   At the metal shop, the rocket frame began to rust.

253   In the quiet autumn Mr. Bittering stood, very dark now, very golden-eyed, upon the slope above his villa, looking at the valley.

254   "It's time to go back," said Cora.

255   "Yes, but we're not going," he said quietly. "There's nothing there any more."

256   "Your books," she said. "Your fine clothes."

257   "Your *Illes* and your fine *ior uele rr*e," she said.

258   "The town's empty. No one's going back," he said. "There's no reason to, none at all."

259   The daughter wove tapestries and the sons played songs on ancient flutes and pipes, their laughter echoing in the marble villa.

260   Mr. Bittering gazed at the Earth settlement far away in the low valley. "Such odd, such ridiculous houses the Earth people built."

261   "They didn't know any better," his wife mused. "Such ugly people. I'm glad they've gone."

262   They both looked at each other, startled by all they had just finished saying. They laughed.

263   "Where did they go?" he wondered. He glanced at his wife. She was golden and slender as his daughter. She looked at him, and he seemed almost as young as their eldest son.

264   "I don't know," she said.

265   "We'll go back to town maybe next year, or the year after, or the year after that," he said, calmly. "Now—I'm warm. How about taking a swim?"

266   They turned their backs to the valley. Arm in arm they walked silently down a path of clear-running spring water.

❊ ❊ ❊

267   Five years later a rocket fell out of the sky. It lay steaming in the valley. Men leaped out of it, shouting.

268   "We won the war on Earth! We're here to rescue you! Hey!"

269   But the American-built town of cottages, peach trees, and theaters was silent. They found a flimsy rocket frame rusting in an empty shop.

270   The rocket men searched the hills. The captain established headquarters in an abandoned bar. His lieutenant came back to report.

CLOSE READ

ANNOTATE Mark details in paragraphs 269–278 that reveal the findings of the rescue mission from Earth.

QUESTION Why has Bradbury chosen to include this scene?

271 "The town's empty, but we found native life in the hills, sir. Dark people. Yellow eyes. Martians. Very friendly. We talked a bit, not much. They learn English fast. I'm sure our relations will be most friendly with them, sir."

272 "Dark, eh?" mused the captain. "How many?"

273 "Six, eight hundred, I'd say, living in those marble ruins in the hills, sir. Tall, healthy. Beautiful women."

274 "Did they tell you what became of the men and women who built this Earth settlement, Lieutenant?"

275 "They hadn't the foggiest notion of what happened to this town or its people."

276 "Strange. You think those Martians killed them?"

277 "They look surprisingly peaceful. Chances are a plague did this town in, sir."

278 "Perhaps. I suppose this is one of those mysteries we'll never solve. One of those mysteries you read about."

279 The captain looked at the room, the dusty windows, the blue mountains rising beyond, the canals moving in the light, and he heard the soft wind in the air. He shivered. Then, recovering, he tapped a large fresh map he had thumbtacked to the top of an empty table.

280 "Lots to be done, Lieutenant." His voice droned on and quietly on as the sun sank behind the blue hills. "New settlements. Mining sites, minerals to be looked for. Bacteriological specimens taken. The work, all the work. And the old records were lost. We'll have a job of remapping to do, renaming the mountains and rivers and such. Calls for a little imagination.

281 "What do you think of naming those mountains the Lincoln Mountains, this canal the Washington Canal, those hills—we can name those hills for you, Lieutenant. Diplomacy. And you, for a favor, might name a town for me. Polishing the apple. And why not make this the Einstein Valley, and farther over . . . are you *listening*, Lieutenant?"

282 The lieutenant snapped his gaze from the blue color and the quiet mist of the hills far beyond the town.

283 "What? Oh, *yes*, sir!"

COMPREHENSION CHECK

What are the lieutenant's impressions of the people he finds on Mars?

BUILD INSIGHT

First Thoughts

Select one of the following questions to answer:
- Do you think the lingering mystery about the colonists' fate at the end of the story improves or weakens the narrative? Explain.
- What aspect of the story do you find to be most interesting? Explain.

Summary

Write a short summary of the story to confirm your comprehension. Remember to include only the story's central ideas and to keep your summary objective and free of personal opinions.

Analysis

1. **(a)** After the Bitterings arrive on Mars, what disaster happens on Earth? **(b) Analyze Cause and Effect** How does this disaster affect the Bitterings?

2. **Make Inferences** In the story, people from Earth renamed the landscape features of Mars, such as the Lincoln Mountains. These names **allude**, or refer, to famous people from history. Why do you think the Earth people did that?

3. **(a) Contrast** How do the houses built by the Earth people differ from the ones built by the Martians? **(b) Draw Conclusions** What can you conclude about Martians and Earth people from this contrast?

4. **(a) Analyze** How does the wind affect the characters in the beginning, middle, and end of the story? **(b) Interpret** What might the wind represent in this story? Use text evidence to support your response.

Exploring the Essential Question

Should we make a home in space?

5. Consider the scenario Bradbury created for a new human home in space. How realistic do you think it is? Explain your thinking in your Evidence Log.

STANDARDS
Reading Literature
- Cite several pieces of textual evidence to support analysis of what the text says explicitly as well as inferences drawn from the text.
- Provide an objective summary of the text.
- Analyze how particular elements of a story or drama interact.

Language
Interpret figures of speech in context.

Dark They Were, and Golden-Eyed 141

ANALYZE AND INTERPRET

DARK THEY WERE, AND GOLDEN-EYED

Close Read

1. The model passage and annotation show how one reader analyzed paragraph 251 of the story. Find another detail in the passage to annotate. Then, write your own question and conclusion.

CLOSE-READ MODEL

> Summer burned the canals dry. Summer moved like flame upon the meadows. In the empty Earth settlement, the painted houses flaked and peeled. Rubber tires upon which children had swung in back yards hung suspended like stopped clock pendulums in the blazing air.

ANNOTATE: I notice that many words contain the letter *m*.

QUESTION: What effect does this repetition of the *m* sound create?

CONCLUDE: The repeated sound creates a drowsy mood and slows down the pace.

MY QUESTION:

MY CONCLUSION:

2. For more practice, answer the Close-Read questions in the selection.

3. Choose a section of the story that you found especially meaningful. Mark important details. Then, jot down questions and write your conclusions in the open space next to the text.

Inquiry and Research

Research and Extend Ray Bradbury's fictional Mars is based on some facts and a lot of imagination. Write down two details about Mars from this story. Using these details, generate two of your own questions about what Mars is really like. Then, conduct research to answer your questions. Use a variety of sources, including government websites, such as NASA's.

Using the knowledge you gained from your research, which of Bradbury's ideas about Mars do you support? What information do you challenge? What is one idea you would expand on?

STANDARDS

Reading Literature
Determine the meaning of words and phrases as they are used in a text, including figurative and connotative meanings; analyze the impact of rhymes and other repetitions of sounds on a specific verse or stanza of a poem or section of a story or drama.

Writing
Conduct short research projects to answer a question, drawing on several sources and generating additional related, focused questions for further research and investigation.

Language
Demonstrate understanding of figurative language, word relationships, and nuances in word meanings.

142 UNIT 2 • LIVING AMONG THE STARS

Essential Question: Should we make a home in space?

Setting and Figurative Language

In this story, the **setting** is important because it creates the characters' conflicts, or problems. To help readers understand what this alien setting is like, Ray Bradbury uses **figurative language,** including similes, metaphors, and personification.

> **EXAMPLES FROM THE STORY**
> **Simile:** *Rubber tires...hung suspended like stopped clock pendulums*
> **Metaphor:** *the rockets had spun a silver web across space*
> **Personification:** *the wind roaring forlorn and changing*

Bradbury uses these **figures of speech** to serve a variety of purposes. They help show how the setting looks and feels, and they give the story a specific mood, or feeling.

PRACTICE Complete the activity and answer the questions.

1. **Analyze** Passages from the story appear in the chart. Identify each as a simile, a metaphor, or personification. In the final column, explain the purpose of each passage—what it shows about the setting and the mood it helps create.

PASSAGE	FIGURATIVE LANGUAGE	PURPOSE
The children, small seeds, might at any instant be sown to all the Martian climes. (paragraph 2)		
They saw the old cities, . . . lying like children's delicate bones … (paragraph 9)		
This was the moment Mars had waited for. Now it would eat them. (paragraph 41)		

2. (a) **Distinguish** Find and write down another example of each type of figurative language in the story.

    Simile:

    Metaphor:

    Personification:

   (b) **Evaluate** Mark the example from item 2 that best helps you understand the setting and its impact on the characters. Explain your choice.

Dark They Were, and Golden-Eyed **143**

STUDY LANGUAGE AND CRAFT

DARK THEY WERE, AND GOLDEN-EYED

Concept Vocabulary

Why These Words? The vocabulary words describe Bradbury's vision of Mars. For example, the Bitterings' house is *submerged* by a river of wind, which also roars "*forlorn* and changing through the old peach tree."

| submerged | canals | atmosphere |
| forlorn | immense | mosaic |

WORD WALL
Note words in the text that are related to the idea of living among the stars. Add them to your Word Wall.

PRACTICE Answer the questions.

1. How do the vocabulary words sharpen the reader's understanding of what life is like for the Bitterings on Mars?

2. What other words in the selection help describe an alien world?

3. Use each concept word in a sentence that demonstrates your understanding of the word's meaning.

4. Challenge yourself to replace the concept word in each sentence with a synonym. How does the change affect the meaning of your sentence? For example, which sentence is stronger? Which has a more positive meaning?

Word Study

Synonyms and Nuance Words that have the same basic meaning are called **synonyms.** Often, however, there are subtle shades of meaning, or **nuances,** between synonyms. For example, the basic meaning of *forlorn* is "sad," but its nuance indicates that it is a type of sadness caused by abandonment or loneliness.

STANDARDS
Language
• Explain the function of phrases and clauses in general and their function in specific sentences.
• Choose among simple, compound, complex, and compound-complex sentences to signal differing relationships among ideas.
• Demonstrate understanding of figurative language, word relationships, and nuances in word meanings.
• Distinguish among the connotations of words with similar denotations.

PRACTICE Compete the following items.

1. Using a print or digital thesaurus, find two other synonyms for the word *forlorn*. Record a precise definition for each synonym, and then describe their differences in nuance.

2. Write a paragraph about something in the story or about Mars. Include the two synonyms you recorded in item 1. Use the nuanced meanings of the words to decide how to use each one correctly in your paragraph.

144 UNIT 2 • LIVING AMONG THE STARS

Essential Question: Should we make a home in space?

Sentence Structures

A sentence is made up of one or more clauses. There are two types of clauses:
- An **independent clause** is a group of words that has a subject and a verb and can stand by itself as a complete thought: *The doorbell rang*
- A **dependent clause** is a group of words that has a subject and a verb but is not a complete thought and cannot stand alone: *But no one answered the door*

The structure of a sentence is determined by the number and types of clauses it contains. Authors use clauses in different ways to combine their ideas and to make their writing interesting. In the chart, the independent clauses are underlined once, and the dependent clauses are underlined twice.

SENTENCE STRUCTURE	EXAMPLE FROM THE STORY
simple sentence: one independent clause	Atom bombs hit New York!
compound sentence: two or more independent clauses linked by a connecting word (conjunction), such as *or*, *and*, or *but*	He felt his heart pounding, and he was afraid.
complex sentence: one independent clause and one or more dependent clauses	If we stay here, we'll all change.
compound-complex sentence: two or more independent clauses and one or more dependent clauses	You see Martian paintings and you wonder what the painter was like.

READ Reread the story, and find another example of a simple sentence, a compound sentence, and a complex sentence. Mark the independent clauses. Then, use another mark to identify the dependent clauses. Finally, write a short explanation of the function of each clause in the sentences you chose.

WRITE / EDIT Write a brief paragraph about the story. Then, revise the paragraph to add greater sentence variety and to signal differing relationships among ideas. Include all four sentence structures in your paragraph, and be sure to maintain consistent verb tense throughout the paragraph.

TIP: When you use a variety of sentence structures to combine your ideas, be sure to maintain consistent verb tense in your writing. Notice how the verbs in the dependent clause and the independent clause are both in the present tense in this complex sentence:

When it rains, we stay inside.

Dark They Were, and Golden-Eyed

PREPARE TO LISTEN

DARK THEY WERE, AND GOLDEN-EYED
(short story)

DARK THEY WERE, AND GOLDEN-EYED
(radio play)

COMPARE: FICTION and DRAMA
The text and audio versions of **Dark They Were, and Golden-Eyed** tell the same story. Pay attention to how experiencing the story is different when you read it and when you listen to it.

About the Producer

Michael McDonough is a professional sound designer and the producer of the *Bradbury 13* series. For *Bradbury 13*, he wrote all the scripts and created spectacular original sound effects. McDonough first learned sound design as a student at Brigham Young University and went on to work on dozens of films and television shows

Media Vocabulary

These words describe characteristics of radio plays. Use them as you analyze, discuss, and write about the selection.

sound effects: sounds produced artificially for a radio production	• Sound effects indicate settings and actions (city noises; the dropping of a book). • Certain sound effects help create mood (the squeak of a rusty door; the screech of an owl).
actors' delivery: the ways in which actors speak their lines	• Voices in a radio play need to be distinct so listeners know which character is speaking. • A speaker's pitch, volume, and pacing take on even more importance in a radio play.
background music: music that is not the focus of the performance	• Background music can signal changes in scene or mood. • Specific melodies might be used with particular characters or settings.

Listening Strategy: Create Mental Images

When you listen to an audio performance, deepen your understanding by **creating mental images.** Envision, or "see," the settings, characters, and action in your mind.

- **Listen for emotion in characters' voices.** For example, fast, breathless speech helps you "see" a character who is afraid or excited.
- **Listen for sound effects** that tell you what characters are doing or what is happening around them. For instance, the sounds of rockets lifting off help you "see" a busy spaceport.
- **Listen to the background music** and notice the mood it creates. Imagine how characters in such a mood might look, feel, and act.

PRACTICE As you listen to the radio play, use the Take Notes section to briefly describe the mental images you create.

STANDARDS
Language
Gather vocabulary knowledge when considering a word or phrase important to comprehension or expression.

146 UNIT 2 • LIVING AMONG THE STARS

MEDIA: RADIO PLAY

 LISTEN

Dark They Were, and Golden-Eyed
Michael McDonough, Producer

BACKGROUND
During the 1930s and 1940s, radio plays were a highly popular form of entertainment. However, with the rise of television, they all but disappeared. In 1984, National Public Radio aired *Bradbury 13*, a series of radio adaptations of Ray Bradbury's works that re-create the feel of classic radio drama.

TAKE NOTES Deepen your understanding of the radio play by taking notes as you listen.

BUILD INSIGHT

DARK THEY WERE, AND GOLDEN-EYED (radio play)

First Thoughts

Respond to one of the following options.

- What do you think works well in the audio version? What doesn't work well? Give reasons for your opinions.
- How do you think you would have responded to the radio play if you had not read the original story? Explain.

Comprehension

1. What does the spaceship pilot announce at the beginning of the play?

2. **(a)** In the short story, how does the author let readers know that bombs have blown up all of Earth's rockets? **(b)** What audio elements does the radio play add to that scene?

3. Which elements of the radio play helped you the most to "see" the characters, settings, and action in your mind? Explain, citing at least one specific example.

Analysis

4. **Compare and Contrast (a)** In what way is the opening scene of the radio play similar to that of the story? **(b)** In what way does the opening scene differ? **(c)** What effects do the techniques used in each medium have on the stories?

5. **(a)** Note at least two items the Bitterings leave behind when they move to the villa in the hills. **(b) Interpret** Why are these items no longer important to them?

6. **Evaluate** Some critics believe that science fiction stories like this one are *not* about the future. They think the stories are actually about concerns people have in the present. If that is true, what aspects of present-day life do you think this story might address? Explain.

Exploring the Essential Question

Should we make a home in space?

7. After listening to the radio play, how have your thoughts and feelings about living in space changed? What aspects of the audio caused those changes? Record your reactions in your Evidence Log.

STANDARDS
Reading Literature
Compare and contrast a written story, drama, or poem to its audio, filmed, staged, or multimedia version, analyzing the effects of techniques unique to each medium.

Speaking and Listening
Analyze the main ideas and supporting details presented in diverse media and formats and explain how the ideas clarify a topic, text, or issue under study.

148 UNIT 2 • LIVING AMONG THE STARS

ANALYZE AND INTERPRET

Close Review

Listen to the radio play again, and take notes about how the audio elements clarify topics, ideas, or events from the text. Note time codes so you can find those elements again later. Then, write a question and your conclusion.

MY QUESTION:

MY CONCLUSION:

Inquiry and Research

Research and Extend Choose one of the following topics to research: author Ray Bradbury, the series called *Bradbury 13*, or the history of radio plays in general. Find one interesting fact using an online source. Write it down along with the search terms you used.

STUDY LANGUAGE AND CRAFT

Media Vocabulary

These words describe characteristics of radio plays and other audio presentations. Practice using them in your responses.

| sound effects | actors' delivery | background music |

1. In what ways has the Martian environment been brought to life in the radio play?

2. How would you evaluate the actors' performances?

3. How are changes of scene indicated in the radio play?

Dark They Were, and Golden-Eyed (radio play) 149

TEST PRACTICE

SHORT STORY

DARK THEY WERE, AND GOLDEN-EYED

RADIO PLAY

DARK THEY WERE, AND GOLDEN-EYED

COMPARE: FICTION and DRAMA
Multiple Choice

These questions are based on the short story and radio play versions of "Dark They Were, and Golden-Eyed." Choose the best answer to each question.

1. In both the story and the play, when the family first arrives on Mars, what does Mr. Bittering want to do right away?

   A He wants to visit the ancient Martian cities.

   B He wants to get back on the rocket and return to Earth.

   C He wants to get to work building a rocket.

   D He wants to start building a villa in the mountains.

2. Read paragraphs 118 to 121 from the story and the transcript of a similar section in the radio play. What happens in the story that does *not* happen in the play?

   Short Story

   "Here you are, Harry." Sam handed him a pocket mirror. "Take a look at yourself."

   Mr. Bittering hesitated, and then raised the mirror to his face.

   There were little, very dim flecks of new gold captured in the blue of his eyes.

   "Now look what you've done," said Sam a moment later. "You've broken my mirror."

   Radio Play

   SAM: Is that so? Harry, what color are your eyes?

   HARRY: My eyes? They're blue.

   SAM: Take a look in this mirror. See for yourself.

   HARRY: [gasps] No! They're turning yellow.

   SAM: Welcome to the club, Harry.

   A Harry gasps when he sees himself.

   B Harry looks at himself in a mirror.

   C Harry sees that his eyes are turning yellow.

   D Harry breaks the mirror.

3. At the end of both the story and the play, what do members of the rescue team start to do?

   A They start to repair the houses the colonists left behind.

   B They develop a plan to drive the Martians out of their villas.

   C They start to give Earth names to the mountains, hills, and canals.

   D They prepare to leave Mars because they failed in their mission.

STANDARDS

Reading Literature
Compare and contrast a written story, drama, or poem to its audio, filmed, staged, or multimedia version, analyzing the effects of techniques unique to each medium.

Writing
Write informative/explanatory texts to examine a topic and convey ideas, concepts, and information through the selection, organization, and analysis of relevant content.

Essential Question: Should we make a home in space?

Short Response

1. **(a) Analyze** In the story, how does the author show the importance of the Martian wind? **(b) Compare** How does the radio play show it?

2. **Interpret** In the radio play, after the Bitterings move to the villa, sound effects include bird song. Birds are not mentioned in the story. Why do you think the radio play includes bird sounds at this point?

3. **(a) Describe** What is life like in the Martian villas? **(b) Contrast** How is that lifestyle different from that of the Earth people? **(c) Evaluate** Which version of the story—the text or the radio play—presents a stronger contrast between Martian and Earth ways of living? Explain.

Timed Writing

A **comparison-and-contrast essay** is a piece of writing in which you discuss similarities and differences among two or more topics.

Assignment

Write a **comparison-and-contrast essay** in which you explain how each version of "Dark They Were, and Golden-Eyed" brings the settings, characters, and events to life. Introduce the topic clearly, previewing the concepts and information you'll share. Organize your ideas logically, and maintain a formal style throughout. Conclude with an evaluation that tells which version is more effective.

5-Minute Planner

1. Read the assignment carefully and completely.
2. Decide what you want to say—your central idea, or thesis.
3. Decide which examples you'll use from the story and play.
4. Organize your ideas, making sure to address these points:
   - Explain how the short story and radio play are similar.
   - Point out important differences between the two.
   - Explain which version of the story is more effective and why.

> **EVIDENCE LOG**
>
> Before moving on to a new selection, go to your Evidence Log and record any additional thoughts and observations you may have about the text and audio versions of "Dark They Were, and Golden-Eyed."

Test Practice **151**

PERFORMANCE TASK

Write an Argument: Editorial

Editorials are short persuasive essays that appear in newspapers and on news sites. People write them to express their opinions about current events or problems.

Assignment

Write an **editorial** in which you take a position on this question:

Is space exploration important?

Support your position with evidence from your reading, your background knowledge, and your own observations. Use the elements of an editorial in your writing.

Use Academic Vocabulary

Try to use one or more of the unit's academic vocabulary words in your editorial: *justify, dissent, certainty, discredit, assumption.*

WRITING CENTER

Visit the Writing Center to watch video tutorials and view annotated student models and rubrics.

ELEMENTS OF AN EDITORIAL

Purpose: to explain and defend a position on an issue

Characteristics

- a clear claim that states your position
- logical reasons that support the claim
- relevant evidence from reliable sources
- acknowledgement of a counterclaim
- precise word choices and a formal style
- well-chosen transitions that connect ideas clearly
- standard English conventions, including correct use of complex sentences, punctuation, and spelling

Structure

- a well-organized structure that includes:
  - an interesting introduction that states the claim
  - a logical flow of ideas from paragraph to paragraph
  - a strong conclusion that follows from the information presented

STANDARDS
Writing
- Write arguments to support claims with clear reasons and relevant evidence.
- Support claim(s) with logical reasoning and relevant evidence, using accurate, credible sources and demonstrating an understanding of the topic or text.
- Write routinely over extended time frames and shorter time frames for a range of discipline-specific tasks, purposes, and audiences.

Essential Question: Should we make a home in space?

Take a Closer Look at the Assignment

1. Do I understand the basic vocabulary of the assignment? What is it asking me to do (in my own words)?

2. Is my **purpose** for writing specified in the assignment?
   - ◯ Yes   If "yes," what is the purpose?
   - ◯ No   If "no," why am I writing this editorial (not just because it's an assignment)?

3. (a) Does the assignment ask me to use specific types of **evidence**?
   - ◯ Yes   If "yes," what are they?
   - ◯ No   If "no," what types of evidence do I think I need?

   (b) Where will I get the evidence? What kinds of sources will I consult?

PURPOSE

A specific **purpose**, or reason for writing, will lead to a stronger editorial.

General Purpose: *In this editorial, I'll argue that exploring space is interesting.*

Specific Purpose: *In this editorial, I'll convince readers that exploring space is critical for humans' future survival.*

EVIDENCE

Relevant evidence includes supporting details that relate directly to your topic. Your evidence should come from reliable sources.

Accurate sources give up-to-date information.

Credible sources provide trustworthy information from experts.

Write Your Editorial

Review the assignment and your notes, and then begin writing your editorial. Keep these tips in mind:

- Remember that you are defending a position on a topic. Make your claim clear and support it with logical reasons.
- Provide different types of relevant evidence, such as facts, examples, or quotations from experts.
- Use persuasive language to convince readers that your position is stronger than opposing positions.

Writer's Handbook: If you need help as you plan, draft, revise, and edit, refer to the Writer's Handbook pages that follow.

Performance Task: Write an Argument 153

WRITER'S HANDBOOK | **ARGUMENT: EDITORIAL**

Planning and Prewriting

Before you draft, decide what you want to say and how you want to say it. Consider the texts you have read and listened to in this unit as well as any background reading you have done on your own. Then, complete the activities to get started.

Discover Your Thinking: Freewrite!

Keep your topic in mind as you write quickly and freely for at least three minutes without stopping.

- Don't worry about your spelling and grammar (you'll fix mistakes later).
- When time is up, pause and look at what you wrote. Mark points that seem strong or interesting.
- Repeat the process as many times as necessary to get all your ideas out. For each round, start with a strong idea you marked. Focus on it as you again write quickly and freely.

> **Using the Writer's Handbook**
>
> In this handbook you'll find strategies to support every stage of the writing process—from planning to publishing. As you write, check in with yourself:
> - *What's going well?*
> - *What isn't going well?*
>
> Then, use the handbook items that will best help you craft a strong editorial.

WRITE Is space exploration important?

___

STANDARDS
Writing • Introduce claim(s), acknowledge alternate or opposing claims, and organize the reasons and evidence logically.
• Provide a concluding statement or section that follows from and supports the argument presented.

Structure Ideas: Make a Plan

A **Choose a Focus** Review your freewriting and pull out the main points you want to make. Don't worry about the order.

_____
_____

B **Write a Claim** Briefly state your position on the topic. As you draft and revise, you may change or refine your claim.

_____
_____

C **Plan a Structure** Use an outline to figure out the content for each section of your editorial.

I. **Introduction:** Plan how you'll engage your reader and show that your topic and claim are important. Consider beginning with an interesting fact or quotation.

II. **Body Paragraphs:** Explain your reasons and evidence in a logical order. Remember to acknowledge a **counterclaim** in one of your paragraphs.

III. **Conclusion:** Plan how you can leave your reader convinced about your position. Consider ending with an unusual statement or a memorable image.

_____
_____
_____
_____
_____
_____

STRUCTURE

A clear **structure**, or organization of ideas and evidence, helps readers follow your thinking. These two types of structures work well with arguments:

- **Order of Importance:** Start with your strongest reason, follow with your next strongest reason, and so on.
- **Nestorian Order:** Start with your second strongest reason, add other points, and end with your strongest reason.

COUNTERCLAIM

A **counterclaim** is an opposing position that differs from your own. In your argument, briefly mention a counterclaim and then point out its weaknesses so that readers will agree with your claim. For example, you could write *Some people say..., but that's not true because....*

Writer's Handbook: Argument

WRITER'S HANDBOOK ARGUMENT: EDITORIAL

Drafting

Apply the planning work you've done, and write a first draft. Start with your introduction, which should grab readers' attention and make your claim clear. Then, explore ways to develop your ideas into a coherent editorial.

Read Like a Writer

Mark the writer's claim and details that you think engage readers' interest. One observation has been done for you.

MENTOR TEXT

from **Humans Are Not Meant to Live in Space**

Long before Neil Armstrong and Edwin Aldrin walked on the moon, people wondered whether humans could someday live in space. Eventually that might be a possibility, but right now it's a terrible idea. The physical effects of living in space far outweigh any potential benefits.

Human bodies are made to exist in Earth's environment. They are not designed to live in microgravity. *Microgravity* refers to the near absence of gravity in space. Whenever the downward pull of gravity is removed, bones and muscles weaken because they are no longer being used to support the body. According to studies conducted on astronauts, bone loss accelerates from 3% per *year* on Earth to 1% per *month* in microgravity. Studies also suggest that over time microgravity alters the ability of bones to heal after fractures. Sure, exercising during space travel reduces these negative effects, but it's impossible for space travelers to work out enough to maintain full bone and muscle strength.

> Which details in paragraph 1 grab your attention? Where is the claim stated? Mark them.

> These statistics are interesting and support the writer's point in this paragraph.

WRITE Write your introduction. Follow the Mentor Text structure, and begin by stating your claim and attracting readers' attention. Then, give your first reason supported by evidence.

_____

_____

_____

_____

_____

DEVELOP IDEAS

As you draft, make your writing clear and persuasive.

- **Claim** State your claim clearly.
- **Development** Support your points with relevant evidence, such as data from research studies.
- **Style** Your tone, or attitude, should reinforce your thinking. Use a formal style throughout.

STANDARDS
Writing • Write arguments to support claims with clear reasons and relevant evidence.
• Use words, phrases, and clauses to create cohesion and clarify the relationships among claim(s), reasons, and evidence.

156 UNIT 2 • LIVING AMONG THE STARS

Coherence and Craft

As you draft your editorial, use transitions to clarify connections among your claim, reasons, and evidence.

One strategy for creating coherence is using **subordinating conjunctions** to create **complex sentences.** The particular subordinating conjunction you choose signals the relationship between your ideas.

SAMPLE SUBORDINATING CONJUNCTIONS	
Relationship Between Ideas	**Subordinating Conjunctions**
show contrast	*although, even though, whereas*
show cause	*because, since*
show effect	*in order that, so that*
show place	*where, wherever*
show time	*before, once, until, whenever*

COMPLEX SENTENCES

A **complex sentence** has one independent clause and one dependent clause.

- An independent clause has a subject and a verb and expresses a complete thought.

A dependent clause has a subject and a verb, but it does not express a complete thought. It often begins with a **subordinating conjunction.**

WRITE Write a paragraph for the body of your editorial. Present one of your reasons and the evidence that supports it. Include at least one subordinating conjunction to help create coherence.

SENTENCE STRUCTURE

Too many short, choppy sentences can make your writing repetitive. Use **subordinating conjunctions** to create coherence and to add interest and variety to your writing.

EXAMPLE:
- We need to be more curious. Curiosity can sometimes be dangerous.
- We need to be more curious *even though* curiosity can sometimes be dangerous.

Writer's Handbook: Argument 157

WRITER'S HANDBOOK | ARGUMENT: EDITORIAL

Revising

Now revise your draft to be sure it is as persuasive as possible.

Read Like a Writer

Review the revisions made to the Mentor Text. Then, complete the activities in the white boxes.

MENTOR TEXT

from **Humans Are Not Meant to Live in Space**

An astronaut's body can take up to three years to recover from a four-month period in space. What, then, might happen to a space traveler who spends far more time in space or journeys to another planet? The travel time from Earth to Mars is estimated at about nine months. Therefore, it could take up to seven years for a Mars traveler to recover from the trip alone. The surface gravity on Mars is about 38% of the gravity of Earth. Rather than bouncing back after landing on Mars, travelers would continue to experience the physical impacts of microgravity. ~~That would really stink.~~

* * *

All space travelers will eventually suffer the negative effects of microgravity, but that is not the only hazard they face. ==Exposure to radiation is ten times higher in space than it is on Earth.== Lead insulation could provide protection for travelers, but it is too heavy for use in spacecraft. Because of this, humans are exposed to much higher—and therefore more dangerous—levels of radiation when they journey outside Earth's atmosphere. Radiation can damage the eyes, brain, and other sensitive tissues of the body—and this damage is permanent.

==Some people argue that space travel to other planets is important for the future of the human race. Their ideas are compelling: We must be prepared to colonize other planets if Earth's population continues to increase.== But space colonizers would have to deal with the life-threatening effects of microgravity and radiation. This isn't a reasonable solution to overpopulation on Earth.

> The writer includes evidence to support the main point in this paragraph. Mark the facts and data used.

> Why do you think the writer chose to delete this sentence?

> Why has the writer added this sentence?

> The writer acknowledges a **counterclaim** by mentioning an opposing position that some people may take. Then, the writer explains why that position is not reasonable.

STANDARDS

Writing Write arguments to support claims with clear reasons and relevant evidence. **Language** Choose language that expresses ideas precisely and concisely, recognizing and eliminating wordiness and redundancy.

158 UNIT 2 • LIVING AMONG THE STARS

Take a Closer Look at Your Draft

Use the Revision Checklist for Argument to evaluate and strengthen your editorial.

REVISION CHECKLIST FOR ARGUMENT

EVALUATE	TAKE ACTION
Clarity	
☐ Is my claim strong and clear?	If not, **replace** it with a question. Then, **answer** the question by stating your position in a direct, forceful way.
Development	
☐ Have I given relevant supporting evidence for every reason?	**Mark** each piece of evidence and the reason it supports. **Move** any detail that is not in the same paragraph as the reason it supports. **Add** facts or quotations from accurate, credible sources to strengthen your points.
☐ Have I included a counterclaim?	If not, **add** mention of an opposing argument. **Follow up** with statements that make your position look stronger.
Organization	
☐ Have I organized my reasons in a logical way?	If the structure doesn't work, **reorganize** your reasons and evidence. Print your paper, cut out the paragraphs, and physically **rearrange** them until you find a better order. Then, **add** transitions to make the flow of ideas clear.
☐ Does my introduction engage readers?	**Add** a question, quotation, or fact to interest your audience.
☐ Have I ended in an effective way?	Restate your claim in your conclusion. You may want to **insert** a quotation or strong statement at the end.
Style	
☐ Are my word choices precise and concise?	Review your draft and **mark** any sections that are too wordy or repetitive. **Replace** long explanations with wording that is more direct and to-the-point.
☐ Is my style appropriately formal for an editorial?	**Replace** any slang or overly casual language with more formal options. For example, instead of saying, "Space exploration is cool," say "Space exploration is both necessary and interesting."
☐ Have I used complex sentences correctly?	Check your sentence structure. **Combine** independent and dependent clauses. **Add** subordinating conjunctions to create coherence.

Writer's Handbook: Argument **159**

WRITER'S HANDBOOK — ARGUMENT: EDITORIAL

Editing

Don't let errors distract readers from your ideas. Reread your draft, and fix mistakes to create a finished persuasive work.

Read Like a Writer

Look at how the writer of the Mentor Text edited an early draft. Then, follow the directions in the white boxes.

MENTOR TEXT

from Humans Are Not Meant to Live in Space

Some people argue that space travel ~~too~~ *to* other planets is important for the future of the human race. They're ideas are compelling: We must be prepared to colonize other planets, if Earth's population continues to increase. But space colonizers would have to deal with the life-threatening ~~affects~~ *effects* of microgravity and radiation. This isn't a reasonable solution to overpopulation on Earth.

Perhaps one day scientists will find a way to drastically reduce the negative physical effects of space travel. Until then, however, it doesn't make sense to send humans on long-term trips into space.

- The writer fixed two spelling errors in the text. Find and fix one more the writer missed.
- Fix an error in which the writer used a comma before a dependent clause in the middle of a complex sentence.
- The conclusion restates the writer's claim.

Focus on Sentences

Grammar Minilesson

Complex Sentences In a complex sentence, make sure the subordinating conjunction you have chosen shows the correct logical relationship between ideas. For example:

Incorrect: We've been very determined <u>where</u> we made our decision.

Correct: We've been very determined <u>since</u> we made our decision.

PRACTICE Fix the incorrect subordinating conjunction in each complex sentence. Then, check your own draft for correctness.

1. Trees don't yet grow on Mars when they eventually will.

2. Although I applied to NASA, I waited patiently to hear from them.

3. Before you support my application, I'll surely be admitted.

4. Progress is slow unless space exploration is so expensive.

EDITING TIPS
1. Mark the subordinating conjunction in each sentence.
2. Replace the incorrect subordinating conjunction with one that shows an accurate relationship between ideas.

Focus on Spelling and Punctuation

Spelling: Homophones Words that sound the same but have different spellings and meanings are called **homophones.** Common examples include *to / too / two* and *your / you're.* These words are easily confused, so it's important to make sure you use the correct ones. Check your editorial for homophones and make edits as needed.

Punctuation: Dependent Clauses There are two common patterns of complex sentences. To determine whether you need to use a comma to set off the dependent clause, follow these general rules:

- Dependent Clause + Independent Clause = Comma
  EXAMPLE: *If we don't find another solar system, all that time will have been wasted.*

- Independent Clause + Dependent Clause = No Comma
  EXAMPLE: *All that time will have been wasted if we don't find another solar system.*

> **EDITING TIP**
> If you're typing your editorial, be aware that spell checkers will not catch homophones that are used incorrectly. Look up homophones in a dictionary to ensure you've chosen the right word and spelled it correctly.

> **PRACTICE** In the following sentences, correct spelling and punctuation errors if necessary. Then, review your own draft for correctness.
>
> 1. Before we head too outer space we should improve Earth.
>
> 2. I've wanted two bee an astronaut, since I was a child.
>
> 3. Although they had a rough landing they were happy to be out of the skies.

Publishing and Presenting

Integrate Media

Share your editorial with your class or school community. Choose one of these options:

OPTION 1 Create an **online editorial.** Post your finished work to a class or school website. Provide hyperlinks to the sources you cited so that your readers may access them. Respectfully comment on the editorials of others, and respond politely to the comments yours receives.

OPTION 2 Hold a **discussion,** and record it for posting to your class or school website. Pair up with a classmate whose editorial defends a different position from yours. Take turns presenting your reasons and evidence to the class. Afterwards, respond to questions and comments from the audience.

STANDARDS
Writing
Use technology, including the Internet, to produce and publish writing and link to and cite sources as well as to interact and collaborate with others, including linking to and citing sources.
Language
Spell correctly.

PEER-GROUP LEARNING

Essential Question

Should we make a home in space?

Some people think that space exploration is the way we will transform our dreams of the future into reality. Others think it is a big waste of time and money. You will read selections that examine different aspects of this subject. Work in a small group to continue your investigation into different perspectives on living among the stars.

Peer-Group Learning Strategies

Throughout your life, in school, in your community, and in your career, you will continue to learn and work with others.

Look at these strategies and the actions you can take to practice them as you work in small groups. Add ideas of your own for each category. Use these strategies during Peer-Group Learning.

STRATEGY	MY ACTION PLAN
Prepare	• Bring texts and completed assignments to class. • Have a notebook or device ready to use so you can take notes during group work. •
Participate fully	• Think about comments that others make and whether they change your mind about particular ideas. • When speaking, be sure to address everyone in your group. •
Support others	• Answer classmates' questions to help them better understand the topic or text under discussion. • Keep the conversation going by adding onto comments made by group members. •
Clarify	• If a peer says something you don't understand, ask follow-up questions, such as *What did you mean when you said…?* • Use visual sources of information, such as charts or images, to help you explain ideas more clearly. •

Contents

SCIENCE FEATURE

Japan to Start Research on the Moon and Mars for Humans

Tomoyuki Suzuki

Japan has plans for living beyond Earth.

COMPARE

ARGUMENT

Why We Should Continue to Explore Space

Sheri Buckner

What do we gain from exploring outer space?

ARGUMENT

Why We Should Save Earth Before Colonizing Mars

Bruce Dorminey

Should we solve Earth's problems instead of abandoning our planet?

PERFORMANCE TASK

SPEAKING AND LISTENING

Conduct a Debate

The Peer-Group selections explore the possibility of living beyond Earth. After reading, you will conduct a debate with your group.

Peer-Group Learning **163**

PEER-GROUP LEARNING

Working as a Group

1. Take a Position

Discuss the following question with your group:

> Would you volunteer to be one of the first humans to live on Mars?

As you take turns sharing your positions, be sure to provide reasons to support your ideas. Make sure you understand one another, and ask questions when you need clarification or more detail. If the conversation goes off track, bring it back by responding to the last on-topic comment someone shared. Finally, discuss the challenges you might encounter if you were living on another planet.

2. List Your Rules

As a group, decide on the rules that you will follow as you discuss and work together. Two samples are provided. Add two more of your own. You may add or revise rules as you work through the readings and activities together.

- Respect other people's opinions.
- Do not monopolize the conversation. Let others speak.

_____

_____

3. Apply the Rules

Practice working as a group. Share what you have learned about the possibility of living in space. Make sure each person in the group contributes. Take notes and be prepared to share with the class one thing that you heard from another member of your group.

4. Create a Communication Plan

Decide how you want to communicate with one another. For example, you might use online collaboration tools, email, or instant messaging.

Our group's plan:

_____

_____

STANDARDS

Speaking and Listening • Follow rules for collegial discussions, track progress toward specific goals and deadlines, and define individual roles as needed. • Pose questions that elicit elaboration and respond to others' questions and comments with relevant observations and ideas that bring the discussion back on topic as needed. • Acknowledge new information expressed by others and, when warranted, modify their own views.

Essential Question: Should we make a home in space?

Making a Schedule

First, find out the due dates for the peer-group activities. Then, preview the texts and activities with your group and make a schedule to track your group's progress as you complete the tasks.

SELECTION	ACTIVITIES	DUE DATE
Japan to Start Research on the Moon and Mars for Humans		
Why We Should Continue to Explore Space		
Why We Should Save Earth Before Colonizing Mars		

Reflect On and Modify Your Views

Texts can generate a wide variety of responses in different readers—and that can make working in groups exciting and fun. At the same time, it can be a challenge to engage in collaborative work with people who have many different opinions. Use these tips to get the most from your peer-group work:

Agree to disagree. Disagreement can be as important as agreement. It makes you focus on why you feel or think as you do, and that can sharpen your reasoning.

Pause before you respond. Really reflect on what someone has said or written. Even if you agree, take a moment before you reply or give feedback.

Ask questions. Make sure you understand the points others have made. Ask them to clarify or elaborate on their ideas before you respond.

Other people's perspectives can open your eyes to new understandings. If new ideas from classmates lead you to modify your own views, share your thinking. Your thought process may be instructive for everyone in your group.

LEARN ABOUT GENRE: NONFICTION

Reading Science Features

JAPAN TO START RESEARCH ON THE MOON AND MARS FOR HUMANS

A **science feature** is a type of journalism, or nonfiction reporting, that presents science-related information for a general audience.

The selection you are about to read is a science feature.

SCIENCE FEATURES

Author's Purpose
- to report current news in the areas of science and technology
- to explain information about a particular scientific topic, innovation, or discovery

Characteristics
- a central idea, or the writer's main point
- supporting details, such as data from scientific research or quotations from experts
- scientific or technical language
- visuals, such as images with captions

Structure
- background information followed by deeper explanations
- a logical flow of ideas: introduction, body paragraphs, conclusion

Take a Minute!

FIND IT Conduct an online search to find two science features. Write down their titles.

Where did you find these features?

STANDARDS
Reading Informational Text
Determine an author's point of view or purpose in a text.

166 UNIT 2 • LIVING AMONG THE STARS

Essential Question: Should we make a home in space?

Author's Purpose

 An **author's purpose** is their reason for writing. Authors write with a main purpose in mind: to inform, entertain, persuade, describe, or reflect. Sometimes they have a secondary purpose as well. The following tips will help you determine the author's purpose or purposes in a text:

- Look at the title of the text for clues.
- Examine the types of details the author includes.
- Ask, "For what reason has the author included these details?"

Consider the following example from an article about sleep.

Why Sleep Matters Most young people don't take sleep seriously enough—and they should. Ideally, teens should get between 8 and 10 hours of sleep each night because their bodies and minds are growing quickly. However, research shows that many teens get less than 8 hours. A lack of sleep can lead to problems with mood, memory, concentration, and decision-making.	The title suggests that the article will inform readers by explaining why sleep is important. This paragraph states a claim and provides relevant evidence. The paragraph is mainly informative but also persuasive.

PRACTICE Read the passages and answer the questions.

Tips for Healthy Eating	Put Down That Cookie!
Small choices can lead to a healthier diet. Choose whole grains over white, starchy foods like rice and pasta. Eat lots of fruit and vegetables—either fresh, frozen, or canned. Consume more fish and less red meat.	Sure, it looks innocent enough. And maybe it tastes great. But eating too much sugar can lead to obesity, tooth decay, heart disease, high blood pressure, and type 2 diabetes. Skip the cookie and grab an apple instead!

1. What is the main purpose of each passage? Which details helped you identify each author's purpose?

2. Share and compare your findings with your group. Are there any points of disagreement? If so, work together to discuss and resolve them.

Learn About Genre   167

PREPARE TO READ

Japan to Start Research on the Moon and Mars for Humans

About the Publication

This science article was first published in the *Asahi Shimbun*, one of the three largest newspapers in Japan. Founded in 1879, the family-owned newspaper is published daily and read by around six million subscribers. The *Asahi Shimbun* has correspondents all over the world and is known for its coverage of political topics both inside and outside Japan. The newspaper's name means "Morning Sun Newspaper."

STANDARDS

Reading Informational Text
Cite several pieces of textual evidence to support analysis of what the text says explicitly as well as inferences drawn from the text.

Language
- Consult general and specialized reference materials, both print and digital, to find the pronunciation of a word or determine or clarify its precise meaning or its part of speech.
- Verify the preliminary determination of the meaning of a word or phrase.

Technical Vocabulary

As you read the science article, you will encounter these words. When you finish reading, work with your group to identify what the words have in common.

| habitation | gravity | capsules |

Reference Materials Scientific writing often includes technical vocabulary. You should first guess at the meanings of unfamiliar terms by looking at the context. Then, verify the precise meanings by looking up the words in a print or digital **science dictionary**, a specialized resource with definitions of scientific and technological terms.

EXAMPLE

meteorite (MEE tee uh ryt) *n.* piece of stone or metal from space that enters a planet's atmosphere as a meteor and impacts its surface

PRACTICE Apply the skill of using a science dictionary to check the meanings of technical vocabulary and scientific terms as you read the article. Write definitions in the open space next to the text.

Reading Strategy: Make Inferences

Inferences are informed guesses readers make based on evidence in a text. Textual evidence provides clues that readers can use to fill in ideas that an author doesn't state directly. To make inferences as you read, follow these steps:

1. Note ideas that are explicit, or stated directly, and ones that are implicit, or suggested indirectly.
2. If an idea is not stated directly, make connections between details the author includes and what you already know about the topic.
3. Look for several pieces of evidence that support your analysis.
4. Make your inference.

PRACTICE As you read, ask yourself: *Why does the writer include this detail? Why is it important? How does it connect to other ideas?* Write your inferences in the margin, and mark the text to indicate evidence that supports each one.

SCIENCE FEATURE

Japan to Start Research on the Moon and Mars for Humans

Tomoyuki Suzuki

BACKGROUND
Nations around the world are competing to colonize the moon and Mars, and the competition is no longer limited to individual countries. Wealthy businesspeople and their companies are now in the mix as well. This science feature describes what one nation, Japan, is planning, including the Lunar Glass facility (pictured).

1 Researchers at Kyoto University and contractor Kajima Corp. presented plans to build living facilities required for human **habitation** on the moon and Mars and a transportation system reminiscent of a galaxy express. "There is no plan like this in other countries' space development plans," said Yosuke Yamashiki, director of the SIC Human Spaceology Center of Kyoto University, at a July 5 news conference at the university. "Our plan represents important technologies crucial to ensuring human beings will be able to move to space in the future." They announced that they will undertake a joint study to achieve the plan.

2 However, the plan will only become possible in the 22nd century, at the earliest.

3 At the core of the plan is constructing "artificial **gravity** living facilities." The facilities will be able to generate the same level of gravity as on Earth by using centrifugal force[1] created by rotational motions. One of these facilities, called Lunar Glass, will be built on the moon under the plan. Another called Mars Glass

---
1. **centrifugal** (sehn TRIHF uh guhl) **force** *n.* apparent outward force felt by a mass when it is rotated.

READ TO UNLOCK MEANING

1. First read the text for comprehension and enjoyment. Use the **Reading Strategy** and **Comprehension Check** questions to support your first read.
2. With your group, apply the vocabulary strategy to unlock word meanings.
3. Find other details in the text you find interesting. Ask your own questions and draw your own conclusions.

Use a dictionary or indicate another strategy you used that helped you determine meaning.

habitation (ha bih TAY shuhn) *n.*
MEANING:

gravity (GRA vuh tee) *n.*
MEANING:

will be constructed on Mars. Gravity on the moon and Mars are one-sixth and one-third of that on Earth, respectively. The facilities will help reduce the impact on the health of people living on the moon or Mars that could be caused by low gravity, according to the researchers. They also plan to create space in the living facilities complete with forests or waterfronts by mimicking the biodiversity on Earth.

4   Although they expect constructing the massive facilities will take them around 100 years, they aim to build a simplified version of them on the moon by 2050.

5   The plan also includes building a transportation system called the "Hexagon Space Track System," reminiscent of a galaxy express, to travel between Earth, the moon, and Mars. The system's space train, as large as a Shinkansen,[2] will also generate artificial gravity and travel like trains running on Earth, according to the researchers. It will stop at "stations," which will be built on satellites orbiting the Earth, the moon, or Mars. Linear motors or rocket engines will be used to launch it when it departs from the moon or Mars. Each car of the train will be separated at the stations and be transported in hexagon capsules when traveling between the planets to avoid being exposed to cosmic rays.

6   "As the idea of living in space becomes more realistic, the problem with the low gravity, which I intuitively became aware of when I was a child, is an issue we must overcome," said Takuya Ono, a project associate professor with the center and a senior researcher at Kajima, a major general contractor. "We are committed to achieving the plan so it will be useful for human beings."

MAKE INFERENCES
What can you infer about the biodiversity inside Lunar Glass and Mars Glass after reading paragraph 3?

Use a dictionary or indicate another strategy you used that helped you determine meaning.

capsules (CAP suhlz) *n.*
MEANING:

COMPREHENSION CHECK
According to Japan's plan, where will people live and work, and how will they travel from place to place?

^ An artist's image of an artifical gravity living facility called Mars Glass on Mars.

2. **Shinkansen** (SHIHN kuhn sehn) *n.* train operating on the high-speed railroad system in Japan.

BUILD INSIGHT

First Thoughts

What questions would you most like to ask the Japanese researchers and contractors mentioned in this science feature?

Summary

Write a short objective summary of the text. Remember to include only the central ideas, and do not include your opinions.

Analysis and Discussion

1. **(a)** Reread paragraphs 2 and 3. What issues does the Japanese plan address that are not addressed by space development plans in other countries? **(b) Draw Conclusions** What does this detail suggest about the main concerns of the people behind the plan?

2. **(a) Analyze** What is the central idea of this science feature?
   (b) Support How do the text features—the illustrations and caption—help support this central idea?

3. The author notes that "the plan will only become possible in the 22nd century, at the earliest" and "constructing the massive facilities will take them around 100 years." **(a) Draw Conclusions** Why do you think the author mentions the lengthy timeline for the project twice?
   (b) Speculate What challenges could arise in creating a plan that may not be completed for 100 or more years?

4. **Get Ready for Close Reading** Choose a passage from the text that you find especially interesting or important. You'll discuss the passage with your group during Close-Read activities.

> **WORKING AS A GROUP**
>
> Discuss your responses to the Analysis and Discussion questions with your group.
>
> - Ask follow-up questions of peers to clarify their ideas.
> - Point out new information you learn when others share.
>
> If necessary, revise your original answers to reflect what you learn from your discussion.

Exploring the Essential Question

Should we make a home in space?

5. Reread the quotation that ends the article. If the plan is achieved, what aspects of it will be most "useful for human beings"?

6. How has this science feature changed or added to your ideas about whether humans should make a home in space?

STANDARDS

Reading Informational Text
Provide an objective summary of the text.

Speaking and Listening
Acknowledge new information expressed by others and, when warranted, modify their own views.

ANALYZE AND INTERPRET

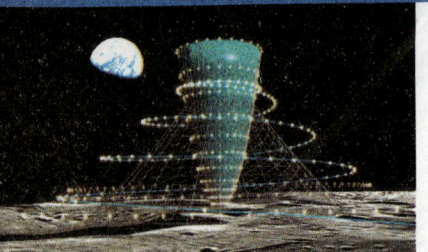

JAPAN TO START RESEARCH ON THE MOON AND MARS FOR HUMANS

Close Read

PRACTICE Complete the following activities, using text evidence.

1. **Present and Discuss** With your group, share passages from the text that you found especially interesting. Discuss what you notice, the questions you have, and the conclusions you reach. For example, you might focus on the following passages:

   • **Paragraph 3:** Why is the construction of "artificial gravity living facilities" so important to the plan?

   • **Paragraph 5:** Discuss the description of the transportation system being developed. In what sense is it a "galaxy express"?

2. **Reflect on Your Learning** What new ideas or insights did you uncover during your second reading of the text?

WORD WALL

Note words in the text that are related to the idea of living among the stars. Add them to your Word Wall.

STUDY LANGUAGE AND CRAFT

Technical Vocabulary

Why These Words? The vocabulary words are related.

| habitation | gravity | capsules |

1. With your group, determine what the words have in common. Discuss your ideas.

2. Add another word that fits the category: _____.

3. Find three other scientific or technical words in the article, and jot down what you think they mean. Verify their meanings in a science dictionary. Then use each word in a sentence.

Word Study

Latin Root: -grav- Many science and technology words have Latin origins. The word *gravity* is built on the Latin root *-grav-*, which means "heavy" or "weighty." *Gravity* can also mean "great seriousness," as in a situation that has serious or "weighty" consequences.

PRACTICE Use a dictionary to find the meanings of the words *gravitate*, *grave*, and *gravitas*. Explain how the root *-grav-* contributes to their meanings. Then, write a sentence using each word.

STANDARDS
Reading Informational Text
Determine an author's point of view or purpose in a text.
Language
Use common, grade-appropriate Greek or Latin affixes and roots as clues to the meaning of a word.

172 UNIT 2 • LIVING AMONG THE STARS

Essential Question: Should we make a home in space?

Author's Purpose

An **author's purpose** is their reason for writing. Authors write for various general purposes: to inform, entertain, persuade, describe, or reflect. Authors of science features directly provide information or convey a central idea about a topic. Usually, though, they don't directly state their purposes for writing. Instead, readers must use strategies to identify author's purpose.

To determine an author's purposes for writing, use these strategies:

- Look at the title of text. Ask: *Does the title provide clues as to author's purpose?*

- Examine details the author includes. Ask: *Do those details entertain, persuade, and/or inform an audience?*

- Think about the author's choices. Ask: *Why does the author include this image? Why does the author quote this person?*

TIP: As you analyze an author's purposes for writing, consider how those purposes target particular readers. Determine whether the author is addressing a group of scientists, the general public, or kids interested in space, and think about how their purposes would differ for each audience.

PRACTICE Complete the activity and answer the questions with your group.

1. **Analyze** Reread each passage identified in the first column of the chart. Then, complete the chart by noting the types of details provided in the text and then telling what purpose those details serve.

PASSAGE	TYPES OF DETAILS PROVIDED	PURPOSE OF THOSE DETAILS
Selection Title and Paragraph 1		
Paragraph 3		
Paragraph 5		

2. **Analyze** Review your responses in the chart. What is the author's overall purpose for writing the science feature?

3. **Speculate** If the author of this article wanted to persuade an audience that Japan's work should be supported by other countries, what changes might be made to the text?

Japan to Start Research on the Moon and Mars for Humans 173

STUDY LANGUAGE AND CRAFT

JAPAN TO START RESEARCH ON THE MOON AND MARS FOR HUMANS

Infinitive Phrases and Gerund Phrases

Writers and speakers use infinitive phrases and gerund phrases to add detail to sentences and to clarify the relationships among ideas.

An **infinitive** is a verb form that acts as a noun, an adjective, or an adverb. It usually begins with the word *to*. An **infinitive phrase** is an infinitive plus its own modifiers, objects, or complements.

- Noun (functioning as a subject): **To travel** to Mars *is my dream.*
- Noun (functioning as an object): *I want* **to explore** other planets.
- Adjective (modifying *error*): *That is the error* **to avoid** at all costs.
- Adverb (modifying *stood*): *We all stood* **to honor** the astronauts.

A **gerund** is a verb form that ends in *-ing* and acts as a noun. It can function as a subject, an object, a predicate noun, or the object of a preposition. A **gerund phrase** is a gerund plus its own modifiers, objects, or complements.

- Subject: **Revising** the plan *was a necessary step.*
- Direct Object: *The shuttle pilot loves* **orbiting** small moons.
- Predicate Noun: *Imani's favorite activity is* low-gravity **leaping**.
- Object of a Preposition: *I am weary of* **reviewing** old NASA videos.

> **TIP:** A **phrase** is a group of words that does not have both a subject and a verb and that functions as one part of speech. A phrase expresses an idea but cannot stand alone.

READ Reread these sentences from the selection with your group. Mark the infinitive phrase or gerund phrase in each one. Then, explain the function each performs in the sentence.

1. They announced that they will undertake a joint study to achieve the plan.

2. The plan also includes building a transportation system called the "Hexagon Space Track System," reminiscent of a galaxy express...

WRITE / EDIT Write an example of each kind of sentence. Share your work with your group and discuss any edits that should be made.

1. A sentence that uses an infinitive phrase as a noun

2. A sentence that uses a gerund phrase as a subject

3. A sentence that uses an infinitive phrase as an adverb

4. A sentence that uses a gerund phrase as a predicate noun

STANDARDS

Writing
Use technology, including the Internet, to produce and publish writing and link to and cite sources as well as to interact and collaborate with others, including linking to and citing sources.

Speaking and Listening
Analyze the main ideas and supporting details presented in diverse media and formats and explain how the ideas clarify a topic, text, or issue under study.

Language
Explain the function of phrases and clauses in general and their function in specific sentences.

SHARE IDEAS

Research

A **summary of research findings** is a document that lists research sources and briefly describes the most important ideas in each one.

Assignment

In the science feature, the author reports on Japan's plans for colonizing the moon and Mars. Work with your group to conduct research to answer this question:

What other organizations are developing plans to colonize the moon and/or Mars? What are their goals and timelines for completion?

Then, work together to create a **summary of research findings** and present it to the class.

Conduct Research Consult several print and digital sources to gather relevant information. Use effective search terms, such as *moon colonization* or *living on Mars*, to get the most useful results.

Summarize and Cite Sources Work with your group to collect your information and develop a summary of your research findings. Your summary should present a clear central idea with evidence that supports it. Use slideshow presentation software to prepare your summary for a class presentation. Be sure to cite the sources you consulted and provide a hyperlink to each one.

Present and Analyze As a group, share your summary with the class. As you listen to other groups, complete the Presentation Analysis Guide to analyze the ideas they present. Then discuss with your group the ways in which each presentation clarified the issue addressed in the research question.

TIP: Make sure the information you gather comes from credible (trustworthy) and accurate (up-to-date) sources.

PRESENTATION ANALYSIS GUIDE

How well did the presentation answer the research question?	
What central idea was presented?	
What supporting evidence was used?	

EVIDENCE LOG

Before moving on to a new selection, go to your Evidence Log and record any additional thoughts or observations you may have about "Japan to Start Research on the Moon and Mars for Humans."

COMPARE WITHIN GENRE

NONFICTION

An **argument** is a work of nonfiction in which the author defends a position on a topic and tries to convince readers to think or do something specific.

ARGUMENT

Author's Purpose
- to argue for or against an idea
- to convince or persuade readers

Characteristics
- a claim, in which the author states their point of view or position on a topic or issue
- sound reasons that support the claim
- relevant and sufficient evidence, such as facts, examples, data, or the writer's personal observations
- a counterclaim, or opposing position, that the author disproves

Structure
- an introduction, a body, and a conclusion that flow in a logical way and make the author's ideas clear

Take a Minute!

MARK Read the list of phrases. Then, mark the ones that you would most likely see in an argument. Discuss your choices with a partner.

I question whether	Great party!	On the other hand
I cannot agree	Equally important	Wait here
First, choose your paint	There is no doubt	Dinner will be served

STANDARDS
Reading Informational Text
- Determine an author's point of view or purpose in a text and analyze how the author distinguishes his or her position from that of others.
- Trace and evaluate the argument and specific claims in a text, assessing whether the reasoning is sound and the evidence is relevant and sufficient to support the claims.

Essential Question: Should we make a home in space?

Claim, Reasoning, and Evidence

In an argument, the author's purpose, or reason for writing, is to convince readers to accept a certain **claim**. The author supports their claim using sound reasoning as well as relevant and sufficient evidence. A successful argument includes these elements:

ELEMENTS OF ARGUMENT	EXPLANATIONS / EXAMPLES
Claim / Addressing counterclaim	• A claim is a statement of the writer's position on a topic. • A counterclaim is a position on a topic that differs from that of the writer making the argument. Counterclaims should be addressed and shown to be weak or of little concern.
Sound reasoning	Reasoning refers to how an argument is put together: how it begins, develops, and ends. There should be no gaps in logic. For example, an argument might show causes and effects or offer a problem and solution format.
Sufficient and revelant evidence	• There is enough evidence, such as facts, examples, data, or observations, to support the points the writer is making. • The evidence is relevant—directly related to the writer's topic and claim.

PRACTICE Read the following argument, and complete the activities with your group.

(a) Our school district must improve its science education program. (b) Right now, our middle schools offer only two and a half hours a week of science instruction. (c) Compare that with our neighboring district, which offers five hours a week, plus a free enrichment program. (d) I know some parents will disagree with me and say that middle school science is not a big deal. (e) But I encourage you to look at the data: Our district has a graduation rate that is 20 percent lower than our neighboring district, and other than science we have the same curriculum. (f) Providing high-interest, hands-on science classes at middle school is vital and will keep our kids in school.

1. Identify the claim, where the counterclaim is addressed, and evidence provided to support the claim.

2. Discuss the writer's reasoning. Is it sound and convincing?

Compare Within Genre **177**

PREPARE TO READ

WHY WE SHOULD CONTINUE TO EXPLORE SPACE

WHY WE SHOULD SAVE EARTH BEFORE COLONIZING MARS

COMPARE NONFICTION
In this lesson, you will read two argumentative essays that offer different perspectives on exploring and colonizing space. You will then compare the authors' arguments.

About the Author

Sheri Buckner is a writer and artist based in Chicago. She holds a degree in English from the University of Nebraska.

Concept Vocabulary

As you read "Why We Should Continue to Explore Space," you will encounter these words. When you finish reading, work with your group to identify what these words have in common.

| improve | striving | persist |

Context Clues Clues in the surrounding text can help you determine the meaning of an unfamiliar word. An **antonym**, or word with an opposite meaning, can provide a clue by indicating contrast.

EXAMPLE
Tomorrow's basketball practice is **mandatory**; the one on Thursday, however, is optional.

PRACTICE As you read, study the context and look for antonyms to help you determine the meanings of unfamiliar words. Mark any antonyms you find.

Reading Strategy: Make Predictions

A **prediction** is an educated guess about a text's main ideas that is made before reading. You can make a prediction about an argument by analyzing the text's structure.

- The **title** often indicates the topic and may suggest the author's opinion about it.
- **Headings** show how the text is organized and how the author develops the argument, section by section.
- **Images,** such as graphs, charts, or photographs, provide supporting evidence and help illustrate certain points.
- **Captions** provide additional information about the images.

PRACTICE Before you read, scan the major sections and features of the text. Then, write your predictions in the open space next to the text.

STANDARDS
Reading Informational Text
Analyze the structure an author uses to organize a text, including how the major sections contribute to the whole and to the development of the ideas.

Language
Use context as a clue to the meaning of a word or phrase.

178 UNIT 2 • LIVING AMONG THE STARS

ARGUMENT

Why We Should Continue to Explore Space

Sheri Buckner

BACKGROUND
This article addresses the topic of space exploration in an era of competing national priorities. It is designed to convince readers that exploring space can help us address pressing issues on our planet.

1   Environmental problems. Public health and safety concerns. Social equality issues. When we face such serious challenges here on Earth, why would we devote precious money, time, and effort to space exploration? The answers are clear and compelling.

Exploring space gives us new insights.

2   Overcoming the challenges of working in space has led to scientific advances that benefit the environment, medicine, transportation, energy, public safety, and information technology. For example, investigating ways to grow food in low-gravity environments, such as on Mars, helps us find strategies for raising crops in extreme conditions on Earth. This information could aid in reducing the negative impacts of worldwide hunger and changing ecosystems. In addition, medical research conducted in space provides fresh understandings about the human body, helping to **improve** our quality of life.

3   The more we learn about what lies beyond Earth, the better we understand our own planet. Space is an endless source of knowledge that helps us answer key questions about the origins of Earth and its place in the universe. Studying the solar system has increased our understanding of our atmosphere, our magnetosphere,[1] gravity, and more. For instance, when we sent

---

1. **magnetosphere** (mag NEE tuh sfeer) *n.* magnetic field that surrounds a planet.

READ TO UNLOCK MEANING
1. First read the text for comprehension and enjoyment. Use the **Reading Strategy** and **Comprehension Check** questions to support your first read.
2. With your group, apply the vocabulary strategy to unlock word meanings.
3. Find other details in the text you find interesting. Ask your own questions and draw your own conclusions.

Mark context clues or indicate another strategy you used that helped you determine meaning.

improve (ihm PROOV) *v.*
MEANING:

Why We Should Continue to Explore Space   **179**

spacecraft to Venus, we were able to see how a habitable planet turned into one with a deadly landscape because of an out-of-control greenhouse effect. Astronauts who travel into space see the fragility of our atmosphere and the delicate balance that keeps our planet livable for humans. This perspective emphasizes the importance of protecting our Earth and encourages efforts to do so.

Space exploration costs less than you realize.

4   Some critics argue that it doesn't make sense to spend money on space exploration when those funds could be used to address pressing problems on Earth. However, the money spent on NASA has a positive impact on the U.S. economy. It generates advancements in technology that have practical applications. It also creates and supports new businesses as well as high-paying, highly skilled jobs. This, in turn, strengthens the overall economy. A stronger economy means there is a larger pool of money we can spend on finding solutions to other important economic, technological, environmental, and social problems.

5   Like many other nations, the U.S. earmarks money for space exploration in the country's annual budget. Most Americans know that funding for NASA is part of the total U.S. budget, but many people significantly overestimate the percentage that is allotted. Opinion polls show that some believe this figure to be as much as

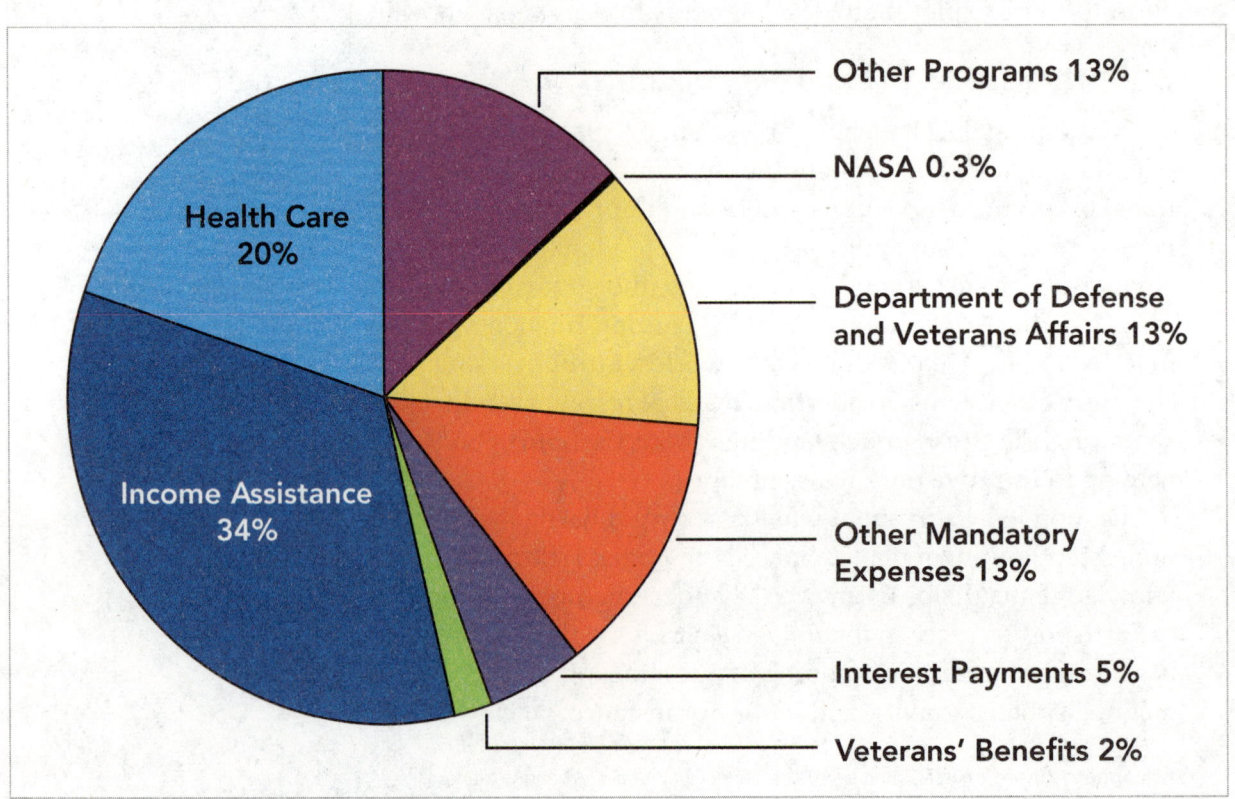

^ Approximate budget for U.S. government for year 2020

180 UNIT 2 • LIVING AMONG THE STARS

25% of federal spending. In reality, however, NASA's funding represents only about 0.3% of the budget.

Outer space fuels our imaginations.

6   For decades, children have imagined life on other planets and voyages through the cosmos. While few of them may ever travel into space, those ideas can motivate kids to pursue scientific careers in medicine or engineering—fields that can benefit society and help resolve or prevent some of our Earthly problems.

7   Adults are inspired by space as well. We marvel at the beauty and enormity of the universe when we stargaze or see images of Mars from NASA's *Perseverance* rover. We consider the possibility that life could exist elsewhere in the galaxy, reminding us that there could be beings on other planets who are struggling with some of the same issues we face on Earth. There is something wonderful and heartening about **striving** to discover something that might forever change the world we live in for the better.

Exploring space benefits Earth.

8   It's true that we need to address many significant problems that affect our world. However, our efforts to confront and conquer those problems shouldn't come at the cost of making new discoveries in space. We can do both. The social and environmental issues we're dealing with do not **persist** because of the money our government spends on space exploration. In fact, such funding may help us solve Earth's most urgent problems.

BUILD INSIGHT

WHY WE SHOULD CONTINUE TO EXPLORE SPACE

First Thoughts

Choose one of the following items to discuss.

- Which parts of the argument about space exploration seem most convincing to you, and why?
- How did you react to the pie chart illustrating the U.S. budget? In your opinion, do any of these programs deserve more—or less—funding? If you were in charge of balancing the budget, how might you change the way funds are allocated?

Summary

Write a brief objective summary of the argument to confirm your comprehension.

Analysis and Discussion

1. **Paraphrase** According to the author, what has space taught us about Earth?

2. (a) **Make Inferences** Why does the author cite statistics in paragraph 5? How are they important to the argument?
   (b) **Evaluate** How effective is the pie chart in illustrating the point the author makes in this paragraph?

3. (a) **Analyze** After commenting on the practical benefits of space exploration, the author includes a section that presents space as inspirational in paragraphs 6–7. What does the discussion on motivation and imagination add to the argument? (b) **Make a Judgment** Which are more important—the practical or the inspirational benefits of space exploration? Explain.

4. (a) Describe the headings in this article. (b) **Evaluate** How effective are the headings in structuring the text? Explain your answer.

5. **Get Ready for Close Reading** Choose a passage from the text that you find especially interesting or important. You'll discuss the passage with your group during Close-Read activities.

Exploring the Essential Question

Should we make a home in space?

6. **Speculate** Do you believe the author would support the idea of living on—and not just exploring—other planets? Explain your ideas in your Evidence Log.

WORKING AS A GROUP

Discuss your responses to the Analysis and Discussion questions with your group.

- Allow time for all group members to respond to the questions.
- If you disagree with a response, politely point out the text evidence that led to your own response.

If necessary, revise your original answers to reflect what you learn from your discussion.

STANDARDS

Reading Informational Text
• Cite several pieces of textual evidence to support analysis of what the text says explicitly as well as inferences drawn from the text.

Language
Demonstrate understanding of figurative language, word relationships, and nuances in word meanings.

---

182 UNIT 2 • LIVING AMONG THE STARS

ANALYZE AND INTERPRET

Close Read

PRACTICE Complete the following activities. Use text evidence to support your responses.

1. **Present and Discuss** With your group, share passages from the article that you found especially interesting. Discuss what you notice, the questions you have, and the conclusions you reach. For example, you might focus on the following passages:

   - **Paragraph 1:** Discuss ways in which the use of fragments helps to attract readers' attention.

   - **Paragraph 8:** Discuss the author's word choice in concluding the text. Is the use of language effective?

2. **Reflect on Your Learning** What new ideas or insights did you uncover during your second reading of the text?

STUDY LANGUAGE AND CRAFT

Concept Vocabulary

Why These Words? The vocabulary words are related.

improve	striving	persist

WORD WALL

Note words in the text that are related to the idea of living among the stars. Add them to your Word Wall.

1. With your group, determine what the words have in common. Write your ideas.

2. Add another word that fits the category _____.

3. Write an answer to this question, using all three of the words: *What advice would you give to someone facing a difficult task?*

Word Study

Synonyms and Nuance Words that have the same basic meaning are known as **synonyms**. Often, synonyms differ in **nuance**, or shades of meaning. For example, these two synonyms both mean "news," but they have different nuances: *scoop / update*.

PRACTICE With your group, look up these words in a print or online dictionary: *improve, refine, upgrade*. Write their definitions, and explain the differences in nuance among them.

Why We Should Continue to Explore Space **183**

ANALYZE AND INTERPRET

WHY WE SHOULD CONTINUE TO EXPLORE SPACE

Claim, Reasoning, and Evidence

In a strong and convincing argument, the author presents a **claim**, or position on an issue, and shows how it is distinct from claims made in other arguments. The author uses **sound reasoning** to demonstrate that the claim is well grounded and provides **evidence** to support the reasons.

TYPE OF EVIDENCE	DEFINITION
facts	information that can be proved true, such as dates
statistics	facts based on numerical data, such as percentages
examples	specific instances that show how an idea works
personal observations	explanations based on the writer's experience

To determine if an argument is valid, readers must trace and evaluate the evidence. Is it **relevant**, or clearly related to the reasoning? Is it **sufficient**—has enough relevant evidence been provided? When a **counterclaim**, or objection to the author's claim, is discussed, is convincing evidence used to address and disprove it?

PRACTICE Work with your group to complete the activities.

1. **(a)** What claim does the author make in "Why We Should Continue to Explore Space"? **(b)** What counterclaim does she address in paragraph 4? **(c) Evaluate** How well does the author point out weaknesses in the counterclaim? Explain.

2. **(a)** Review the paragraphs listed in the chart. Record the types of evidence presented in each one. **(b) Evaluate** Determine whether the evidence is relevant and sufficient to support the reasoning in the paragraph. Explain your answers.

PASSAGE	TYPES OF EVIDENCE	RELEVANT/SUFFICIENT?
paragraph 3		
paragraph 5 and pie chart		

3. **Make a Judgment** Trace and evaluate the argument in this article. Has the author provided enough sound reasoning to convince you that her claim about space exploration is valid? Explain your answer.

STANDARDS

Reading Informational Text
- Determine an author's point of view or purpose in a text and analyze how the author distinguishes his or her position from that of others.
- Trace and evaluate the argument and specific claims in a text, assessing whether the reasoning is sound and the evidence is relevant and sufficient to support the claims.

Language
Explain the function of phrases and clauses in general and their function in specific sentences.

184 UNIT 2 • LIVING AMONG THE STARS

STUDY LANGUAGE AND CRAFT

Dependent Clauses

A **clause** is a group of words with its own subject and verb. Writers use different types of clauses to express their ideas and enliven their writing.

An **independent clause** can stand alone as a complete sentence. A **dependent clause** cannot stand on its own. The chart shows different types of dependent clauses and provides an example of each.

TYPE OF DEPENDENT CLAUSE	EXAMPLE
An **adverb clause** acts as an adverb. It begins with a subordinating conjunction, such as *although*, *if*, or *because*.	Because their equipment needed repairs, the astronauts delayed the spacewalk for two weeks. (The underlined clause modifies the verb *delayed*, telling *why*.)
An **adjective clause** acts as an adjective. It usually begins with a relative pronoun, such as *who*, *whom*, or *which*.	The technician who fixed the equipment had years of experience in the space program. (The underlined clause modifies the noun *technician*, telling *which one*.)
A **noun clause** acts as a noun. It begins with a word such as *what*, *where*, *that*, *how*, or *why*.	What the team accomplished impressed everyone. (The underlined clause acts as the subject of the sentence.)

READ Work on your own to complete the activities.

1. Underline the dependent clause in each sentence. Then identify its function and the type of dependent clause it is.

   a. Do you know where the astronauts are waiting?

   b. The spaceflight, which was threatened by bad weather, began only slightly behind schedule.

2. Find this sentence in paragraph 3 of the article: *Astronauts who travel into space see the fragility of our atmosphere and the delicate balance that keeps our planet livable for humans.* Underline the two dependent clauses. Then, write in the margin what types of dependent clause they are.

WRITE / EDIT Work with your group to write three complete sentences, one with an adverb clause, one with an adjective clause, and one with a noun clause. Label each clause with its type. Then, check your work together.

Why We Should Continue to Explore Space 185

PREPARE TO READ

WHY WE SHOULD CONTINUE TO EXPLORE SPACE

WHY WE SHOULD SAVE EARTH BEFORE COLONIZING MARS

COMPARE NONFICTION
The argumentative essay you are about to read offers a different perspective on exploring and colonizing space. Pay attention to the similarities and differences in how this author advances his argument.

About the Author

Bruce Dorminey (b. 1959) is a longtime journalist from Georgia who has written extensively about science and space exploration. His work has appeared in *Scientific American*, *Astronomy*, *Forbes*, and several other publications. Dorminey is the author of the book *Distant Wanderers: The Search for Planets Beyond the Solar System*.

STANDARDS
Reading Informational Text Analyze the interactions between individuals, events, and ideas in a text.
Language Consult general and specialized reference materials, both print and digital, to find the pronunciation of a word or determine or clarify its precise meaning or its part of speech.

Concept Vocabulary

As you read, you will encounter these words. After reading, work with your group to identify what these words have in common.

| ominously | anxious | calamitous |

Reference Materials A **thesaurus** provides a word's part of speech, its synonyms (words with similar meanings), and its antonyms (words with opposite meanings). When you encounter an unfamiliar word, looking up these details can help you determine its meaning.

EXAMPLE
verdant *adj. synonyms:* lush, leafy, green; *antonyms:* barren, leafless

In this example, familiar synonyms (*leafy*, *green*) and antonyms (*barren*, *leafless*) give clues to the meaning of the less familiar word *verdant*. The abbreviation *adj.* indicates the word's part of speech: adjective.

PRACTICE As you read the article, use a print or online thesaurus to help you determine the meanings of unfamiliar words. Write the definitions in the open space next to the text.

Reading Strategy: Make Connections

You can gain insight into a text by **making connections** to other texts you have read on the same subject. Analyze the text by asking yourself, *How is this text similar to and different from other texts?* These connections will deepen your understanding of the text you are reading now and the subject as a whole.

Consider these textual elements as you make connections:
- claims, reasoning, and supporting evidence
- how individuals, events, and ideas interact in a text
- writing style and word choice

PRACTICE As you read the article, use the open space next to the text to note connections you make to other texts.

186 UNIT 2 • LIVING AMONG THE STARS

Why We Should Save Earth Before Colonizing Mars

Bruce Dorminey

ARGUMENT

BACKGROUND

This article was written for *Forbes* magazine just after the European Space Agency announced the building of a new telescope. Bruce Dorminey, who has written a great deal about space science, chose this moment to publish his thoughts about space settlement. He quotes a well-known twentieth-century actor, Charlton Heston.

1   Upon hearing NASA's confirmation that Mars has complex organics, a reader took heart that someday soon we would be colonizing the world next door. But my first thought was why don't we simply start by cleaning up this one? That is, ridding our oceans of the islands of plastic and our planet's atmosphere of its sulfuric acid rain and nitrogen dioxide.

2   That includes becoming smarter about how and why we build infrastructure and the resulting traffic congestion that usually goes with unbridled development.

3   What's with this guy, you may be thinking? Why would someone who's long advocated space exploration and astronomy suddenly turn inward?

4   Maybe it's because no matter how we spin the data, of the several thousand planets now confirmed to be circling other suns, precious few seem to resemble our own. And although Mars might eventually be a candidate for terraforming,[1] why not simply take that energy and rectify our own Earth back to its former glory?

5   Although we may be capable of searching out biosignatures[2] of life on nearby extrasolar earths, we won't be capable of journeying there anytime soon.

---

1. **terraforming** (TEHR uh fawr mihng) *v.* transforming a planet so that it can support human life.
2. **biosignatures** (by oh SIG nuh churz) *n. pl.* chemical or physical markers that provide scientific evidence of past or present life.

READ TO UNLOCK MEANING

1. First read the text for comprehension and enjoyment. Use the **Comprehension Check** question to support your first read.
2. With your group, apply the vocabulary strategy to unlock word meanings.
3. Find other details in the text you find interesting. Ask your own questions and draw your own conclusions.

Use a thesaurus or indicate another strategy you used that helped you determine meaning.

ominously (O muh nuhs lee) *adv.*
MEANING:

anxious (ANGK shuhs) *adj.*
MEANING:

calamitous (kuh LA muh tuhs) *adj.*
MEANING:

COMPREHENSION CHECK
According to the author, why don't we need to worry about an impactor destroying life on Earth?

From *Forbes*. © 2018 Forbes. All rights reserved. Used under license.

6   Thus, I'm increasingly becoming more and more appreciative of what Earth offers and why we should be doing more to protect it; including its disappearing species of rhinos, elephants, tigers, lions, dolphins and whales.

7   This generation is certainly the tip of the spear that's ever slowly moving its way into the cosmos. But we live in an era of strange dichotomies. We remain fixated on finding life off-planet when we still haven't cataloged all of our own Earth's biota.[3]

8   We also need to think about planetary defense.

9   As the late Charlton Heston intoned during the opening moments of the 1998 film *Armageddon*, during the age of the dinosaurs, Earth was lush and verdant. Then their reign was interrupted by a six-mile-wide rock that unleashed the force of 10,000 nuclear weapons in our atmosphere; kicking up a trillion tons of dirt and dust to go with it. A thousand years of nuclear winter followed. And then most **ominously,** Heston pauses for effect and repeats: "It happened before. It will happen again."

10   As the B612 Foundation[4] and others like it warn, humanity must get off this planet for good. Perhaps. But arguably in the nearer term, we need to ensure that the planet we are so **anxious** to leave is also one in which we would want to return.

11   As for tracking potential space hazards?

12   NASA's Jet Propulsion Laboratory (JPL) already tracks some 7,000 potentially hazardous Near-Earth Objects (NEOs). But just today, the European Space Agency (ESA) announced plans for a new automated telescope, the first in a future network that would completely scan the sky to identify NEOs for follow up. ESA says that like the insect, the "Flyeye," can expand and compound its field of view into a diameter some 13 times that of the Moon, as seen from Earth.

13   Thus, the biggest current blindside may be simply not taking care of planet Earth. In terms of **calamitous** impactors, the odds remain in our favor. After all, it's been 65 million years since such a civilization-ending impactor.

14   Our species is less than 250,000 years old. What we learn from cleaning up our own planet and preserving its flora and fauna will only help us when terraforming the world next door.

15   And if we aren't out terraforming nearby star systems in another half million years, our civilization may have long disappeared anyway. Thus, we should deal with our own environmental issues here first. Then worry about terraforming Mars.

---

3   **biota** (by OH tuh) *n.* plant and animal life of a particular place, habitat, or time.
4   **B612 Foundation** nonprofit foundation dedicated to planetary science and planetary defense against asteroid and other near-Earth object impacts.

BUILD INSIGHT

First Thoughts

Select one of the following items to discuss:

- What do you think of the author's writing style? How does it affect you as a reader?
- Does the author's use of a movie reference strengthen or weaken the article? Explain.

Summary

Write a short objective summary of the text to confirm your comprehension. Remember to include only the main ideas, and do not include your opinions.

Analysis and Discussion

1. **Analyze Cause and Effect** In paragraph 3, the author states that he once strongly supported space exploration but now has "turned inward" to focus on Earth. What caused this change?

2. **Generalize** Reread paragraphs 4 and 5. What is the author's main point about how much effort should be invested in space settlement?

3. **Interpret** Reread paragraph 7. What is meant by "an era of strange dichotomies"? (Dichotomies are contradictions.)

4. **Assess** In paragraph 14, the author suggests that humans should learn to care for Earth before they even try terraforming. Is this judgment fair? Explain your answer.

5. **Get Ready for Close Reading** Choose a passage from the text that you find especially interesting or important. You'll discuss the passage with your group during Close-Read activities.

> **WORKING AS A GROUP**
>
> Discuss your responses to the Analysis and Discussion questions with your group.
>
> - Support your ideas by citing evidence from the text.
> - Follow the rules for respectful peer-group discussions.
>
> If necessary, revise your original answers to reflect what you learn from your discussion.

Exploring the Essential Question

Should we make a home in space?

6. Might making a home in space have negative consequences for Earth? Record your ideas in your Evidence Log.

STANDARDS

Reading Informational Text
Cite several pieces of textual evidence to support analysis of what the text says explicitly as well as inferences drawn from the text.

ANALYZE AND INTERPRET

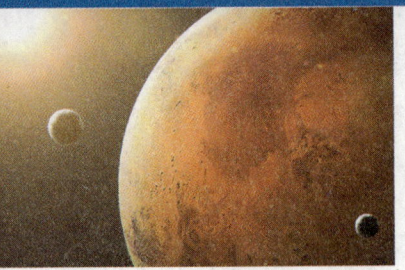

WHY WE SHOULD SAVE EARTH BEFORE COLONIZING MARS

Close Read

PRACTICE Complete the following activities.

1. **Present and Discuss** With your group, share passages from the text that you found especially interesting. For example, you might focus on the following passages:

   - **Paragraphs 9–10:** Determine the author's position and point of view, and discuss how the author distinguishes his position from those of Charlton Heston and the B612 Foundation.

   - **Paragraphs 11–13:** Trace and evaluate the specific claims the author makes about the danger of asteroids.

2. **Reflect on Your Learning** What new ideas or insights did you uncover during your second reading of the text?

WORD WALL
Note words in the text that are related to the idea of living among the stars. Add them to your Word Wall.

STUDY LANGUAGE AND CRAFT

Concept Vocabulary

Why These Words? The vocabulary words are related.

| ominously | anxious | calamitous |

1. With your group, write down what the words have in common.

2. Add another word that fits the category. _____

3. Use each word in a sentence. Include synonyms that hint at each word's meaning.

Word Study

Connotation and Denotation The **denotation** of a word is its dictionary definition. The **connotation** is the shade of meaning or emotion that the word suggests. Words with similar denotations can have different connotations. For example, the word *calamitous* is similar in meaning to *unfortunate*, but *calamitous* has a more negative connotation.

PRACTICE Use a thesaurus to find other synonyms for *calamitous*. In your group, discuss the different synonyms and their connotations.

STANDARDS
Reading Informational Text
- Determine an author's point of view or purpose in a text and analyze how the author distinguishes his or her position from that of others.
- Trace and evaluate the argument and specific claims in a text, assessing whether the reasoning is sound and the evidence is relevant and sufficient to support the claims.

Language
Distinguish among the connotations of words with similar denotations.

190 UNIT 2 • LIVING AMONG THE STARS

Essential Question: Should we make a home in space?

Claim, Reasoning, and Evidence

A **claim** is the position that an author takes in a piece of argumentative writing. It cannot stand alone; a claim must be supported with sound **reasoning.** When a writer uses sound reasoning, they present information in a logical, sensible way and support their points with solid evidence.

Readers should trace the argument and evaluate the quality of the evidence presented. Relevant and sufficient evidence raises the author's credibility; unrelated evidence or a lack of evidence lowers credibility.

- **Relevant evidence** is clearly related to the claim and does not stray from the topic.

- **Sufficient evidence** has enough quantity and variety to convince readers that a reason is valid.

An author assembles the parts of an argument in a way that best suits the topic and the audience. The author may anticipate that some readers will object to their claim. To address a **counterclaim,** or an opposing view, the author presents reasoning and evidence that disproves it and supports their own claim.

TIP: Evidence may consist of facts, examples, quotations, expert opinions, or other pieces of information.

PRACTICE Work with your group to complete the activities.

1. **Analyze** Reread each passage listed in the chart. What specific evidence does the author give in each passage to support the claim that we need to focus more on Earth than on space? Write the evidence and then explain why the author's reasoning is or is not sound.

PASSAGE	EVIDENCE	IS IT SOUND?
Paragraphs 1–2		
Paragraphs 6–7		
Paragraph 10		
Paragraph 13		

2. **Analyze** Reread paragraphs 8–13. Explain how the author disproves this counterclaim: *Danger from asteroids means that humans must leave Earth to live on a different planet.*

3. **Evaluate** Which piece of evidence in the text do you find most convincing? Explain your answer.

Why We Should Save Earth Before Colonizing Mars **191**

STUDY LANGUAGE AND CRAFT

WHY WE SHOULD SAVE EARTH BEFORE COLONIZING MARS

Diction, Meaning, and Tone

Diction is the type of language—the words and expressions—that an author chooses. Diction may be informal, formal, technical, sophisticated, and so on. Authors of arguments often use scholarly diction and a serious tone to show that their position is credible, or trustworthy.

Tone is the author's attitude toward their subject and audience, and this attitude has an emotional quality. For example, the tone might be hopeful, hostile, friendly, stern, or playful. An author's diction affects both the meaning of what they write and the tone it conveys to readers.

EXAMPLES
Two sentences that use different words will mean slightly different things and express different emotions. Notice how diction affects meaning and tone in these examples.

Sentence 1
People who indulge the idea of living on Mars are not being sensible.

Sentence 2
I'd have to say that anyone who wants to live on Mars is pretty crazy!

TIP:
- The formal diction in sentence 1 (*indulge; sensible*) has a serious tone.
- The informal diction in sentence 2 (*I'd have to say; pretty crazy*) has a casual tone.

PRACTICE Work on your own to complete the activities. Then discuss your responses with your group.

1. Read this passage from the selection, and mark words and phrases that create the tone, or the author's attitude toward the subject.

   Upon hearing NASA's confirmation that Mars has complex organics, a reader took heart that someday soon we would be colonizing the world next door. But my first thought was why don't we simply start by cleaning up this one? That is, ridding our oceans of the islands of plastic and our planet's atmosphere of its sulfuric acid rain and nitrogen dioxide.

2. **Interpret** Mark the answer choice that best describes the text's overall tone.

   ○ engaging and conversational
   ○ formal and distant
   ○ sarcastic and funny

3. **Support** Explain the reasons for your answer to item 2. Cite specific words and phrases from the passage that support your response.

STANDARDS

Reading Informational Text
Determine the meaning of words and phrases as they are used in a text, including figurative, connotative, and technical meanings; analyze the impact of a specific word choice on meaning and tone.

Speaking and Listening
• Analyze the main ideas and supporting details presented in diverse media and formats and explain how the ideas clarify a topic, text, or issue under study.
• Delineate a speaker's argument and specific claims, evaluating the soundness of the reasoning and the relevance and sufficiency of the evidence.

SHARE IDEAS

Speaking and Listening

In a **debate**, two individuals or teams present opposing arguments.

Assignment

With your group, pair up with another group to conduct a brief **debate** about one of the following ideas from the article:

- ○ Dealing with environmental problems on Earth is more important than exploring space.
- ○ Working to create space settlements is not a practical, worthwhile undertaking right now.

Work with your group to plan and deliver your argument. Listen and take notes as the other group presents the opposing argument.

USE NEW WORDS
Academic Vocabulary
Use the unit's academic vocabulary words during your debate.
- justify
- dissent
- certainty
- discredit
- assumption

Organize the Argument With the other group, determine which idea to debate, which group will support the idea, and which group will oppose it.

Then, meet with your own group to outline your side of the argument. Include these features:

- An introduction that includes a clearly stated claim
- At least two logical reasons that support the claim and show your understanding of the issue
- Convincing evidence that shows why your reasons are valid
- Relevant evidence from accurate (current) and credible (trustworthy) sources
- A conclusion that restates the claim in an interesting way

Conduct and Discuss the Debate Deliver your side of the argument with your group. As the other team delivers its argument, listen politely and take notes.

After both presentations are complete, meet with your team to evaluate the opposing team's argument. Discuss the following points:

- What was the group's argument and specific claim?
- Did the group use logical and sound reasoning to support their argument?
- Did the group provide relevant supporting evidence?
- Did the group provide sufficient supporting evidence?
- Was the argument convincing?

Finally, bring both groups together to share the evaluations and discuss the debate as a whole.

TEST PRACTICE

ARGUMENT

WHY WE SHOULD CONTINUE TO EXPLORE SPACE

WHY WE SHOULD SAVE EARTH BEFORE COLONIZING MARS

COMPARE NONFICTION
Multiple Choice

These questions are based on the two argumentative texts you have read. Choose the best answer to each question.

1. Each text bases its argument upon a claim. Which statement best describes how the two claims are related?

   A The two claims are almost identical.

   B The two claims take opposing views on the same topic.

   C The two claims take similar views on different topics.

   D The two claims are completely unrelated.

2. Read these passages. Which statement best describes the authors' perspectives on space exploration?

   from "Why We Should Continue to Explore Space"

   . . . investigating ways to grow food in low-gravity environments, such as on Mars, helps us find strategies for raising crops in extreme conditions on Earth.

   from "Why We Should Save Earth Before Colonizing Mars"

   Thus, we should deal with our own environmental issues here first. Then worry about terraforming Mars.

   A Both authors believe space should be the top priority for humans.

   B Both authors believe space should be a low priority for humans.

   C Neither author makes a clear statement about how high a priority space should be.

   D One author thinks space should be a higher priority; the other thinks Earth should be.

3. Both authors cite evidence about environmental problems on Earth. Which statement best describes how each uses this evidence?

   A One uses it to prove the merits of space exploration, and the other uses it to prove that we should focus on Earth, not space.

   B Both authors cite evidence about Earth's environment, but it does not form an important part of either argument.

   C Both authors cite evidence about the environment to support the idea that space exploration is urgently needed.

   D One author uses this evidence to tell an interesting personal story, and the other uses it to criticize the use of government funds.

STANDARDS

Reading Informational Text
Analyze how two or more authors writing about the same topic shape their presentations of key information by emphasizing different evidence or advancing different interpretations of facts.

Writing
Write arguments to support claims with clear reasons and relevant evidence.

194 UNIT 2 • LIVING AMONG THE STARS

Essential Question: Should we make a home in space?

Short Response

1. **Analyze** Identify the types of evidence each author uses to support their position. Which argument is more effectively supported with relevant and sufficient evidence? Explain your response.

2. **Make Inferences** How might Sheri Buckner respond to Bruce Dorminey's position that we will not be colonizing space for a very, very long time, if ever?

3. **Connect** Describe an area of agreement between the two authors. Include details from each article.

Timed Writing

An **argumentative essay** is a brief work of nonfiction in which the author's goal is to persuade readers to take a specific action or agree with a certain opinion about a situation or an idea.

> **Assignment**
>
> Write an **argumentative essay** in which you analyze and compare the arguments in the two texts. Clearly state a claim about which argument is more inspiring. Support your opinion with evidence from both texts.

5-Minute Planner

1. Read the assignment carefully and completely.
2. Decide on your claim—the position you will take in your essay.
3. Choose relevant supporting evidence from both articles.
4. In an informal outline, organize your ideas logically. Make sure to include supporting reasons and evidence. Keep these points in mind:
   - Briefly summarize each author's point of view on space exploration and the different information each one emphasizes.
   - Clearly connect the relevant evidence you cite from each text with your claim about which argument is more inspiring.

EVIDENCE LOG

Before moving on, go to your Evidence Log and record any additional thoughts or observations you may have about "Why We Should Continue to Explore Space" and "Why We Should Save Earth Before Colonizing Mars."

Test Practice **195**

PERFORMANCE TASK

SOURCES

- Space Settlement Art
- Dark They Were, and Golden-Eyed (short story)
- Dark They Were, and Golden-Eyed (radio play)
- Japan to Start Research on the Moon and Mars for Humans
- Why We Should Continue to Explore Space
- Why We Should Save Earth Before Colonizing Mars

Conduct a Debate

Assignment

With your group, pair up with another group to conduct a **debate** in which each team takes a position on this statement:

The risks of building a human home in space outweigh the benefits.

Prepare for the Debate

Assign Teams There are two teams in a debate. The "Pro" team supports the statement, and the "Con" team opposes it. Assign at least two people to each team and one person to act as the debate judge. You don't have to personally agree with the position you are assigned.

Follow Debate Structure A formal debate follows this order:

1. Opening Arguments: Each team speaks for an agreed-upon amount of time and presents its position. This is followed by a short break that gives each team time to prepare a rebuttal.
2. Rebuttals: Each team argues against the points the other team made.
3. Closing Statements: Each team reinforces why their position is best.
4. The judge decides which team won the debate.

Build Arguments and Gather Evidence With your team, discuss the texts from the unit. Identify three clear reasons that support your position, arrange them in a logical order, and gather evidence from the texts to support each reason. Be sure to prepare for possible rebuttals too. Use the chart to organize your ideas. Then, work as a group to write your argument.

POSITION (choose one): PRO or CON	
Reason 1:	Evidence:
Reason 2:	Evidence:
Reason 3:	Evidence:
Possible Rebuttals:	Evidence:

196 UNIT 2 • LIVING AMONG THE STARS

Essential Question: Should we make a home in space?

Rehearse

Practice With Your Group Decide which team members will present each stage of the debate, and then rehearse. Use the checklist to evaluate your argument and delivery. Then, work together to strengthen your team's position by rewriting or trying a new approach.

DEBATE CHECKLIST		
CONTENT	**DEBATE TECHNIQUE**	**PRESENTATION TECHNIQUE**
◯ Reasons and evidence clearly support the pro or con argument. ◯ Reasoning shows clear understanding of the topic and texts. ◯ Evidence includes relevant descriptions, facts, details, or examples. ◯ Opposing arguments are anticipated and addressed effectively.	◯ Each speaker keeps within agreed-upon time limits. ◯ Each speaker presents ideas in an organized way.	Each team member communicates effectively: ◯ enunciates, pronouncing words clearly ◯ speaks loudly enough to be heard but does not shout ◯ looks up to make occasional eye contact with listeners ◯ speaks formally, following the conventions of standard English

Hold the Debate

Speak Effectively When it is your turn to speak, present your position in an organized manner and do not rush. Use a steady tone that shows you're in control. Choose precise words that communicate exactly what you mean to say.

Listen Attentively While the other team presents their arguments, listen carefully. Note their claim and evaluate the quality of their reasons and evidence. Is their reasoning sound? Is their evidence relevant and sufficient? If you see flaws in logic or credibility, plan to challenge the team during the rebuttal, but remember to be respectful.

Discuss and Evaluate

Once both teams have presented, discuss the following points:

- What was the team's specific claim?
- Did the argument include sound reasoning?
- Did the team include relevant and sufficient evidence for their claim?

Provide time for the judge to decide which team had the stronger argument and the more persuasive delivery.

STANDARDS

Speaking and Listening
- Delineate a speaker's argument and specific claims, evaluating the soundness of the reasoning and the relevance and sufficiency of the evidence.
- Present claims and findings, emphasizing salient points in a focused, coherent manner with pertinent descriptions, facts, details, and examples; use appropriate eye contact, adequate volume, and clear pronunciation.

INDEPENDENT LEARNING

Essential Question

Should we make a home in space?

Some people imagine a future in which humans live on other planets, while others see one in which humanity improves life on Earth. In this section, you will choose a selection about living among the stars to read independently. Get the most from this section by establishing a purpose for reading. Ask yourself, "What do I hope to gain from my independent reading?" Here are just a few purposes you might consider:

Read to Learn Think about the selections you have already read. What questions do you still have about the unit topic?

Read to Enjoy Read the descriptions of the texts. Which one seems most interesting and appealing to you?

Read to Form a Position Consider your thoughts and feelings about the Essential Question. Are you still undecided about some aspect of the topic?

Independent Learning Strategies

Throughout your life, in school, in your community, and in your career, you will need to rely on yourself to learn and work on your own. Use these strategies to keep your focus as you read independently for sustained periods of time. Add ideas of your own for each category.

STRATEGY	MY ACTION PLAN
Create a schedule	• Think about all of your assignments when planning out how you'll spend your time. • Keep track of your progress toward meeting goals and deadlines. •
Read with purpose	• Read the text more than once. For a longer text, revisit key sections. • Apply different reading strategies to monitor your comprehension. •
Take notes	• Use a note-taking strategy that works for you, such as using sticky notes or different colors. • Mark key details in the text, such as specific dates, names, places, and events. •

Contents

Choose one selection. Selections are available online only.

SCIENCE FEATURE

Beyawned Earth: Pillownauts and the Downside of Space Travel

Jennifer Mason

Volunteers spend days in bed for science.

MAGAZINE ARTICLE

Danger! This Mission to Mars Could Bore You to Death!

Maggie Koerth

Could space travel actually be boring?

SHORT STORY

Time Capsule Found on the Dead Planet

Margaret Atwood

The author imagines what might become of Earth… eventually.

MEDIA: COMIC STRIPS

Space Comics

Various cartoonists

Cartoonists portray the silly side of space.

SHARE YOUR INDEPENDENT LEARNING

SHARE • LEARN • REFLECT

Reflect on and evaluate the information you gained from your Independent Reading selection. Then, share what you learned with others.

Independent Learning 199

INDEPENDENT LEARNING

Close-Read Guide

Establish your purpose for reading. Then, read the selection through at least once. Use this page to record your close-read ideas.

> A Close-Read Guide and Annotation Model are available online.

Selection Title: _____

Purpose for Reading: _____ Minutes Read: _____

Close Read the Text

Zoom in on sections you found interesting. **Annotate** what you notice. Ask yourself **questions** about the text. What can you **conclude**?

_____
_____
_____
_____
_____
_____
_____
_____

Analyze the Text

Think about the author's choices of literary elements, techniques, and structures. Select one and record your thoughts.

_____
_____
_____
_____
_____
_____
_____
_____

QuickWrite

Choose a paragraph from the text that grabbed your interest. Explain the power of this passage.

_____
_____
_____
_____
_____
_____
_____

Share Your Independent Learning

Essential Question

Should we make a home in space?

When you read something independently, your understanding continues to grow as you share what you have learned with others.

Prepare to Share

WRITE One of the most important ways to respond to a text is to notice and describe your personal reactions. Think about the text you explored independently and the ways in which it connects to your own experiences.

- What similarities and differences do you see between the text and your own life? Describe your observations.
- How do you think this text connects to the Essential Question? Describe your ideas.

Learn From Your Classmates

DISCUSS Share your ideas about the text you explored on your own. As you talk with others, take notes about new information that seems important, and consider whether it changes your views about particular ideas.

Reflect

EXPLAIN Review your notes, and mark the most important insight you gained from these writing and discussion activities. Explain how this idea adds to your understanding of living in outer space.

STANDARDS
Speaking and Listening • Come to discussions prepared, having read or researched material under study.
• Acknowledge new information expressed by others and, when warranted, modify their own views.

UNIT 2 REFLECT AND RESPOND

In this unit, you encountered many different perspectives on making a home in space. Now, take some time to reflect on the texts you explored and to express your own ideas.

Reflect on Your Unit Goals

Review your Unit Goals chart from the beginning of the unit. Then, complete the activity and answer the question.

1. In the Unit Goals chart, rate how well you meet each goal now.
2. In which goals were you most and least successful?

Reflect on the Texts

Space Visit If you could visit one place from this unit, where would it be? In the chart, list the locations connected to each text. Be specific. Then, imagine you could go to one of these places today, and mark your first choice for a visit. Briefly explain the reason for your choice.

TITLE	LOCATIONS	REASON
Space Settlement Art		
Dark They Were, and Golden-Eyed		
Japan to Start Research on the Moon and Mars for Humans		
Why We Should Continue to Explore Space		
Why We Should Save Earth Before Colonizing Mars		
Independent Learning Selection:		

Essential Question: Should we make a home in space?

Develop Your Perspective: Unit Projects

Choose one of the following Unit Project ideas.

LIST

Make a packing list for a trip to Mars. Jot down at least ten items you would bring onboard the spacecraft. For each item, write a sentence explaining why it will be useful on your trip. Include at least two concept vocabulary words from the unit in your list.

HOME DESIGN

Design your new home in outer space. Imagine you have moved to another planet and now live there. Create a visual representation of your new home to share with your loved ones back on Earth. You may sketch, paint, use software, or include other multimedia components to develop your image. Once you have a finished product, give it a title, and write a brief explanation to clarify what it shows and to point out important features. Include at least two academic or concept vocabulary words.

COMMERCIAL

Imagine you work for a travel company that offers trips to the moon. With a partner or small group, **create and present a commercial** for one of your company's vacations. Work together to write a radio or TV ad that is clear, easy to follow, and includes at least two academic vocabulary words. Make your ad convincing by emphasizing the best features of the trips you're selling.

Then, present your commercial to your class. Keep in mind that you are trying to sell vacation packages to a general audience (the public). Be sure to use your voice in an animated way to grab listeners' attention and to persuade them to purchase a trip.

USE NEW WORDS
Academic Vocabulary
Use the academic vocabulary from the unit as you plan, draft, and discuss your project:

- justify
- dissent
- certainty
- discredit
- assumption

Concept Vocabulary
Review your Word Wall and write down any words you want to use in your project:

STANDARDS
Writing
Produce clear and coherent writing in which the development, organization, and style are appropriate to task, purpose, and audience.

Speaking and Listening
Include multimedia components and visual displays in presentations to clarify claims and findings and emphasize salient points.

Unit 2 Reflect and Respond 203

PERFORMANCE-BASED ASSESSMENT

SOURCES

- Whole-Class Selections
- Peer-Group Selections
- Independent Learning Selection
- Your own experiences and observations

Argument

Assignment

In this unit, you read different perspectives about whether we should live among the stars. You also practiced writing editorials and other arguments. Now, apply what you have learned.

Write an **argument** in which you state and defend a claim in response to the Essential Question.

Essential Question

Should we make a home in space?

Review and Evaluate Evidence

Review your Evidence Log and your QuickWrite from the beginning of the unit. Has your position changed?

○ Yes	○ No
Identify at least three pieces of evidence that convinced you to change your mind.	Identify at least three pieces of evidence that reinforced your initial position.
1.	1.
2.	2.
3.	3.

State your position now:

What other evidence might you need to support your position?

204 UNIT 2 • LIVING AMONG THE STARS

Essential Question: Should we make a home in space?

Share Your Perspective

The **Argument Checklist** will help you stay on track.

PLAN Before you write, read the Argument Checklist and make sure you understand all the items.

DRAFT As you write, pause occasionally to make sure you're meeting the checklist requirements.

Use New Words Refer to your Word Wall to vary your word choice. Also, consider using one or more of the academic vocabulary terms you learned at the beginning of the unit: *justify, dissent, certainty, discredit, assumption.*

REVIEW AND EDIT After you have written a first draft, evaluate it against the checklist. Make any changes needed to strengthen your claim, structure, transitions, and language. Then, reread your argument and fix any errors you find.

EVIDENCE LOG
Make sure you have pulled in details from your Evidence Log to support your claim.

ARGUMENT CHECKLIST

My argument clearly contains . . .

- ○ a claim that states a clear position.
- ○ reasons that support the claim, organized logically.
- ○ relevant and sufficient evidence, such as data and examples, that supports the claim and shows my understanding of the topic.
- ○ a counterclaim with a statement of rebuttal against it.
- ○ transitional words, phrases, and clauses that clearly show the relationships among my claim, reasons, and evidence.
- ○ a conclusion that restates my claim.
- ○ standard English grammar and usage, including subordinating conjunctions and complex sentences.
- ○ precise and concise word choices that help create a formal style.
- ○ no capitalization, punctuation, or spelling errors.

STANDARDS
Writing
• Write arguments to support claims with clear reasons and relevant evidence.

• Introduce claim(s), acknowledge alternate or opposing claims, and organize the reasons and evidence logically.

• Support claim(s) with logical reasoning and relevant evidence.

• Use words, phrases, and clauses to create cohesion and clarify the relationships among claim(s), reasons, and evidence.

• Establish and maintain a formal style.

• Provide a concluding statement or section that follows from and supports the argument presented.

Transformations

WATCH THE ViDEO

DISCUSS How can people change to overcome their fears?

Write your response before sharing your ideas.

UNIT 3

INTRO

Essential Question
Can people really change?

SHORT STORY
The Golden Windows

MENTOR TEXT

WHOLE-CLASS LEARNING

COMPARE

A Christmas Carol: Scrooge and Marley, Acts I and II
based on the novella by Charles Dickens

DRAMA

from A Christmas Carol
Charles Dickens

▶ MEDIA CONNECTION:
from Scrooge

NOVELLA EXCERPT

Write a Short Story

WRITING: PERFORMANCE TASK

PEER-GROUP LEARNING

Thank You, M'am
Langston Hughes

SHORT STORY

Learning Rewires the Brain
Alison Pearce Stevens

SCIENCE JOURNALISM

Trying to Name What Doesn't Change
Naomi Shihab Nye

I Myself
Ángel González

Do not trust the eraser
Rosamond S. King

POETRY COLLECTION

Makeup Artist Mimi Choi's Mesmerizing Art-Inspired Beauty Looks • Mimi Choi Brings Fear to Life With Her Makeup Artistry
Ryma Chikhoune • True Calling Media

HUMAN INTEREST STORY | MEDIA: VIDEO

Deliver a Dramatic Adaptation

SPEAKING AND LISTENING: PERFORMANCE TASK

INDEPENDENT LEARNING

Little Things Are Big
Jesús Colón

REFLECTIVE ESSAY

The Story of Victor d'Aveyron, the Wild Child
Eloise Montalban

HISTORICAL NARRATIVE

A Retrieved Reformation
O. Henry

SHORT STORY

The Old Man and His Grandson
Jacob and Wilhelm Grimm

FABLE

SHARE • LEARN • REFLECT

SHARE INDEPENDENT LEARNING

REFLECT AND RESPOND

GOALS • TEXTS • UNIT PROJECTS

PERFORMANCE-BASED ASSESSMENT

Short Story
You will write a short story that explores the Essential Question for the unit.

UNIT 3 INTRODUCTION

Unit Goals

Throughout this unit you will deepen your perspective about transformations by reading, writing, speaking, listening, and presenting. These goals will help you succeed on the Unit Performance-Based Assessment.

SET GOALS Use a scale of 1 to 5 to rate how well you meet these goals right now. You will revisit your ratings later, when you reflect on your growth during this unit.

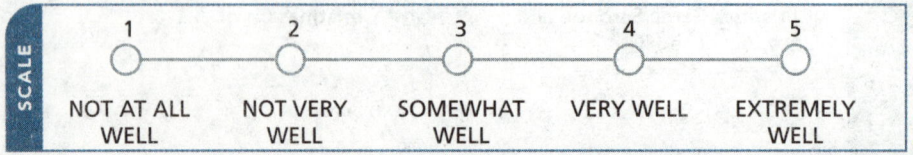

SCALE: 1 NOT AT ALL WELL — 2 NOT VERY WELL — 3 SOMEWHAT WELL — 4 VERY WELL — 5 EXTREMELY WELL

	Unit Introduction	Unit Reflection
ESSENTIAL QUESTION		
I can read selections that express different points of view about transformations and develop my own perspective.	1 2 3 4 5	1 2 3 4 5
READING		
I can understand and use academic vocabulary words related to fiction.	1 2 3 4 5	1 2 3 4 5
I can recognize elements of different genres, especially drama, fiction, and poetry.	1 2 3 4 5	1 2 3 4 5
I can read a selection of my choice independently and make meaningful connections to other texts.	1 2 3 4 5	1 2 3 4 5
WRITING		
I can write an engaging and meaningful short story.	1 2 3 4 5	1 2 3 4 5
I can complete Timed Writing tasks with confidence.	1 2 3 4 5	1 2 3 4 5
SPEAKING AND LISTENING		
I can prepare and deliver a dramatic adaptation.	1 2 3 4 5	1 2 3 4 5
MY GOALS		

STANDARDS

Language
- Use common, grade-appropriate Greek or Latin affixes and roots as clues to the meaning of a word.
- Acquire and use accurately grade-appropriate general academic and domain-specific words and phrases; gather vocabulary knowledge when considering a word or phrase important to comprehension or expression.

Essential Question: Can people really change?

Academic Vocabulary: Fiction

Academic terms can help you read, write, and discuss with precision. Many of these words have roots, or key parts, that come from Latin and Greek.

PRACTICE Academic terms are used routinely in classrooms. Build your knowledge of these words by completing the chart.

1. **Review** each word, its root, and the mentor sentences.
2. **Determine** the meaning and usage of each word using the mentor sentences and a dictionary, if needed.
3. **List** at least two related words for each academic term. Then, challenge yourself to write a sentence that contains two of the academic terms.

WORD	MENTOR SENTENCES	PREDICT MEANING	RELATED WORDS
ingenious LATIN ROOT: -gen- "birth"; "produce"	1. No one else could have imagined the new, *ingenious* invention. 2. Julia came up with an *ingenious* solution to the problem.		generation; genuine genius
omniscient LATIN ROOT: -omni- "all"; "every"	1. An *omniscient* narrator can tell the reader what all the characters in a story are thinking. 2. Anyone who claims to be *omniscient* must be lying because no one knows everything.		
envision LATIN ROOT: -vis- "see"	1. I *envision* a future in which everyone lives in harmony. 2. The writer's description helped me *envision* the beautiful scenery.		
lucid LATIN ROOT: -luc- "light"	1. Elena's *lucid* explanation made the complex process seem simple. 2. Octavio wasn't *lucid* until his fever finally died down.		
sensation LATIN ROOT: -sens- "feel"; "think"	1. The new action-adventure movie became an instant *sensation*. 2. As she boarded the plane, Eve had a nagging *sensation* that she had forgotten something important.		

UNIT 3 INTRODUCTION

MENTOR TEXT

SHORT STORY MODEL

READ As you read, notice the author's choice of words that paint a vivid picture of the setting.

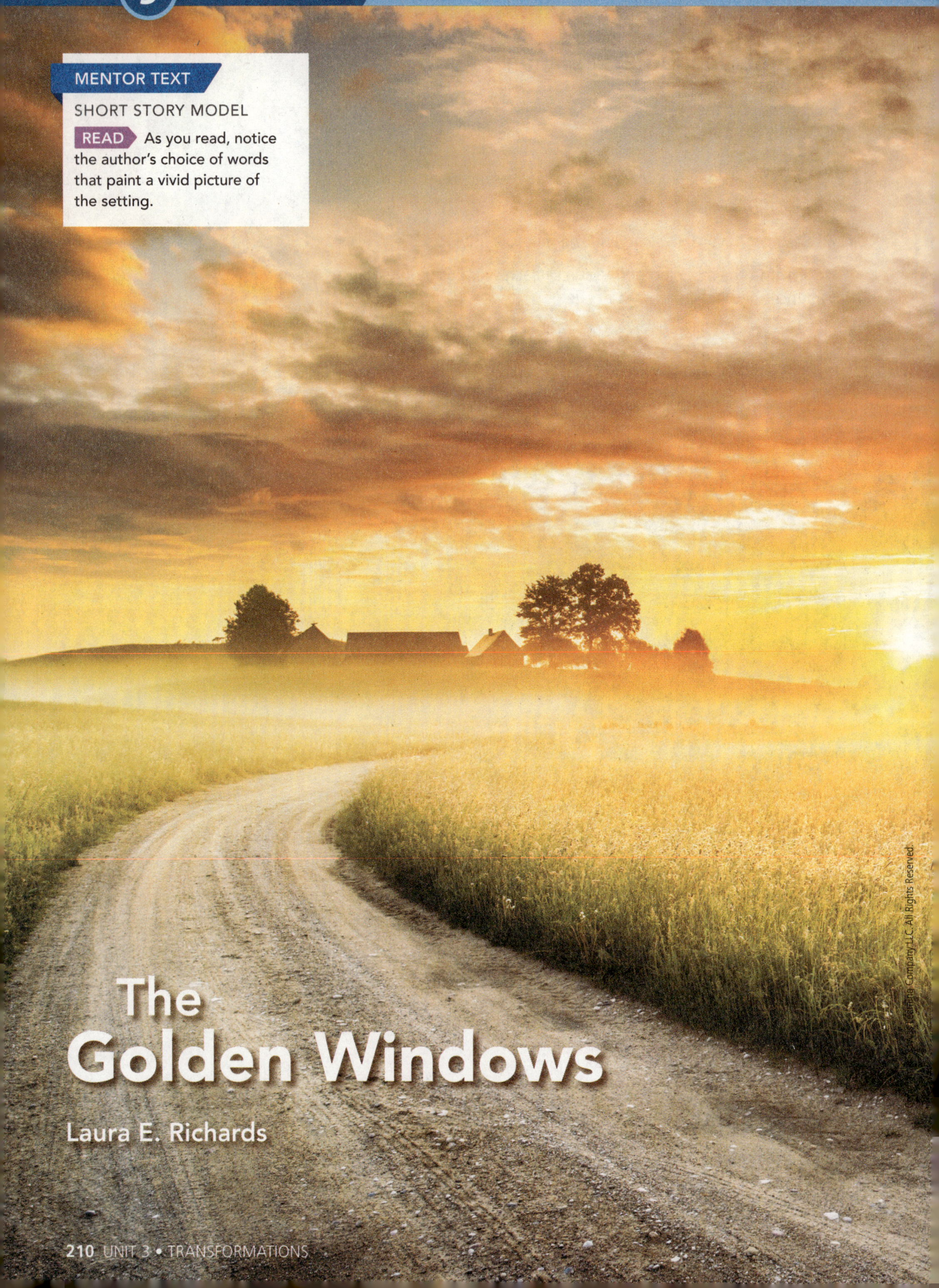

The Golden Windows

Laura E. Richards

Essential Question: Can people really change?

1. All day long the little boy had worked hard, in field and barn and shed, for his people were poor farmers, and could not pay a workman; but at sunset there came an hour that was all his own, for his father had given it to him. Then the boy would go up to the top of a hill and look across at another hill that rose some miles away. On this far hill stood a house with windows of clear gold and diamonds. They shone and blazed so that it made the boy wink to look at them: but after a while the people in the house put up shutters, as it seemed, and then it looked like any common farmhouse. The boy supposed they did this because it was supper-time; and then he would go into the house and have his supper of bread and milk, and so to bed.

2. One day the boy's father called him and said: "You have been a good boy, and have earned a holiday. Take this day for your own; but remember that God gave it, and try to learn some good thing."

3. The boy thanked his father and kissed his mother; then he put a piece of bread in his pocket, and started off to find the house with the golden windows.

4. It was pleasant walking. His bare feet made marks in the white dust, and when he looked back, the footprints seemed to be following him, and making company for him. His shadow, too, kept beside him, and would dance or run with him as he pleased; so it was very cheerful.

5. By and by he felt hungry; and he sat down by a brown brook that ran through the alder hedge by the roadside, and ate his bread, and drank the clear water. An apple tree, which nestled beside wildflowers, was heavy with fruit. Then he scattered the crumbs for the birds, as his mother had taught him to do, and went on his way.

6. After a long time he came to a high green hill; and when he had climbed the hill, there was the house on the top; but it seemed that the shutters were up, for he could not see the golden windows. He came up to the house, and then he could well have wept, for the windows were of clear glass, like any others, and there was no gold anywhere about them.

7. A woman came to the door, and looked kindly at the boy, and asked him what he wanted.

8. "I saw the golden windows from our hilltop," he said, "and I came to see them, but now they are only glass."

9. The woman shook her head and laughed.

10. "We are poor farming people," she said, "and are not likely to have gold about our windows; but glass is better to see through."

11. She bade the boy sit down on the broad stone step at the door, and brought him a cup of milk and a cake, and bade him rest; then

The Golden Windows 211

UNIT 3 INTRODUCTION

    she called her daughter, a child of his own age, and nodded kindly at the two, and went back to her work.

12   The little girl was barefooted like himself, and wore a brown cotton gown, but her hair was golden like the windows he had seen, and her eyes were blue like the sky at noon. She led the boy about the farm, and showed him her black calf with the white star on its forehead, and he told her about his own at home, which was red like a chestnut, with four white feet. Then when they had eaten an apple together, and so had become friends, the boy asked her about the golden windows. The little girl nodded, and said she knew all about them, only he had mistaken the house.

13   "You have come quite the wrong way!" she said. "Come with me, and I will show you the house with the golden windows, and then you will see for yourself."

14   They went to a knoll that rose behind the farmhouse, and as they went the little girl told him that the golden windows could only be seen at a certain hour, about sunset.

15   "Yes, I know that!" said the boy.

212 UNIT 3 • TRANSFORMATIONS

Essential Question: Can people really change?

16   When they reached the top of the knoll, the girl turned and pointed; and there on a hill far away stood a house with windows of clear gold and diamond, just as he had seen them. And when they looked again, the boy saw that it was his own home.

17   Then he told the little girl that he must go; and he gave her his best pebble, the white one with the red band, that he had carried for a year in his pocket; and she gave him three horse-chestnuts, one red like satin, one spotted, and one white like milk. He kissed her, and promised to come again, but he did not tell her what he had learned; and so he went back down the hill, and the little girl stood in the sunset light and watched him.

18   The way home was long, and it was dark before the boy reached his father's house; but the lamplight and firelight shone through the windows, making them almost as bright as he had seen them from the hilltop; and when he opened the door, his mother came to kiss him, and his little sister ran to throw her arms about his neck, and his father looked up and smiled from his seat by the fire.

19   "Have you had a good day?" asked his mother.

20   Yes, the boy had had a very good day.

21   "And have you learned anything?" asked his father.

22   "Yes!" said the boy. "I have learned that our house has windows of gold and diamond."

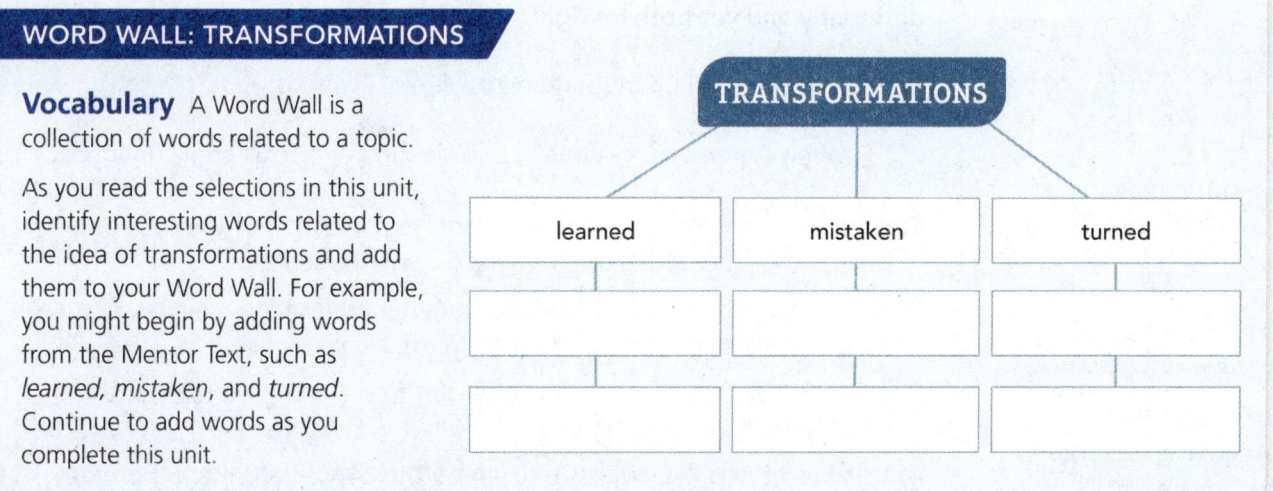

WORD WALL: TRANSFORMATIONS

Vocabulary A Word Wall is a collection of words related to a topic.

As you read the selections in this unit, identify interesting words related to the idea of transformations and add them to your Word Wall. For example, you might begin by adding words from the Mentor Text, such as *learned*, *mistaken*, and *turned*. Continue to add words as you complete this unit.

The Golden Windows 213

UNIT 3 INTRODUCTION

Summary

A **summary** is a brief, complete overview of a text that maintains the meaning and logical order of ideas of the original work. It should be objective and should not include your personal opinions.

WRITE Write a summary of "The Golden Windows."

_____
_____
_____
_____
_____
_____
_____
_____
_____
_____

Icebreaker

Conduct a Four-Corner Debate

Consider this statement: **It's possible for two people to see things differently and yet both be right.**

Record your position on the statement.

◯ Strongly Agree ◯ Agree ◯ Disagree ◯ Strongly Disagree

1. Form a group with like-minded students in one corner of the classroom. Discuss your choice and give reasons for your position.

2. Ask others in your group questions to better understand their views, such as "What examples can you provide to explain your ideas?"

3. After your discussion, choose one person to present a summary of the group's position to the class.

4. Listen as groups give evidence to support their positions. Reflect on that evidence and modify your own position as needed.

5. After all groups have presented their views, move into the four corners again. If you have changed your corner, be ready to explain why.

STANDARDS

Reading Literature
Provide an objective summary of the text.

Writing
Write routinely over extended time frames and shorter time frames for a range of discipline-specific tasks, purposes, and audiences.

Speaking and Listening
• Pose questions that elicit elaboration.

• Acknowledge new information expressed by others and, when warranted, modify their own views.

214 UNIT 3 • TRANSFORMATIONS

Essential Question: Can people really change?

QuickWrite

Consider class discussions, presentations, the video, and the Mentor Text as you think about the Essential Question.

Essential Question

Can people really change?

At the end of the unit, you will respond to the Essential Question again and see if your perspective has deepened or changed.

WRITE Record your first thoughts here.

___

EVIDENCE LOG

Can people really change?

As you read the selections in this unit, use a chart like the one shown to record your ideas and list details from the texts that support them. Taking notes as you go will help you clarify your thinking, gather relevant information, and be ready to respond to the Essential Question.

TITLE	MY IDEAS / OBSERVATIONS	TEXT EVIDENCE / INFORMATION

Unit Introduction **215**

WHOLE-CLASS LEARNING

Essential Question

Can people really change?

It's a common expression that "people change"—but do they? If so, how? You will work with your whole class to explore the concept of transformation and what it means to truly change.

Whole-Class Learning Strategies

Throughout your life, in school, in your community, and in your career, you will continue to learn and work in large-group environments.

Review these strategies and the actions you can take to practice them as you work with your whole class. Add ideas of your own for each category. Get ready to use these strategies during Whole-Class Learning.

STRATEGY	MY ACTION PLAN
Listen actively	• Track the speaker with your eyes and listen closely. • Listen for details that remind you of things you've previously learned about or experienced. •
Demonstrate respect	• Recognize that any new thought that is added to a conversation can be valuable. • If you disagree with a speaker's point, take a moment to consider why. •
Show interest	• Take notes about ideas or details that spark your curiosity. • If you find yourself losing interest, stay engaged by writing down a related question that matters to you. •
Interact and share ideas	• Remember that the more you actively participate in group discussions, the more you'll get out of them. • Consider what else you would like to know about the topic; then, share those ideas. •

Contents

COMPARE

DRAMA

A Christmas Carol: Scrooge and Marley, Acts I and II

based on the novella by Charles Dickens

Can visions of the past, present, and future change a miserable miser?

NOVELLA EXCERPT

from A Christmas Carol

Charles Dickens

Can a humble family's Christmas celebration inspire Ebenezer Scrooge to change?

▶ MEDIA CONNECTION: from Scrooge

PERFORMANCE TASK

WRITING PROMPT • WRITER'S HANDBOOK

Write a Short Story

The Whole-Class selections dramatize moments of truth for Ebenezer Scrooge. After reading, you will write a short story about a character who has a significant, possibly transformative, life experience.

Whole-Class Learning 217

LEARN ABOUT GENRE: DRAMA

A CHRISTMAS CAROL: SCROOGE AND MARLEY, ACTS I AND II

Reading Drama

A **drama,** or play, is a narrative written to be performed by actors.

The selection you are about to read is a drama.

COMPARE ACROSS GENRES

This play is a dramatic adaptation of the novella **A Christmas Carol**, a classic book by Charles Dickens. After reading the play, you will read an excerpt from the novella and compare it to the dramatic adaptation.

DRAMA

Author's Purpose
- to tell a story meant to be performed by actors in front of an audience

Characteristics
- characters who take part in the story's action
- a setting, or the time and place in which the story's action occurs; may have multiple settings
- various types of dramatic speeches, including dialogue and monologue
- stage directions that describe how characters look, speak, and behave
- stage directions may indicate other performance elements, such as sets, lighting, and costumes

Structure
- written in script form and organized in sections called *acts* and *scenes*
- a plot, or related sequence of events, driven by one or more conflicts

STANDARDS
Reading Literature
- Analyze how particular elements of a story or drama interact.
- Analyze how a drama's or poem's form or structure contributes to its meaning.
- By the end of the year, read and comprehend literature, including stories, dramas, and poems.

Take a Minute!

DISCUSS With a partner, discuss whether you prefer to read a script of a play and imagine it coming to life or if you prefer to see someone else's vision come to life in a production of a play.

218 UNIT 3 • TRANSFORMATIONS

Essential Question: Can people really change?

Character Development in Drama

Plays are stories that are brought to life by a script, a director, and actors. A script contains information about the characters and their development. Here are two basic elements of a script:

- **Dialogue** is the conversation among characters. Most plays convey characters' personalities and thoughts through dialogue—the words they say. Analyzing dialogue can help you understand how characters interact and how they respond to events in a play.

- **Stage directions** are the playwright's instructions in a script. They indicate how characters should behave and include information about the setting, sound effects, and costumes. As a result, they directly contribute to the meaning of the play.

EXAMPLE Notice how the stage directions affect the characters' development.

[A backstage dressing room. Kate *sits in front of a mirror.* Peg *is pinning up Kate's hair.*]

Version 1

Kate. [*barely able to contain her excitement*] Oh, I feel grand! I can just see my reviews tomorrow—"Kate West! Huge Star!"

Version 2

Kate. [*slumped; with sarcasm*] Oh, I feel grand! I can just see my reviews tomorrow—"Kate West! Huge Star!"

PRACTICE Read the passage and analyze how the characters, dialogue, and stage directions interact in the scene. Then, answer the questions.

[Kate's *dressing room, later that night.* Kate *sits before a mirror while* Peg *brushes her hair.*]

Kate. [*suddenly angry*] What are you doing? My hair looks awful!

Peg. [*wearily*] It's fine, Miss West. You always look fine.

Kate. [*narrowing her eyes*] This isn't fine. You've ruined me! I'm going to look terrible tonight!

Peg. [*makes a face and then catches herself*] Yes, Miss West. I mean, of course not, Miss West.

1. What do you learn about the characters from the dialogue?

2. How do the stage directions affect the meaning of the scene?

PREPARE TO READ

A Christmas Carol: Scrooge and Marley, Act I

About Adaptations

During his lifetime, British novelist **Charles Dickens** (1812–1870) was one of the best-selling writers in England. Readers loved his vivid stories, which are full of unforgettable characters, realistic settings, dark humor, and social commentary. Since Dickens's death, his popularity has only grown. His many novels have served as the basis for countless other works, including movies, plays, operas, and ballets. This dramatic adaptation of his novella *A Christmas Carol* retells the famous tale of the miser Ebenezer Scrooge in two powerful acts.

Concept Vocabulary

Predict The words here appear in the play. Judging from these words, explain the kinds of characters and events you think this play will be about.

WORDS FROM THE PLAY	MY EXPECTATIONS
covetous (KUHV uh tuhs) *adj.* greedy and jealous	
morose (muh ROHS) *adj.* gloomy; ill-tempered	
resolute (REHZ uh loot) *adj.* determined	
impossible (ihm POS uh buhl) *adj.* disagreeable; unreasonable	
malcontent (MAL kuhn tehnt) *n.* person who is always unhappy	
miser (MY zuhr) *n.* greedy person who keeps and refuses to spend money, even at the expense of their own comfort	

Reading Strategy: Paraphrase

When you **paraphrase** a text, you restate it in your own words while maintaining the meaning and logical order of the original. Doing so can help you better understand what you read. When you encounter a complex passage, paraphrase to clarify its meaning.

EXAMPLE

Consider this passage from Scene 2, paragraph 15:

> **Nephew.** There are many things from which I have derived good, by which I have not profited, I daresay.

Paraphrase: There are many things that have done me good but not made me money, I have to say.

PRACTICE As you read, use the open space next to the text to write paraphrases of challenging passages.

STANDARDS
Language
Gather vocabulary knowledge when considering a word or phrase important to comprehension or expression.

DRAMA

A Christmas Carol: Scrooge and Marley

Act I

a drama based on the novella by Charles Dickens

BACKGROUND
Charles Dickens's novella, *A Christmas Carol,* from which this play was adapted, shows sympathy for the struggles of the poor. The story is set in England during the nineteenth century, a time of rapid industrial growth. In this booming economy, the wealthy lived in luxury, but the poor and the working class suffered.

CHARACTERS

Jacob Marley, a specter
Ebenezer Scrooge, not yet dead, which is to say still alive
Bob Cratchit, Scrooge's clerk
Fred, Scrooge's nephew
Thin Do-Gooder
Portly Do-Gooder
Specters (Various), carrying money-boxes
The Ghost of Christmas Past
Four Jocund Travelers
A Band of Singers
A Band of Dancers
Little Boy Scrooge
Young Man Scrooge
Fan, Scrooge's little sister
The Schoolmaster
Schoolmates

Fezziwig, a fine and fair employer
Dick, young Scrooge's co-worker
Young Scrooge
A Fiddler
More Dancers
Scrooge's Lost Love
Scrooge's Lost Love's Daughter
Scrooge's Lost Love's Husband
The Ghost of Christmas Present
Some Bakers
Mrs. Cratchit, Bob Cratchit's wife
Belinda Cratchit, a daughter
Martha Cratchit, another daughter

Peter Cratchit, a son
Tiny Tim Cratchit, another son
Scrooge's Niece, Fred's wife
The Ghost of Christmas Future, a mute Phantom
Three Men of Business
Drunks, Scoundrels, Women of the Streets
A Charwoman
Mrs. Dilber
Joe, an old second-hand goods dealer
A Corpse, very like Scrooge
An Indebted Family
Adam, a young boy
A Poulterer
A Gentlewoman
Some More Men of Business

READ TO UNLOCK MEANING

1. First read the text for comprehension and enjoyment. Use the **Reading Strategy** and **Comprehension Check** questions to support your first read.
2. Go back and respond to the Close-Read notes.
3. Identify other details in the text you find interesting. Ask your own questions and draw your own conclusions.

1. **counting-house** *n.* office for keeping financial records and writing business letters.

covetous (KUHV uh tuhs) *adj.* greedy and jealous

CLOSE READ

ANNOTATE Mark the use of descriptive words in paragraph 4.

QUESTION How do the playwright's word choices affect the reader's understanding of Scrooge?

THE PLACE OF THE PLAY Various locations in and around the City of London, including Scrooge's Chambers and Offices; the Cratchit Home; Fred's Home; Scrooge's School; Fezziwig's Offices; Old Joe's Hide-a-Way.

THE TIME OF THE PLAY The entire action of the play takes place on Christmas Eve, Christmas Day, and the morning after Christmas, 1843.

Scene 1

1 [*Ghostly music in auditorium. A single spotlight on* Jacob Marley, D.C. *He is ancient; awful, dead-eyed. He speaks straight out to auditorium.*]

2 **Marley.** [*Cackle-voiced*] My name is Jacob Marley and I am dead. [*He laughs.*] Oh, no, there's no doubt that I am dead. The register of my burial was signed by the clergyman, the clerk, the undertaker... and by my chief mourner... Ebenezer Scrooge... [*Pause; remembers*] I am dead as a doornail.

3 [*A spotlight fades up, Stage Right, on* Scrooge, *in his counting-house*[1] *counting. Lettering on the window behind* Scrooge *reads: "Scrooge and Marley, Ltd." The spotlight is tight on* Scrooge's *head and shoulders. We shall not yet see into the offices and setting. Ghostly music continues, under.* Marley *looks across at* Scrooge; *pitifully. After a moment's pause*]

4 I present him to you: Ebenezer Scrooge... England's most tightfisted hand at the grindstone, Scrooge! a squeezing, wrenching, grasping, scraping, clutching, **covetous**, old sinner! secret, and self-contained, and solitary as an oyster. The cold within him freezes his old features, nips his pointed nose, shrivels his cheek, stiffens his gait; makes his eyes red, his thin lips blue; and speaks out shrewdly in his grating voice. Look at him. Look at him...

5 [Scrooge *counts and mumbles.*]

6 **Scrooge.** They owe me money and I will collect. I will have them jailed, if I have to. They owe me money and I will collect what is due me.

7 [Marley *moves towards* Scrooge; *two steps. The spotlight stays with him.*]

222 UNIT 3 • TRANSFORMATIONS

8. **Marley.** [*Disgusted*] He and I were partners for I don't know how many years. Scrooge was my sole executor, my sole administrator, my sole assign, my sole residuary legatee,[2] my sole friend and my sole mourner. But Scrooge was not so cut up by the sad event of my death, but that he was an excellent man of business on the very day of my funeral, and solemnized[3] it with an undoubted bargain. [*Pauses again in disgust*] He never painted out my name from the window. There it stands, on the window and above the warehouse door: Scrooge and Marley. Sometimes people new to our business call him Scrooge and sometimes they call him Marley. He answers to both names. It's all the same to him. And it's cheaper than painting in a new sign, isn't it? [*Pauses; moves closer to* Scrooge] Nobody has ever stopped him in the street to say, with gladsome looks, "My dear Scrooge, how are you? When will you come to see me?" No beggars implored him to bestow a trifle, no children ever ask him what it is o'clock, no man or woman now, or ever in his life, not once, inquire the way to such and such a place. [Marley *stands next to* Scrooge *now. They share, so it seems, a spotlight.*] But what does Scrooge care of any of this? It is the very thing he likes! To edge his way along the crowded paths of life, warning all human sympathy to keep its distance.

9. [*A ghostly bell rings in the distance.* Marley *moves away from* Scrooge, *now, heading* D. *again. As he does, he "takes" the light:* Scrooge *has disappeared into the black void beyond.* Marley *walks* D.C., *talking directly to the audience. Pauses*]

10. The bell tolls and I must take my leave. You must stay a while with Scrooge and watch him play out his scroogey life. It is now the story: the once-upon-a-time. Scrooge is busy in his counting-house. Where else? Christmas eve and Scrooge is busy in his counting-house. It is cold, bleak, biting weather outside: foggy withal: and, if you listen closely, you can hear the people in the court go wheezing up and down, beating their hands upon their breasts, and stamping their feet upon the pavement stones to warm them . . .

11. [*The clocks outside strike three.*]

12. Only three! and quite dark outside already: it has not been light all day this day.

13. [*This ghostly bell rings in the distance again.* Marley *looks about him. Music in.* Marley *flies away.*]

14. [*N.B.* Marley's *comings and goings should, from time to time, induce the explosion of the odd flash-pot, I.H.*]

---

2. **sole residuary legatee** *n.* legal term for a person who inherits someone's home after they die.

3. **solemnized** *v.* honored or remembered. Marley is being sarcastic.

PARAPHRASE

Paraphrase passages you find confusing. For example, how would you paraphrase the first three sentences in paragraph 8?

COMPREHENSION CHECK

Where and when does Scene 1 take place?

Scene 2

1 [*Christmas music in, sung by a live chorus, full. At conclusion of song, sound fades under and into the distance. Lights up in set: offices of Scrooge and Marley, Ltd. Scrooge sits at his desk, at work. Near him is a tiny fire. His door is open and in his line of vision, we see Scrooge's clerk, Bob Cratchit, who sits in a dismal tank of a cubicle, copying letters. Near Cratchit is a fire so tiny as to barely cast a light: perhaps it is one pitifully glowing coal? Cratchit rubs his hands together, puts on a white comforter[4] and tries to heat his hands around his candle. Scrooge's Nephew enters, unseen.*]

2 **Scrooge.** What are you doing, Cratchit? Acting cold, are you? Next, you'll be asking to replenish your coal from my coal-box, won't you? Well, save your breath, Cratchit! Unless you're prepared to find employ elsewhere!

3 **Nephew.** [*Cheerfully; surprising* Scrooge] A merry Christmas to you, Uncle! God save you!

4 **Scrooge.** Bah! Humbug![5]

5 **Nephew.** Christmas a "humbug," Uncle? I'm sure you don't mean that.

6 **Scrooge.** I do! Merry Christmas? What right do you have to be merry? What reason have you to be merry? You're poor enough!

7 **Nephew.** Come, then. What right have you to be dismal? What reason have you to be **morose**? You're rich enough.

8 **Scrooge.** Bah! Humbug!

9 **Nephew.** Don't be cross, Uncle.

10 **Scrooge.** What else can I be? Eh? When I live in a world of fools such as this? Merry Christmas? What's Christmastime to you but a time of paying bills without any money; a time for finding yourself a year older, but not an hour richer. If I could work my will, every idiot who goes about with "Merry Christmas" on his lips, should be boiled with his own pudding, and buried with a stake of holly through his heart. He should!

11 **Nephew.** Uncle!

12 **Scrooge.** Nephew! You keep Christmas in your own way and let me keep it in mine.

13 **Nephew.** Keep it! But you don't keep it, Uncle.

14 **Scrooge.** Let me leave it alone, then. Much good it has ever done you!

---

4. **comforter** *n.* long, woolen scarf.

5. **Humbug** *interj.* nonsense.

morose (muh ROHS) *adj.* gloomy; ill-tempered

CLOSE READ

ANNOTATE Mark words in paragraph 10 that show Scrooge's attitude toward Christmas.

QUESTION What does Scrooge think of people who celebrate the holiday? What does this attitude tell you about Scrooge himself?

15 **Nephew.** There are many things from which I have derived good, by which I have not profited, I daresay. Christmas among the rest. But I am sure that I always thought of Christmas time, when it has come round—as a good time: the only time I know of, when men and women seem to open their shut-up hearts freely, and to think of people below them as if they really were fellow-passengers to the grave, and not another race of creatures bound on other journeys. And therefore, Uncle, though it has never put a scrap of gold or silver in my pocket, I believe that it has done me good, and that it *will* do me good; and I say, God bless it!

16 [*The Clerk in the tank applauds, looks at the furious* Scrooge *and pokes out his tiny fire, as if in exchange for the moment of impropriety.* Scrooge *yells at him.*]

17 **Scrooge.** [*To the clerk*] Let me hear another sound from *you* and you'll keep your Christmas by losing your situation. [*To the nephew*] You're quite a powerful speaker, sir. I wonder you don't go into Parliament.[6]

18 **Nephew.** Don't be angry, Uncle. Come! Dine with us tomorrow.

19 **Scrooge.** I'd rather see myself dead than see myself with your family!

20 **Nephew.** But, why? Why?

21 **Scrooge.** Why did you get married?

22 **Nephew.** Because I fell in love.

23 **Scrooge.** That, sir, is the only thing that you have said to me in your entire lifetime which is even more ridiculous than "Merry Christmas!" [*Turns from* Nephew] Good afternoon.

24 **Nephew.** Nay, Uncle, you never came to see me before I married either. Why give it as a reason for not coming now?

25 **Scrooge.** Good afternoon, Nephew!

26 **Nephew.** I want nothing from you; I ask nothing of you; why cannot we be friends?

27 **Scrooge.** Good afternoon!

28 **Nephew.** I am sorry with all my heart, to find you so **resolute**. But I have made the trial in homage to Christmas, and I'll keep my Christmas humor to the last. So A Merry Christmas, Uncle!

29 **Scrooge.** Good afternoon!

30 **Nephew.** And a Happy New Year!

PARAPHRASE

In your own words, what does Scrooge's nephew say in paragraph 15, and what does it indicate about his attitude toward Christmas?

6. **Parliament** national legislative body of Great Britain, in some ways like the U.S. Congress.

resolute (REHZ uh loot) *adj.* determined

COMPREHENSION CHECK

Why has Scrooge's nephew come to see Scrooge?

31 **Scrooge.** Good afternoon!

32 **Nephew.** [*He stands facing* Scrooge.] Uncle, you are the most . . . [*Pauses*] No, I shan't. My Christmas humor is intact . . . [*Pause*] God bless you, Uncle . . . [Nephew *turns and starts for the door; he stops at* Cratchit's *cage.*] Merry Christmas, Bob Cratchit . . .

33 **Cratchit.** Merry Christmas to you sir, and a very, very happy New Year . . .

34 **Scrooge.** [*Calling across to them*] Oh, fine, a perfection, just fine . . . to see the perfect pair of you; husbands, with wives and children to support . . . my clerk there earning fifteen shillings a week . . . and the perfect pair of you, talking about a Merry Christmas! [*Pauses*] I'll retire to Bedlam![7]

35 **Nephew.** [*To* Cratchit] He's **impossible**!

36 **Cratchit.** Oh, mind him not, sir. He's getting on in years, and he's alone. He's noticed your visit. I'll wager your visit has warmed him.

37 **Nephew.** Him? Uncle Ebenezer Scrooge? *Warmed?* You are a better Christian than I am, sir.

38 **Cratchit.** [*Opening the door for* Nephew; *two Do-Gooders will enter, as* Nephew *exits*] Good day to you, sir, and God bless.

39 **Nephew.** God bless . . . [*One man who enters is portly, the other is thin. Both are pleasant.*]

40 **Cratchit.** Can I help you, gentlemen?

41 **Thin Man.** [*Carrying papers and books; looks around* Cratchit *to* Scrooge] Scrooge and Marley's, I believe. Have I the pleasure of addressing Mr. Scrooge, or Mr. Marley?

42 **Scrooge.** Mr. Marley has been dead these seven years. He died seven years ago this very night.

43 **Portly Man.** We have no doubt his liberality[8] is well represented by his surviving partner . . . [*Offers his calling card*]

44 **Scrooge.** [*Handing back the card; unlooked at*] . . . Good afternoon.

45 **Thin Man.** This will take but a moment, sir . . .

46 **Portly Man.** At this festive season of the year, Mr. Scrooge, it is more than usually desirable that we should make some slight provision for the poor and destitute, who suffer greatly at the present time. Many thousands are in want of common necessities; hundreds of thousands are in want of common comforts, sir.

---

7. **Bedlam** *n.* hospital in London for the mentally ill.

impossible (ihm POS uh buhl) *adj.* disagreeable; unreasonable

8. **liberality** *n.* generosity.

47 **Scrooge.** Are there no prisons?

48 **Portly Man.** Plenty of prisons.

49 **Scrooge.** And aren't the Union workhouses still in operation?

50 **Thin Man.** They are. Still, I wish that I could say that they are not.

51 **Scrooge.** The Treadmill[9] and the Poor Law[10] are in full vigor, then?

52 **Thin Man.** Both very busy, sir.

53 **Scrooge.** Ohhh, I see. I was afraid, from what you said at first, that something had occurred to stop them from their useful course. [*Pauses*] I'm glad to hear it.

54 **Portly Man.** Under the impression that they scarcely furnish Christian cheer of mind or body to the multitude, a few of us are endeavoring to raise a fund to buy the Poor some meat and drink, and means of warmth. We choose this time, because it is a time, of all others, when Want is keenly felt, and Abundance rejoices. [*Pen in hand; as well as notepad*] What shall I put you down for, sir?

55 **Scrooge.** Nothing!

56 **Portly Man.** You wish to be left anonymous?

57 **Scrooge.** I wish to be left alone! [*Pauses; turns away; turns back to them*] Since you ask me what I wish, gentlemen, that is my answer. I help to support the establishments that I have mentioned: they cost enough: and those who are badly off must go there.

58 **Thin Man.** Many can't go there; and many would rather die.

59 **Scrooge.** If they would rather die, they had better do it, and decrease the surplus population. Besides—excuse me—I don't know that.

60 **Thin Man.** But you might know it!

61 **Scrooge.** It's not my business. It's enough for a man to understand his own business, and not to interfere with other people's. Mine occupies me constantly. Good afternoon, gentlemen!

62 [*Scrooge turns his back on the gentlemen and returns to his desk.*]

63 **Portly Man.** But, sir, Mr. Scrooge . . . think of the poor.

64 **Scrooge.** [*Turns suddenly to them. Pauses*] Take your leave of my offices, sirs, while I am still smiling.

65 [*The* Thin Man *looks at the* Portly Man. *They are undone. They shrug. They move to the door.* Cratchit *hops up to open it for them.*]

9. **the Treadmill** mill wheel turned by the weight of people treading steps arranged around it; this device was used to punish prisoners.

10. **Poor Law** the original 16th-century Poor Laws called for overseers in each neighborhood to provide relief for the needy. The New Poor Law of 1834 made the workhouses in which the poor sometimes lived and worked extremely harsh places.

CLOSE READ

ANNOTATE Mark the words in paragraph 54 that describe the Portly Man's reasons for asking for help.

QUESTION What do these details reveal about the setting of the drama?

COMPREHENSION CHECK

What is Scrooge's attitude toward people who are in need?

66 **Thin Man.** Good day, sir . . . [*To* Cratchit] A merry Christmas to you, sir . . .

67 **Cratchit.** Yes. A Merry Christmas to both of you . . .

68 **Portly Man.** Merry Christmas . . .

69 [Cratchit *silently squeezes something into the hand of the* Thin Man.]

70 **Thin Man.** What's this?

71 **Cratchit.** Shhhh . . .

72 [Cratchit *opens the door; wind and snow whistle into the room.*]

73 **Thin Man.** Thank you, sir, thank you.

74 [Cratchit *closes the door and returns to his workplace.* Scrooge *is at his own counting table. He talks to* Cratchit *without looking up.*]

75 **Scrooge.** It's less of a time of year for being merry, and more a time of year for being loony . . . if you ask me.

76 **Cratchit.** Well, I don't know, sir . . . [*The clock's bell strikes six o'clock.*] Well, there it is, eh, six?

77 **Scrooge.** Saved by six bells, are you?

78 **Cratchit.** I must be going home . . . [*He snuffs out his candle and puts on his hat.*] I hope you have a . . . very very lovely day tomorrow, sir . . .

79 **Scrooge.** Hmmm. Oh, you'll be wanting the whole day tomorrow, I suppose?

80 **Cratchit.** If quite convenient, sir.

81 **Scrooge.** It's not convenient, and it's not fair. If I was to stop half-a-crown for it, you'd think yourself ill-used, I'll be bound?

82 [Cratchit *smiles faintly.*]

83 **Cratchit.** I don't know, sir . . .

84 **Scrooge.** And yet, you don't think me ill-used when I pay a day's wages for no work . . .

85 **Cratchit.** It's only but once a year . . .

86 **Scrooge.** A poor excuse for picking a man's pocket every 25th of December! But I suppose you must have the whole day. Be here all the earlier the next morning!

87 **Cratchit.** Oh, I will, sir. I will. I promise you. And, sir . . .

CLOSE READ

ANNOTATE Mark details in paragraphs 78–95 that show Cratchit's attitude toward Scrooge.

QUESTION What does this conversation between Cratchit and Scrooge reveal about Cratchit's character?

88 **Scrooge.** Don't say it, Cratchit.

89 **Cratchit.** But let me wish you a . . .

90 **Scrooge.** Don't say it, Cratchit. I warn you . . .

91 **Cratchit.** Sir!

92 **Scrooge.** Cratchit!

93 [Cratchit *opens the door.*]

94 **Cratchit.** All right, then, sir . . . well . . . [*Suddenly*] Merry Christmas, Mr. Scrooge!

95 [*And he runs out the door, shutting same behind him.* Scrooge *moves to his desk; gathering his coat, hat, etc. A* Boy *appears at his window . . . .*]

96 **Boy.** [*Singing*] "Away in a manger . . ."

97 [Scrooge *seizes his ruler and whacks at the image of the* Boy *outside. The* Boy *leaves.*]

98 **Scrooge.** Bah! Humbug! Christmas! Bah! Humbug! [*He shuts out the light.*]

99 *A note on the crossover, following Scene 2:*

COMPREHENSION CHECK

In paragraph 69, what does Cratchit give to the Thin Man?

A Christmas Carol: Scrooge and Marley, Act I **229**

100 [*Scrooge will walk alone to his rooms from his offices. As he makes a long slow cross of the stage, the scenery should change. Christmas music will be heard, various people will cross by Scrooge, often smiling happily.*]

101 *There will be occasional pleasant greetings tossed at him.*

102 *Scrooge, in contrast to all, will grump and mumble. He will snap at passing boys, as might a horrid old hound.*

103 *In short, Scrooge's sounds and movements will define him in contrast from all other people who cross the stage: he is the misanthrope,[11] the **malcontent**, the **miser**. He is Scrooge.*

104 *This statement of Scrooge's character, by contrast to all other characters, should seem comical to the audience.*

105 *During Scrooge's crossover to his rooms, snow should begin to fall. All passers-by will hold their faces to the sky, smiling, allowing snow to shower them lightly. Scrooge, by contrast, will bat at the flakes with his walking-stick, as might an insomniac swat at a sleep-stopping, middle-of-the-night swarm of mosquitoes. He will comment on the blackness of the night, and, finally, reach his rooms and his encounter with the magical specter:[12] Marley, his eternal mate.*]

Scene 3

1 **Scrooge.** No light at all . . . no moon . . . *that* is what is at the center of Christmas Eve: dead black: void . . .

2 [*Scrooge puts his key in the door's keyhole. He has reached his rooms now. The door knocker changes and is now Marley's face. A musical sound: quickly: ghostly. Marley's image is not at all angry, but looks at Scrooge as did the old Marley look at Scrooge. The hair is curiously stirred; eyes wide open, dead: absent of focus. Scrooge stares wordlessly here. The face, before his very eyes, does deliquesce.[13] It is a knocker again. Scrooge opens the door and checks the back of same, probably for Marley's pigtail. Seeing nothing but screws and nuts, Scrooge refuses the memory.*]

3 Pooh, pooh!

4 [*The sound of the door closing resounds throughout the house as thunder. Every room echoes the sound. Scrooge fastens the door and walks across the hall to the stairs, trimming his candle as he goes; and then he goes slowly up the staircase. He checks each room: sitting room, bedrooms, lumber-room. He looks under the sofa, under the table: nobody there. He fixes his evening gruel on the hob,[14] changes his jacket. Scrooge sits near the tiny low-flamed fire, sipping his gruel. There are various pictures on the walls: all of them now show likenesses of Marley. Scrooge blinks his eyes.*]

---

11. **misanthrope** (MIHS uhn throhp) *n.* person who hates or distrusts everyone.

malcontent (MAL kuhn tehnt) *n.* person who is always unhappy

miser (MY zuhr) *n.* greedy person who keeps and refuses to spend money, even at the expense of their own comfort

12. **specter** *n.* ghost.

13. **deliquesce** (dehl ih KWEHS) *v.* melt away.

14. **gruel on the hob** thin broth warming on a ledge at the back or side of the fireplace.

5 Bah! Humbug!

6 [Scrooge *walks in a circle about the room. The pictures change back into their natural images. He sits down at the table in front of the fire. A bell hangs overhead. It begins to ring, of its own accord. Slowly, surely, begins the ringing of every bell in the house. They continue ringing for nearly half a minute. Scrooge* is stunned by the phenomenon. *The bells cease their ringing all at once. Deep below* Scrooge, *in the basement of the house, there is the sound of clanking, of some enormous chain being dragged across the floors; and now up the stairs. We hear doors flying open.*]

7 Bah still! Humbug still! This is not happening! I won't believe it!

8 [Marley's Ghost *enters the room. He is horrible to look at: pigtail, vest, suit as usual, but he drags an enormous chain now, to which is fastened cash-boxes, keys, padlocks, ledgers, deeds, and heavy purses fashioned of steel. He is transparent.* Marley *stands opposite the stricken* Scrooge.]

9 How now! What do you want of me?

10 **Marley.** Much!

11 **Scrooge.** Who are you?

12 **Marley.** Ask me who I was.

13 **Scrooge.** Who were you then?

14 **Marley.** In life, I was your business partner: Jacob Marley.

15 **Scrooge.** I see . . . can you sit down?

16 **Marley.** I can.

17 **Scrooge.** Do it then.

18 **Marley.** I shall. [Marley *sits opposite* Scrooge, *in the chair across the table, at the front of the fireplace.*] You don't believe in me.

19 **Scrooge.** I don't.

20 **Marley.** Why do you doubt your senses?

21 **Scrooge.** Because every little thing affects them. A slight disorder of the stomach makes them cheat. You may be an undigested bit of beef, a blot of mustard, a crumb of cheese, a fragment of an underdone potato. There's more of gravy than of grave about you, whatever you are!

22 [*There is a silence between them.* Scrooge *is made nervous by it. He picks up a toothpick.*]

23 Humbug! I tell you: humbug!

COMPREHENSION CHECK

What reason does Scrooge give for not believing Marley is actually in the room?

24 [*Marley opens his mouth and screams a ghostly, fearful scream. The scream echoes about each room of the house. Bats fly, cats screech, lightning flashes.* Scrooge *stands and walks backwards against the wall.* Marley *stands and screams again. This time, he takes his head and lifts it from his shoulders. His head continues to scream. Marley's face again appears on every picture in the room: all screaming.* Scrooge, *on his knees before* Marley.]

15. **apparition** *n.* ghost.

25 Mercy! Dreadful apparition,[15] mercy! Why, O! why do you trouble me so?

PARAPHRASE

In your own words, what is Marley saying about himself in paragraph 28?

that he walked in wrong path and is stuck forever

26 **Marley.** Man of the worldly mind, do you believe in me, or not?

27 **Scrooge.** I do. I must. But why do spirits such as you walk the earth? And why do they come to me?

28 **Marley.** It is required of every man that the spirit within him should walk abroad among his fellow-men, and travel far and wide; and if that spirit goes not forth in life, it is condemned to do so after death. [Marley *screams again; a tragic scream; from his ghostly bones.*]

time?

I wear the chain I forged in life. I made it link by link, and yard by yard. Is its pattern strange to you? Or would you know, you, Scrooge, the weight and length of the strong coil you bear yourself? It was full as heavy and long as this, seven Christmas Eves ago. You have labored on it, since. It is a ponderous chain.

29 [*Terrified that a chain will appear about his body,* Scrooge *spins and waves the unwanted chain away. None, of course, appears. Sees* Marley *watching him dance about the room.* Marley *watches* Scrooge; *silently.*]

30 **Scrooge.** Jacob. Old Jacob Marley, tell me more. Speak comfort to me, Jacob . . .

31 **Marley.** I have none to give. Comfort comes from other regions, Ebenezer Scrooge, and is conveyed by other ministers, to other kinds of men. A very little more, is all that is permitted to me. I cannot rest, I cannot stay, I cannot linger anywhere . . . [*He moans again.*] My spirit never walked beyond our counting-house—mark me!—in life my spirit never roved beyond the narrow limits of our moneychanging hole; and weary journeys lie before me!

32 **Scrooge.** But you were always a good man of business, Jacob.

33 **Marley.** [*Screams word "business"; a flash-pot explodes with him.*] BUSINESS!!! Mankind was my business. The common welfare was my business; charity, mercy, forbearance, benevolence, were, all, my business. [Scrooge is *quaking.*] Hear me, Ebenezer Scrooge! My time is nearly gone.

34 **Scrooge.** I will, but don't be hard upon me. And don't be flowery, Jacob! Pray!

35 **Marley.** How is it that I appear before you in a shape that you can see, I may not tell. I have sat invisible beside you many and many a day. That is no light part of my penance. I am here tonight to warn you that you have yet a chance and hope of escaping my fate. A chance and hope of my procuring, Ebenezer.

36 **Scrooge.** You were always a good friend to me. Thank'ee!

37 **Marley.** You will be haunted by Three Spirits.

38 **Scrooge.** Would that be the chance and hope you mentioned, Jacob?

39 **Marley.** It is.

40 **Scrooge.** I think I'd rather not.

41 **Marley.** Without their visits, you cannot hope to shun the path I tread. Expect the first one tomorrow, when the bell tolls one.

42 **Scrooge.** Couldn't I take 'em all at once, and get it over, Jacob?

CLOSE READ

ANNOTATE Mark the words in paragraphs 30–34 that show Scrooge's reaction to Marley.

QUESTION What do these words reveal about Scrooge at this point in the play?

COMPREHENSION CHECK

What is Marley's purpose in visiting Scrooge?

A Christmas Carol: Scrooge and Marley, Act I

43 **Marley.** Expect the second on the next night at the same hour. The third upon the next night when the last stroke of twelve has ceased to vibrate. Look to see me no more. Others may, but you may not. And look that, for your own sake, you remember what has passed between us!

44 [*Marley places his head back upon his shoulders. He approaches the window and beckons to* Scrooge *to watch. Outside the window, specters fly by, carrying money-boxes and chains. They make a confused sound of lamentation.* Marley, *after listening a moment, joins into their mournful dirge. He leans to the window and floats out into the bleak, dark night. He is gone.*]

45 **Scrooge.** [*Rushing to the window*] Jacob! No, Jacob! Don't leave me! I'm frightened! [*He sees that* Marley *has gone. He looks outside. He pulls the shutter closed, so that the scene is blocked from his view. All sound stops. After a pause, he re-opens the shutter and all is quiet, as it should be on Christmas Eve. Carolers carol out of doors, in the distance.* Scrooge *closes the shutter and walks down the stairs. He examines the door by which* Marley *first entered.*] No one here at all! Did I imagine all that? Humbug! [*He looks about the room.*] I did imagine it. It only happened in my foulest dream-mind, didn't it? An undigested bit of . . . [*Thunder and lightning in the room; suddenly*] Sorry! Sorry!

46 [*There is silence again. The lights fade out.*]

Scene 4

1 [*Christmas music, choral, "Hark the Herald Angels Sing," sung by an onstage choir of children, spotlighted,* D.C. *Above,* Scrooge *in his bed, dead to the world, asleep, in his darkened room. It should appear that the choir is singing somewhere outside of the house, of course, and a use of scrim*[16] *is thus suggested. When the singing is ended, the choir should fade out of view and* Marley *should fade into view, in their place.*]

2 **Marley.** [*Directly to audience*] From this point forth . . . I shall be quite visible to you, but invisible to him. [*Smiles*] He will feel my presence, nevertheless, for, unless my senses fail me completely, we are—you and I—witness to the changing of a miser: that one, my partner in life, in business, and in eternity: that one: Scrooge. [*Moves to staircase, below* Scrooge] See him now. He endeavors to pierce the darkness with his ferret eyes.[17] [*To audience*] See him, now. He listens for the hour.

3 [*The bells toll.* Scrooge *is awakened and quakes as the hour approaches one o'clock, but the bells stop their sound at the hour of twelve.*]

---

16. **scrim** *n.* see-through fabric backdrop used to create special effects in the theater.

17. **ferret eyes** A ferret is a small, weasel-like animal used for hunting rabbits. This expression means to stare continuously, the way a ferret hunts.

4 **Scrooge.** [*Astonished*] Midnight! Why this isn't possible. It was past two when I went to bed. An icicle must have gotten into the clock's works! I couldn't have slept through the whole day and far into another night. It isn't possible that anything has happened to the sun, and this is twelve at noon! [*He runs to window; unshutters same; it is night.*] Night, still. Quiet, normal for the season, cold. It is certainly not noon. I cannot in any way afford to lose my days. Securities come due, promissory notes,[18] interest on investments: these are things that happen in the daylight! [*He returns to his bed.*] Was this a dream?

5 [Marley *appears in his room. He speaks to the audience.*]

6 **Marley.** You see? He does not, with faith, believe in me fully, even still! Whatever will it take to turn the faith of a miser from money to men?

7 **Scrooge.** Another quarter and it'll be one and Marley's ghostly friends will come. [*Pauses; listens*] Where's the chime for one? [*Ding, dong*] A quarter past [*Repeats*] Half-past! [*Repeats*] A quarter to it! But where's the heavy bell of the hour one? This is a game in which I lose my senses! Perhaps, if I allowed myself another short doze . . .

8 **Marley.** . . . Doze, Ebenezer, doze.

9 [*A heavy bell thuds its one ring; dull and definitely one o'clock. There is a flash of light.* Scrooge *sits up, in a sudden. A hand draws back the curtains by his bed. He sees it.*]

10 **Scrooge.** A hand! Who owns it! Hello!

11 [*Ghostly music again, but of a new nature to the play. A strange figure stands before* Scrooge—*like a child, yet at the same time like an old man: white hair, but unwrinkled skin, long, muscular arms, but delicate legs and feet. Wears white tunic; lustrous belt cinches waist. Branch of fresh green holly in its hand, but has its dress trimmed with fresh summer flowers. Clear jets of light spring from the crown of its head. Holds cap in hand. The Spirit is called* Past.]

12 Are you the Spirit, sir, whose coming was foretold to me?

13 **Past.** I am.

14 **Marley.** Does he take this to be a vision of his green grocer?

15 **Scrooge.** Who, and what are you?

16 **Past.** I am the Ghost of Christmas Past.

17 **Scrooge.** Long past?

18 **Past.** Your past.

CLOSE READ

ANNOTATE Mark details in paragraph 4 that describe the setting.

QUESTION How do these details work together to increase the tension in the scene?

18. **promissory notes** *n.* written promises to pay someone a certain sum of money.

COMPREHENSION CHECK

At the beginning of Scene 4, who can see and hear Marley?

A Christmas Carol: Scrooge and Marley, Act I **235**

19 **Scrooge.** May I ask, please, sir, what business you have here with me?

20 **Past.** Your welfare.

21 **Scrooge.** Not to sound ungrateful, sir, and really, please do understand that I am plenty obliged for your concern, but, really, kind spirit, it would have done all the better for my welfare to have been left alone altogether, to have slept peacefully through this night.

22 **Past.** Your reclamation, then. Take heed!

23 **Scrooge.** My what?

24 **Past.** [*Motioning to* Scrooge *and taking his arm*] Rise! Fly with me! [*He leads* Scrooge *to the window.*]

25 **Scrooge.** [*Panicked*] Fly, but I am a mortal and cannot fly!

26 **Past.** [*Pointing to his heart*] Bear but a touch of my hand here and you shall be upheld in more than this!

27 [Scrooge *touches the spirit's heart and the lights dissolve into sparkly flickers. Lovely crystals of music are heard. The scene dissolves into another. Christmas music again*]

Scene 5

1 [Scrooge *and the* Ghost of Christmas Past *walk together across an open stage. In the background, we see a field that is open; covered by a soft, downy snow: a country road.*]

2 **Scrooge.** Good Heaven! I was bred in this place. I was a boy here!

3 [Scrooge *freezes, staring at the field beyond.* Marley's *ghost appears beside him; takes* Scrooge's *face in his hands, and turns his face to the audience.*]

4 **Marley.** You see this Scrooge: stricken by feeling. Conscious of a thousand odors floating in the air, each one connected with a thousand thoughts, and hopes, and joys, and care long, long forgotten. [*Pause*] This one—this Scrooge—before your very eyes, returns to life, among the living. [*To audience, sternly*] You'd best pay your most careful attention. I would suggest rapt.[19]

5 [*There is a small flash and puff of smoke and* Marley *is gone again.*]

6 **Past.** Your lip is trembling, Mr. Scrooge. And what is that upon your cheek?

---

19. **rapt** *adj.* giving complete attention; totally carried away by something.

7 **Scrooge.** Upon my cheek? Nothing . . . a blemish on the skin from the eating of overmuch grease . . . nothing . . . [*Suddenly*] Kind Spirit of Christmas Past, lead me where you will, but quickly! To be stagnant in this place is, for me, unbearable!

8 **Past.** You recollect the way?

9 **Scrooge.** Remember it! I would know it blindfolded! My bridge, my church, my winding river! [*Staggers about, trying to see it all at once. He weeps again.*]

10 **Past.** These are but shadows of things that have been. They have no consciousness of us.

11 [*Four jocund travelers enter, singing a Christmas song in four-part harmony—"God Rest Ye Merry Gentlemen."*]

12 **Scrooge.** Listen! I know these men! I remember the beauty of their song!

13 **Past.** But, why do you remember it so happily? It is Merry Christmas that they say to one another! What is Merry Christmas to you, Mr. Scrooge? Out upon Merry Christmas, right? What good has Merry Christmas ever done you, Mr. Scrooge? . . .

14 **Scrooge.** [*After a long pause*] None. No good. None . . . [*He bows his head.*]

15 **Past.** Look, you, sir, a school ahead. The schoolroom is not quite deserted. A solitary child, neglected by his friends, is left there still.

16 [*Scrooge falls to the ground; sobbing as he sees, and we see, a small boy, the young Scrooge, sitting and weeping, bravely, alone at his desk: alone in a vast space, a void.*]

17 **Scrooge.** I cannot look on him!

18 **Past.** You must, Mr. Scrooge, you must.

19 **Scrooge.** It's me. [*Pauses; weeps*] Poor boy. He lived inside his head . . . alone . . . [*Pauses; weeps*] poor boy. [*Pauses; stops his weeping*] I wish . . . [*Dries his eyes on his cuff*] ah! it's too late!

20 **Past.** What is the matter?

21 **Scrooge.** There was a boy singing a Christmas Carol outside my door last night. I should like to have given him something: that's all.

22 **Past.** [*Smiles; waves his hand to* Scrooge] Come. Let us see another Christmas.

CLOSE READ

ANNOTATE Mark words in paragraphs 15–19 that describe Scrooge's emotions and behavior.

QUESTION What does the playwright reveal through these words?

23 [*Lights out on a little boy. A flash of light. A puff of smoke. Lights up on older boy*]

24 **Scrooge.** Look! Me, again! Older now! [*Realizes*] Oh, yes . . . still alone.

25 [*The boy—a slightly older* Scrooge—*sits alone in a chair, reading. The door to the room opens and a young girl enters. She is much, much younger than this slightly older* Scrooge. *She is, say, six, and he is, say, twelve. Elder* Scrooge *and the* Ghost of Christmas Past *stand watching the scene, unseen.*]

26 **Fan.** Dear, dear brother, I have come to bring you home.

27 **Boy.** Home, little Fan?

28 **Fan.** Yes! Home, for good and all! Father is so much kinder than he ever used to be, and home's like heaven! He spoke so gently to me one dear night when I was going to bed that I was not afraid to ask him once more if you might come home; and he said "yes" . . . you should; and sent me in a coach to bring you. And you're to be a man and are never to come back here, but first, we're to be together all the Christmas long, and have the merriest time in the world.

29 **Boy.** You are quite a woman, little Fan!

30 [*Laughing; she drags at boy, causing him to stumble to the door with her. Suddenly we hear a mean and terrible voice in the hallway. Off. It is the* Schoolmaster.]

31 **Schoolmaster.** Bring down Master Scrooge's travel box at once! He is to travel!

32 **Fan.** Who is that, Ebenezer?

33 **Boy.** O! Quiet, Fan. It is the Schoolmaster, himself!

34 [*The door bursts open and into the room bursts with it the* Schoolmaster.]

35 **Schoolmaster.** Master Scrooge?

36 **Boy.** Oh, Schoolmaster, I'd like you to meet my little sister, Fan, sir . . .

37 [*Two boys struggle on with* Scrooge's *trunk.*]

38 **Fan.** Pleased, sir . . . [*She curtsies.*]

39 **Schoolmaster.** You are to travel, Master Scrooge.

40 **Scrooge.** Yes, sir, I know sir . . .

41 [*All start to exit, but* Fan *grabs the coattail of the mean old* Schoolmaster.]

42 **Boy.** Fan!

43 **Schoolmaster.** What's this?

44 **Fan.** Pardon, sir, but I believe that you've forgotten to say your goodbye to my brother, Ebenezer, who stands still now awaiting it . . . [*She smiles, curtsies, lowers her eyes.*] pardon, sir.

45 **Schoolmaster.** [*Amazed*] I . . . uh . . . harumph . . . uhh . . . well, then . . . [*Outstretches hand*] Goodbye, Scrooge.

46 **Boy.** Uh, well, goodbye, Schoolmaster . . .

47 [*Lights fade out on all but* Boy *looking at* Fan; *and* Scrooge *and* Past *looking at them.*]

48 **Scrooge.** Oh, my dear, dear little sister, Fan . . . how I loved her.

49 **Past.** Always a delicate creature, whom a breath might have withered, but she had a large heart . . .

50 **Scrooge.** So she had.

COMPREHENSION CHECK

Who is Fan, and why does she come to see Scrooge at the school?

A Christmas Carol: Scrooge and Marley, Act I **239**

51 **Past.** She died a woman, and had, as I think, children.

52 **Scrooge.** One child.

53 **Past.** True. Your nephew.

54 **Scrooge.** Yes.

55 **Past.** Fine, then. We move on, Mr. Scrooge. That warehouse, there? Do you know it?

56 **Scrooge.** Know it? Wasn't I apprenticed[20] there?

57 **Past.** We'll have a look.

58 [*They enter the warehouse. The lights crossfade with them, coming up on an old man in Welsh wig:* **Fezziwig**.]

59 **Scrooge.** Why, it's old Fezziwig! Bless his heart; it's Fezziwig, alive again!

60 [**Fezziwig** *sits behind a large, high desk, counting. He lays down his pen; looks at the clock: seven bells sound.*]

61 Quittin' time . . .

62 **Fezziwig.** Quittin' time . . . [*He takes off his waistcoat and laughs: calls off*] Yo ho, Ebenezer! Dick!

63 [**Dick Wilkins** *and* **Ebenezer Scrooge**—*a young man version*—*enter the room.* **Dick** *and* **Ebenezer** *are* **Fezziwig**'*s apprentices.*]

64 **Scrooge.** Dick Wilkins, to be sure! My fellow-'prentice! Bless my soul, yes. There he is. He was very much attached to me, was Dick. Poor Dick! Dear, dear!

65 **Fezziwig.** Yo ho, my boys. No more work tonight. Christmas Eve, Dick. Christmas, Ebenezer!

66 [*They stand at attention in front of* **Fezziwig**; *laughing*]

67 Hilli-ho! Clear away, and let's have lots of room here! Hilliho, Dick! Chirrup, Ebenezer!

68 [*The young men clear the room, sweep the floor, straighten the pictures, trim the lamps, etc. The space is clear now. A fiddler enters, fiddling.*]

69 Hi-ho, Matthew! Fiddle away . . . where are my daughters?

70 [*The fiddler plays. Three young daughters of* **Fezziwig** *enter followed by six young adult male suitors. They are dancing to the music. All employees come in: workers, clerks, housemaids, cousins, the baker, etc. All dance. Full number wanted here. Throughout the dance, food is brought*

20. **apprenticed** (uh PREHN tihst) *v.* received instruction in a trade as well as food and housing or wages in return for work.

into the feast. It is "eaten" in dance, by the dancers. Ebenezer *dances with all three of the daughters, as does* Dick. *They compete for the daughters, happily, in the dance.* Fezziwig *dances with his daughters.* Fezziwig *dances with* Dick *and* Ebenezer. *The music changes:* Mrs. Fezziwig *enters. She lovingly scolds her husband. They dance. She dances with* Ebenezer, *lifting him and throwing him about. She is enormously fat. When the dance is ended, they all dance off, floating away, as does the music.* Scrooge *and the* Ghost of Christmas Past *stand alone now. The music is gone.*]

CLOSE READ

ANNOTATE Mark details in paragraphs 70–76 that describe young Scrooge's behavior and personality.

QUESTION How do these details deepen your understanding of Scrooge?

71 **Past.** It was a small matter, that Fezziwig made those silly folks so full of gratitude.

72 **Scrooge.** Small!

73 **Past.** Shhh!

74 [*Lights up on* Dick *and* Ebenezer]

75 **Dick.** We are blessed, Ebenezer, truly, to have such a master as Mr. Fezziwig!

76 **Young Scrooge.** He is the best, best, the very and absolute best! If ever I own a firm of my own, I shall treat my apprentices with the same dignity and the same grace. We have learned a wonderful lesson from the master, Dick!

77 **Dick.** Ah, that's a fact, Ebenezer. That's a fact!

78 **Past.** Was it not a small matter, really? He spent but a few pounds[21] of his mortal money on your small party. Three or four pounds, perhaps. Is that so much that he deserves such praise as you and Dick so lavish now?

21. **pounds** *n.* type of money used in Great Britain.

79 **Scrooge.** It isn't that! It isn't that, Spirit. Fezziwig had the power to make us happy or unhappy; to make our service light or burdensome; a pleasure or a toil. The happiness he gave is quite as great as if it cost him a fortune.

80 **Past.** What is the matter?

81 **Scrooge.** Nothing particular.

82 **Past.** Something, I think.

83 **Scrooge.** No, no. I should like to be able to say a word or two to my clerk just now! That's all!

84 [Ebenezer *enters the room and shuts down all the lamps. He stretches and yawns. The* Ghost of Christmas Past *turns to* Scrooge *all of a sudden.*]

COMPREHENSION CHECK

Who is Fezziwig, and what is he like?

85 **Past.** My time grows short! Quick!

A Christmas Carol: Scrooge and Marley, Act I **241**

86 [*In a flash of light,* Ebenezer *is gone, and in his place stands an* Older Scrooge, *this one a man in the prime of his life. Beside him stands a young woman in a mourning dress. She is crying. She speaks to the man, with hostility.*]

87 **Woman.** It matters little . . . to you, very little. Another idol has displaced me.

88 **Man.** What idol has displaced you?

89 **Woman.** A golden one.

90 **Man.** This is an even-handed dealing of the world. There is nothing on which it is so hard as poverty; and there is nothing it professes to condemn with such severity as the pursuit of wealth!

91 **Woman.** You fear the world too much. Have I not seen your nobler aspirations fall off one by one, until the masterpassion, Gain, engrosses you? Have I not?

92 **Scrooge.** No!

93 **Man.** What then? Even if I have grown so much wiser, what then? Have I changed towards you?

94 **Woman.** No . . .

95 **Man.** Am I?

96 **Woman.** Our contract is an old one. It was made when we were both poor and content to be so. You are changed. When it was made, you were another man.

97 **Man.** I was not another man: I was a boy.

98 **Woman.** Your own feeling tells you that you were not what you are. I am. That which promised happiness when we were one in heart is fraught with misery now that we are two . . .

99 **Scrooge.** No!

100 **Woman.** How often and how keenly I have thought of this, I will not say. It is enough that I have thought of it, and can release you . . .

101 **Scrooge.** [*Quietly*] Don't release me, madame . . .

102 **Man.** Have I ever sought release?

103 **Woman.** In words. No. Never.

104 **Man.** In what then?

105 **Woman.** In a changed nature: in an altered spirit. In everything that made my love of any worth or value in your sight. If this has never been between us, tell me, would you seek me out and try to win me now? Ah, no!

106 **Scrooge.** Ah, yes!

107 **Man.** You think not?

108 **Woman.** I would gladly think otherwise if I could, heaven knows! But if you were free today, tomorrow, yesterday, can even I believe that you would choose a dowerless girl[22]—you who in your very confidence with her weigh everything by Gain; or, choosing her, do I not know that your repentance and regret would surely follow? I do; and I release you. With a full heart, for the love of him you once were.

22. **a dowerless girl** girl without a dowry, the property or wealth a woman brings to her husband in marriage.

109 **Scrooge.** Please, I . . . I . . .

110 **Man.** Please, I . . . I . . .

111 **Woman.** Please. You may—the memory of what is past half makes me hope you will—have pain in this. A very, very brief time, and you will dismiss the memory of it, as an unprofitable dream, from which it happened well that you awoke. May you be happy in the life that you have chosen for yourself . . .

112 **Scrooge.** No!

113 **Woman.** Yourself . . . alone . . .

114 **Scrooge.** No!

115 **Woman.** Goodbye, Ebenezer . . .

116 **Scrooge.** Don't let her go!

117 **Man.** Goodbye.

118 **Scrooge.** No!

119 [*She exits. Scrooge goes to younger man: himself.*]

120 You fool! Mindless loon! You fool!

121 **Man.** [*To exited woman*] Fool. Mindless loon. Fool . . .

122 **Scrooge.** Don't say that! Spirit, remove me from this place.

123 **Past.** I have told you these were shadows of the things that have been. They are what they are. Do not blame me, Mr. Scrooge.

124 **Scrooge.** Remove me! I cannot bear it!

CLOSE READ

ANNOTATE In paragraphs 116–122, mark Scrooge's words to his younger self.

QUESTION What do these words reveal about the ways in which Scrooge's feelings have changed?

125 [*The faces of all who appeared in this scene are now projected for a moment around the stage: enormous, flimsy, silent.*]

126 Leave me! Take me back! Haunt me no longer!

127 [*There is a sudden flash of light: a flare. The Ghost of Christmas Past is gone. Scrooge is, for the moment, alone onstage. His bed is turned down, across the stage. A small candle burns now in* Scrooge's *hand. There is a child's cap in his other hand. He slowly crosses the stage to his bed, to sleep.* Marley *appears behind* Scrooge, *who continues his long, elderly cross to bed.* Marley *speaks directly to the audience.*]

128 **Marley.** Scrooge must sleep now. He must surrender to the irresistible drowsiness caused by the recognition of what was. [*Pauses*] The cap he carries is from ten lives past: his boyhood cap . . . donned atop a hopeful hairy head . . . askew, perhaps, or at a rakish angle.[23] Doffed now in honor of regret. Perhaps even too heavy to carry in his present state of weak remorse . . .

129 [Scrooge *drops the cap. He lies atop his bed. He sleeps. To audience*]

130 He sleeps. For him, there's even more trouble ahead. [*Smiles*] For you? The play house tells me there's hot cider, as should be your anticipation for the specter Christmas Present and Future, for I promise you both. [*Smiles again*] So, I pray you hurry back to your seats refreshed and ready for a miser—to turn his coat of gray into a blazen Christmas holly-red. [*A flash of lightning. A clap of thunder. Bats fly. Ghostly music.* Marley *is gone.*]

---

23. **donned . . . angle**. To *don* and *doff* a hat means to put it on and take it off, *askew* means "crooked," and *at a rakish angle* means "having a dashing or jaunty look."

COMPREHENSION CHECK

What thoughts and feelings have his visits to the past aroused in Scrooge?

BUILD INSIGHT

First Thoughts

Select one of the following items to answer.
- Scrooge could afford to live a luxurious life, yet he denies himself the comforts his wealth could offer. Does the fact that he treats himself as badly as he treats others make him a more or a less sympathetic character? Explain.
- At the beginning of the play, what attitude does Scrooge express toward the poor? Who might be a Scrooge-like figure in our society today?

Summary

Write a short summary of Act I to confirm your comprehension. Remember to include only the key ideas and to keep your summary objective and free of personal opinions.

Analysis

1. **(a) Connect** In Scene 3, why is Marley dragging a chain of cash-boxes and other metal objects? **(b) Make Inferences** What does the chain suggest about the life Marley lived? Explain.

2. **(a)** What scenes from his past does Scrooge visit? **(b) Draw Conclusions** How did each event in his life contribute to his current attitude and personality? Explain.

3. **Interpret** Why is the past painful to Scrooge? Cite details from the text to support your interpretation.

Exploring the Essential Question
Can people really change?

4. Given what you've learned about Scrooge in Act I, do you think he might change his ways? If so, how? If not, why not? Provide specific details from the drama to support your response. Record your thinking in your Evidence Log.

STANDARDS
Reading Literature
- Cite several pieces of textual evidence to support analysis of what the text says explicitly as well as inferences drawn from the text.
- Provide an objective summary of the text.

A Christmas Carol: Scrooge and Marley, Act I 245

ANALYZE AND INTERPRET

A CHRISTMAS CAROL:
SCROOGE AND MARLEY, ACT I

Close Read

1. The model passage shows how one reader analyzed part of Scene 5, paragraph 4. Find another detail in the passage to annotate. Then, write your own question and conclusion.

CLOSE-READ MODEL

Marley. You **s**ee thi**s S**crooge: **s**tricken by feeling. Con**s**ciou**s** of a thou**s**and odor**s** floating in the air, each one connected with a thou**s**and thought**s**, and hope**s**, and joy**s**, and care long, long forgotten. [*Pause*] Thi**s** one—thi**s S**crooge—before your very eye**s**, return**s** to life, among the living.

ANNOTATE: I notice that the playwright uses lots of *s*'s in this monologue.

QUESTION: Why might the playwright have made this choice?

CONCLUDE: The repeated *s* sound makes it seem as if Marley were hissing or whispering, creating an eerie mood.

MY QUESTION:

MY CONCLUSION:

2. For more practice, answer the questions in the Close-Read notes in the selection.

3. Choose a section of the drama that you found especially meaningful. Mark important details. Then, jot down questions and write your conclusions in the open space next to the text.

Inquiry and Research

Research and Extend In Act I, Scene 2, Scrooge refers to workhouses and the Poor Law. Generate a research question to find out how these topics are related and to make connections between them. Then, research the Poor Law and workhouses in Victorian England, using those words as search terms. Identify at least two credible, or reliable, online sources and gather relevant information. How does your research increase your understanding of the play's setting?

STANDARDS

Reading Literature
• Analyze how particular elements of a story or drama interact.
• Analyze the impact of rhymes and other repetitions of sounds on a specific verse or stanza of a poem or section of a story or drama.

Writing
Gather relevant information from multiple print and digital sources, using search terms effectively.

246 UNIT 3 • TRANSFORMATIONS

Essential Question: Can people really change?

Dialogue and Character Development

In a play, some information about characters is provided in stage directions. However, most of the details that develop each character's personality come through **dialogue.** What characters say and how they say it shows readers or viewers what they are like. Consider how the example reveals the nephew's friendly, forgiving nature. Even though Scrooge is cold and unkind to him, he continues to speak gently.

EXAMPLE

Scrooge. Why did you get married?

Nephew. Because I fell in love.

Scrooge. That, sir, is the only thing that you have said to me in your entire lifetime which is even more ridiculous than "Merry Christmas!" *[Turns from Nephew]* Good afternoon.

Nephew. Nay, Uncle, you never came to see me before I married either. Why give it as a reason for not coming now?

Scrooge. Good afternoon, Nephew!

Nephew. I want nothing from you; I ask nothing of you; why cannot we be friends?

PRACTICE Complete the activity and answer the questions.

1. **Analyze** Reread the passages indicated in the chart. Then, analyze how each example of dialogue helps develop the characters' personalities.

EXAMPLE OF DIALOGUE	WHAT DIALOGUE SHOWS
Cratchit. *I must be going ... Merry Christmas, Mr. Scrooge!* (Scene 2, paragraphs 78–94)	*his bidding a farewell to his assistant.*
Scrooge. *Oh, my dear, dear little sister ... it's Fezziwig, alive again!* (Scene 5, paragraphs 48–59)	*it's bringing him joy.*

2. **(a) Distinguish** Identify a passage of dialogue from Act I that you think is especially effective in developing Scrooge's character. Mark it in the text. **(b) Analyze** Explain your choice, noting specific character traits the passage reveals.

STUDY LANGUAGE AND CRAFT

A CHRISTMAS CAROL: SCROOGE AND MARLEY, ACT I

Concept Vocabulary

Why These Words? The vocabulary words relate to Scrooge's personality in Act I of the play. For example, Scrooge shows he is a *miser* by refusing to give a donation to the poor.

| covetous | resolute | malcontent |
| morose | impossible | miser |

WORD WALL

Note words in the text that are related to the idea of transformations. Add them to your Word Wall.

PRACTICE Answer the questions.

1. What other words in Act I help you better understand Scrooge and his personality?

2. What might someone do if he or she were *covetous*?

3. How might a person behave if he or she were *morose*?

4. Describe a situation in which someone might be *resolute*.

5. What character traits might cause a person to be viewed as *impossible*?

6. How would a *malcontent* behave at a party?

7. What actions and behaviors might be expected of a *miser*?

Word Study

Latin Prefix: *mal-* The Latin prefix *mal-* means "bad." As an adjective, the word *malcontent* means "dissatisfied with current conditions or circumstances." As a noun, *malcontent* means "a discontented, or unhappy, person."

PRACTICE Complete the activities.

1. Write your own sentence that correctly uses the word *malcontent*, as either a noun or an adjective. Indicate which part of speech you used.

2. Use a print or digital dictionary to find three other words that have the prefix *mal-*. For each word, note its precise meaning and part of speech. Then, write a sentence in which you correctly use each word.

STANDARDS

Reading Literature
Analyze how an author develops and contrasts the points of view of different characters or narrators in a text.

Language
Use common, grade-appropriate Greek or Latin affixes and roots as clues to the meaning of a word.

248 UNIT 3 • TRANSFORMATIONS

Essential Question: Can people really change?

Subjective and Objective Points of View

In this play, the playwright develops a dual role for Marley. He is both a character in the story and a narrator of the action. Marley is the figure that starts the conflict and moves the plot forward, but he also steps away from the story in order to give background information and explain situations. These contrasting roles represent two different types of point of view—subjective and objective.

- As a character, Marley has a **subjective point of view**. This means he expresses only his own ideas, thoughts, and experiences.

- As a narrator, he has an **objective point of view**. He expresses attitudes that many characters share and gives information that is widely known within the setting of the play. Consider this example from Scene 4:

EXAMPLE
Marley. *[Directly to audience]* From this point forth ... I shall be quite visible to you, but invisible to him. *[Smiles]* He will feel my presence, nevertheless, for, unless my senses fail me completely, we are—you and I— witness to the changing of a miser: that one, my partner in life, in business, and in eternity: that one: Scrooge. *[Moves to staircase, below Scrooge]* See him now. He endeavors to pierce the darkness with his ferret eyes. *[To audience]* See him, now. He listens for the hour.

Marley delivers a number of long speeches in the play. Sometimes, they show just one of these points of view. In some cases, they show both.

EVIDENCE LOG

Before moving on to a new selection, go to your Evidence Log and record any additional thoughts or observations you may have about *A Christmas Carol: Scrooge and Marley,* Act I.

PRACTICE Complete the activity and answer the questions.

1. **(a) Analyze** Which point of view, subjective or objective, is used in each of the passages listed in the chart? **(b) Connect** Explain what each passage tells you about characters or situations in the play.

PASSAGE	POINT OF VIEW	EXPLANATION
I present him to you: ... Look at him ... (Scene 1, paragraph 4)		
I have none to give ... weary journeys lie before me! (Scene 3, paragraph 31)		

2. **Evaluate** Analyze the role Marley plays in this drama. Do you find his contrasting roles as both a character and a narrator effective? Why or why not?

A Christmas Carol: Scrooge and Marley, Act I

PREPARE TO READ

A Christmas Carol: Scrooge and Marley, Act II

Concept Vocabulary

Preview and Write Listed below are some words that appear in Act II of the drama. Read the words and context sentences and mark the ones you already know. Challenge yourself to use the words you know in new sentences of your own.

parallel Juan and Andy had parallel experiences in elementary school. ☐ Know it ☐ Don't know it	**altered** I altered the way I study for tests, and now I'm doing much better. ☐ Know it ☐ Don't know it
strive Will you strive to become a better chess player next year? ☐ Know it ☐ Don't know it	**dispelled** Making the team dispelled my doubts about my skills on the court. ☐ Know it ☐ Don't know it
earnest Yin made an earnest attempt to convince the audience but was unsuccessful. ☐ Know it Don't know it	**infinitely** Brianna was infinitely grateful for your help. ☐ Know it ☐ Don't know it

My Sentences

_____
_____
_____
_____
_____
_____

Reading Strategy: Annotate

If you find you do not fully understand a section of text, pause to **annotate,** or take notes about, details that seem important. Doing so can help you understand challenging language or break down complex ideas. Here are some ways you might annotate a text:

- highlight, underline, or circle key words, phrases, and ideas
- signal important passages with symbols such as arrows or stars
- take notes about your observations or reactions in the margins

PRACTICE As you read, annotate long or difficult sections of text to clarify the most important ideas.

STANDARDS
Reading Literature
By the end of the year, read and comprehend literature, including stories, dramas, and poems.
Language
Acquire and use accurately grade-appropriate general academic and domain-specific words and phrases; gather vocabulary knowledge when considering a word or phrase important to comprehension or expression.

DRAMA

A Christmas Carol: Scrooge and Marley

Act II

a drama based on the novella by Charles Dickens

BACKGROUND

In mid-nineteenth-century England, millions of peasants moved to the cities. There, they lived in overcrowded slums. Adults and many children worked up to 12 hours a day, 6 days a week. In contrast, factory owners and professionals lived in grand houses with at least one—and often many—servants. These differences in social conditions play a part in *A Christmas Carol*.

Scene 1

1 [*Lights. Choral music is sung. Curtain.* Scrooge, *in bed, sleeping, in spotlight. We cannot yet see the interior of his room.* Marley, *opposite, in spotlight equal to* Scrooge's. Marley *laughs. He tosses his hand in the air and a flame shoots from it, magically, into the air. There is a thunder clap, and then another; a lightning flash, and then another. Ghostly music plays under. Colors change.* Marley's *spotlight has gone out and now reappears, with* Marley *in it, standing next to the bed and the sleeping* Scrooge. Marley *addresses the audience directly.*]

2 **Marley.** Hear this snoring Scrooge! Sleeping to escape the nightmare that is his waking day. What shall I bring to him now? I'm afraid nothing would astonish old Scrooge now. Not after what he's seen. Not a baby boy, not a rhinoceros, nor anything in between would astonish Ebenezer Scrooge just now. I can think of nothing . . . [*Suddenly*] that's it! Nothing! [*He speaks confidentially.*]

READ TO UNLOCK MEANING

1. First read the text for comprehension and enjoyment. Use the **Reading Strategy** and **Comprehension Check** questions to support your first read.
2. Go back and respond to the Close Read notes.
3. Identify other details in the text you find interesting. Ask your own questions and draw your own conclusions.

I'll have the clock strike one and, when he awakes expecting my second messenger, there will be no one . . . nothing. Then I'll have the bell strike twelve. And then one again . . . and then nothing. Nothing . . . [*Laughs*] nothing will . . . astonish him. I think it will work.

3 [*The bell tolls one.* Scrooge *leaps awake.*]

4 **Scrooge.** One! One! This is it; time! [*Looks about the room*] Nothing!

5 [*The bell tolls midnight.*]

6 Midnight! How can this be? I'm sleeping backwards.

7 [*One again*]

8 Good heavens! One again! I'm sleeping back and forth! [*A pause.* Scrooge *looks about.*] Nothing! Absolutely nothing!

9 [*Suddenly, thunder and lightning.* Marley *laughs and disappears. The room shakes and glows. There is suddenly springlike music.* Scrooge *makes a run for the door.*]

10 **Marley.** Scrooge!

11 **Scrooge.** What?

12 **Marley.** Stay you put!

13 **Scrooge.** Just checking to see if anyone is in here.

14 [*Lights and thunder again: more music.* Marley *is of a sudden gone. In his place sits the* Ghost of Christmas Present—*to be called in the stage directions of the play,* Present—*center of room. Heaped up on the floor, to form a kind of throne, are turkeys, geese, game, poultry, brawn, great joints of meat, suckling pigs, long wreaths of sausages, mince-pies, plum puddings, barrels of oysters, red hot chestnuts, cherry-cheeked apples, juicy oranges, luscious pears, immense twelfth cakes, and seething bowls of punch, that make the chamber dim with their delicious steam. Upon this throne sits* Present, *glorious to see. He bears a torch, shaped as a Horn of Plenty.*[1] Scrooge *hops out of the door, and then peeks back again into his bedroom.* Present *calls to* Scrooge.]

15 **Present.** Ebenezer Scrooge. Come in, come in! Come in and know me better!

16 **Scrooge.** Hello. How should I call you?

17 **Present.** I am the Ghost of Christmas Present. Look upon me.

18 [Present *is wearing a simple green robe. The walls around the room are now covered in greenery, as well. The room seems to be a perfect grove now: leaves of holly, mistletoe and ivy reflect the stage lights. Suddenly, there is a mighty roar of flame in the fireplace and now the hearth burns*

1. **Horn of Plenty** horn overflowing with fruits, flowers, and grain, representing wealth and abundance.

with a lavish, warming fire. There is an ancient scabbard girdling the Ghost's middle, but without sword. The sheath is gone to rust.]

19. You have never seen the like of me before?

20. **Scrooge.** Never.

21. **Present.** You have never walked forth with younger members of my family: my elder brothers born on Christmases past.

22. **Scrooge.** I don't think I have. I'm afraid I've not. Have you had many brothers, Spirit?

23. **Present.** More than eighteen hundred.

24. **Scrooge.** A tremendous family to provide for! [Present *stands*] Spirit, conduct me where you will. I went forth last night on compulsion, and learnt a lesson which is working now. Tonight, if you have aught to teach me, let me profit by it.

25. **Present.** Touch my robe.

26. [Scrooge *walks cautiously to* Present *and touches his robe. When he does, lightning flashes, thunder claps, music plays. Blackout*]

Scene 2

1. [PROLOGUE: Marley *stands spotlit, L. He speaks directly to the audience.*]

2. **Marley.** My ghostly friend now leads my living partner through the city's streets.

3. [*Lights up on* Scrooge *and* Present]

4. See them there and hear the music people make when the weather is severe, as it is now.

5. [*Winter music. Choral group behind scrim, sings. When the song is done and the stage is re-set, the lights will fade up on a row of shops, behind the singers. The choral group will hum the song they have just completed now and mill about the streets,[2] carrying their dinners to the bakers' shops and restaurants. They will, perhaps, sing about being poor at Christmastime, whatever.*]

6. **Present.** These revelers, Mr. Scrooge, carry their own dinners to their jobs, where they will work to bake the meals the rich men and women of this city will eat as their Christmas dinners. Generous people these . . . to care for the others, so . . .

CLOSE READ

ANNOTATE Mark the details in paragraphs 5–6 that describe the setting.

QUESTION How does this information help you better understand the play?

2. **mill about the streets** walk around aimlessly.

A Christmas Carol: Scrooge and Marley, Act II **253**

3. **incense** (IHN sehns) *n.* substance that produces a pleasant odor when burned.

7 [*Present walks among the choral group and a sparkling incense[3] falls from his torch on to their baskets, as he pulls the covers off of the baskets. Some of the choral group become angry with each other.*]

8 **Man #1.** Hey, you, watch where you're going.

9 **Man #2.** Watch it yourself, mate!

10 [*Present sprinkles them directly, they change.*]

11 **Man #1.** I pray go in ahead of me. It's Christmas. You be first!

12 **Man #2.** No, no. I must insist that YOU be first!

13 **Man #1.** All right, I shall be, and gratefully so.

14 **Man #2.** The pleasure is equally mine, for being able to watch you pass, smiling.

15 **Man #1.** I would find it a shame to quarrel on Christmas Day . . .

16 **Man #2.** As would I.

17 **Man #1.** Merry Christmas then, friend!

18 **Man #2.** And a Merry Christmas straight back to you!

19 [*Church bells toll. The choral group enter the buildings: the shops and restaurants; they exit the stage, shutting their doors closed behind them. All sound stops. Scrooge and Present are alone again.*]

20 **Scrooge.** What is it you sprinkle from your torch?

21 **Present.** Kindness.

22 **Scrooge.** Do you sprinkle your kindness on any particular people or on all people?

23 **Present.** To any person kindly given. And to the very poor most of all.

24 **Scrooge.** Why to the very poor most?

25 **Present.** Because the very poor need it most. Touch my heart . . . here, Mr. Scrooge. We have another journey.

26 [*Scrooge touches the Ghost's heart and music plays, lights change color, lightning flashes, thunder claps. A choral group appears on the street, singing Christmas carols.*]

Scene 3

1 [*Marley stands spotlit in front of a scrim on which is painted the exterior of Cratchit's four-roomed house. There is a flash and a clap and Marley is gone. The lights shift color again, the scrim flies away, and we are in the*

interior of the Cratchit *family home.* Scrooge *is there, with the spirit* (Present), *watching* Mrs. Cratchit *set the table, with the help of* Belinda Cratchit *and* Peter Cratchit, *a baby, pokes a fork into the mashed potatoes on his highchair's tray. He also chews on his shirt collar.*]

2 **Scrooge.** What is this place, Spirit?

3 **Present.** This is the home of your employee, Mr. Scrooge. Don't you know it?

4 **Scrooge.** Do you mean Cratchit, Spirit? Do you mean this is Cratchit's home?

5 **Present.** None other.

6 **Scrooge.** These children are his?

7 **Present.** There are more to come presently.

8 **Scrooge.** On his meager earnings! What foolishness!

9 **Present.** Foolishness, is it?

10 **Scrooge.** Wouldn't you say so? Fifteen shillings[4] a week's what he gets!

11 **Present.** I would say that he gets the pleasure of his family, fifteen times a week times the number of hours a day! Wait, Mr. Scrooge. Wait, listen and watch. You might actually learn something . . .

12 **Mrs. Cratchit.** What has ever got your precious father then? And your brother, Tiny Tim? And Martha warn't as late last Christmas by half an hour!

13 [Martha *opens the door, speaking to her mother as she does.*]

14 **Martha.** Here's Martha, now, Mother! [*She laughs. The* Cratchit Children *squeal with delight.*]

15 **Belinda.** It's Martha, Mother! Here's Martha!

16 **Peter.** Marthmama, Marthmama! Hullo!

17 **Belinda.** Hurrah! Martha! Martha! There's such an enormous goose for us, Martha!

18 **Mrs. Cratchit.** Why, bless your heart alive, my dear, how late you are!

19 **Martha.** We'd a great deal of work to finish up last night, and had to clear away this morning, Mother.

20 **Mrs. Cratchit.** Well, never mind so long as you are come. Sit ye down before the fire, my dear, and have a warm, Lord bless ye!

21 **Belinda.** No, no! There's Father coming. Hide, Martha, hide!

4. **fifteen shillings** small amount of money for a week's work.

COMPREHENSION CHECK

Several new characters are introduced in Scene 3. Who are the members of the Cratchit family?

22 [Martha *giggles and hides herself.*]

23 **Martha.** Where? Here?

24 **Peter.** Hide, hide!

25 **Belinda.** Not there! THERE!

26 [Martha *is hidden.* Bob Cratchit *enters, carrying* Tiny Tim *atop his shoulder. He wears a threadbare and fringeless comforter hanging down in front of him.* Tiny Tim *carries small crutches and his small legs are bound in an iron frame brace.*]

27 **Bob and Tiny Tim.** Merry Christmas.

28 **Bob.** Merry Christmas my love, Merry Christmas Peter, Merry Christmas Belinda. Why, where is Martha?

29 **Mrs. Cratchit.** Not coming.

30 **Bob.** Not coming: Not coming upon Christmas Day?

31 **Martha.** [*Pokes head out*] Ohhh, poor Father. Don't be disappointed.

32 **Bob.** What's this?

33 **Martha.** 'Tis I!

34 **Bob.** Martha! [*They embrace.*]

35 **Tiny Tim.** Martha! Martha!

36 **Martha.** Tiny Tim!

37 [Tiny Tim *is placed in* Martha's *arms.* Belinda *and* Peter *rush him offstage.*]

38 **Belinda.** Come, brother! You must come hear the pudding singing in the copper.

39 **Tiny Tim.** The pudding? What flavor have we?

40 **Peter.** Plum! Plum!

41 **Tiny Tim.** Oh, Mother! I love plum!

42 [*The children exit the stage giggling.*]

43 **Mrs. Cratchit.** And how did little Tim behave?

44 **Bob.** As good as gold, and even better. Somehow he gets thoughtful sitting by himself so much, and thinks the strangest things you ever heard. He told me, coming home, that he hoped people saw him in the church, because he was a cripple, and it might be pleasant to them to remember upon Christmas Day, who made lame beggars walk and blind men see. [*Pauses*] He has the oddest ideas sometimes, but he seems all the while to be growing stronger and

CLOSE READ

ANNOTATE Mark the pause in paragraph 44.

QUESTION What purpose might the pause serve? Reread Bob's lines following the pause. What important information is he sharing?

more hearty . . . one would never know. [*Hears Tim's crutch on floor outside door*]

45 **Peter.** The goose has arrived to be eaten!

46 **Belinda.** Oh, mama, mama, it's beautiful.

47 **Martha.** It's a perfect goose, Mother!

48 **Tiny Tim.** To this Christmas goose, Mother and Father I say . . . [*Yells*] Hurrah! Hurrah!

49 **Other Children.** [*Copying* Tim] Hurrah! Hurrah!

50 [*The family sits round the table.* Bob *and* Mrs. Cratchit *serve the trimmings, quickly. All sit; all bow heads; all pray.*]

51 **Bob.** Thank you, dear Lord, for your many gifts . . . our dear children; our wonderful meal; our love for one another; and the warmth of our small fire—[*Looks up at all*] A merry Christmas to us, my dear. God bless us!

52 **All.** [*Except* Tim] Merry Christmas! God bless us!

53 **Tiny Tim.** [*In a short silence*] God bless us every one.

COMPREHENSION CHECK

What do you know about Tiny Tim so far?

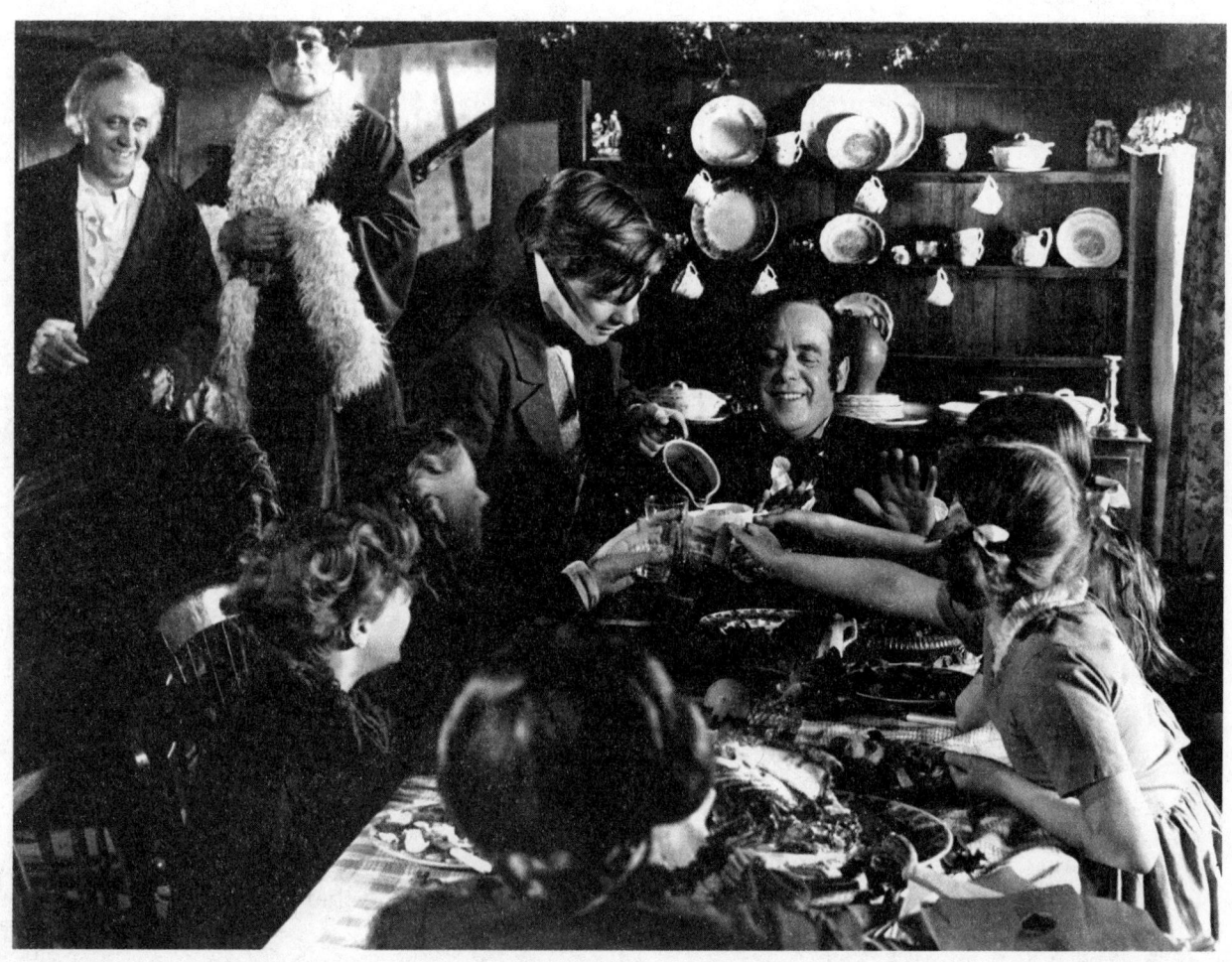

54 [*All freeze. Spotlight on* Present *and* Scrooge]

55 **Scrooge.** Spirit, tell me if Tiny Tim will live.

56 **Present.** I see a vacant seat . . . in the poor chimney corner, and a crutch without an owner, carefully preserved. If these shadows remain unaltered by the future, the child will die.

57 **Scrooge.** No, no, kind Spirit! Say he will be spared!

58 **Present.** If these shadows remain unaltered by the future, none other of my race will find him here. What then? If he be like to die, he had better do it, and decrease the surplus population.

59 [Scrooge *bows his head. We hear* Bob's *voice speak* Scrooge's *name.*]

60 **Bob.** Mr. Scrooge . . .

61 **Scrooge.** Huh? What's that? Who calls?

62 **Bob.** [*His glass raised in a toast*] I'll give you Mr. Scrooge, the Founder of the Feast!

63 **Scrooge.** Me, Bob? You toast *me*?

64 **Present.** Save your breath, Mr. Scrooge. You can't be seen or heard.

65 **Mrs. Cratchit.** The Founder of the Feast, indeed! I wish I had him here, that miser Scrooge. I'd give him a piece of my mind to feast upon, and I hope he'd have a good appetite for it!

66 **Bob.** My dear! Christmas Day!

67 **Mrs. Cratchit.** It should be Christmas Day, I am sure, on which one drinks the health of such an odious, stingy, unfeeling man as Mr. Scrooge . . .

68 **Scrooge.** Oh. Spirit, must I? . . .

69 **Mrs. Cratchit.** You know he is, Robert! Nobody knows it better than you do, poor fellow!

70 **Bob.** This is Christmas Day, and I should like to drink to the health of the man who employs me and allows me to earn my living and our support and that man is Ebenezer Scrooge . . .

71 **Mrs. Cratchit.** I'll drink to his health for your sake and the day's, but not for his sake . . . a Merry Christmas and a Happy New Year to you, Mr. Scrooge, wherever you may be this day!

72 **Scrooge.** Just here, kind madam . . . out of sight, out of sight . . .

73 **Bob.** Thank you, my dear. Thank you.

74 **Scrooge.** Thank you, Bob . . . and Mrs. Cratchit, too. No one else is toasting me, . . . not now . . . not ever. Of that I am sure . . .

CLOSE READ

ANNOTATE In paragraphs 62–71, mark words and phrases that highlight the differences between Mrs. Cratchit's and Bob Cratchit's attitudes toward Scrooge.

QUESTION What does this contrast reveal about each character's personality and point of view?

75 **Bob.** Children . . .

76 **All.** Merry Christmas to Mr. Scrooge.

77 **Bob.** I'll pay you sixpence, Tim, for my favorite song.

78 **Tiny Tim.** Oh, Father, I'd so love to sing it, but not for pay. This Christmas goose—this feast—you and Mother, my brother and sisters close with me: that's my pay—

79 **Bob.** Martha, will you play the notes on the lute, for Tiny Tim's song.

80 **Belinda.** May I sing, too, Father?

81 **Bob.** We'll all sing.

82 [*They sing a song about a tiny child lost in the snow—probably from Wordsworth's poem.* Tim *sings the lead vocal; all chime in for the chorus. Their song fades under, as the* Ghost of Christmas Present *speaks.*]

83 **Present.** Mark my words, Ebenezer Scrooge. I do not present the Cratchits to you because they are a handsome, or brilliant family. They are not handsome. They are not brilliant. They are not well-dressed, or tasteful to the times. Their shoes are not even waterproofed by virtue of money or cleverness spent. So when the pavement is wet, so are the insides of their shoes and the tops of their toes. These are the Cratchits, Mr. Scrooge. They are not highly special. They are happy, grateful, pleased with one another, contented with the time and how it passes. They don't sing very well, do they? But, nonetheless, they do sing . . . [*Pauses*] think of that, Scrooge. Fifteen shillings a week and they do sing . . . hear their song until its end.

84 **Scrooge.** I am listening. [*The chorus sings full volume now, until . . . the song ends here.*] Spirit, it must be time for us to take our leave. I feel in my heart that it is . . . that I must think on that which I have seen here . . .

85 **Present.** Touch my robe again . . .

86 [Scrooge *touches* Present's *robe. The lights fade out on the* Cratchits, *who sit, frozen, at the table.* Scrooge *and* Present *in a spotlight now. Thunder, lightning, smoke. They are gone.*]

Scene 4

1 [Marley *appears D.L. in single spotlight. A storm brews. Thunder and lightning.* Scrooge *and* Present *"fly" past, U. The storm continues, furiously, and, now and again,* Scrooge *and* Present *will zip past in their travels.* Marley *will speak straight out to the audience.*]

COMPREHENSION CHECK
Why does Tiny Tim refuse the sixpence his father offers to pay him to sing his favorite song?

2 **Marley.** The Ghost of Christmas Present, my co-worker in this attempt to turn a miser, flies about now with that very miser, Scrooge, from street to street, and he points out partygoers on their way to Christmas parties. If one were to judge from the numbers of people on their way to friendly gatherings, one might think that no one was left at home to give anyone welcome . . . but that's not the case, is it? Every home is expecting company and . . . [*He laughs.*] Scrooge is amazed.

3 [Scrooge *and* Present *zip past again. The lights fade up around them. We are in the* Nephew's *home, in the living room.* Present *and* Scrooge *stand watching the* Nephew: Fred *and his wife, fixing the fire.*]

4 **Scrooge.** What is this place? We've moved from the mines!

5 **Present.** You do not recognize them?

6 **Scrooge.** It is my nephew! . . . and the one he married . . .

7 [Marley *waves his hand and there is a lightning flash. He disappears.*]

8 **Fred.** It strikes me as sooooo funny, to think of what he said . . . that Christmas was a humbug, as I live! He believed it!

9 **Wife.** More shame for him, Fred!

10 **Fred.** Well, he's a comical old fellow, that's the truth.

11 **Wife.** I have no patience with him.

12 **Fred.** Oh, I have! I am sorry for him; I couldn't be angry with him if I tried. Who suffers by his ill whims? Himself, always . . .

13 **Scrooge.** It's me they talk of, isn't it, Spirit?

14 **Fred.** Here, wife, consider this. Uncle Scrooge takes it into his head to dislike us, and he won't come and dine with us. What's the consequence?

15 **Wife.** Oh . . . you're sweet to say what I think you're about to say, too, Fred . . .

16 **Fred.** What's the consequence? He don't lose much of a dinner by it, I can tell you that!

17 **Wife.** Ooooooo, Fred! Indeed, I think he loses a very good dinner . . . ask my sisters, or your bachelor friend, Topper . . . ask any of them. They'll tell you what old Scrooge, your uncle, missed: a dandy meal!

18 **Fred.** Well, that's something of a relief, wife. Glad to hear it! [*He hugs his wife. They laugh. They kiss.*] The truth is, he misses much yet. I mean to give him the same chance every year, whether he likes it or not, for I pity him. Nay, he is my only uncle and I feel for the old

miser . . . but, I tell you, wife: I see my dear and perfect mother's face on his own wizened cheeks and brow: brother and sister they were, and I cannot erase that from each view of him I take . . .

19 **Wife.** I understand what you say, Fred, and I am with you in your yearly asking. But he never will accept, you know. He never will.

20 **Fred.** Well, true, wife. Uncle may rail at Christmas till he dies. I think I shook him some with my visit yesterday . . . [*Laughing*] I refused to grow angry . . . no matter how nasty he became . . . [*Whoops*] It was HE who grew angry, wife! [*They both laugh now.*]

21 **Scrooge.** What he says is true, Spirit . . .

22 **Fred and Wife.** Bah, humbug!

23 **Fred.** [*Embracing his wife*] There is much laughter in our marriage, wife. It pleases me. You please me . . .

24 **Wife.** And you please me, Fred. You are a good man . . . [*They embrace.*] Come now. We must have a look at the meal . . . our guests will soon arrive . . . my sisters, Topper . . .

25 **Fred.** A toast first . . . [*He hands her a glass*] A toast to Uncle Scrooge . . . [*Fills their glasses*]

26 **Wife.** A toast to him?

27 **Fred.** Uncle Scrooge has given us plenty of merriment, I am sure, and it would be ungrateful not to drink to his health. And I say . . . Uncle Scrooge!

28 **Wife.** [*Laughing*] You're a proper loon,[5] Fred . . . and I'm a proper wife to you . . . [*She raises her glass.*] Uncle Scrooge! [*They drink. They embrace. They kiss.*]

29 **Scrooge.** Spirit, please, make me visible! Make me audible! I want to talk with my nephew and my niece!

30 [*Calls out to them. The lights that light the room and Fred and wife fade out. Scrooge and Present are alone, spotlit.*]

31 **Present.** These shadows are gone to you now, Mr. Scrooge. You may return to them later tonight in your dreams. [*Pauses*] My time grows short, Ebenezer Scrooge. Look you on me! Do you see how I've aged?

32 **Scrooge.** Your hair has gone gray! Your skin, wrinkled! Are spirits' lives so short?

33 **Present.** My stay upon this globe is very brief. It ends tonight.

34 **Scrooge.** Tonight?

5. **a proper loon** silly person.

COMPREHENSION CHECK

Why does Fred invite Scrooge to Christmas dinner every year, even though Scrooge never accepts?

35 **Present.** At midnight. The time is drawing near!

36 [*Clock strikes 11:45.*]

37 Hear those chimes? In a quarter hour, my life will have been spent! Look, Scrooge, man. Look you here.

38 [*Two gnarled baby dolls are taken from* Present's *skirts.*]

39 **Scrooge.** Who are they?

40 **Present.** They are Man's children, and they cling to me, appealing from their fathers. The boy is Ignorance; the girl is Want. Beware them both, and all of their degree, but most of all beware this boy, for on his brow I see that written which is Doom, unless the writing be erased.

41 [*He stretches out his arm. His voice is now amplified: loudly and oddly.*]

42 **Scrooge.** Have they no refuge or resource?

43 **Present.** Are there no prisons? Are there no workhouses? [*Twelve chimes*] Are there no prisons? Are there no workhouses?

44 [*A* Phantom, *hooded, appears in dim light,* D., *opposite.*]

ANNOTATE

What is the Ghost of Christmas Present's main message to Scrooge in paragraph 40? Mark key words in the paragraph and then jot the message in the margin.

45 Are there no prisons? Are there no workhouses?

46 [Present *begins to deliquesce.* Scrooge *calls after him.*]

47 **Scrooge.** Spirit, I'm frightened! Don't leave me! Spirit!

48 **Present.** Prisons? Workhouses? Prisons? Workhouses . . .

49 [*He is gone.* Scrooge *is alone now with the* Phantom, *who is, of course, the* Ghost of Christmas Future. *The* Phantom *is shrouded in black. Only its outstretched hand is visible from under his ghostly garment.*]

50 **Scrooge.** Who are you, Phantom? Oh, yes. I think I know you! You are, are you not, the Spirit of Christmas Yet to Come? [*No reply*] And you are about to show me the shadows of the things that have not yet happened, but will happen in time before us. Is that not so, Spirit? [*The* Phantom *allows* Scrooge *a look at his face. No other reply wanted here. A nervous giggle here.*] Oh, Ghost of the Future, I fear you more than any Specter I have seen! But, as I know that your purpose is to do me good and as I hope to live to be another man from what I was, I am prepared to bear you company. [Future *does not reply, but for a stiff arm, hand and finger set, pointing forward.*] Lead on, then, lead on. The night is waning fast, and it is precious time to me. Lead on, Spirit!

51 [Future *moves away from* Scrooge *in the same rhythm and motion employed at its arrival.* Scrooge *falls into the same pattern, a considerable space apart from the* Spirit. *In the space between them,* Marley *appears. He looks to* Future *and then to* Scrooge. *He claps his hands. Thunder and lightning. Three* Businessmen *appear, spotlighted singularly: One is D.L.; one is D.R.; one is U.C. Thus, six points of the stage should now be spotted in light.* Marley *will watch this scene from his position,* C. Scrooge *and* Future *are R. and L. of C.*]

52 **First Businessman.** Oh, no, I don't know much about it either way, I only know he's dead.

53 **Second Businessman.** When did he die?

54 **First Businessman.** Last night, I believe.

55 **Second Businessman.** Why, what was the matter with him? I thought he'd never die, really . . .

56 **First Businessman.** [*Yawning*] Goodness knows, goodness knows . . .

57 **Third Businessman.** What has he done with his money?

58 **Second Businessman.** I haven't heard. Have you?

59 **First Businessman.** Left it to his Company, perhaps. Money to money; you know the expression . . .

CLOSE READ

ANNOTATE Mark the words and phrases that the Ghost of Christmas Present repeats in paragraphs 43–48.

QUESTION Why might the playwright have included this repetition, and what effect does it have on the reader or viewer?

COMPREHENSION CHECK

How does the Ghost of Christmas Future respond to Scrooge's many questions and comments?

60 **Third Businessman.** He hasn't left it to *me*. That's all I know . . .

61 **First Businessman.** [*Laughing*] Nor to me . . . [*Looks at* Second Businessman] You, then? You got his money???

62 **Second Businessman.** [*Laughing*] Me, me, his money? Nooooo!

63 [*They all laugh.*]

64 **Third Businessman.** It's likely to be a cheap funeral, for upon my life, I don't know of a living soul who'd care to venture to it. Suppose we make up a party and volunteer?

65 **Second Businessman.** I don't mind going if a lunch is provided, but I must be fed, if I make one.

66 **First Businessman.** Well, I am the most disinterested among you, for I never wear black gloves, and I never eat lunch. But I'll offer to go, if anybody else will. When I come to think of it, I'm not all sure that I wasn't his most particular friend: for we used to stop and speak whenever we met. Well, then . . . bye, bye!

67 **Second Businessman.** Bye, bye . . .

68 **Third Businessman.** Bye, bye . . .

69 [*They glide offstage in three separate directions. Their lights follow them.*]

70 **Scrooge.** Spirit, why did you show me this? Why do you show me businessmen from my streets as they take the death of Jacob Marley? That is a thing past. You are future!

71 [Jacob Marley *laughs a long, deep laugh. There is a thunder clap and lightning flash, and he is gone. Scrooge faces* Future, *alone on stage now.* Future *wordlessly stretches out his arm-hand-and-finger-set, pointing into the distance,* U. *There, above them, scoundrels "fly" by, half-dressed and slovenly. When this scene has passed, a woman enters the playing area. She is almost at once followed by a second woman; and then a man in faded black; and then, suddenly, an old man, who smokes a pipe. The old man scares the other three. They laugh, anxious.*]

72 **First Woman.** Look here, old Joe, here's a chance! If we haven't all three met here without meaning it!

73 **Old Joe.** You couldn't have met in a better place. Come into the parlor. You were made free of it long ago, you know; and the other two ain't strangers [*He stands; shuts a door. Shrieking*] We're all suitable to our calling. We're well matched. Come into the parlor. Come into the parlor . . . [*They follow him* D. Scrooge *and* Future *are now in their midst, watching; silent. A truck comes in on which is set a small wall with fireplace and a screen of rags, etc. All props for the scene.*] Let me just rake this fire over a bit . . .

74 [*He does. He trims his lamp with the stem of his pipe. The First Woman throws a large bundle on to the floor. She sits beside it, crosslegged, defiantly.*]

75 **First Woman.** What odds then? What odds, Mrs. Dilber? Every person has a right to take care of themselves. HE always did!

76 **Mrs. Dilber.** That's true indeed! No man more so!

77 **First Woman.** Why, then, don't stand staring as if you was afraid, woman! Who's the wiser? We're not going to pick holes in each other's coats, I suppose?

78 **Mrs. Dilber.** No, indeed! We should hope not!

79 **First Woman.** Very well, then! That's enough. Who's the worse for the loss of a few things like these? Not a dead man, I suppose?

80 **Mrs. Dilber.** [*Laughing*] No, indeed!

81 **First Woman.** If he wanted to keep 'em after he was dead, the wicked old screw, why wasn't he natural in his lifetime? If he had been, he'd have had somebody to look after him when he was struck with Death, instead of lying gasping out his last there, alone by himself.

82 **Mrs. Dilber.** It's the truest word that was ever spoke. It's a judgment on him.

83 **First Woman.** I wish it were a heavier one, and it should have been, you may depend on it, if I could have laid my hands on anything else. Open that bundle, old Joe, and let me know the value of it. Speak out plain. I'm not afraid to be the first, nor afraid for them to see it. We knew pretty well that we were helping ourselves, before we met here, I believe. It's no sin. Open the bundle, Joe.

84 **First Man.** No, no, my dear! I won't think of letting you being the first to show what you've . . . earned . . . earned from this. I throw in mine.

85 [*He takes a bundle from his shoulder, turns it upside down, and empties its contents out on to the floor.*]

86 It's not very extensive, see . . . seals . . . a pencil case . . . sleeve buttons . . .

87 **First Woman.** Nice sleeve buttons, though . . .

88 **First Man.** Not bad, not bad . . . a brooch there . . .

89 **Old Joe.** Not really valuable, I'm afraid . . .

90 **First Man.** How much, old Joe?

91 **Old Joe.** [*Writing on the wall with chalk*] A pitiful lot, really. Ten and six and not a sixpence more!

COMPREHENSION CHECK

Scrooge listens to the three businessmen discussing a recent death. Whose death does Scrooge think they are referring to? Whose death are they actually discussing?

92 **First Man.** You're not serious!

93 **Old Joe.** That's your account and I wouldn't give another sixpence if I was to be boiled for not doing it. Who's next?

94 **Mrs. Dilber.** Me! [*Dumps out contents of her bundle*] Sheets, towels, silver spoons, silver sugar-tongs . . . some boots . . .

95 **Old Joe.** [*Writing on wall*] I always give too much to the ladies. It's a weakness of mine and that's the way I ruin myself. Here's your total comin' up . . . two pounds-ten . . . if you asked me for another penny, and made it an open question, I'd repent of being so liberal and knock off half-a-crown.

96 **First Woman.** And now do MY bundle, Joe.

97 **Old Joe.** [*Kneeling to open knots on her bundle*] So many knots, madam . . . [*He drags out large curtains; dark*] What do you call this? Bed curtains!

98 **First Woman.** [*Laughing*] Ah, yes, bed curtains!

99 **Old Joe.** You don't mean to say you took 'em down, rings and all, with him lying there?

100 **First Woman.** Yes, I did, why not?

101 **Old Joe.** You were born to make your fortune and you'll certainly do it.

102 **First Woman.** I certainly shan't hold my hand, when I can get anything in it by reaching it out, for the sake of such a man as he was. I promise you, Joe. Don't drop that lamp oil on those blankets, now!

103 **Old Joe.** His blankets?

104 **First Woman.** Whose else's do you think? He isn't likely to catch cold without 'em, I daresay.

105 **Old Joe.** I hope that he didn't die of anything catching? Eh?

106 **First Woman.** Don't you be afraid of that. I ain't so fond of his company that I'd loiter about him for such things if he did. Ah! You may look through that shirt till your eyes ache, but you won't find a hole in it, nor a threadbare place. It's the best he had, and a fine one, too. They'd have wasted it, if it hadn't been for me.

107 **Old Joe.** What do you mean "They'd have wasted it"?

108 **First Woman.** Putting it on him to be buried in, to be sure. Somebody was fool enough to do it, but I took it off again . . .

109 [*She laughs, as do they all, nervously.*]

110 If calico[6] ain't good enough for such a purpose, it isn't good enough then for anything. It's quite as becoming to the body. He can't look uglier than he did in that one!

111 **Scrooge.** [*A low-pitched moan emits from his mouth; from the bones.*] OOOOOOOooooOOOOOooooOOOOOOOO ooooOOOOOOooooOO!

112 **Old Joe.** One pound six for the lot. [*He produces a small flannel bag filled with money. He divvies it out. He continues to pass around the money as he speaks. All are laughing.*] That's the end of it, you see! He frightened every one away from him when he was alive, to profit us when he was dead! Hah ha ha!

113 **All.** HAHAHAHAhahahahahahah!

114 **Scrooge.** OOoooOOoooOOOoooOOOoooOOoooOOoooOOOooo! [*He screams at them.*] Obscene demons! Why not market the corpse itself, as sell its trimming??? [*Suddenly*] Oh, Spirit, I see it, I see it! This unhappy man—this stripped-bare corpse . . . could very well be my own. My life holds **parallel**! My life ends that way now!

115 [*Scrooge backs into something in the dark behind his spotlight. Scrooge looks at Future, who points to the corpse. Scrooge pulls back the blanket. The corpse is, of course, Scrooge, who screams. He falls aside the bed; weeping.*]

116 Spirit, this is a fearful place. In leaving it, I shall not leave its lesson, trust me. Let us go!

117 [*Future points to the corpse.*]

118 Spirit, let me see some tenderness connected with a death, or that dark chamber, which we just left now, Spirit, will be forever present to me.

119 [*Future spreads his robes again. Thunder and lightning. Lights up, U., in the Cratchit home setting. Mrs. Cratchit and her daughters, sewing*]

120 **Tiny Tim's Voice.** [*Off*] And He took a child and set him in the midst of them.

121 **Scrooge.** [*Looking about the room; to Future*] Huh? Who spoke? Who said that?

122 **Mrs. Cratchit.** [*Puts down her sewing*] The color hurts my eyes. [*Rubs her eyes*] That's better. My eyes grow weak sewing by candlelight. I shouldn't want to show your father weak eyes when he comes home . . . not for the world! It must be near his time . . .

6. **calico** (KAL ih koh) *n.* coarse and inexpensive cotton cloth.

CLOSE READ
ANNOTATE Mark the sounds and sound effects in paragraphs 111–114.
QUESTION What is the effect of including these sounds in the stage directions?

parallel (PAR uh lehl) *adj.* having the same direction or nature; similar

COMPREHENSION CHECK
What items does First Woman bring to Old Joe, and where does she get them from?

ANNOTATE
In paragraphs 123 and 124, mark details that describe a contrast in Bob's behavior. Explain the reason for the contrast.

123 **Peter.** [*In corner, reading. Looks up from book*] Past it, rather. But I think he's been walking a bit slower than usual these last few evenings, Mother.

124 **Mrs. Cratchit.** I have known him walk with . . . [*Pauses*] I have known him walk with Tiny Tim upon his shoulder and very fast indeed.

125 **Peter.** So have I, Mother! Often!

126 **Daughter.** So have I.

127 **Mrs. Cratchit.** But he was very light to carry and his father loved him so, that it was not trouble—no trouble. [*Bob, at door*]

128 And there is your father at the door.

129 [*Bob Cratchit enters. He wears a comforter. He is cold, forlorn.*]

130 **Peter.** Father!

131 **Bob.** Hello, wife, children . . .

132 [*The daughter weeps; turns away from Cratchit.*]

133 Children! How good to see you all! And you, wife. And look at this sewing! I've no doubt, with all your industry, we'll have a quilt to set down upon our knees in church on Sunday!

134 **Mrs. Cratchit.** You made the arrangements today, then, Robert, for the . . . service . . . to be on Sunday.

135 **Bob.** The funeral. Oh, well, yes, yes, I did. I wish you could have gone. It would have done you good to see how green a place it is. But you'll see it often. I promised him that I would walk there on Sunday, after the service. [*Suddenly*] My little, little child! My little child!

136 **All Children.** [*Hugging him*] Oh, Father . . .

137 **Bob.** [*He stands*] Forgive me. I saw Mr. Scrooge's nephew, who you know I'd just met once before, and he was so wonderful to me, wife . . . he is the most pleasant-spoken gentleman I've ever met . . . he said "I am heartily sorry for it and heartily sorry for your good wife. If I can be of service to you in any way, here's where I live." And he gave me this card.

138 **Peter.** Let me see it!

139 **Bob.** And he looked me straight in the eye, wife, and said, meaningfully, "I pray you'll come to me, Mr. Cratchit, if you need some help. I pray you do." Now it wasn't for the sake of anything that he might be able to do for us, so much as for his kind way. It seemed as if he had known our Tiny Tim and felt with us.

140 **Mrs. Cratchit.** I'm sure that he's a good soul.

141 **Bob.** You would be surer of it, my dear, if you saw and spoke to him. I shouldn't be at all surprised, if he got Peter a situation.

142 **Mrs. Cratchit.** Only hear that, Peter!

143 **Martha.** And then, Peter will be keeping company with someone and setting up for himself!

144 **Peter.** Get along with you!

145 **Bob.** It's just as likely as not, one of these days, though there's plenty of time for that, my dear. But however and whenever we part from one another, I am sure we shall none of us forget poor Tiny Tim—shall we?—or this first parting that was among us?

146 **All Children.** Never, Father, never!

147 **Bob.** And when we recollect how patient and mild he was, we shall not quarrel easily among ourselves, and forget poor Tiny Tim in doing it.

148 **All Children.** No, Father, never!

149 **Little Bob.** I am very happy, I am. I am. I am very happy.

150 [Bob *kisses his little son, as does* Mrs. Cratchit, *as do the other children. The family is set now in one sculptural embrace. The lighting fades to a gentle pool of light, tight on them.*]

151 **Scrooge.** Specter, something informs me that our parting moment is at hand. I know it, but I know not how I know it.

152 [Future *points to the other side of the stage. Lights out on* Cratchits. Future *moves slowing, gliding.* Scrooge *follows.* Future *points opposite.* Future *leads* Scrooge *to a wall and a tombstone. He points to the stone.*]

153 Am I that man those ghoulish parasites[7] so gloated over? [*Pauses*] Before I draw nearer to that stone to which you point, answer me one question. Are these the shadows of things that will be, or the shadows of things that MAY be, only?

154 [Future *points to the gravestone.* Marley *appears in light well U. He points to grave as well. Gravestone turns front and grows to ten feet high. Words upon it:* Ebenezer Scrooge: *Much smoke billows now from the grave. Choral music here.* Scrooge *stands looking up at gravestone.* Future *does not at all reply in mortals' words, but points once more to the gravestone. The stone undulates and glows. Music plays, beckoning* Scrooge. Scrooge *reeling in terror*]

155 Oh, no. Spirit! Oh, no, no!

156 [Future's *finger still pointing*]

7. **ghoulish parasites** (GOOL ish PAR uh syts) referring to the men and women who stole and divided Scrooge's goods after he died. Scrooge is saying that they are evil people who exploit others and give nothing in return.

COMPREHENSION CHECK

What does Bob want his family to remember about Tiny Tim?

A Christmas Carol: Scrooge and Marley, Act II **269**

157 Spirit! Hear me! I am not the man I was. I will not be the man I would have been but for this intercourse. Why show me this, if I am past all hope?

158 [Future *considers* Scrooge's logic. *His hand wavers.*]

159 Oh. Good Spirit, I see by your wavering hand that your good nature intercedes for me and pities me. Assure me that I yet may change these shadows that you have shown me by an **altered** life!

160 [Future's *hand trembles; pointing has stopped*.]

161 I will honor Christmas in my heart and try to keep it all the year. I will live in the Past, the Present, and the Future. The Spirits of all Three shall **strive** within me. I will not shut out the lessons that they teach. Oh, tell me that I may sponge away the writing that is upon this stone!

162 [Scrooge *makes a desperate stab at grabbing* Future's *hand. He holds firm for a moment, but* Future, *stronger than* Scrooge, *pulls away.* Scrooge *is on his knees, praying.*]

altered (AWL tuhrd) *adj.* changed

strive (STRYV) *v.* make a great effort; try very hard

163 Spirit, dear Spirit, I am praying before you. Give me a sign that all is possible. Give me a sign that all hope for me is not lost. Oh, Spirit, kind Spirit, I beseech thee: give me a sign . . .

164 [Future *deliquesces, slowly, gently. The* Phantom's *hood and robe drop gracefully to the ground in a small heap. Music in. There is nothing in them. They are mortal cloth. The* Spirit *is elsewhere.* Scrooge *has his sign.* Scrooge *is alone. Tableau. The light fades to black.*]

Scene 5

1 [*The end of it.* Marley, *spotlighted, opposite* Scrooge, *in his bed, spotlighted.* Marley *speaks to audience, directly.*]

2 **Marley.** [*He smiles at* Scrooge.] The firm of Scrooge and Marley is doubly blessed; two misers turned; one, alas, in Death, too late; but the other miser turned in Time's penultimate nick.[8] Look you on my friend, Ebenezer Scrooge . . .

3 **Scrooge.** [*Scrambling out of bed; reeling in delight*] I will live in the Past, in the Present, and in the Future! The Spirits of all Three shall strive within me!

4 **Marley.** [*He points and moves closer to* Scrooge's *bed.*] Yes, Ebenezer, the bedpost is your own. Believe it! Yes, Ebenezer, the room is your own. Believe it!

5 **Scrooge.** Oh, Jacob Marley! Wherever you are, Jacob, know ye that I praise you for this! I praise you . . . and heaven . . . and Christmastime! [*Kneels facing away from* Marley] I say it to you on my knees, old Jacob, on my knees! [*He touches his bed curtains.*] Not torn down. My bed curtains are not at all torn down! Rings and all, here they are! They are here: I am here: the shadows of things that would have been, may now be **dispelled**. They will be, Jacob! I know they will be!

6 [*He chooses clothing for the day. He tries different pieces of clothing and settles, perhaps, on a dress suit, plus a cape of the bed clothing: something of color.*]

7 I am light as a feather, I am happy as an angel. I am as merry as a schoolboy. [*Yells out window and then out to audience*] Merry Christmas to everybody! Merry Christmas to everybody! A Happy New Year to all the world! Hallo here! Whoop! Whoop! Hallo! Hallo! I don't know what day of the month it is! I don't care! I don't know anything! I'm quite a baby! I don't care! I don't care a fig! I'd much rather be a baby than be an old wreck like me or Marley! (Sorry, Jacob. wherever ye be!) Hallo! Hallo there!

8. **in Time's penultimate nick** just at the last moment.

dispelled (dihs PEHLD) *v.* driven away; scattered

COMPREHENSION CHECK

Whom does Scrooge thank for giving him a chance to change his ways?

CLOSE READ

ANNOTATE In paragraphs 12–22, mark words that show Scrooge's attitude and behavior toward Adam.

QUESTION How does the interaction between Scrooge and Adam reveal a transformation in Scrooge's character?

9. **poulterer's** (POHL tuhr uhrz) *n.* British term for a person or a store that sells poultry.

earnest (UR nihst) *n.* serious mental state.

8 [*Church bells chime in Christmas Day. A small boy, named* Adam, *is seen now* D.R., *as a light fades up on him.*] Hey, you boy! What's today? What day of the year is it?

9 **Adam.** Today, sir? Why, it's Christmas Day!

10 **Scrooge.** It's Christmas Day, is it? Whoop! Well, I haven't missed it after all, have I? The Spirits did all they did in one night. They can do anything they like, right? Of course they can! Of course they can!

11 **Adam.** Excuse me, sir?

12 **Scrooge.** Huh? Oh, yes, of course. What's your name, lad?

13 [Scrooge *and* Adam *will play their scene from their own spotlights.*]

14 **Adam.** Adam, sir.

15 **Scrooge.** Adam! What a fine, strong name! Do you know the poulterer's[9] in the next street but one, at the corner?

16 **Adam.** I certainly should hope I know him, sir!

17 **Scrooge.** A remarkable boy! An intelligent boy! Do you know whether the poulterer's have sold the prize turkey that was hanging up there? I don't mean the little prize turkey, Adam. I mean the big one!

18 **Adam.** What, do you mean the one they've got that's as big as me?

19 **Scrooge.** I mean, the turkey the size of Adam: that's the bird!

20 **Adam.** It's hanging there now, sir.

21 **Scrooge.** It is? Go and buy it! No, no. I am absolutely in **earnest**. Go and buy it and tell 'em to bring it here, so that I may give them the directions to where I want it delivered, as a gift. Come back here with the man, Adam, and I'll give you a shilling. Come back here with him in less than five minutes, and I'll give you half-a-crown!

22 **Adam.** Oh, my sir! Don't let my brother in on this.

23 [Adam *runs offstage.* Marley *smiles.*]

24 **Marley.** An act of kindness is like the first green grape of summer: one leads to another and another and another. It would take a queer man indeed to not follow an act of kindness with an act of kindness. One simply whets the tongue for more . . . the taste of kindness is too too sweet. Gifts—goods—are lifeless. But the gift of goodness one feels in the giving is full of life. It . . . is . . . a . . . wonder.

25 [*Pauses; moves closer to* Scrooge, *who is totally occupied with his dressing and arranging of his room and his day. He is making lists,* etc. Marley *reaches out to* Scrooge.]

26 **Adam.** [*Calling, off*] I'm here! I'm here!

27 [Adam *runs on with a man, who carries an enormous turkey.*]

28 Here I am, sir. Three minutes flat! A world record! I've got the poultryman and he's got the poultry! [*He pants, out of breath.*] I have earned my prize, sir, if I live . . .

29 [*He holds his heart, playacting.* Scrooge *goes to him and embraces him.*]

30 **Scrooge.** You are truly a champion, Adam . . .

31 **Man.** Here's the bird you ordered, sir . . .

32 **Scrooge.** Oh, my, MY!!! Look at the size of that turkey, will you! He never could have stood upon his legs, that bird! He would have snapped them off in a minute, like sticks of sealingwax! Why you'll never be able to carry that bird to Camden-Town, I'll give you money for a cab . . .

COMPREHENSION CHECK

What type of gift does Marley say is "full of life"?

A Christmas Carol: Scrooge and Marley, Act II 273

33 **Man.** Camden-Town's where it's goin', sir?

34 **Scrooge.** Oh, I didn't tell you? Yes, I've written the precise address down just here on this . . . [*Hands paper to him*] Bob Cratchit's house. Now he's not to know who sends him this. Do you understand me? Not a word . . . [*Handing out money and chuckling*]

35 **Man.** I understand, sir, not a word.

36 **Scrooge.** Good. There you go then . . . this is for the turkey . . . [*Chuckle*] . . . and this is for the taxi. [*Chuckle*] . . . and this is for your world-record run, Adam . . .

37 **Adam.** But I don't have change for that, sir.

38 **Scrooge.** Then keep it, my lad. It's Christmas!

39 **Adam.** [*He kisses* Scrooge's *cheek, quickly.*] Thank you, sir. Merry, Merry Christmas! [*He runs off.*]

40 **Man.** And you've given me a bit overmuch here, too, sir . . .

41 **Scrooge.** Of course I have, sir. It's Christmas!

42 **Man.** Oh, well, thanking you, sir. I'll have this bird to Mr. Cratchit and his family in no time, sir. Don't you worry none about that. Merry Christmas to you, sir, and a very happy New Year, too . . .

43 [*The man exits.* Scrooge *walks in a large circle about the stage, which is now gently lit. A chorus sings Christmas music far in the distance. Bells chime as well, far in the distance. A gentlewoman enters and passes.* Scrooge *is on the streets now.*]

44 **Scrooge.** Merry Christmas, madam . . .

45 **Woman.** Merry Christmas, sir . . .

46 [*The portly businessman from the first act enters.*]

47 **Scrooge.** Merry Christmas, sir.

48 **Portly Man.** Merry Christmas, sir.

49 **Scrooge.** Oh, you! My dear sir! How do you do? I do hope that you succeeded yesterday! It was very kind of you. A Merry Christmas.

50 **Portly Man.** Mr. Scrooge?

51 **Scrooge.** Yes, Scrooge is my name though I'm afraid you may not find it very pleasant. Allow me to ask your pardon. And will you have the goodness to—[*He whispers into the man's ear.*]

CLOSE READ

ANNOTATE In paragraphs 49–56, mark words and phrases that indicate the Portly Man's reaction to Scrooge.

QUESTION What does this reaction show about Scrooge's character at this point in the play?

52 **Portly Man.** Lord bless me! My dear Mr. Scrooge, are you *serious!?!*

53 **Scrooge.** If you please. Not a farthing[10] less. A great many back payments are included in it, I assure you. Will you do me that favor?

54 **Portly Man.** My dear sir, I don't know what to say to such munifi—

55 **Scrooge.** [*Cutting him off*] Don't say anything, please. Come and see me. Will you?

56 **Portly Man.** I will! I will! Oh I will, Mr. Scrooge! It will be my pleasure!

57 **Scrooge.** Thank'ee, I am much obliged to you. I thank you fifty times. Bless you!

58 [Portly Man *passes offstage, perhaps by moving backwards.* Scrooge *now comes to the room of his* Nephew *and* Niece. *He stops at the door, begins to knock on it, loses his courage, tries again, loses his courage again, tries again, fails again, and then backs off and runs at the door, causing a tremendous bump against it. The* Nephew *and* Niece *are startled.* Scrooge, *poking head into room*]

59 Fred!

60 **Nephew.** Why, bless my soul! Who's that?

61 **Nephew and Niece.** [*Together*] How now? Who goes?

62 **Scrooge.** It's I. Your Uncle Scrooge.

63 **Niece.** Dear heart alive!

64 **Scrooge.** I have come to dinner. May I come in, Fred?

65 **Nephew.** *May you come in???!!!* With such pleasure for me you may, Uncle!!! What a treat!

66 **Niece.** What a treat, Uncle Scrooge! Come in, come in!

67 [*They embrace a shocked and delighted* Scrooge: Fred *calls into the other room.*]

68 **Nephew.** Come in here, everybody, and meet my Uncle Scrooge! He's come for our Christmas party!

69 [*Music in. Lighting here indicates that day has gone to night and gone to day again. It is early, early morning.* Scrooge *walks alone from the party, exhausted, to his offices, opposite side of the stage. He opens his offices. The offices are as they were at the start of the play.* Scrooge *seats himself with his door wide open so he can see into the tank, as he awaits* Cratchit, *who enters, head down, full of guilt.* Cratchit, *starts writing almost before he sits.*]

10. **farthing** (FAHR thihng) *n.* small British coin.

70 **Scrooge.** What do you mean by coming in here at this time of day, a full eighteen minutes late, Mr. Cratchit? Hallo, sir? Do you hear me?

71 **Bob.** I am very sorry, sir. I *am* behind my time.

72 **Scrooge.** You are? Yes, I certainly think you are. Step this way, sir, if you please . . .

73 **Bob.** It's only but once a year, sir . . . It shall not be repeated. I was making rather merry yesterday and into the night . . .

74 **Scrooge.** Now, I'll tell you what, Cratchit. I am not going to stand this sort of thing any longer. And therefore . . .

75 [*He stands and pokes his finger into* Bob's *chest.*]

76 I am . . . about . . . to . . . raise . . . your salary.

77 **Bob.** Oh, no, sir. I . . . [*Realizes*] what did you say, sir?

78 **Scrooge.** A Merry Christmas, Bob . . . [*He claps* Bob's *back.*] A merrier Christmas, Bob, my good fellow! than I have given you for many a year. I'll raise your salary and endeavor to assist your struggling family and we will discuss your affairs this very afternoon over a bowl of smoking bishop.[11] Bob! Make up the fires and buy another coal scuttle before you dot another i, Bob. It's too cold in this place! We need warmth and cheer, Bob Cratchit! Do you hear me? DO . . . YOU . . . HEAR . . . ME?

79 [Bob Cratchit *stands, smiles at* Scrooge: Bob Cratchit *faints. Blackout. As the main lights black out, a spotlight appears on* Scrooge: C. *Another on* Marley: *He talks directly to the audience.*]

80 **Marley.** Scrooge was better than his word. He did it all and **infinitely** more; and to Tiny Tim, who did NOT die, he was a second father. He became as good a friend, as good a master, as good a man, as the good old city knew, or any other good old city, town, or borough in the good old world. And it was always said of him that he knew how to keep Christmas well, if any man alive possessed the knowledge. [*Pauses*] May that be truly said of us, and all of us. And so, as Tiny Tim observed . . .

81 **Tiny Tim.** [*Atop* Scrooge's *shoulder*] God Bless Us, Every One . . .

82 [*Lights up on chorus, singing final Christmas Song.* Scrooge *and* Marley *and all spirits and other characters of the play join in. When the song is over, the lights fade to black.*]

---

11. **smoking bishop** type of mulled wine or punch that was popular in Victorian England at Christmas time.

infinitely (IHN fuh niht lee) *adv.* enormously; remarkably

COMPREHENSION CHECK

What causes Bob to faint in this scene?

BUILD INSIGHT

First Thoughts

Choose one of the following items to answer.

- Is it fair that Scrooge gets a chance to live a happy life? Does he deserve to be forgiven for his past actions and attitudes? Explain your response.
- Consider which spirit makes the greatest impact on Scrooge. Do you think we learn more from examining the past or contemplating the future?

Summary

Write a short summary of two scenes in Act II. Remember to include only the main ideas and to keep your summary free of personal opinions.

Analysis

1. **(a)** In Scene 3, what does Scrooge learn about the Cratchit family? **(b) Analyze** Why does Scrooge care about Tiny Tim's fate? **(c) Make Inferences** In what ways does this scene suggest that Scrooge is changing? Explain.

2. **(a)** In Scene 4, what happens to Scrooge's belongings in Christmas future? **(b) Analyze Cause and Effect** How do Scrooge's observations of his possible future affect him? Explain, citing text evidence.

3. **(a) Make Inferences** Why do you think the Ghost of Christmas Future doesn't speak? **(b) Analyze** What effect does Future's silence have on Scrooge? How might it affect an audience? Explain.

4. **Take a Position** Do you think Bob Cratchit and Scrooge's nephew do the right thing by forgiving Scrooge immediately? Explain.

Exploring the Essential Question

Can people really change?

5. In your opinion, how realistic are the events of Act II, Scene 5? Consider Scrooge's behavior towards others as well as other people's reactions to him. Record your ideas in your Evidence Log.

STANDARDS
Reading Literature
- Cite several pieces of textual evidence to support analysis of what the text says explicitly as well as inferences drawn from the text.
- Provide an objective summary of the text.

A Christmas Carol: Scrooge and Marley, Act II **277**

ANALYZE AND INTERPRET

A CHRISTMAS CAROL: SCROOGE AND MARLEY, ACT II

Close Read

1. The model passage and annotation show how one reader analyzed part of Scene 1, paragraph 18. Find another detail in the passage to annotate. Then, write your own question and conclusion.

CLOSE-READ MODEL

[*Present is wearing a simple green robe.... Suddenly, there is a mighty roar of flame in the fireplace and now the hearth burns with a lavish, warming fire.* There is an ancient scabbard girdling the Ghost's middle, but without sword. The sheath is gone to rust.]

ANNOTATE: The Ghost of Christmas Present wears a rusty scabbard, and there is no sword in it.

QUESTION: What idea do these details suggest?

CONCLUDE: The empty scabbard symbolizes the abandoning of weapons. The Ghost of Christmas Present represents peace.

MY QUESTION:

MY CONCLUSION:

2. For more practice, answer the Close-Read questions in the selection.

3. Choose a section of the drama that you found especially meaningful. Mark important details. Then, jot down questions and write your conclusions in the open space next to the text.

Inquiry and Research

Research and Extend This drama is based on *A Christmas Carol* by Charles Dickens. When Dickens was twelve, his father was jailed for debt, and young Dickens was forced to leave school and work at a factory. Such circumstances were not uncommon in Victorian England, and they gave Dickens great sympathy for people who had experiences similar to his own.

Conduct research to find out how the life and times of Dickens shaped the stories he wrote. Gather relevant information from at least two credible online sources. Share your findings with your classmates.

STANDARDS

Reading Literature
- Analyze how particular elements of a story or drama interact.
- Analyze how a drama's or poem's form or structure contributes to its meaning.

Writing
Gather relevant information from multiple print and digital sources, using search terms effectively.

278 UNIT 3 • TRANSFORMATIONS

Essential Question: Can people really change?

Stage Directions and Character Development

The written text of a play is called a **script**. The structure of a script consists of two main parts: dialogue and stage directions. **Stage directions** are the playwright's instructions to the director and actors to guide them in interpreting the script and staging the performance for an audience. These directions affect the meaning conveyed in the play.

TIP: If you are reading a script instead of watching a play's performance, you get certain information only from stage directions. Stage directions are usually printed in italics and set off by brackets or parentheses.

| INFORMATION GIVEN IN STAGE DIRECTIONS ||
STORY ELEMENT	TYPES OF DETAILS
character development, or the personalities of the characters	• characters' feelings and thoughts • how actors should move or speak in order to portray characters accurately
setting, or the time and place of the action	• scenery • music • lighting • sound • sets • costumes

PRACTICE Complete the activity and answer the questions.

1. **Analyze** Reread the paragraphs indicated in the chart. Then, analyze how each example of stage directions helps develop the characters and scenes.

EXAMPLE OF STAGE DIRECTIONS	DEVELOPMENT OF CHARACTERS / SCENE
[*Lights and thunder ... Present calls to Scrooge.*] (Scene 1, paragraph 14)	
[*Scrooge backs into ... the bed; weeping.*] (Scene 4, paragraph 115)	
[*Hands paper to ... money and chuckling*] (Scene 5, paragraph 34)	

2. **(a) Distinguish** Choose a different example of stage directions from Act II that you think contributes strongly to a scene. Mark it in the text.
   (b) Interpret Explain your choice, noting how the stage directions affect the scene's meaning.

A Christmas Carol: Scrooge and Marley, Act II

STUDY LANGUAGE AND CRAFT

A CHRISTMAS CAROL: SCROOGE AND MARLEY, ACT II

Concept Vocabulary

Why These Words? The vocabulary words relate to Scrooge's transforming character and personality. For example, after the Spirits' visits, he is an *altered* man who is *infinitely* more pleasant and willing to help other people.

| parallel | strive | earnest |
| altered | dispelled | infinitely |

PRACTICE Answer the questions.

1. How do the vocabulary words sharpen your understanding of the ways in which Scrooge changes?

2. What other words in the selection describe Scrooge's changing personality?

3. Use each vocabulary word in a sentence that shows your understanding of the word's meaning.

4. Challenge yourself to replace the vocabulary word in each sentence you wrote with a **synonym,** or word that has a similar meaning. Explain how the replacement word affects the meaning of each sentence.

Word Study

Greek Prefix: *para-* The Greek prefix *para-* means "beside." In the word *parallel*, the prefix is combined with a Greek root that means "of another." So, *parallel* means "beside another." Lines that are *parallel* extend in the same direction beside one another and are always the same distance apart.

PRACTICE Complete the activities.

1. Use a dictionary to find another word that contains the Greek prefix *para-*. Jot down the definition of the word you found.

2. Explain how the prefix *para-* contributes to the word's meaning.

WORD WALL

Note words in the text that are related to the idea of transformations. Add them to your Word Wall.

STANDARDS

Reading Literature
• Determine a theme or central idea of a text and analyze its development over the course of the text.
• Analyze how particular elements of a story or drama interact.

Language
• Use common, grade-appropriate Greek or Latin affixes and roots as clues to the meaning of a word.
• Use the relationship between particular words to better understand each of the words.
• Acquire and use accurately grade-appropriate general academic and domain-specific words and phrases.

280 UNIT 3 • TRANSFORMATIONS

Essential Question: Can people really change?

Multiple Themes

A **theme** is a message or insight expressed in a literary work. Many works express more than one theme. Usually, writers do not state themes directly. Instead, they develop thematic meaning over the course of a text through the following types of details:

- **characters:** characters' actions, statements, and emotions; the ways in which characters grow or change; what characters learn

- **conflicts:** the problems characters face and the ways in which they resolve them

- **settings:** important or dramatic places or time periods

Readers analyze how these details interact to infer the work's themes. While readers' interpretations may vary, any valid statement of a theme must reflect all the work's important details.

> **TIP:** A theme is not a statement about specific characters or events. It is a message or insight that applies to life in general.
> **Not a theme:** The main character learns to overcome fear of moving away.
> **Possible theme:** By overcoming fears, it's possible to see the world in new ways.
> **Possible theme:** Moving away can deepen family connections.

PRACTICE Consider both Act I and Act II of the drama as you answer the questions and complete the activity.

1. **Interpret** Consider this possible theme for the drama: *Anyone can change if they decide to do so*. Cite at least three details from the play that help develop this theme. Explain your choices.

2. **Interpret** Consider this possible theme for the drama: *We can't change the past, but we can learn from it*. Cite at least three details from the play that help develop this theme. Explain your choices.

3. **(a) Analyze** Use the chart to gather details about Scrooge's relationship with his nephew and to analyze how it changes over the course of the play. **(b) Make Inferences** What theme about compassion and forgiveness is suggested by these details?

SCROOGE AND NEPHEW	DETAILS AND THEME
Act I, Scene 2	
Act II, Scene 4	
Act II, Scene 5	

4. **Draw Conclusions** What theme about happiness does the play express? Explain, citing specific details to support your thinking.

A Christmas Carol: Scrooge and Marley, Act II **281**

SHARE IDEAS

A CHRISTMAS CAROL: SCROOGE AND MARLEY, ACT II

Writing

A **friendly letter** is an informal written message addressed to a specific person or group of people.

Assignment

Write a **friendly letter** to Scrooge in which you express your opinion about his transformation and the lessons readers can learn from his story. Share your thoughts in a personal but respectful way.

- Write the date in the top right corner of your letter, and begin with a greeting, such as "Dear Mr. Scrooge."
- In the body of your letter, discuss the two key events that you think contribute the most to Scrooge's transformation.
- Next, share your opinion about the life lessons you feel Scrooge teaches by example. Support your ideas with details from the text.
- End your letter with a polite closing, such as "Yours truly" or "Sincerely." Then, sign your name.

Use New Words
Refer to your Word Wall to use new vocabulary you have learned. Also, try to include one or more of these vocabulary words in your writing: *parallel, altered, strive, dispelled, earnest, infinitely*

Reflect on Your Writing

PRACTICE Think about the choices you made as you wrote. Also consider what you learned by writing. Share your experiences by responding to these questions.

1. Was it easy or difficult to write a letter to Scrooge? Explain.

2. Have your ideas about personal transformation changed after writing this letter? Why, or why not?

3. **Why These Words?** Review your letter. Which words did you specifically choose to create a friendly tone, and why?

STANDARDS
Writing
• Gather relevant information from multiple print and digital sources, using search terms effectively.
• Write routinely over extended time frames and shorter time frames for a range of discipline-specific tasks, purposes, and audiences.

Speaking and Listening
• Present claims and findings, emphasizing salient points in a focused, coherent manner with pertinent descriptions, facts, details, and examples.
• Include multimedia components and visual displays in presentations to clarify claims and findings and emphasize salient points.

Essential Question: Can people really change?

Speaking and Listening

Costume plans provide descriptions and images of the clothing that actors will wear on stage during a performance.

> **Assignment**
>
> With a partner, research the clothing that was worn in Victorian England. Then, create and present **costume plans** for two different characters from *A Christmas Carol: Scrooge and Marley*.

Conduct Research Work with your partner to review the play's characters and select two to focus on. Then, gather information and visuals to develop realistic costume plans for both characters. When researching online, use effective search terms, such as "winter clothes in Victorian England," to get the most useful results. Look for answers to these questions:

- What types of clothing would the characters have worn based on their social positions?
- What types of clothing were typically worn during the season?

Develop Your Costume Plans Use the information you've gathered to describe the clothing, including colors and fabrics. Include multimedia components, such as diagrams, digital images, or hand-drawn sketches, to illustrate your descriptions.

Present Your Costume Plans Share your costume plans with the class, emphasizing specific details about each one and displaying your visuals. Then, ask classmates for feedback about whether your costumes reflect what they imagined as they read the play.

> **USE NEW WORDS**
> **Academic Vocabulary**
> As you write your descriptions, consider using one or more of these words.
>
> - ingenious
> - omniscient
> - envision
> - lucid
> - sensation

PRESENTATION EVALUATION GUIDE

Rate each statement on a scale of 1 (not demonstrated) to 4 (fully demonstrated). Write your scores in the boxes.

- [ ] The costume plans accurately reflected both the characters and the time period.
- [ ] The speakers clearly explained the decisions behind each costume.
- [ ] The presentation was illustrated with pictures or sketches.

> **EVIDENCE LOG**
>
> Before moving on to a new selection, go to your Evidence Log and record any additional thoughts or observations you may have about *A Christmas Carol: Scrooge and Marley*, Act II.

PREPARE TO READ

A CHRISTMAS CAROL: SCROOGE AND MARLEY, ACTS I AND II

from **A CHRISTMAS CAROL**

COMPARE: DRAMA and FICTION
This excerpt from Charles Dickens's novella focuses on the Cratchit family dinner, a scene that also appears in the play you studied earlier. Pay attention to similarities and differences between the two versions of the same scene.

About the Author

Charles Dickens (1812–1870) was the author of many novels, novellas, short stories, articles, and letters. He is considered one of the best English writers of all time. In his stories, he created memorable characters and often expressed concern for children and the poor. His novels include *Oliver Twist*, *Nicholas Nickleby*, *David Copperfield*, *A Tale of Two Cities*, and *Great Expectations*.

Concept Vocabulary

Preview You will encounter the following words as you read the excerpt from *A Christmas Carol*. Before reading, note how familiar you are with each word. Using a scale of 1 (do not know it at all) to 4 (know it very well), indicate your knowledge of each word.

WORD	YOUR RATING
dreaded	
penitence	
grief	
rebuke	
trembling	
plaintive	

Reading Strategy: Make Connections

To deepen your understanding of a text, **make connections** to other texts you have read. As you read, ask yourself questions, such as *What does this remind me of?* and *How is this different from other texts with similar characters or situations?* To make connections, consider the following elements:

- ideas, themes, or messages in other texts
- characters, settings, and events in other texts
- the style and language of other texts

PRACTICE As you read the novella excerpt, use the open space next to the text to note connections you make to the drama as well as to ideas in other texts you have read.

STANDARDS
Reading Literature
By the end of the year, read and comprehend literature, including stories, dramas, and poems.

284 UNIT 3 • TRANSFORMATIONS

NOVELLA EXCERPT

from
A Christmas Carol
Charles Dickens

BACKGROUND
Charles Dickens wrote *A Christmas Carol* in six weeks in 1843. The novella has since inspired many stage, screen, and radio versions. It gave the term Scrooge to the English language and popularized the expression "Merry (instead of *Happy*) Christmas." It also highlighted the struggle against hunger and illness faced by poor children, represented by sweet but sickly Tiny Tim. In this excerpt, the Cratchit family enjoys Christmas dinner while Scrooge and the Ghost of Christmas Present look on.

1   At last the dinner was all done, the cloth was cleared, the hearth swept, and the fire made up. The compound in the jug being tasted, and considered perfect, apples and oranges were put upon the table, and a shovelful of chestnuts on the fire. Then all the Cratchit family drew round the hearth, in what Bob Cratchit called a circle, meaning half a one; and at Bob Cratchit's elbow stood the family display of glass. Two tumblers, and a custard-cup without a handle.

READ TO UNLOCK MEANING
1. First read the text for comprehension and enjoyment. Use the **Comprehension Check** question to support your first read.
2. Go back and respond to the Close-Read notes.
3. Identify other details in the text you find interesting. Ask your own questions and draw your own conclusions.

2   These held the hot stuff from the jug, however, as well as golden goblets would have done; and Bob served it out with beaming looks, while the chestnuts on the fire sputtered and cracked noisily. Then Bob proposed:

3   "A Merry Christmas to us all, my dears. God bless us!"

4   Which all the family re-echoed.

5   "God bless us every one!" said Tiny Tim, the last of all.

6   He sat very close to his father's side upon his little stool. Bob held his withered little hand in his, as if he loved the child, and wished to keep him by his side, and **dreaded** that he might be taken from him.

7   "Spirit," said Scrooge, with an interest he had never felt before, "tell me if Tiny Tim will live."

8   "I see a vacant seat," replied the Ghost, "in the poor chimney-corner, and a crutch without an owner, carefully preserved. If these shadows remain unaltered by the Future, the child will die."

9   "No, no," said Scrooge. "Oh, no, kind Spirit! Say he will be spared."

10 "If these shadows remain unaltered by the Future, none other of my race," returned the Ghost, "will find him here. What then? If he be like to die, he had better do it, and decrease the surplus population."

11 Scrooge hung his head to hear his own words quoted by the Spirit, and was overcome with **penitence** and **grief**.

12 "Man," said the Ghost, "if man you be in heart, not adamant,[1] forbear that wicked cant[2] until you have discovered What the surplus is, and Where it is. Will you decide what men shall live, what men shall die? It may be, that in the sight of Heaven, you are more worthless and less fit to live than millions like this poor man's child. Oh God! To hear the insect on the leaf pronouncing on the too much life among his hungry brothers in the dust!"

13 Scrooge bent before the Ghost's **rebuke**, and **trembling** cast his eyes upon the ground. But he raised them speedily, on hearing his own name.

14 "Mr. Scrooge!" said Bob; "I'll give you Mr. Scrooge, the Founder of the Feast!"

15 "The Founder of the Feast indeed!" cried Mrs. Cratchit, reddening. "I wish I had him here. I'd give him a piece of my mind to feast upon, and I hope he'd have a good appetite for it."

16 "My dear," said Bob, "the children! Christmas Day."

17 "It should be Christmas Day, I am sure," said she, "on which one drinks the health of such an odious, stingy, hard, unfeeling man as Mr. Scrooge. You know he is, Robert! Nobody knows it better than you do, poor fellow!"

---

1. **adamant** (AD uh mant) *n.* legendary stone believed to be unbreakable.
2. **forbear that wicked cant** hold back from such morally bad, insincere talk.

---

dreaded (DREHD uhd) *v.* felt great fear or extreme reluctance

penitence (PEHN ih tuhns) *n.* sorrow for one's sins or faults

grief (GREEF) *n.* deep sadness

CLOSE READ

ANNOTATE Mark the words and phrases in paragraph 12 that relate to judgments on Scrooge's worth or value as a person.

QUESTION How do these words challenge Scrooge's sense of his own importance?

rebuke (ree BYOOK) *n.* severe or stern criticism; scolding

trembling (TREHM blihng) *v.* shaking uncontrollably

▲ This illustration shows Scrooge in spirit form looking on as the Cratchit family enjoys their holiday dinner. The inset image is of the author, Charles Dickens.

18   "My dear," was Bob's mild answer, "Christmas Day."

19   "I'll drink his health for your sake and the Day's," said Mrs. Cratchit, "not for his. Long life to him! A merry Christmas and a happy new year! He'll be very merry and very happy, I have no doubt!"

20   The children drank the toast after her. It was the first of their proceedings which had no heartiness. Tiny Tim drank it last of all, but he didn't care twopence[3] for it. Scrooge was the Ogre of the family. The mention of his name cast a dark shadow on the party, which was not dispelled for full five minutes.

21   After it had passed away, they were ten times merrier than before, from the mere relief of Scrooge the Baleful being done with. Bob Cratchit told them how he had a situation in his eye for Master Peter, which would bring in, if obtained, full five-and-sixpence weekly. The two young Cratchits laughed tremendously at the idea of Peter's being a man of business;

---

3. **twopence** *n.* British sum of money equal to two pennies.

COMPREHENSION CHECK

What is Mrs. Cratchit's attitude toward Scrooge?

from A Christmas Carol **287**

and Peter himself looked thoughtfully at the fire from between his collars, as if he were deliberating what particular investments he should favor when he came into the receipt of that bewildering income. Martha, who was a poor apprentice at a milliner's,[4] then told them what kind of work she had to do, and how many hours she worked at a stretch, and how she meant to lie abed tomorrow morning for a good long rest; tomorrow being a holiday she passed at home. Also how she had seen a countess and a lord some days before, and how the lord "was much about as tall as Peter" at which Peter pulled up his collars so high that you couldn't have seen his head if you had been there. All this time the chestnuts and the jug went round and round; and by-and-by they had a song, about a lost child traveling in the snow, from Tiny Tim, who had a **plaintive** little voice, and sang it very well indeed.

22 There was nothing of high mark in this. They were not a handsome family; they were not well dressed; their shoes were far from being waterproof; their clothes were scanty; and Peter might have known, and very likely did, the inside of a pawnbroker's. But, they were happy, grateful, pleased with one another, and contented with the time; and when they faded, and looked happier yet in the bright sprinklings of the Spirit's torch at parting, Scrooge had his eye upon them, and especially on Tiny Tim, until the last.

---

4. **milliner's** *n.* a milliner is a person who makes hats for women.

plaintive (PLAYN tihv) *adj.* sounding sad and mournful

CLOSE READ

ANNOTATE Mark words and phrases in paragraph 22 that relate to the Cratchit family's outward appearance. Mark other words and phrases that relate to their emotions and attitudes.

QUESTION What does the contrast between these sets of words show about this family?

MEDIA CONNECTION

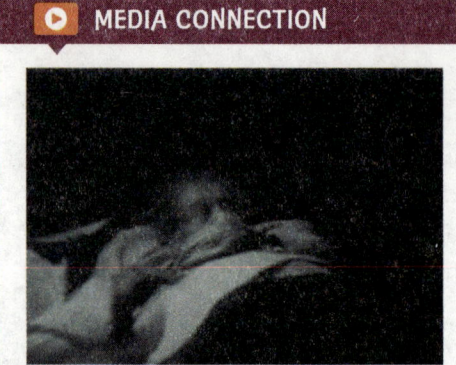

from **Scrooge**

DISCUSS Does the feature-film clip reflect what you imagined the characters and setting to be like when you were reading the text? Why or why not?

Write your response before sharing your ideas.

BUILD INSIGHT

First Thoughts

Select one of the following questions to answer.
- Whom do you agree with about toasting Scrooge—Mr. Cratchit or Mrs. Cratchit? State your choice and explain why.
- Charles Dickens chose supernatural spirits, rather than real people, to inspire Scrooge's transformation. Do you think this was an effective choice? Explain.

Summary

Write a short summary of the excerpt to confirm your comprehension. Include only the central ideas and keep your summary objective.

Analysis

1. **(a) Connect** In paragraph 1, the narrator mentions the items the family uses to hold drinks. What point does the narrator make about these items in paragraph 2? **(b) Interpret** What theme, or message, about the importance of wealth do these details support? Explain.

2. **Interpret** In paragraph 10, the Ghost repeats words Scrooge said earlier in the story. Why do these words affect Scrooge so deeply now? What has changed for him?

3. **(a) Analyze Cause and Effect** How does the mention of Scrooge affect the family? **(b) Deduce** Given this reaction, what kinds of conversations do you think the family has had about Scrooge in the past? Explain.

4. **Contrast** In the last paragraph, the narrator describes the Cratchit family. Why do you think the author presents this description? What point about Scrooge's life does this passage make by contrast?

Exploring the Essential Question

Can people really change?

5. Do you think people can really transform overnight like Scrooge did? Is it possible to change your life so quickly and drastically? Explain your thinking in your Evidence Log.

STANDARDS
Reading Literature
- Cite several pieces of textual evidence to support analysis of what the text says explicitly as well as inferences drawn from the text.
- Provide an objective summary of the text.
- Compare and contrast a written story, drama, or poem to its audio, filmed, staged, or multimedia version.

from A Christmas Carol

ANALYZE AND INTERPRET

Close Read

from A CHRISTMAS CAROL

1. The model passage and annotation show how one reader analyzed paragraphs 5–6 of the novella excerpt. Find another detail in the passage to annotate. Then, write your own question and conclusion.

CLOSE-READ MODEL

"God bless us every one!" said Tiny Tim, the last of all.

He sat very close to his father's side upon his little stool. Bob held his ==withered== little hand in his, as if he ==loved== the child, and ==wished== to keep him by his side, and ==dreaded== that he might be taken from him.

ANNOTATE: These are powerful words that show strong contrasts.

QUESTION: Why might the author have chosen to use these powerful, contrasting words in a single sentence?

CONCLUDE: These words show that Bob is experiencing many strong, complex feelings at the same time.

MY QUESTION:

MY CONCLUSION:

1. For more practice, answer the Close-Read questions in the selection.
2. Choose a section of the novella excerpt you found especially meaningful. Mark important details. Then, jot down questions and write your conclusions in the open space next to the text.

Inquiry and Research

Research and Extend How historically accurate is the Cratchit family dinner scene? Conduct short online research to answer this question. Be sure to use effective search terms that will give you relevant results. For instance, you could enter "Christmas dinner in Victorian England" into a search engine. Consult several reliable sources and take notes.

Share your findings with a partner. Discuss how the fictional portrayal of the holiday meal compares with historical accounts. Does Dickens stay true to history or alter it in some way?

STANDARDS

Reading Literature
• Analyze how an author develops and contrasts the points of view of different characters or narrators in a text.
• Compare and contrast a fictional portrayal of a time, place, or character and a historical account of the same period as a means of understanding how authors of fiction use or alter history.

Writing
• Conduct short research projects to answer a question, drawing on several sources and generating additional related, focused questions for further research and investigation.
• Gather relevant information from multiple print and digital sources, using search terms effectively.

290 UNIT 3 • TRANSFORMATIONS

Essential Question: Can people really change?

Narrative Point of View: Omniscient Narrator

Narrative point of view is a key ingredient in all fiction. A **narrator** is the voice that tells a story. The **narrative point of view** is the perspective from which a story is told. The excerpt from *A Christmas Carol* uses the **third-person omniscient point of view**, which has these qualities:

THIRD-PERSON OMNISCIENT POINT OF VIEW	
The narrator...	is an observer and not a character in the story.
	shows how *at least two* characters feel, think, and perceive the events. (Note: If the narrator shows the thoughts and feelings of only one character, the point of view is **third-person limited**.)
	has the ability to reveal the inner thoughts and feelings of all the characters but most often reveals the thoughts of just two or maybe three characters.
	uses third-person pronouns, such as *he, she*, and *they* to refer to all the characters.

TIP: If the narrator describes aspects of a character that any observer could see by looking, that doesn't reflect omniscience.

For example,

- **Not omniscient:** Maria sat in her chair, tapping her foot and looking anxious. Reg smiled gently at Maria.
- **Omniscient:** Marie sat in her chair, thinking *How will I survive this interview?* Reg looked at Marie and felt sorry for her.

PRACTICE Answer the questions.

1. **(a) Analyze** Which character's thoughts and feelings does the narrator share in paragraphs 1–19 of the excerpt? **(b) Contrast** How does this change in paragraph 20, showing the use of an omniscient narrator? Explain.

2. **Analyze** In paragraph 6, the narrator describes Bob Cratchit's gesture toward Tiny Tim. Does Dickens use third-person omniscient narration or third-person limited narration here? Explain your answer.

3. **Interpret** Reread paragraph 22. Could the excerpt have ended this way if the author had not used an omniscient narrator? Explain.

from A Christmas Carol **291**

STUDY LANGUAGE AND CRAFT

from A CHRISTMAS CAROL

Concept Vocabulary

Why These Words? The vocabulary words are all related to fear and guilt. For example, a person who *dreaded* auditioning for a role in a play might *rebuke* herself later for not trying out.

| dreaded | penitence | grief |
| rebuke | trembling | plaintive |

> **WORD WALL**
> Note words in the text that are related to the idea of transformations. Add them to your Word Wall.

PRACTICE Answer the question and complete the activity.

1. How do the vocabulary words help show the emotions Scrooge experiences and ways in which he changes?

2. Use the vocabulary words to complete the paragraph in a way that makes sense. Use each word only once.

When I was a kid, I liked TV shows about history, but my little brother _____ them. We would often argue about what to watch. Sometimes, he got so mad he'd start _____ a little. Later, my mom would give me a stern _____, saying how disappointed she was. I'd apologize in a _____ voice. I did feel _____ and _____ for my actions, but I still wanted to watch the shows I liked.

Word Study

Synonyms and Nuance: *dread* Words that have the same or similar meanings are **synonyms.** Synonyms often have subtle **nuances,** or slight differences, in their meanings. These nuances may relate to degrees of intensity. For example, one synonym may be more negative, neutral, or positive than another.

PRACTICE The vocabulary word *dreaded* is built on the base word *dread*. *Dread* can be a noun that means "great fear" or a verb that means "experience great fear."

1. Use a thesaurus to find three synonyms for the word *dread*.

2. Use a dictionary to verify the definition of each synonym you find. Explain the nuances in their meanings.

3. Identify which synonyms have the most intense or negative meanings and which are more neutral.

> **STANDARDS**
> **Language**
> • Demonstrate command of the conventions of standard English grammar and usage when writing.
> • Verify the preliminary determination of the meaning of a word or phrase.
> • Demonstrate understanding of figurative language, word relationships, and nuances in word meanings.
> • Use the relationship between particular words to better understand each of the words.

292 UNIT 3 • TRANSFORMATIONS

Essential Question: Can people really change?

Conjunctions

Words that join other words, phrases, or clauses together are called **conjunctions**. There are three types of conjunctions:

TYPE OF CONJUNCTION	EXAMPLES	SAMPLE SENTENCES
Coordinating Conjunctions: join words or groups of words of equal importance	and, or, but, nor, for, yet, so	• Scrooge <u>and</u> the Ghost of Christmas Present watched the Cratchits celebrate. • Bob Cratchit wanted to toast Scrooge, <u>so</u> the rest of the family agreed.
Subordinating Conjunctions: introduce a dependent clause in a complex sentence	after, although, because, since, unless, when, while, where	• Bob Cratchit poured the drinks <u>while</u> chestnuts roasted on the fire. • <u>After</u> the Cratchits toasted Scrooge, Tiny Tim sang a song.
Correlative Conjunctions: come in pairs and join two equal grammatical terms	both/and; either/or; neither/nor; not only/but also; whether/or	• <u>Neither</u> Scrooge <u>nor</u> the Ghost were visible to the Cratchit family. • Scrooge felt <u>both</u> sorrow <u>and</u> remorse as the Ghost talked of Tiny Tim's bleak future.

READ Identify the conjunctions used in these sentences. Label each conjunction as *coordinating, subordinating,* or *correlative.*

1. Mrs. Cratchit was reluctant to toast Scrooge because she thinks he is selfish.

2. The Cratchits were neither rich nor refined, but they were content.

3. Unless the future is altered, Tiny Tim will suffer a very sad fate.

WRITE/EDIT Write a paragraph about a holiday celebration. Then, edit your draft to use at least one coordinating conjunction, one subordinating conjunction, and one set of correlative conjunctions.

from A Christmas Carol **293**

TEST PRACTICE

DRAMA

A CHRISTMAS CAROL: SCROOGE AND MARLEY, ACTS I AND II

NOVELLA EXCERPT

from A CHRISTMAS CAROL

COMPARE: DRAMA and FICTION
Multiple Choice

These questions are based on the play *A Christmas Carol: Scrooge and Marley* and the excerpt from the novella *A Christmas Carol*. Choose the best answer to each question.

1. In both the play and the novella, what does the Ghost tell Scrooge about Tiny Tim's future?

   A Tiny Tim will survive and regain his health.

   B Unless the family's situation changes, Tiny Tim will die.

   C Tiny Tim's situation will remain the same no matter what.

   D Tiny Tim, who is currently well, will become sick.

2. Which statement is true of both the character of Jacob Marley in the play and the narrator in the novella?

   A In the play, Marley is a character, and in the novella he is the narrator.

   B Marley is not an important character in the play, but he is very important in the novella.

   C Both Marley and the narrator express opinions about the characters and action.

   D Neither Marley nor the narrator expresses an opinion about the characters and action.

3. Read Act II, Scene 3, paragraph 84 from the play and part of paragraph 22 from the novella excerpt. What idea is implied in the novella but stated more directly in the play?

Play

Scrooge. I am listening. [*The chorus sings full volume now, until . . . the song ends here.*] Spirit, it must be time for us to take our leave. I feel in my heart that it is . . . that I must think on that which I have seen here . . .

Novella

But, they were happy, grateful, pleased with one another, and contented with the time; and when they faded, and looked happier yet in the bright sprinklings of the Spirit's torch at parting, Scrooge had his eye upon them, and especially on Tiny Tim, until the last.

A Scrooge knows exactly what he will do to help the Cratchits.

B Scrooge feels powerless to change the Cratchits' circumstances.

C Scrooge will think deeply about the events he has just witnessed.

D Scrooge has not been affected by the events he has just seen.

STANDARDS
Writing
• Write arguments to support claims with clear reasons and relevant evidence.

• Apply grade 7 Reading standards to literature.

Essential Question: Can people really change?

Short Response

1. **Compare** One key feature of literary style during the Victorian era—when Dickens wrote—was to portray daily life in a realistic way. How is this style present in both versions of the story?

2. **Contrast** In both the play and the novella, Tiny Tim sings a song. How is that moment in the play different from the same moment in the novella? Why do think the playwright changed it?

3. (a) **Compare and Contrast** Reread Act II, Scene 3, paragraph 83 of the play and paragraph 22 of the novella excerpt. How did the playwright adapt the text from the novella to suit the purposes of a play? (b) **Make a Judgment** Which version do you think is more effective? Explain your choice.

Timed Writing

A **critical review** is a form of argumentative writing in which you analyze and evaluate a literary or other artistic work.

> **Assignment**
>
> Write a **critical review** in which you discuss how the play and the novella present the Cratchit family dinner scene. Then, take a stance on whether the play represents the novella well in this scene.

5-Minute Planner

1. Read the assignment carefully and completely.
2. Decide on your claim—the position you will take in your essay.
3. Decide which details from the texts you will use as evidence to support your claim.
4. Organize your ideas logically. Make sure to include clear reasons and relevant evidence. Keep these points in mind:
   - Explain how the dinner scene in the two works is similar and different.
   - Defend your position about whether the scene from the play accurately reflects the novella on which it is based.

EVIDENCE LOG

Before moving on to a new selection, go to your Evidence Log and record any additional thoughts or observations you may have about the drama *A Christmas Carol: Scrooge and Marley* and the excerpt from the novella *A Christmas Carol*.

PERFORMANCE TASK

Write a Short Story

Short stories are brief works of fiction. They may be realistic or even based on real people and events, but they are still works of imagination.

Assignment

Write a **short story** about a character who has a significant life-changing experience. Shape your story to answer this question:

Does your character *truly* change?

You may write a science-fiction story, a realistic story, or another type of story you like to read. Include the elements of a short story in your writing.

Use Academic Vocabulary Try to use one or more of the unit's academic vocabulary words in your short story: *ingenious, omniscient, envision, lucid, sensation.*

> **WRITING CENTER**
> Visit the Writing Center to watch video tutorials and view annotated student models and rubrics.

ELEMENTS OF A SHORT STORY

Purpose: to entertain readers with a tale that expresses an insight

Characteristics

- an effective narrative point of view
- well-developed, interesting characters
- a clearly described setting
- a theme, or an insight about life
- precise word choices, descriptive details, and sensory language
- narrative elements and techniques, such as dialogue, pacing, and description
- transitions that indicate changes in time or location

Structure

- a plot that centers on a conflict and includes a logical, well-structured sequence of events
- a conclusion that follows from the events in the story

STANDARDS
Writing
• Write narratives to develop real or imagined experiences or events using effective technique, relevant descriptive details, and well-structured event sequences.
• Engage and orient the reader by establishing a context and point of view and introducing a narrator and/or characters.

Essential Question: Can people really change?

Take a Closer Look at the Assignment

1. What does the assignment ask me to do (in my own words)?

2. (a) Which type of story, or **genre**, interests me the most—realism, science fiction, adventure, fantasy, or another type of fiction? Why?

   (b) Which genre will best help me develop the experiences or events I want to portray?

3. What **narrative point of view** do I want to use?
   - ◯ Do I want a character to tell the story?
   - ◯ Do I want an outside narrator to tell the story?
   - ◯ Do I want the narrator to share the thoughts and feelings of everyone or just one character?

GENRE

Different **genres** create different possibilities.
- **Realistic Fiction:** true-to-life characters, settings, and events
- **Science Fiction:** futuristic settings; time travel; space travel; robots; aliens
- **Adventure:** physical challenges and danger; action-filled
- **Fantasy:** magical settings; characters with special powers; imaginary beings

NARRATIVE POINT OF VIEW

Point of view refers to the type of narrator you use.
- **First-Person:** narrator is a character in the story
- **Third-Person Limited:** narrator is not a character; shares the thoughts and feelings of one character only
- **Third-Person Omniscient:** narrator is not a character; shares the thoughts and feelings of all the characters

Write Your Short Story

Review the assignment and your notes, and then begin writing your short story. Keep these tips in mind:
- Keep in mind your narrative point of view and tell your story from that perspective.
- Include dialogue and description to help readers envision your characters.
- Use descriptive details and sensory language to develop settings and plot events.
- End in a way that reflects on the experiences in your story.

Writer's Handbook If you need help as you plan, draft, revise, and edit, refer to the Writer's Handbook pages that follow.

Performance Task: Write a Short Story **297**

WRITER'S HANDBOOK | **SHORT STORY**

Planning and Prewriting

Before you start to draft, generate first thoughts for a story you truly want to tell. For example, consider a place you've visited that might be a good story setting or an experience you've had that suggests an interesting conflict you could turn into fiction.

Discover Your Thinking: Freewrite!

Keep your first thoughts in mind as you write quickly and freely for at least three minutes without stopping. If it helps you, fill in this sentence to start your freewrite:

What if [character] _____ suddenly [action] _____?

- Don't worry about spelling and grammar. You'll fix mistakes later.

- When time is up, pause and read what you wrote. Mark ideas that seem strong or interesting.

- Repeat the process as many times as necessary to get all your ideas out. For each new round, start with the strong ideas you marked earlier.

WRITE Does your character *truly* change?

_____
_____
_____
_____
_____
_____
_____
_____
_____
_____
_____
_____
_____
_____

Using the Writer's Handbook

In this handbook you'll find strategies to support every stage of the writing process—from planning to publishing. As you write, check in with yourself:
- What's going well?
- What isn't going well?

Then, use the handbook items that will best help you craft a strong short story.

STANDARDS
Writing • Engage and orient the reader by establishing a context and point of view and introducing a narrator and/or characters; organize an event sequence that unfolds naturally and logically. • Use narrative techniques, such as dialogue, pacing, and description, to develop experiences, events, and/or characters.

Structure Ideas: Make a Plan

A **Collect Your Ideas** Reread your freewriting and pull out your most compelling ideas—the ones that fire up your imagination.

B **Focus on Character and Context** Write a sentence or two about the main character and their situation—the **setting** and circumstances of the character's life.

C **Organize Events** Consider the **conflict** your characters face and the **pacing** of events in your story.

1. What event sparks the conflict or brings it to characters' awareness?
2. How does the conflict develop? Does it build quickly to excite readers or slowly to build suspense?
3. At what point is the conflict most intense?
4. How does the conflict end?

SETTING

Consider the **setting,** or time and place, of your story's events:

- Where and when does the story take place?
- Does the setting have any special features?
- Will the setting affect the story's events? If so, how?

CONFLICT

Every plot is driven by a **conflict**, or problem, that characters deal with. Establish a definite conflict and show how it develops and resolves through a clear sequence of events.

PACING

Pacing refers to the speed at which your story unfolds. Scenes with lots of action and dialogue move quickly while descriptive passages move more slowly.

WRITER'S HANDBOOK **SHORT STORY**

Drafting

Apply your planning work to write a first draft. Use narrative techniques to develop your characters and show how they think, feel, and interact.

Read Like a Writer

Reread these paragraphs of the Mentor Text. Mark details that help develop the characters. One observation has been done for you.

MENTOR TEXT

from **The Golden Windows**

A woman came to the door, and looked kindly at the boy, and asked him what he wanted.

"I saw the golden windows from our hilltop," he said, "and I came to see them, but now they are only glass."

==The woman shook her head and laughed.==

=="We are poor farmers," she said, "and are not likely to have gold about our windows; but glass is better to see through."==

She bade the boy sit down on the broad stone step at the door, and brought him a cup of milk and a cake, and bade him rest; then she called her daughter, a child of his own age, and nodded kindly at the two, and went back to her work.

> The author uses dialogue and description to develop the character of the woman at the door.

> Mark descriptive details the author uses in this paragraph to capture the events of the scene.

> How does the author introduce yet another new character in the scene?

WRITE Write a scene for your short story. Use dialogue and description to develop characters' experiences.

_____
_____
_____
_____
_____
_____

DEVELOP IDEAS

Use narrative elements and techniques to bring your story to life.

- **dialogue** that gives each character a unique voice
- **sensory details** that appeal to the five senses
- **precise language** that conveys events clearly

STANDARDS

Writing • Use narrative techniques, such as dialogue, pacing, and description, to develop experiences, events, and/or characters. • Use a variety of transition words, phrases, and clauses to convey sequence and signal shifts from one time frame or setting to another. • Use precise words and phrases, relevant descriptive details, and sensory language to capture the action and convey experiences and events. **Language** Demonstrate command of the conventions of standard English grammar and usage when writing or speaking.

300 UNIT 3 • TRANSFORMATIONS

Coherence and Craft

In a **coherent** story, events unfold naturally and ideas connect logically. Use these strategies to enhance the coherence of your story.

- Don't overload one paragraph with too many actions. Instead, describe separate events in separate paragraphs.
- With rare exceptions (see TIP), use complete sentences that show logical sequences of ideas or actions. A **complete sentence** contains a subject and a verb and expresses a complete thought, using proper punctuation. Sentence fragments and run-ons, including comma splices, are two common errors that you should avoid.

TIPS In narrative writing, fragments cand run-ons can be used in dialogue or to develop style and tone. Be sure you can explain the purpose of any fragments or run-ons in your story.

TYPE OF SENTENCE ERROR	INCORRECT	CORRECT
Sentence Fragment: group of words that is missing a subject, a verb, or both but is punctuated like a complete sentence	*Enjoys hiking in the forest.* (missing subject) *Alice never at the lake.* (missing verb)	**Add missing subject:** *Rosita enjoys hiking in the forest.* **Add missing verb:** *Alice never swims at the lake.*
Run-on Sentence: two or more complete sentences that are incorrectly punctuated **Comma Splice:** a type of run-on; two or more complete sentences joined by a comma without a conjunction	*Sparrows stay all winter they don't fly south.* *Sparrows stay all winter, they don't fly south.*	**Make two sentences:** *Sparrows stay all winter. They don't fly south.* **Add a conjunction and a comma:** *Sparrows stay all winter, and they don't fly south.* **Add a semicolon:** *Sparrows stay all winter; they don't fly south.*

WRITE Write a paragraph of your story here. Use transitions to organize the sequence of events and to signal changes in timeframes or settings. Then, edit your paragraph to correct any fragments or run-ons.

USE TRANSITIONS

Include **transitional words, phrases, and clauses** to guide readers from one event, location, or time period to the next. Examples include *afterward, the next day,* and *After I got home.*

Writer's Handbook: Short Story

WRITER'S HANDBOOK | SHORT STORY

Revising

Now that you have a first draft, revise it to be sure the characters and other details come to life for your readers.

Read Like a Writer

Review the revisions made to the Mentor Text. Then, answer the questions in the white boxes.

MENTOR TEXT

from **The Golden Windows**

All day long the little boy had worked hard ==in field and barn and shed, for his people were poor farmers, and could not pay a workman== but ==at sunset== there came an hour that was all his own, for his father had given it to him. Then the boy would go up to the top of a hill and look across at another hill that rose some miles away. On this far hill stood a house with windows. ~~It~~ ==of clear gold and diamonds. They shone and blazed so that it== made the boy wink to look at them: but after a while the people in the house put up shutters, as it seemed, and then it looked like any common farmhouse. The boy supposed they did this because it was suppertime; and then we would go into the house and have his supper of bread and milk, and so to bed.

One day the boy's father called him and said: =="You have been a good boy, and have earned a holiday. Take this day for your own, but remember that God gave it, and try to learn some good thing."== ~~he could take the day as a holiday. He told him to remember it was a gift and to use the day wisely.~~

> Adding these precise words and details conveys more information about the boy's life and experiences.

> The author uses a transition to organize events and to signal a change in time. Mark at least three other transitions in these paragraphs.

> Why do you think the writer added these sensory details? How do they help the author convey meaning?

> Why do you think the writer replaced the explanation with dialogue? What impact does this change have on readers?

STANDARDS

Writing • Engage and orient the reader by establishing a context and point of view and introducing a narrator and/or characters; organize an event sequence that unfolds naturally and logically. • Use precise words and phrases, relevant descriptive details, and sensory language to capture the action and convey experiences and events. • Provide a conclusion that follows from and reflects on the narrated experiences or events. • Produce clear and coherent writing in which the development, organization, and style are appropriate to task, purpose, and audience.

Take a Closer Look at Your Draft

Use the Revision Checklist for Fiction to evaluate and strengthen your short story.

REVISION CHECKLIST FOR FICTION

EVALUATE	TAKE ACTION
Clarity	
☐ Is my point of view consistent?	**Check** that you maintained the same narrative point of view (first-person, third-person limited, or third-person omniscient) throughout your story. If not, **rewrite** paragraphs to be consistent.
☐ Does my story clearly convey a theme?	If your message is unclear, **say** it aloud. Then, **look for** points in the story where characters can express the insight or where details can suggest it.
Development	
☐ Are my characters believable and well-drawn?	**List** each character's traits. **Mark** descriptions, actions, and dialogue that reveal those traits. If there are too few, **add** details.
☐ Do characters' actions and dialogue fit their personalities?	**List** each character's traits. **Note** what each character does and says. If an action or line of dialogue does not reflect a character's personality, **delete** or **change** it.
Organization	
☐ Is the conflict clear?	**Mark** the points at which the conflict begins and gets most intense. If those two points are not clear, **add** details that better show the problem.
☐ Is the sequence of events logical?	**List** the story's events in time order. **Reorder** any that are confusing or out of place. **Insert** transitions to make the sequence clear.
☐ Is my pacing effective?	To make story events more fast-paced, **break up** long, descriptive sentences into shorter ones. Consider **replacing** descriptions of characters' words into actual dialogue.
☐ Does my conclusion wrap up the events of the story?	If the ending seems unfinished or leaves readers hanging, **add** details that follow naturally from the events and experiences in the story.
Style and Tone	
☐ Have I used vivid descriptive and sensory details to bring my story to life?	**Replace** vague words with precise ones that appeal to the five senses. Be sure to use appropriate parts of speech. For example, instead of saying, "The pie tasted great," use precise adjectives and say, "The pie tasted sweet, spicy, and buttery."

Editing

Don't let errors distract readers from your story. Reread your draft and fix mistakes to create a finished work.

Read Like a Writer

Look at how the writer of the Mentor Text edited her draft. Then, follow the directions in the white boxes.

MENTOR TEXT

from **The Golden Windows**

By and by he felt hungry; and he sat down by a brown brook that ran through the alder hegde by the roadside, and ate his bread and drank the clear water. An apple tree, which nestled beside wildflowers, were heavy with fruit. Then he scattered the crumbs for the birds, as his mother had taught him to do, and went on his way.

- Find and fix a spelling error.
- The writer added commas before and after an adjective clause.
- Find and fix an error in subject-verb agreement in a complex sentence.

Focus on Sentences

Grammar Minilesson

Subject-Verb Agreement in Complex Sentences A complex sentence may include an adjective clause in the middle of the independent clause. The adjective clause adds detail but can lead to problems with subject-verb agreement. Make sure the subject and verb of the independent clause agree.

EXAMPLE:

Incorrect: The <u>boy</u>, whose parents are poor farmers, <u>help</u> his family.

Correct: The <u>boy</u>, whose parents are poor farmers, <u>helps</u> his family.

PRACTICE Correct the subject-verb agreement in the following sentences. Then, check your own draft for correctness.

1. The window that faces the mountains begin to shine.
2. The farmers, who are working in the field, waves at the boy.
3. The food, which cooks for several hours, are delicious.
4. The families who come for the picnic is happy.

EDITING TIPS

1. Cover the adjective clause in the sentence.
2. Mark the subject of the independent clause.
3. If the verb in the independent clause does not agree with the subject, replace it with the correct form of the verb.

STANDARDS

Writing Use technology, including the Internet, to produce and publish writing. **Language** • Use a comma to separate coordinate adjectives.
• Use knowledge of language and its conventions when writing, speaking, reading, or listening. • Spell correctly.

Focus on Spelling and Punctuation

Spelling Patterns: Use *dge* or *ge* for Ending *j* Sound In English, any word that has an ending *j* sound is spelled with *dge* or *ge*. The *e* is silent.

hedge   bridge   carriage   knowledge

Check your story for words that have an ending *j* sound and make sure you have spelled them correctly.

Commas with Adjectives When you place two or more adjectives before a noun they describe, make sure to use commas correctly.

- **Use commas to separate coordinate adjectives.** Test whether adjectives are coordinate, or of equal rank, by switching their order or placing the word *and* between them. If the meaning stays the same, the adjectives are equal, and you need to include a comma.
  Incorrect: Bianca asked in a civil polite way.
  Correct: Bianca asked in a civil, polite way.

- **Don't use commas to separate adjectives that have a specific order.**
  Incorrect Order: There are large two birds in the yard.
  Correct Order: There are two large birds in the yard.

- **Don't use a comma after the last adjective in a series.**
  Incorrect: The boy walked the winding, narrow, and rocky, path.
  Correct: The boy walked the winding, narrow, and rocky path.

> **EDITING TIPS**
> - Read your work out loud to hear any missing or repeated words.
> - Set your story aside for a while before you proofread it. This will help you notice errors more efficiently.

> **PRACTICE** In the following sentences, fix any spelling or punctuation errors. Then, review your own draft for correctness.
>
> 1. The children live in a tiny remote villedge.
>
> 2. The trees are full of sweet crisp bright, apples.
>
> 3. The boy loved the imaje of four, golden, windows.

Publishing and Presenting

Integrate Media

Choose an option to publish your work.

OPTION 1 Create a **digital version** of your short story. Type your story and either insert free online images or scan and upload hand-drawn illustrations. Then, post your digital story to your class or school website.

OPTION 2 Record yourself giving a **dramatic reading** of your story. Add music or sound effects. Then, play the recording for your class or upload it to your school website.

Writer's Handbook: Short Story

PEER-GROUP LEARNING

Essential Question

Can people really change?

Is it truly possible to change—either over time or in an instant? If so, what can cause us to change? You will read selections that talk about changes, both big and small. Work in a small group to continue your exploration of transformations.

Peer-Group Learning Strategies

Throughout your life, in school, in your community, and in your career, you will continue to learn and work with others.

Look at these strategies and the actions you can take to practice them as you work in small groups. Add ideas of your own for each category. Use these strategies during Peer-Group Learning.

STRATEGY	MY ACTION PLAN
Prepare	• Organize your thinking so you can contribute to your group's discussion. • Get the facts. Mark key details—such as dates, names, places, and events—that you can refer to later. •
Participate fully	• Keep in mind that the more you participate in group activities, the more comfortable you will be doing so. • Share your thoughts and ask questions to stay fully engaged in discussions. •
Support others	• Encourage others to speak up, acknowledging that it might be hard for them to do so. • Come up with a way to show agreement, such as snapping fingers or gently tapping on the desk. •
Clarify	• Think about where else you might use or apply this information. • Check in with group members to make sure everyone understands. •

Contents

SHORT STORY

Thank You, M'am
Langston Hughes

A chance encounter has a powerful impact.

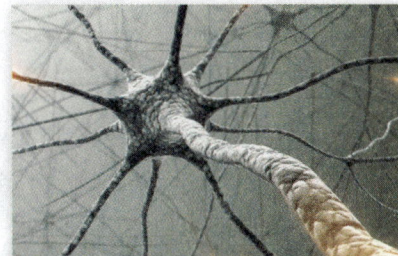

SCIENCE JOURNALISM

Learning Rewires the Brain
Alison Pearce Stevens

Some behaviors can enhance changes in brain cells and improve learning.

POETRY COLLECTION

Trying to Name What Doesn't Change
Naomi Shihab Nye

I Myself
Ángel González

Do not trust the eraser
Rosamond S. King

Change comes in many different forms.

HUMAN INTEREST STORY | MEDIA: VIDEO

Makeup Artist Mimi Choi's Mesmerizing Art-Inspired Beauty Looks • Mimi Choi Brings Fear to Life With Her Makeup Artistry
Ryma Chikhoune • True Calling Media

Are some changes only skin deep?

PERFORMANCE TASK

SPEAKING AND LISTENING

Deliver a Dramatic Adaptation

The Peer-Group readings feature different perspectives on transformations and what it means to truly change. After reading the selections, your group will plan and deliver a dramatic adaptation of one of the fictional texts in this unit.

Peer-Group Learning 307

PEER-GROUP LEARNING

Working as a Group

1. Discuss the Topic

In your group, discuss the following question:

What might cause a sudden change in someone's life?

As you take turns sharing your ideas, refer to evidence from texts you have read to dive deeper into the topic. After all group members have shared, discuss the personality traits that would be necessary to make a sudden and permanent change.

2. List Your Rules

As a group, decide on the rules that you will follow to ensure your discussion is friendly and collaborative. Two samples are provided. Add two more of your own. You may add or revise rules as you work through the readings and activities together.

- Be respectful, even when you don't agree.
- If you notice the discussion going off-topic, respond to the last relevant comment someone made to get the group back on track.

_____

_____

3. Apply the Rules

Practice working as a group. Share what you have learned about personal change. Make sure every person in the group has a role to play and gets a chance to contribute. Take notes, and be prepared to share with the class one new thing that you learned from another member of your group.

4. Name Your Group

Choose a name for your group that reflects the unit topic.

Our group's name: _____

Create a Communication Plan

Decide how you want to communicate with one another. For example, you might use online collaboration tools, email, or instant messaging.

Our group's plan: _____

STANDARDS

Speaking and Listening Follow rules for collegial discussions, track progress toward specific goals and deadlines, and define individual roles as needed. **Language** Acquire and use accurately grade-appropriate general academic and domain-specific words and phrases; gather vocabulary knowledge when considering a word or phrase important to comprehension or expression.

Essential Question: Can people really change?

Making a Schedule

First, find out the due dates for the peer-group activities. Then, preview the texts and activities with your group, and make a schedule for completing the tasks. Use the chart to help you track your group's progress.

SELECTION	ACTIVITIES	DUE DATE
Thank You, M'am		
Learning Rewires the Brain		
Trying to Name What Doesn't Change I Myself Do not trust the eraser		
Makeup Artist Mimi Choi's… • Mimi Choi Brings Fear…		

Building Your Vocabulary

Words are powerful. When you have a strong vocabulary, you can better understand what you read and hear, and you can write and speak more effectively.

Use these strategies to expand your vocabulary:

Use Academic Words You use academic language when you discuss a subject, explain a topic, or read a textbook in school. Examples of such language include *analyze, objective, demonstrate,* and *evidence*. Use these words in class to help broaden your vocabulary.

Use Domain-Specific Terms Some words are specialized and relate to particular subjects, such as mathematics, archaeology, or biology. Build your vocabulary by learning and using these words and the fields they pertain to.

Listen to Audio: Play the audio versions of the selections to hear words in context and how they are pronounced.

Use Resources: Regularly consult dictionaries, glossaries, and thesauri to build your word knowledge.

Peer-Group Learning 309

LEARN ABOUT GENRE: FICTION

THANK YOU, M'AM

Reading Short Stories

A **short story** is a brief work of fiction. **Realistic short stories** are works of imagination that feature true-to-life characters, events, and situations.

The selection you are about to read is a realistic short story.

REALISTIC SHORT STORIES

Author's Purpose
- to entertain and express insights

Characteristics
- settings that are realistic and may even be real places
- characters that seem like real people
- conflicts, or problems, that are like those people face in real life
- a theme about life or human nature
- natural-sounding dialogue
- a narrator who tells the story

Structure
- a plot, centered on a conflict; often, uses foreshadowing to generate curiosity or suspense

Take a Minute!

CHOOSE From the following list, choose at least three characters and events you might find in a work of realistic fiction and three you would not. Discuss your choices with a partner.

alien being	fairy godmother	twelve-year-old chess champion
loss of a loved one	circus performer	dragons flaming a village
objects that come to life	monsters	boy who discovers a crime

STANDARDS
Reading Literature
- Analyze how particular elements of a story or drama interact.
- By the end of the year, read and comprehend literature, including stories, dramas, and poems.

310 UNIT 3 • TRANSFORMATIONS

Essential Question: Can people really change?

Plot Elements

A **plot** is the related sequence of events in a story. All plots center on a **conflict**, or problem. The ways in which various characters address the conflict help drive the plot, which develops in stages.

STAGES OF PLOT	
Exposition	introduces the characters, setting, and situation
Rising Action	presents the incident that starts the conflict; may also include some events that explain characters' actions
Climax	point at which the conflict becomes most intense
Falling Action	shows events that follow the climax
Resolution	point at which the conflict ends

TIP: Analyzing how the elements of a story interact—such as how characters' actions affect plot events—can help you better understand a text.

The plots of well-crafted fiction seem logical and unified to readers, even if some events are surprising. One way writers can create this unified quality is by using **foreshadowing,** or clues that hint at later events. These clues also build readers' interest and may create a feeling of **suspense,** or anxious curiosity about the fates of the characters.

PRACTICE Work on your own to read the passage and answer the questions.

[1] It was a spring-green day as the boy walked home, but he was lost in visions of the girl and didn't notice. [2] That morning, his father had smiled bleakly when the boy asked if he could take the girl to prom: "Sorry, son. Can't afford it." [3] Troubled by dark thoughts, the boy nearly missed the wallet, fat with cash, lying on the sidewalk. [4] *It belongs to someone*, he thought, and paused. [5] But a vision of the girl in a golden gown filled his mind. [6] Ignoring the guilt hammering at his heart, he picked up the wallet....

1. What conflicts does the boy in this passage face?

2. Which sentences are part of the exposition?

3. Which details foreshadow events that might come later and may cause readers to feel curiosity or suspense? Explain.

PREPARE TO READ

Thank You, M'am

About the Author

Langston Hughes (1902–1967) published his first work just a year after his high school graduation. Though he wrote in many genres, Hughes is best known for his poetry. He was one of the main figures in the Harlem Renaissance, a creative movement among African Americans that took place during the 1920s in Harlem, an area in New York City.

Concept Vocabulary

As you read "Thank You, M'am," you will encounter these words. After reading, work with your group to identify what the words have in common.

| permit | release | contact |

Context Clues The **context** of a word consists of the other words and phrases that appear close to it in a text. Clues in the context can help you determine the meanings of unfamiliar words.

Cause-and-effect clues suggest a word's meaning by showing how one thing leads to, or causes, another.

EXAMPLE The medicine **alleviated** Kiara's flu symptoms, so she was able to return to school.

Analysis: Since Kiara was able to return to school after taking medicine, *alleviated* must mean "helped" or "relieved."

PRACTICE As you read "Thank You, M'am," study the context to determine the meanings of unfamiliar words. Mark your observations in the open space next to the text.

Reading Strategy: Establish a Purpose

When you are assigned texts, setting a purpose for reading can help you focus and learn more. It can also add to your enjoyment of reading. Set a purpose by thinking about the text and your goals—what do you want to gain from your reading experience?

- **Genre:** Consider the type of text. For example, your purposes for reading a story and an essay will probably be different.

- **Background:** You may already know something about a text. For example, you might be familiar with an author's work and want to read more, or you might want to read works set in a particular place. These kinds of elements can direct your purpose for reading.

PRACTICE Before you begin to read the story, establish a purpose. Write your purpose here.

STANDARDS
Language
- Determine or clarify the meaning of unknown and multiple-meaning words and phrases based on grade 7 reading and content, choosing flexibly from a range of strategies.
- Use context as a clue to the meaning of a word or phrase.

SHORT STORY

Thank You, M'am

Langston Hughes

BACKGROUND
In this story, published in 1958, Roger, the protagonist, really wants a pair of blue suede shoes. This particular fashion item became popular after Carl Perkins released his hit song "Blue Suede Shoes" in 1956. Elvis Presley also famously covered the song in the same year.

1   She was a large woman with a large purse that had everything in it but hammer and nails. It had a long strap, and she carried it slung across her shoulder. It was about eleven o'clock at night, dark, and she was walking alone, when a boy ran up behind her and tried to snatch her purse. The strap broke with the sudden single tug the boy gave it from behind. But the boy's weight and the weight of the purse combined caused him to lose his balance. Instead of taking off full blast as he had hoped, the boy fell on his back on the sidewalk and his legs flew up. The large woman simply turned around and kicked him right square in his blue-jeaned sitter. Then she reached down, picked the boy up by his shirt front, and shook him until his teeth rattled.

READ TO UNLOCK MEANING

1. First read the text for comprehension and enjoyment. Use the **Reading Strategy** and **Comprehension Check** questions to support your first read.
2. With your group, apply the vocabulary strategy to unlock word meanings.
3. Find other details in the text you find interesting. Ask your own questions and draw your own conclusions.

Mark context clues or indicate another strategy you used that helped you determine meaning.

permit (puhr MIHT) *v.*

MEANING:

Mark context clues or indicate another strategy you used that helped you determine meaning.

release (rih LEES) *v.*

MEANING:

Mark context clues or indicate another strategy you used that helped you determine meaning.

contact (KON takt) *n.*

MEANING:

2   After that the woman said, "Pick up my pocketbook, boy, and give it here."

3   She still held him tightly. But she bent down enough to **permit** him to stoop and pick up her purse. Then she said, "Now ain't you ashamed of yourself?"

4   Firmly gripped by his shirt front, the boy said, "Yes'm."

5   The woman said, "What did you want to do it for?"

6   The boy said, "I didn't aim to."

7   She said, "You a lie!"

8   By that time two or three people passed, stopped, turned to look, and some stood watching.

9   "If I turn you loose, will you run?" asked the woman.

10   "Yes'm," said the boy.

11   "Then I won't turn you loose," said the woman. She did not **release** him.

12   "Lady, I'm sorry," whispered the boy.

13   "Um-hum! Your face is dirty. I got a great mind to wash your face for you. Ain't you got nobody home to tell you to wash your face?"

14   "No'm," said the boy.

15   "Then it will get washed this evening," said the large woman starting up the street, dragging the frightened boy behind her.

16   He looked as if he were fourteen or fifteen, frail and willow-wild, in tennis shoes and blue jeans.

17   The woman said, "You ought to be my son. I would teach you right from wrong. Least I can do right now is to wash your face. Are you hungry?"

18   "No'm," said the being-dragged boy. "I just want you to turn me loose."

19   "Was I bothering *you* when I turned that corner?" asked the woman.

20   "No'm."

21   "But you put yourself in **contact** with *me*," said the woman. "If you think that that contact is not going to last awhile, you got another thought coming. When I get through with you, sir, you are going to remember Mrs. Luella Bates Washington Jones."

22   Sweat popped out on the boy's face and he began to struggle. Mrs. Jones stopped, jerked him around in front of her, put a half nelson[1] about his neck, and continued to drag him up the street. When she got to her door, she dragged the boy inside, down a hall, and into a large kitchenette-furnished room at the rear of the house. She switched on the light and left the door open. The boy could hear other roomers laughing and talking in the large house. Some of their doors were open, too, so he knew he and the woman

---

1. **half nelson** wrestling hold in which an arm is placed under the opponent's armpit from behind with the palm of the hand pressed against the back of the neck.

314   UNIT 3 • TRANSFORMATIONS

were not alone. The woman still had him by the neck in the middle of her room.

23   She said, "What is your name?"

24   "Roger," answered the boy.

25   "Then, Roger, you go to that sink and wash your face," said the woman, whereupon she turned him loose—at last. Roger looked at the door—looked at the woman—looked at the door—*and went to the sink.*

26   "Let the water run until it gets warm," she said. "Here's a clean towel."

27   "You gonna take me to jail?" asked the boy, bending over the sink.

28   "Not with that face, I would not take you nowhere," said the woman. "Here I am trying to get home to cook me a bite to eat and you snatch my pocketbook! Maybe, you ain't been to your supper either, late as it be. Have you?"

29   "There's nobody home at my house," said the boy.

30   "Then we'll eat," said the woman, "I believe you're hungry—or been hungry—to try to snatch my pocketbook."

31   "I wanted a pair of blue suede shoes," said the boy.

32   "Well, you didn't have to snatch *my* pocketbook to get some suede shoes," said Mrs. Luella Bates Washington Jones. "You could of asked me."

33   "M'am?"

34   The water dripping from his face, the boy looked at her. There was a long pause. A very long pause. After he had dried his face and not knowing what else to do dried it again, the boy turned around, wondering what next. The door was open. He could make a dash for it down the hall. He could run, run, run, *run*!

35   The woman was sitting on the day bed. After a while she said, "I were young once and I wanted things I could not get."

36   There was another long pause. The boy's mouth opened. Then he frowned, not knowing he frowned.

37   The woman said, "Um-hum! You thought I was going to say *but*, didn't you? You thought I was going to say, *but I didn't snatch people's pocketbooks*. Well, I wasn't going to say that." Pause. Silence. "I have done things, too, which I would not tell you, son—neither tell God, if He didn't already know. Everybody's got something in common. So you set down while I fix us something to eat. You might run that comb through your hair so you will look presentable."

38   In another corner of the room behind a screen was a gas plate[2] and an icebox. Mrs. Jones got up and went behind the screen. The woman did not watch the boy to see if he was going to run now, nor did she watch her purse, which she left behind her on the day

---

2. **gas plate** hot plate heated by gas that is used for cooking.

COMPREHENSION CHECK

Why does Roger try to steal Mrs. Jones's purse?

Thank You, M'am **315**

ESTABLISH A PURPOSE

Has your purpose for reading changed since the beginning of the story? If so, how?

bed. But the boy took care to sit on the far side of the room, away from her purse, where he thought she could easily see him out of the corner of her eye if she wanted to. He did not trust the woman *not* to trust him. And he did not want to be mistrusted now.

39 "Do you need somebody to go to the store," asked the boy, "maybe to get some milk or something?"

40 "Don't believe I do," said the woman, "unless you just want sweet milk yourself. I was going to make cocoa out of this canned milk I got here."

41 "That will be fine," said the boy.

42 She heated some lima beans and ham she had in the icebox, made the cocoa, and set the table. The woman did not ask the boy anything about where he lived, or his folks, or anything else that would embarrass him. Instead, as they ate, she told him about her job in a hotel beauty-shop that stayed open late, what the work was like, and how all kinds of women came in and out, blondes, redheads, and Spanish. Then she cut him a half of her ten-cent cake.

43 "Eat some more, son," she said.

44 When they were finished eating she got up and said, "Now, here, take this ten dollars and buy yourself some blue suede shoes. And next time, do not make the mistake of latching onto *my* pocketbook *nor nobody else's*—because shoes got by devilish ways will burn your feet. I got to get my rest now. But from here on in, son, I hope you will behave yourself."

45 She led him down the hall to the front door and opened it. "Good night! Behave yourself, boy!" she said, looking out into the street.

46 The boy wanted to say something else other than "Thank you, m'am" to Mrs. Luella Bates Washington Jones, but although his lips moved, he couldn't even say that as he turned at the foot of the barren stoop and looked up at the large woman in the door. Then she shut the door. ❧

COMPREHENSION CHECK

Does Roger ever thank Mrs. Jones for everything she does for him?

316 UNIT 3 • TRANSFORMATIONS

BUILD INSIGHT

First Thoughts

Choose one of the following items to discuss with your group.

- What view of human nature does this story present? Is it realistic? Is it naive? Explain your thinking.
- Does this story seem to uphold or challenge any stereotypes? Explain.

Summary

Confirm your comprehension by writing a short summary of the story. Remember to include only the story's central ideas and to keep your summary objective and free of personal opinions.

Analysis and Discussion

1. **Interpret** In paragraph 37, Mrs. Jones says, "Everybody's got something in common." What does she mean? Explain.

2. **Make Inferences** Why do you think Mrs. Jones deliberately leaves Roger alone with her purse as she makes dinner? Explain, citing evidence from the story.

3. **(a) Draw Conclusions** Why is Roger unable to speak as he is leaving Mrs. Jones's apartment? **(b) Speculate** What do you think Roger wanted to say? Explain.

4. **Get Ready for Close Reading** Choose a passage from the text that you find especially interesting or important. You'll discuss the passage with your group during Close-Read activities.

Exploring the Essential Question

Can people really change?

5. Do you think Roger changes his ways after his encounter with Mrs. Jones? If so, why, and how does he change? If not, why not? Go to your Evidence Log and record your thoughts.

WORKING AS A GROUP

Discuss your responses to the Analysis and Discussion questions with your group.

- Pose and respond to questions from others in your group.
- If the discussion starts to go off track, reply to the last comment someone made to bring the conversation back on topic.

If necessary, modify your original answers to reflect what you learn from your discussion.

STANDARDS

Reading Literature
Provide an objective summary of the text.

Speaking and Listening
Pose questions that elicit elaboration and respond to others' questions and comments with relevant observations and ideas that bring the discussion back on topic as needed.

ANALYZE AND INTERPRET

THANK YOU, M'AM

Close Read

PRACTICE Complete the following activities. Use text evidence to support your responses.

1. **Present and Discuss** With your group, share the passages from the story that you found especially interesting. Discuss what you notice, the questions you have, and the conclusions you reach. For example, you might focus on the following passages.

   - **Paragraph 37:** Discuss what this passage reveals about Mrs. Jones's character, in both the past and the present.
   - **Paragraph 44:** Discuss why Mrs. Jones gives Roger money for the blue suede shoes.

2. **Reflect on Your Learning** What new ideas or insights did you uncover during your second reading of the text?

WORD WALL
Note words in the text that are related to the idea of transformations. Add them to your Word Wall.

STUDY LANGUAGE AND CRAFT

Concept Vocabulary

Why These Words? Complete the activities with your group.

| permit | release | contact |

1. The concept vocabulary words are related. With your group, determine what the words have in common. Write your ideas.

2. Add another word that fits the category. _____

3. Write one sentence that contains all three words.

Word Study

Multiple-Meaning Words The concept vocabulary words are all multiple-meaning words: they each have more than one definition. Readers can use context clues or check in a dictionary to determine which meaning is correct in a particular text.

PRACTICE Write the meaning and part of speech of each vocabulary word as it is used in the story. Then, make a guess at another meaning and part of speech for each word. Check your answers in a print or digital dictionary.

STANDARDS
Reading Literature
Analyze how particular elements of a story or drama interact.

Language
- Determine or clarify the meaning of unknown and multiple-meaning words and phrases based on grade 7 reading and content.
- Verify the preliminary determination of the meaning of a word or phrase.

318 UNIT 3 • TRANSFORMATIONS

Essential Question: Can people really change?

Plot Elements

A story's plot is made up of a series of connected events. Nearly all plots center on one or more **conflicts**, or problems. There are two main types of conflict: external and internal.

CONFLICT TYPE	DEFINITION	EXAMPLE FROM THE STORY
External	struggle between a character and an outside force, such as another character, nature, or society	…a boy ran up behind her and tried to snatch her purse.
Internal	struggle caused by a character's own opposing feelings	…the boy turned around, wondering what next.

To engage readers in a story's plot, an author may drop hints or clues about upcoming events. These clues raise questions for readers, building curiosity and suspense about the fates of the characters. This is called *foreshadowing*.

PRACTICE Work with your group to complete the activity and answer the questions.

1. **(a)** What external conflict opens the story? **(b) Analyze** How does Mrs. Jones's reaction to that conflict create new conflicts? Explain.

2. **Analyze** Reread the passages listed in the chart. Name the type of conflict (external or internal) in each one. Then, explain how each conflict, and the way the character interacts with it, helps propel the plot.

PASSAGE	CONFLICT	EXPLANATION
Paragraph 22		
Paragraph 25		
Paragraph 34		

3. **(a)** In paragraphs 9–10, what question does Mrs. Jones ask, and how does Roger answer? **(b) Connect** Given Roger's answer, what do you expect might happen in the course of the story?

4. **Analyze** At what points in the story did you feel suspense about the outcome of the conflicts? What specific plot events helped to create that suspense and move the plot along?

Thank You, M'am **319**

STUDY LANGUAGE AND CRAFT

THANK YOU, M'AM

Prepositions and Prepositional Phrases

A **preposition** relates a noun or a pronoun that follows it to another word in the sentence. For example, in the sentence *The car is in the garage*, the preposition *in* relates the noun *car* to another word in the sentence, *garage*.

A **prepositional phrase** is a group of words that:

- begins with a preposition and ends with either a noun or a pronoun, which is the *object of the preposition*.

- functions as an adjective by telling *which one* or *what kind* or as an adverb by telling *how*, *when*, or *where*.

Note that if a prepositional phrase begins a sentence, it must be followed by a comma. In addition, the verb of a sentence must always agree with the subject of the sentence, not with the object of the preposition.

> **TIP:** There are more than 100 prepositions in English. Some of the most common ones are: *at, after, between, for, from, in, of, on, to, through, above*, and *with*.

EXAMPLES:

SENTENCE	EXPLANATION
Mrs. Jones got up and went <u>behind the screen</u>.	The prepositional phrase begins with the preposition *behind* and ends with the noun *screen*, which is the object of the preposition. It tells *where* Mrs. Jones went.
<u>After dinner</u>, Mrs. Jones gave Roger ten dollars.	The prepositional phrase begins with the preposition *After* and ends with the noun *dinner*, which is the object of the preposition. It tells *when* Mrs. Jones gave Roger the money. A comma is needed after the last word of the prepositional phrase.

READ ▶ Reread the story and mark three prepositional phrases. In the margin, indicate whether each one functions as an adjective or an adverb. With your group, discuss whether the prepositions you found tell *which one, how, when,* or *where*.

WRITE/EDIT ▶ Write a paragraph in which you describe someone who is important to you. Use at least two prepositional phrases. Then, edit your draft, making sure you have applied correct subject-verb agreement and included commas correctly after any prepositional phrase at the beginning of a sentence. Share your paragraph with your group.

STANDARDS

Reading Literature
Analyze how an author develops and contrasts the points of view of different characters or narrators in a text.

Writing
With some guidance and support from peers and adults, develop and strengthen writing as needed by planning, revising, editing, rewriting, or trying a new approach.

Language
Explain the function of phrases and clauses in general and their function in specific sentences.

320 UNIT 3 • TRANSFORMATIONS

SHARE IDEAS

Writing

A **journal entry** is a brief autobiographical record of a day's events.

Assignment

Write **journal entries** from the points of view of each of the characters in "Thank You, M'am." Focus on the following:

- Mrs. Jones's perspective on meeting Roger
- Roger's perspective on meeting Mrs. Jones

Work on your own to complete this assignment. Then, share and discuss your journal entries with your group.

Plan and Write Use the characteristics of journal writing:

- List the date, place, and time of each entry.
- Write from the first-person point of view, using the pronouns *I, me, my* and *mine*.
- Retell the events of the day from each character's perspective, including reflections or explanations.

Reread the story to analyze how the author develops each character's point of view. Find examples that show how they contrast, or differ, and note them in the chart. Then, write your journal entries, using your imagination and details from the text to create each character's unique voice.

NOTES FOR MY JOURNAL ENTRIES	
Mrs. Jones	
Roger	

Guide and Support Share your journal entries as a group and engage in a meaningful discussion about the choices you made. Offer and accept feedback on one another's work in a helpful and respectful manner. Afterwards, revise, edit, or rewrite your entries based on comments you received. You could also try a new approach suggested by a peer.

EVIDENCE LOG

Before moving on to a new selection, go to your Evidence Log and record any additional thoughts or observations you may have about "Thank You M'am."

Thank You, M'am **321**

LEARN ABOUT GENRE: NONFICTION

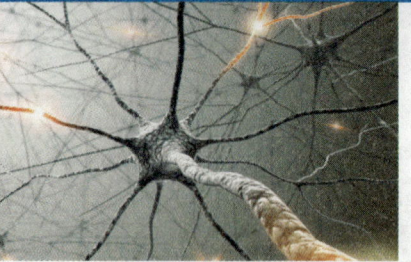

LEARNING REWIRES THE BRAIN

Reading Science Journalism

Journalism is nonfiction in which a writer (journalist) reports on current events. **Science journalism** focuses on scientific topics, issues, or discoveries.

The selection you are about to read is an example of science journalism.

SCIENCE JOURNALISM

Author's Purpose
- to report and explain current news about science for a general audience

Characteristics
- a central idea, or thesis, supported with evidence and sound reasoning
- scientific or technical terms
- examples and comparisons that clarify unfamiliar concepts

Structure
- an engaging first sentence or section
- a logical order of ideas that creates a clear path through a complex subject
- print and graphic features that help illustrate concepts and show how the text is organized

Take a Minute!

CHOOSE Scan the listed topics. Identify at least three that could be the subject of science journalism. Discuss the reasons for your choices with a partner.

elections in Europe
landing your dream job
Mars colonization
a cure for the common cold

fall fashions
high-tech artificial limbs
healthy holiday recipes
how lightbulbs work

STANDARDS
Reading Informational Text
Analyze the structure an author uses to organize a text, including how the major sections contribute to the whole and to the development of the ideas.

322 UNIT 3 • TRANSFORMATIONS

Essential Question: Can people really change?

Print and Graphic Features

Print and graphic features are structural elements of texts that authors use to develop and organize their ideas. These features enable readers to grasp complex information by breaking it into sections and by showing concepts visually.

TIP: Text features help readers locate specific information and see how the sections of a text fit together.

STRUCTURAL ELEMENTS

FEATURE	EXAMPLES	PURPOSE
Print Features	title, headings	break text into chunks that show sections
	bulleted lists; numbered lists	organize data or other information into logical or numeric order
	inset boxes; sidebars	highlight interesting aspects of the topic
Graphic Features	photos, illustrations, diagrams	provide visuals for reference; label parts and pieces
	maps, blueprints	provide information about geography, distances, and layouts
	charts, tables, graphs	organize data into categories

PRACTICE Work on your own to read the passage. Then, answer the questions with your group.

The Science Behind Erosion

Have you ever heard the expression "solid as a rock"? The fact is, not even rock can resist the power of erosion.

What is erosion?

Erosion is a natural process in which Earth's surface is worn away by wind, water, and ice. This gradual process is destructive but results in dramatic landscapes.

Natural sculptures

Bryce Canyon National Park in Utah is the site of dozens of spectacular rock formations known as *hoodoos*. These towering columns were formed when water and other natural elements eroded the softer sandstone beneath the limestone caps.

1. What purpose do the headings in this text serve?

2. What type of graphic feature might best help readers understand the "Natural sculptures" section? Explain your thinking.

Learn About Genre **323**

PREPARE TO READ

Learning Rewires the Brain

About the Author

Alison Pearce Stevens is fascinated with science and its ability to explain how the world works. She specializes in writing about science and nature topics for kids and teens. In addition to writing, Stevens teaches Environmental Curriculum at the University of Nebraska.

Technical Vocabulary

As you read the article, you will encounter these words. After reading, work with your group to identify what the words have in common.

| signals | transmit | relay |

Digital Resources A **digital dictionary** is a reference source you access online or through a mobile device. It provides information about words and often includes audio pronunciations.

SAMPLE DIGITAL DICTIONARY ENTRY

neuroscience [nur oh SIH ehns] *n.* 🔊

Examples   Word Origin   Synonyms

1. scientific study of the nervous system and its effects

Analysis: This entry provides a definition and shows that *neuroscience* is a noun with four syllables. To hear the word pronounced, you would click the audio icon. To see it in sentences, you would click *Examples*. To learn its origins and synonyms, you would click the appropriate links.

PRACTICE As you read, use a digital dictionary to find the precise meanings, syllabication, pronunciations, word origins, and parts of speech of technical terms and other unfamiliar words. Use the open space next to the text to note this information.

Reading Strategy: Make Connections

Deepen your understanding of a text by **making connections** as you read. You may connect with a text in several different ways:

- Consider how ideas in a text connect to your personal experiences.
- Notice how ideas in a text connect to ideas in other texts you have read, including both fiction and nonfiction.
- Analyze how ideas in a text connect to society, or to the world around you, including your own school or community.

PRACTICE As you read, use the open space next to the text to write down connections you make to personal experiences, ideas in other texts, and society.

STANDARDS

Reading Informational Text
Determine the meaning of words and phrases as they are used in a text, including figurative, connotative, and technical meanings.

Language
Consult general and specialized reference materials, both print and digital, to find the pronunciation of a word or determine or clarify its precise meaning or its part of speech.

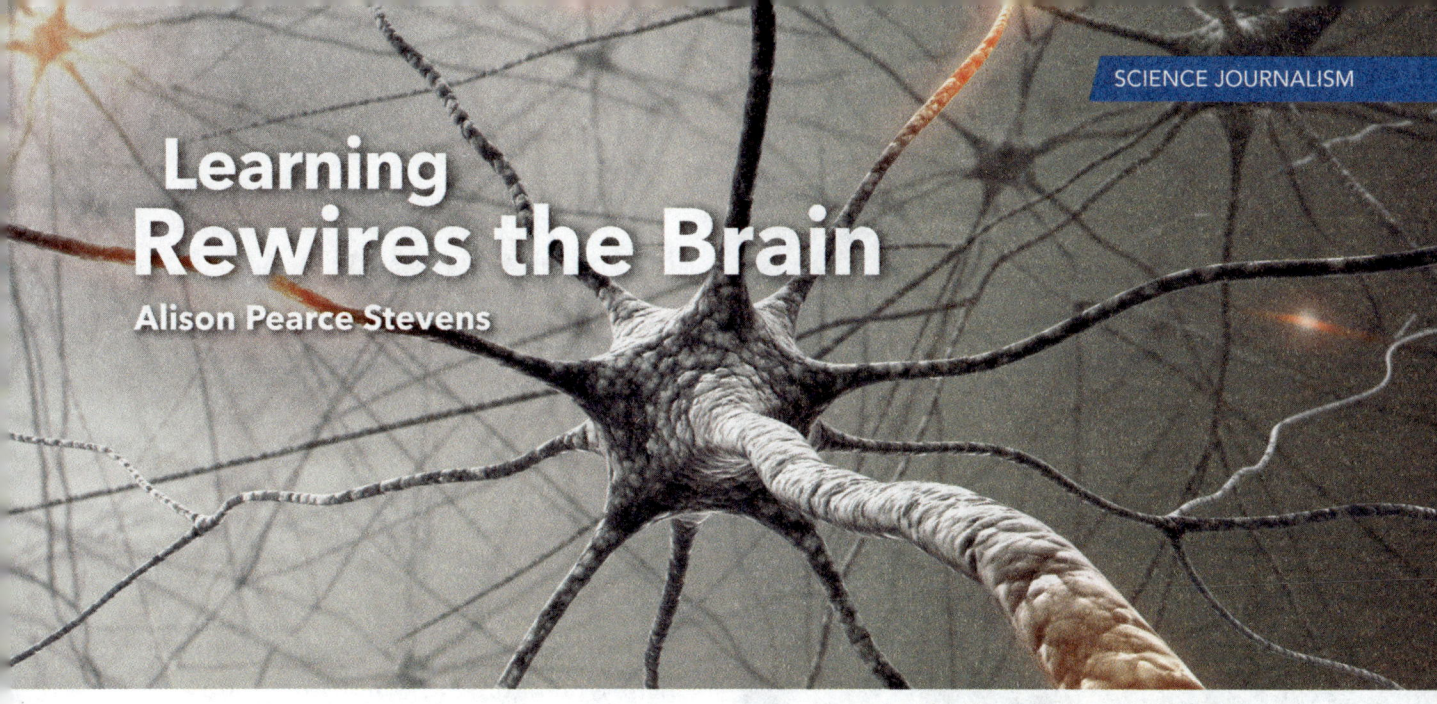

SCIENCE JOURNALISM

Learning Rewires the Brain

Alison Pearce Stevens

∧ An artist's depiction of an electrical signal (yellow-orange regions) shooting down a nerve cell and then off to others in the brain. Learning strengthens the paths that these signals take, essentially "wiring" certain common paths through the brain.

BACKGROUND

In this science article, the author reports a research finding that is truly life-changing—the discovery that as we learn, our brain cells undergo physical changes. This cause-and-effect process, much of which takes place as we sleep, helps us retain knowledge.

1 Musicians, athletes, and quiz bowl champions all have one thing in common: training. Learning to play an instrument or a sport requires time and patience. It is all about steadily mastering new skills. The same is true when it comes to learning information—preparing for that quiz bowl, say, or studying for a big test.

2 As teachers, coaches and parents everywhere like to say: Practice makes perfect.

3 Doing something over and over again doesn't just make it easier. It actually changes the brain. That may not come as a surprise. But exactly how that process happens has long been a mystery. Scientists have known that the brain continues to develop through our teenage years. But these experts used to think that those changes stopped once the brain matured.

4 No more.

5 Recent data have been showing that the brain continues to change over the course of our lives. Cells grow. They form connections with new cells. Some stop talking to others. And it's not just nerve cells that shift and change as we learn. Other brain cells also get into the act.

6 Scientists have begun unlocking these secrets of how we learn, not only in huge blocks of tissue, but even within individual cells.

READ TO UNLOCK MEANING

1. First read the text for comprehension and enjoyment. Use the **Reading Strategy** and **Comprehension Check** questions to support your first read.
2. With your group, apply the vocabulary strategy to unlock word meanings.
3. Find other details in the text you find interesting. Ask your own questions and draw your own conclusions.

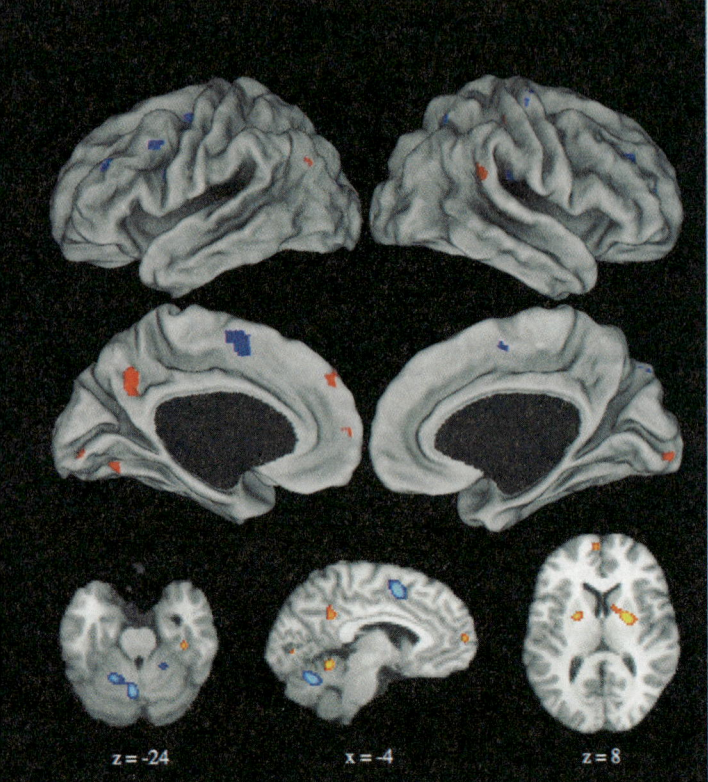

∧ Blood flow reveals activity in the brain. Here, blue highlights attention-related areas that had greater blood flow when people first learned a task. Blood flow decreased in those areas as they became more familiar with the task. Red areas became more active as the task was mastered, suggesting these regions may be associated with lower externally-directed attention demands.

Rewiring

7   The brain is not one big blob of tissue. Just six to seven weeks into the development of a human embryo, the brain starts to form into different parts. Later, these areas will each take on different roles. Consider the prefrontal cortex. It's the region right behind your forehead. That's where you solve problems. Other parts of the cortex (the outer layer of the brain) help process sights and sounds. Deep in the brain, the hippocampus helps store memories. It also helps you figure out where things are located around you.

8   Scientists can see what part of the brain is active by using functional magnetic resonance imaging, or fMRI. At the heart of every fMRI device is a strong magnet. It allows the device to detect changes in blood flow. Now, when a scientist asks a volunteer to perform a particular task—such as playing a game or learning something new—the machine reveals where blood flow within the brain is highest. That boost in blood flow highlights which cells are busy working.

9   Many brain scientists use fMRI to map brain activity. Others use another type of brain scan, known as positron emission tomography, or PET. Experts have performed dozens of such studies. Each looked at how specific areas of the brain responded to specific tasks.

10   Nathan Spreng did something a little different: He decided to study the studies. Spreng is a neuroscientist at Cornell University in Ithaca, N.Y. A neuroscientist studies the brain and nervous system. Spreng wanted to know how the brain changes—how it morphs a little bit—as we learn.

11   He teamed up with two other researchers. Together, they analyzed 38 of those earlier studies. Each study had used an fMRI or PET scan to probe which regions of the brain turn on when people learn new tasks.

12   Areas that allow people to pay attention became most active as someone began a new task. But those attention areas became less active over time. Meanwhile, areas of the brain linked with daydreaming and mind-wandering became more active as people became more familiar with a task.

13   "At the beginning, you require a lot of focused attention," Spreng says. Learning to swing a bat requires a great deal of focus when you first try to hit a ball. But the more you practice, Spreng says, the less you have to think about what you're doing.

14   Extensive practice can even allow a person to perform a task while thinking about other things—or about nothing at all. A professional pianist, for example, can play a complex piece of music without thinking about which notes to play next. In fact, stopping to think about the task can actually interfere with a flawless performance. This is what musicians, athletes and others often refer to as being "in the zone."

Cells that fire together, wire together

15   Spreng's findings involve the whole brain. However, those changes actually reflect what's happening at the level of individual cells.

16   The brain is made up of billions of nerve cells, called neurons. These cells are chatty. They "talk" to each other, mostly using chemical messengers. Incoming **signals** cause a listening neuron to *fire* or send signals of its own. A cell fires when an electrical signal travels through it. The signal moves away from what is called the *cell body*, down through a long structure called an *axon*. When the signal reaches the end of the axon, it triggers the release of those chemical messengers. The chemicals then leap across a tiny gap. This triggers the next cell to fire. And on it goes.

17   As we learn something new, cells that send and receive information about the task become more and more efficient. It

---

Use a dictionary or indicate another strategy you used that helped you determine meaning.

signals (SIHG nuhlz) *n.*
MEANING:

COMPREHENSION CHECK
According to Nathan Spreng, when do people's brains become most active?

∧ Chemical messengers—called neurotransmitters—leave the end of one nerve cell and jump across a gap to stimulate the next nerve cell.

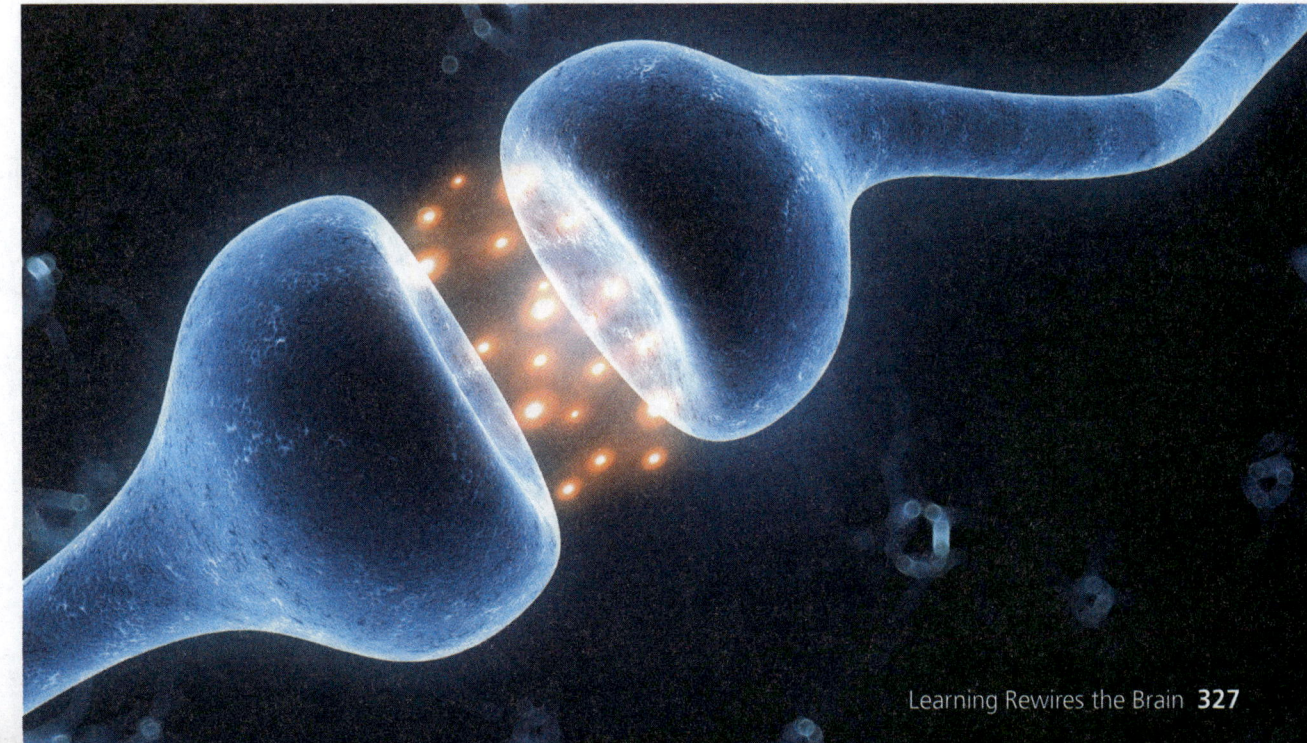

Learning Rewires the Brain 327

takes less effort for them to signal the next cell about what's going on. In a sense, the neurons become wired together.

18   Spreng detected that wiring. As cells in a brain area related to some task became more efficient, they used less energy to chat. This allowed more neurons in the "daydreaming" region of the brain to rev up their activity.

19   Neurons can signal to several neighbors at once. For example, one neuron might **transmit** information about the location of a baseball pitch that's flying toward you. Meanwhile, other neurons alert your muscles to get ready to swing the bat. When those neurons fire at the same time, connections between them strengthen. That improves your ability to connect with the ball.

Learning while you slumber

20   The brain doesn't shut down overnight. In fact, catching some zzz's can dramatically improve learning. That's because as we sleep, our brains store memories and new information from the previous day. So a poor night's sleep can hurt our ability to remember new things. Until recently, however, researchers didn't know why.

21   A group of scientists at the University of Heidelberg in Germany provided the first clues. Specific cells in the hippocampus—that region involved in storing memories—fired when mice slept, the scientists found. But the cells didn't fire normally. Instead, electrical signals spontaneously fired near the middle of an axon, then traveled back in the direction of the cell body. In other words, the cells fired in reverse.

22   This boosted learning. It did so by making connections between cells stronger. Again, the action sort of wired together the cells. Research by Olena Bukalo and Doug Fields showed how it happens. They are neuroscientists at the National Institutes of Child Health and Human Development in Bethesda, MD.

23   Working with tissue from rat brains, the scientists electrically stimulated nerve axons. Carefully, they stimulated them just in the middle. The electrical signals then traveled in reverse. That is just what the German scientists had seen.

24   This reverse signaling made the neuron less sensitive to signals from its neighbors, the experts found. This made it harder for the cell to fire, which gave the neuron a chance to recharge, Bukalo explains. When she then applied electric stimulation near the cell body, the neuron fired. And it did so even more strongly than it had before.

25   Cells involved in learning new information are most likely to fire in reverse during sleep, Bukalo says. The next day, they will be wired more tightly to each other. Although scientists don't know for certain, it is likely that repeated cycles of reverse firing create a

---

Use a dictionary or indicate another strategy you used that helped you determine meaning.

transmit (TRANZ miht) *v.*

MEANING:

strong network of neurons. The neurons **relay** information faster and more efficiently, just as Spreng found in his study. As a result, those networks reflect an improvement in understanding or physical skill.

Firing faster

26 Neurons are the best-known cells in the brain. But they are far from the only ones. Another type, called glia, actually makes up a whopping 85 percent of brain cells. For a long time, scientists thought that glia simply held neurons together. (Indeed, "glia" take their name from the Greek word for glue.) But recent research by Fields, Bukalo's colleague at the National Institutes of Child Health and Human Development, reveals that glial cells also become active during learning.

27 One type of glial cell wraps around nerve axons. (Note: Not all axons have this wrapping.) These wrapping cells create what's known as a myelin sheath. Myelin is made of protein and fatty substances. It insulates the axons. Myelin is a bit like the plastic coating that jackets the copper wires in your home. That insulation prevents electrical signals from inappropriately leaking out of one wire (or axon) and into another.

28 In axons, the myelin sheath has a second role: It actually speeds the electrical signals along. That's because glial cells force a signal to jump from one spot on the axon to the next. As it hops between glial cells, the signal moves faster. It's kind of like flying from one spot to the next, instead of taking the train.

29 Fields has found that when new skills are learned, the amount of myelin insulating an axon increases. This happens as the size of individual glial cells increases. New glial cells also may be added to bare axons. These changes improve the ability of a neuron to signal. And that leads to better learning.

30 A thicker myelin sheath helps improve all types of brainy tasks. These include reading, creating memories, playing a musical instrument and more. A thicker sheath is also linked with better decision-making.

31 Nerve cells continue to add myelin well into adulthood, as our brains continue to grow and develop. The prefrontal cortex, for example—that area where decisions are made—gains myelin well into a person's 20s. This may explain why teens don't always make the best decisions. They're not finished sheathing their nerve cells. But there is hope. And getting enough sleep certainly can help. Glial cells, like neurons, seem to change most during certain stages of sleep.

32 Exactly what causes the glial cells to change remains a mystery. Fields and his colleagues are hard at work to figure that out. It's exciting, he says, to launch into a whole new field of research.

Use a dictionary or indicate another strategy you used that helped you determine meaning.

relay (ree LAY) *v.*
MEANING:

COMPREHENSION CHECK

What happens to myelin when new skills are learned?

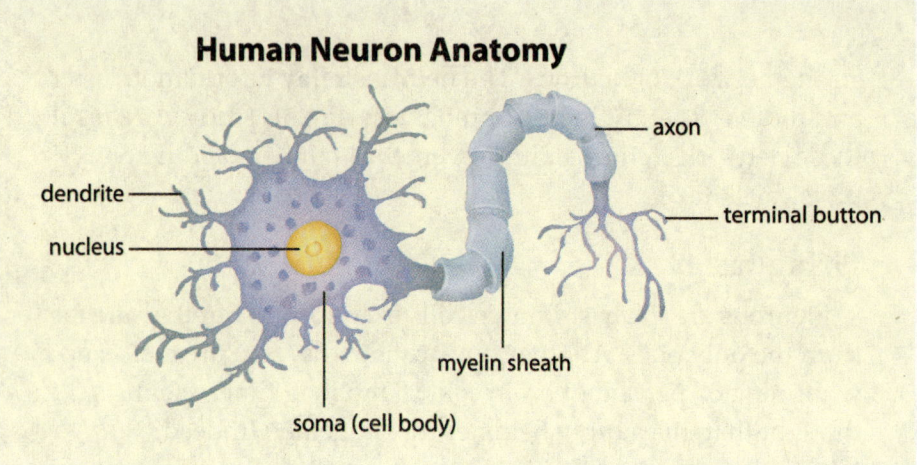

▲ Artist's depiction of a nerve cell in the brain. Glial cells wrap around the axon like a blanket, forming the myelin sheath. As people learn, brain cells change in ways that increase the speed and efficiency with which signals travel down the nerve cells.

Slow and steady

33 These changes in the brain allow for faster, stronger signaling between neurons as the brain gains new skills. But the best way to speed up those signals is to introduce new information to our noggins—slowly.

34 Many students instead try to memorize lots of information the night before a test. Cramming may get them through the test. But the students won't remember the information for very long, says Hadley Bergstrom. He is a neuroscientist at the National Institutes of Alcohol Abuse and Alcoholism in Rockville, MD.

35 It's important to spread out learning over many days, his work shows. That means learning a little bit at a time. Doing so allows links between neurons to steadily strengthen. It also allows glial cells time to better insulate axons.

36 Even an "aha!" moment—when something suddenly becomes clear — doesn't come out of nowhere. Instead, it is the result of a steady accumulation of information. That's because adding new information opens up memories associated with the task. Once those memory neurons are active, they can form new connections, explains Bergstrom. They also can form stronger connections within an existing network. Over time, your level of understanding increases until you suddenly "get" it.

37 Like Fields and Bukalo, Bergstrom stresses the importance of sleep in forming the new memories needed to gain knowledge. So the next time you study for a test, start learning new information a few days ahead of time. The night before, give your brain a break and go to bed early. It will allow your brain a chance to cement that new information into its cells. And that should boost your chances of doing well.

MAKE CONNECTIONS
What personal experiences do you have related to paragraphs 34 and 35?

COMPREHENSION CHECK
According to Hadley Bergstrom, what is the most important thing a person can do to improve their learning?

BUILD INSIGHT

First Thoughts

Given what you've read about learning and your brain, will you change the way you prepare for an important test? If so, how? If not, why not?

Summary

Write a short summary of the text that includes only the central ideas. Keep your summary objective and free of personal opinions.

Analysis and Discussion

1. **Analyze** How do our brain cells "talk" to each other, or send information?

2. Review paragraph 14. **(a)** What do athletes, musicians, and other experts mean when they say they are "in the zone"? **(b) Compare and Contrast** How does the function of the brain of someone who is "in the zone" compare to the function of the brain of a person learning a new task?

3. **(a)** What does research suggest about the learning achievements of those who get enough sleep and those who don't? Explain.
(b) Extend Cite two ways in which the information in this article might affect people's lives. Explain your thinking, citing evidence from the text.

4. **Get Ready for Close Reading** Choose a passage from the text that you find especially interesting or important. You'll discuss the passage with your group during Close-Read activities.

Exploring the Essential Question

Can people really change?

5. What does this article reveal about people's ability to change their brains, and therefore their lives? Go to your Evidence Log and record your thoughts.

WORKING AS A GROUP

Discuss your responses to the Analysis and Discussion questions with your group.

- Refer to specific evidence in the text to dive deeper into the ideas you are exploring.
- Ask follow-up questions to clarify others' comments.

If necessary, modify your original answers to reflect new information you learn from others.

STANDARDS
Speaking and Listening
• Come to discussions prepared, having read or researched material under study; explicitly draw on that preparation by referring to evidence on the topic, text, or issue to probe and reflect on ideas under discussion.

• Acknowledge new information expressed by others and, when warranted, modify their own views.

ANALYZE AND INTERPRET

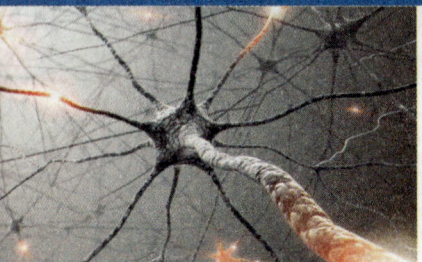

LEARNING REWIRES THE BRAIN

Close Read

PRACTICE Complete the following activities. Use text evidence to support your responses.

1. **Present and Discuss** With your group, share the passages from the science article that you found especially interesting. For example, you might focus on the following passages:

    - **Paragraphs 12–14:** Discuss the science behind the expression "practice makes perfect."

    - **Paragraphs 17–18:** Discuss the idea that neurons "chat." Consider why the author uses that comparison.

2. **Reflect on Your Learning** What new ideas or insights did you uncover during your second reading of the text?

WORD WALL

Note words in the text that are related to the idea of transformations. Add them to your Word Wall.

STUDY LANGUAGE AND CRAFT

Technical Vocabulary

Why These Words? The vocabulary words are related.

| signals | transmit | relay |

1. With your group, determine what the words have in common. Write your ideas.

2. Add another word that fits the category. _____

3. Write a paragraph that contains all three technical vocabulary words. Include context clues that hint at each word's meaning.

Word Study

Latin Root: -sign- The word *signals* includes the root *-sign-*. This root comes from the Latin word *signum*, meaning "identifying mark."

PRACTICE Use a print or online dictionary to determine the meanings, parts of speech, and pronunciations of these words: *signature, insignia, design*. Explain how the meaning of the Latin root *-sign-* is evident in each word. Also, note when the *g* sound is pronounced and when it is silent.

STANDARDS

Reading Informational Text
- Determine the meaning of words and phrases as they are used in a text, including figurative, connotative, and technical meanings.
- Analyze the structure an author uses to organize a text, including how the major sections contribute to the whole and to the development of the ideas.

Language
- Use common, grade-appropriate Greek or Latin roots as clues to the meaning of a word.
- Consult general and specialized reference materials, both print and digital, to find the pronunciation of a word or determine or clarify its precise meaning or its part of speech.

Essential Question: Can people really change?

Organizational Patterns

Many works of science journalism feature organizational patterns that break down complex topics into sections that make them easier to understand. **Print and graphic features** help show how the text is organized. These features also illustrate concepts, add information in compact ways, and help readers navigate the text to better understand how ideas are related.

EXAMPLE
- Complex science topic, indicated by title
  - Major sections, indicated by headings
    - Print and graphic features that further explain and illustrate information

PRACTICE Work with your group to complete the activity and answer the questions.

1. **Analyze** Use the chart to make an outline of the article.

Topic:
Sections:
Features:

2. **Analyze** Review the graphic features in each section. How does the information in each graphic feature relate to the text in the section? Using your observations, explain the role graphic features play in the organizational pattern of the article.

3. **Distinguish** Which heading in the article indicates that it's a section about why it's best to learn a little bit every day? Explain.

4. **Analyze** In what ways does the image with the caption beginning "Blood flow reveals..." clarify information presented elsewhere in the article? Explain.

Learning Rewires the Brain 333

STUDY LANGUAGE AND CRAFT

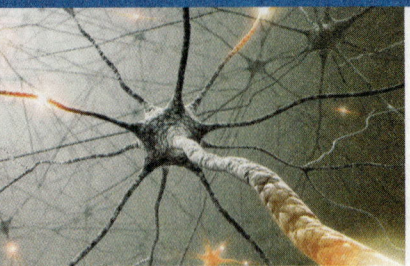

LEARNING REWIRES THE BRAIN

Rhetorical Devices and Logical Fallacies

Rhetorical devices are patterns of words writers may use to stress certain ideas and engage readers' interest. These devices show sound, careful reasoning. Writers may also use **logical fallacies**, or language that shows faulty reasoning. Rhetorical devices strengthen informational texts; in many cases, logical fallacies weaken them. Readers should trace an author's reasoning in a text and evaluate whether it is sound.

PURPOSES OF RHETORICAL DEVICES AND LOGICAL FALLACIES		
TERM AND DEFINITION	**RHETORICAL DEVICE OR LOGICAL FALLACY?**	**PURPOSE**
Direct Address: use of "you" to speak directly to the reader	Rhetorical Device	engage readers; make them feel a connection to the text and author
Analogy: extended comparison between an unfamiliar concept and a familiar one	Rhetorical Device	explain unfamiliar ideas by showing connections to things readers already know
Sweeping Generalization: statement that applies a general rule too broadly	Logical Fallacy	pull readers in with a dramatic statement; can be used unfairly to present information in a false way or to create a stereotype

STANDARDS

Reading Informational Text
Trace and evaluate the argument and specific claims in a text, assessing whether the reasoning is sound.

Writing
- Include formatting, graphics, and multimedia when useful to aiding comprehension.
- Quote or paraphrase the data and conclusions of others while avoiding plagiarism and following a standard format for citation.

Speaking and Listening
- Define individual roles as needed.
- Include multimedia components and visual displays in presentations to clarify claims and findings and emphasize salient points.

PRACTICE Work on your own to answer the questions. Then, share your responses with your group.

1. **(a) Analyze** Explain how the first sentence of the article could be considered a sweeping generalization. **(b) Evaluate** What purpose does this generalization serve? **(c) Analyze** What examples of sound reasoning in paragraph 1 make the sentence less of a fallacy?

2. **(a) Analyze** Explain why paragraph 2 could also be considered a sweeping generalization. **(b) Evaluate** What purpose does this generalization serve?

3. **(a) Analyze** Explain the analogy used in paragraph 27—what two concepts are compared? **(b) Evaluate** Does this comparison show sound reasoning? Explain why or why not.

4. **Analyze** What rhetorical device does the author use in paragraph 37? What purpose does this device serve? Explain.

334 UNIT 3 • TRANSFORMATIONS

SHARE IDEAS

Research

A **research report** is a type of nonfiction that presents information gathered from a variety of sources and conveys a clear central idea, or thesis.

> ### Assignment
>
> Work with your group to prepare a **research report** related to text features or information from "Learning Rewires the Brain." Choose one of the following options:
>
> ○ **The Art of Scientific Illustration:**
> Review the images in the article and conduct research to learn about the history and use of scientific illustrations.
>
> ○ **Origins of Science Words:**
> Choose three scientific terms from the article and conduct research about their Latin or Greek origins and roots.
>
> Make sure every group member has a significant role to play in researching, planning, writing, and presenting the finished product.

Choose a Mode of Delivery After you gather information about the topic your group chose, discuss the best way to present it. The formatting, graphics, and multimedia you choose should emphasize your most important points and help the audience understand your research findings. Mark your choice.

○ **Written Report**: Type a polished report that includes an introduction, body paragraphs with specially formatted headings, and a conclusion.

○ **Oral Presentation**: Create detailed notecards and posters with graphics to deliver your findings orally.

○ **Multimedia Presentation**: Use presentation software to present your report. Enhance it with media elements, such as images, videos, or music.

Don't Plagiarize Plagiarism is the act of using the language or ideas of another person without permission. Follow these steps to avoid plagiarism:

- Properly cite information and ideas that are not common knowledge. Follow a standard format for citation, provided by your teacher.

- **Paraphrase**, or restate the ideas of others in your own words. Note that even when you paraphrase, you must still cite the source because the ideas are not your own.

- If you want to **quote** an author, or use their exact words, set the words in quotation marks and cite the source accurately.

EVIDENCE LOG

Before moving on to a new selection, go to your Evidence Log and record any additional thoughts or observations you may have about "Learning Rewires the Brain."

LEARN ABOUT GENRE: POETRY

POETRY COLLECTION

The selections you are about to read are examples of different types of poetry.

Reading Poetry

Poetry is a form of literature that uses concise, musical, or emotionally charged language to convey messages.

POETRY

Author's Purpose
- to use focused, imaginative language to express thoughts, feelings, or insights

Characteristics
- has a speaker, or voice that "tells" the poem
- conveys a theme; often has multiple layers of meaning
- uses imagery, or sensory language that creates word pictures
- lyric poems have a musical quality and capture the emotions of a moment
- narrative poems tell a story
- free-verse poems do not follow any particular "rules"

Structure
- often arranges words into lines and stanzas
- different types of poems follow different structures, or none at all

Take a Minute!

DISCUSS With a partner, discuss poems you have enjoyed. Are they lyric, narrative, or free verse? How do you know?

STANDARDS
Reading Literature
- Determine a theme or central idea of a text and analyze its development over the course of the text.
- Determine the meaning of words and phrases as they are used in a text, including figurative and connotative meanings.
- By the end of the year, read and comprehend literature, including stories, dramas, and poems.

336 UNIT 3 • TRANSFORMATIONS

Essential Question: Can people really change?

Imagery and Themes

One of the most powerful ways in which poets convey meaning is through imagery. **Imagery** is figurative language that creates word pictures using details that appeal to the senses. Readers can determine a poem's **theme**, or insight about life, by analyzing its title, imagery, and statements made by the speaker.

TIP: A theme is not just a word or phrase. It is a statement that can be applied to other literary works or to life in general.

EXAMPLE
Winter Blooms

At summer's end, sunflowers set,
their petals browned and scattered.
Husks of wildflowers rustle,
their seeds a feast for hungry jays

who cry, "Eat, eat!"
They cry, "Me! Mine!"

Their feathers are the dark blue
of sky as night falls early, of shadows
on fields locked in snow,
of the cold as winter blooms.

Images of dead flowers, hungry birds, and the coming of winter create a timeline of seasonal change.
Two themes the reader may infer:
1. *The cycle of the seasons is part of nature's power.*
2. *Endings and beginnings are connected.*

PRACTICE Read the poems and answer the questions. Then, discuss your responses with your group.

Child in Rain	I Left Her Behind
If you see a child who scrambles wide-eyed	During the sudden storms
And wondering across fields of grass,	of time's passage,
Just to watch a rainstorm passing,	I left her behind.
Applauding the raindrops with laughter,	Now she pauses
Tasting rain on her tongue like licorice tea,	with caution at every corner,
Please, won't you send her home to me?	Worry-eyed and wondering,
I have not forgotten who I am.	The girl I was does not know me,
	and I no longer know her.

1. What shared theme about identity do both poems develop? Which details help express that theme?

2. What theme about becoming an adult do both poems express? How are the themes of the two poems different? Explain.

Learn About Genre 337

PREPARE TO READ

POETRY COLLECTION
Trying to Name What Doesn't Change • I Myself • Do not trust the eraser

Concept Vocabulary

As you read the poems, you will encounter these words. After reading, work with your group to identify what the words have in common.

| shrinking | distorting | discards |

Print Resources A **thesaurus** is a reference book about words. A typical thesaurus entry gives a word's part of speech and, more importantly, lists its synonyms and antonyms. Readers can examine the words with similar and opposite meanings to better understand a new word.

SAMPLE THESAURUS ENTRY

vivify *v.* synonyms: energize, enliven, animate, revive, invigorate
antonyms: deaden, dull, kill

Here, synonyms *(energize, revive)* and antonyms *(deaden, dull)* clarify the meaning of the verb *vivify*, which is "give life to."

PRACTICE As you read, use a thesaurus to determine the precise meanings and parts of speech of unfamiliar words by looking at their synonyms and antonyms.

Reading Strategy: Create Mental Images

When you read, deepen your understanding by creating mental images, or envisioning scenes in your mind. To do so, notice details that relate to the senses: sight, hearing, taste, touch, and smell. Allow these details to form pictures in your mind.

EXAMPLE

Notice details related to sight and smell in these lines. Use them to imagine the scene in your mind.

The widow *in the tilted house / spices her soup with cinnamon.*

PRACTICE As you read, look for details that help you create mental images and deepen your understanding. Mark the details and jot down notes in the open space next to the text.

STANDARDS
Language
• Determine or clarify the meaning of unknown and multiple-meaning words and phrases based on grade 7 reading and content, choosing flexibly from a range of strategies.
• Consult general and specialized reference materials, both print and digital, to find the pronunciation of a word or determine or clarify its precise meaning or its part of speech.
• Use the relationship between particular words to better understand each of the words.

338 UNIT 3 • TRANSFORMATIONS

Essential Question: Can people really change?

About the Poems

Trying to Name What Doesn't Change

BACKGROUND

"Trying to Name What Doesn't Change" was first published in Naomi Shihab Nye's 1995 collection *The Words Under the Words*. It is an example of the poet's interest in what she has called "local life, random characters met on the streets . . ." In this poem, which begins simply and gradually becomes more complex, the speaker shares different perspectives on the same subject: change.

Naomi Shihab Nye was born in St. Louis, Missouri, in 1952. Her father was a Palestinian refugee and her mother an American of German and Swiss descent. Her poetry offers a fresh perspective on ordinary people and everyday events. She lives in San Antonio, Texas.

I Myself

BACKGROUND

"I Myself," or "Yo Mismo" in the original Spanish, was translated into English in 1977. In 1985, as he accepted the Prince of Asturias Award for Literature, Ángel González spoke of himself as two people: "Here stands only the man who has contrived the words that give life to the poet." He also observed that "the way we are . . . depends on others more than we usually think." Similar ideas about human nature and identity echo in this powerful poem.

Ángel González (1925–2008) was a major 20th-century Spanish poet. He was born in Oviedo, Spain, and grew up during the Spanish Civil War and the rule of the military dictator Francisco Franco. González trained and worked as a lawyer but eventually began writing poetry. His work earned immediate critical acclaim. González went on to publish numerous poetry collections and to win many important literary honors. For almost 20 years, he was a professor of contemporary Spanish literature at the University of New Mexico, dividing his time between the United States and Spain.

Do not trust the eraser

BACKGROUND

"Do not trust the eraser" was written by Rosamond S. King in 2022. It is an example of free-verse poetry, which breaks "free" from the rules and forms typically associated with poetry.

Rosamond S. King is a writer, performer, and artist. She was born in the United States to a Trinidadian mother and a Gambian father. King attended Cornell University and New York University and studied literature in Gambia on a Fulbright scholarship. She has been a professor of literature at Brooklyn College since 2008.

Poetry Collection **339**

LYRIC POETRY

Trying to Name What Doesn't Change

Naomi Shihab Nye

READ TO UNLOCK MEANING

1. First read the text for comprehension and enjoyment. Use the **Reading Strategy** question to support your first read.
2. With your group, apply the vocabulary strategy to unlock word meanings.
3. Find other details in the text you find interesting. Ask your own questions and draw your own conclusions.

Roselva says the only thing that doesn't change
is train tracks. She's sure of it.
The train changes, or the weeds that grow up spidery
by the side, but not the tracks.
5   I've watched one for three years, she says,
and it doesn't curve, doesn't break, doesn't grow.

Peter isn't sure. He saw an abandoned track
near Sabinas, Mexico, and says a track without a train
is a changed track. The metal wasn't shiny anymore.
10 The wood was split and some of the ties were gone.

Every Tuesday on Morales Street
butchers crack the necks of a hundred hens.
The widow in the tilted house
spices her soup with cinnamon.
15 Ask her what doesn't change.

Stars explode.
The rose curls up as if there is fire in the petals.
The cat who knew me is buried under the bush.

The train whistle still wails its ancient sound
20 but when it goes away, **shrinking** back
from the walls of the brain,
it takes something different with it every time.

Use a thesaurus or indicate another strategy you used that helped you determine meaning.
shrinking (SHRINK ihng) *v.*
MEANING:

340 UNIT 3 • TRANSFORMATIONS

NARRATIVE POETRY

I Myself

Ángel González
translated by Donald D. Walsh

I myself
met me face to face at a crossing.
I saw on me
a stubborn expression, and a hardness
5   in the eyes, like
a man who'd stop at nothing.

The road was narrow, and I said to me:
"Stand aside, make
way,
10 for I have to get to such and such a place."

But I was not strong, and my enemy
fell upon me with all the weight of my flesh,
and I was left defeated in the ditch.

That's the way it happened, and I never could
15 reach that place, and ever since
my body walks by itself, getting lost,
distorting whatever plans I make.

CREATE MENTAL IMAGES
What do you picture in your mind after reading lines 1–2?

Use a thesaurus or indicate another strategy you used that helped you determine meaning.

distorting (dih STAWRT ihng) *v.*
MEANING:

Poetry Collection **341**

FREE-VERSE POETRY

Do not trust the eraser

Rosamond S. King

Use a thesaurus or indicate another strategy you used that helped you determine meaning.

discards (DIHS cahrdz) *n.*
MEANING:

Do not trust the eraser. Prefer
crossed out, scribbled over monuments
to something once thought correct
. Instead: colors, transparencies
5   track changes, versions, iterations
. How else might you return
after **discards,** attempts
and mis takes, to your
original genius
10   ?

BUILD INSIGHT

First Thoughts

Which poem do you relate to the most? What makes it meaingful to you?

Comprehension

1. **Comprehension Check** (a) In "Trying to Name...," what does Roselva say is the one thing that doesn't change? (b) Whom does the speaker meet in "I Myself"? (c) In "Do not trust...," whom is the speaker addressing?

2. **Strategy: Create Mental Images** (a) Which passages in each poem were you able to picture most clearly? Why? (b) In what ways did this strategy deepen your understanding of the poems?

Analysis and Discussion

3. (a) In "Trying to Name...," what different details do Roselva and Peter notice about train tracks? (b) **Analyze** Explain how these contrasting details support the conclusions each character draws about the tracks.

4. (a) **Analyze** In the third stanza of "I Myself," why is the speaker defeated? (b) **Analyze Cause and Effect** What happens to the speaker as a result? (c) **Interpret** What does this poem suggest about the reasons people fail? Explain.

5. (a) **Analyze** In "Do not trust...," what are the cross-outs, scribbles, discards, and "mis takes" the speaker refers to? (b) **Interpret** Why does the speaker encourage you to prefer these over an eraser? Explain.

6. **Get Ready for Close Reading** Choose a passage from each poem that you find especially interesting or important. You'll discuss the passages with your group during Close-Read activities.

> **WORKING AS A GROUP**
>
> Discuss your responses to the Analysis and Discussion questions with your group.
>
> • Support your responses with text evidence.
>
> • Adapt your speech to be appropriate for a group discussion about literature. Decide whether you should use a speaking style that is informal and friendly, formal and serious, or a combination of both. Then, apply your style as you discuss the poems.

Exploring the Essential Question

Can people really change?

7. What have you learned about different perspectives and attitudes related to change from reading the poems? Explore your ideas in your Evidence Log.

STANDARDS

Reading Literature
Cite several pieces of textual evidence to support analysis of what the text says explicitly as well as inferences drawn from the text.

Speaking and Listening
Adapt speech to a variety of contexts and tasks.

ANALYZE AND INTERPRET

POETRY COLLECTION

Close Read

PRACTICE Complete the following activities. Use text evidence to support your responses.

1. **Present and Discuss** With your group, share the passages from the poems that you found especially interesting. For example, you might focus on the following passages:

   - **Lines 19–22 of "Trying to Name…":** Discuss the effect of the train whistle and what it might be taking away from the speaker.

   - **Lines 1–6 of "I Myself":** Discuss what the speaker's other self is like and why he might be that way.

   - **Line 8 of "Do not trust…":** Discuss why the poet may have written *mis takes* instead of *mistakes*.

2. **Reflect on Your Learning** What new ideas or insights did you uncover during your second reading of the texts?

WORD WALL

Note words in the poems that are related to the idea of transformations. Add them to your Word Wall.

STUDY LANGUAGE AND CRAFT

Concept Vocabulary

Why These Words? The vocabulary words are related.

| shrinking | distorting | discards |

1. With your group, determine what the words have in common. Write your ideas.

2. Add another word that fits the category. _____

3. Write a stanza of a poem, using all three concept vocabulary words.

Word Study

Latin Root: -tort- In "I Myself," the speaker says his body is *distorting* his plans. The word *distorting* contains the Latin root -tort-, which means "twist."

PRACTICE Using this knowledge, write a definition for *distorting*. Then, use a dictionary to find meanings for the words *retort* and *contort*. Explain how the Latin root -tort- gives a clue to the meaning of each word.

STANDARDS

Reading Literature
Determine a theme or central idea of a text and analyze its development over the course of the text.

Language
Use common, grade-appropriate Greek or Latin affixes and roots as clues to the meaning of a word.

344 UNIT 3 • TRANSFORMATIONS

Essential Question: Can people really change?

Imagery and Themes

Imagery is figurative language that appeals to the senses and creates vivid pictures in your mind. As you read poetry, analyze uses of imagery you find. The use of related images within a poem may help you to interpret its **themes**, or insights about life.

EXAMPLES: Related Images

POEM	EXAMPLES FROM THE POEMS	RELATED IDEAS
Trying to Name What Doesn't Change	abandoned track; track without a train	absence, emptiness, being left behind
I Myself	a stubborn expression; a hardness in the eyes	harshness, hostility
Do not trust the eraser	eraser; crossed out; scribbled over	replacement, removal

PRACTICE Work with your group to complete the activity and answer the questions.

1. **Analyze** Use the chart to analyze the ideas suggested by the imagery in "Trying to Name What Doesn't Change." One item has been done for you. What similar ideas connect all of these images? Explain.

IMAGERY	IDEAS SUGGESTED
weeds that grow up spidery (line 3)	weeds = decay and neglect; spidery makes the image more visual and scarier
metal wasn't shiny anymore. / The wood was split and some of the ties were gone. (lines 9–10) tilted house (line 13)	
Stars explode. (line 16) The rose curls up as if there is fire in the petals. (line 17)	

2. **Interpret** In "I Myself," the speaker refers to his other self as "a man who'd stop at nothing" and "my enemy." What theme do these details suggest? Explain.

3. **Interpret** In "Do not trust the eraser," the speaker refers to "something once thought correct" and "your original genius." What theme do these details suggest? Explain.

Poetry Collection 345

STUDY LANGUAGE AND CRAFT

POETRY COLLECTION

Poetic Structures and Meaning

The most basic structure in a poem is a **line,** or horizontal group of words. **Stanzas** are groups of lines that are separated by space. The structures of lines and stanzas help shape a poem's meaning and fulfill the poet's purpose for writing.

STANZA TRAITS	DETAILS
Stanzas are named for the number of lines they contain and may be as short as one line.	two lines = *couplet*; three lines = *tercet*; four lines = *quatrain*; five lines = *cinquain*; six lines = *sestet*
Each stanza usually expresses a single, focused idea.	• In a lyric poem, each stanza may offer a new thought. • In a narrative poem, each stanza may show a new stage in the plot. (See TIP box.) • In a free-verse poem, as in all poems, each stanza may reflect on a new thought or build upon a previous one.

TIP: A narrative poem tells a story that includes all the stages of a plot:
- *Exposition:* background
- *Rising Action:* start of the conflict
- *Climax:* point of greatest tension
- *Resolution:* end of the conflict

PRACTICE Work with your group to complete the activities.

1. **(a) Label** Identify each type of stanza (tercet, etc.) in "Trying to Name…" **(b) Analyze** Explain the key idea expressed in each stanza.

STANZA TYPE	KEY IDEA EXPRESSED
Stanza 1:	One point of view:
Stanza 2:	Another point of view:
Stanza 3:	Speaker's Observations:
Stanza 4:	Speaker's Observations:
Stanza 5:	Speaker's Insight:

2. **(a) Analyze** What structures in "I Myself" indicate that it is a narrative poem? **(b) Evaluate** Do you find the narrative structure to be effective? Why, or why not?

3. **(a)** What do you notice about the structure of lines 4, 6, and 10 in "Do not trust…"? **(b) Analyze** How does this unique feature affect the meaning of the poem?

STANDARDS

Reading Literature
Analyze how a drama's or poem's form or structure contributes to its meaning.

Speaking and Listening
• Use appropriate eye contact, adequate volume, and clear pronunciation.
• Adapt speech to a variety of contexts and tasks.

SHARE IDEAS

Speaking and Listening

To perform a **dramatic reading** of poetry, a presenter reads aloud a poem with emotion and gestures to convey the thoughts and feelings of the speaker.

Assignment

Choose one of the poems in this collection and deliver to your group a **dramatic reading** that brings the poem to life.

- ○ Trying to Name What Doesn't Change
- ○ I Myself
- ○ Do not trust the eraser

Prepare Imagine you are the speaker in your chosen poem. Use the following suggestions to adapt your speech for a dramatic reading.

- Read aloud the poem repeatedly to become familiar with it.
- Practice pronouncing words clearly, especially if they are new to you.
- Mark words you will speak loudly or softly and places where you will speak quickly or slowly.
- Vary your tone of voice to express different feelings at different points in the poem.
- Plan the gestures you will use to express emotions as you speak.
- Make occasional eye contact to fully engage audience members.

Present Deliver your dramatic reading to your group. Remember to present the poem as if you are the speaker.

Evaluate Use a guide like the one shown to evaluate your own dramatic reading as well as those of your classmates.

PRESENTATION EVALUATION GUIDE

Rate each statement on a scale of 1 (not demonstrated) to 4 (fully demonstrated).

Statement	1	2	3	4
The presenter's delivery was vivid and brought the poem to life.	○	○	○	○
The presenter used appropriate eye contact, adequate volume, and clear pronunciation.	○	○	○	○
The presenter's tone of voice, volume, pacing, and gestures effectively expressed the poem's meaning and the speaker's emotions.	○	○	○	○

EVIDENCE LOG

Before moving on to a new selection, go to your Evidence Log and record any additional thoughts and observations you may have about the Poetry Collection.

LEARN ABOUT GENRE: NONFICTION

MAKEUP ARTIST MIMI CHOI'S... •
MIMI CHOI BRINGS FEAR...

Reading Human Interest Stories

A **human interest story** is a popular form of journalism that focuses on the more personal side of current events.

The selection you are about to read is a human interest story. After reading, you will view a video related to the topic.

HUMAN INTEREST STORIES

Author's Purpose
- to inform readers about a person in an engaging way

Characteristics
- one or more central ideas, or main points, about the person profiled
- supporting evidence, such as direct quotations or images
- details that appeal to readers' emotions

Structure
- may be published as written text, images, videos, or a combination of these elements
- information that answers basic questions: *who, what, where, when, why,* and *how*

Take a Minute!

FIND Work with a partner to find a human interest story in a daily newspaper or magazine, either in print or online. Jot down the title.

Why do you think this is a human interest story?

STANDARDS
Reading Informational Text
• Determine two or more central ideas in a text and analyze their development over the course of the text.

• By the end of the year, read and comprehend literary nonfiction.

348 UNIT 3 • TRANSFORMATIONS

Essential Question: Can people really change?

Central Ideas

A **central idea** is an author's main point—the message they want readers to understand. A nonfiction text often contains multiple central ideas. The author develops each one with supporting evidence or details, such as direct quotations and images.

- **Direct quotations** are the exact words a person says. Authors of human interest stories may include quotations to show specific details about the subject.
- **Images** convey information visually. They can be still images, such as photographs, or moving images, such as videos. Images grab a viewer's attention and convey information in a way that is different from written text.

Sometimes authors state their central ideas directly. Often, however, readers must determine central ideas by making **inferences**, or educated guesses, based on evidence in the text.

> **PRACTICE** Complete the activity on your own. Then share your responses with your group.
>
> Imagine you are writing a story about a local hero who rescued someone in danger. Complete the chart by describing a quotation or an image that would help develop each central idea in your story. The first item has been done for you.
>
> | HUMAN INTEREST STORY ABOUT A LOCAL HERO ||
> |---|---|
> | **CENTRAL IDEA** | **DESCRIPTION OF QUOTATION OR IMAGE** |
> | a. The opportunity to play a heroic role is rare. | quotation from the local police chief about how unusual the dangerous situation was |
> | b. A hero is often an ordinary person faced with an extraordinary situation. | |
> | c. A heroic act may affect many people. | |
> | d. A heroic act may change the hero's life in a profound way. | |

Learn About Genre **349**

PREPARE TO READ

Makeup Artist Mimi Choi's Mesmerizing Art-Inspired Beauty Looks • Mimi Choi Brings Fear to Life With Her Makeup Artistry

About the Author

Ryma Chikhoune is a beauty reporter for *Women's Wear Daily*, a fashion-trade journal. Her articles have also appeared in such magazines as *Vanity Fair*, *The Hollywood Reporter*, and *Interview*. She received a Bachelor of Arts degree in journalism from the University of Maryland.

STANDARDS

Speaking and Listening
Analyze the main ideas and supporting details presented in diverse media and formats and explain how the ideas clarify a topic, text, or issue under study.

Language
Consult general and specialized reference materials, both print and digital, to find the pronunciation of a word or determine or clarify its precise meaning or its part of speech.

Concept Vocabulary

As you read "Makeup Artist Mimi Choi's...," you will encounter these words. When you finish reading, work with your group to identify what the words have in common.

| intricate | illusion | inspiration |

Reference Materials A **dictionary** is a print or digital reference source that provides information about words, including their precise meanings, parts of speech, spellings, pronunciations, and word origins.

SAMPLE DIGITAL DICTIONARY ENTRY

embellishment   [ihm BEH lihsh mehnt] *n.* 🔊

Examples   Word Origin   Synonyms

1. decoration; adornment
2. detail, perhaps imaginary, added to make a story more interesting

Analysis: This entry shows that *embellishment* is a noun with four syllables. To hear the word pronounced, you would click the audio icon. To see it in sentences, you would click *Examples*. To learn about its origins and synonyms, you would click the appropriate links.

PRACTICE As you read the article and watch the video that follows, use a print or online dictionary to find the pronunciations, precise meanings, and parts of speech of unfamiliar words. Note this information in the open space next to the selections.

Viewing Strategy: Listen Actively

When you watch a video, **listen actively** and pay attention to both the spoken words and the onscreen images. Notice language and scenes that express the speaker's emotions or that show connections, such as cause and effect. Doing so will help you analyze the video's main ideas and better understand its topic.

PRACTICE As you watch the video, listen actively. Use the Take Notes space to jot down main ideas and supporting details presented in both words and images. Then, work with your group to explain how the ideas you noted help clarify the topic of the video.

HUMAN INTEREST STORY

Makeup Artist Mimi Choi's Mesmerizing Art-Inspired Beauty Looks

Ryma Chikhoune

BACKGROUND

Mimi Choi is a makeup artist who works in an artistic tradition called surrealism that deliberately distorts reality. One of surrealism's most famous artists is the Spanish painter Salvador Dalí. His work depicts objects in bizarre ways, as if seen in a dream.

1 Makeup transforms, inside and out. It's what attracted makeup artist Mimi Choi to the art form as a child. She was fascinated by the power of makeup. She said: "I would watch my mom put on mascara and red lipstick, and eventually, I snuck into her makeup collection and tried things out on myself."

2 Choi began experimenting with looks while in college, but it was just a hobby then, and she went on to become a preschool teacher for several years.

READ TO UNLOCK MEANING

1. First read the text for comprehension and enjoyment.
2. With your group, apply the vocabulary strategy to unlock word meanings.
3. Find other details in the text you find interesting. Ask your own questions and draw your own conclusions.

Use a dictionary or indicate another strategy you used that helped you determine meaning.

intricate (IHN trih cuht) *adj.*
MEANING:

illusion (ih LOO zhuhn) *n.*
MEANING:

inspiration (ihn spuh RAY shuhn) *n.*
MEANING:

3   "I enjoyed doing **intricate** nail art during my free time as a creative outlet," she explained. "This is when I decided to enroll in makeup school and pursue my passion."

4   It's at Blanche Macdonald, the beauty school in Vancouver, Canada—where she's based—that Choi began to explore **illusion** makeup looks. In 2013, she started sharing them on Instagram, and today, she has 1.6 million followers on the platform, where she's known as @mimles.

5   "My audience has grown organically," she said. "As I created more looks and my technique improved, I would be featured by makeup brands and various media outlets around the world.

6   "Honestly, I don't pay much attention to my follower count," she continued. "I paint for myself, but I am grateful that others enjoy my work as well."

7   Finding **inspiration** from "everything" around her, "including paintings, textures, patterns and even my dreams," she said, the art world has had "a huge" influence on her work. "When I travel, I like to explore museums, which is where I gain much of my inspiration." Maurits Cornelis Escher, Salvador Dalí and Giuseppe Arcimboldo are artists she particularly loves. "They go beyond simply painting what they see," Choi said. "Their illusional interpretations are so inspiring to me, and their works challenge me to achieve their level of creativity." 🐝

©Mimi Choi Makeup Artistry Inc.

MEDIA: VIDEO

WATCH AND LISTEN ▶

Mimi Choi Brings Fear to Life With Her Makeup Artistry

True Calling Media

BACKGROUND

Artists find inspiration in many places, such as the work of other artists, nature, and personal experiences. For some artists, their dreams are a particularly rich source of inspiration. The artistic creations that have originated in dreams encompass many art forms, including movies, songs, paintings, and novels.

TAKE NOTES As you watch and listen, take notes to record main ideas and supporting details that help explain the topic.

BUILD INSIGHT

MAKEUP ARTIST MIMI CHOI'S... •
MIMI CHOI BRINGS FEAR...

First Thoughts

Select one of the following items to discuss with your group.

- How did you react to the transformed faces that Mimi Choi creates? What, if anything, do they remind you of? What feelings do they call up in you?

- Do you think transforming yourself as drastically as Choi does reveals or hides your true self? Explain your response.

Summary

Write a short objective summary of the human interest story and video to describe Mimi Choi and her work. Remember to include only the main ideas, and do not include your opinions.

Analysis and Discussion

1. **(a) Make Inferences** Reread paragraphs 5 and 6 of the human interest story. What inference can you make about Choi's values as an artist from these paragraphs? **(b) Connect** Replay the video and listen carefully to what Choi says between time codes 2:12 and 2:19. Do her statements support the inference you made about her artistic values? Cite evidence from the selections to explain your response.

2. **Analyze Cause and Effect** In the video, Choi describes an interaction between herself and another person that causes Choi to make a big change. Describe the interaction and explain its effect on Choi.

3. **(a)** The human interest story describes experiences in Choi's life that led to her career as an illusion makeup artist. What were those experiences? **(b) Analyze** What specific words and phrases in the text reveal that those experiences were important to Choi? **(c) Speculate** Where do you think Choi's passion for makeup art might take her next in her career?

4. **Get Ready for Close Reading** Choose a passage from the human interest story or the video that you find especially interesting. You'll discuss the passage with your group during Close-Read activities.

Exploring the Essential Question

Can people really change?

5. What do the human interest story and video reveal about what it takes to transform one's life? Record your ideas in your Evidence Log.

WORKING AS A GROUP

Discuss your responses to the Analysis and Discussion questions with your group.

- Note points of agreement and disagreement.
- Ask follow-up questions of peers, as needed, to clarify their ideas.

If necessary, revise your original answers to reflect what you learn from your discussion.

STANDARDS

Reading Informational Text
• Cite several pieces of textual evidence to support analysis of what the text says explicitly as well as inferences drawn from the text.
• Compare and contrast a text to an audio, video, or multimedia version of the text.

Language
Use the relationship between particular words to better understand each of the words.

354 UNIT 3 • TRANSFORMATIONS

ANALYZE AND INTERPRET

Close Read

PRACTICE Complete the following activities. Use text evidence to support your responses.

1. **Present and Discuss** With your group, share passages from the human interest story or the video that you found especially interesting. For example, you might focus on the following passages:

   - **Paragraph 7 of the article:** Discuss what Choi finds inspiring in other artists' work.
   - **Passage from 2:19 to 2:36 of the video:** Discuss what fear means to Choi as an artist.

2. **Reflect on Your Learning** What new ideas or insights did you uncover during your second review of the text and video?

STUDY LANGUAGE AND CRAFT

Concept Vocabulary

Why These Words? The vocabulary words are related.

| intricate | illusion | inspiration |

WORD WALL

Note words in the text that are related to the concept of transformations. Add them to your Word Wall.

1. With your group, determine what the words have in common. Write your ideas.

2. Add another word that fits the category. _____

3. Discuss each question: **(a)** Could an *intricate* jigsaw puzzle be done in a few minutes? **(b)** What sort of *illusion* might you create for a school carnival? **(c)** What is a source of *inspiration* for you?

Word Study

Synonyms and Antonyms A **synonym** is a word that has the same or nearly the same meaning as another word. *Complex* and *elaborate* are synonyms of *intricate*. An **antonym** is a word that has the opposite meaning of another word. *Simple* and *uncomplicated* are antonyms of *intricate*.

PRACTICE Consult a thesaurus to find two synonyms and two antonyms for the vocabulary words *illusion* and *inspiration*. Then, explain how the relationship between the words helps you understand each word.

ANALYZE AND INTERPRET

MAKEUP ARTIST MIMI CHOI'S... • MIMI CHOI BRINGS FEAR...

Central Ideas

Informational texts, whether written or multimedia, convey **central ideas**. When you read, hear, or view an informational selection, analyzing the following elements can help you determine its central ideas:

- direct statements
- quotations
- repeated ideas
- vivid images

When reading two or more pieces on the same topic, you may want to compare the central ideas they contain and analyze how they are conveyed. Ask yourself questions like these:

- Which presentation provides more detailed information?
- Which provides better visual support for ideas?
- Which conveys emotions more effectively?

PRACTICE Work on your own to complete the activities. Then, share your responses with your group.

1. **Compare and Contrast** Describe the similarities and differences in the use of media and in the information presented in the two selections.

2. **Analyze** Review the selections and determine two central ideas developed in each one. Write them in the chart. In the last row, write a central idea that is common to both selections.

Human Interest Story	Video
Common Central Idea:	

3. **Evaluate** Explain which of the two selections you think is more effective at developing its central ideas and portraying its subject, Mimi Choi. In your explanation, consider these questions: *Which selection portrays Choi more vividly? Which has a stronger impact on the reader or viewer?*

STANDARDS

Reading Informational Text
- Determine two or more central ideas in a text and analyze their development over the course of the text.
- Compare and contrast a text to an audio, video, or multimedia version of the text, analyzing each medium's portrayal of the subject.

Speaking and Listening
Include multimedia components and visual displays in presentations to clarify claims and findings and emphasize salient points.

Language
Use knowledge of language and its conventions when writing, speaking, reading, or listening.

356 UNIT 3 • TRANSFORMATIONS

SHARE IDEAS

Speaking and Listening

A **multimedia presentation** is a speech that incorporates multiple forms of media—text, charts, images, video, and sound—to convey information.

Assignment

With your group, create and deliver a **multimedia presentation** that portrays someone or something that has undergone a transformation. For example, you might depict a person, an object, or a location that has changed over time, such as an empty lot that has been converted into a community garden.

Choose one of these formats:

○ an oral presentation that explains the transformation using text and images

○ a video presentation that shows the transformation using video and audio

Plan Work with your group to identify your subject and its transformation. Then, consider the media and visuals you'll use to emphasize your main points.

- For an oral presentation, brainstorm images, captions, and direct quotations that could provide evidence of the transformation.
- For a video presentation, determine how you will obtain or create audio and video recordings to show the transformation.

Make a list of tasks that your group will need to complete, and then assign roles to individual group members.

Prepare Follow these steps to prepare your presentation:

- Create and assemble your various media components.
- Write a script to organize the presentation. Include speakers' lines and media cues.
- Reread and edit the script and any text that appears in the presentation to clarify ideas and fix errors in grammar, usage, or conventions.
- Rehearse your presentation before sharing it with your class.

Speak and Listen Present your work. As you speak, use your knowledge of standard English grammar, usage, and conventions to express your ideas clearly. Listen actively as other groups present. Ask questions after the presentations if anything is unclear.

> **EVIDENCE LOG**
>
> Before moving on, go to your Evidence Log and record any additional thoughts or observations you may have about "Makeup Artist Mimi Choi's…" and "Mimi Choi Brings Fear…."

PERFORMANCE TASK

SOURCES

- *from* A Christmas Carol
- Thank You, M'am
- Trying to Name What Doesn't Change
- I Myself

Deliver a Dramatic Adaptation

A **dramatic adaptation** is a play that is based on another literary work, such as a novel, work of literary nonfiction, short story, or poem. An adaptation brings a text to life and interprets it in a new way.

Assignment

You have read different selections about the possibilities of change. With your group, write and deliver a **dramatic adaptation** of one of the following texts:

- ○ the novella excerpt *A Christmas Carol*
- ○ the short story "Thank You, M'am"
- ○ the poem "Trying to Name What Doesn't Change"
- ○ the poem "I Myself"

Plan With Your Group

Choose a Text Discuss the selections with your group and choose one to interpret as a play. Focus on how to bring the text to life for an audience:

- What aspects of the text need to be explained by a narrator?
- How can you convey the thoughts of characters who do not speak aloud in the text?
- What language from the text do you want to use exactly? What vocabulary will you modify?
- What props and costumes will you need?

Write and Rehearse

Write the Script Develop parts for a narrator and characters, and organize your script to follow play format. Include stage directions that tell actors how to deliver their lines. Make sure every group member has a defined role to play, and support each other as you develop the script.

When your script is complete, ask a teacher or drama coach for feedback. Use their comments to determine how you can revise, edit, or rewrite your script—or approach it differently—to produce a strong, coherent adaptation.

STANDARDS

Writing
- Produce clear and coherent writing in which the development, organization, and style are appropriate to task, purpose, and audience.
- With some guidance and support from peers and adults, develop and strengthen writing as needed by planning, revising, editing, rewriting, or trying a new approach, focusing on how well purpose and audience have been addressed.

Speaking and Listening
Pose questions that elicit elaboration and respond to others' questions and comments with relevant observations and ideas.

Essential Question: Can people really change?

Rehearse Practice your delivery as a group. Adapt your speech to suit the character you will portray and request feedback about your performance. Keep your audience and purpose in mind as you consider these questions:

- Does each performer's tone, or emotional attitude, fit the character and situation?
- Does each performer use their voice, gestures, and movements to show a character's unique personality?
- Can changes be made to the script, such as revisions to vocabulary or stage directions, that would improve the performance?

Use your rehearsal to revise the script and strengthen your delivery.

Deliver Your Adaptation

Present to the Class Use the following tips to make your presentation effective and engaging.

- Vary the highs and lows of your voice to express emotion and convey an appropriate attitude, or tone.
- Vary the volume of your voice and the speed at which you speak to stress important words, create suspense, and convey emotions.
- Use body language that reinforces the meaning of your lines and adds to the interest and emotional impact of the performance.

Discuss and Evaluate

Explain Your Adaptation After presenting, work with your group to discuss your performance with the audience. Address the following:

- how you interpreted the text
- what purposes you wanted to fulfill
- which elements you wanted to emphasize
- how you used your voice
- why you chose the props and costumes you used

Listen Actively Pay close attention as other groups present their adaptations. Focus on the performers as you listen to the words they speak. Prepare for the discussion by taking notes, jotting down words that will remind you of relevant observations you may share or questions you might ask.

Participate in Discussion When it's time to discuss a group's performance, express your thoughts in a respectful and helpful manner. Begin by saying what you liked or thought worked well, and then ask a question or make an observation about a less successful element. Offer a suggestion for improving the performance.

Performance Task: Deliver a Dramatic Adaptation

INDEPENDENT LEARNING

Essential Question

Can people really change?

As we go through life, we change physically. We also become more responsible and learn new skills. However, is there something inside all of us that does *not* change? In this section, you will choose a selection about transformations to read independently. Get the most from this section by establishing a purpose for reading. Ask yourself, "What do I hope to gain from my independent reading?" Here are just a few purposes you might consider:

Read to Learn Think about the selections you have already studied. What questions do you still have about the unit topic?

Read to Enjoy Read the descriptions of the texts. Which one seems most interesting and appealing to you?

Read to Form a Position Consider your thoughts and feelings about the Essential Question. Are you still undecided about some aspect of the unit topic?

Independent Learning Strategies

Throughout your life, in school, in your community, and in your career, you will need to rely on yourself to learn and work on your own. Use these strategies to keep your focus as you read independently for sustained periods of time. Add ideas of your own for each category.

STRATEGY	MY ACTION PLAN
Create a schedule	• Plan a time to read so you can give the selection your full attention. • Be realistic about how long it will take to complete activities. •
Read with purpose	• Notice how you respond to the text. What do you like? What don't you like? Why? • Keep a reference source on hand, such as a print or online dictionary, to check the meanings of words you don't know. •
Take notes	• Remember that the act of taking notes can help you recall details and information. • Jot down only a few key words that will jog your memory; don't try to write everything. •

360 UNIT 3 • TRANSFORMATIONS

Contents

Choose one selection. Selections are available online only.

REFLECTIVE ESSAY

Little Things Are Big
Jesús Colón

Can one subway ride change a person forever?

HISTORICAL NARRATIVE

The Story of Victor d'Aveyron, the Wild Child
Eloise Montalban

Does Victor hold the key to defining what is human?

SHORT STORY

A Retrieved Reformation
O. Henry

Jimmy Valentine finally proves himself in a matter of life or death.

FABLE

The Old Man and His Grandson
Jacob and Wilhelm Grimm

Sometimes adults can learn important lessons from a child.

SHARE YOUR INDEPENDENT LEARNING

SHARE • LEARN • REFLECT

Reflect on and evaluate the information you gained from your Independent Reading selection. Then, share what you learned with others.

Independent Learning **361**

INDEPENDENT LEARNING

Close-Read Guide

A Close-Read Guide and Annotation Model are available online.

Establish your purpose for reading. Then, read the selection through at least once. Use this page to record your close-read ideas.

Selection Title: _____

Purpose for Reading: _____   Minutes Read: _____

Close Read the Text

Zoom in on sections you found interesting. **Annotate** what you notice. Ask yourself **questions** about the text. What can you **conclude**?

_____
_____
_____
_____
_____
_____
_____
_____
_____

Analyze the Text

Think about the author's choices of literary elements, techniques, and structures. Select one and record your thoughts.

_____
_____
_____
_____
_____
_____
_____
_____
_____

QuickWrite

Choose a paragraph from the text that grabbed your interest. Explain the power of this passage.

_____
_____
_____
_____
_____
_____
_____
_____

Essential Question: Can people really change?

Share Your Independent Learning

Essential Question

Can people really change?

When you read something independently, your understanding continues to grow as you share what you have learned with others.

Prepare to Share

WRITE Think about the text you explored independently and the ways in which it connects to your own experiences.

- What similarities and differences do you see between the text and your own life? Describe your observations.
- How do you think this text connects to the Essential Question? Describe your ideas.

Learn From Your Classmates

DISCUSS Hold a collaborative discussion about the texts. Build on your classmates' ideas as they share their selections, and express your own ideas about the one you chose. As you discuss, acknowledge new information expressed by your classmates. Take notes on points that seem important and consider whether they cause you to modify your views about particular ideas.

Reflect

EXPLAIN Review your notes, and mark the most important insight you gained from these writing and discussion activities. Explain how this idea adds to your understanding of transformations.

STANDARDS
Speaking and Listening • Engage effectively in a range of collaborative discussions with diverse partners on grade 7 topics, texts, and issues, building on others' ideas and expressing their own clearly. • Acknowledge new information expressed by others and, when warranted, modify their own views.

UNIT 3 REFLECT AND RESPOND

In this unit, you encountered many different perspectives on transformations. Now, take some time to reflect on the texts you explored and to express your own ideas.

Reflect on Your Unit Goals

Review your Unit Goals chart from the beginning of the unit. Then, complete the activity and answer the question.

1. In the Unit Goals chart, rate how well you meet each goal now.

2. In which goals were you most and least successful?

Reflect on the Texts

Guest Panel Imagine you are hosting a podcast episode about transformations. If you could put together a guest panel of three people from this unit, who would you choose, and why? In the chart, list one person connected to each text—an author, a character, or a real person. Then, mark your top three choices. Briefly explain what each person would contribute to a conversation about transformations and write at least one question you'd like to ask the panel.

TITLE	PODCAST GUEST	REASON AND QUESTION
A Christmas Carol: Scrooge and Marley, Act I		
A Christmas Carol: Scrooge and Marley, Act II		
from A Christmas Carol		
Thank You, M'am		
Learning Rewires the Brain		
• Trying to Name What Doesn't Change • I Myself • Do not trust the eraser		
Makeup Artist Mimi Choi's… • Mimi Choi Brings Fear…		
Independent Learning Selection:		

364 UNIT 3 • TRANSFORMATIONS

Essential Question: Can people really change?

Develop Your Perspective: Unit Projects

Choose one of the following Unit Project ideas.

POEM

Write a lyric, narrative, or free-verse poem about transformation. Use one of the unit poems as a model, and include at least two concept vocabulary words. In your poem, be sure to include imagery that will appeal to the readers' senses and create vivid pictures in their minds. Finally, give your poem an interesting title that will engage your audience.

SOCIAL MEDIA POST

Write a social media post as a character or subject from a unit selection. Discuss the way you have transformed and one positive aspect of that transformation. Use at least two concept vocabulary words in your post.

INFORMAL DEBATE

In small groups, **hold an informal debate** about the Essential Question: *Can people really change?*

Divide into two teams to represent the two sides of the issue. With your team, prepare several reasons that support your side of the argument, and note evidence from the unit that strengthens your position. Incorporate at least two academic vocabulary words from the unit into your presentation.

As teams take turns defending their positions, remember to be respectful of others' ideas and opinions, even if you don't agree with them.

USE NEW WORDS

Academic Vocabulary

Use the academic vocabulary from the unit as you plan, draft, and discuss your project:

- ingenious
- omniscient
- envision
- lucid
- sensation

Concept Vocabulary

Review your Word Wall and write down any words you want to use in your project:

STANDARDS

Writing

- Produce clear and coherent writing in which the development, organization, and style are appropriate to task, purpose, and audience.

- Draw evidence from literary or informational texts to support analysis, reflection, and research.

- Write routinely over shorter time frames for a range of discipline-specific tasks, purposes, and audiences.

PERFORMANCE-BASED ASSESSMENT

SOURCES
- Whole-Class Selections
- Peer-Group Selections
- Independent Learning Selection
- Your own experiences and observations

Short Story

Assignment

In this unit, you have read about change and transformation from different perspectives. You have also practiced writing a short story. Now, apply what you have learned.

Imagine one of the characters from this unit ten years later. What has happened to this person? Have they changed? Write a **short story** that explores the Essential Question.

Essential Question
Can people really change?

Review and Evaluate Evidence

Review your Evidence Log and your QuickWrite from the beginning of the unit and complete the chart. Have your ideas changed?

⬤ Yes	⬤ No
Identify at least three examples or details that made you think differently about people's ability to change.	Identify at least three examples or other details that reinforced your initial ideas about people's ability to change.
1.	1.
2.	2.
3.	3.

State your ideas now:

How might you reflect on your thinking about people's ability to change in a short story?

Essential Question: Can people really change?

Share Your Perspective

The **Short Story Checklist** will help you stay on track.

PLAN Before you write, read the Short Story Checklist and make sure you understand all the items.

DRAFT As you write, pause occasionally to make sure you're meeting the checklist requirements.

Use Academic Vocabulary Refer to your Word Wall to vary your word choice. Also, consider using one or more of the academic vocabulary terms you learned at the beginning of the unit: *omniscient, ingenious, envision, lucid, sensation.*

REVIEW AND EDIT After you have written a first draft, evaluate it against the checklist. Make any changes needed to clarify the sequence of events or to make your characters more vivid. Then, reread your story and fix any errors you find.

EVIDENCE LOG

Make sure you have pulled in details from your Evidence Log to support your insights about transformations.

SHORT STORY CHECKLIST

My short story clearly contains…

- ○ well-described characters and dialogue that reveals what they are like.
- ○ a natural and logical sequence of events driven by a meaningful conflict.
- ○ vivid settings and actions described using precise words and sensory language.
- ○ a consistent narrative point of view, whether first-person, third-person limited, or third-person omniscient.
- ○ pacing that develops experiences, events, and characters in an intentional way.
- ○ transitions that lead from event to event and to the conclusion that follows.
- ○ correct use of standard English grammar, usage, and conventions, including avoidance of run-ons and strictly intentional use of sentence fragments.
- ○ no capitalization, punctuation, or spelling errors.

STANDARDS
Writing
- Engage and orient the reader by establishing a context and point of view and introducing a narrator and/or characters; organize an event sequence that unfolds naturally and logically.
- Use narrative techniques, such as dialogue, pacing, and description, to develop experiences, events, and/or characters.
- Use precise words and phrases, relevant descriptive details, and sensory language to capture the action and convey experiences and events.

Learning From Nature

WATCH THE ViDEO

DISCUSS In what ways do people, plants, and animals depend on each other?

Write your response before sharing your ideas.

UNIT 4

INTRO

Essential Question

What is the relationship between people and nature?

RESEARCH-BASED ESSAY
Wildlife Rehabbers Are Here to Help

MENTOR TEXT

WHOLE-CLASS LEARNING

The Bee Highway: Making a Place for Bees in the City
Kathryn Hulick

FEATURE ARTICLE

from **Silent Spring**
Rachel Carson

DESCRIPTIVE ESSAY

COMPARE

How Grandmother Spider Stole the Sun
Michael J. Caduto and Joseph Bruchac

CREATION STORY

Coyote Steals the Sun and Moon
Richard Erdoes and Alfonso Ortiz

CREATION STORY

Write a Research Paper

WRITING: PERFORMANCE TASK

PEER-GROUP LEARNING

COMPARE

Our Purpose in Poetry: Or, Earthrise
Amanda Gorman

LYRIC POETRY

Earthrise
Amanda Gorman

MEDIA: SPOKEN-WORD POETRY

Creature Comforts: Three Biology-Based Tips for Builders
Mary Beth Cox

SCIENCE FEATURE

He—y, Come On Ou—t!
Shinichi Hoshi, translated by Stanleigh Jones

MAGICAL REALISM

Give and Follow Instructions

SPEAKING AND LISTENING: PERFORMANCE TASK

INDEPENDENT LEARNING

from **My Side of the Mountain**
Jean Craighead George

ADVENTURE STORY

How the Teens of St. Pete Youth Farm Fight Food Insecurity, One Harvest at a Time
Gabrielle Calise

FEATURE ARTICLE

Rice University Researchers Are Turning Dead Spiders Into "Necrobots"
Ariana Garcia

SCIENCE ARTICLE

Turtle Watchers
Linda Hogan

Jaguar
Francisco X. Alarcón

The Sparrow
Paul Laurence Dunbar

LYRIC POETRY

SHARE • LEARN • REFLECT

SHARE INDEPENDENT LEARNING

REFLECT AND RESPOND

GOALS • TEXTS • UNIT PROJECTS

PERFORMANCE-BASED ASSESSMENT

Research-Based Essay
You will write a research-based essay in response to the Essential Question for the unit.

UNIT 4 INTRODUCTION

Unit Goals

Throughout this unit, you will deepen your perspective about the relationship between people and nature by reading, writing, speaking, listening, and presenting. These goals will help you succeed on the Unit Performance-Based Assessment.

SET GOALS Use a scale of 1 to 5 to rate how well you meet these goals right now. You will revisit your ratings later, when you reflect on your growth during this unit.

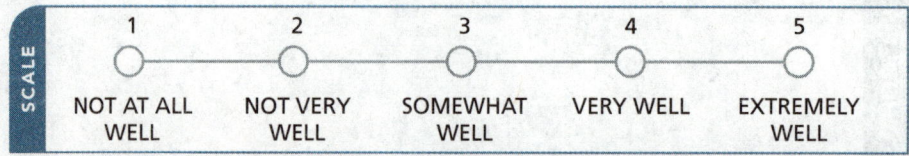

SCALE:
1 — NOT AT ALL WELL
2 — NOT VERY WELL
3 — SOMEWHAT WELL
4 — VERY WELL
5 — EXTREMELY WELL

	Unit Introduction	Unit Reflection
ESSENTIAL QUESTION		
I can read selections that explore the interactions between people and nature and use what I learn as a springboard for future research.	1 2 3 4 5	1 2 3 4 5
READING	Unit Introduction	Unit Reflection
I can understand and use academic vocabulary words related to research writing.	1 2 3 4 5	1 2 3 4 5
I can recognize elements of different genres, especially descriptive essays, informational texts, and magical realism.	1 2 3 4 5	1 2 3 4 5
I can read a selection of my choice independently and make connections to other texts.	1 2 3 4 5	1 2 3 4 5
WRITING	Unit Introduction	Unit Reflection
I can write a well-documented research paper.	1 2 3 4 5	1 2 3 4 5
SPEAKING AND LISTENING	Unit Introduction	Unit Reflection
I can research, give, and follow instructions.	1 2 3 4 5	1 2 3 4 5
MY GOALS	Unit Introduction	Unit Reflection

STANDARDS

Language
- Use common, grade-appropriate Greek or Latin affixes and roots as clues to the meaning of a word.
- Acquire and use accurately grade-appropriate general academic and domain-specific words and phrases; gather vocabulary knowledge when considering a word or phrase important to comprehension or expression.

Essential Question: What is the relationship between people and nature?

Academic Vocabulary: Research

Academic terms can help you read, write, and discuss with precision. Many of these words have roots, or key parts, that come from Latin and Greek.

PRACTICE Academic terms are used routinely in classrooms. Build your knowledge of these words by completing the chart.

1. **Review** each word, its root, and the mentor sentences.
2. **Determine** the meaning and usage of each word using the mentor sentences and a dictionary, if needed.
3. **List** at least two related words for each academic term. Then, challenge yourself to write a sentence that contains two of the academic terms.

WORD	MENTOR SENTENCES	PREDICT MEANING	RELATED WORDS
logical GREEK ROOT: -log- "reason"; "idea"	1. The speaker's statement made no sense; it was not *logical*. 2. There must be a *logical* reason for her strange actions.		logic; illogical; logically
generate LATIN ROOT: -gen- "origin"; "race"; "family"	1. The committee wanted to *generate* enthusiasm for their project. 2. Is it possible to *generate* new life from old DNA?		
philosophy GREEK ROOTS: -phil- + -soph- "love" + "wisdom"	1. In our *philosophy* class, we study the connections between knowledge and truth. 2. The company's *philosophy* is, "the customer comes first."		
evident LATIN ROOT: -vid- "see"	1. No clues were *evident* at the crime scene; the detectives were stumped. 2. It is *evident* that the new drug cured the disease.		
elucidate LATIN ROOT: -luc- "bright"; "clear"	1. The mathematician attempted to *elucidate* his theory for his peers. 2. Can you *elucidate* your ideas for the class?		

Unit Introduction 371

UNIT 4 INTRODUCTION

MENTOR TEXT

RESEARCH-BASED ESSAY MODEL

READ As you read, think about the way the writer presents information. Notice how facts and specific details are used to support ideas.

Wildlife Rehabbers Are Here to Help

1 Most people live in areas that were once home only to wildlife. Direct contact between humans and wild animals is bound to happen, and sometimes that contact can be a problem. According to Maine's state wildlife rehabilitation website, "In most cases, when humans and wildlife collide, wildlife suffers." That's where wildlife rehabilitators come in. Rehabbers provide valuable services to injured animals and also assist the professionals who treat them.

2 According to Cornell University's Wildlife Health Lab (CWHL), there are more than 400 professional wildlife rehabilitators (Peaslee 5). The number of volunteers is even greater. Some estimates put that figure at more than 1,600 across the United States. But even volunteers must get licenses to conduct wildlife rehab work. In North Carolina, for example, rehabilitators are required to work with mentors for a full year before they can get their own licenses.

3 Wildlife rehabbers care for injured and orphaned animals and then return them to their natural habitats. Wild animals can be cute, especially when they are babies, but people should not try to take them in as pets. Becoming comfortable around humans is not safe for them. PAWS, an animal rehab organization, points out that the work that wildlife rehabilitators do is not about trying to tame the animals under their care. The animals are held in captivity only until they are healthy enough to return to the wild. During this rehab period, contact between humans and the animals is kept to a minimum.

4 Some rehabilitators also educate the public about wildlife. For instance, they advise people on what to do if they encounter a wild animal. They also teach people to recognize when an animal needs help. "Education is an important part of wildlife rehabilitation," according to Urban Utopia Wildlife Rehabilitation

Essential Question: What is the relationship between people and nature?

in New York. They believe that teaching people about wildlife keeps both animals and humans safe.

5   In addition, rehabbers receive calls from people who need help. One caller may want to report an injured animal. Another might have a wild animal inside their home. Rehabilitators help the callers stay calm. They advise them about what to do and where to take the animals. At times, qualified rehabbers may remove animals and take them to a wildlife rehab center for treatment. Calls like these can come at any time, so rehabilitators must always be prepared. According to CWHL, animals are most often brought to wildlife rehab centers between the months of May and July (Peaslee 9).

6   On a typical day, a wildlife rehabilitator feeds and waters the animals in their care. They also clean the animals' cages and change their bedding. In addition, the rehabilitator will consult with a veterinarian and administer any medications the animals might need. Most rehabbers will accept donations to help pay for food and supplies. However, they often take on much of the expense themselves.

7   Working in animal rehab is enjoyable, but it can also be difficult or even dangerous. Those who work with certain types of animals, such as raccoons or bats, are required to have a rabies vaccination. This is to protect them in case they are bitten by an infected animal. But for those involved in wildlife rehabilitation, the rewards are worth it.

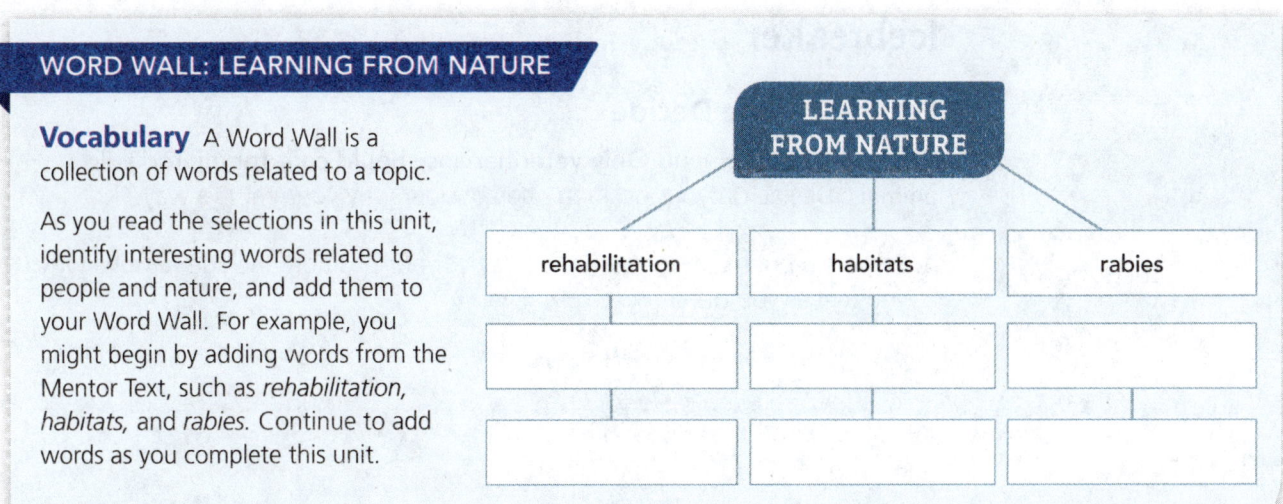

WORD WALL: LEARNING FROM NATURE

Vocabulary A Word Wall is a collection of words related to a topic.

As you read the selections in this unit, identify interesting words related to people and nature, and add them to your Word Wall. For example, you might begin by adding words from the Mentor Text, such as *rehabilitation*, *habitats*, and *rabies*. Continue to add words as you complete this unit.

LEARNING FROM NATURE: rehabilitation, habitats, rabies

UNIT 4 INTRODUCTION

Summary

A **summary** is a brief, complete overview of a text that maintains the meaning and logical order of ideas in the original work. It should be objective and should not include your personal opinions.

WRITE Write a summary of "Wildlife Rehabbers Are Here to Help."

_____
_____
_____
_____
_____
_____
_____
_____
_____
_____
_____

Icebreaker

Let the People Decide

Consider this statement: **Only veterinarians should care for injured wild animals.** Decide on your position and consider why you feel this way.

1. Prepare a brief statement that expresses your position. Include reasons why you feel as you do.

_____
_____

2. As a class, take turns sharing the statements you wrote.
3. When it's your turn, read your statement and try to persuade your classmates to agree with your position.
4. After everyone has had a chance to share, vote on whether veterinarians are the only people who shoud take care of injured wild animals. Tally the votes, and discuss the results.

STANDARDS
Reading Informational Text
Provide an objective summary of the text.

Speaking and Listening
Engage effectively in a range of collaborative discussions with diverse partners on grade 7 topics, texts, and issues.

374 UNIT 4 • LEARNING FROM NATURE

Essential Question: What is the relationship between people and nature?

QuickWrite

Consider the introductory video, the Icebreaker activity, your own knowledge, and the Mentor Text as you think about the Essential Question.

Essential Question

What is the relationship between people and nature?

At the end of the unit, you will respond to the Essential Question again and see if your perspective has deepened or changed.

WRITE Record your first thoughts here.

_____
_____
_____
_____
_____
_____
_____
_____
_____
_____

EVIDENCE LOG

What is the relationship between people and nature?

As you read the selections in this unit, use a chart like the one shown to record your ideas and list details from the texts that support them. Taking notes as you go will help you clarify your thinking, gather relevant information, and be ready to respond to the Essential Question.

TITLE	MY IDEAS / OBSERVATIONS	TEXT EVIDENCE / INFORMATION

Unit Introduction 375

WHOLE-CLASS LEARNING

Essential Question

What is the relationship between people and nature?

Nature provides us with the necessities we need to survive—air, water, and soil in which to grow food. However, our relationship with nature goes far beyond the needs of survival. The natural world can be a mirror in which we see ourselves, a friend that gives us gifts, and even an enemy that we fight and that fights us back.

Whole-Class Learning Strategies

Throughout your life, in school, in your community, and in your career, you will continue to learn and work in large-group environments.

Review these strategies and the actions you can take to practice them as you work with your whole class. Add ideas of your own for each strategy. Get ready to use these strategies during Whole-Class Learning.

STRATEGY	MY ACTION PLAN
Listen actively	• Listen to the speaker's full message before planning a response. • Be ready to take notes when you hear key details, such as important names or dates. •
Demonstrate respect	• Be open to new ideas and information. • Avoid side conversations while in class. •
Make connections	• Ask yourself how the ideas being presented could be applied to your personal life or to life in general. • Link the information you're learning now to things you've learned in other subject areas. • Notice details that remind you of something you've experienced. •

Contents

FEATURE ARTICLE

The Bee Highway: Making a Place for Bees in the City

Kathryn Hulick

How can we help pollinators in big cities?

DESCRIPTIVE ESSAY

from Silent Spring

Rachel Carson

This essay comes from the powerful book that inspired a new public awareness about the dangers of pollution.

COMPARE

CREATION STORY

How Grandmother Spider Stole the Sun

Michael J. Caduto and Joseph Bruchac

A Native American creation story explains the origin of the sun.

CREATION STORY

Coyote Steals the Sun and Moon

Richard Erdoes and Alfonso Ortiz

Coyote causes mischief in this Native American creation story.

PERFORMANCE TASK

WRITING PROMPT • WRITER'S HANDBOOK

Write a Research Paper

Throughout history, people have observed nature, tried to understand it, and told stories about it. The Whole-Class readings illustrate some of these different perspectives. After reading, you will further explore this topic by writing a research paper.

Whole-Class Learning 377

LEARN ABOUT GENRE: NONFICTION

THE BEE HIGHWAY

Reading Feature Articles

A **feature article** is a work of journalism that educates readers about a topic.

The selection you are about to read is a feature article.

FEATURE ARTICLE

Author's Purpose
- to inform readers about recent events and issues and to explain why they are relevant and important

Characteristics
- a title that grabs readers' attention
- a clear central idea, or main point
- supporting information, such as images, quotations, and examples
- factual information reported in an interesting way

Structure
- an engaging introduction that draws readers in
- paragraphs, headings, and other types of text features that organize the information

Take a Minute!

FIND IT Think of a topic you like reading about, such as games or animals. Quickly search online to find a feature article related to that topic. Write down its title and source.

STANDARDS
Reading Informational Text
Analyze the structure an author uses to organize a text, including how the major sections contribute to the whole and to the development of the ideas.

378 UNIT 4 • LEARNING FROM NATURE

Essential Question: What is the relationship between people and nature?

Informational Text Features

The main purpose of an informational text is to present factual information accurately. A feature article is one type of informational text. It provides an in-depth look at an issue, an event, or a person.

The **central idea** of an informational text is its main message or main point. To support their central ideas, authors provide various types of details, such as quotations, statistics, and examples.

To ensure their central ideas are clear, authors provide structure to their writing in various ways.

- **Section headings** may be used to organize information.
- **Paragraphs** may be arranged by chronological order, cause and effect, comparison and contrast, or problem and solution.
- **Topic sentences** within paragraphs are supported by various types of details, such as facts, quotations, and statistics.
- **Special features**—such as sidebars, graphs or images, bulleted or numbered lists, and footnotes or glossaries—provide additional details.

> **TIP:** A central idea is not a topic. Instead, it conveys an insight about the topic. Some texts convey more than one central idea. Here's an example.
>
> **Topic:** Forests
>
> **Central Idea 1:** Forests provide homes to various forms of wildlife.
>
> **Central Idea 2:** Forests offer many different foods for animals and humans.

PRACTICE Read the passage from an informational text. Then, answer the questions.

> According to the World Wildlife Fund (WWF), as many as 41,000 animal species around the world are in danger of dying off. They include large creatures, such as leopards and rhinos, and smaller ones, such as beavers and bees. Carter Roberts, the president of the WWF, states that "the world is waking up to the fact that our future depends on reversing the loss of nature." Fortunately, a number of individuals, businesses, and governments are taking action to address this problem.

1. What is the topic of this paragraph? What details support the topic sentence?

2. This passage presents a problem to readers: Animal species are in danger of dying off. What sentence in the passage hints that a solution will be proposed?

3. Write a short heading the author could include to signal to readers what this section is about.

Learn About Genre **379**

PREPARE TO READ

The Bee Highway

About the Author

Kathryn Hulick writes books and articles about science. Her favorite part of the process is interviewing experts on different topics. Before she began her writing career, she served in the Peace Corps in Kyrgyzstan in central Asia, teaching English without access to the internet.

STANDARDS

Reading Informational Text
Analyze the structure an author uses to organize a text, including how the major sections contribute to the whole and to the development of the ideas.

Language
Acquire and use accurately grade-appropriate general academic and domain-specific words and phrases; gather vocabulary knowledge when considering a word or phrase important to comprehension or expression.

Concept Vocabulary

Preview The words listed below appear in the feature article. Write a paragraph that includes at least four of the words. If necessary, you can alter a word's form (for example, *pollinate* instead of *pollinators*).

pesticides (PEHS tuh sydz) *n.* chemicals used to kill animals, especially insects
The farmer uses pesticides to keep beetles from destroying his crop.

herbicides (UHR buh sydz) *n.* chemicals used to kill unwanted plants
Juana sprayed herbicides on the weeds growing in her lawn.

pollinators (PAH lih nay tuhrz) *n.* creatures who spread pollen, a fine powder produced by flowers
Bees are pollinators of plants all over the world.

colonies (KAH luh neez) *n.* groups of individuals settled together in one place
She discovered several colonies of ants in the backyard.

parasites (PAR uh syts) *n.* creatures that survive by living on or in a host creature
Some types of parasites are not harmful to their hosts.

extinction (ehk STINGK shuhn) *n.* the act of permanently dying out
The extinction of some species could have been prevented.

Reading Strategy: Make Predictions

Before you read a feature article, **make predictions** about its content. Predictions are guesses you make by previewing the article's organizational structure and text features. Here are some features to look for:

- **Title and subtitle:** These may state the topic and suggest a central idea.
- **Headings:** These may indicate the type of information included in the major sections of the text.
- **Images:** These may illustrate important ideas.
- **Sidebars:** These give additional information about some aspect of the topic.

PRACTICE Before you read, scan the article's text features, and use your observations to write a prediction. Then, read on to determine whether your prediction was accurate.

380 UNIT 4 • LEARNING FROM NATURE

FEATURE ARTICLE

The Bee Highway: Making a Place for Bees in the City

Kathryn Hulick

BACKGROUND

The honey bee is known as a keystone species—one whose activities help support all the living things in a particular location. The loss of a keystone species can have a negative effect on the plants and wild animals in that environment—and on humans, too. This feature article discusses threats to honey bees and what can be done to help them thrive.

1   The sound of bees surrounds Helena Arondoski as she approaches a pair of hives. She looks like an outer space explorer, dressed from head to toe in a bee suit that's just the right size for an 11-year-old. "It's like a big bulky sweatshirt with MC Hammer pants,"[1] she says. The suit helps protect against stings, but it's not perfect. So she moves slowly and uses a small, handheld smoke machine to calm the bees.

---
1   **M.C. Hammer pants** long, baggy pants, tapered at the ankle, that were popularized in the late 1980s and early 1990s by American rapper M.C. Hammer.

READ TO UNLOCK MEANING

1. First read the text for comprehension and enjoyment. Use the **Reading Strategy** and **Comprehension Check** questions to support your first read.
2. Go back and respond to the Close-Read note.
3. Identify other details in the text you find interesting. Ask your own questions and draw your own conclusions.

MAKE PREDICTIONS

Based on what you've read so far, what kind of work do you think "Bees in the D" might do to help bees?

2   Carefully, Helena lifts out a frame from one of the hives, smelling sweet beeswax and seeing the glint of fresh honey. Bees climb over and around the frame, going about their work as she checks to make sure they are healthy. Her family helps care for these hives and many others as volunteers for the organization Bees in the D. The "D" stands for Detroit, Michigan. The hives Helena is checking today are located right outside the Downtown Boxing Gym in the middle of the city.

From Factories to Rooftops

3   Those hives are just one stop on a bee highway that winds through Detroit. The highway isn't just one road, though. "It's more of a web," explains Brian Peterson-Roest, co-founder of Bees in the D. The goal of the highway is to make sure bees will be able to find food, water, and shelter, no matter where they go in the city. So far, Bees in the D cares for 175 hives in 60 different locations in and around the city. And they add more new ones every year. There are beehives at schools, community gardens, and just outside a factory where Chrysler makes cars. Many of the beehives are up on rooftops, including those of the Shinola hotel, TCF Convention Center, a parking garage, and many other local businesses. "Our bees have some of the best views of the city," says Peterson-Roest.

4   Putting beehives on a city roof transforms a mostly wasted space into something useful for the community and for nature. Some of the rooftops, like the convention center, were already green, with plantings or gardens built in. So the beehives fit right in. But most of the roofs don't have any flowers or plants. And the bees don't mind. Honey bees typically fly 2 to 3 miles (3 to 5 km) or farther to find food. In fact, compared to the bees that live elsewhere, "my city bees do the best," says Peterson-Roest.

5   A city, it turns out, offers a greater variety of plants than a suburb or rural area. In sidewalk cracks, vacant lots, along roads, and in parks, people often allow weeds and wild plants to grow. "Weeds are a great thing for bees," says Peterson-Roest. In the suburbs and farmland, people tend to control growth more carefully with **pesticides** and **herbicides**. These chemicals harm bees and the food they depend on. Truly, the easiest way to make a space more welcoming for bees is to leave nature alone: let grass and weeds grow. Also, leave old sticks, leaves, and logs where they fall. Some species of wild bee use brush piles or hollow logs as homes.

Bee Baths and Gardens

6   Bees may love tall grass, weeds, and fallen leaves or logs, but most humans don't. Thankfully, people can create beautiful outdoor spaces that bees also love. Girl Scouts Georgia Basch and Charlotte Wilder are both fourth graders who live in the Detroit area. They

pesticides (PEHS tuh sydz) *n.* chemicals used to kill animals, especially insects

herbicides (UHR buh sydz) *n.* chemicals used to kill unwanted plants

made a special space for bees in Georgia's backyard, beside a tomato and a basil plant. "It's a bee drinking fountain," says Georgia. Bees can't easily drink from open water, such as a bird bath or pond. If they fall in, they drown. So the girls decorated a flower pot, flipped it upside down, placed the base on top, filled it with rocks, then added water. The bees stand on the rocks to safely take a drink.

7   Georgia, Charlotte, and nine other girls in troop number 76424 earned beekeeping patches in 2020. It was part of a special partnership between Bees in the D and the Girl Scouts of South East Michigan. Each girl came up with her own project idea. Lily Saier, a fifth grader, made beeswax candles. After learning what types of flowers bees like best, her family added some to their garden. "We planted lavender." Whenever she went outside after that, "I'd see at least two bees on the lavender," she says. Sisters Molly and Libby Urquhart, who are in third and sixth grade,

COMPREHENSION CHECK

Why are cities better places for bees than suburbs or farmlands?

The Bee Highway 383

pollinators (PAH lih nay tuhrz) *n.* creatures who spread pollen, a fine powder produced by flowers

made posters about bee awareness and shared them online. The posters asked people to plant more flowers and not kill bees. Molly says that before she started working on her patch, she didn't like bees. "I was really scared of them," she says. Now, Molly says, "I know they help the planet."

8   How do bees help the planet? Of course, honey tastes great, but there is a far more important reason to build homes and gardens and water fountains for bees: They are **pollinators**. That means they carry pollen from flower to flower as they harvest nectar. A plant or tree needs pollinators to thrive and grow fruit. Some of the plants that bees pollinate, like apple trees or blueberry bushes, produce foods humans love to eat. Others, like alfalfa, feed the livestock we eat as meat. So directly and indirectly, bees help us grow our food. Roughly one-third of all the food you eat, or "every third bite you put in your mouth," was made possible by pollinators, says Peterson-Roest. And most of those pollinators are honey bees. The plants and trees that bees pollinate also feed wildlife and help entire ecosystems thrive.

A World of Trouble

colonies (KAH luh neez) *n.* groups of individuals settled together in one place

9   Unfortunately, the world's bees face some serious threats. The winter is always a tough time for bees. Some **colonies** don't survive. But starting in 2006, beekeepers noticed that many more

honey bee colonies than usual were dying over the winter, and they didn't know why. All the adult worker bees would die, leaving the queen and a few larvae behind. These bees couldn't support themselves and would eventually die too. This became known as Colony Collapse Disorder (CCD). In the beginning of 2020, beekeepers in the U.S. lost over 100,000 colonies.

10   No one knows exactly why CCD happens. Most likely, a wide number of different problems play a role. Diseases and **parasites** have affected many bees. Pesticides and herbicides sicken bees. In addition, bee colonies get stressed when they can't find enough food or enough variety of food or when their habitat changes. Any of these problems alone may not be enough to kill an entire colony. But when multiple problems happen at once, bees can't easily cope. And it's not only honey bees under threat. Wild bees are dying too. "They are struggling to find places to nest and enough food sources," says Ane Johnsen. She's the managing director at ByBi, an organization that manages a bee highway in Oslo, Norway.

parasites (PAR uh syts) *n.* creatures that survive by living on or in a host creature

WHERE THE WILD BEES ARE

The organization ByBi began building one of the world's first bee highways in 2016 in Oslo, Norway. Though they do raise honey bees, the organization focuses on saving wild bees. In a city, "it's easier to be a honey bee than to be a wild bee," says managing director Ane Johnsen. Honey bees can fly far from their hive and often feed on a wide variety of flowers. Wild bees travel much shorter distances and may specialize only in certain types of flowers. Wild bees also need different sorts of homes. Many wild bees like to dig their homes in sand or dirt. Other species, such as the mason bee, don't live in colonies. These solitary bees usually like to lay their eggs in holes inside branches or tree trunks. You can make or buy an insect hotel that provides holes for these pollinators to use. ByBi has set up several wild bee homes that turn old logs and twigs into art. It looks beautiful, and bees love it too!

11   Climate change is worsening many of these problems. Higher temperatures mean more parasites survive the winter and more bees get sick. Warmer temperatures also mean that bees may wake up from hibernation before flowers have begun blooming. Even a few days' difference in this timing can harm bee health, a 2017 study found. It may not be possible for bees to migrate to places where the climate is closer to what they are used to. When bees are in danger, "our whole food system is in danger," says Johnsen.

12   Thankfully, groups like Bees in the D, ByBi, and many others like them aren't just going to sit around and do nothing. "Bees are the new panda," says Peterson-Roest. Panda bears were once at the brink of **extinction**, but people refused to let the animals die out. The same thing is happening now for bees—both honey bees

CLOSE READ

ANNOTATE In paragraph 11, mark scientific terms the author uses to describe some of the problems bees face.

QUESTION Why do you think the author uses technical terms here?

extinction (ehk STINGK shuhn) *n.* the act of permanently dying out

The Bee Highway   **385**

and wild species. "Everyone wants to help the bees," says Peterson-Roest. Johnsen adds, "We need everyone to participate. Children, teens, and grownups. We have a huge challenge ahead of us."

How You Can Help

13   Even if your city or town doesn't have its own bee highway, you can still help. The first thing to do is learn as much as you can about bees, says Peterson-Roest. He always teaches people the difference between bees and wasps. They may look similar, but they are totally different animals. If there's something with a stinger bothering you, it's almost definitely a wasp and not a bee. Wasps are generally considered pests.

14   The second thing to do is to make your home friendlier to bees. If you have a yard, you could let part of it grow wild. This part of your yard may look untidy, but if you put up a sign that you're letting weeds grow to help pollinators, Johnsen says, people tend to understand.

15   If your family doesn't want a wild lawn, that's perfectly OK. You can ask your parents to avoid chemicals that kill weeds or pests. You can also plant flowers that bees love in your yard or in planters on a deck or balcony. Honey bees love black-eyed Susans, herbs such as mint, asters, goldenrod, sunflowers, and many more. Ornamental flowers such as mums or roses aren't great for bees. You could also make a water stop for bees similar to the one described in this article.

16   The most important thing to do, though, is to help spread the word. Educate others about how important bees are and tell them that bees need our help and protection. "Spread the love for nature, for the Earth, and for the animals," says Johnsen. When you fall in love with bees, you'll do what it takes to protect them.

COMPREHENSION CHECK

According to the article, what are some things people can do around their homes to help bees?

BUILD INSIGHT

First Thoughts

Choose one of the following items to answer.
- Would you enjoy working with bees like the kids in this article do? Why or why not?
- Did you learn anything new about bees from reading this article? What surprised, puzzled, or interested you most?

Summary

Write a short summary of the text to confirm your comprehension. Remember to include only the central ideas.

Analysis

1. **Speculate** Reread paragraphs 1–2. The author could have started the article with basic information about different threats to bees. Why do you think she began instead with a descriptive passage about Helena?

2. **Compare** In paragraphs 6–7, the author gives examples of young people involved in activities to support bees. What character traits do these kids share? Include an example from the text.

3. (a) **Analyze Causes and Effects** What causes and effects does the author describe in paragraph 8? (b) **Draw Conclusions** Without honey bees, what might happen to the food supply?

4. **Analyze** Review the final section of the article. Is it mostly informational or mostly persuasive? Support your response with text evidence.

Exploring the Essential Question

What is the relationship between people and nature?

5. The article discusses several people who have taken action to support bees. What insight about people and nature does it share? Write your response in your Evidence Log.

STANDARDS

Reading Informational Text
- Cite several pieces of textual evidence to support analysis of what the text says explicitly as well as inferences drawn from the text.
- Provide an objective summary of the text.

The Bee Highway 387

ANALYZE AND INTERPRET

THE BEE HIGHWAY

Close Read

1. The model passage and annotation show how one reader analyzed part of paragraph 3. Find another detail in the passage to annotate. Then, write your own question and conclusion.

CLOSE-READ MODEL

Those hives are just one stop on a bee highway that winds through Detroit. The highway isn't just one road, though. "It's more of a web," explains Brian Peterson-Roest, co-founder of Bees in the D. The goal of the highway is to make sure bees will be able to find food, water, and shelter, no matter where they go in the city.

ANNOTATE: The author compares the pathway of bees to a highway. Peterson-Roest compares it to a web.

QUESTION: What is the purpose of these two comparisons?

CONCLUDE: Comparing unfamiliar things to familiar things helps readers understand new ideas.

MY QUESTION:

MY CONCLUSION:

2. For more practice, answer the Close Read note in the selection.

3. Choose a section of the feature article you found especially meaningful. Mark important details. Then jot down questions, and write your conclusions in the open space next to the text.

Inquiry and Research

Research and Extend Extend your learning by answering this question: *What other efforts are being made to help honey bees?* Answer the question by conducting research. Use at least three online sources.

Then, generate two additional questions for further investigation. Your questions should focus on honey bees or pollinators or on a related topic from the article. Write your questions here:

STANDARDS

Reading Informational Text
• Determine two or more central ideas in a text and analyze their development over the course of the text.
• Analyze the structure an author uses to organize a text, including how the major sections contribute to the whole and to the development of the ideas.

Writing
Conduct short research projects to answer a question, drawing on several sources and generating additional related, focused questions for further research and investigation.

388 UNIT 4 • LEARNING FROM NATURE

Essential Question: What is the relationship between people and nature?

Informational Text Features

Authors of nonfiction articles often use **informational text features** to develop and organize their ideas. These features include headings, sidebars, and images or graphics.

In texts that have a number of **central ideas,** or essential messages, headings can be especially important. They state or suggest these different ideas to readers. Here is an example from "The Bee Highway":

> **Heading:** "From Factories to Rooftops"
> **Central Idea:** Cities can sustain bee populations in unlikely places, such as factories and rooftops.

Another useful feature is the **sidebar.** Set off from the main text, with its own title, a sidebar discusses a closely related, interesting topic. A sidebar may contain its own informational text features such as a heading, quotations, examples, or images.

PRACTICE Complete the activities.

1. **Analyze** Review the headings from "The Bee Highway" in the chart. Write the central idea of the paragraph that each one introduces.

HEADING	CENTRAL IDEA
"Bee Baths and Gardens"	
"A World of Trouble"	
"How You Can Help"	

2. **Analyze** Reread the sidebar "Where the Wild Bees Are." Identify its topic (what it's about) and its central idea (what it says about that topic).

Topic: _____

Central Idea: _____

3. **Synthesize** Review the central ideas of each individual section, including the sidebar. What is the central idea of the article as a whole?

The Bee Highway **389**

STUDY LANGUAGE AND CRAFT

THE BEE HIGHWAY

Concept Vocabulary

Why These Words? All the vocabulary words relate to the lives of bees and the threats that endanger them.

pesticides	pollinators	parasites
herbicides	colonies	extinction

PRACTICE Answer the question and complete the activity.

1. How might your knowledge of the vocabulary words help you explain to someone why bees are in danger?

2. Use the vocabulary words to complete the sentences.

   (a) Some kinds of bees live in _____ , but others shelter by themselves.

   (b) Bees are called _____ because they spread pollen.

   (c) Scientists want bees to survive and are working to prevent their _____ .

   (d) Some farmers use _____ and _____ to protect their crops from weeds and bugs that might cause damage.

   (e) Diseases and _____ , which depend on bees to survive, put stress on bees.

Word Study

Spelling Patterns: -tion, -sion Some verbs that describe actions can be turned into nouns that express the results of those actions.

- When a verb ends in *-ate*, the related noun will usually end in *-tion*. For example, *pollinate* becomes *pollination* (the final *e* is dropped before adding *-tion*).

- When a verb ends in *-d, -de, -se,* or *-t,* the related noun will end in *-sion*. For example, *decide* becomes *decision* (the final *de* is dropped before adding *-sion*).

PRACTICE Complete the activities.

1. Form a noun from each of the following verbs: *invade, hibernate, supervise, locate*. Follow the spelling guidelines above.

2. Write a paragraph using the nouns you formed in item 1. Be sure to spell the words correctly.

WORD WALL

Note words in the text that are related to the idea of learning from nature. Add them to your Word Wall.

STANDARDS

Reading Informational Text
Analyze the impact of a specific word choice on meaning and tone.

Language
- Spell correctly.
- Acquire and use accurately grade-appropriate general academic and domain-specific words and phrases; gather vocabulary knowledge when considering a word or phrase important to comprehension or expression.

390 UNIT 4 • LEARNING FROM NATURE

Essential Question: What is the relationship between people and nature?

Diction, Meaning, and Tone

The term **diction** refers to an author's choice of words and phrasing. An author's diction may be richly descriptive, simple and straightforward, or mainly technical. The **tone** of a piece of writing expresses the author's attitude toward the subject. Tone can be described with adjectives such as *solemn*, *humorous*, or *friendly*.

The author of "The Bee Highway" uses a range of diction. Some passages contain descriptive words; others feature technical terms.

> **EXAMPLES**
> **Descriptive phrasing:** Carefully, Helena lifts out a frame from one of the hives, smelling sweet beeswax and seeing the glint of fresh honey.
>
> **Technical phrasing:** All the adult worker bees would die, leaving the queen and a few larvae behind . . . This became known as Colony Collapse Disorder (CCD).

The first example helps readers imagine the scent of the beeswax and the sight of the honey. The second example includes technical terms, such as "larvae" and "Colony Collapse Disorder." Descriptive and technical word choices work together to convey different types of information about bees.

> **PRACTICE** Complete the activities.
>
> 1. **Analyze** Read each passage from the selection. Mark words and phrases that you consider descriptive or technical.
>
>   **Paragraph 6:** Bees may love tall grass, weeds, and fallen leaves or logs, but most humans don't. Thankfully, people can create beautiful outdoor spaces that bees also love. Girl Scouts Georgia Basch and Charlotte Wilder . . . made a special space for bees in Georgia's backyard, beside a tomato and a basil plant.
>
>   **Paragraph 10:** Diseases and parasites have affected many bees. Pesticides and herbicides sicken bees. In addition, bee colonies get stressed when they can't find enough food or enough variety of food or when their habitat changes. Any of these problems alone may not be enough to kill an entire colony.
>
> 2. (a) **Interpret** Mark the answer that best describes the tone of "The Bee Highway."
>
>   ○ Friendly and engaging
>
>   ○ Formal and serious
>
>   ○ Academic and neutral
>
>   (b) **Support** Explain how the author's word choices affect the meaning of the article.

SHARE IDEAS

THE BEE HIGHWAY

TIP: Check your formal letter for correct capitalization, punctuation, and spelling.

Writing

A **formal letter** can be used to conduct business, make a complaint or an official request, or deal with other serious issues.

Assignment

Imagine that your school administration is considering adding rooftop beehives to your school building. Write a **formal letter** to your principal, expressing your opinion on the matter.

- First, consider pros and cons. For example, beehives will help support important pollinators, and tending to them would provide a meaningful science project for students. However, being on a roof presents safety concerns, along with the risk of bee stings, especially for people who are allergic.
- Begin the letter with an introduction that presents your opinion.
- Organize an argument supporting your opinion with reasons and evidence from the article and other accurate, credible sources. Be sure to use a formal style throughout.
- Conclude by restating your opinion and thanking your principal for considering it.

Use New Words
Refer to your Word Wall to use new vocabulary you have learned. Also, try to include one or more of these concept vocabulary words in your writing: *pesticides, herbicides, pollinators, colonies, parasites, extinction.*

Reflect on Your Writing

PRACTICE Think about the choices you made as you wrote. Also, consider what you learned by writing. Share your experiences by responding to these questions.

1. What was the most challenging part of this assignment?

2. When might you write a formal letter in the future?

3. **Why These Words?** The words you choose make a difference in your writing. Which words helped you convey your ideas clearly?

STANDARDS
Writing
• Write arguments to support claims with clear reasons and relevant evidence.
• Draw evidence from literary or informational texts to support analysis, reflection, and research.
Speaking and Listening
• Present claims and findings, emphasizing salient points in a focused, coherent manner with pertinent descriptions, facts, details, and examples.
• Include multimedia components and visual displays in presentations to clarify claims and findings and emphasize salient points.

Essential Question: What is the relationship between people and nature?

Speaking and Listening

A **multimedia presentation** is a speech supported with different types of media, such as audio clips, photos, charts, graphs, or videos.

Assignment

Choose an endangered plant or animal, and conduct research on it using reliable print and online sources. Organize the information in an outline that will be easy to follow as you speak. Gather a variety of media to emphasize important points. Then, deliver a **multimedia presentation** to your class.

- Write your speech using a formal style. State the reason why you chose your topic; develop the topic with facts, details, and examples; and provide a conclusion.
- Make sure your visuals are formatted in a way that the audience will find easy to understand. Avoid graphics that are overly complicated or flashy.
- Check that your media player is working properly. Cue up audio and video clips to the right time codes to support your main points.
- Coordinate your speech with your presentation of media, and practice it several times.

USE NEW WORDS

Academic Vocabulary
Consider using one or more of the unit's academic vocabulary words as you write your presentation.

- logical
- generate
- philosophy
- evident
- elucidate

Evaluate Presentations

Use a guide like the one shown to evaluate the presentations.

PRESENTATION EVALUATION GUIDE

Rate each statement on a scale of 1 (not demonstrated) to 4 (fully demonstrated).

Statement	1	2	3	4
The speaker presented well-organized, well-researched information.	○	○	○	○
The speaker included a variety of media that supported the spoken ideas.	○	○	○	○
The speaker used a formal style to make the presentation clear to listeners.	○	○	○	○

EVIDENCE LOG

Before moving on to a new selection, go to your Evidence Log and record any additional thoughts or observations you may have about "The Bee Highway."

LEARN ABOUT GENRE: NONFICTION

from SILENT SPRING

Reading Descriptive Essays

A **descriptive essay** is a work of nonfiction that uses words that convey a vivid picture of a subject.

The selection you are about to read is a descriptive essay.

DESCRIPTIVE ESSAY

Author's Purpose
- to show the importance of a subject through vivid and precise language

Characteristics
- a central idea, or main point
- vivid sensory details that appeal to the five senses
- imagery, or mental word pictures, and figurative language
- concrete details that help readers visualize abstract ideas
- a mood, or emotional quality, created by details and word choices

Structure
- a clear organization that enables readers to "see" what is being described
- usually contains an introduction, body, and conclusion, but may be structured by describing aspects of a person or thing

Take a Minute!

LIST With a partner, list three subjects you think would be good for a descriptive essay. What qualities make these good subjects?

STANDARDS
Reading Informational Text
Determine the meaning of words and phrases as they are used in a text, including figurative, connotative, and technical meanings; analyze the impact of a specific word choice on meaning and tone.

394 UNIT 4 • LEARNING FROM NATURE

Essential Question: What is the relationship between people and nature?

Language and Mood

Authors of descriptive texts often use **sensory language**—words and phrases that appeal to the five senses. Such language produces **imagery** by describing how a subject looks, sounds, feels, tastes, and smells.

The use of imagery can create **mood,** or an atmosphere that evokes feelings in readers. Other elements that contribute to mood include the **connotations,** or emotional associations, of words, as well as their **figurative,** or nonliteral, meanings. Here is an example:

LANGUAGE AND MOOD

PASSAGE WITH IMAGERY & FIGURATIVE LANGUAGE	DESCRIPTION OF MOOD
The icy sharp landscape glistened in the sun, piercing the eyes of the lone onlooker. The only sound was the cracking of the ice-encrusted snow. The air hurt to breathe, as if it were an enemy and as dangerous as the knife-like shards of ice.	The landscape is described as threatening and hostile, which creates an ominous mood and helps develop a central idea about the dangers of nature.

PRACTICE Mark examples of imagery and figurative language in the passage. Then, choose the description of the mood that best fits the passage, and explain your answer.

PASSAGE WITH IMAGERY & FIGURATIVE LANGUAGE	DESCRIPTION OF MOOD
The door gently opened, and Delia stepped into the home of her past. The old wooden floor shone dully, polished by footsteps of her beloved family. The scent of lavender still hung in the air, and the grandfather clock ticked with slow confidence, the heartbeat of the home.	○ warm and gentle ○ carefree and uplifting ○ exciting and electric

Explanation:

Learn About Genre **395**

PREPARE TO READ

from Silent Spring

About the Author

Even as a child, **Rachel Carson** (1907–1964) wanted to be a writer. In college, she majored in marine biology and later earned a master's degree in zoology. Carson had long been worried about the overuse of pesticides and wanted to raise awareness about this problem. Her book *Silent Spring* became one of the most influential environmental texts ever written.

Concept Vocabulary

Predict The words below appear in the essay. Judging from these words, what kinds of things do you think the author will describe?

WORDS FROM THE TEXT	MY EXPECTATIONS
blight (BLYT) *n.* something that spoils, prevents growth, or destroys	
maladies (MAL uh deez) *n.* illnesses or diseases	
puzzled (PUHZ uhld) *adj.* confused and unable to understand something	
stricken (STRIHK uhn) *adj.* very badly affected by trouble or illness	
stillness (STIHL nihs) *n.* absence of noise or motion	
deserted (dih ZUR tihd) *adj.* abandoned; empty	

Reading Strategy: Make Connections

During reading, when you **make connections to society,** you use your background knowledge about the world and look for relationships between ideas in the text and the larger community. For example, you might connect the author's ideas to local or national events or issues.

EXAMPLE

Passage: ...no enemy action had silenced the rebirth of new life in this stricken world. The people had done it themselves.

Connection to Society: This passage includes the war-like word *enemy*. It suggests a hostile relationship between society and nature.

PRACTICE As you read, make connections between ideas in the text and society. Jot down your thoughts in the page margins.

STANDARDS

Reading Informational Text
By the end of the year, read and comprehend literary nonfiction.

Language
Gather vocabulary knowledge when considering a word or phrase important to comprehension or expression.

DESCRIPTIVE ESSAY

from
Silent Spring

Rachel Carson

BACKGROUND
Pesticides are chemical compounds designed to destroy crop-eating insects. Pesticides can be deadly to many species—including humans—in addition to the insects and other pests they are intended to kill. In 1962, Rachel Carson published *Silent Spring*, which revealed to the public the dangers of DDT, a pesticide in wide use at the time. The awareness raised by *Silent Spring* eventually led the United States to ban DDT entirely in 1972. This excerpt comes from the opening pages of the book.

1   There was once a town in the heart of America where all life seemed to live in harmony with its surroundings. The town lay in the midst of a checkerboard of prosperous farms, with fields of grain and hillsides of orchards where, in spring, white clouds of bloom drifted above the green fields. In autumn, oak and maple and birch set up a blaze of color that flamed and flickered across a backdrop of pines. Then foxes barked in the hills and deer silently crossed the fields, half hidden in the mists of the fall mornings.

2   Along the roads, laurel, viburnum and alder, great ferns and wildflowers delighted the traveler's eye through much of the year. Even in winter the roadsides were places of beauty, where countless birds came to feed on the berries and on the seed heads of the dried weeds rising above the snow. The countryside was, in fact, famous for the abundance and variety of its bird life, and when the flood of migrants was pouring through in spring and fall people traveled from great distances to observe them. Others came to fish the streams, which flowed clear and cold out of the

READ TO UNLOCK MEANING
1. First read the text for comprehension and enjoyment. Use the **Reading Strategy** question to support your first read.
2. Go back and respond to the Close-Read note.
3. Identify other details in the text you find interesting. Ask your own questions and draw your own conclusions.

CLOSE READ
ANNOTATE: Mark vivid details in paragraph 2 that the author uses to describe the environment of the town.

QUESTION: What can you conclude about the town from these details?

blight (BLYT) *n.* something that spoils, prevents growth, or destroys

maladies (MAL uh deez) *n.* illnesses or diseases

puzzled (PUHZ uhld) *adj.* confused and unable to understand something

stricken (STRIHK uhn) *adj.* very badly affected by trouble or illness

stillness (STIHL nihs) *n.* absence of noise or motion

hills and contained shady pools where trout lay. So it had been from the days many years ago when the first settlers raised their houses, sank their wells, and built their barns.

3   Then a strange **blight** crept over the area and everything began to change. Some evil spell had settled on the community: mysterious **maladies** swept the flocks of chickens; the cattle and sheep sickened and died. Everywhere was a shadow of death. The farmers spoke of much illness among their families. In the town the doctors had become more and more **puzzled** by new kinds of sickness appearing among their patients. There had been several sudden and unexplained deaths, not only among adults but even among children, who would be **stricken** suddenly while at play and die within a few hours.

4   There was a strange **stillness**. The birds, for example—where had they gone? Many people spoke of them, puzzled and disturbed. The feeding stations in the backyards were deserted. The few birds seen anywhere were moribund; they trembled violently and could not fly. It was a spring without voices. On the mornings that had once throbbed with the dawn chorus of robins, catbirds, doves, jays, wrens, and scores of other bird voices, there was now no sound; only silence lay over the fields and woods and marsh.

5   On the farms the hens brooded, but no chicks hatched. The farmers complained that they were unable to raise any pigs—the litters were small and the young survived only a few days. The apple trees were coming into bloom but no bees droned among the blossoms, so there was no pollination and there would be no fruit.

6   The roadsides, once so attractive, were now lined with browned and withered vegetation as though swept by fire. These, too, were silent, **deserted** by all living things. Even the streams were now lifeless. Anglers[1] no longer visited them, for all the fish had died.

deserted (dih ZUR tihd) *adj.* abandoned; empty

7   In the gutters under the eaves and between the shingles of the roofs, a white granular powder still showed a few patches; some weeks before it had fallen like snow upon the roofs and the lawns, the fields and streams.

MAKE CONNECTIONS

Cite one connection you made to society as you read the essay. Explain how the connection deepened your understanding of the text.

8   No witchcraft, no enemy action had silenced the rebirth of new life in this stricken world. The people had done it themselves.

9   This town does not actually exist, but it might easily have a thousand counterparts in America or elsewhere in the world. I know of no community that has experienced all the misfortunes I describe. Yet every one of these disasters has actually happened somewhere, and many real communities have already suffered a substantial number of them. A grim specter has crept upon us almost unnoticed, and this imagined tragedy may easily become a stark reality we all shall know.

From *Silent Spring* by Rachel Carson. Copyright © 1962 by Rachel L. Carson. Copyright © renewed 1990 by Roger Christie. Reprinted by permission of Frances Collin, Trustee. All copying, including electronic, or re-distribution of this text, is expressly forbidden.

---

1   **anglers** (ANG gluhrz) *n.* people who fish with a line and hook.

BUILD INSIGHT

First Thoughts

Choose one of the following items to answer.

- What aspect of the text do you find interesting or surprising?
- Is this how you would expect a famous book about the dangers of DDT to begin? Why, or why not?

Comprehension

1. **Comprehension Check** (a) What two animals attracted visitors to the town? (b) What happened to the people and animals in the town? (c) What fell on the roofs, lawns, fields, and streams?

Analysis

2. (a) **Interpret** In paragraph 1, what does the phrase "the heart of America" suggest? (b) **Speculate** Why do you think Carson uses this phrase in the first paragraph?

3. **Analyze** State the central idea of paragraph 2 in one sentence. What specific details support this central idea?

4. **Contrast** Review paragraphs 1 and 7. How do they differ? Consider the author's word choice in each paragraph.

5. (a) **Analyze** Mark all the references to people in the essay. How does the experience of the people change over time? (b) **Draw Conclusions** How does this change emphasize the author's central idea?

6. **Make Inferences** In the book, this essay is titled "A Fable for Tomorrow." Why might Carson have chosen this title for this section of the book?

Exploring the Essential Question

What is the relationship between people and nature?

7. What does the text suggest about the relationship between people and nature? Record your ideas in your Evidence Log.

STANDARDS
Reading Informational Text
Cite several pieces of textual evidence to support analysis of what the text says explicitly as well as inferences drawn from the text.

ANALYZE AND INTERPRET

from SILENT SPRING

Close Read

1. The model passage and annotation show how one reader analyzed part of paragraph 3 of the text. Find another detail in the passage to annotate. Then, write your own question and conclusion.

CLOSE-READ MODEL

Then a **strange blight** crept over the area and everything began to change. Some **evil spell** had settled on the community: **mysterious maladies** swept the flocks of chickens; the cattle and sheep **sickened and died.**

ANNOTATE: The author uses descriptive details to show the changes in the town.

QUESTION: What mood, or feeling, do these words create?

CONCLUDE: This description creates a mood of destruction and despair.

MY QUESTION:

MY CONCLUSION:

2. For more practice, answer the Close-Read note in the selection.
3. Choose a section of the essay you found especially meaningful. Mark important details. Then, jot down questions and write your conclusions in the open space next to the text.

Inquiry and Research

Research and Extend Conduct online research to answer these questions: *How did different groups respond to* Silent Spring *when it was first published? Why were the reactions so varied?* Use search terms effectively, entering words from the questions into a search engine. Then, gather relevant information from at least two different digital sources. Remember to assess each source's credibility and accuracy. It should be both trustworthy and up-to-date.

STANDARDS

Reading Informational Text
Determine the meaning of words and phrases as they are used in a text, including figurative, connotative, and technical meanings; analyze the impact of a specific word choice on meaning and tone.

Writing
• Conduct short research projects to answer a question.
• Gather relevant information from multiple print and digital sources, using search terms effectively; assess the credibility and accuracy of each source.

400 UNIT 4 • LEARNING FROM NATURE

Essential Question: What is the relationship between people and nature?

Language and Mood

In the essay from *Silent Spring*, Rachel Carson uses language that creates a very specific **mood,** or overall feeling. To create this mood, Carson employs different kinds of descriptive details:

- Imagery, or words that appeal to the senses: *Then foxes barked in the hills and deer silently crossed the fields . . .*

- Concrete details, or specific details that help readers visualize an abstract concept or idea: *Along the roads, laurel, viburnum and alder, great ferns and wildflowers delighted the traveler's eye . . .*

- Figurative language, or non-literal language, such as metaphor and personification: *Everywhere was a shadow of death.*

- Nuanced words, or the use of words that have specific positive or negative connotations: *A grim specter has crept upon us . . .*

PRACTICE Complete the activity and answer the questions.

1. Analyze Read the passages and identify details that create mood.

PASSAGES FROM *SILENT SPRING*	DETAILS THAT CREATE MOOD
There was once a town in the heart of America where all life seemed to live in harmony with its surroundings. The town lay in the midst of a checkerboard of prosperous farms, with fields of grain and hillsides of orchards where, in spring, white clouds of bloom drifted above the green fields. (paragraph 1)	
Then a strange blight crept over the area and everything began to change. Some evil spell had settled on the community: mysterious maladies swept the flocks of chickens; the cattle and sheep sickened and died. Everywhere was a shadow of death. (paragraph 3)	

2. (a) Contrast Review your completed chart. How has the mood changed between paragraphs 1 and 3? **(b) Interpret** What idea is Carson conveying through this change in mood?

3. Review the final paragraph of Carson's essay. Here, the author is speaking directly to readers. **(a) Interpret** What tone, or attitude, is created by the connotations of words such as *disaster, grim,* and *specter*? **(b) Draw Conclusions** For what reason might Carson have decided on this narrative shift?

from Silent Spring

STUDY LANGUAGE AND CRAFT

from SILENT SPRING

Concept Vocabulary

Why These Words? The vocabulary words are related to unwelcome change—in this case, to a town's landscape. For example, after the town is *stricken* with the mysterious *blight*, there is a strange *stillness*.

| blight | puzzled | stillness |
| maladies | stricken | deserted |

PRACTICE Answer the questions.

1. What other words in the selection are related to this concept?

2. Correctly complete each sentence using a vocabulary word.

   (a) When she returned home from the music festival, the woman found the _____ of her apartment strange in comparison.

   (b) Before the return of their lost pet, the family had been _____ with worry and fear.

   (c) Alfredo was _____ by his friend's confusing remark.

   (d) The _____ destroyed the potatoes grown in the county.

   (e) Common _____, such as colds and flus, affect the most people during the winter.

   (f) When the concert hall was _____, you could hear a pin drop from across the room.

Word Study

Long *i* Spelling Patterns In English, the long *i* sound can be spelled in a number of different ways. One way is with the letter sequence *igh*, as in the vocabulary word *blight*. The sound can also be spelled with the letter combinations *ig* (sign), *y* (cry), and *ie* (tie; die).

PRACTICE Complete the following activity.

Work with a partner to identify and write two additional words that use each of the four letter combinations (*igh*, *ig*, *y*, and *ie*) to create the long *i* sound.

WORD WALL

Note words in the text that are related to the relationship between people and nature. Add them to your Word Wall.

STANDARDS

Reading Informational Text
Determine an author's point of view or purpose in a text and analyze how the author distinguishes his or her position from that of others.

Language
Spell correctly.

402 UNIT 4 • LEARNING FROM NATURE

Essential Question: What is the relationship between people and nature?

Author's Point of View

All writing expresses a point of view, or perspective. In fiction and poetry, the narrator or speaker usually speaks from a first-person or third-person point of view. In nonfiction pieces like *Silent Spring*, the author speaks directly to you, the reader, using either an **objective point of view** or a **subjective point of view**. Here's how to distinguish between the two:

POINT OF VIEW	PASSAGE FROM *SILENT SPRING*	CHARACTERISTICS
Subjective: Writers using this point of view express primarily their own ideas, thoughts, experiences, and beliefs. This perspective is used often in narrative nonfiction, informal essays, blog posts, and some persuasion.	Then a strange blight crept over the area and everything began to change. Some evil spell had settled on the community: mysterious maladies swept the flocks of chickens; the cattle and sheep sickened and died.	• personal ideas and feelings are represented • based more on opinions than on facts
Objective: Writers using this point of view express the ideas, thoughts, and beliefs of multiple people. This perspective is used often in formal essays, research papers, and official documents.	The farmers complained that they were unable to raise any pigs—the litters were small and the young survived only a few days.	• balanced ideas • absence of bias • based more on facts than on emotions or opinions

PRACTICE Complete the activities.

1. **Analyze** Reread the essay and decide if it is written mostly from the objective or the subjective point of view. List evidence from the text that supports your analysis.

2. **Modify** Rewrite this subjective passage from the text to be objective: *The roadsides, once so attractive, were now lined with browned and withered vegetation as though swept by fire. These, too, were silent, deserted by all living things. Even the streams were now lifeless. Anglers no longer visited them, for all the fish had died.*

from *Silent Spring* 403

SHARE IDEAS

from SILENT SPRING

Writing

In an **argument,** a writer presents a claim, or position, on an issue and supports it with reasons and evidence.

Assignment

In *Silent Spring*, Rachel Carson paints a harsh picture of the future. Write a brief **argument** in which you answer this question:

Does Carson's description discourage or inspire people to act?

As you draft, be sure to do the following:

- State your claim and support it with clear, logical reasons and relevant textual evidence, using a formal style.
- Use transitions to show the relationships among your claim, reasons, and evidence.
- Conclude by restating your position.

After writing, trade arguments with a partner. Evaluate your partner's work by answering these questions:

- Did the writer state the claim clearly?
- Did the writer use sound, logical reasoning?
- Did the writer include evidence that relates to and supports the claim?

Use Academic Vocabulary

Challenge yourself to use one or more of the unit's academic vocabulary words in your argument: *logical, generate, philosophy, evident, elucidate.*

> **TIP:** As you write, select your words carefully. In an argument, you can appeal to your audience by including language that sparks their emotions. Consider the **connotations,** or emotional associations, of words, and intentionally choose words that will persuade your readers.

Reflect on Your Writing

PRACTICE Think about the choices you made as you wrote. Also, consider what you learned by writing. Share your experiences by responding to these questions.

1. Where in your argument did you state your position?

2. What aspect of writing the argument did you most enjoy?

3. **Why These Words?** Which words did you specifically choose to make your argument strong?

STANDARDS
Writing
- Write arguments to support claims with clear reasons and relevant evidence.
- Gather relevant information from multiple print and digital sources, using search terms effectively; assess the credibility and accuracy of each source; and quote or paraphrase the data and conclusions of others while avoiding plagiarism and following a standard format for citation.

404 UNIT 4 • LEARNING FROM NATURE

Essential Question: What is the relationship between people and nature?

Research

A **research report** is an informational text in which you explain a topic using facts, quotations, and examples from a variety of sources.

> ### Assignment
>
> Write a **research report** about one of the following topics:
> - ○ the importance of *Silent Spring* and the impact it had
> - ○ the struggle to ban DDT and the ban's eventual victory

Conduct Research

Generate Questions To focus your research, write at least two questions about your chosen topic. Enter key terms from your questions into a search engine to get the most relevant results. Then, identify a variety of print and digital sources you will use to gather useful information.

Examine Sources Read your sources critically and evaluate their reliability.

- Is each source credible? Make sure statements are supported with balanced, unbiased evidence.
- Is each source accurate? Check that the information is current and not outdated.
- Who published each source? Record the author, title, date, and publication information.
- Revise your research plan and consult difference sources, as needed.

TIP: Here are some ways to use **search terms** effectively:
- Put quotation marks around a phrase or name to search for the words in that exact order: "Rachel Carson"
- Type OR between two words if you're searching for something that two sites might phrase differently or if you want options: DDT OR pesticides

Paraphrase, Quote, and Cite Sources

Use Sources Ethically Follow these steps to use source materials ethically and to avoid plagiarism:

- Cite sources of information and ideas that are not common knowledge.
- Paraphrase by using your own words to restate the ideas of others. Make sure your paraphrases reflect the meaning and order of ideas of the original text. Note that even when you paraphrase, you must still cite the source because the ideas are not your own.
- If you want to quote an author, set their exact words in quotation marks and cite the source accurately.
- To avoid plagiarism, always cite all of your sources. Follow a format for citation provided by your teacher.

EVIDENCE LOG

Before moving on to a new selection, go to your Evidence Log and record any additional thoughts or observations you may have about this essay from *Silent Spring*.

from Silent Spring

COMPARE WITHIN GENRE

FICTION
A **creation story** explains the actions of divine beings, the origins of natural phenomena, or a combination of the two.

CREATION STORY

Purpose
- to explain an aspect of the world and how it came to be
- to share cultural beliefs and customs with future generations

Characteristics
- characters that may be humans, animals, or gods that have magical or supernatural abilities
- settings that may be imaginary or real and are centered in a particular culture
- themes, or insights about life, that are important to the culture the story comes from
- details (plants, animals, foods, dances, ceremonies, and so on) that reflect the culture the story comes from

Structure
- a conflict-driven plot, or series of events
- often involves tests or obstacles characters must overcome

Take a Minute!
LIST With a partner, identify other stories you're familiar with (graphic novels, movies, cartoons, and so on) that are based on creation stories. What elements of creation stories do they have?

STANDARDS
Reading Literature
Determine a theme or central idea of a text and analyze its development over the course of the text.

406 UNIT 4 • LEARNING FROM NATURE

Essential Question: What is the relationship between people and nature?

Multiple Themes

In literature, a **theme** is a message or an insight about life that the author expresses. It is different from a text's topic. For example, if crime and punishment are the topics of a text, one theme might be, "Crime doesn't pay." A text can have multiple themes related to its topic.

In creation stories, themes about big ideas like love and hate or good and evil are often **universal,** meaning that they relate to people in all times and places. Creation stories also reflect a culture's values.

An author develops themes over the course of a text, but generally these themes are not **explicitly,** or directly, stated. Instead, they are **implicitly** suggested. Readers must infer implicit themes by analyzing literary details, such as characters' actions and the ways they respond to conflicts.

Compare these topics and related themes.

TIP: Modern writers who adapt creation stories or ancient myths into their own works maintain the themes conveyed in the original versions, such as good versus evil or the origin of natural phenomena.

EXAMPLE: DISTINGUISHING TOPIC FROM THEME

TOPIC	THEME
family relationships	Family helps us define ourselves.
bravery	Being brave doesn't mean being unafraid.
war and peace	Some things are worth fighting for.

PRACTICE With a partner, discuss and complete each activity.

1. Which of the items are topics, and which are themes?

		TOPIC	THEME
A	Love can triumph over hate.	○	○
B	Jealousy	○	○
C	Greed can destroy lives.	○	○
D	Mysteries of the universe	○	○

2. Make up a possible theme for the topic of kindness.

Compare Within Genre **407**

PREPARE TO READ

HOW GRANDMOTHER SPIDER STOLE THE SUN

COYOTE STEALS THE SUN AND MOON

COMPARE: FICTION

In this lesson, you will read and compare two creation stories: **How Grandmother Spider Stole the Sun** and **Coyote Steals the Sun and Moon.**

Concept Vocabulary

Preview You will encounter the following words as you read the selections. Before reading, note how familiar you are with each word. Using a scale of 1 (do not know it at all) to 4 (know it very well), indicate your knowledge of each word.

WORD	YOUR RANKING
benefit	
chosen	
honored	
pestering	
fault	
mischief	

Reading Strategy: Adjust Your Reading Rate

When you set a purpose for reading, you decide what your focus will be. Then, you **adjust your reading rate,** or the speed at which you read, to meet that goal. Consider these two purposes:

- **For Analysis or Information:** Read slowly. After you finish reading a complex passage, pause to think about the ideas and make sure you fully understand them. Mark important details, and reread if necessary.

- **For Enjoyment:** Read more quickly. You may want to linger over passages you like, but studying the text is less important.

PRACTICE As you read and analyze the texts, adjust your reading rate to suit your reading purpose.

STANDARDS
Reading Literature
By the end of the year, read and comprehend literature, including stories, dramas, and poems.

Essential Question: What is the relationship between people and nature?

About the Creation Stories

How Grandmother Spider Stole the Sun

BACKGROUND
"How Grandmother Spider Stole the Sun" is a Native American creation story that explains how the world became the way it is. Grandmother Spider appears in the stories of many Native American groups, such as the Hopi, Navajo, and Cherokee, as an important creator who is also a powerful teacher and helper. This story comes from the Muskogee, or Creek, people.

Michael J. Caduto (b. 1955) is an award-winning author, storyteller, educator, poet, and musician. His work emphasizes respect for the earth and the environment, as well as the scientific knowledge and cultural traditions that underline the importance of the natural world.

Joseph Bruchac (b. 1942) is a novelist, poet, and storyteller of Abenaki descent. He lives in the foothills of New York's Adirondack Mountains, where his ancestors also lived. Bruchac has written more than 70 books for children and has performed worldwide as a teller of Native American folk tales.

Coyote Steals the Sun and Moon

BACKGROUND
"Coyote Steals the Sun and Moon" is a Zuni creation story. The Zuni belong to a group of Native American peoples known as the Pueblos. According to their beliefs, the Great Spirit and other sacred beings guided the people to their homelands, showed them how to plant corn, and taught them to live in peace with each other. Zuni stories often involve the sun and the moon, with daylight symbolizing life. Coyote, who is usually full of mischief, is a popular character in them.

Richard Erdoes (1912–2008) was born in Frankfurt, Germany, and was educated in Vienna, Berlin, and Paris. As a young boy, he became fascinated by American Indian cultures. In 1940, he moved to the United States to escape Nazi rule and became a well-known author, photographer, and illustrator. He wrote several books on Native Americans and the American West.

Alfonso Ortiz (1939–1997) was a Tewa Pueblo, born in New Mexico. He became a professor of anthropology at the University of New Mexico and was a leading expert on Pueblo culture.

CREATION STORY

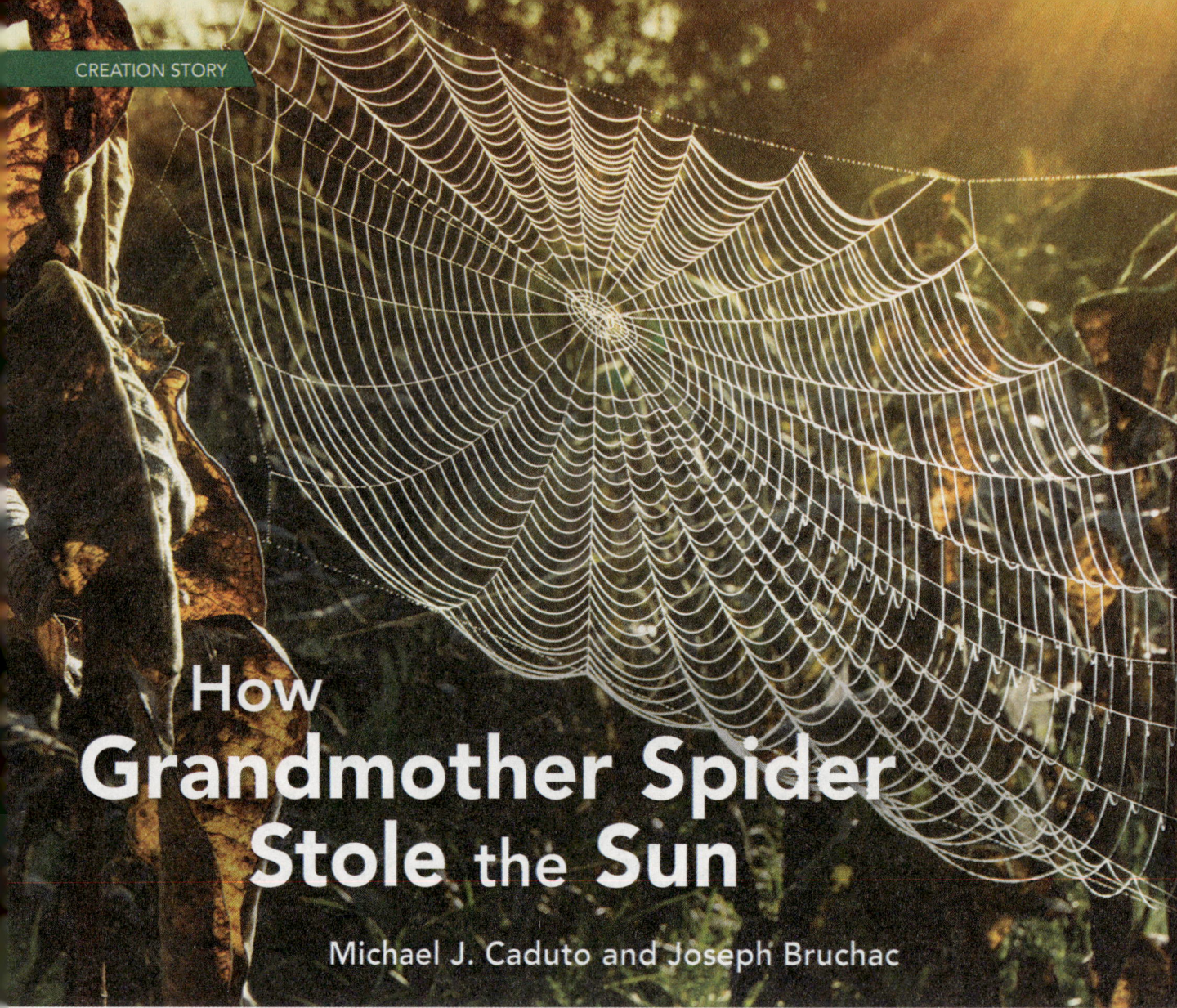

How Grandmother Spider Stole the Sun

Michael J. Caduto and Joseph Bruchac

READ TO UNLOCK MEANING

1. First read the text for comprehension and enjoyment. Use the **Reading Strategy** and **Comprehension Check** questions to support your first read.
2. Go back and respond to the Close-Read note.
3. Identify other details in the text you find interesting. Ask your own questions and draw your own conclusions.

1   When the Earth was first made, there was no light. It was very hard for the animals and the people in the darkness. Finally the animals decided to do something about it.

2   "I have heard there is something called the Sun," said the Bear. "It is kept on the other side of the world, but the people there will not share it. Perhaps we can steal a piece of it."

3   All the animals agreed that it was a good idea. But who would be the one to steal the Sun?

4   The Fox was the first to try. He sneaked to the place where the Sun was kept. He waited until no one was looking. Then he grabbed a piece of it in his mouth and ran. But the Sun was so hot it burned his mouth and he dropped it. To this day all foxes have black mouths because that first fox burned his carrying the Sun.

5   The Possum tried next. In those days Possum had a very bushy tail. She crept up to the place where the Sun was kept, broke off a piece, and hid it in her tail. Then she began to run, bringing the Sun back to the animals and the people. But the Sun was so hot it

burned off all the hair on her tail and she lost hold of it. To this day all possums have bare tails because the Sun burned away the hair on that first possum.

6   Then Grandmother Spider tried. Instead of trying to hold the Sun herself, she wove a bag out of her webbing. She put the piece of the Sun into her bag and carried it back with her. Now the question was where to put the Sun.

7   Grandmother Spider told them, "The Sun should be up high in the sky. Then everyone will be able to see it and **benefit** from its light."

8   All the animals agreed, but none of them could reach up high enough. Even if they carried it to the top of the tallest tree, that would not be high enough for everyone on the Earth to see the Sun. Then they decided to have one of the birds carry the Sun up to the top of the sky. Everyone knew the Buzzard could fly the highest, so he was **chosen.**

9   Buzzard placed the Sun on top of his head, where his feathers were the thickest, for the Sun was still very hot, even inside Grandmother Spider's bag. He began to fly, up and up toward the top of the sky. As he flew the Sun grew hotter. Up and up he went, higher and higher, and the Sun grew hotter and hotter still. Now the Sun was burning through Grandmother Spider's bag, but the Buzzard still kept flying up toward the top of the sky. Up and up he went and the Sun grew hotter. Now it was burning away the feathers on top of his head, but he continued on. Now all of his feathers were gone, but he flew higher. Now it was turning the bare skin of his head all red, but he continued to fly. He flew until he reached the top of the sky, and there he placed the Sun where it would give light to everyone.

10   Because he carried the Sun up to the top of the sky, Buzzard was **honored** by all the birds and animals. Though his head was naked and ugly because he was burned carrying the Sun, he is still the highest flyer of all, and he can be seen circling the Sun to this day. And because Grandmother Spider brought the Sun in her bag of webbing, at times the Sun makes rays across the sky that are shaped like the rays in Grandmother Spider's web. It reminds everyone that we are all connected, like the strands of Grandmother Spider's web, and it reminds everyone of what Grandmother Spider did for all the animals and the people. 🕷

---

benefit (BEH nuh fiht) *v.* get good or helpful results; gain

chosen (CHOH zuhn) *v.* selected; decided on

CLOSE READ
ANNOTATE Mark the repeated words in the first seven sentences of paragraph 9.
QUESTION Why might the authors have chosen to use so much repetition in this passage? What effect does it create?

honored (AH nuhrd) *v.* given special recognition

COMPREHENSION CHECK
How does Grandmother Spider make it possible to transport the Sun?

CREATION STORY

Coyote Steals the Sun and Moon

Richard Erdoes and Alfonso Ortiz

1   Coyote is a bad hunter who never kills anything. Once he watched Eagle hunting rabbits, catching one after another—more rabbits than he could eat. Coyote thought, "I'll team up with Eagle so that I can have enough meat." Coyote is always up to something.

2   "Friend," Coyote said to Eagle, "we should hunt together. Two can catch more than one."

3   "Why not?" Eagle said, and so they began to hunt in partnership. Eagle caught many rabbits, but all Coyote caught was some little bugs.

4   At this time the world was still dark; the sun and moon had not yet been put in the sky. "Friend," Coyote said to Eagle, "no wonder I can't catch anything; I can't see. Do you know where we can get some light?"

5   "You're right, friend, there should be some light," Eagle said. "I think there's a little toward the west. Let's try and find it."

6. And so they went looking for the sun and moon. They came to a big river, which Eagle flew over. Coyote swam and swallowed so much water that he almost drowned. He crawled out with his fur full of mud, and Eagle asked, "Why don't you fly like me?"

7. "You have wings, I just have hair," Coyote said. "I can't fly without feathers.

8. At last they came to a pueblo, where the Kachinas happened to be dancing. The people invited Eagle and Coyote to sit down and have something to eat while they watched the sacred dances. Seeing the power of the Kachinas, Eagle said, "I believe these are the people who have light."

9. Coyote, who had been looking all around, pointed out two boxes, one large and one small, that the people opened whenever they wanted light. To produce a lot of light, they opened the lid of the big box, which contained the sun. For less light, they opened the lid of the small box, which held the moon.

10. Coyote nudged Eagle. "Friend, did you see that? They have all the light we need in the big box. Let's steal it."

11. "You always want to steal and rob. I say we should just borrow it."

12. "They won't lend it to us."

13. "You may be right," said Eagle. "Let's wait till they finish dancing and then steal it."

14. After a while the Kachinas went home to sleep, and Eagle scooped up the large box and flew off. Coyote ran along trying to keep up, panting, his tongue hanging out. Soon he yelled up to Eagle, "Ho, friend, let me carry the big box a little way."

15. "No, no," said Eagle, "you never do anything right."

16. He flew on, and Coyote ran after him. After a while Coyote shouted again: "Friend, you're my chief, and it's not right for you to carry the box; people will call me lazy. Let me have it."

17. "No, no, you always mess everything up." And Eagle flew on and Coyote ran along.

18. So it went for a stretch, and then Coyote started again. "Ho, friend, it isn't right for you to do this. What will people think of you and me?"

19. "I don't care what people think. I'm going to carry this box."

20. Again Eagle flew on and again Coyote ran after him. Finally Coyote begged for the fourth time: "Let me carry it. You're the chief, and I'm just Coyote. Let me carry it."

21. Eagle couldn't stand any more **pestering**. Also, Coyote had asked him four times, and if someone asks four times, you better give him what he wants. Eagle said, "Since you won't let up on me, go ahead and carry the box for a while. But promise not to open it."

---

pestering (PEH stur ihng) *n.* constant bothering

COMPREHENSION CHECK

Why do Eagle and Coyote want to steal the boxes from the Kachinas?

ADJUST YOUR READING RATE

How does the rate at which you read change between paragraphs of dialogue and paragraphs of description and explanation?

22   "Oh, sure, oh yes, I promise." They went on as before, but now Coyote had the box. Soon Eagle was far ahead, and Coyote lagged behind a hill where Eagle couldn't see him. "I wonder what the light looks like, inside there, he said to himself. Why shouldn't I take a peek? Probably there's something extra in the box, something good that Eagle wants to keep to himself."

23   And Coyote opened the lid. Now, not only was the sun inside, but the moon also. Eagle had put them both together, thinking that it would be easier to carry one box than two.

24   As soon as Coyote opened the lid, the moon escaped, flying high into the sky. At once all the plants shriveled up and turned brown. Just as quickly, all the leaves fell off the trees, and it was winter. Trying to catch the moon and put it back in the box, Coyote ran in pursuit as it skipped away from him. Meanwhile the sun flew out and rose into the sky. It drifted far away, and the peaches, squashes, and melons shriveled up with cold.

25   Eagle turned and flew back to see what had delayed Coyote. "You fool! Look what you've done!" he said. "You let the sun and moon escape, and now it's cold." Indeed, it began to snow, and Coyote shivered. "Now your teeth are chattering." Eagle said, "and it's your **fault** that cold has come into the world."

26   It's true. If it weren't for Coyote's curiosity and **mischief** making, we wouldn't have winter; we could enjoy summer all the time.

fault (FAWLT) *n.* responsibility for a bad result

mischief (MIS chuhf) *n.* trouble; naughtiness

BUILD INSIGHT

First Thoughts

Which story resonated with you, or spoke to you, more strongly? Explain your reaction, citing details from the text.

Summary

Confirm your understanding by writing a short objective summary of one of the creation stories. Be sure to include only the central ideas and to keep your summary free from personal opinions.

Analysis

1. **Analyze** In "How Grandmother…", which descriptions of the animals seem true to life? Which are more imaginative? Explain.

2. (a) **Make Inferences** What do the story details suggest about Grandmother Spider? (b) **Connect** Why do you think the story is titled as it is?

3. (a) **Compare and Contrast** In "Coyote Steals…", how do Coyote and Eagle differ in their points of view about stealing and carrying the box of light? (b) **Analyze** What conflict does this difference develop?

4. (a) **Analyze** What idea about the world does "Coyote Steals . . ." share with readers? (b) **Draw Conclusions** Why do you think eternal summer might be a good thing for some cultures? (c) **Make a Judgment** Do you think eternal summer is a good thing or a bad thing? Explain your opinion.

5. **Evaluate** Why do you think people still read and share creation stories? What qualities do these stories have that continue to give them meaning and impact? Explain, citing details from the texts.

Exploring the Essential Question

What is the relationship between people and nature?

6. What have these creation stories revealed about how people relate to the natural world? Write your ideas in your Evidence Log.

STANDARDS
Reading Literature
• Cite several pieces of textual evidence to support analysis of what the text says explicitly as well as inferences drawn from the text.

• Provide an objective summary of the text.

ANALYZE AND INTERPRET

HOW GRANDMOTHER SPIDER STOLE THE SUN • COYOTE STEALS THE SUN AND MOON

Close Read

1. The model passage and annotation show how one reader analyzed part of paragraph 10 of "How Grandmother Spider Stole the Sun." Find another detail in the passage to annotate. Then, write your own question and conclusion.

CLOSE-READ MODEL

Because he carried the Sun up to the top of the sky, Buzzard was honored by all the birds and animals. Though his head was naked and ugly because he was burned carrying the Sun, he is still the highest flyer of all. . . . And because Grandmother Spider brought the Sun in her bag of webbing…

ANNOTATE: I notice that many sentences in this paragraph include clauses that contain *because*.

QUESTION: What is the effect of that pattern?

CONCLUDE: The author deliberately chose this pattern to emphasize the causes of different events in the story.

MY QUESTION:

MY CONCLUSION:

2. For more practice, answer the Close-Read note in the selection.

3. Choose a section of the creation stories that you found especially meaningful. Mark important details. Then, jot down questions and write your conclusions in the open space next to the texts.

Inquiry and Research

Research and Extend Conduct brief research in a few different sources to find answers to this question: *What other cultures have creation stories about the sun, and how do they portray it?*

STANDARDS

Reading Literature
• Determine a theme or central idea of a text and analyze its development over the course of the text.
• Analyze how particular elements of a story or drama interact.

Writing
Conduct short research projects to answer a question, drawing on several sources.

416 UNIT 4 • LEARNING FROM NATURE

Essential Question: What is the relationship between people and nature?

Multiple Themes

Creation stories often express themes that comment on human nature and our relationship to the world we live in. Themes are rarely **explicitly**, or directly, stated in a text. Instead, they are **implicitly**, or indirectly, expressed through details in the work. One text can express multiple themes, and different texts can express similar themes.

How to Interpret Themes To determine the implicit themes of a text, analyze how characters, settings, and events interact.

- Notice how the setting affects characters or causes events to occur.
- Look for ways in which the characters grow or change.
- Analyze ways in which characters resolve conflicts.

How to State Themes Once you have analyzed the story elements, formulate two or three themes that apply to the text. Be sure to state themes in sentence format. They should be worded to apply to the world, not to the text alone. Read these examples:

- **Theme:** Greed leads to misery.
- **Not a theme:** In this story, Tania's greed makes her miserable.
- **Not a theme:** Misery

> **TIP:** You can also use these strategies to infer a text's **universal themes**, or insights that are meaningful to people in all time periods, places, and cultures. The universal themes conveyed in creation stories remain true even in modern adaptations.

PRACTICE Complete the activity and answer the questions.

1. **Interpret** Complete the chart by filling in two themes from each selection. Record text evidence that supports each theme. Then, with a partner, discuss how characters, settings, and events interact to develop the themes over the course of the text.

SELECTION	POSSIBLE THEMES	TEXT EVIDENCE
How Grandmother Spider Stole the Sun		
Coyote Steals the Sun and Moon		

2. **Interpret** Study the themes you identified in item 1. What universal theme might both creation stories share? What evidence supports this shared theme?

STUDY LANGUAGE AND CRAFT

HOW GRANDMOTHER SPIDER
STOLE THE SUN • COYOTE
STEALS THE SUN AND MOON

Concept Vocabulary

Why These Words? The vocabulary words describe positive and negative acts or situations. For example, all the animals *honored* Buzzard in "How Grandmother…"

| benefit | chosen | honored |
| pestering | fault | mischief |

WORD WALL

Note words in the texts that are related to the relationship between people and nature. Add them to your Word Wall.

PRACTICE Answer the questions and complete the activities.

1. How do the vocabulary words contribute to your understanding of the characters' conflicts in these creation stories?

2. Find two other words in each selection that relate to positive or negative actions or consequences.

3. Write a paragraph that includes all six vocabulary words.

Word Study

Denotation and Connotation A word's **denotation** is its dictionary definition. Its **connotation** consists of the ideas and feelings that the word brings to mind. Connotations may be positive, negative, or neutral. Words with similar denotations (synonyms) can have different connotations. For instance, *pestering* has a similar denotation to *annoying*, but its connotation is not as strongly negative.

PRACTICE Complete the activities.

1. With a partner, use a thesaurus to identify two more synonyms for the vocabulary word *pestering*. Jot them down and discuss the different connotation of each word. Then, put all three words in order from least to most negative.

2. Find two synonyms for the vocabulary word *mischief*—one with a more positive connotation and one with a more negative connotation. Then, write a sentence using each synonym.

STANDARDS
Language
• Place phrases and clauses within a sentence, recognizing and correcting misplaced and dangling modifiers.
• Distinguish among the connotations of words with similar denotations.
• Acquire and use accurately grade-appropriate general academic and domain-specific words and phrases; gather vocabulary knowledge when considering a word or phrase important to comprehension or expression.

418 UNIT 4 • LEARNING FROM NATURE

Essential Question: What is the relationship between people and nature?

Misplaced and Dangling Modifiers

A **modifier** is a word or phrase that gives information about another word in the sentence. When you are writing, it is important to place every modifier in its correct location—usually, directly next to the word or phrase it modifies.

A **misplaced modifier** seems to modify the wrong word in a sentence because it is too far away from the word it really modifies.

> **Misplaced:** Burning hot, Fox dropped the sun.
> (The sun is hot, not Fox.)
>
> **Corrected:** Fox dropped the burning hot sun.

A **dangling modifier** seems to modify the wrong word or no word at all because the word it should modify is not in the sentence.

> **Dangling:** Instead of trying to hold the Sun herself, a bag was woven out of webbing.
> (The sentence is missing the noun that goes with the modifier—Grandmother Spider.)
>
> **Corrected:** Instead of trying to hold the Sun herself, Grandmother Spider wove a bag out of webbing.

TIP: Misplaced and dangling modifiers can be single words, phrases, or clauses. Dangling modifiers most often appear as introductory phrases or clauses.

WRITE / EDIT Rewrite each sentence to correct the misplaced or dangling modifier. You may need to change the wording to make the sentences clear.

1. Creation stories around the world exist in every culture.

2. Possessing magical powers, creation stories have interesting characters.

3. To overcome the darkness, a plan was developed to steal a piece of the Sun.

4. The Kachinas communicate with the spirit world performing sacred dances.

5. Happy, the sunlight warmed the people.

TEST PRACTICE

CREATION STORY

HOW GRANDMOTHER SPIDER STOLE THE SUN

CREATION STORY

COYOTE STEALS THE SUN AND MOON

COMPARE: FICTION
Multiple Choice

These questions are based on the creation stories "How Grandmother Spider Stole the Sun" and "Coyote Steals the Sun and Moon." Choose the best answer to each question.

1. Which statement is accurate?
   - A Both texts describe people's conflicts with animals.
   - B Both texts describe people's triumphs over nature.
   - C Both texts include characters that have both animal and human traits.
   - D Both texts depict people who are overpowered by nature.

2. Why might these two stories represent the sun so differently?
   - A The stories come from cultures that each believe the sun contains both good and evil.
   - B The stories come from cultures with different beliefs.
   - C The stories come from cultures that originated on opposite sides of the planet.
   - D The stories come from cultures that were at war.

3. Read paragraph 1 from "How Grandmother Spider Stole the Sun" and paragraph 4 from "Coyote Steals the Sun and Moon." Which does neither paragraph do?

---

from **How Grandmother...**

When the Earth was first made, there was no light. It was very hard for the animals and the people in the darkness. Finally the animals decided to do something about it.

---

from **Coyote Steals...**

At this time the world was still dark; the sun and moon had not yet been put in the sky. "Friend," Coyote said to Eagle, "no wonder I can't catch anything; I can't see. Do you know where we can get some light?"

- A refer to a time long ago
- B indicate something the characters will seek out
- C indicate which character or characters face hardship
- D state morals or messages

STANDARDS

Reading Literature
Cite several pieces of textual evidence to support analysis of what the text says explicitly as well as inferences drawn from the text.

Writing
Draw evidence from literary or informational texts to support analysis, reflection, and research.

420 UNIT 4 • LEARNING FROM NATURE

Essential Question: What is the relationship between people and nature?

Short Response

1. **(a) Compare** What traits are shared by Buzzard from "How Grandmother . . . " and Eagle from "Coyote Steals . . . "? **(b) Analyze** In what ways do the two birds act as heroes in their creation stories? Include textual evidence in your response.

2. **Interpret** Write a theme that the two creation stories share.

3. **(a) Analyze** What qualities make the animal characters successful in each story? **(b) Draw Conclusions** What do these qualities suggest about the values of the cultures that first told these stories?

Timed Writing

A **comparison-and-contrast essay** is a piece of writing in which you discuss similarities and differences among two or more topics.

Assignment

Write a **comparison-and-contrast essay** in which you analyze the characters' need for light in each creation story. What makes light so important? Does the value of light justify the stealing that takes place in each story?

5-Minute Planner

1. Read the assignment carefully and completely.
2. Decide what you want to say—your central idea.
3. Decide what examples you'll use from each creation story.
4. Organize your ideas, making sure to address these points:
   - Why is light important in each story?
   - How is light obtained in each story?
   - Does the value of light justify its theft?

EVIDENCE LOG

Before moving on to a new selection, go to your Evidence Log and record any additional thoughts or observations you may have about "How Grandmother Spider Stole the Sun" and "Coyote Steals the Sun and Moon."

Test Practice **421**

PERFORMANCE TASK

Write a Research Paper

Research papers are reports in which a writer synthesizes research from outside sources with their own critical thinking and analysis to answer a research question.

Assignment

Write a research paper in which you answer a focused research question about the following broad topic:

specific ways that humans are trying to solve a problem faced by animals

Synthesize information to create an engaging and informative text. Include the elements of research writing in your paper.

WRITING CENTER

Visit the Writing Center to watch video tutorials and view annotated student models and rubrics.

ELEMENTS OF RESEARCH WRITING

Purpose: to answer a focused research question

Characteristics

- a clear thesis statement that expresses the central idea
- relevant evidence, such as facts, definitions, concrete details, quotations, and examples
- information from several credible and accurate sources, both print and digital
- citations that follow a standard format
- a formal style with precise language and specific vocabulary
- correct grammar, spelling, capitalization, and punctuation

Structure

- an introduction that clearly conveys the thesis and previews what is to follow
- well-organized body paragraphs with transitions that create cohesion and clarity
- a conclusion that supports the information presented

STANDARDS
Writing
• Write informative/explanatory texts to examine a topic and convey ideas, concepts, and information through the selection, organization, and analysis of relevant content.
• Gather relevant information from multiple print and digital sources, using search terms effectively; assess the credibility and accuracy of each source; and quote or paraphrase the data and conclusions of others while avoiding plagiarism and following a standard format for citation.

422 UNIT 4 • LEARNING FROM NATURE

Essential Question: What is the relationship between people and nature?

Checklist: Am I Ready to Research and Write?

1. Topic: Do I have a clear central idea for my topic?

◯ yes   If "yes," what are my topic and central idea?

◯ no   If "no," what do I want to learn about the problems facing pollinators?

2. Research Question: Do I have a strong research question?

◯ yes   If "yes," what is my research question?

◯ no   If "no," what are 2–3 questions related to my central idea, and which is the strongest or most interesting?

3. Sources: Do I know what types of sources I'll consult, how to locate them (online or at the library), and whether I'll conduct original research, such as interviews?

◯ yes   If "yes," what are my source types?

◯ no   If "no," where will I find the information I need, and how will I access it?

SOURCES

Use various types of **sources** to make your research paper accurate, credible, and interesting.

- **Primary sources** are firsthand accounts of events, such as diaries, letters, or oral histories.
- **Secondary sources** discuss information originally presented in primary sources and include articles, reference book entries, and biographies.

Research and Write Your Paper

If you've made decisions about all the items on the checklist, get started with your research. Keep these tips in mind:

- **Research Question:** Make sure your research question is interesting to you and neither too broad nor too narrow.
- **Quality and Variety of Sources:** Consult a variety of high-quality sources that are both credible and accurate. Be wary of sources that do not offer proper citations, are poorly written, or show bias.
- **Citation Information:** Be sure to gather source information as part of your notetaking and to cite the sources properly.

Writer's Handbook: If you answered "no" to any of the checklist items, refer to the Writer's Handbook pages that follow.

WRITER'S HANDBOOK | RESEARCH PAPER

Planning and Prewriting

In order to choose your topic and generate a meaningful research question, you need to do some preliminary work.

Generate Questions to Develop a Plan

A. Choose a Topic Conduct quick online research to gather background information about the broad topic, using effective search terms. In the chart, take notes on what you learn in the left column, and write what else you want to know in the right column. List aspects of the topic that spark your curiosity. Write them as "how" and "why" questions.

Topic: _____

WHAT I LEARNED	WHAT I STILL WANT TO KNOW

B. Review Your Questions Review your list of questions and mark the ones you find most exciting. Cross out the ones that don't interest you.

Using the Writer's Handbook

In this handbook you'll find strategies to support every stage of the writing process—from planning to publishing. As you write, check in with yourself:
- *What's going well?*
- *What isn't going well?*

Then, use the handbook items that will best help you craft a strong research paper.

STANDARDS

Writing Conduct short research projects to answer a question, drawing on several sources and generating additional related, focused questions for further research and investigation.

424 UNIT 4 • LEARNING FROM NATURE

Refine Your Research Question

A. Write Your Question Pick the question you like the most from the ones you generated. Write it here:

> **Sample Research Questions**
> - How do pesticides affect honey bee colonies?
> - Why are monarch butterflies facing extinction?

B. Evaluate Your Question A strong question will provide a clear path for your research. A weak question will result in too much or too little information. Read the chart. Answer the questions in the Evaluate column to make sure your question is interesting and answerable. If you answer "no" to an Evaluate item, then follow the instructions in the Take Action column.

EVALUATE	TAKE ACTION
Complexity The answer to your research question should require explanation. You should not be able to answer it with a simple *yes* or *no*. Does my answer require explanation? ○ yes ○ no	If "no," add elements to your question or rephrase it to ask *why* or *how*.
Significance Your research question should be important and interesting. It should matter to you. Do I care about my question? ○ yes ○ no	If "no," find an aspect of the topic that sparks your curiosity or choose another topic.
Scope Your research question should not be too narrow (too specific) nor too broad (too general). Is the scope of my question appropriate for this project? ○ yes ○ no	Test the scope of your question with quick research. If sources are hard to find, broaden your question. If the number of sources is overwhelming, narrow your question.

C. Refine Your Question If you had to revise or change your research question based on your answers in the chart, write your new question here:

WRITER'S HANDBOOK | **RESEARCH PAPER**

Planning and Prewriting

Gather your research sources from a library, reliable websites, and local experts, such as science teachers or nature preserve workers.

Identify and Gather a Variety of Sources

List multiple print and digital sources you might use to gather information that is relevant to your research question. Plan to use at least one source from each category.

Type of Source	Source Information
Primary Sources: texts created at the time the event actually happened • diaries or journals • original newspaper articles • eyewitness accounts • public records • research studies	
Secondary Sources: information shared by writers and researchers after the events occurred; secondary sources often interpret primary sources • newspaper or magazine articles • encyclopedia entries • historical writing • media (documentaries, TV shows, podcasts or radio programs)	
Your Own Research: information you gather on your own • online surveys • in-person surveys • interviews	

STANDARDS
Writing Gather relevant information from multiple print and digital sources, using search terms effectively; assess the credibility and accuracy of each source.

Evaluate Sources

Plan to use only those sources that are relevant, accurate, and credible. Fill out the form to evaluate the quality of each source and the information it offers.

- For any question you answer "yes" to, you should also be able to answer the question in the last column. Write your answers in the chart.
- If you answer "no" to any question, the source may not be strong or reliable enough. You should discard it.

Is the information **relevant**—does it relate directly to my research question?	◯ yes ◯ no	How does the information relate to my question?
Is the information **accurate**—does it provide recent facts and data?	◯ yes ◯ no	How does the information connect to other research I have gathered?
Is the information **credible**—does it come from a trustworthy source?	◯ yes ◯ no	Is this information similar to what I have read in other sources? How can I tell that the author's views are fair and unbiased?

CHECK ONLINE SOURCES

Some websites are reliable, but some are not.

- Go to websites of established institutions and those with expertise (.edu, .gov).
- Avoid commercial sites (.com).
- Question personal blogs.
- Avoid anonymous sites or pages.

Revise Your Plan Allow enough time for your initial research. Then, review your findings and decide if you need more information. Leave time to visit the library, research online, or ask local experts additional questions.

WRITER'S HANDBOOK **RESEARCH PAPER**

Drafting

Now that you've gathered the information you need, organize it and write a first draft of your research paper.

Write Your Thesis

Your **thesis** is a statement of the central idea you will explain and prove in your research paper. Generally, a thesis statement has three parts: 1. an introduction of the topic; 2. the point you will develop; and, 3. a preview of your reasoning or evidence.

EXAMPLE:
Recent research shows that monarch butterflies have become [1] endangered because their primary food source is being killed [2] [3] off by pesticides.

1 = the topic
2 = the point to develop or explain
3 = the reasoning / evidence

Note that your thesis may change as you research, draft, and revise. Write a **working thesis** here:

Make an Outline

List the points you want to make and the evidence that will support each one.

WRITE Make an outline for your paper.

_____
_____
_____
_____
_____
_____
_____
_____

DEVELOP IDEAS

- **Organize** the evidence you gathered in a logical way. Group related information into paragraphs.
- **Develop** each paragraph with relevant facts, definitions, concrete details, quotations, or examples from your research.

STANDARDS
Writing • Organize ideas, concepts, and information, using strategies such as definition, classification, comparison/contrast, and cause/effect.
• Quote or paraphrase the data and conclusions of others while avoiding plagiarism and following a standard format for citation.

Incorporate Evidence

There are different ways to include information from sources in your writing. Regardless of the method you choose, you must credit your sources. Decide how you will use each piece of evidence.

METHOD	DEFINITION	EXAMPLE
Direct Quotation	a source's exact words, set off in quotation marks	According to Dr. Yang, "Sadly, monarch butterflies may soon be extinct" (74).
Paraphrase	a restatement of another person's ideas in your own words (Note: Restated ideas are still not yours and must be cited.)	Biologists fear that the monarch butterfly may become extinct (Yang 74).
Summary	a brief statement of the main ideas and key details from a text	"Good-bye Butterfly" presents one biologist's findings about threats to monarch butterflies (Yang).

In-Text Citations:

Place in-text citations in parentheses.
- Author Indicated: cite the page number
- Author Not Indicated: cite the author's last name and page number
- No Author: cite short version of the title and the page number
- No Page Number: cite short title or author only

When to Cite Sources

As you use information from sources, be sure to create citations. Otherwise, you risk plagiarizing, or presenting someone else's words or ideas as your own.
- **Citation Not Needed:** your own ideas; common knowledge (facts that most people know)
- **Citation Needed:** direct quotation, paraphrase, or summary of someone else's ideas; specialized information (facts that only experts or specialists know)

When you finish drafting, provide full publication information about your sources in a Works Cited list at the end of your paper. Follow the format your teacher prefers.

WRITE Write a paragraph of your paper. Include evidence using both a direct quotation and a paraphrase, and cite both methods correctly.

USE TRANSITIONS

Once you have included evidence, use **transitions** within the paragraph to clarify the connection to your ideas. Use transitions between paragraphs to guide readers from one idea to the next.

WRITER'S HANDBOOK — RESEARCH PAPER

Revising

Now that you have a first draft, revise it to be sure it is as clear and informative as possible.

Read Like a Writer

Review the revisions made to the Mentor Text. Then, answer the questions in the white boxes.

MENTOR TEXT

from Wildlife Rehabbers Are Here to Help

Most people live in areas that were once home only to wildlife. Direct contact between humans and wild animals is bound to happen, and sometimes that contact can be a problem. *According to Maine's state wildlife rehabilitation website, "In most cases, when humans and wildlife collide, wildlife suffers."* That's where wildlife rehabilitators come in. Rehabbers provide valuable services to injured animals and also assist the professionals treating them.

According to Cornell University's Wildlife Health Lab (CWHL), there are more than 400 professional wildlife rehabilitators *(Peaslee 5)*. The number of volunteers is even greater. Some estimates put that figure at more than 1,600 across the United States. But even volunteers ~~have to know what they're doing~~ *must get licenses to conduct wildlife rehab work*. In North Carolina, for example, rehabilitators are required to work with mentors for a full year before they can get their own licenses.

> The writer added a memorable quotation to the first paragraph to engage readers.

> Where does the writer present the thesis statement? Mark it in the paragraph.

> The writer inserted a missing citation.

> Why do you think the writer changed this sentence?

WORK WITH A PEER

Partner with a classmate to review and provide feedback on each other's drafts. Follow these steps:

- Work through the Revision Checklist and discuss with your partner any areas that could be strengthened.
- Give your partner suggestions for revising instances of redundancy and wordiness.

   Redundancy is the unnecessary repetition of ideas. Revise phrases or longer passages that repeat words with similar meanings. Omit repetitive word pairs, such as *important essentials* or *past history*.

   Wordiness is the use of too many words to express an idea. Eliminate unnecessary words, such as *basically* or *actually*. Revise unnecessarily wordy phrases, such as *due to the fact that* or *by means of*.

Help your partner find the clearest, simplest way to communicate their ideas.

STANDARDS

Writing • Introduce a topic clearly, previewing what is to follow. • Use precise language and domain-specific vocabulary to inform about or explain the topic. **Language** Choose language that expresses ideas precisely and concisely, recognizing and eliminating wordiness and redundancy.

Take a Closer Look at Your Draft

Use the Revision Checklist for Research Writing to evaluate and improve your research paper.

REVISION CHECKLIST FOR RESEARCH WRITING

EVALUATE	TAKE ACTION
Clarity	
☐ Is my thesis statement clear?	**Check** that your thesis statement introduces your topic and main point and previews your reasoning or evidence.
☐ Have I explained any specialized terms?	**Define** specialized terms in parentheses or within the sentence with a set-off clause.
Development	
☐ Have I balanced researched information with my own ideas?	**Mark** researched information with one color and your own ideas with another color. Then, **add** more sourced information or original ideas, as needed.
☐ Do I rely too much on one source?	If most of the evidence you use is from the same source, **add** variety. Review your source list and **integrate** relevant evidence from a different text.
Organization	
☐ Does every paragraph add meaningfully to my thesis?	**Write** your thesis in the margin beside the first sentence of each paragraph. Is the connection of that sentence to the thesis clear? If not, **revise** it.
☐ Are all the sentences within each paragraph related?	**Delete** any sentence that is unrelated or **revise** it to clarify its relationship to the topic. **Insert** transitions to show the connections between ideas.
Style and Tone	
☐ Does my introduction engage readers?	**Add** a question, anecdote, quotation, or vivid detail to interest your audience.
☐ Is my conclusion strong and memorable?	**Add** a quotation, a call to action, an insight, or a strong statement that supports the information presented.
☐ Is my word choice precise, concise, and formal?	**Replace** slang or vague words, such as *cool* or *good* with more precise, formal words. Make sure the new words are in the same parts of speech as the words you replaced.

WRITER'S HANDBOOK | RESEARCH PAPER

Editing

Don't let errors weaken the power of your research paper. Reread your draft and fix mistakes to create a finished work.

Read Like a Writer

Look at how the writer of the Mentor Text edited an early draft. Then, follow the directions in the white boxes.

MENTOR TEXT

from *Wildlife Rehabbers Are Here to Help*

In addition, rehabbers ~~Rehabbers~~ receive calls from people who need help. One caller may want to report an injured animal. Another might have a wild animal inside their home. Rehabilitators help the callers stay calm. They advise them about what to do and where to take the animals. At times, qualified rehabbers may remove animals and take them to a wildlife rehab center for treatment. ~~They may also remove animals for treatment.~~ Calls like these can come at any time, so rehabilitators must always be prepared. According to CWHL, animals are most often brought to wildlife rehab centers between the months of May and July. (Peaslee 9).

> Why do you think the writer changed this sentence?

> The writer rewrote this sentence to make it clearer.

Focus on Sentences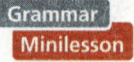

Subject-Verb Agreement With Prepositional Phrases Subjects and verbs must agree (for example, *the gorillas swim* and *the gorilla swims*), even when you insert a prepositional phrase between them (*the gorillas* in the water *swim gracefully*).

PRACTICE Fix the errors in subject-verb agreement in these sentences with prepositional phrases. Then, check your own draft for correctness.

1. Everything about the costumes are wrong.
2. Each of the pumpkins have been decorated.
3. A box of crayons were found in a drawer.

EDITING TIPS
1. Mark the subject in each sentence and note whether it is singular or plural.
2. Read the sentence, omitting the prepositional phrase. Make sure the verb agrees with the subject in number.

STANDARDS
Writing • Use technology, including the Internet, to produce and publish writing and link to and cite sources. • Quote or paraphrase the data and conclusions of others while avoiding plagiarism and following a standard format for citation.

Rules for Proper Citation

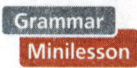

Works Cited List A Works Cited list is just what the name suggests—a list of all the sources you cite in your paper. There are different styles for the formatting of these lists. The rules shown here represent MLA style.

- **Capitalization of Titles:** Don't capitalize articles (*a, an, the*), prepositions, or conjunctions unless they are the first words in a title.
  Book Title: *The Incredible Complexity of Bee Colonies*
  Magazine Article Title: "Talking to a Butterfly"

- **Punctuation of Author Names:** Follow these models to punctuate author names correctly.
  Full-Length Book, Single Author: Becker, Ron. *Pollinators*. Plano Publications, 2022.
  Full-Length Book, Multiple Authors: Becker, Ron, and Dawn Smith. *Why We Love Pollinators*. Plano Publications, 2023.

- **Formatting Titles:** Place the titles of shorter works (short stories, articles, poems, songs, episodes) in quotation marks. Set the titles of full-length works in italics.
  Shorter Work: Landen, John. "Butterflies and Bees." *Our Natural World*, 2023, pp. 9–13.
  Full-Length Work: Rand, Susan. *Pollination Matters*. 2nd ed., KJ Press, 2021.

> **PRACTICE** Refer to the rules and use the information shown here to write a correct citation.
>
> | Information: Full-Length Book | Citation |
> |---|---|
> | Title: Pollinator Problems | |
> | Date of Publication: 2022 | |
> | Author: Marie Gonzalez | |
> | Publisher: Red Hawk Books | |

Publishing and Presenting

Integrate Media

Share your research paper with your class. Choose from these options:

OPTION 1 Publish your research paper to the **school or class website,** including links to the sources you cited. Comment on classmates' papers and respond to feedback on yours.

OPTION 2 Turn your research paper into a **slideshow** and present it to the class. Include an image, video, or audio clip with each section.

PEER-GROUP LEARNING

Essential Question

What is the relationship between people and nature?

The natural world is full of amazing creatures that we interact with in countless ways—from feeling awe at their beauty to finding inspiration in their solutions to the challenges of survival. In this section, you will work in a group to continue your exploration of the relationship between people and nature.

Peer-Group Learning Strategies

Throughout your life, in school, in your community, and in your career, you will continue to learn and work with others.

Look at these strategies and the actions you can take to practice them as you work in small groups. Add ideas of your own for each category. Use these strategies during Peer-Group Learning.

STRATEGY	MY ACTION PLAN
Prepare	• Complete your assignments so that you are prepared for group work. • Organize your thinking so you can contribute meaningfully to your group's discussion. •
Participate fully	• Respond to others' questions and comments with relevant observations and ideas. • Refer to evidence in the text when making a point. •
Support others	• Build off ideas from others in your group. • Encourage others who have not yet spoken to do so. •
Clarify	• If someone uses a word you don't understand, ask for a definition or explanation: "What do you mean by _____?" • Ask follow-up questions to dive deeper into the topic. •

Contents

COMPARE

LYRIC POETRY

Our Purpose in Poetry: Or, Earthrise
Amanda Gorman

The speaker encourages us to come together to protect the natural world.

MEDIA: SPOKEN-WORD POETRY

Earthrise
Amanda Gorman

The poet gives a moving performance of her work.

SCIENCE FEATURE

Creature Comforts: Three Biology-Based Tips for Builders
Mary Beth Cox

What can human architects learn from nature?

MAGICAL REALISM

He—y, Come On Ou—t!
Shinichi Hoshi, translated by Stanleigh Jones

It might be a bad idea to ignore the obvious.

PERFORMANCE TASK

SPEAKING AND LISTENING

Give and Follow Instructions

The Peer-Group selections present different perspectives on the ways in which people interact with and learn from nature. After reading, your group will give and follow instructions on how to create something related to the natural world.

Peer-Group Learning **435**

PEER-GROUP LEARNING

Working as a Group

1. Take a Position

In your group, discuss the following question:

What is our relationship with the natural world?

As you share your position, speak in a manner appropriate for small-group discussion: pronounce words correctly, speak clearly but not too loudly, and make eye contact. As others share, notice their position on the question, and listen carefully for main ideas and supporting details they provide. After all group members have participated, work together to explain how your shared ideas clarify the relationship between people and nature.

2. List Your Rules

As a group, decide on the rules that you will follow as you work together. Read the two samples provided. Notice that these rules use both basic and academic words. Write two rules of your own. As you write, pay attention to the basic and academic words you use to communicate.

- Come prepared for group discussions.
- Acknowledge other people's opinions.

_____

_____

3. Apply the Rules

Practice working as a group. Share what you have learned about the relationship between people and nature. Make sure each person in the group contributes. Take notes and be prepared to share with the class one thing that you heard from another member of your group.

4. Name Your Group

Choose a name that reflects the unit topic.

Our group's name: _____

5. Create a Communication Plan

Decide how you want to communicate with one another. For example, you might use online collaboration tools, email, or instant messaging.

Our group's plan: _____

STANDARDS

Reading Literature Cite several pieces of textual evidence to support analysis of what the text says explicitly as well as inferences drawn from the text. **Speaking and Listening** Analyze the main ideas and supporting details presented in diverse media and formats and explain how the ideas clarify a topic, text, or issue under study.

Essential Question: What is the relationship between people and nature?

Making a Schedule

First, find out the due dates for the peer-group activities. Then, preview the texts and activities with your group and make a schedule for completing the tasks.

SELECTION	ACTIVITIES	DUE DATE
Our Purpose in Poetry: Or, Earthrise		
Earthrise (video)		
Creature Comforts: Three Biology-Based Tips for Builders		
He—y, Come On Ou—t!		

Analyzing Explicit and Implicit Meanings

Literature is rich in meanings that are both explicit and implicit. You will be asked to discuss and write about both types of meaning as you work with your group.

Explicit meanings don't require interpretation. They are directly stated. Informational texts and arguments may convey explicit meanings more often than implicit ones.

Implicit meanings are suggested by details. Readers make inferences and draw connections to figure them out. Literary genres, such as short stories, may include some explicit meanings, but the key meanings are usually implicit.

Apply these strategies to identify and interpret both kinds of meaning:
- *To identify explicit meanings,* mark passages that directly state or explain ideas. Paraphrase these ideas, restating them in your own words, to make sure you understand them.
- *To interpret implicit meanings,* mark details that stand out. Then, consider how the details relate to one another and whether other details have similar or different qualities. Make inferences about the deeper ideas the details suggest.

Peer-Group Learning 437

COMPARE ACROSS GENRES

POETRY and MEDIA
Lyric poetry refers to poems with musical qualities that typically express feelings or emotions. **Spoken-word poetry** is an oral presentation in which a poet gives a dramatic performance of a poem.

LYRIC POETRY

Author's Purpose
- to use focused, imaginative language and form to capture emotion and thought

Characteristics
- a speaker that narrates the poem
- conveys themes, or insights about life
- imagery and other figurative language that describes things in fresh new ways
- language that creates a musical effect
- multiple layers of meaning

Structure
- expresses ideas in lines, which are grouped into stanzas
- may use visual elements, such as nontraditional spacing, to reinforce meaning

SPOKEN-WORD POETRY

Purpose
- to express a message or raise awareness through performance

Characteristics
- recited aloud with great emotion
- may be memorized or read from a text
- conveys themes, or insights about life

Effects
- emphasizes rhyme, rhythm, repetition, and alliteration
- performer uses gestures and elements of voice, such as intonation and volume

Essential Question: What is the relationship between people and nature?

Theme in Lyric Poetry

 A **lyric poem** expresses thoughts and feelings about a person, a place, a moment in time, or an idea. The voice that "speaks" the words of a poem belongs to the **speaker.** This speaker communicates ideas that may or may not reflect those of the poet.

A lyric poem expresses a **theme**, or an insight about life, related to the subject of the poem. You can determine a poem's theme by reading it closely and answering questions like these:

- What is the subject of the poem?
- What vivid words, descriptions, or statements seem important?
- What emotion is expressed?

> **TIP:** A poem's **speaker** functions like the narrator of a story or novel. Often, the speaker is an unidentified voice. At times, however, the speaker is a clearly identified person, presence, or character.

PRACTICE Read the poem. Then complete the activity and answer the question.

> Clouds, in the distance
> rolling slowly toward
> where I stand. Others
> might frown or even run
> because a storm is at hand,
> but after drought so long
> few plants could sprout, I wait
> for the rain, I welcome it
> over my face, my shoulders,
> like joy pouring down
> to let the good earth drink.

1. Complete the chart, referring to the poem.

QUESTION	TEXT EVIDENCE AND ANALYSIS
What is the poem's subject?	
What vivid words or descriptions does the speaker use?	
What emotion is expressed?	
What possible theme related to the subject do these features suggest?	

2. Write a title for the poem that reinforces its theme. Explain why you chose it.

STANDARDS
Reading Literature
Determine a theme or central idea of a text and analyze its development over the course of the text.

Compare Across Genres **439**

PREPARE TO READ

OUR PURPOSE IN POETRY: OR, EARTHRISE

EARTHRISE

COMPARE: POETRY and MEDIA
In this lesson, you will read Amanda Gorman's poem **Our Purpose in Poetry: Or, Earthrise** and watch her spoken-word performance of the same poem. You will then compare the print version and the video.

About the Poet

Amanda Gorman (b. 1998) recited her poem "The Hill We Climb" at the inauguration of President Joseph Biden in 2021, when she was twenty-two years old. By then, she was already an accomplished poet. At age sixteen, she became Youth Poet Laureate of Los Angeles, and at nineteen, the first U.S. Youth Poet Laureate. A graduate of Harvard University, Gorman published the book *The One for Whom Food Is Not Enough* in 2015.

STANDARDS
Language
Consult general and specialized reference materials, both print and digital, to find the pronunciation of a word or determine or clarify its precise meaning or its part of speech.

Concept Vocabulary

As you read the poem, you will encounter these words. When you finish reading, work with your group to identify what the words have in common.

advocating	implores	uncompromising

Reference Materials A **digital dictionary** is a reference source you access online. Like a print dictionary, it provides information about words, including precise meanings, parts of speech, and pronunciations.

SAMPLE DIGITAL DICTIONARY ENTRY

celestial (suh LEHS chuhl) *adj.* 🔊

Examples   Word Origin   Synonyms

1. related to the sky or the heavens

Analysis: This entry for *celestial* provides the word's definition and part of speech. It also has an audio icon to access the word's pronunciation and hyperlinks to additional information about the word.

PRACTICE ▶ As you read, use a digital dictionary to find the meaning, pronunciation, and part of speech for each unfamiliar word you encounter. Use the open space next to the text to record this information.

Reading Strategy: Annotate

Instead of trying to understand a poem *after* you finish reading, **annotate** it as you go. Pause now and then as you read to mark words or sections that seem important. Doing this can help you understand complex ideas one detail at a time. Here are some ways to annotate a text:

- Star, underline, or highlight important words or ideas.
- Write your reactions and questions in the margin.

PRACTICE ▶ As you read, mark details in the poem and take notes in the margin. Then review your annotations to determine key ideas.

LYRIC POETRY

Our Purpose in Poetry: Or, Earthrise

Amanda Gorman

BACKGROUND
In December 1968, the first astronauts to orbit the moon saw a memorable sight: Earth rising over the moon's horizon. Our planet had never before been seen from that perspective.

Dedicated to Al Gore and The Climate Reality Project

On Christmas Eve, 1968, astronaut Bill Anders
Snapped a photo of the earth
As Apollo 8 orbited the moon.

Those three guys
5 Were surprised
To see from their eyes
Our planet looked like an earthrise
A blue orb hovering over the moon's gray horizon,
with deep oceans and silver skies.

10 It was our world's first glance at itself
Our first chance to see a shared reality,
A declared stance and a commonality;

A glimpse into our planet's mirror,
And as threats drew nearer,
15 Our own urgency became clearer,
As we realize that we hold nothing dearer
than this floating body we all call home.

READ TO UNLOCK MEANING

1. First read the text for comprehension and enjoyment. Use the **Reading Strategy** and **Comprehension Check** questions to support your first read.
2. With your group, apply the vocabulary strategy to unlock word meanings.
3. Find other details in the text you find interesting. Ask your own questions and draw your own conclusions.

ANNOTATE

Read lines 18–35 and mark the line that you think communicates the poet's most important idea. Why did you choose this line?

We've known
That we're caught in the throes
20 Of climactic changes some say
Will just go away,
While some simply pray
To survive another day;
For it is the obscure, the oppressed, the poor,
25 Who when the disaster
Is declared done,
Still suffer more than anyone.

Climate change is the single greatest challenge of our time,

Of this, you're certainly aware.
30 It's saddening, but I cannot spare you
From knowing an inconvenient fact, because
It's getting the facts straight that gets us to act and not to wait.

So I tell you this not to scare you,
but to prepare you, to dare you
35 To dream a different reality,

Where despite disparities
We all care to protect this world,
This riddled blue marble, this little true marvel
To muster the verve and the nerve
40 To see how we can serve
Our planet. You don't need to be a politician
To make it your mission to conserve, to protect,
To preserve that one and only home
That is ours,
45 To use your unique power
To give next generations the planet they deserve.

We are demonstrating, creating, **advocating**

We heed this inconvenient truth, because we need to be anything but lenient
With the future of our youth.

50 And while this is a training
in sustaining the future of our planet,
There is no rehearsal. The time is
Now
Now
55 Now,

Use a digital dictionary or indicate another strategy you used that helped you determine meaning.

advocating (AD vuh kay tihng) *v.*

MEANING:

442 UNIT 4 • LEARNING FROM NATURE

Because the reversal of harm,
And protection of a future so universal
Should be anything but controversial.

So, earth, pale blue dot
60 We will fail you not.

Just as we chose to go to the moon
We know it's never too soon
To choose hope.
We choose to do more than cope
65 With climate change
We choose to end it—
We refuse to lose.
Together we do this and more
Not because it's very easy or nice
70 But because it is necessary,
Because with every dawn we carry
the weight of the fate of this celestial body orbiting a star.
And as heavy as that weight sounded, it doesn't hold us down,
But it keeps us grounded, steady, ready,
75 Because an environmental movement of this size
Is simply another form of an earthrise.

To see it, close your eyes.
Visualize that all of us leaders in this room
and outside of these walls or in the halls, all
80 of us changemakers are in a spacecraft,
Floating like a silver raft
in space, as we see the face of our planet anew.
We relish the view;
We witness its round green and brilliant blue,
85 Which inspires us to ask deeply, wholly:
What can we do?
Open your eyes.
Know that the future of
this wise planet
90 Lies right in sight:
Right in all of us. Trust
this earth uprising.
All of us bring light to exciting solutions never tried before
For it is our hope that **implores** us, at our **uncompromising**
core,
95 To keep rising up for an earth more than worth fighting for.

Use a digital dictionary or indicate another strategy you used that helped you determine meaning.

implores (ihm PLAWRZ) *v.*
MEANING:

uncompromising (un KOM pruh my zihng) *adj.*
MEANING:

COMPREHENSION CHECK
What does the speaker want readers to do?

Our Purpose in Poetry: Or, Earthrise **443**

BUILD INSIGHT

OUR PURPOSE IN POETRY: OR, EARTHRISE

First Thoughts

Choose one of the following items to discuss with your group.

- This poem is a call to action. Do you think poetry is a good genre for inspiring people to act? Why, or why not?
- In line 49, Gorman refers to "the future of our youth." Do you think your generation will manage environmental issues better than previous generations have? Why, or why not?

Summary

Write a short objective summary of the first four stanzas of the poem. Include only the main ideas, and avoid stating your opinions.

> **WORKING AS A GROUP**
> Discuss your responses to the Analysis and Discussion questions with your group. Support your ideas with evidence from the text.

Analysis and Discussion

1. **Analyze** The first nine lines of the poem depict a moment in an important space mission. What is the purpose of this reference to history?

2. **Interpret** Reread lines 61–66. What effect does the use of repetition create?

3. **Interpret** Describe the speaker's **tone**, or attitude toward the poem's subject. Give details to support your answer.

4. **Get Ready for Close Reading** Choose a passage from the poem that you find especially interesting or important. You'll discuss this passage with your group during Close Read activities.

STANDARDS
Reading Literature
- Cite several pieces of textual evidence to support analysis of what the text says explicitly as well as inferences drawn from the text.
- Provide an objective summary of the text.

Language
Use common, grade-appropriate Greek or Latin affixes and roots as clues to the meaning of a word.

Exploring the Essential Question

What is the relationship between people and nature?

5. How successful is this poem in depicting the relationship between people and nature? Give reasons for your response in your Evidence Log.

444 UNIT 4 • LEARNING FROM NATURE

ANALYZE AND INTERPRET

Close Read

PRACTICE Complete the following activities. Use text evidence to support your responses.

1. **Present and Discuss** With your group, share passages from the poem that you found especially interesting. Discuss what you notice, the questions you have, and the conclusions you reach. For example, you might focus on the following passages:

   - **Lines 4–7:** Discuss Gorman's use of casual language and its effect.
   - **Lines 36-46:** Read this stanza aloud and discuss the effects of the rhythm in these lines.

2. **Reflect on Your Learning** What new ideas or insights did you uncover during your second reading of the poem?

STUDY LANGUAGE AND CRAFT

Concept Vocabulary

Why These Words? The vocabulary words are related.

| advocating | implores | uncompromising |

WORD WALL

Note words in the poem that are related to the concept of learning from nature. Add them to your Word Wall.

1. With your group, determine what the words have in common. Write your ideas.

2. Add another word that fits the category. _____

3. List as many related words as you can for each vocabulary word.

Word Study

Latin Root: -voc- The word *advocating* includes the Latin root *-voc-*, which means "voice" or "to call."

PRACTICE Use a print or digital dictionary to look up these words: *vocalist, vocation, vocabulary*. Explain how the root *-voc-* contributes to the meaning of each one. Then, write a sentence for each word, using phrasing that shows you understand the word's meaning.

Our Purpose in Poetry: Or, Earthrise **445**

STUDY LANGUAGE AND CRAFT

OUR PURPOSE IN POETRY: OR, EARTHRISE

TIP: A literary theme states an insight about life. A theme is not the same as a topic or a summary. Note the differences in this example:

Topic: Music

Summary: The poem is about the importance of music.

Themes: Music frees your mind; Music has the power to reach across generations.

Theme in Lyric Poetry

A **lyric poem** is a creative expression of thoughts and feelings, often including descriptive details related to the five senses. As with all poems, lyric poems convey one or more themes.

A poem's **theme** is the insight about life that it expresses. To determine a poem's theme, note these details:

- the poem's title and subject
- a speaker's direct statements or particular observations
- repeated or emphasized ideas
- images or descriptive details that may suggest ideas that are not directly stated

Interpret this textual evidence to arrive at the theme. Ask yourself, "What idea about life is this poem sharing with readers?" Some poems, especially longer ones, may have more than one theme.

PRACTICE Complete the activity and answer the questions.

1. Read each passage from "Our Purpose in Poetry: Or, Earthrise" and mark details that help develop its theme. Take notes in the column to the right.

PASSAGES	MY NOTES
. . . with every dawn we carry / the weight of the fate of this celestial body orbiting a star. / And as heavy as that weight sounded, it doesn't hold us down, / But it keeps us grounded . . .	
All of us bring light to exciting solutions never tried before / For it is our hope that implores us, at our uncompromising core, / To keep rising up for an earth more than worth fighting for.	

2. **Interpret** Review the chart and your notes from item 1. What theme do the details you marked help to develop?

3. **Analyze** What details in the poem help to develop the possible theme that "Young people of today are tomorrow's leaders"?

4. **Interpret** Review the poem and your annotations. Then, state the theme of the poem as a whole.

STANDARDS

Reading Literature

- Determine a theme or central idea of a text and analyze its development over the course of the text.
- Analyze the impact of rhymes and other repetitions of sounds on a specific verse or stanza of a poem or section of a story or drama.

446 UNIT 4 • LEARNING FROM NATURE

Essential Question: What is the relationship between people and nature?

Repetition, Rhyme, and Alliteration

Poets use language to create a wide range of effects.

- **Repetition** of words or phrases emphasizes ideas and creates patterns of sound.

- **Rhyme** is a kind of repetition. It is the use of words with the same ending sound, such as *believe / receive / achieve*.

- **Alliteration** is the repetition of the initial consonant sound in a set of nearby words: *summer's sun / moody melody*

EXAMPLE
Notice the repetition in these lines from Gorman's poem. The rhymed words are underlined, and the repeated words are in boldface.

> There is no rehearsal. The time is
> **Now**
> **Now**
55 **Now**,
> Because the reversal of harm,
> And protection of a future so universal
> Should be anything but controversial.

Note that "controversial" does not exactly rhyme with the other underlined words—but it almost does. This type of rhyme is known as *slant rhyme*.

TIP: Rhymed words don't always appear at the ends of lines. They can also fall within lines, as in line 56 of the example.

READ Complete the chart on your own. For each passage, identify the type(s) of repetition you find as *rhyme, alliteration,* or *repeated words*. Some passages have more than one type. Then, record the words that show the pattern of repetition in the poem. The first item has been done for you.

PASSAGE	TYPE OF REPETITION	WORDS THAT SHOW THE PATTERN
line 8	alliteration	hovering, horizon
lines 10–12		
lines 26–27		
lines 33–37		
lines 61–67		

WRITE Work with your group to find another passage that includes patterns of repetition. Write a paragraph analyzing the types of repetition and the way they add emphasis or interest to the poem.

Our Purpose in Poetry: Or, Earthrise

PREPARE TO VIEW

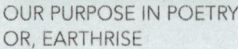
OUR PURPOSE IN POETRY: OR, EARTHRISE

EARTHRISE

COMPARE: POETRY and MEDIA

This spoken-word performance of Amanda Gorman's **Our Purpose in Poetry: Or, Earthrise** allows you to hear the poem in the poet's own voice. Pay attention to what makes a spoken performance different from experiencing the poem on the page.

About the Organization

In 2011, the nonprofit organization Climate Reality Project was created by joining two environmental action groups founded by former U.S. Vice President Al Gore.

Media Vocabulary

These terms describe features of videos. Use them as you analyze, discuss, and write about the video selection.

close-up: type of camera shot done at close range	• In a close-up, the camera comes in close to a person, an object, or a place so that it fills the frame. • A close-up can capture a person's facial expressions, gestures, and emotions.
cut: editing of a video that produces an abrupt shift	• After a video has been shot, an editor may make a cut to create a sharp transition between images or scenes. • Cuts can improve pacing by removing less interesting action or speech.
incidental music: background music that enhances a video	• Incidental music helps set a video's mood, or the overall feeling it conveys. • The music's volume, tempo, and types of sound (instruments, voices, or electronic effects) help build a sense of excitement, sadness, wonder, or some other mood.

Listening Strategy: Listen Actively

To get the most out of a spoken-word performance like the one in this video, **listen actively** to analyze the poet's main ideas. Pay close attention, noting important supporting details the poet presents.

- Remove distractions, such as your cell phone.
- Focus on the performer's message, noting details that are emphasized.
- Notice tone of voice, which may suggest the speaker's feelings.
- If necessary, pause the video and use a dictionary to clarify the meanings of unfamiliar words.

PRACTICE As you view the video, listen actively. Jot down your thoughts while keeping your attention on the speaker.

STANDARDS

Speaking and Listening
Analyze the main ideas and supporting details presented in diverse media and formats.

Language
Gather vocabulary knowledge when considering a word or phrase important to comprehension or expression.

448 UNIT 4 • LEARNING FROM NATURE

MEDIA: SPOKEN-WORD POETRY

WATCH AND LISTEN ▶

Earthrise
Amanda Gorman

BACKGROUND
In 2018, Amanda Gorman presented "Earthrise" at the Los Angeles Climate Reality Leadership Corps Training conference. She dedicated the poem to former Vice President Al Gore and the Climate Reality Project. The poem briefly references Gore's book *An Inconvenient Truth* and the documentary film of the same title.

TAKE NOTES As you watch and listen, take notes to record key ideas.

BUILD INSIGHT

EARTHRISE

First Thoughts

Choose one of these items to discuss with your group.

- How would you describe Gorman's spoken presentation of the poem? Which parts of the video stood out to you the most? Why?

- What comments do you have on your experience of listening to a poem such as this one?.

Analysis and Discussion

1. **Compare and Contrast** For you, what was the biggest difference between reading the poem and watching it performed by the poet?

2. **Evaluate** Do the images shown in the video enhance the poem's meaning? Support your response with details from both the video and the poem.

3. **Speculate** Imagine you listened to an audio recording of the poet's presentation without the visuals or incidental music. What might be especially interesting about hearing the words alone?

4. **Get Ready for Close Reading** Choose a clip from the video that you find especially interesting or important. Note its time code so you can find it again easily. You'll discuss that part of the video with your group during the Close Review activity.

Exploring the Essential Question

What is the relationship between people and nature?

5. What do you think Amanda Gorman's main purpose was for making this video? What point does she make about people and nature? Explain your ideas in your Evidence Log.

> **WORKING AS A GROUP**
>
> Discuss your responses to the Analysis and Discussion questions with your group.
>
> - Refer to specific details in the poem to support your ideas.
> - Ask follow-up questions of peers to clarify their ideas.

STANDARDS

Speaking and Listening
- Explicitly draw on that preparation by referring to evidence on the topic, text, or issue to probe and reflect on ideas under discussion.
- Acknowledge new information expressed by others and, when warranted, modify their own views.

Language
Acquire and use accurately grade-appropriate general academic and domain-specific words and phrases.

450 UNIT 4 • LEARNING FROM NATURE

ANALYZE AND INTERPRET

Close Review

Watch the spoken-word performance again. As you watch, take notes about important details, and jot down your observations. Note the time codes so you can find specific elements again later. Then, write a question and your conclusion.

MY QUESTION:

MY CONCLUSION:

STUDY LANGUAGE AND CRAFT

Media Vocabulary

These words describe features of videos. Practice using them as you write and discuss your responses.

| close-up | cut | incidental music |

1. Most of Gorman's performance was shot in close-up. What effect does this technique have on the presentation?

2. What kinds of cuts did the editor make? Do you think the cuts are effective? Explain.

3. **(a)** Describe the video's incidental music. **(b)** What overall effect does it have on the poem and on the listener?

Earthrise **451**

TEST PRACTICE

LYRIC POETRY

OUR PURPOSE IN POETRY: OR, EARTHRISE

SPOKEN-WORD POETRY

EARTHRISE

COMPARE: POETRY and MEDIA

Multiple Choice

These questions are based on the printed poem "Our Purpose in Poetry: Or, Earthrise" and the spoken-word performance by Amanda Gorman. Choose the best answer to each question.

1. What is one way that the spoken-word poem differs from the printed poem?

   A The spoken-word poem is longer than the printed poem.

   B The spoken-word poem conveys the poem's rhythm more clearly than the printed poem does.

   C The spoken-word poem omits some important details that are in the printed poem.

   D The spoken-word poem is a call to action, but the printed poem is not.

2. Watch time codes 0:55–1:00 of the video. How does this portion of the video help clarify lines 18–23 of the printed poem?

   > *from* **Earthrise**
   > We've known
   > That we're caught in the throes
   > Of climactic changes some say
   > Will just go away,
   > While some simply pray
   > To survive another day;

   A The incidental music in the video clip reinforces the rhyme scheme of these lines.

   B In the video clip, Gorman's face is blurred, showing that she does not feel strongly about these lines.

   C The image in the video clip shows one of the "climactic changes" Gorman refers to.

   D In the video clip, Gorman uses physical gestures to reinforce important words in the poem.

3. Which idea is emphasized both in lines 83–86 of the printed poem and at time codes 3:28–3:44 of the video?

   A Seeing the beauty of our planet makes us want to find ways to save it.

   B When viewed from space, our planet looks as if it has a face.

   C Looking at the beautiful colors of our planet brings us great joy.

   D Each time we look at our planet, it's as if we're seeing it for the first time.

STANDARDS

Reading Literature
Compare and contrast a written story, drama, or poem to its audio, filmed, staged, or multimedia version, analyzing the effects of techniques unique to each medium.

Writing
Write informative/explanatory texts to examine a topic and convey ideas, concepts, and information through the selection, organization, and analysis of relevant content.

Essential Question: What is the relationship between people and nature?

Short Response

1. **Connect** How does watching the video affect your understanding of the poem? Explain using details from both versions.

2. **Evaluate** What are some advantages of reading this poem over listening to it? Cite details that support your response.

3. **Make a Judgment** If you were to recommend this poem to a friend, would you recommend the printed version or the spoken-word version? Explain your choice.

Timed Writing

A **comparison-and-contrast essay** is a piece of writing that discusses the similarities and differences between two or more topics.

Assignment

Write a **comparison-and-contrast essay** in which you explain ways in which the printed version and spoken-word version of the poem are similar and different. Then, tell which version more effectively conveys the poet's message.

- Which version is more engaging?
- Which version more clearly expresses the poet's ideas?

5-Minute Planner

1. Read the assignment carefully and completely.
2. Decide what you want to say—your thesis statement. State this in your introduction, develop it in your body paragraphs, and restate it in your conclusion.
3. Choose examples from each version of the poem to support your thesis.
4. Organize your ideas by classifying them as similarities, differences, and the poet's message.

> **EVIDENCE LOG**
>
> Before moving on to a new selection, go to your Evidence Log and record any additional thoughts and observations you may have about "Our Purpose in Poetry: Or, Earthrise" and the spoken-word performance.

Test Practice 453

LEARN ABOUT GENRE: NONFICTION

Reading Science Features

A **science feature** is a type of journalism that presents scientific information for general readers.

CREATURE COMFORTS: THREE BIOLOGY-BASED TIPS FOR BUILDERS

The selection you are about to read is a science feature.

SCIENCE FEATURE

Author's Purpose
- to explain technical or scientific information to nonscientists

Characteristics
- a central idea, or thesis
- supporting details and evidence, often from scientific studies, experiments, and experts
- citations and acknowledgments
- may contain visual elements (sidebars, charts, diagrams, images)

Structure
- an engaging introduction and body paragraphs, and a memorable conclusion
- internal text structures, such as cause-and-effect statements or comparison-and-contrast organization

Take a Minute!

LIST With a partner, make a list of possible subjects and titles for science features. Assume that the audience is nonscientists. What interests you most among the topics you listed?

STANDARDS
Reading Informational Text
Analyze the structure an author uses to organize a text.

454 UNIT 4 • LEARNING FROM NATURE

Essential Question: What is the relationship between people and nature?

Informational Text Features

Science features are a type of informational text. They typically contain a wealth of facts and data. Writers of these articles use text features to organize their ideas in ways that help readers follow complex ideas. There are a wide variety of **informational text features.**

- Related ideas are grouped under headings.
- Bulleted lists (such as this one!) present data, definitions, and explanations in an easy-to-read format.
- Glossaries or listings of scientific terms may be provided for readers.
- Sidebars provide detailed information, often through the use of images and graphics.
- Captions provide information about photos, diagrams, graphs, maps, and other types of images.
- Specialized information, such as references to source materials, appears within parentheses following quoted material and in Works Cited lists.

PRACTICE Read the text and answer the questions. Then, share and discuss your responses with your group.

Types of Camels

Camels are interesting creatures. They are working animals, used to transport people and goods. There are three types of camels in the world today.

- Dromedary camels, or Arabian camels, have a single hump. They are found in the Middle East and in South Asia.
- Bactrian camels have two humps. They are found in Central Asia.
- Wild Bactrian camels are found in China and Mongolia and are on the critically endangered list (Britannica).

1. What is the purpose of the heading?

2. Why might the writer have chosen to present information about the camels in a bulleted list?

3. If you were to provide an image or a graphic to enhance this article, what would it show and what purpose would it serve?

Learn About Genre 455

PREPARE TO READ

Creature Comforts: Three Biology-Based Tips for Builders

About the Author

Mary Beth Cox is a chemist from Texas. She is a frequent contributor to Cricket Media, a global education company that publishes award-winning magazines for children on a variety of subjects.

Concept Vocabulary

As you read this science feature, you will encounter these words. After reading, work with your group to identify what these words have in common.

| incorporate | melded | affinity |

Reference Materials A **thesaurus** is a print or digital resource that provides synonyms and antonyms for words and some expressions. This information can help you infer the meanings of unfamiliar words. For example, consider how the synonyms and antonyms for the adjective *pet* clarify the word's precise meaning, which is "favorite; preferred."

Synonyms for *pet*: beloved, cherished, dear

Antonyms for *pet*: hated, unimportant

PRACTICE As you read the article, use a thesaurus to determine the meanings of unfamiliar words. Write your notes in the margins of the text.

Reading Strategy: Make Predictions

When you **make predictions**, you use what you know about a text to guess at the types of ideas it might include. Use these aspects of informational texts to make predictions:

- **Genre:** Informational texts include fact-based content. If you know the topic of a text, you can predict the kinds of facts and ideas it contains.
- **Text Features:** Headings, images, and captions can help you make predictions about the focus of the text.
- **Structures:** Informational texts use organizational structures, such as cause-and-effect. Recognizing these structures can help you make predictions. For example, if you see that an author discusses a cause, you can predict that they will also discuss an effect.

PRACTICE Scan the article before you read it fully. Use what you know about the genre, text features, and organizational structures to write at least one prediction.

STANDARDS

Reading Informational Text
Analyze the structure an author uses to organize a text, including how the major sections contribute to the whole and to the development of the ideas.

Language
Consult general and specialized reference materials, both print and digital, to find the pronunciation of a word or determine or clarify its precise meaning or its part of speech.

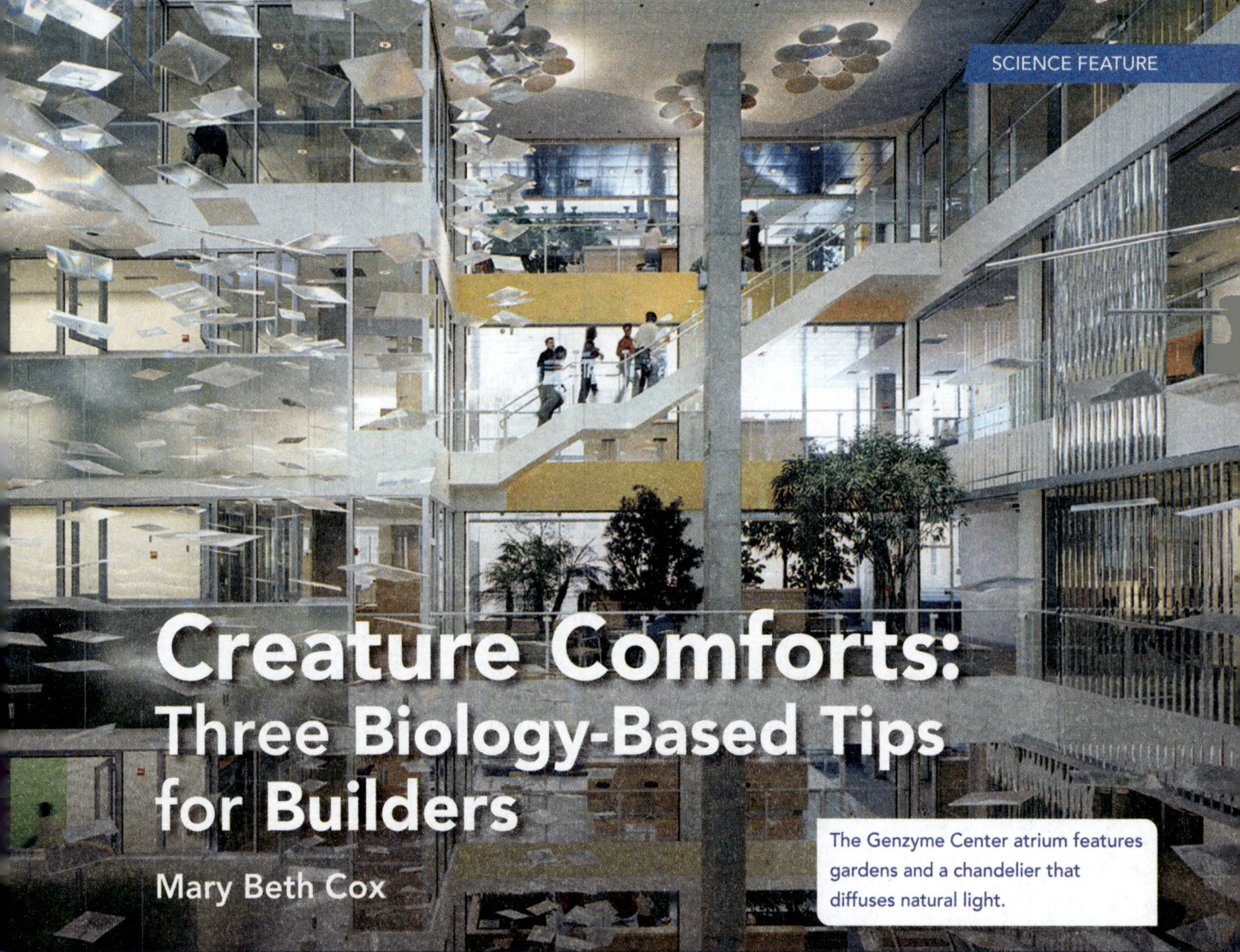

SCIENCE FEATURE

Creature Comforts: Three Biology-Based Tips for Builders

Mary Beth Cox

The Genzyme Center atrium features gardens and a chandelier that diffuses natural light.

BACKGROUND

Nature is full of examples of amazing solutions to the challenges of survival. From wings that are strong and light to shelters that are comfortable and cool, the creativity of nature results in designs that work incredibly well. They are also, often, beautiful. These natural solutions inspire people, who are also seeking ways to solve difficult problems. This feature explores how architects, engineers, and other designers working today look to nature for inspiration.

1   Human architects are the new kids on the block. They've been shaping their surroundings for only a few thousand years. Other life forms have done so for quite a bit longer. Life first appeared on planet Earth four *billion* years ago. Over that staggering stretch of time, creatures turned this moist rocky planet into a home. They adapted to diverse environments. They coped with fluctuating conditions. They endured tricky survival situations. So it behooves human builders to borrow what they can from the B's. Not from the hive-building insects, though they too are instructive. The B's are three biology-based ideas: biophilia, biomorphism, and biomimicry.

biophilia an appreciation for life and the living world

biomorphism act of using the forms, shapes, or patterns of living things

biomimicry act of developing systems by imitating actual living processes

Creature Comforts: Three Biology-Based Tips for Builders   457

Spanish architect Santiago Calatrava designed the Milwaukee Art Museum's Quadracci Pavilion.

READ TO UNLOCK MEANING

1. First read the text for comprehension and enjoyment. Use the **Reading Strategy** and **Comprehension Check** questions to support your first read.
2. With your group, apply the vocabulary strategy to unlock word meanings.
3. Find other details in the text you find interesting. Ask your own questions and draw your own conclusions.

Use a thesaurus or indicate another strategy that helped you determine meaning.

incorporate (ihn COHR puh rayt) *v.*
MEANING:

melded (MEL dihd) *v.*
MEANING:

The Company of Nature

2   Biophilia is a term coined by the esteemed biologist E. O. Wilson. *Bio* means life, and *philia* means love. According to Wilson, biophilia is an instinctive fondness humans feel for other living things (1–2). People find comfort in the company of nature. Biophilic architects build accordingly. They **incorporate** sunlight, fresh air, water, and plants into their designs. They preserve the native sense of a place by blending buildings into surroundings. They landscape appropriately for the ecosystems of their sites. They provide views of the wider outside world. Frank Lloyd Wright's Fallingwater is an example of biophilic architecture. The rough stone home is intimately **melded** with its woods and waterfall. At Fallingwater, the indoors feels like it's outside. Sometimes biophilic architects do things the other way round. They bring the great out-of-doors in. Natural light floods the atrium of Boston's Genzyme Center. A water feature splish-splashes pleasantly. Specimen trees thrive in scattered mini-gardens.

Living Shapes and Patterns

3   The second B, biomorphism, is a term best defined by a quote from the naturalist Charles Darwin. Darwin famously observed that living things adopt "endless forms most beautiful and wonderful" (867). Architects who design biomorphically couldn't agree more. They are inspired by the shapes and patterns of the living world. Life forms differ from human-made forms. Humans engineer rigid structures with lots of right angles. They frequently build with inorganic materials such as metal and stone. Life tends to be more flexible. It prefers bends and curves to squared-off angles. Some creatures have inorganic bones or shells, but most are composed of organic, carbon-based materials. Biomorphic architects model their work on those wonderful forms that humans happen to enjoy. The Milwaukee Art Museum bears a

striking example. The museum's roof is outfitted with an adjustable sunscreen, or *brise soleil*. The screen looks like a pair of giant wings that grace the Wisconsin sky. A few states to the east, a Connecticut campus sports a biomorphic building. The cetacean-style[1] hockey rink is fondly known as the "Yale Whale."

Sustainable Structures

4   Biophilia and biomorphism are about **affinity** and appearance. Biomimicry is concerned with action. Biomimetic architects are interested in life's processes, mechanisms, and strategies. Their designs don't necessarily look lifelike—they *act* lifelike. Such is the case with the famed Eiffel Tower. The Parisian landmark is among the most familiar structures in the world, and yet few realize the debt it owes to biomimicry. Monsieur Eiffel's source of inspiration was his own species. His iconic tower handles off-center stresses in the same manner as the human thighbone ("Human Anatomy").

5   Biomimicry offers a wealth of ideas to architects who are interested in sustainability. It shows them how to minimize any negative impacts their structures might have on the environment. Living things have spent four billion years researching sustainable strategies. They've achieved some enviable results. They rely solely on locally available resources. They're efficient recyclers—one creature's waste is often another's raw material. Photosynthetic[2] green plants are even solar powered! Eco-sensitive biomimicry is what keeps the Eastgate Centre in Harare, Zimbabwe, cool and

---

1. **cetacean-style** (sih TAY shun STY uhl) *adj.* modeled after a certain group of marine mammals that includes whales, dolphins, and porpoises.
2. **photosynthetic** (foh toh sihn THEH tihk) *adj.* characterized by the ability to turn water and carbon dioxide into food when exposed to light—the process by which plants make their food.

Use a thesaurus or indicate another strategy that helped you determine meaning.

affinity (uh FIHN ih tee) *n.*
MEANING:

COMPREHENSION CHECK
What are the three B's and what does each one mean?

Yale University's Ingalls Rink has been nicknamed the "Yale Whale."

comfortable. The office complex is ventilated by an air-handling system that is inspired by termite mounds. The system features hollow horizontal floors, vertical vent shafts, and high-volume fans. Cool night air drawn in at the building's base pushes the day's hot air up and out. Termites use a similar strategy to control temperatures in the chambers of their mounds (except the bugs do it without the fans). The Eastgate Centre uses 90 percent less energy than comparable human-made structures (Doan).

Thoughtful Design

6   When architects borrow from the B's, they take life's lessons in new directions. Biology focuses on one goal and one goal only: Survive long enough to reproduce. It is restricted to testing random, incremental changes. It can build only on previous success. Its main advantage is eons of time.

7   Human architects get to choose their own various projects. Their work is not usually a matter of life or death (though at times it can be stressful). Architects are freer to experiment. They can build on established traditions, but they can also start from scratch. They plan with logical insight. They create with leaps of imagination. Of course, their deadlines are much tighter!

8   But the innovations of humans are not isolated from the environment shaped by other living things. All Earthlings cope with the same planetary conditions. We contend with the same ecological consequences. Humans just meet the challenges with an odd adaptation called intelligence. Intelligence improves our chances of survival. It also lets us learn from the hard-won experience of others. The value of that is impossible to overestimate. Our fellow creatures have been making themselves comfortable here for a very, very long time.

MAKE PREDICTIONS
What do you think the "Thoughtful Design" section will be about, based on that heading, the image, and the caption?

French engineer Gustave Eiffel studied the way the human femur (thigh bone) supports off-center weight while designing the Paris landmark.

The termite-inspired Eastgate Centre is a renowned example of green architecture.

Acknowledgments

In writing this article, I received help from people all over the world. I wish to thank Janine Benyus and her team at the Biomimicry Institute. They see biomimicry as a way to build environments that help people live in harmony with nature rather than against it. I am also grateful to the wonderful people at The Genzyme Center in Boston, Massachusetts, and the Milwaukee Art Museum in Milwaukee, Wisconsin. The staff at both organizations spent a great deal of time with me and generously gave me tours of their facilities. They also answered my many questions with vast patience. I also wish to thank my college friend, Tenley Harper, who teaches in Harare, Zimbabwe. She alerted me to the fascinating, biomimetic design of the Eastgate Centre in that country. Finally, I would like to express my gratitude to all the visionary scientists, architects, and engineers who are including elements of the natural world in their designs. I believe their efforts will create a brighter future for everyone.

COMPREHENSION CHECK

What living creatures or things in the natural environment inspired the structures discussed in this article?

Works Cited

Benyus, Janine M. *Biomimicry: Innovation Inspired by Nature.* HarperCollins, 1997.

Brooks, Michael. "Nature Designs It Better." *The Guardian,* 5 Apr. 2000, http://www.url-website. Accessed 29 June 2017.

Darwin, Charles. *On the Origin of Species.* 1st ed., John Murray, 1859. *Project Gutenberg E-book,* http://www.url-website. Accessed 30 June 2017.

Delgado, Jacinto. Personal interview. 1 June 2017.

Doan, Abigail. "Biomimetic Architecture: Green Building in Zimbabwe Modeled After Termite Mounds." *Inhabit,* 29 Nov. 2012, http://www.url-website. Accessed 20 June 2017.

Holland, Mirabai. "What Does Your Thigh Bone Have in Common with the Eiffel Tower?" *HuffPost News: The Blog*, 3 July 2013, http://www.url-website. Accessed 25 June 2017.

"Human Anatomy and Biomimicry." *CSDT Community*, Rensselaer Polytechnic Institute, http://www.url-website. Accessed 22 June 2017.

Lee, Dora. *Biomimicry: Inventions Inspired by Nature*. Kids Can Press, 2011.

Pearce, Mick. "Biomimicry Video - 02." *Mick Pearce*, 2016, http://www.url-website. Accessed 27 June 2017.

Pearce, Mick. "Eastgate." *Mick Pearce*, 2016, http://www.url-website. Accessed 1 July 2017.

Wilson, Edward O. *Biophilia*. Harvard UP, 1984.

BUILD INSIGHT

First Thoughts

Select one of the following items to discuss with your group.

- Which building or structure from the article would you most like to visit? Explain your choice.
- Do you think it's valuable to design buildings and structures to mimic the natural world, or should people develop new design strategies the world has never seen before? Explain your response.

Summary

Write a short summary of the text to confirm your comprehension. Remember to include only the central ideas and to keep your summary objective and free from personal opinions.

Analysis and Discussion

1. **(a)** What is the writer's central idea, or thesis? **(b) Analyze** How does her introduction make that idea understandable to nonscientists?

2. **Compare and Contrast** How are the three biology-based ideas similar and different?

3. **Analyze** Reread the section of the article titled "Thoughtful Design." What purpose does this section serve?

4. **Get Ready for Close Reading** Choose a passage from the text that you find especially interesting or important. You will discuss the passage with your group during Close-Read activities.

> **WORKING AS A GROUP**
> Discuss your responses to the Analysis and Discussion questions with your group.
> - Support your responses with evidence from the text.
> - When listening, ask questions as needed to understand others' ideas well.

Exploring the Essential Question

What is the relationship between people and nature?

5. If you could design a building based on something in nature, what natural thing would you choose and why? Describe your idea in your Evidence Log.

STANDARDS

Reading Informational Text
- Cite several pieces of textual evidence to support analysis of what the text says explicitly as well as inferences drawn from the text.
- Provide an objective summary of the text.

Creature Comforts: Three Biology-Based Tips for Builders **463**

ANALYZE AND INTERPRET

CREATURE COMFORTS: THREE BIOLOGY-BASED TIPS FOR BUILDERS

Close Read

PRACTICE Complete the following activities. Use text evidence to support your responses.

1. **Present and Discuss** With your group, share the passages from the science feature that you find especially interesting. For example, you might focus on the following passages:

   - **Paragraph 2:** Discuss why people might "find comfort in the company of nature."
   - **Paragraph 5:** Discuss why sustainability is an important issue in building design.

2. **Reflect on Your Learning** What new ideas or insights did you uncover during your second reading of the text?

WORD WALL

Note words in the text that are related to the relationship between people and nature. Add them to your Word Wall.

STUDY LANGUAGE AND CRAFT

Concept Vocabulary

Why These Words? The vocabulary words are related.

incorporate	melded	affinity

1. With your group, discuss these words and determine what they have in common.

2. Add another word that fits the category. _____

3. On your own, use a thesaurus to find antonyms for each vocabulary word. Then, compare the words you found with your group.

Word Study

Latin Root: -fin- The word *affinity*, which means a "liking of or sympathy with something; similarity of characteristics suggesting a relationship," is built from the prefix *af-*, which means "add," and the Latin root *-fin-*, which means "border" or "end." Literally speaking, an *affinity* is a natural drawing together of two or more things across a border.

PRACTICE Use a dictionary to find the meanings of other words built from the root *-fin-*: *finish*, *infinite*, and *define*. Explain how the meaning of "end" or "border" is evident in each word.

STANDARDS

Reading Informational Text
Analyze the structure an author uses to organize a text.

Language
Use common, grade-appropriate Greek or Latin affixes and roots as clues to the meaning of a word.

Essential Question: What is the relationship between people and nature?

Informational Text Features

A key characteristic of science features is the inclusion of references and acknowledgments. **References** cite sources used by the writer; an **acknowledgments** section recognizes the contributions that other people and organizations made to the writer's work.

The author of "Creature Comforts" uses different types of references within the body of the text. At the end of the article, she compiles all the references into a Works Cited list.

FROM THE TEXT	FROM THE WORKS CITED LIST
Darwin famously observed that living things adopt "endless forms most beautiful and wonderful" (867).	Darwin, Charles. *On the Origin of Species*. 1st ed., John Murray, 1859. *Project Gutenberg E-book*, http://www.url-website. Accessed 30 June 2017.
His iconic tower handles off-center stresses in the same manner as the human thighbone ("Human Anatomy").	"Human Anatomy and Biomimicry." *CSDT Community*, Rensselaer Polytechnic Institute, http://www.url-website. Accessed 22 June 2017.

PRACTICE Answer the questions to analyze the use of references and acknowledgments in this article. Work on your own, and then discuss your responses with your group.

1. **Analyze** Mark references that appear within the body of the text. Why does the writer note her sources at these points?

2. **Make Inferences** Reread the acknowledgments at the end of the article. What does the information in this section suggest about the writer's research process?

3. **Make a Judgment** Scan the Works Cited list. Has the author consulted a variety of trustworthy sources? Explain why or why not.

4. **Evaluate** Does the inclusion of references and acknowledgments affect your attitude toward the information in the text? Explain.

STUDY LANGUAGE AND CRAFT

CREATURE COMFORTS: THREE BIOLOGY-BASED TIPS FOR BUILDERS

Verb Tenses

A **verb** expresses an action or a state of being. A verb's **tense** indicates when an action happens or when a state exists.

VERB TENSE	EXAMPLE
Present tense indicates an action that is happening now or happens regularly.	I plan a project.
Past tense indicates an action that has already happened.	You planned the last project.
Future tense indicates an action that will happen.	We will plan a project.
Present perfect tense indicates an action that happened in the past and may still be happening now.	They have planned many projects.
Past perfect tense indicates an action that ended before another action in the past.	He had planned the project before he left.
Future perfect tense indicates an action that will have ended before a specific time.	She will have planned the project by next week.

When writing and speaking, be sure to avoid incorrectly changing verb tenses in the middle of a sentence. If events happen in the same time frame, use the same verb tense. For example: *Paul observes animals and designs buildings,* not *Paul observes animals and designed buildings.*

READ With your group, identify examples of present, past, and future tense verbs in "Creature Comforts." Write them in the chart.

Present	
Past	
Future	

WRITE/EDIT Choose a verb from the article, such as *find, provide, design,* or *build*. Write an original sentence using the verb in the present tense. Then, edit your sentence, changing your verb to the other five tenses. Share your work with a partner and challenge them to identify the verb tense you used in each of your sentences.

STANDARDS
Writing
• Include formatting, graphics, and multimedia when useful to aiding comprehension.
• Gather relevant information from multiple print and digital sources, using search terms effectively; assess the credibility and accuracy of each source.

Language
Use knowledge of language and its conventions when writing, speaking, reading, or listening.

SHARE IDEAS

Research

In a **research report,** you present information gathered from sources to support your own explanations and insights on a focused topic.

> **Assignment**
>
> Work with your group to write a **research report** about some aspect of biomimicry. You may choose one of these options, or pick a different topic that you prefer.
>
> ○ transportation (for example, airplanes, trains, or cars)
>
> ○ athletic clothing (for example, sharkskin swimsuits)

Plan Your Work Begin by making a plan to guide your work. List the tasks you will need to complete—such as researching, organizing, writing, and editing. Make sure everyone has a role to play.

Gather Information Record facts, details, quotations, and examples from reliable sources. Then, use the questions listed here to evaluate their relevance and quality. If any information gets a "No" answer, it may not be useful for this project.

Evaluate Information		
Does the information relate directly to the topic?	○ No	○ Yes
Does the information fill a specific gap in knowledge, such as background?	○ No	○ Yes
Is the information current and from a trustworthy source?	○ No	○ Yes

Synthesize Information Integrate ideas, examples, and facts from a variety of sources to develop your topic and offer your own new insight. That insight is your thesis. Work together to prepare your report, including a strong thesis.

Choose a Mode of Delivery Discuss the best way to organize and present your information and ideas. Mark your choice.

○ **Written Report:** Type a polished, well-structured text. Use formatting, such as boldface headings, to organize your ideas. Include graphics and visuals—such as images, diagrams, or charts—to convey information or data visually.

○ **Multimedia Presentation:** Create and present a digital slideshow. Include media elements—such as videos, music, or 3D diagrams—to make your information clear for your audience.

> **EVIDENCE LOG**
>
> Before moving on to a new selection, go to your Evidence Log and record any additional thoughts or observations you may have about "Creature Comforts: Three Biology-Based Tips for Builders."

Creature Comforts: Three Biology-Based Tips for Builders **467**

LEARN ABOUT GENRE: FICTION

Reading Magical Realism

Magical realism is a literary genre that combines both realistic and magical, or fantastic, elements.

HE—Y, COME ON OU—T!

The selection you are about to read is magical realism.

MAGICAL REALISM

Author's Purpose
- to tell a story that weaves together realistic and magical elements

Characteristics
- ordinary settings (the real world) with extraordinary elements that break natural law or logic
- characters who are ordinary but who accept or expect magical events
- strange or magical events conveyed with an unsurprised tone
- dialogue
- irony, or unexpected outcomes

Structure
- plots that often center on a major, fantasy-like change or transformation

Take a Minute!

LIST With a partner, think of television shows or movies that you've seen or know about that might belong to the genre of magical realism. Make a list and discuss why you chose each item.

STANDARDS
Reading Literature
Analyze how particular elements of a story or drama interact.

468 UNIT 4 • LEARNING FROM NATURE

Essential Question: What is the relationship between people and nature?

Setting and Plot

A story's **setting** is the time and place in which the events occur. The **plot** is the sequence of those events. In magical realism, the interactions between setting, plot, and characters are important. The setting is grounded in the real world but includes fantastic, or magical, details. The plot in magical realist stories is built around the fantastic elements and characters' reactions to them.

REALISM VERSUS MAGICAL REALISM		
ELEMENT	REALISM	MAGICAL REALISM
setting	a classroom	a classroom that fades in and out of sight
plot	initiated by a conflict between characters	initiated by a magical event
characters	react typically to the extraordinary (for example, with shock or surprise)	accept the extraordinary as normal

PRACTICE Mark each item as an example of realism or magical realism. Give a reason for each response. Then, discuss your answers with your group.

EXAMPLE	REALISM?	MAGICAL REALISM?
1. A boy has a conversation with a talking horse.		
2. In an ancient church, light streams in through stained-glass windows.		
3. A legal decision gives a woman justice.		
4. A hidden doorway leads to a world in which time moves backwards.		

Learn About Genre **469**

PREPARE TO READ

He—y, Come On Ou—t!

About the Author

Shinichi Hoshi (1926–1997), a Japanese writer, is best known for his "short-short stories," in which he makes observations about human nature and society. Hoshi wrote more than a thousand short-short stories, as well as longer fantasy stories, detective stories, biographies, and travel articles. In addition, he was one of the first Japanese science-fiction writers. Hoshi's stories have been translated into many languages, and devoted readers enjoy their unexpected plot twists.

STANDARDS
Reading Literature
By the end of the year, read and comprehend literature, including stories, dramas, and poems.
Language
Use context as a clue to the meaning of a word or phrase.

Concept Vocabulary

As you read "He—y, Come On Ou—t!" you will encounter these words. After reading, work with your group to identify what the words have in common.

| disposal | consequences | resolved |

Context Clues If a word is unfamiliar to you, try using **context clues**—or words and phrases that appear nearby in the text—to help you determine its meaning. There are various types of context clues that you may encounter as you read.

- **Synonyms:** A *throng* gathered around the hole, so the village built a fence to keep the crowd from getting too close.
- **Restatement of an Idea:** People traveled to the village to see the hole, and when they arrived, they were so impressed by its depth that they *gawked* at it.
- **Contrast of Ideas:** The scientist was able to keep his *composure* despite the fact that he was afraid of the deep hole.

PRACTICE As you read "He—y, Come On Ou—t!" use context clues to determine meanings of unfamiliar words. Write your definitions in the open space next to the text.

Reading Strategy: Make Connections

You can **make connections** to society while reading by looking for relationships between ideas in a text and the larger world. For example, you might consider how characters, aspects of a setting, and the events of a story connect to real-life social issues. Then, think about the author's intentions—does the author seem to be commenting directly on society?

- Think about what a situation in a story might represent or symbolize in society.
- Consider how characters' actions and reactions reflect the attitudes people in the real world take toward the issue.

PRACTICE As you read, make connections between the story and society. Mark your observations in the open space next to the text.

470 UNIT 4 • LEARNING FROM NATURE

MAGICAL REALISM

He—y, Come On Ou—t!

Shinichi Hoshi
translated by Stanleigh Jones

BACKGROUND
Each year, the world generates billions of tons of waste. Much of that waste is disposed of in landfills, where heavy metals and toxins can leak into the environment. The oceans have also been polluted with vast amounts of trash because for many decades it was common practice to dump chemicals, garbage, and even nuclear waste directly into the sea.

1   The typhoon had passed and the sky was a gorgeous blue. Even a certain village not far from the city had suffered damage. A little distance from the village and near the mountains, a small shrine had been swept away by a landslide.
2   "I wonder how long that shrine's been here."
3   "Well, in any case, it must have been here since an awfully long time ago."
4   "We've got to rebuild it right away."
5   While the villagers exchanged views, several more of their number came over.
6   "It sure was wrecked."
7   "I think it used to be right here."
8   "No, looks like it was a little more over there."
9   Just then one of them raised his voice. "Hey what in the world is this hole?"

READ TO UNLOCK MEANING

1. First read the text for comprehension and enjoyment. Use the **Reading Strategy** and **Comprehension Check** questions to support your first read.
2. With your group, apply the vocabulary strategy to unlock word meanings.
3. Find other details in the text you find interesting. Ask your own questions and draw your own conclusions.

He—y, Come On Ou—t! **471**

10 Where they had all gathered there was a hole about a meter in diameter. They peered in, but it was so dark nothing could be seen. However, it gave one the feeling that it was so deep it went clear through to the center of the earth.

11 There was even one person who said, "I wonder if it's a fox's hole."

12 "He—y, come on ou—t!" shouted a young man into the hole. There was no echo from the bottom. Next he picked up a pebble and was about to throw it in.

13 "You might bring down a curse on us. Lay off," warned an old man, but the younger one energetically threw the pebble in. As before, however, there was no answering response from the bottom. The villagers cut down some trees, tied them with rope and made a fence which they put around the hole. Then they repaired to the village.

14 "What do you suppose we ought to do?"

15 "Shouldn't we build the shrine up just as it was over the hole?"

16 A day passed with no agreement. The news traveled fast, and a car from the newspaper company rushed over. In no time a scientist came out, and with an all-knowing expression on his face he went over to the hole. Next, a bunch of gawking curiosity seekers showed up; one could also pick out here and there men of shifty glances who appeared to be concessionaires.[1] Concerned that someone might fall into the hole, a policeman from the local substation kept a careful watch.

17 One newspaper reporter tied a weight to the end of a long cord and lowered it into the hole. A long way down it went. The cord ran out, however, and he tried to pull it out, but it would not come back up. Two or three people helped out but when they all pulled too hard, the cord parted at the edge of the hole. Another reporter, a camera in hand, who had been watching all of this, quietly untied a stout rope that had been wound around his waist.

18 The scientist contacted people at his laboratory and had them bring out a high-powered bull horn, with which he was going to check out the echo from the hole's bottom. He tried switching through various sounds, but there was no echo. The scientist was puzzled, but he could not very well give up with everyone watching him so intently. He put the bull horn right up to the hole, turned it to its highest volume, and let it sound continuously for a long time. It was a noise that would have carried several dozen kilometers above ground. But the hole just calmly swallowed up the sound.

19 In his own mind the scientist was at a loss, but with a look of apparent composure he cut off the sound and, in a manner

---

1. **concessionaires** (kuhn sehsh uh NAIRZ) *n.* businesspeople.

suggesting that the whole thing had a perfectly plausible explanation, said simply, "Fill it in."

20 Safer to get rid of something one didn't understand.

21 The onlookers, disappointed that this was all that was going to happen, prepared to disperse. Just then one of the concessionaires, having broken through the throng and come forward, made a proposal.

22 "Let me have that hole. I'll fill it in for you."

23 "We'd be grateful to you for filling it in," replied the mayor of the village, "but we can't very well give you the hole. We have to build a shrine there."

24 "If it's a shrine you want, I'll build you a fine one later. Shall I make it with an attached meeting hall?"

25 Before the mayor could answer, the people of the village all shouted out.

26 "Really? Well, in that case, we ought to have it closer to the village."

27 "It's just an old hole. We'll give it to you!"

28 So it was settled. And the mayor, of course, had no objection.

29 The concessionaire was true to his promise. It was small, but closer to the village he did build for them a shrine with an attached meeting hall.

30 About the time the autumn festival was held at the new shrine, the hole-filling company established by the concessionaire hung out its small shingle at a shack near the hole.

31 The concessionaire had his cohorts mount a loud campaign in the city. "We've got a fabulously deep hole! Scientists say it's at least five thousand meters deep! Perfect for the disposal of such things as waste from nuclear reactors."

32 Government authorities granted permission. Nuclear power plants fought for contracts. The people of the village were a bit worried about this, but they consented when it was explained that there would be absolutely no above-ground contamination[2] for several thousand years and that they would share in the profits. Into the bargain, very shortly a magnificent road was built from the city to the village.

33 Trucks rolled in over the road, transporting lead boxes. Above the hole the lids were opened, and the wastes from nuclear reactors tumbled away into the hole.

34 From the Foreign Ministry and the Defense Agency boxes of unnecessary classified documents were brought for disposal. Officials who came to supervise the disposal held discussions on golf. The lesser functionaries, as they threw in the papers, chatted about pinball.

---

2. **contamination** (kuhn tam uh NAY shuhn) *n.* pollution caused by poison or another dangerous substance.

Use context clues or indicate another strategy you used that helped you determine meaning.

disposal (dihs POH zuhl) *n.*
MEANING:

COMPREHENSION CHECK
What deal do the mayor and the concessionaire agree to?

35 The hole showed no signs of filling up. It was awfully deep, thought some; or else it might be very spacious at the bottom. Little by little the hole-filling company expanded its business.

36 Bodies of animals used in contagious disease experiments at the universities were brought out and to these were added the unclaimed corpses of vagrants. Better than dumping all of its garbage in the ocean, went the thinking in the city, and plans were made for a long pipe to carry it to the hole.

37 The hole gave peace of mind to the dwellers of the city. They concentrated solely on producing one thing after another. Everyone disliked thinking about the eventual **consequences**. People wanted only to work for production companies and sales corporations; they had no interest in becoming junk dealers. But, it was thought, these problems too would gradually be **resolved** by the hole.

38 Young girls whose betrothals[3] had been arranged discarded old diaries in the hole. There were also those who were inaugurating new love affairs and threw into the hole old photographs of themselves taken with former sweethearts. The police felt comforted as they used the hole to get rid of accumulations of expertly done counterfeit bills. Criminals breathed easier after throwing material evidence into the hole.

39 Whatever one wished to discard, the hole accepted it all. The hole cleansed the city of its filth; the sea and sky seemed to have become a bit clearer than before.

40 Aiming at the heavens, new buildings went on being constructed one after another.

41 One day, atop the high steel frame of a new building under construction, a workman was taking a break. Above his head he heard a voice shout:

42 "He—y, come on ou—t!"

43 But, in the sky to which he lifted his gaze there was nothing at all. A clear blue sky merely spread over all. He thought it must be his imagination. Then, as he resumed his former position, from the direction where the voice had come, a small pebble skimmed by him and fell on past.

44 The man, however, was gazing in idle reverie[4] at the city's skyline growing ever more beautiful, and he failed to notice.

Use context clues or indicate another strategy you used that helped you determine meaning.

consequences (KON suh kwehns ihz) *n.*

MEANING:

resolved (rih ZOLVD) *v.*

MEANING:

MAKE CONNECTIONS
Reread paragraph 37 and make a connection to a real-life issue we face in society today.

---

3. **betrothals** (bih TROTH uhlz) *n.* promises of marriage.
4. **idle reverie** (Y duhl REHV uh ree) *n.* daydreaming.

BUILD INSIGHT

First Thoughts

Select one of the following items to discuss with your group.

- What do you find most interesting or surprising about the story? Would you recommend it to a friend? Why, or why not?
- Paragraph 20 says, "Safer to get rid of something one didn't understand." Do you agree with this statement? Explain.

Summary

Confirm your comprehension by writing a summary of the story. Be sure to include only the central ideas and to keep your summary objective.

> **WORKING AS A GROUP**
>
> Discuss your responses to the Analysis and Discussion questions with your group.
>
> - As your peers share, ask follow-up questions to gain more information about their ideas.
> - If necessary, modify your original responses to reflect new information you learn during the discussion.

Analysis and Discussion

1. **(a) Analyze** Which character do you think is most responsible for the sequence of events that leads to the story's conclusion? Why?
   (b) Interpret How do that person's actions shape your understanding of the conclusion?

2. **(a)** What things do people in the story throw into the hole? **(b) Draw Conclusions** What can you conclude about their society based on these details?

3. **Interpret** What comment does the author seem to be making about the idea of a "disposable society"? Explain, citing text evidence.

4. **Get Ready for Close Reading** Choose a passage from the text that you find especially interesting or important. You'll discuss the passage with your group during Close-Read activities.

Exploring the Essential Question

What is the relationship between people and nature?

5. If the events of this story were to happen in real life, do you think people would behave similarly? Why or why not? Record your idea in your Evidence Log.

STANDARDS

Reading Literature
Provide an objective summary of the text.

Speaking and Listening
Pose questions that elicit elaboration.

He—y, Come On Ou—t!

ANALYZE AND INTERPRET

HE—Y, COME ON OU—T!

Close Read

PRACTICE Complete the following activities. Use text evidence to support your responses.

1. **Present and Discuss** With your group, share the passages from the story that you found especially interesting. You might focus on the following passages:

   - **Paragraphs 18 and 19:** Discuss the scientist's reactions. Explain how he might have reacted if the story were realistic.

   - **Paragraphs 41 and 42:** Discuss possible explanations for what happens in these paragraphs.

2. **Reflect on Your Learning** What new ideas or insights did you uncover during your second reading of the text?

WORD WALL

Note words in the text that are related to the relationship between people and nature. Add them to your Word Wall.

STUDY LANGUAGE AND CRAFT

Concept Vocabulary

Why These Words? The vocabulary words are related.

| disposal | consequences | resolved |

1. With your group, discuss what the words have in common.

2. Add another word that fits the category. _____

3. Write a paragraph that contains all three vocabulary words. Include context clues that hint at each word's meaning. Share and discuss your paragraphs with your group.

Word Study

Analogies In an **analogy**, pairs of words share a relationship. Types of relationships expressed in analogies include synonym, antonym, part to whole, and cause and effect. In this example, the relationship shown is synonym: *sinkhole* is to *crater* as *pollution* is to *contamination*.

PRACTICE Use one of the concept vocabulary words to complete each analogy.

1. *throw* is to *pitch* as _____ is to *settled*
2. *earthquakes* are to *damage* as *actions* are to _____
3. *easy* is to *effortless* as *removal* is to _____

STANDARDS
Reading Literature
Analyze how particular elements of a story or drama interact.

Language
Use the relationship between particular words to better understand each of the words.

476 UNIT 4 • LEARNING FROM NATURE

Essential Question: What is the relationship between people and nature?

Setting and Plot

In magical realism, the limitations of real-life settings don't apply. The magical qualities of the setting spur characters' reactions and develop the plot. Often, the interaction between the magical events and the plot that results hint at real social problems. Consider the following examples from "He—y, Come on Ou—t!"

EXAMPLES: Characteristics of Magical Realism

CHARACTERISTICS	STORY EXAMPLES	NOTES
Individuals are less important than society as a whole.	"You might bring down a curse on us. Lay off," warned an old man, but the younger one energetically threw the pebble in.	Characters are not given names.
Magical events suggest a problem or issue in society.	It was a noise that would have carried several dozen kilometers above ground. But the hole just calmly swallowed up the sound.	A large hole in the earth appears from nowhere and is seemingly bottomless.
A magical event creates conflicts, and characters' reactions drive the plot.	Where they had all gathered there was a hole about a meter in diameter. They peered in, but it was so dark nothing could be seen.	The story's plot revolves around the discovery of a bottomless hole and how various characters react to it.

PRACTICE Work on your own to answer the questions and complete the activity. Then, discuss your responses with your group.

1. **(a) Analyze** What details of the setting make this story an example of magical realism? Explain. **(b) Connect** How does the setting influence the story's plot? Cite specific details that support your response.

2. **Interpret** Complete the chart, describing the significance of key events in the story. One row has been completed for you.

EVENT	INTERPRETATION/SIGNIFICANCE
loss of shrine in a landslide	The villagers have ignored the shrine for so long, they no longer know its meaning. This allows for their next dangerous move.
young man yells into the hole and throws in a pebble	
scientist's direction: "Fill it in."	
concessionaire's business decisions and government responses and actions	

STUDY LANGUAGE AND CRAFT

HE—Y, COME ON OU—T!

Irony and Theme

In literature, **situational irony** occurs when something happens that is the opposite of what the reader or character expects. Such ironic moments provide clues to the text's **themes**, or insights about life.

EXAMPLES

SITUATIONAL IRONY	SUGGESTED THEME
expecting the adult to take charge of a chaotic situation and then discovering that a child restores order	Children can be wiser than adults.
expecting an act of kindness to have positive consequences but finding that it has negative ones instead	Being kind may not solve life's problems.

PRACTICE Answer these questions on your own. Then, discuss them with your group.

1. **(a) Analyze** In what way is the beginning of the story an example of situational irony? **(b) Connect** What did you expect, and what is the significance of what happens instead?

2. **(a) Draw Conclusions** In what way is the story's ending ironic, or unexpected? **(b) Generalize** Can a story's ending be both ironic and logical? Explain why or why not.

3. **(a) Interpret** What theme or themes does the story's ironic ending convey about people and how we interact with the world around us? **(b) Support** How does the author develop this theme throughout the text? Use specific details from the story to support your interpretation.

STANDARDS

Reading Literature
Determine a theme or central idea of a text and analyze its development over the course of the text.

Writing
- Use narrative techniques, such as dialogue, pacing, and description, to develop experiences, events, and/or characters.
- Use a variety of transition words, phrases, and clauses to convey sequence and signal shifts from one time frame or setting to another.
- Provide a conclusion that follows from and reflects on the narrated experiences or events.

SHARE IDEAS

Writing

An **alternate ending** is a new conclusion that explores a different way in which the conflicts in a work of fiction might be resolved.

Assignment

Develop an **alternate ending** for "He—y, Come on Ou—t!" Write at least three paragraphs that begin where the story ends. Choose one of the following styles for your ending:

○ realistic fiction, that provides an explanation for the bottomless hole

○ magical realism, that continues the fantastic elements of the original story

Brainstorm for ideas with your group. Then, write an alternate ending on your own.

Plan Your Ending With your group, brainstorm for different directions the alternate endings could take and decide which style of writing you will use. Make sure your choices reflect the world of the story, including the nature of the setting and the ways characters interact. Then, on your own, choose which characters will be involved, what events will take place, and what will happen as a result. Remember that the conclusion should follow from the experiences and events of the story and reflect on it in some way.

Draft Your Alternate Ending On your own, draft at least three new paragraphs that provide a satisfying end to the story. Follow these guidelines:

- Use strong descriptive details that capture the action and help readers visualize the scene.

- Use a variety of transitions—such as *later that day, meanwhile,* or *after he had left*—to show the sequence of events and to shift from the place and time of the original ending to your new version. Continue to use transitions to link sentences and paragraphs in a clear, coherent way.

- Determine the pacing for your new ending. **Pacing** is the rate at which a story unfolds. Scenes with dialogue and action tend to build quickly and are exciting. Passages of description and explanation move more slowly but can help to develop background and explain characters' behaviors.

Reflect on Your Writing Share your draft with your group and ask for feedback on your form and content. Then, strengthen your ending by revising, editing, or rewriting it based on the guidance from your peers.

EVIDENCE LOG

Before moving on, go to your Evidence Log and record any additional thoughts or observations you may have about "He—y, Come on Ou—t!"

PERFORMANCE TASK

Give and Follow Instructions

Assignment

With your group, research how to perform a specific task or activity related to the natural world. Then, teach the rest of your class that task, using **instructions** to guide them step by step. Groups should alternate giving and following instructions until all groups have done both.

Use Academic Vocabulary
Try to use one or more of the unit's academic vocabulary words in your instructions: *logical, generate, philosophy, evident, elucidate.*

Plan and Rehearse With Your Group

Choose a Topic As a group, choose one of the topics listed or come up with your own topic. Make sure it involves only readily available items from home or school. Mark your choice.

- ○ how to create crystal eggshell geodes
- ○ how to draw a natural resources/landscape map (water, trees, parks, etc.) of your city or town
- ○ how to create a balloon greenhouse
- ○ how to build a bottle terrarium
- ○ how to purify water using the sun
- ○ our own topic: _____

Conduct Research Identify print or digital sources that describe the activity. You need at least two sources in case one of them contains any gaps. As you gather information, consult with group members. Ask each other questions to clarify the research process, your project goals, or the content you find.

Develop the Instructions Determine the steps necessary to complete the task. Then, write the instructions. Be sure to include transitions, such as *before, next,* and *finally,* to guide your listeners from one step to the next. After your instructions are complete, find or create visual aids that will help your audience understand each step. In addition, gather the materials they will need to complete the task.

Plan and Rehearse the Presentation Decide how to present the steps clearly so that the audience can follow them easily. Make sure everyone in your group has a role to play in the presentation.

STANDARDS
Writing
Produce clear and coherent writing in which the development, organization, and style are appropriate to task, purpose, and audience.

Speaking and Listening
Present claims and findings, emphasizing salient points in a focused, coherent manner with pertinent descriptions, facts, details, and examples; use appropriate eye contact, adequate volume, and clear pronunciation.

Essential Question: What is the relationship between people and nature?

Use this chart to plan your presentation. List the steps of your instructions, the materials needed to complete them, and a group member's name and responsibilities for each step. Add rows if you need them. Then, rehearse as a group.

INSTRUCTIONS	MATERIALS	GROUP MEMBER
Step 1:		
Step 2:		
Step 3:		

Give Instructions

Present As a group, present your instructions to the class, following your plan. Keep these tips in mind:

- Speak loudly and slowly, and pronounce words clearly.
- Make sure everyone in the audience can see your visual aids.
- Make eye contact with listeners as you explain each step. Then, watch as they perform each step to be sure they are following along.

Evaluate Once your group has finished presenting, have audience members compare their final products. Did your instructions produce the expected results? If not, how could they be revised to be clearer?

Follow Instructions

Listen Actively Watch and listen closely as other groups present. Apply these strategies to follow instructions accurately:

- Check to be sure you have all the necessary materials.
- Ask clarifying questions of the presenters as needed.
- Look at the visual aids to help you to understand the steps.

Evaluate Once you have finished following instructions, evaluate how well you completed the task. What could you have done to ensure a better result? What constructive feedback do you have for the presenters?

Performance Task: Give and Follow Instructions

INDEPENDENT LEARNING

Essential Question

What is the relationship between people and nature?

The natural world affects everyone and everything on the planet. In this section, you will choose one additional selection that explores the relationship between people and nature to read independently. Get the most from this section by establishing a purpose for reading. Ask yourself, "What do I hope to gain from my independent reading?" Here are just a few purposes you might consider:

Read to Learn Think about the selections you have already read. What questions do you still have about the unit topic?

Read to Enjoy Read the descriptions of the texts. Which one seems most interesting and appealing to you?

Read to Form a Position Consider your thoughts and feelings about the Essential Question. Are you still undecided about some aspect of the topic?

Independent Learning Strategies

Throughout your life, in school, in your community, and in your career, you will need to rely on yourself to learn and work on your own. Use these strategies to keep your focus as you read independently for sustained periods of time. Add ideas of your own for each category.

STRATEGY	MY ACTION PLAN
Create a schedule	• Be aware of your deadlines and make a plan to meet them. • Find a quiet place to read where you can really focus on the text. •
Read with purpose	• Use a variety of reading strategies to deepen your understanding. • Read the first time for understanding, the second time for detail. •
Take notes	• Record important details, such as specific dates, names, places, and events. • Review your notes before sharing what you've learned. •

Contents

Choose one selection. Selections are available online only.

ADVENTURE STORY

from My Side of the Mountain
Jean Craighead George

Can you imagine living in a tree?

FEATURE ARTICLE

How the Teens of St. Pete Youth Farm Fight Food Insecurity, One Harvest at a Time
Gabrielle Calise

Students grow food to give back to their community.

SCIENCE ARTICLE

Rice University Researchers Are Turning Dead Spiders Into "Necrobots"
Ariana Garcia

How much weight can a dead spider lift?

LYRIC POETRY

Turtle Watchers
Linda Hogan

Jaguar
Francisco X. Alarcón

The Sparrow
Paul Laurence Dunbar

Take another look at the world around us, through poets' eyes.

SHARE YOUR INDEPENDENT LEARNING

SHARE • LEARN • REFLECT

Reflect on and evaluate the information you gained from your Independent Reading selection. Then, share what you learned with others.

Independent Learning 483

INDEPENDENT LEARNING

Close-Read Guide

A Close-Read Guide and Annotation Model are available online.

Establish your purpose for reading. Then, read the selection through at least once. Use this page to record your close-read ideas.

Selection Title: _____

Purpose for Reading: _____ Minutes Read: _____

Close Read the Text

Zoom in on sections you found interesting. **Annotate** what you notice. Ask yourself **questions** about the text. What can you **conclude**?

Analyze the Text

Think about the author's choices of literary elements, techniques, and structures. Select one and record your thoughts.

QuickWrite

Choose a paragraph from the text that grabbed your interest. Explain the power of this passage.

Essential Question: What is the relationship between people and nature?

Share Your Independent Learning

Essential Question
What is the relationship between people and nature?

When you read something independently, your understanding continues to grow as you share what you have learned with others.

Prepare to Share

WRITE One of the most important ways to respond to a text is to notice and describe your personal reactions. Think about the text you explored independently and the ways in which it connects to your own experiences.

- What similarities and differences do you see between the text and your own life? Describe your observations.
- How do you think this text connects to the Essential Question? Describe your ideas.

Learn From Your Classmates

DISCUSS Share your ideas about the text you explored on your own. As you talk with others in your class, jot down a few ideas and take notes about new ideas that seem important.

Reflect

EXPLAIN Review your notes, and mark the most important insight you gained from these writing and discussion activities. Draw on that idea to explain how it adds to your understanding of the relationship between people and nature.

STANDARDS
Speaking and Listening Come to discussions prepared, having read or researched material under study; explicitly draw on that preparation by referring to evidence on the topic, text, or issue to probe and reflect on ideas under discussion.

UNIT 4 REFLECT AND RESPOND

In this unit, you encountered many different perspectives on learning from nature. Now, take some time to reflect on the texts you explored and to express your own ideas.

Reflect on Your Unit Goals

Review your Unit Goals chart from the beginning of the unit. Then, complete the activity and answer the question.

1. In the Unit Goals chart, rate how well you meet each goal now.
2. In which goals were you most and least successful?

Reflect on the Texts

Enter the Texts If you could enter the world of one of the selections in this unit, which one would it be? Describe the setting or situation of each selection listed in the chart. Then, mark your top choice for the text you'd like to put yourself in. Briefly explain the reason for your choice.

TITLE	SETTING/SITUATION	REASON
The Bee Highway: Making a Place for Bees in the City		
from Silent Spring		
How Grandmother Spider Stole the Sun		
Coyote Steals the Sun and Moon		
• Our Purpose in Poetry: Or, Earthrise • Earthrise (video)		
Creature Comforts: Three Biology-Based Tips for Builders		
He—y, Come On Ou—t!		
Independent Learning Selection:		

486 UNIT 4 • LEARNING FROM NATURE

Essential Question: What is the relationship between people and nature?

Develop Your Perspective: Unit Projects

Choose one of the following Unit Project ideas.

T-SHIRT DESIGN

Create a t-shirt design that depicts one idea from the unit about the relationship between people and nature. Consider which ideas might reasonably be represented on a t-shirt and whether you mean to send a message to others or merely illustrate something you read about. Your design should include both visual elements and a small amount of text. Use at least one concept or academic vocabulary word from the unit on your shirt.

COMIC STRIP

With a partner, **develop a comic strip** that shows or comments on the relationship between humans and nature. Create three or four panels using simple drawings and either speech bubbles or captions to convey your ideas. Your comic strip may be funny or serious, but it must show at least one person interacting with the natural world in some way. Include at least two concept vocabulary words in your comic.

RADIO AD

Team up with a classmate to **write a radio advertisement** for an upcoming event (real or imaginary) that connects people and nature in your local area.

In the script for your on-air ad, announce the name of the event and its location. Then, give a brief explanation of how the event is an opportunity for people to interact with, learn from, or protect plants or animals in your community.

Develop an enthusiastic tone, and be sure to include at least two academic vocabulary words. If possible, perform your ad for your class or another audience.

USE NEW WORDS

Academic Vocabulary

Use the academic vocabulary from the unit as you plan, draft, and discuss your project:

- logical
- generate
- philosophy
- evident
- elucidate

Concept Vocabulary

Review your Word Wall and write down any words you want to use in your project:

STANDARDS
Writing
• Produce clear and coherent writing in which the development, organization, and style are appropriate to task, purpose, and audience.
• Draw evidence from literary or informational texts to support analysis, reflection, and research.

PERFORMANCE-BASED ASSESSMENT

SOURCES

- Whole-Class Selections
- Peer-Group Selections
- Independent Learning Selection
- Your own experiences and observations

Research-Based Essay

Assignment

In this unit, you read different perspectives on people's relationship with nature. You also practiced writing research reports and papers. Now, apply what you have learned.

Write a **research-based essay** that explores an answer to the Essential Question.

Essential Question

What is the relationship between people and nature?

Review and Evaluate Evidence

Review your Evidence Log and your QuickWrite from the beginning of the unit. Have your ideas changed?

○ Yes	○ No
Identify at least three pieces of evidence that caused you to think differently.	Identify at least three pieces of evidence that reinforced your initial views.
1.	1.
2.	2.
3.	3.

State your ideas now:

What other evidence might you need to develop a central idea?

488 UNIT 4 • LEARNING FROM NATURE

Essential Question: What is the relationship between people and nature?

Share Your Perspective

The **Research-Based Essay Checklist** will help you stay on track.

PLAN Before you write, read the checklist and make sure you understand all the items. Gather information from outside sources that you'll use to support your ideas.

DRAFT As you write, pause occasionally to make sure you're meeting the checklist requirements.

Use New Words Refer to your Word Wall to vary your word choice. Also, consider using one or more of the academic vocabulary terms you learned at the beginning of the unit: *logical, generate, philosophy, evident, elucidate.*

REVIEW AND EDIT After you have written a first draft, evaluate it against the checklist. Make any changes needed to strengthen your thesis, structure, transitions, and language. Then, reread your essay and fix any errors you find.

EVIDENCE LOG

Make sure you have pulled in details from your Evidence Log to support your thesis.

RESEARCH-BASED ESSAY CHECKLIST

My essay clearly contains…

- [ ] a clear central idea, or thesis, that answers the Essential Question.
- [ ] relevant information from a variety of print and digital sources, as well as my own ideas and insights.
- [ ] an organized structure with an introduction, a conclusion, and appropriate transitions among all paragraphs.
- [ ] precise, topic-specific words that explain my ideas clearly.
- [ ] quotations, paraphrases, and references to sources integrated into the body of the essay.
- [ ] a standard format for references and citations.
- [ ] correct use of standard English grammar and usage, including subject-verb agreement.
- [ ] correct use of standard English conventions, including capitalization, punctuation, and spelling.

STANDARDS

Writing
Write informative/explanatory texts to examine a topic and convey ideas, concepts, and information through the selection, organization, and analysis of relevant content.

Language
Demonstrate command of the conventions of standard English grammar and usage when writing or speaking.

Facing Adversity

WATCH THE ViDEO

DISCUSS What types of challenges are the hardest to overcome?

Write your response before sharing your ideas.

UNIT 5

INTRO

Essential Question
How do we overcome life's challenges?

 INFORMATIONAL ESSAY
Against the Odds
MENTOR TEXT

WHOLE-CLASS LEARNING

COMPARE

Black Sunday: The Storm That Gave Us the Dust Bowl
Erin Blakemore
HISTORICAL NONFICTION

from **Survival in the Storm: The Dust Bowl Diary of Grace Edwards**
Katelan Janke

▶ MEDIA CONNECTION: **The Dust Bowl**
HISTORICAL FICTION

A More Accessible World
Lisa Christensen
INFORMATIONAL ARTICLE

Write an Informational Essay
WRITING: PERFORMANCE TASK

PEER-GROUP LEARNING

COMPARE

The Circuit
Francisco Jiménez
SHORT STORY

How This Son of Migrant Farm Workers Became an Astronaut
José Hernández and Octavio Blanco
INTERVIEW

A Work in Progress
Aimee Mullins
ORAL HISTORY

Simile: Willow and Ginkgo
Eve Merriam

Four Skinny Trees from **The House on Mango Street**
Sandra Cisneros
POETRY • VIGNETTE

Present an Informational Text
SPEAKING AND LISTENING: PERFORMANCE TASK

INDEPENDENT LEARNING

The Girl Who Fell From the Sky
Juliane Koepcke
PERSONAL NARRATIVE

Malala Yousafzai: Speech to United Nations Security Council
Malala Yousafzai
PERSUASIVE SPEECH

from **The Story of My Life**
Helen Keller
AUTOBIOGRAPHY

Rikki-tikki-tavi
Rudyard Kipling
SHORT STORY

SHARE • LEARN • REFLECT
SHARE INDEPENDENT LEARNING

REFLECT AND RESPOND
GOALS • TEXTS • UNIT PROJECTS

PERFORMANCE-BASED ASSESSMENT
Informational Essay
You will write an informational essay in response to the Essential Question for the unit.

491

UNIT 5 INTRODUCTION

Unit Goals

Throughout this unit you will deepen your perspective about facing adversity by reading, writing, speaking, listening, and presenting. These goals will help you succeed on the Unit Performance-Based Assessment.

SET GOALS Use a scale of 1 to 5 to rate how well you meet these goals right now. You will revisit your ratings later when you reflect on your growth during this unit.

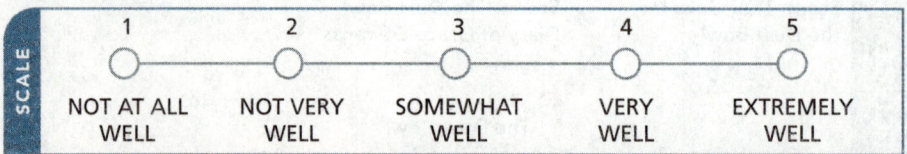

SCALE
1 NOT AT ALL WELL
2 NOT VERY WELL
3 SOMEWHAT WELL
4 VERY WELL
5 EXTREMELY WELL

	Unit Introduction	Unit Reflection
ESSENTIAL QUESTION		
I can read selections that reflect the experience of facing adversity and develop my own perspective.	1 2 3 4 5	1 2 3 4 5
READING	Unit Introduction	Unit Reflection
I can understand and use academic vocabulary words related to informational texts.	1 2 3 4 5	1 2 3 4 5
I can recognize elements of different genres, especially historical nonfiction and fiction, informational texts, and poetry.	1 2 3 4 5	1 2 3 4 5
I can read a selection of my choice independently and make connections to other texts.	1 2 3 4 5	1 2 3 4 5
WRITING	Unit Introduction	Unit Reflection
I can write a focused, well-organized informational essay.	1 2 3 4 5	1 2 3 4 5
I can complete Timed Writing tasks with confidence.	1 2 3 4 5	1 2 3 4 5
SPEAKING AND LISTENING	Unit Introduction	Unit Reflection
I can prepare and deliver an informational presentation.	1 2 3 4 5	1 2 3 4 5
MY GOALS	Unit Introduction	Unit Reflection

STANDARDS
Language
• Use common, grade-appropriate Greek or Latin affixes and roots as clues to the meaning of a word.
• Acquire and use accurately grade-appropriate general academic and domain-specific words and phrases; gather vocabulary knowledge when considering a word or phrase important to comprehension or expression.

Essential Question: How do we overcome life's challenges?

Academic Vocabulary: Informational Text

Academic terms can help you read, write, and discuss with precision. Many of these words have roots, or key parts, that come from Latin and Greek.

PRACTICE Academic terms are used routinely in classrooms. Build your knowledge of these words by completing the chart.

1. **Review** each word, its root, and the mentor sentences.
2. **Determine** the meaning and usage of each word using the mentor sentences and a dictionary, if needed.
3. **List** at least two related words for each academic term. Then, challenge yourself to write a sentence that contains two of the academic terms.

WORD	MENTOR SENTENCES	PREDICT MEANING	RELATED WORDS
deviate LATIN ROOT: -via- "way"	1. Don't *deviate* from the route I gave you or you'll get lost! 2. She was making an important point, but she allowed herself to *deviate* into side issues.		viable; viaduct
persevere LATIN ROOT: -sever- "strict"; "serious"	1. Despite the difficult deadline, Diego's dedication helped him *persevere* and get his paper in on time. 2. Though the soccer team was losing in the first half, they were able to *persevere* and win the game.		
determination LATIN ROOT: -term- "end"	1. Because of his *determination* to do well on the test, Robert studied for many hours. 2. Despite the heavy rain, Jenny's *determination* allowed her to complete her first marathon.		
diversity LATIN ROOT: -ver- "turn"	1. There is cultural *diversity* in the United States because people come from many different places. 2. The oceans are filled with a *diversity* of marine life.		
observation LATIN ROOT: -serv- "watch over"	1. Mastery of a skill requires more than *observation*; you have to do the activity yourself. 2. Any *observation* of the moon was impossible because it was such a cloudy night.		

Unit Introduction 493

UNIT 5 INTRODUCTION

MENTOR TEXT

INFORMATIONAL ESSAY MODEL

READ As you read, notice that the author presents facts without offering opinions or arguments.

Against the Odds

1   "If you have to ditch a commercial aircraft in the Hudson River," the news anchor joked, "this is the guy you want."

2   That guy was Chesley Sullenberger. As a 29-year veteran of US Airways and a former Air Force fighter pilot, he had what it took to land his plane safely and save his passengers' lives.

3   On January 15, 2009, Sullenberger was the pilot on US Airways Flight 1549 from New York's LaGuardia Airport to Charlotte, North Carolina. Flight 1549 left the tarmac at 3:25 p.m. Sullenberger thought he was in for an average flight—a routine, everyday trip.

4   The flight was unremarkable for the first 90 seconds. Then something caught the eye of copilot Jeff Skiles. At 3,000 feet, he saw a flock of Canada geese headed toward the plane. Moments later the geese struck the fuselage, wings, and engine.

5   The 150 passengers felt a powerful thud against the airplane, followed by severe vibrations from the engine. One passenger said it sounded like sneakers thumping around in a dryer. There was a loud explosion. The cabin filled up with smoke. There was a horrible smell and then an eerie quiet: both engines were disabled.

6   Sullenberger made a Mayday radio call to air traffic control and calmly explained the situation. They discussed the options: The plane could either return to LaGuardia or land at Teterboro Airport in New Jersey.

7   Sullenberger knew the situation was too dire for the plane to stay in the air long enough for either plan to be successful. He had about 30 seconds to find an alternative. The pilot decided on a

494 UNIT 5 • FACING ADVERSITY

Essential Question: How do we overcome life's challenges?

radical move: He'd ditch the plane in the Hudson River—despite the fact that passenger jets are not built to land on water.

8 "Brace for impact!" came the captain's voice over the intercom. A hush fell over the passengers. They thought they were going to die.

9 Sullenberger lowered the plane's nose in a gradual glide toward the river. The plane managed to clear the George Washington Bridge and, against the odds, land safely on the Hudson. It skidded across the water at 145 mph and finally slowed to a stop.

10 "He was thinking in nanoseconds," said a former airline pilot, speaking of Sullenberger. "He made all the right choices at all the right times. He might have been staring at the instruments, but he was feeling that airplane in his hands. He picked his landing spot and went for it."

11 Now Sullenberger's job was to get the people off the plane, which was quickly filling up with water. In this as well, he showed his tremendous capacity for calm leadership.

12 Witnesses were convinced that everyone on Flight 1549 was dead. What they couldn't see was that passengers were already exiting the plane. With water seeping into the plane, Sullenberger and Skiles walked the length of the cabin twice, calling "Is anyone there?" The water was so cold they had to walk on top of the seats. But they would not leave the plane until they were sure everyone was out.

13 "He's the man," said one of the rescued passengers. "If you want to talk to a hero, get a hold of him."

14 After all the thanking was over, Sullenberger was humble. "You're welcome," he said simply. Like most heroes, he didn't want the label. According to him, he was just doing his job.

15 But 154 men, women, and children owed their lives to a modest man who faced adversity with cool competence on one of the most remarkable days in aviation history.

WORD WALL: FACING ADVERSITY

Vocabulary A Word Wall is a collection of words related to a topic.

As you read the selections in this unit, identify interesting words related to facing adversity and add them to your Word Wall. For example, you might begin by adding words from the Mentor Text, such as *dire, humble,* and *competence.* Continue to add words as you complete this unit.

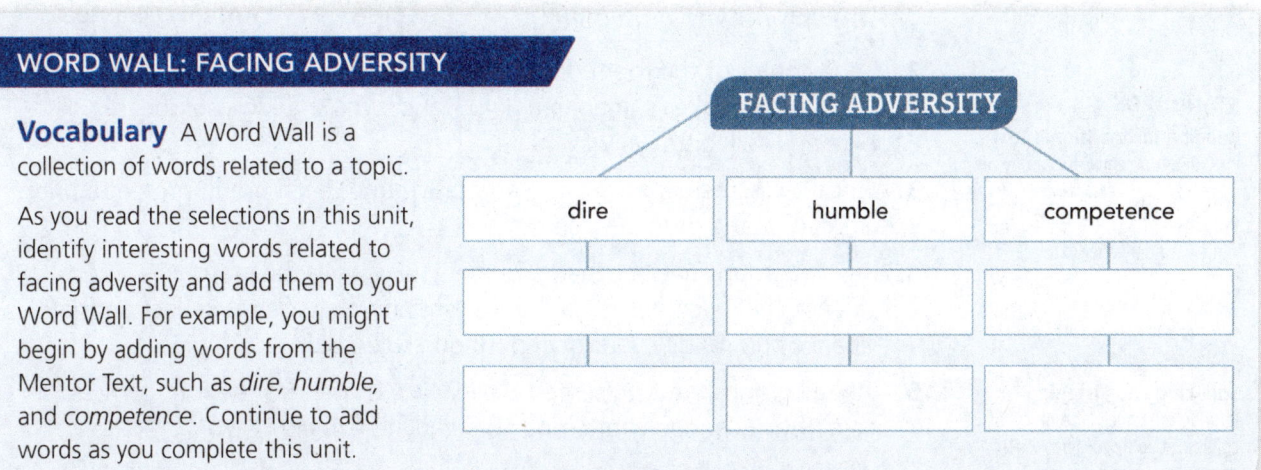

Against the Odds   495

UNIT 5 INTRODUCTION

Summary

A **summary** is a brief, complete overview of a text that maintains the meaning and logical order of ideas of the original work. It should be objective and should not include your personal opinions.

WRITE Write a summary of "Against the Odds."

Icebreaker

Conduct a Four-Corner Debate

Consider this statement: **Chesley Sullenberger wasn't really a hero because, as he himself said, facing adversity was part of his job.**

1. Identify your position on the statement.

   ◯ Strongly Agree   ◯ Agree   ◯ Disagree   ◯ Strongly Disagree

2. In one corner of the room, form a group with like-minded students, and discuss what makes someone a hero. Take turns sharing your ideas in a polite and collaborative way.

3. After the discussion, have a representative from each group present a brief summary of the group's position.

4. Listen as groups present their arguments. Evaluate the reasoning and evidence that each group provides to support their claim. Reflect on that evidence and modify your own position as needed.

5. After all groups have presented their views, move into the four corners again. If you change your corner, be ready to explain why.

STANDARDS

Reading Informational Text
Provide an objective summary of the text.

Writing
Write routinely over extended time frames and shorter time frames for a range of discipline-specific tasks, purposes, and audiences.

Speaking and Listening
Engage effectively in a range of collaborative discussions with diverse partners on grade 7 topics, texts, and issues.

Essential Question: How do we overcome life's challenges?

QuickWrite

Consider class discussions, presentations, the video, and the Mentor Text as you think about the Essential Question.

Essential Question
How do we overcome life's challenges?

At the end of the unit, you will respond to the Essential Question again and see if your perspective has deepened or changed.

WRITE Record your first thoughts here.

___

EVIDENCE LOG

How do we overcome life's challenges?

As you read the selections in this unit, use a chart like the one shown to record your ideas and list details from the texts that support them. Taking notes as you go will help you clarify your thinking, gather relevant information, and be ready to respond to the Essential Question.

TITLE	MY IDEAS / OBSERVATIONS	TEXT EVIDENCE / INFORMATION

WHOLE-CLASS LEARNING

Essential Question

How do we overcome life's challenges?

Everyone has a bad day now and then. Most of the time we take a deep breath and keep going—but what happens when we meet a challenge we don't think we can overcome? You will work with your whole class to explore the concept of facing adversity. The selections you are going to read present different examples of the ways in which people cope with challenges and face adversity.

Whole-Class Learning Strategies

Throughout your life, in school, in your community, and in your career, you will continue to learn and work in large-group environments. Read the strategies and the actions you can take to practice them as you work with your whole class. Add ideas of your own for each category. Get ready to use these strategies during Whole-Class Learning.

STRATEGY	MY ACTION PLAN
Listen actively	• Make eye contact with the speaker to show you are listening. • Eliminate distractions; for example, put notifications on mute. •
Demonstrate respect	• Do not interrupt others when they are speaking. • Stay open-minded about the ideas your classmates share. •
Make personal connections	• Consider how characters' actions and reactions can help you understand your own experiences. • Think about where you might apply the information you're learning to your own life. • Remember that literature explores the human experience—the themes are universal even though the details differ. •

498 UNIT 5 • FACING ADVERSITY

Contents

COMPARE

HISTORICAL NONFICTION

Black Sunday: The Storm That Gave Us the Dust Bowl
Erin Blakemore

A storm to end all storms rolls in.

HISTORICAL FICTION

from Survival in the Storm: The Dust Bowl Diary of Grace Edwards
Katelan Janke

How do you survive a killer storm?

MEDIA CONNECTION: The Dust Bowl

INFORMATIONAL ARTICLE

A More Accessible World
Lisa Christensen

How do people with blindness or low vision overcome everyday challenges?

PERFORMANCE TASK

WRITING PROMPT • WRITER'S HANDBOOK

Write an Informational Essay

The Whole-Class readings describe the challenges people must overcome when dealing with tremendous adversity. After reading, you will write an informational essay on what it means to face adversity.

Whole-Class Learning **499**

COMPARE ACROSS GENRES

NONFICTION and FICTION

Historical nonfiction presents true stories that happened in the past, including details about real events and the experiences of real people. In contrast, **historical fiction** tells stories that are set in a real time and place from the past, but the details about people's personal experiences are made up.

HISTORICAL NONFICTION

Author's Purpose
- to explain real-life past events by providing facts and analysis

Characteristics
- one or more central ideas supported by varied evidence, including information from primary sources
- an objective point of view
- in addition to explanation, can include elements of storytelling, description, and argument

Structure
- a logical progression of information
- may use a variety of organizational structures, such as chronological order or cause and effect

HISTORICAL FICTION

Author's Purpose
- to tell a story that combines historical and made-up elements

Characteristics
- a setting that is a real place and time
- characters who are real historical figures or are modeled on real people from the past
- conflicts that reflect historical situations
- a theme, or insight
- dialogue that shows how people spoke in the past or in a specific place

Structure
- a plot that combines real-life historical events with made-up events

500 UNIT 5 • FACING ADVERSITY

Essential Question: How do we overcome life's challenges?

Theme and Central Idea

 When you read any work of fiction or nonfiction, think about what it reveals about life or about a topic.

• A work of fiction conveys an insight about life, or **theme**. Themes are usually implied, or unstated. Readers interpret themes by thinking about what the story details reveal about life.

• A work of nonfiction conveys a **central idea** about a topic. Central ideas are usually explicitly stated and supported by details. Readers identify central ideas by looking for an idea that is directly stated and then repeated or emphasized throughout the text.

SIMILARITIES AND DIFFERENCES	
THEME	**CENTRAL IDEA**
insight about life or human nature	specific statement about a topic
usually implied and not stated directly	often stated directly
developed and suggested by all the story details	developed with supporting evidence and details
one work may have multiple themes	one work may have more than one central idea

In most literary texts, readers connect details to interpret the theme. In most informational texts, readers evaluate the strength of the central ideas and the author's reasoning.

PRACTICE Determine whether each item most likely expresses a theme in historical fiction or a central idea in historical nonfiction. Explain your thinking.

1. Money cannot buy love or happiness.

2. Jazz is a truly American form of music that is influenced by various musical traditions.

3. Many early women's rights activists were inspired by abolitionists.

4. One person's trash is another person's treasure.

STANDARDS

Reading Literature
Determine a theme or central idea of a text and analyze its development over the course of the text.

Reading Informational Text
Determine two or more central ideas in a text and analyze their development over the course of the text.

Compare Across Genres 501

PREPARE TO READ

BLACK SUNDAY: THE STORM THAT GAVE US THE DUST BOWL

from SURVIVAL IN THE STORM: THE DUST BOWL DIARY OF GRACE EDWARDS

COMPARE: NONFICTION and FICTION
In this lesson, you will read **Black Sunday**, a nonfiction text about the Dust Bowl, and an excerpt from **Survival in the Storm**, a work of historical fiction on the same subject. You will then compare and contrast how the texts portray the historical events and time period.

About the Author

Erin Blakemore is a freelance journalist and author of *The Heroine's Bookshelf*, a Colorado Book Award winner. Her writing has appeared in many print and online publications, including *TIME, The Washington Post, Smithsonian Magazine, Popular Science,* and *National Geographic.*

Concept Vocabulary

Predict The words in the chart appear in the text. Judging from these words, what kinds of things do you think the author will describe?

plight (PLYT) *n.* serious or harmful condition or situation	**unending** (uhn EHN dihng) *adj.* never stopping; constant
ravaged (RAV ihjd) *v.* destroyed or damaged badly	**demoralized** (dih MAWR uh lyzd) *adj.* discouraged; defeated
widespread (WYD sprehd) *adj.* occurring in many places	**impoverished** (ihm POV uhr ihsht) *adj.* extremely poor; miserable and exhausted

My Expectations:

Reading Strategy: Establish a Purpose

Establishing a **purpose for reading** will help you get more meaning from a text. Answer the following questions to set a purpose for reading:

- **What is the genre?** Your purpose should reflect the type of text you are reading.
- **What is the title?** The title can help you determine what the text might be about, which will help you set your purpose.
- **What do the text features tell me?** Quickly scan the text to help you set your purpose. Look for text features, such as images, headings, and key terms.

> **PRACTICE** Before you begin the selection, establish your purpose for reading and write it here.

STANDARDS
Reading Informational Text
By the end of the year, read and comprehend literary nonfiction.
Language
Gather vocabulary knowledge when considering a word or phrase important to comprehension or expression.

502 UNIT 5 • FACING ADVERSITY

HISTORICAL NONFICTION

Black Sunday:
The Storm That Gave Us the Dust Bowl

Erin Blakemore

An enormous dust storm descends on the town of Springfield, Colorado, during the Dust Bowl in the 1930s.

BACKGROUND
Since the mid-nineteenth century, farmers had been flocking to the Great Plains of the American Midwest, which offered large plots of land for raising crops and livestock. This migration changed the landscape of the region, replacing the native prairie grasses with plowed fields. In 1930, a severe drought hit this altered environment creating dust storms that raged for nearly a decade. This selection recounts one of the worst dust storms in the era known as the Dust Bowl.

1   It seemed like an ordinary day at first. Like any other day, folks on the Great Plains were struggling to get by. People walked to church, swept up from the dust storm that had blown through the week before, perhaps discussed the Congressional hearings that had brought the **plight** of the region, which had been **ravaged** by drought and the economic effects of the Great Depression, to the attention of the rest of the nation.

2   But Black Sunday—April 14, 1935—was no ordinary day.

3   That afternoon, a gigantic cloud swept across the Great Plains. It was 1,000 miles long and blew at speeds up to 100 miles per hour. It was made of 300,000 tons of dust whipped from the ground of northern farmlands, where poor soil conservation techniques[1] had led to **widespread** erosion made worse by the **unending** drought.

   1. **soil conservation techniques** methods that farmers can use to stop soil from being removed by natural forces.

plight (PLYT) *n.* serious or harmful condition or situation

ravaged (RAV ihjd) *v.* destroyed or damaged badly

widespread (WYD sprehd) *adj.* occurring in many places

unending (uhn EHN dihng) *adj.* never stopping; constant

READ TO UNLOCK MEANING

1. First read the text for comprehension and enjoyment. Use the **Comprehension Check** question to support your first read.
2. Go back and respond to the Close-Read note.
3. Identify other details in the text you find interesting. Ask your own questions and draw your own conclusions.

CLOSE READ

ANNOTATE In paragraph 6, mark details that describe the reactions of humans and animals.

QUESTION What effect do these details have?

demoralized (dih MAWR uh lyzd) *adj.* discouraged; defeated

impoverished (ihm POV uhr ihsht) *adj.* extremely poor; miserable and exhausted

COMPREHENSION CHECK

How did this period in time come to be known as the Dust Bowl?

---

4 Great Plains residents were used to dust, but they had never seen anything like this. One observer compared it to "the Red Sea closing in on the Israel children[2] . . . it got so dark that you couldn't see your hand before your face, you couldn't see anybody in the room."

5 "You couldn't see the street lights," recalled Jim Williams, who watched the storm from his home in Dodge City, Kansas. "It rolled over and over and over and over and over when it came in," another witness remembered, "and it was coal black; it was coal black, and it was terrible that afternoon. It was hot and dry."

6 Humans weren't the only ones terrified by the storm. Birds fled ahead of the cloud. Confused by the dark, chickens started to go inside to roost. Cows ran in circles.

7 Once the storm subsided, a simple spring day had become the worst day in recent memory. The "black blizzard" that swept across the plains states left a trail of devastation in its wake—leveled fields, crashed cars, reports of people who had been blinded or given pneumonia by the storm. Everything was covered in dust, which choked wells and killed cattle. "Black Sunday," as the storm became known, was the death knell[3] for the poor farmers of Oklahoma and Texas. **Demoralized** and **impoverished**, thousands of so-called "Okies" cut their losses[4] and began the long migration to more favorable locations like California.

8 In Boise City, Oklahoma, an Associated Press reporter named Robert E. Geiger had weathered the storm with photographer Harry G. Eisenhard. "Three little words achingly familiar on a Western farmer's tongue," he wrote after the storm, "rule life in the dust bowl of the continent—if it rains." Some speculate that Geiger meant to say, "dust belt," a term he used to refer to the devastated region before and after Black Sunday.

9 Inadvertent or no, the term was picked up almost immediately. Geiger had given name to a phenomenon that would come to define the economic and social impacts of the Great Depression. But though Black Sunday and the Dust Bowl it helped name drew attention to the plight of the plains and turned soil conservation into a national priority, its effects were best summed up by a folk singer, not a reporter or politician. These are some of the lyrics to Woody Guthrie's "Dust Storm Disaster," which tells the story of the "deathlike black" cloud that enveloped America that day in 1935:

> *It covered up our fences, it covered up our barns,*
> *It covered up our tractors in this wild and dusty storm.*
> *We loaded our jalopies and piled our families in,*
> *We rattled down that highway to never come back again.*

---

2. **the Red Sea closing in on the Israel children** According to the Bible, the Red Sea opened up for the escaping children of Israel and then closed in on the Egyptians who were chasing them. The term "children of Israel" refers to both adults and children.
3. **death knell** *n.* sound signaling an end or failure.
4. **cut their losses** abandoned an unsuccessful occupation or activity before anyone suffered more harm.

BUILD INSIGHT

First Thoughts

Select one of the following items to answer.
- How does this description of the dust storm compare with other natural disasters you've experienced or read about?
- Which effects of the dust storm seem most devastating to you? Why?

Summary

Confirm your understanding of the text by writing a short summary. Include only the text's central ideas, and keep your summary objective.

Analysis

1. **(a) Analyze Cause and Effect** What combination of factors caused the historic dust storm of Black Sunday? **(b) Support** What details from the text support your response?

2. **(a)** Cite one example of a quotation from an eyewitness and one example of numerical data in the text. **(b) Analyze** Why do you think the author chose to include each one? Explain.

3. **(a) Analyze** What qualities of the storm are described in paragraphs 3–5? Cite three examples of words and phrases that help convey these qualities. **(b) Draw Conclusions** What conclusion can you draw from this description about the nature of dust storms during the Dust Bowl era?

4. **(a) Interpret** Why might the author have chosen to end the article by quoting a song? Explain. **(b) Evaluate** Do you agree with the author's statement that the "effects [of Black Sunday] were best summed up by a folk singer, not a reporter or politician"? Why, or why not?

Exploring the Essential Question

How do we overcome life's challenges?

5. Which part of the storm or its effects would be the biggest challenge to overcome? Why? Record your ideas in your Evidence Log.

STANDARDS
Reading Informational Text
- Cite several pieces of textual evidence to support analysis of what the text says explicitly as well as inferences drawn from the text.
- Provide an objective summary of the text.

Black Sunday: The Storm That Gave Us the Dust Bowl **505**

ANALYZE AND INTERPRET

BLACK SUNDAY: THE STORM THAT GAVE US THE DUST BOWL

Close Read

1. The model passage and annotation show how one reader analyzed paragraph 4 of the text. Find another detail in the passage to annotate. Then, write your own question and conclusion.

TIP: An **allusion** is a reference to a well-known person, place, event, or literary work that helps a writer express complex ideas. Common allusions refer to well-known myths, the Bible, and famous works of art or literature.

CLOSE-READ MODEL

Great Plains residents were used to dust, but they had never seen anything like this. One observer compared it to "the Red Sea closing in on the Israel children[2] . . . it got so dark that you couldn't see your hand before your face, you couldn't see anybody in the room."

ANNOTATE: This quote contains an allusion to a story in the Bible.
QUESTION: Why does the author include this allusion?
CONCLUDE: The allusion describes the situation in a vivid and dramatic way.

MY QUESTION:

MY CONCLUSION:

2. For more practice, answer the Close-Read question in the selection.

3. Choose a section of the text that you found especially meaningful. Mark important details. Then, jot down questions and write your conclusions in the open space next to the text.

Inquiry and Research

Research and Extend The text ends with lines from the song "Dust Storm Disaster" by Woody Guthrie. Find the song online and either read the lyrics or listen to a recording. Then, write two questions about details in the song that you would be interested in answering through additional research.

STANDARDS
Reading Informational Text
Determine two or more central ideas in a text and analyze their development over the course of the text.
Writing
Conduct short research projects to answer a question, drawing on several sources and generating additional related, focused questions for further research and investigation.
Language
Interpret figures of speech in context.

506 UNIT 5 • FACING ADVERSITY

Essential Question: How do we overcome life's challenges?

Central Ideas and Supporting Evidence

Authors of historical nonfiction often develop multiple **central ideas**, or main points, in their work. They use many types of **supporting evidence**, or details and information, to support these central ideas. Authors of historical nonfiction may use evidence from both primary and secondary sources to develop their central ideas over the course of a text.

TYPE OF SOURCE	EXAMPLES
Primary Source: • original account of an event or time period from a person who experienced it directly • does not include interpretations	• personal letters, diaries, blogs, and emails • interviews and direct quotations • photographs and video or audio recordings • original art, music, or literature
Secondary Source: • analyzes, evaluates, or interprets primary sources • "one step removed" from the events or time period	• nonfiction books such as biographies and textbooks; reference books such as encyclopedias • journalism written after the event or time period • reviews and criticisms • documentaries

PRACTICE Complete the items.

1. **(a) Classify** How can you tell that "Black Sunday" is a secondary source?

   (b) Distinguish Identify three types of primary sources the author refers to in the text.

2. **Analyze** In your own words, state two central ideas of the text:
   (a) State a central idea about the causes of the storm. Then, mark two details in the text that provide supporting evidence and develop that central idea.

   (b) State a central idea about the storm's impact on the people and the land. Then, mark two details in the text that provide supporting evidence and develop that central idea.

Black Sunday: The Storm That Gave Us the Dust Bowl

STUDY LANGUAGE AND CRAFT

BLACK SUNDAY: THE STORM THAT GAVE US THE DUST BOWL

Concept Vocabulary

Why These Words? The vocabulary words relate to the idea of an overwhelming problem. For example, the farmers were already *impoverished,* or struggling to get by economically, when the storm hit.

| plight | widespread | demoralized |
| ravaged | unending | impoverished |

WORD WALL
Note words in the text that are related to the idea of facing adversity. Add them to your Word Wall.

PRACTICE Answer the questions, and complete the activities.

1. How do the vocabulary words deepen your understanding of what life was like for people during the Dust Bowl?

2. Use each vocabulary word in a sentence that demonstrates your understanding of the word's meaning.

3. Choose three of your sentences, and replace the vocabulary word with a **synonym,** or word with a similar meaning. How does the synonym affect the meaning of each sentence? Explain.

Word Study

Denotation and Connotation **Denotation** is the dictionary definition of a word. **Connotation** refers to the emotional quality of a word and the feelings it brings up. For instance, the denotation of *ravaged* is similar to that of *damaged,* but *ravaged* has a stronger, more negative connotation. A house that is *damaged* in a storm suffers harm, but one that is *ravaged* is harmed violently or even destroyed.

PRACTICE Complete the items.

1. Use a dictionary to find the precise meaning of the vocabulary word *demoralized*. Record its denotation and then write a sentence using the word.

2. Use a thesaurus to identify a synonym for *demoralized* that has a different connotation. Record the synonym and its denotation, and explain how its connotation differs. Then, write a sentence using the word.

STANDARDS
Reading Informational Text
• Determine the meaning of words and phrases as they are used in a text, including figurative, connotative, and technical meanings; analyze the impact of a specific word choice on meaning and tone.

• Determine an author's point of view or purpose in a text.

Language
Distinguish among the connotations of words with similar denotations.

Essential Question: How do we overcome life's challenges?

Author's Point of View

There are two main points of view from which authors of nonfiction typically write. **Objective point of view** presents information that is all or mostly based on fact and excludes the author's personal perspective on the topic. **Subjective point of view** presents information through the lens of the author's own ideas about the topic.

POINT OF VIEW	EXAMPLE PASSAGE
Objective • factual information and ideas without the author's personal opinions or feelings • used in research reports, expository articles, informational texts, and official documents	A gigantic cloud swept across the Great Plains, where poor soil conservation techniques had led to widespread erosion made worse by the unending drought.
Subjective • may include factual information but is based largely on the author's personal opinions, thoughts, and emotions • used in diaries, biographies, blog posts, and arguments	A monster was on the horizon, taunting the unsuspecting farmers of the Great Plains. Their soil conservation efforts had been poor, but it wasn't their fault. The terrible drought had made their lives miserable.

PRACTICE Complete the activities.

1. **Analyze** Reread the selection and determine whether it is written mainly from the objective or subjective point of view. Mark evidence in the text that supports your analysis.

2. **Modify** Rewrite each objective sentence to be subjective.

   a. In 1930, a drought covered the Great Plains and led to dust storms that lasted for a decade.

   b. The Dust Bowl affected not only farmers but also their crops, livestock, and homes.

   c. Black Sunday is the name given to April 14, 1935, when a particularly bad dust storm hit the Great Plains.

EVIDENCE LOG

Before moving on to a new selection, go to your Evidence Log and record any additional thoughts or observations you may have about "Black Sunday: The Storm That Gave Us the Dust Bowl."

PREPARE TO READ

BLACK SUNDAY

from SURVIVAL IN THE STORM

COMPARE: NONFICTION and FICTION
As you read, pay attention to similarities and differences between the dust storm described in this excerpt from **Survival in the Storm** and in **Black Sunday**.

About the Author
Katelan Janke was only fifteen when her novel *Survival in the Storm* was published. The novel resulted from her winning entry in the 1998 Arrow Book Club/ Dear America Student Writing Contest. After winning the contest, Janke was given the opportunity to turn her entry into a book. She set the story in Dalhart, Texas, where she grew up. Her research for the book included interviews with local people who lived through the Dust Bowl period.

Concept Vocabulary

Write The words listed here appear in the story. Write a mini story of your own using all four vocabulary words.

WORDS FROM THE STORY	
stammering (STA muh rihng) *v.* speaking hesitantly, with starts and stops They were stammering as they described the accident.	**frantically** (FRAN tihk lee) *adv.* in a hurried, wild, or desperate way The survivors searched frantically through the fallen building.
shuddered (SHUH duhrd) *v.* trembled or quivered The frightened dog shuddered with each burst of fireworks.	**exhaustion** (ehg ZAWS chuhn) *n.* extreme tiredness or fatigue. After hiking all day, we collapsed with exhaustion.

MY MINI STORY

Reading Strategy: Use Background Knowledge

If you are struggling to understand a text, use your **background knowledge,** or what you already know, to improve your grasp of new ideas and challenging passages.

- Read the Background note and consider what you already know about the subject.
- As you read, mark new ideas and details. Determine whether they add to, change, or contradict your background knowledge.
- If you are unclear about the meaning of a passage, draw on your previous experiences and the ideas in the text that you *do* understand.

PRACTICE As you read, use the open space to note places where you used your background knowledge.

STANDARDS
Reading Literature
Cite several pieces of textual evidence to support analysis of what the text says explicitly as well as inferences drawn from the text.
Language
Acquire and use accurately grade-appropriate general academic and domain-specific words and phrases; gather vocabulary knowledge when considering a word or phrase important to comprehension or expression.

510 UNIT 5 • FACING ADVERSITY

HISTORICAL FICTION

from
Survival in the Storm:
The Dust Bowl Diary of Grace Edwards

Katelan Janke

BACKGROUND
In the 1930s, severe dust storms blew over drought-stricken areas of the Great Plains region of the United States. A dust storm is a mass of dust and debris that is carried by the strong winds produced by a thunderstorm. Dust storms can develop suddenly and threaten both people and animals. The reduced visibility caused by a dust storm can cause accidents, and inhaled dust can damage health, particularly the health of people who have asthma.

Thursday, March 7, 1935

1   A duster hit today.
2   The afternoon had been beautifully warm, and Mama had even opened several windows in the house to let in the fresh air. Several ladies from church were over to discuss what could be done to help the community's less fortunate. After arriving home from school, I sat and listened to the conversation; Mama and the ladies seem to know every single family's needs.
3   Mrs. Mayfield's daughter Hannah came along with her to the meeting. She is Ruth's age, and they are two peas in a pod. The girls spent the whole afternoon out on the porch with their dolls.

READ TO UNLOCK MEANING
1. First read the text for comprehension and enjoyment. Use the **Reading Strategy** and **Comprehension Check** questions to support your first read.
2. Go back and respond to the Close-Read note.
3. Identify other details in the text you find interesting. Ask your own questions and draw your own conclusions.

from Survival in the Storm 511

stammering (STA muh rihng) *v.* speaking hesitantly with starts and stops

shuddered (SHUH duhrd) *v.* trembled or quivered

frantically (FRAN tihk lee) *adv.* in a hurried, wild, or desperate way

USE BACKGROUND KNOWLEDGE

What previous experience do you have with events that sent chills down your back or created a deafening roar? How does this background knowledge help you understand what's happening in paragraph 7?

From time to time their laughter floated through the windows, and several ladies commented how nice it is to see carefree little girls like Hannah and Ruth.

4   Mama had just risen from her seat to make more coffee for the ladies when Ruth and Hannah burst in the front door, **stammering** about a big dark cloud coming fast. Looks of alarm traveled quickly around the room as the buzzing women grabbed their pocketbooks and rushed out to the porch.

5   Sure enough, an enormous cloud of yellowish-brown sand was sweeping toward the hill just beyond our farm. I gasped as the women ran to their automobiles and hurriedly drove away. Mama cried, "Dear Lord, help them make it home before it hits!" I **shuddered**, taking one last look at the cloud of sand—it was barreling ahead like a train, never slowing down.

6   Somehow, Ruth was once again absorbed with her doll, and I **frantically** grabbed her and stumbled into the house, shutting the door tightly. I had to urge her to help Mama and me soak sheets in water to hang over the windows and doors. We stuffed towels and rags along the windowsills to catch and filter out as much dirt as possible; without them, it's nearly impossible to breathe.

7   While Ruth placed sheets over our beds and pillows, I pushed a towel tightly under the last window, which was facing the wall of the coming storm. It sent chills down my back as I witnessed the mass of churning dust-fog hit the window right before my eyes with a deafening roar.

8   Ruth and I ran to the kitchen to join Mama, my hands trembling as the winds whipped against the walls, howling and whistling. There was no telling how long it would last, and as I sat down across the table from Mama, the room grew darker and darker, until finally I had to help Mama light the lamps.

9   Even though we had stuffed as many rags and towels against the panes as was possible, the windows still rattled noisily, and I feared any moment they would burst, letting in clouds of choking dust. As it was, there was dirt already seeping in through the cracks, and the room began to fill with foggy darkness. The glow of the lamp grew steadily dimmer, and Mama instructed Ruth and me to cover our noses. I was having trouble breathing even after I placed a damp handkerchief over my nose and mouth. One of these days, I fear our house will outright blow away with the rest of the swirling sand.

10 The door suddenly banged open in the wind, and I heard Daddy stumble in. I was so relieved he was safe; even though I knew he was just putting up the livestock, I'd worried he'd lost his way trying to make it to the house. He sat at the table with us to wait out the storm.

11   We sat in silence as the gusts of wind pounded our little house. It then became so dark, I couldn't see my hand as I stretched it out in front of my face. I kept drawing it nearer and nearer, but I couldn't see my fingers until they were only inches from my face. I knew that if I tried to talk no one would hear me over the deafening roar of the wind. I shut my stinging, burning eyes and buried my head in my arms—I could barely breathe, my eyes were on fire, and everything tasted and smelled like dust. I felt as if I were all alone.

12   I guess I fell asleep, because the next thing I knew, Mama was gently shaking me. I knew right away by the silence that the storm was over. Relief washed over me, like **exhaustion** after running a long, long race. Mama told me it was past 10:00 P.M. She gave me a piece of cornbread that she had wrapped up when the storm first hit, and told me we'll begin cleanup first thing in the morning. Tomorrow will be a day of hard work.

Friday, March 8, 1935

13   I ache all over so much; I don't even know exactly what it is that's aching. Mama called us early. I immediately got out of bed and was dressed soon after, but Ruth didn't even want to wake up. I dreaded having to spend a whole day away from school cleaning with Ruth and Mama.

14   First we strained the water. So much dirt and grit gets mixed in during a duster; it's impossible to get it all out. We had to pour it through a dishcloth several times to filter out the larger grains of

CLOSE READ

ANNOTATE Mark sensory language, or words and phrases related to the five senses, that the author uses in paragraph 11.

QUESTION How does this language contribute to your understanding of the dust storm?

exhaustion (ehg ZAWS chuhn) *n.* extreme tiredness or fatigue

from Survival in the Storm 513

sand. We then set it aside, allowing most of the remaining dirt to settle to the bottom. By suppertime, it was fit for use. It was still a little cloudy, but at least it tasted more like water than dust.

15   Dust covered the floor, and I spent nearly two hours sweeping every last corner, and whisking it out the door. Then Ruth and I proceeded to the front steps, which were completely covered in a huge sand dune. We scooped away, filling our buckets slowly. It didn't really matter where we dumped them, because most of the yard was covered with ripply waves of sand, anyway.

16   It seemed as if no matter how hard I worked, it was never satisfactory for Mama. I shoveled and swept the dirt off the porch, using lots of elbow grease. When Mama came to inspect, she said I needed to sweep the porch all over again, to rid it of the still-lingering grime. Sometimes I don't know which is worse: The dust storms or the cleaning.

17   Daddy spent a good deal of time unblocking the barn doors—the wind had blown a great mound of dirt right up to the door handles. He reported that his wheat had somehow stayed put in the ground, but he didn't know how. Meanwhile, Mama said the cupboards needed to be scrubbed, the sheets aired, and on and on her list continued. By nightfall, we had just completed the last chore, and we were more than ready for bed. At least with Ruth already asleep beside me, I can write in my diary undisturbed.

18   Daddy said if the sandstorms keep coming this bad, we'll have to start going down to the cellar. I think these dusters wear down the people just as much as they wear down the land.

COMPREHENSION CHECK

What do the various members of the family do to prepare for the dust storm to hit?

MEDIA CONNECTION

"The Dust Bowl"

DISCUSS How does the video help you understand the period of American history known as the Dust Bowl in a way that is different from "Black Sunday" and the excerpt from *Survival in the Storm*?

Write your response before sharing your ideas.

BUILD INSIGHT

First Thoughts

Choose one of the following items to answer.
- What part of the description of the dust storm did you find most frightening? Why?
- Which would you find more difficult to cope with—the dust storm or the cleanup? Explain your thinking.

Summary

Write a short objective summary of the text to confirm your comprehension. Remember to include only the main ideas, and do not include your opinions.

Analysis

1. **(a) Compare and Contrast** Reread paragraphs 2 and 3 of the diary entry for Thursday, March 7. How do these paragraphs contrast with the rest of that day's entry? **(b) Speculate** Why do you think the author chose to begin this part of her historical fiction account the way she did?

2. **Analyze** How would you describe Grace, based on her thoughts and actions before and after the dust storm? Cite text evidence to support your answer.

3. **(a) Analyze** The author presents this work of historical fiction in diary form. How does the organizational structure help readers understand events in the story? **(b) Evaluate** Do you think using a diary structure is a good way to present historical fiction? Explain your response.

4. **Compare and Contrast** How does author Katelan Janke use or alter the real-life events shown in the video "The Dust Bowl" in her fictional story *Survival in the Storm*? How true to history is her story?

5. **(a) Draw Conclusions** Is this Grace's first experience with a dust storm? Support your conclusion with text evidence. **(b) Speculate** This selection is an excerpt from a novel. What future events do you think Grace might experience as the novel progresses?

Exploring the Essential Question

How do we overcome life's challenges?

6. What have you learned about overcoming life's challenges by reading this story? What personal qualities help Grace and her family deal with a challenging situation? Record your ideas in your Evidence Log.

STANDARDS
Reading Literature
- Provide an objective summary of the text.
- Compare and contrast a fictional portrayal of a time, place, or character and a historical account of the same period as a means of understanding how authors of fiction use or alter history.

Reading Informational Text
Compare and contrast a text to an audio, video, or multimedia version of the text.

from *Survival in the Storm* 515

ANALYZE AND INTERPRET

from SURVIVAL IN THE STORM

Close Read

1. The model passage and annotation show how one reader analyzed part of paragraph 5. Find another detail in the passage to annotate. Then, write your own question and conclusion.

CLOSE-READ MODEL

… I **gasped** as the women ran to their automobiles and **hurriedly drove away.** Mama **cried**, "Dear Lord, help them make it home before it hits!" I **shuddered**, taking one last look at the cloud of sand—it was **barreling ahead** like a train, **never slowing down.**"

ANNOTATE: The author uses vivid verbs and adverbs to describe the storm and people's reactions to it.

QUESTION: What idea do these words convey?

CONCLUDE: The words show that people are terrified of the storm because it is powerful and unstoppable.

MY QUESTION:

MY CONCLUSION:

2. For more practice, answer the Close-Read question in the selection.

3. Choose a section of the story you found especially important. Mark key details. Then, jot down questions and write your conclusions in the open space next to the text.

Inquiry and Research

Research and Extend Conduct online research to answer this question: *How did photography affect public understanding of the Dust Bowl?* Consult several different sources to answer the question, and identify one photographer whose work is especially noteworthy. Share your findings with a classmate.

STANDARDS

Reading Literature
Determine a theme or central idea of a text and analyze its development over the course of the text.

Writing
Conduct short research projects to answer a question, drawing on several sources.

516 UNIT 5 • FACING ADVERSITY

Essential Question: How do we overcome life's challenges?

Multiple Themes

Every successful literary work develops at least one **theme,** or insight. Themes are expressed as general truths about people or life. You can interpret a story's themes by paying attention to its setting and how characters function within that setting.

Setting: Think about how the physical, cultural, and historical settings affect the story's plot and characters.

- **Physical setting:** Where the story takes place: in a house, in the countryside, during a blizzard, in springtime?
- **Cultural setting:** The mindset, beliefs, and attitudes typical of the people living in the physical setting.
- **Historical setting:** The time or era in which the story events unfold. Where do people work? Are unfair laws in place? Do doctors exist? Is a war raging?

Characters: Think about how characters' actions, attitudes, and experiences may reveal insights about life.

- What conflicts do characters face? Is the main conflict resolved? How?
- Do characters undergo changes in attitude during the story?
- What lessons do characters learn in the course of the story? What ideas about life do the characters' experiences suggest?

PRACTICE Complete the activity.

(a) Distinguish Use the chart to record details from the text that describe the story's physical, cultural, and historical settings and characters' actions, attitudes, and experiences. **(b) Connect** Analyze the story elements you described to identify two different themes. Write the themes as complete sentences in the chart.

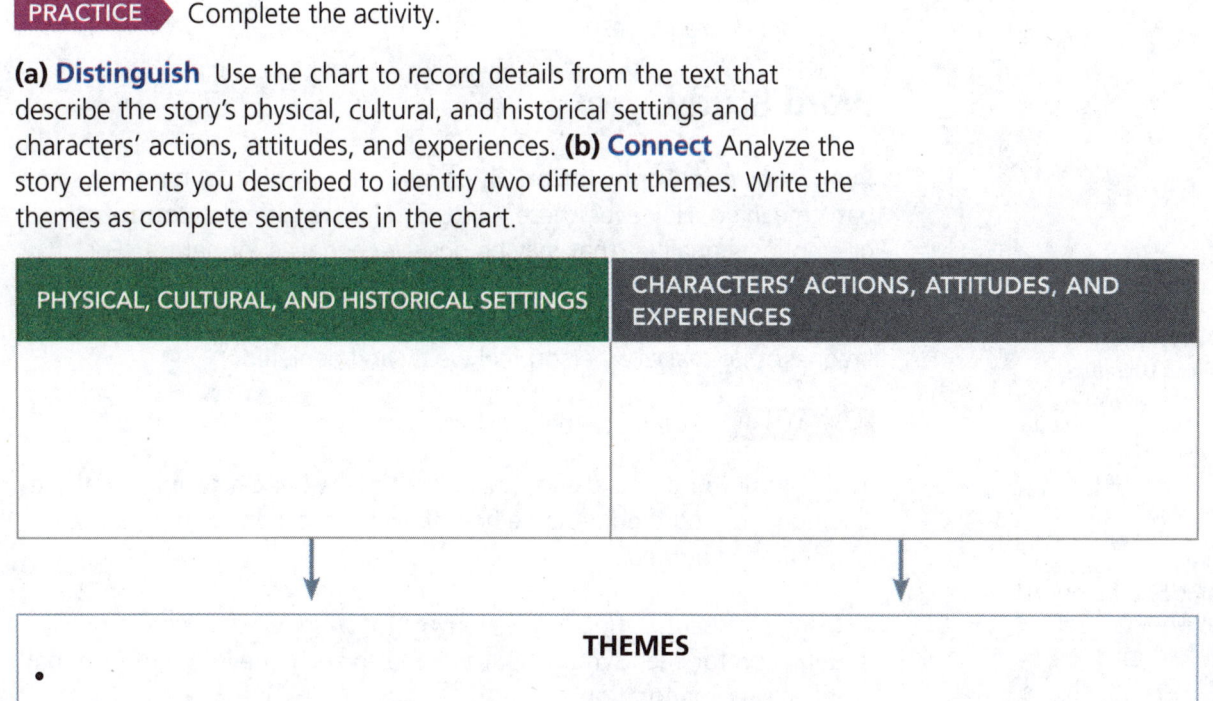

PHYSICAL, CULTURAL, AND HISTORICAL SETTINGS	CHARACTERS' ACTIONS, ATTITUDES, AND EXPERIENCES

THEMES
-
-

from Survival in the Storm

STUDY LANGUAGE AND CRAFT

from SURVIVAL IN THE STORM

Concept Vocabulary

Why These Words? All the vocabulary words relate to how people feel and act when dealing with a disaster or crisis. For example, in an approaching storm, farmers work *frantically* to make their livestock as safe as possible.

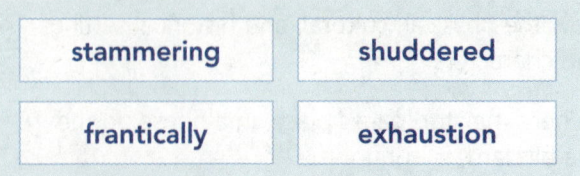

> **WORD WALL**
>
> Note words in the text that are related to the idea of facing adversity. Add them to your Word Wall.

PRACTICE Answer the questions.

1. How do the vocabulary words help you understand how people respond to dust storms?

2. Answer the questions to show your knowledge of the vocabulary words.

   (a) What might cause a person to act *frantically*?

   (b) If someone is *stammering*, what does their speech sound like?

   (c) How does *exhaustion* make someone look and act?

   (d) What kind of story might someone be listening to if they *shuddered* in response?

Word Study

Synonyms and Connotation **Synonyms** are words that have the same basic meaning. However, these words often have different **connotations,** or emotional qualities that may be positive, negative, or neutral. For instance, the vocabulary word *exhaustion* is a synonym for *tiredness,* but *exhaustion* has a more negative connotation. It is a type of extreme tiredness that makes a person feel weary and depleted.

PRACTICE Complete the activities.

1. Use a print or digital dictionary to identify the basic meanings of these synonyms, and then describe how their connotations differ: *frantically / hurriedly*

2. Using a thesaurus, find two synonyms for *shuddered*. Record a precise definition for each synonym, and then use each one in a sentence that reflects its connotation.

> **STANDARDS**
>
> **Reading Literature**
> Determine the meaning of words and phrases as they are used in a text, including figurative and connotative meanings.
>
> **Language**
> • Demonstrate understanding of figurative language, word relationships, and nuances in word meanings.
> • Interpret figures of speech in context.
> • Distinguish among the connotations of words with similar denotations.

518 UNIT 5 • FACING ADVERSITY

Essential Question: How do we overcome life's challenges?

Figurative Language

Writers often use **figurative language**—language that is not intended to be taken literally—to describe and compare things in imaginative ways. Types of figurative language are called **figures of speech.** The chart shows three types that are often found in stories.

FIGURES OF SPEECH		
TYPE	**DEFINITION**	**EXAMPLE**
metaphor	a comparison of seemingly unlike things that says one thing *is* the other	The wind *was a steamroller* flattening everything in its path.
simile	a comparison of seemingly unlike things that points out a similarity using the words *like* or *as*	The dark room felt *like the inside of a tomb*.
idiom	an expression that has meaning particular to a language or region; its meaning can't be figured out by defining its words	They *hit the sack* after finishing the exhausting cleanup.

PRACTICE Complete the activity and answer the questions.

1. **Analyze** Read each passage from the selection. In the chart, identify the figure of speech in the passage as a *metaphor,* a *simile,* or an *idiom*. In the last column, explain the effect of each figure of speech.

PASSAGE	FIGURE OF SPEECH	EFFECT
Paragraph 12: Relief washed over me, like exhaustion after running a long, long race.		
Paragraph 15: ...most of the yard was covered with ripply waves of sand, anyway.		
Paragraph 16: I shoveled and swept the dirt off the porch, using lots of elbow grease.		

2. **Analyze** Review the figures of speech used by the narrator. What do these word choices suggest about her world?

from Survival in the Storm

TEST PRACTICE

HISTORICAL NONFICTION

BLACK SUNDAY

HISTORICAL FICTION

from SURVIVAL IN THE STORM

COMPARE: NONFICTION and FICTION
Multiple Choice

These questions are based on the article "Black Sunday" and the excerpt from *Survival in the Storm*. Choose the best answer to each question.

1. Which victims of the Dust Bowl are featured in both texts?

   A folk singers   **B** farmers

   C politicians   **D** newspaper reporters

2. Read paragraph 7 of the nonfiction selection and paragraph 8 of the fiction excerpt. How does the first passage compare to the second?

Historical Nonfiction
"Black Sunday," as the storm became known, was the death knell for the poor farmers of Oklahoma and Texas. Demoralized and impoverished, thousands of so-called "Okies" cut their losses and began the long migration to more favorable locations like California.

Historical Fiction
Daddy said if the sandstorms keep coming this bad, we'll have to start going down to the cellar. I think these dusters wear down the people just as much as they wear down the land.

   A The nonfiction passage contradicts the opinion expressed in the fiction passage.

   B Both passages state a fact that is supported by evidence.

   C The passages refer to different, unrelated effects of the Dust Bowl.

   D The nonfiction passage supports the opinion expressed in the fiction passage.

3. Erin Blakemore wrote the historical nonfiction piece, and Katelan Janke wrote the historical fiction piece. Which answer choice best describes the difference in the authors' approaches to writing about the Dust Bowl?

   A Blakemore focuses on the events and effects of Black Sunday. Janke focuses on how a family survives a dust storm.

   B Blakemore focuses on how folk songs made the dust storms widely known. Janke focuses on how hard Grace has to work.

   C Blakemore focuses on how the term "Dust Bowl" came into use. Janke focuses on how fast dust storms can travel.

   D Blakemore focuses on the events and effects of Black Sunday. Janke focuses on how Grace's family will survive the *next* dust storm.

STANDARDS

Reading Literature
Compare and contrast a fictional portrayal of a time, place, or character and a historical account of the same period as a means of understanding how authors of fiction use or alter history.

Reading Informational Text
Analyze how two or more authors writing about the same topic shape their presentations of key information by emphasizing different evidence or advancing different interpretations of facts.

Writing
Write informative/explanatory texts to examine a topic and convey ideas, concepts, and information through the selection, organization, and analysis of relevant content.

Essential Question: How do we overcome life's challenges?

Short Response

1. **(a) Distinguish** Cite two examples of descriptive language from each text that help paint a vivid picture of the Dust Bowl. Explain the reasons for your choices. **(b) Evaluate** Which text does a more effective job at bringing to life the living conditions during the Dust Bowl period? Explain.

2. **(a) Analyze** How does the genre of each text affect the way in which the author presents historical facts? **(b) Make a Judgment** Which form of writing did you prefer reading, the historical nonfiction text or the historical fiction text? Explain your choice.

3. **Synthesize** How does the information presented in the nonfiction text help you understand the fiction text, and vice versa? Explain.

Timed Writing

A **comparison-and-contrast essay** is an informational text that analyzes the similarities and differences between two or more subjects.

Assignment

Write a **comparison-and-contrast essay** in which you explore how authors Blakemore and Janke use different genres to express insights about the Dust Bowl and its effects. In what ways do both genres present truths about historical events? How are the truths they express alike? How are they different?

5-Minute Planner

1. Read the assignment carefully and underline key words.
2. Decide what you want to say—your central idea, or thesis.
3. Decide which details and examples you'll use from each text to develop your ideas.
4. Organize your ideas, making sure to address these points:
   - Explain how the insights in each text are similar.
   - Explain how the insights in each text are different.
   - Explain how the author of each text uses characteristics of its genre to convey ideas.

> **EVIDENCE LOG**
>
> Before moving on to a new selection, go to your Evidence Log and record any additional thoughts and observations you may have about "Black Sunday" and *Survival in the Storm*.

LEARN ABOUT GENRE: NONFICTION

Reading Informational Articles

An **informational article** is a short nonfiction piece that informs readers about a particular topic.

A MORE ACCESSIBLE WORLD

The selection you are about to read is an informational article.

INFORMATIONAL ARTICLE

Author's Purpose
- to inform readers about real people, situations, and events

Characteristics
- presents factual information about a topic
- expresses a central, or main, idea
- uses varied types of supporting evidence
- typically includes text features, such as headings, sidebars, and images with captions
- often includes references to research studies or experts in the field

Structure
- follows a logical organizational pattern that clarifies ideas and information
- may use text features to help provide structure

Take a Minute!

FIND IT Think of a topic you like reading and learning about, such as a particular interest or hobby. Conduct a brief internet search to find an informational article related to that topic. Jot down its title and publication details.

STANDARDS
Reading Informational Text
Analyze the structure an author uses to organize a text, including how the major sections contribute to the whole and to the development of the ideas.

Essential Question: How do we overcome life's challenges?

Organizational Structure: Text Features

Authors of nonfiction carefully organize information in a way that makes the content easy for readers to follow. A well-structured informational article will often include **text features** that clarify information and help develop the author's ideas.

TEXT FEATURE	EXPLANATION
Headings	Headings help identify the topic of each major section. They also give readers a place to pause before reading on.
Illustrations	Complicated ideas can be illustrated, making them easier to understand.
Pull-Quotes	Brief passages from the text itself can be displayed off to the side, highlighting key information in an engaging way.
Images and Captions	Photos, graphs, diagrams, and other images add visual information to support the ideas in an article. Captions explain what the images show.
Sidebars	Sidebars are mini-articles on a topic related to the main article. Often set off in a box, a sidebar may have its own headings, examples, quotations, images, and captions.

PRACTICE Answer the questions about organizational structure. Explain each of your answers.

1. An author has drafted an article and is disappointed that an interesting, related topic doesn't fit well in the body text. To include this information, which text feature might the author use?

2. An author has drafted an article that includes a complex scientific idea. To make sure readers grasp it, which text feature might the author include?

3. An author has drafted an article that has several paragraphs. To help readers follow the development of ideas, which text feature might the author include?

Learn About Genre 523

PREPARE TO READ

A More Accessible World

About the Author

Lisa Christensen is a writer living in Salt Lake City, Utah. She writes for *Muse* magazine and other publications.

Concept Vocabulary

Predict The words here appear in the article. Judging from these words, predict what kind of information the article might contain.

WORDS FROM THE ARTICLE	MY EXPECTATIONS
accessible (ihk SEH suh buhl) *adj.* easy to use; *Will the steep stairs be accessible to everyone?*	
tactile (TAK tuhl) *adj.* relating to the sense of touch; *We felt the surface of each sculpture in the tactile exhibition.*	
audibly (AW duh blee) *adv.* in a way that can be heard; *The woman who gave us directions spoke audibly, despite the noisy traffic.*	
sensors (SEHN suhrz) *n.* devices that respond to a physical event, such as heat or pressure; *The sensors respond to high heat with a series of beeps.*	
navigate (NA vuh gayt) *v.* find a way through; *You must navigate many paths to reach the lake.*	
embossed (ehm BAWST) *v.* marked with a raised pattern; *A design was embossed on each card.*	

Reading Strategy: Preview and Predict

When you **preview** a text, you skim quickly through it. Doing so will enable you to **predict**, or anticipate, what kinds of information you will be reading about. After you preview and predict, decide on a reading rate that suits the text you will be studying. For example, you may want to read a science article more slowly than you might read a short story.

PRACTICE Preview the text, and predict what it will cover. Then, decide on a reading rate that suits the text.

STANDARDS
Reading Informational Text
Cite several pieces of textual evidence to support analysis of what the text says explicitly as well as inferences drawn from the text.
Language
Gather vocabulary knowledge when considering a word or phrase important to comprehension or expression.

524 UNIT 5 • FACING ADVERSITY

INFORMATIONAL ARTICLE

A More Accessible World

Lisa Christensen

BACKGROUND
Many people in the United States have blindness or low vision. According to the National Federation of the Blind, in 2016 more than seven million people aged sixteen through seventy-five experienced visual disabilities. Yet we have a long way to go in designing public places and devices that these individuals can use with ease. This article suggests several ways of meeting this challenge.

1   What do you think about when you wait at a crosswalk? What about browsing the internet? Chances are, if you're not visually impaired, you don't think much about these everyday activities as you're doing them. But for people with blindness or low vision, these sorts of things can be difficult if the people designing them don't take steps to make them **accessible**.

2   About 90 percent of people who are "legally blind" have some sight—they can make out some amount of light or movement. But

READ TO UNLOCK MEANING

1. First read the text for comprehension and enjoyment. Use the **Comprehension Check** question to support your first read.
2. Go back and respond to the Close Read note.
3. Identify other details in the text you find interesting. Ask your own questions, and draw your own conclusions.

accessible (ihk SEH suh buhl) *adj.* easy to use

their vision isn't good enough to allow them to interact with the world in the same ways as seeing people. They might use a seeing-eye dog or white cane to get around, or use a text reader to help them access written material. Audio descriptions of scenes in TV shows and movies also let blind people enjoy the latest streaming hit and blockbuster.

Some Surprising Obstacles

3   In stores and restaurants, automatic kiosks are convenient options for many people, but can make life more difficult for people who are blind if they're not designed with accessibility in mind. Those kiosks often use a touch screen, which is harder for blind people to use than something with **tactile** buttons.

4   Delivery apps can be inconvenient, too, says Everette Bacon, president of the Utah chapter of the National Federation of the Blind. "Delivery is something you would think blind people would welcome and we do, but a lot of the delivery applications were very inaccessible, and they also weren't thought of with us in mind at all," he says.

5   To be more accessible, those apps need tools like descriptions of an item or dish rather than relying on a picture to do the trick. Pictures on apps and websites can create barriers for those who are visually impaired. Text readers can **audibly** deliver text and describe pictures—but only if the site or app developer followed accessibility standards such as the Web Content Accessibility Guidelines. Unfortunately, those guidelines aren't always followed.

Don't Make Assumptions

6   One big problem blind people persistently face is the assumptions of sighted people about what they can and can't do. Bacon says more than once he's had a stranger grab his elbow, thinking he needs help.

7   "It's impressions about blindness that are far more threatening to blind people than the blindness itself," says Daniel Kish, president of World Access for the Blind.

8   Assumptions about capability contribute to a low number of blind and low-vision people working in or studying STEM (science, technology, engineering, and math) fields. People with low or no vision have a lot to offer in these fields. They are just as capable as anyone else at experimenting and making new discoveries. They just need accessible ways to interact with data and scientific equipment.

9   One device helping give those students that experience is the Sci-Voice Talking LabQuest 2, a tool that reads aloud data from over 70 **sensors** commonly used in science experiments. Cary Supalo

---

tactile (TAK tuhl) *adj.* relating to the sense of touch

audibly (AW duh blee) *adv.* in a way that can be heard

sensors (SEHN suhrz) *n.* devices that respond to a physical event such as heat or pressure

invented this device to help students experience hands-on science learning. He is the founder of Independence Science and has been blind since the age of seven. "For kids who are blind or vision impaired, before this technology existed, they had to be told what happened," he says.

How You Can Help

10   Making the world more accessible isn't limited to inventing a cool new piece of technology, though. If you're posting a picture or meme on social media, adding a specific description of what's happening in the picture, called alt text, can help people who are blind understand your post without having to rely on sight. If you're building a website, or know someone who is, follow accessibility guidelines.

COMPREHENSION CHECK

According to the author, what keeps people with blindness or low vision from participating in STEM fields?

A More Accessible World   527

11   And if you see something that could be inaccessible to blind people—in a store, at school, online—contacting someone in charge and asking them to make it more readily available to others can go a long way, says Bacon. Understanding how blind and vision-impaired people **navigate** the world can be a first step in helping to make it more accessible for them.

navigate (NA vuh gayt) *v.* find a way through

SCIENCE WITHOUT SIGHT

In October, a group of teens who are blind gathered in Salt Lake City to make some thermite reactions—that is, some fireballs! They measured ingredients and assembled three aluminum cans for the experiment. A device called Sci-Voice Talking LabQuest 2 helped them audibly keep track of their measurements.

Then—outside, under the supervision of several scientists—they set off three fireballs on different surfaces: concrete, a steel plate, and a pile of sand. Instruments measured the heat transfer the fireballs sent through each surface and read the rising temperatures aloud. That data was **embossed** on paper so the students could feel the graph to notice how dramatically each experiment affected the temperature of each surface. Students could also feel the residual heat and touch the cooled-down stony waste, called slag. By examining the results of the experiment and hypothesizing about how the differences between the three fireballs could have changed the results, the teens participated in the scientific process. "Most blind kids in public schools are given very little science learning," says Ned Lindholm, a chemist and professor at Salt Lake Community College who is blind. "Hands-on learning is vital in science. That's being kept away from most blind kids."

Ashley Neybert, a curriculum designer for Independence Science who is blind and also helped with the event, says she's hoping devices like the Sci-Voice Talking LabQuest used in this experiment can fix that. "We don't want students of the future to struggle like we did."

embossed (ehm BAWST) *v.* marked with a raised pattern

CLOSE READ

ANNOTATE Mark quotations the author includes in the sidebar.

QUESTION Why do you think the author included these quotations? How do they affect the quality and reliability of the information in the article?

BUILD INSIGHT

First Thoughts

Choose one of the following items to answer.

- If you have full vision, what questions do you have after reading this article? What would you like to ask a person with blindness or low vision so that you better understand their needs?
- If you have blindness or low vision, what information would you want to add to this article?

Summary

Write a short objective summary of the article that could help someone understand the challenges faced by people with blindness or low vision.

Analysis

1. **(a) Analyze** How does the author begin paragraph 1? **(b) Evaluate** Do you find that an effective way to begin the article? Why, or why not?

2. **Speculate** Reread paragraph 3. How do you envision a kiosk that would be accessible to people who are blind?

3. **(a)** What does the author say about common assumptions concerning individuals who are blind? **(b) Evaluate** Does the author provide convincing evidence that these assumptions are widespread? Explain.

4. **Analyze** What seems to be the author's purpose in paragraphs 10 and 11? Cite details that support your response.

5. **Connect** Reread the sidebar "Science Without Sight." How might a device similar to Sci-Voice Talking LabQuest 2 help students who are blind in classes other than science?

Exploring the Essential Question

How do we overcome life's challenges?

6. What have you learned about overcoming life's challenges by reading "A More Accessible World"? For example, does the article make you consider situations and circumstances you have not considered before? Record your ideas in your Evidence Log.

STANDARDS

Reading Informational Text
- Cite several pieces of textual evidence to support analysis of what the text says explicitly as well as inferences drawn from the text.
- Provide an objective summary of the text.

ANALYZE AND INTERPRET

A MORE ACCESSIBLE WORLD

Close Read

1. The model passage and annotation show how one reader analyzed the second paragraph of the sidebar "Science Without Sight." Find another detail in the passage to annotate. Then, write your own question and conclusion.

CLOSE-READ MODEL

Then—outside, under the supervision of several scientists— they set off three fireballs on different surfaces: concrete, a steel plate, and a pile of sand. Instruments measured the heat transfer the fireballs sent through each surface and read the rising temperatures aloud.

ANNOTATE: The author includes information set off by dashes in this description of a student experiment.

QUESTION: Why does she include this extra information?

CONCLUDE: She wants to show that the experiment's organizers took precautions to ensure the students' safety.

MY QUESTION:

MY CONCLUSION:

2. For more practice, answer the Close Read question in the selection.
3. Choose a section of the informational article you found especially meaningful. Mark important details. Then, jot down questions and write your conclusions in the open space next to the text.

Inquiry and Research

Research and Extend Extend your learning by choosing one of the questions below. Perform brief online research to find the answer.

- How can a person write effective alt text?
- When and by whom were the Web Content Accessibility Guidelines developed?

STANDARDS

Reading Informational Text
Analyze the structure an author uses to organize a text, including how the major sections contribute to the whole and to the development of the ideas.

Writing
Conduct short research projects to answer a question.

Essential Question: How do we overcome life's challenges?

Organizational Structure: Text Features

Informational articles often include complex ideas. To make these ideas easy for readers to follow, an author develops an **organizational structure** that will often include various **text features.** In "A More Accessible World," the author uses these types of text features:

- **Headings** that organize text sections and state or hint at the topic of each section.

- **Images**, in the form of photographs, that provide visual information to accompany the text.

- A **sidebar**, or special feature, that relates to the information in the article but is set off from it.

PRACTICE Complete the activity and answer the questions.

1. **Analyze** List the headings within the article, and then provide a summary of the information found in each section.

HEADING	SUMMARY

2. **(a) Analyze** To what extent do the images help you understand the text? **(b) Evaluate** Would the article be as effective without the images? Why, or why not?

3. **(a)** What information in the article does the sidebar relate to? **(b) Analyze** How does the sidebar contribute to your understanding of that information?

STUDY LANGUAGE AND CRAFT

A MORE ACCESSIBLE WORLD

Concept Vocabulary

Why These Words? All the vocabulary words are related to things that can help people with low or no vision. For example, a device's *tactile* features can make it easier to use.

| accessible | tactile | audibly |
| sensors | navigate | embossed |

PRACTICE Answer the question and complete the activity.

1. How do the vocabulary words help you understand the concept of accessibility for people with blindness?

2. Use one vocabulary word to complete each sentence.

   (a) Because the actor did not speak _____, I misunderstood some of his lines.

   (b) The alarm went off when _____ detected smoke.

   (c) Knitting with soft, silky yarns is a _____ pleasure.

   (d) Parts of this collage are _____ with star-shaped details.

   (e) App designers can use features that make content _____ to people who are blind.

   (f) This detailed map will help as I _____ these hiking trails.

Word Study

Antonyms and Latin Prefix: *in-* The prefix *in-* means "not." Adding this prefix to an adjective or adverb produces an **antonym**, or word with the opposite meaning. For example, *accessible* + *in-* = *inaccessible*, meaning "not accessible" or "not easy to use."

PRACTICE Complete the following items.

1. Add the prefix *in-* to each word. Then write a definition for the antonym you created. Check a print or online dictionary to confirm the antonym's meaning.

   (a) audibly
   (b) capable
   (c) expensive

2. Choose one of the antonyms you created and use it in a sentence that shows you understand its meaning.

> **WORD WALL**
> Note words in the text that are related to the idea of facing adversity. Add them to your Word Wall.

STANDARDS
Language
• Use a comma to separate coordinate adjectives.
• Use common, grade-appropriate Greek or Latin affixes and roots as clues to the meaning of a word.
• Use the relationship between particular words to better understand each of the words.

532 UNIT 5 • FACING ADVERSITY

Essential Question: How do we overcome life's challenges?

Adjectives

An **adjective** is a word that modifies, or describes, a noun or pronoun. Different adjectives answer different kinds of questions, as shown in the chart. The adjectives are underlined. Notice that possessive nouns and pronouns can be used as adjectives too.

What kind?	You'll enjoy this <u>useful</u> app.	Which one?	Has Kate finished reading <u>that</u> manual?
How many?	They need <u>eight</u> volunteers.	Whose?	We joined <u>Ron's</u> team.

Coordinate adjectives are two or more adjectives that modify the same noun and are separated by a comma. You can tell whether adjectives are coordinate if the word *and* could be used in place of the comma and you could reverse the adjectives. **Cumulative adjectives** also modify the same noun, but they are not separated by a comma and cannot be reversed.

COORDINATE ADJECTIVES	CUMULATIVE ADJECTIVES
It was a brilliant, simple design. You could say: *It was a brilliant and simple design.* or: *It was a simple, brilliant design.*	We used pale yellow paint in the bedroom. It is not correct to say: *We used yellow pale paint in the bedroom.*

READ Underline the adjectives in each sentence, and circle the nouns they modify. Identify the adjectives as *coordinate* or *cumulative*.

1. Is there a way to solve this puzzling technological problem?

2. The team is trying to develop an effective, inexpensive solution.

3. Users experience frequent technical glitches when using this software.

WRITE / EDIT Underline the adjectives in each sentence. Add or delete a comma between the adjectives if needed. Write "no change" if no change is necessary.

1. The friendly, seeing-eye dog is about to begin work.

2. A devoted caring trainer taught the dog to act as a guide.

3. The owner grasps the dog's bright blue harness.

4. Together they make a capable energetic team.

SHARE IDEAS

A MORE ACCESSIBLE WORLD

TIP: Remember that *accurate sources* provide correct, up-to-date information, and *credible sources* provide trustworthy information from experts.

STANDARDS
Writing
• Support claim(s) with logical reasoning and relevant evidence, using accurate, credible sources and demonstrating an understanding of the topic or text.

• Use technology, including the Internet, to produce and publish writing and link to and cite sources.

Speaking and Listening
• Present claims and findings, emphasizing salient points in a focused, coherent manner with pertinent descriptions, facts, details, and examples; use appropriate eye contact, adequate volume, and clear pronunciation.

• Include multimedia components and visual displays in presentations to clarify claims and findings and emphasize salient points.

Writing

A **persuasive email** is a formal text that is typed and sent to make a request or solve a problem. It must include convincing reasons that will encourage the reader to take action.

Assignment

Write a **persuasive email** to a business owner, encouraging them to add specific accessibility options to the company's website, kiosk, menu, or building. To find ideas, reread paragraphs 10–11 of the article. In addition, conduct research using accurate and credible sources. Then draft your email.

- Start with a respectful greeting.
- Clearly state your claim—what you would like the business owner to do and why it is important.
- Provide support for your request. Give clear reasons that show you understand the issue. Include relevant evidence to support each reason, organized in a logical way.
- Maintain a formal style as you write. Be polite and use correct English. Avoid making demands or finding fault.
- End with a conclusion that restates your request.

After writing, trade arguments with a partner. Evaluate your partner's work by answering these questions:

- Did the writer state the claim clearly?
- Did the writer use sound, logical reasoning?
- Did the writer include evidence that relates to and supports the claim?

Reflect on Your Writing

PRACTICE Respond to these questions.

1. What was the most enjoyable part of the assignment?

2. What could you add to your email to make it more convincing?

3. **Why These Words?** The words you choose make a difference in your writing. Which words did you select to persuade your reader?

Essential Question: How do we overcome life's challenges?

Speaking and Listening

A **multimedia research presentation** offers information about a carefully researched topic. The presentation includes both spoken words and visual elements.

> ### Assignment
>
> Prepare a **multimedia research presentation** on one of these topics:
>
> ○ a specific accessible device or assistive technology (such as a text-to-speech tool or portable captioning)
>
> ○ a person who has fought for the rights of people with disabilities (such as Judy Heumann or Alan Reich)
>
> Then, deliver your presentation to your class or a small group.

Conduct Research Choose your topic, and use several reliable, up-to-date print and online resources to gather information about it. Take notes, and then organize your findings in an outline that will guide your presentation. Include citations and links for your sources so that you or your listeners can access the information later, if desired.

Prepare Visuals Decide which visuals to use to emphasize your main points, such as a poster, a labeled diagram, photos, or a time line of events. Consider producing a slideshow with audio and visual elements. Use graphics and formatting that will make information easy to grasp. On your outline, indicate when you will present each visual.

Present and Evaluate As you give your presentation, speak clearly and loudly enough for listeners to hear. Introduce each visual as you present it, and allow time for the audience to take it in. When it is your turn to listen, be attentive and respectful. Use a guide like the one shown to evaluate your presentation as well as those of your classmates.

TIP: Evaluate sources for research. Make sure they are credible and accurate. Avoid those that seem biased or unfair.

PRESENTATION EVALUATION GUIDE

Rate each statement on a scale of 1 (not demonstrated) to 4 (fully demonstrated).

Statement	1	2	3	4
The speaker presented relevant facts, details, and examples from their research.	○	○	○	○
The visuals were clear and easy to understand.	○	○	○	○
The speaker used clear pronunciation and appropriate volume.	○	○	○	○

EVIDENCE LOG

Before moving on to a new selection, go to your Evidence Log and record any additional thoughts and observations you may have about "A More Accessible World."

PERFORMANCE TASK

Write an Informational Essay

An **informational essay** is a brief work of nonfiction in which a writer educates readers about a topic.

Assignment

Write an **informational essay** in which you respond to the following question:

What does it mean to overcome adversity?

Support your ideas with details from your reading, background knowledge, and personal observations. Use the elements of informational essays in your writing.

Use Academic Vocabulary Try to use one or more of the unit's academic vocabulary words in your informational essay: *deviate, persevere, determination, diversity, observation*.

WRITING CENTER
Visit the Writing Center to watch video tutorials and view annotated student models and rubrics.

ELEMENTS OF INFORMATIONAL ESSAYS

Purpose: to provide information and explanations about a topic

Characteristics
- a clear thesis statement, or central idea
- relevant supporting evidence, such as facts, examples, and quotations
- precise language and well-chosen transitions
- definitions of unfamiliar or technical terms
- a formal style and an objective point of view
- standard English conventions, including correct use of conjunctive adverbs

Structure
- an engaging introduction that previews the content of the essay
- a coherent and focused flow of ideas within and across paragraphs
- a strong conclusion that supports the information presented

STANDARDS
Writing
• Write informative/explanatory texts to examine a topic and convey ideas, concepts, and information through the selection, organization, and analysis of relevant content.
• Develop the topic with relevant facts, definitions, concrete details, quotations, or other information and examples.
• Use precise language and domain-specific vocabulary to inform about or explain the topic.

536 UNIT 5 • FACING ADVERSITY

Essential Question: How do we overcome life's challenges?

Take a Closer Look at the Assignment

1. What is the assignment asking me to do (in my own words)?

2. Is a specific **audience** mentioned in the assignment?
- ◯ Yes   If "yes," who is my main audience?
- ◯ No   If "no," who do I think my audience is or should be?

3. (a) Does the assignment ask me to provide specific types of **relevant evidence**?
- ◯ Yes   If "yes," what are they?
- ◯ No   If "no," what types of evidence do I think I need?

(b) Where will I get the evidence? What details can I pull from my Evidence Log?

> **AUDIENCE**
>
> Always keep your **audience**, or readers, in mind when you write. Define specialized terms or other information that they may not know.

> **EVIDENCE**
>
> **Relevant evidence,** or details related to your topic, will make your essay stronger.
> - **Facts:** information that can be proved true
> - **Definitions:** explanations of unfamiliar terms
> - **Examples:** specific instances or brief narratives that illustrate facts or concepts
> - **Direct Quotations:** people's exact words set off with quotation marks

Write Your Informational Essay

Review the assignment and your notes, and then begin writing your informational essay. Keep these tips in mind:

- Introduce your topic clearly, and organize your ideas in a logical way.
- Use evidence to develop the topic and support your ideas.
- Include transitions to show the relationships between ideas and supporting evidence.
- End with a conclusion that reinforces the information you presented.

Writer's Handbook: If you need help as you plan, draft, revise, and edit, refer to the Writer's Handbook pages that follow.

WRITER'S HANDBOOK | INFORMATIONAL ESSAY

Planning and Prewriting

Before you draft, decide what you want to say and how you want to say it. Complete the activities to get started.

Discover Your Topic: Freewrite!

Keep your topic in mind as you write quickly and freely for at least three minutes without stopping.

- Don't worry about your spelling or grammar (you'll fix mistakes later).
- When time is up, pause and reread what you wrote. Mark ideas or details that seem strong or interesting.
- Repeat the process several times. When you begin a new round, start with the strong ideas you marked earlier.

Using the Writer's Handbook

In this handbook you'll find strategies to support every stage of the writing process—from planning to publishing. As you write, check in with yourself:
- *What's going well?*
- *What isn't going well?*

Then, use the handbook items that will best help you craft a strong informational essay.

WRITE What does it mean to overcome adversity?

_____
_____
_____
_____
_____
_____
_____
_____
_____
_____
_____
_____

STANDARDS

Wrtiting • Introduce a topic clearly, previewing what is to follow; organize ideas, concepts, and information, using strategies such as definition, classification, comparison/contrast, and cause/ effect; include formatting, graphics, and multimedia when useful to aiding comprehension.
• Use appropriate transitions to create cohesion and clarify the relationships among ideas and concepts. • Provide a concluding statement or section that follows from and supports the information or explanation presented.

Structure Ideas: Make a Plan

A **Collect Your Ideas** Review your freewriting and decide which ideas and details you want to include in your essay. Don't worry about the order yet.

_____
_____
_____
_____

B **Write a Thesis Statement** Write one sentence that expresses the central idea, or main point, of your essay.

_____
_____

THESIS STATEMENT

Your **thesis statement** should present your topic clearly. Begin by writing one key idea, avoiding any unnecessary words. As you draft and revise, you can clarify your thesis statement.

C **Plan a Structure** Figure out what you want to say in each section of your essay so that your ideas build in a focused way.

I. Introduction: Consider how to blend your thesis statement into your introduction. This paragraph should preview the information your essay will discuss and show that your topic is interesting and important.

II. Body Paragraphs: Write a topic sentence for each paragraph and list the evidence you will use to support it. Think about transitions, formatting, and graphics you might include to guide readers and organize information.

III. Conclusion: Remind readers of your thesis, and leave them with a strong impression.

STRUCTURE

A clear **structure,** or organization of ideas, strengthens the focus of your essay and helps readers follow your thinking. These two types of structures work well in informational writing:

- **Subtopic:** Break a topic into smaller, related subtopics and then give each subtopic a heading.
- **Cause-and-Effect:** Examine how a particular situation leads to another, which in turn leads to another.

_____
_____
_____
_____
_____
_____
_____
_____

Writer's Handbook: Informational Essay

WRITER'S HANDBOOK | **INFORMATIONAL ESSAY**

Drafting

Apply the planning work you've done and write a first draft. Start with your introduction, which should grab your reader's attention and hint at some of the information you will cover in your essay.

Read Like a Writer

Reread the first few paragraphs of the Mentor Text. Mark details that make you want to find out more. One observation has been done for you.

MENTOR TEXT

from **Against the Odds**

"If you have to ditch a commercial aircraft in the Hudson River," the news anchor joked, "this is the guy you want." That guy was Chesley Sullenberger. As a 29-year veteran of US Airways and a former Air Force fighter pilot, he had what it took to land his plane safely and save his passengers' lives.

On January 15, 2009, Sullenberger was the pilot on US Airways Flight 1549 from New York's LaGuardia Airport to Charlotte, North Carolina.

> This quotation is dramatic and also gives important facts. Readers will want to know more.

> Mark key facts the author has provided.

WRITE Write your introduction. Follow the Mentor Text example, and start with a dramatic quotation that also presents key facts you will discuss later in your essay.

_____
_____
_____
_____
_____
_____
_____
_____
_____

DEVELOP IDEAS

As you draft the rest of your essay, make your writing thoughtful and informative.

- **Audience** Give your audience the background information they need to understand your ideas.
- **Style** Use formal language; avoid slang.
- **Development** Support your ideas with relevant evidence, including facts, details, and strong examples.

STANDARDS
Writing • Introduce a topic clearly, previewing what is to follow. • Use appropriate transitions to create cohesion and clarify the relationships among ideas and concepts. • Establish and maintain a formal style.

540 UNIT 5 • FACING ADVERSITY

Coherence and Craft

As you draft your essay, use transitions to create coherence. A **coherent** essay "holds together" within and across paragraphs. Use **transitions** to show how ideas are related and how they build on one another. There are two basic types of transitions:

- **Transitional words and phrases** create smooth connections between sentences and paragraphs, making your essay easy to follow.
- **Conjunctive adverbs** connect ideas in two independent clauses.

SAMPLE TRANSITIONS

Relationship Between Ideas	Transitional Words and Phrases	Conjunctive Adverbs
time sequence	before; by the time that	eventually; next
contrast	but; on the contrary	however; conversely
comparison	as; like; in the same way	similarly; likewise
cause-and-effect	because; under the circumstances	therefore; consequently
add information	also; for example	additionally; moreover

TRANSITIONS AND PUNCTUATION

- When you use a conjunctive adverb to connect two independent clauses, place a semicolon before the adverb and a comma after it.
- When you use a conjunctive adverb at the beginning of a sentence, follow it with a comma.

WRITE Write a paragraph of your essay here. Include transitions that show the connections between sentences. Then, write the first sentence of the next paragraph, using a transition. Consider different sentence types, and be sure to punctuate correctly.

SENTENCE VARIETY

Add variety by choosing different sentence types and varying your transitions.

EXAMPLE:
Use conjunctive adverbs to form compound sentences. *He spent decades in the military; subsequently, he became a successful pilot.*

EXAMPLE:
Use a transitional word or phrase, but keep two simple sentences. *He spent decades in the military. After that, he became a successful pilot.*

Writer's Handbook: Informational Essay

WRITER'S HANDBOOK INFORMATIONAL ESSAY

Revising

Now that you have a first draft, revise it to to be sure it conveys information as effectively as possible.

Read Like a Writer

Review the revisions made to the Mentor Text. Then, answer the questions in the white boxes.

MENTOR TEXT

from **Against the Odds**

The 150 passengers felt a powerful thud against the airplane, followed by vibrations from the engine. *One passenger said it sounded like sneakers thumping around in a dryer.* ~~There was a loud explosion.~~ The cabin filled up with smoke. ~~There was a loud explosion.~~ There was a horrible smell and then an eerie quiet: both engines were disabled.

Sullenberger made a Mayday radio call to air traffic control and ~~he's like all calm!~~ *calmly explained the situation.* They discussed the options: The plane could either return to LaGuardia or land at Teterboro Airport in New Jersey.

> Why do you think the writer added this detail?

> Why do you think the writer moved this sentence?

> The writer changed some words to maintain a formal style.

Peer Review Partner with a classmate to review your completed drafts. When you review:

- Locate and evaluate the thesis statement. Is the thesis clear?
- Review the body paragraphs. Do they appear in logical order? Do they support the thesis statement?
- Do any statements lack support? Suggest adding evidence, as needed.
- Evaluate your peer's use of language. Is their writing style appropriate and formal? Mark instances of informal and vague language that should be replaced with precise words.

Once your partner returns your draft, review their suggestions. Refer to the Revision Checklist as you revise your essay.

STANDARDS
Writing • Develop the topic with relevant facts, definitions, concrete details, quotations, or other information and examples. • Use precise language and domain-specific vocabulary to inform about or explain the topic. • Establish and maintain a formal style. • Provide a concluding statement or section that follows from and supports the information or explanation presented.

Take a Closer Look at Your Draft

Use the Revision Checklist for Informational Essays to evaluate and strengthen your writing.

REVISION CHECKLIST FOR INFORMATIONAL ESSAYS

EVALUATE	TAKE ACTION
Clarity	
☐ Is my thesis statement clear?	If your thesis isn't clear, **say** your main point out loud as though you were speaking to a friend. Use that statement to help **clarify** the idea you want to express.
Development	
☐ Have I provided enough information to explain the topic?	**List** your main ideas—the topic sentence of each paragraph. • **Add** evidence for ideas that need more support. • **Delete** details that are not relevant.
☐ Have I used a variety of relevant evidence?	• **Add** facts or quotations to support your thesis. • **Add** examples or definitions to illustrate your facts.
Organization	
☐ Have I organized ideas in a logical way to create a focused text?	• Do readers need to understand some ideas before others? If so, **reorder** to build background or to show cause and effect. • Do events feature prominently in your essay? If so, make sure the sequence is clear and **rearrange** if necessary.
☐ Is my essay coherent?	Does each sentence have a clear relationship to the ones that come before and after it? Does each paragraph? If not, **add** transitions to clarify the connections.
Style	
☐ Does my introduction engage readers?	**Add** a question, quotation, or interesting detail to engage your audience and to preview what's to follow.
☐ Is my style appropriate for an informational essay?	**Substitute** formal language for informal language. • **Replace** vague words, slang, and improper grammar with precise, topic-specific terms and standard English. • **Revise** short, simple sentences into more complex ones.
☐ Does my conclusion revisit my thesis?	**Restate** your central idea in an interesting way.

Writer's Handbook: Informational Essay 543

WRITER'S HANDBOOK | INFORMATIONAL ESSAY

Editing

Don't let errors distract readers from your ideas. Reread your draft and fix mistakes to create a finished informative work.

Read Like a Writer

Look at how the writer of the Mentor Text edited an early draft. Then, follow the directions in the white boxes.

MENTOR TEXT

from **Against the Odds**

Sullenberger knew the situation was too dire for the plane to stay in the air long enough for either plan to be successful, he had about 30 seconds to find an ~~alternateive~~ *alternative*. The pilot decided on a radical move: He'd ditch the plane in the Hudson River—despite the fact that passenger jets are not built to land on water....

Sullenberger lowered the plane's nose in a gradual glide toward the ~~river the~~ *river. The* plane managed to clear the George Washington Bridge and, against the odds, land safly on the surface of the Hudson.

- Fix the comma splice.
- The writer fixed a spelling error.
- The writer fixed a run-on sentence.
- Find and correct a spelling error.

Focus on Sentences

Grammar Minilesson

Run-Ons and Splices A **run-on sentence** is a sentence in which two or more independent clauses (complete sentences) are connected with incorrect or missing punctuation. A **comma splice** is a run-on in which a comma incorrectly joins independent clauses. One way to fix run-ons and splices is to create complex sentences. Turn one of the independent clauses into a dependent clause by adding a subordinating conjunction. Then, connect the dependent clause to the independent clause.

Run-On: *The pilot is a hero he saved the passengers.*

Splice: *The pilot is a hero, he saved the passengers.*

Corrected as a Complex Sentence: *The pilot is a hero because he saved the passengers.*

PRACTICE Correct each run-on or comma splice by creating a complex sentence with a subordinating conjunction.

1. Some people are afraid of flying air travel is very safe.
2. It was an impressive feat, the pilot landed a huge jet on a river.
3. The pilot thought he was doing his job others thought he was a hero.

EDITING TIP
Subordinating conjunctions include the words *because*, *although*, and *until*. They begin subordinate, or dependent, clauses that cannot stand alone as sentences. Instead, you must connect them to independent clauses to create complex sentences.

Focus on Spelling and Punctuation

Spelling: Adding Suffixes Many words in English—such as *change, note,* and *hope*—end with a silent *e*. Follow two rules when adding suffixes to such words:

- Drop the final silent *e* if the suffix begins with a vowel.
- Keep the silent *e* if the suffix begins with a consonant.

EXAMPLE: *care + -ing = caring; care + -ful = careful*

Punctuation with Conjunctive Adverbs Follow these rules:

- If you use a conjunctive adverb to begin a sentence, follow it with a comma. Examples of conjunctive adverbs include: *eventually, also, however,* and *furthermore*.

  EXAMPLE: *Eventually, Mia turned in her paper.*

- If you use a conjunctive adverb to connect two independent clauses, place a semicolon before the conjunctive adverb, and place a comma after it.

  EXAMPLE: *Eventually, Mia worked hard; however, her paper was late.*

> **PRACTICE** Fix any spelling or punctuation errors in the following sentences. Then, review your own draft for correctness.
>
> 1. Certainly people at the waterfront found it amazeing to watch the jet land on the river.
>
> 2. Staying calm makes a difference during a crisis furthermore Captain Sullenberger had flown for US Airways for 29 years.
>
> 3. The situation looked hopless, fortunatly; the pilot knew just what to do.

Publishing and Presenting

Integrate Media

Share your informational essay with your class. Choose one of these options.

OPTION 1 Work with your class to publish your essays in a **digital anthology**. Include visuals, formatting, and graphics—such as headings, diagrams, maps, or captioned images—to emphasize important points.

OPTION 2 With a classmate, produce a **podcast**. Take turns briefly introducing each other and reading your essays. End the podcast with a conversation in which you compare the central ideas of the two essays.

STANDARDS
Writing
Use technology, including the Internet, to produce and publish writing and link to and cite sources as well as to interact and collaborate with others, including linking to and citing sources.

Language
- Demonstrate command of the conventions of standard English grammar and usage when writing or speaking.
- Demonstrate command of the conventions of standard English capitalization, punctuation, and spelling when writing.
- Spell correctly.

PEER-GROUP LEARNING

Essential Question

How do we overcome life's challenges?

You've hit a bump in the road and face an unexpected challenge. Now, what should you do? In this section, you will read selections that describe challenges that people have faced and how they were able to overcome them. You will work in a group to continue your exploration of the topic of facing adversity.

Peer-Group Learning Strategies

Throughout your life, in school, in your community, and in your career, you will continue to learn and work with others.

Review these strategies and the actions you can take to practice them as you work in small groups. Add ideas of your own for each category. Use these strategies during Peer-Group Learning.

STRATEGY	MY ACTION PLAN
Prepare	• Bring all materials to class. • Review your completed assignment so you are ready to participate in group activities. •
Participate fully	• Make eye contact to signal that you are paying attention. • Remember that the more you participate in group discussions, the more comfortable you will be doing so. •
Support others	• Recognize that any new thought that is added to a conversation can be valuable. • Find a way to show agreement within your group, such as giving a thumbs-up. •
Clarify	• Rephrase the comments of others to confirm your understanding. • Ask your classmates questions to better understand what they say: "What did you mean when you said _____?" •

Contents

COMPARE

SHORT STORY

The Circuit

Francisco Jiménez

Why does a cardboard box fill the narrator with dread?

INTERVIEW

How This Son of Migrant Farm Workers Became an Astronaut

José Hernández and Octavio Blanco

What can this success story teach all of us?

ORAL HISTORY

A Work in Progress

Aimee Mullins

Why be "normal" when you can be extraordinary?

POETRY COLLECTION

Simile: Willow and Ginkgo

Eve Merriam

Four Skinny Trees from **The House on Mango Street**

Sandra Cisneros

What can trees teach us about overcoming challenges?

PERFORMANCE TASK

SPEAKING AND LISTENING

Present an Informational Text

The Peer-Group readings demonstrate how people can overcome tremendous adversity. After reading, your group will plan and present biographical profiles about people who faced huge challenges but overcame them in creative ways.

Peer-Group Learning **547**

PEER-GROUP LEARNING

Working as a Group

1. Take a Position

In your group, discuss the following question:

Are any challenges impossible to overcome?

As you share your position, adapt your speech for a small-group discussion: make eye contact, speak up, enunciate, and use standard English without being overly formal. As others share, notice their position on the question. Analyze the main ideas and supporting details they present. Then, work together to explain how the ideas shared by the group clarify the topic of overcoming challenges.

2. Use Text Evidence

Make sure everyone in the group uses relevant evidence to support their responses in both speaking and writing activities. If needed, ask a teacher or writing coach for guidance in using textual evidence to develop and strengthen your work. Identify different types of evidence that reflect the demands of a question or activity:

- **Comprehension:** Identify specific, explicitly stated details.
- **Analysis:** Examine details thoroughly to see if they are relevant.
- **Inference:** Identify clues that hint at meaning but do not directly state it.
- **Interpretation:** Draw connections among multiple details and show how they lead to deeper meanings.
- **Evaluation:** Identify textual evidence and consider it in relationship to other texts, your own values, or another measure.

3. Name Your Group

Choose a name that reflects the unit topic.

Our group's name: _____

4. Create a Communication Plan

Decide how you want to communicate with one another. For example, you might use online collaboration tools, email, or instant messaging.

Our group's plan: _____

STANDARDS

Writing With some guidance and support from peers and adults, develop and strengthen writing as needed.
Speaking and Listening • Analyze the main ideas and supporting details presented in diverse media and formats and explain how the ideas clarify a topic, text, or issue under study. • Adapt speech to a variety of contexts and tasks, demonstrating command of formal English when indicated or appropriate

Essential Question: How do we overcome life's challenges?

Making a Schedule

First, find out the due dates for the peer-group activities. Then, preview the texts and activities with your group, and make a schedule for completing the tasks.

SELECTION	ACTIVITIES	DUE DATE
The Circuit		
How This Son of Migrant Farm Workers Became an Astronaut		
A Work in Progress		
• Simile: Willow and Ginkgo • Four Skinny Trees from The House on Mango Street		

Giving and Receiving Constructive Feedback

As you complete writing tasks and other projects with your group, make sure everyone produces the best possible work by giving and receiving constructive feedback.

- **Give constructive feedback** by being insightful and supportive. Focus on *what works, what does not work,* and most importantly, *why.* Lead off with positive comments, and always mention specific examples.
- **Receive constructive feedback** by listening carefully. Remember that the comments are about your work, not about you personally. You may not agree with every point; apply the comments that are most valuable to you when you revise.
- **Seek constructive feedback** from both peers and adults. Asking for guidance and support from others will help you strengthen your work.

Constructive and Nonconstructive Feedback

Constructive: helpful; offers specific suggestions

- *The main character is very believable, but the other characters are less vivid. You could add some description or dialogue.*
- *This explanation is great, but you might want to include a graphic to help readers understand it better.*

Nonconstructive: not helpful; focuses on the person, not the writing; expresses unsupported opinions

- *I just don't like it that much.*
- *Can't you make it more exciting? I was bored.*

Peer-Group Learning **549**

COMPARE ACROSS GENRES

FICTION and NONFICTION
Short stories are brief works of fiction that have characters, settings, events, and themes. An **interview** is a structured conversation in which one person asks questions and the other person answers them.

SHORT STORY

Author's Purpose
- to entertain readers and provide an insight about life or human nature

Characteristics
- a setting that may influence characters' behaviors and play a key role in the story's events
- characters whose actions affect the events in the story
- conflicts, or problems, that characters face and need to resolve
- dialogue that shows characters' personalities
- a theme, or insight about life

Structure
- a plot, or series of related events, that centers around the conflict

INTERVIEW

Author's Purpose
- to share the experiences and knowledge of a noteworthy person

Characteristics
- an interviewer who asks questions
- an interview subject who answers questions
- open-ended questions that invite thoughtful responses
- the subject's experience often reflects a sense of place as well as historical and cultural influences

Structure
- a question-and-answer format
- an introduction that provides background information about the interview subject

STANDARDS
Reading Literature
Analyze how particular elements of a story or drama interact.

Reading Informational Text
Analyze the interactions between individuals, events, and ideas in a text (e.g., how ideas influence individuals or events, or how individuals influence ideas or events).

Essential Question: How do we overcome life's challenges?

Influence of Setting

 No one exists in a vacuum. We all live in a place and time, traveling from home to school across fields or city blocks. Our beliefs and actions are formed by the people with whom we interact and the events that shape our lives. For example, skilled interviewers ask questions of notable people to discover how a person's background and relationships have led to success. In short stories, narrators develop characters through descriptions of settings and interactions with other characters.

Here are some ways in which setting can affect a narrative:

EXAMPLES: Influence of Setting

ELEMENT OF SETTING	EXAMPLE	EFFECT ON CHARACTER AND PLOT
Historical: country, year, political events	U.S.; The Great Depression	Jacob leaves home and gets a railroad job to lift a burden from his family.
Cultural: attitudes, beliefs, customs	Mexican-American family	Luz, a 14-year-old girl, prepares for her upcoming quinceañera.
Location (for example, a specific city; a theater; a rainforest)	San Francisco; Market Street	Emily races a historic street car on foot to see if she can beat it.
Climate/Weather	Midwest prairie; tornado alert	Pat lived through a tornado two years ago and is now terrified of them.

PRACTICE Read the passage and complete the activity. Use different marks for items 1 and 2. Share your responses with your group.

PASSAGE	INFLUENCE OF SETTING
As a hiding place, it could be worse. At least it was dry and bug-free. Hal was tired of running. He prayed that mama bear would go away and that the shed would keep him safe. A loud crack came out of nowhere. Hal ducked and grabbed a shovel. He fervently wished he were somewhere else. Anywhere else. It had been a lousy idea to hike in the woods alone, and he had no cell phone and no map. Hal started to make a plan.	1. Which details reveal the setting? Mark them. 2. Which details reveal how Hal reacts to the setting? Mark them. 3. How do details of the setting help to propel the story's plot?

Compare Across Genres **551**

PREPARE TO READ

THE CIRCUIT

HOW THIS SON OF MIGRANT FARM WORKERS BECAME AN ASTRONAUT

COMPARE: FICTION and NONFICTION
In this lesson, you will read a short story, **The Circuit**, and an interview, **How This Son of Migrant Farm Workers Became an Astronaut.** You will then compare and contrast the two selections.

About the Author

Francisco Jiménez (b. 1943) was born in Mexico and came to the United States with his family when he was four years old. The family settled in California and became migrant workers. Although he could not go to school before the harvest ended, Jiménez studied in the fields. His hard work paid off as he went on to become an outstanding teacher and award-winning writer.

STANDARDS
Reading Literature
By the end of the year, read and comprehend literature, including stories, dramas, and poems.
Language
Determine or clarify the meaning of unknown and multiple-meaning words and phrases based on grade 7 reading and content, choosing flexibly from a range of strategies.

Concept Vocabulary

As you read the short story, you will encounter these words. After reading, work with your group to identify what these words have in common.

| instinctively | enthusiastically | hesitantly |

Base Words Base, or "inside," words can help you clarify the meanings of unfamiliar words.

EXAMPLE

Unfamiliar Word in Context: Louisa was *energetic*: She rarely took a break from work.

Base word: energy, or "great physical power"

Conclusion: Adding *-etic* turns the noun *energy* into an adjective. *Energetic* must mean "filled with energy."

PRACTICE As you read, look for base words in unfamiliar words to help you determine their meanings. Mark the base words in the open space next to the text.

Reading Strategy: Make Predictions

When you **make predictions** while reading a story, you use what you know about how plots work to anticipate, or guess, what will happen later. You then read on to see if your predictions were correct. For example, most stories have these structural qualities that can help you make predictions:

- A story's main character is introduced; readers learn about that character's situation and hopes or goals.
- The main character faces conflict as they strive to achieve a goal.

PRACTICE Make predictions as you read this story. Write your predictions in the margins of the text.

552 UNIT 5 • FACING ADVERSITY

SHORT STORY

The Circuit
Francisco Jiménez

BACKGROUND
This selection is from *The Circuit: Stories from the Life of a Migrant Child*, a collection of autobiographical short stories by Francisco Jiménez. In this story, the narrator, Panchito, tells of his difficult early years as part of a family of migrant farm workers. To him, life consisted of constant moving and work, with school wedged in around harvesting jobs. The "circuit" in the title refers to the path migrant workers take every year to find jobs.

1   It was that time of year again. Ito, the strawberry sharecropper,[1] did not smile. It was natural. The peak of the strawberry season was over and the last few days the workers, most of them braceros,[2] were not picking as many boxes as they had during the months of June and July.

---
1. **sharecropper** (SHAIR krop uhr) *n.* one who works for a share of a crop; tenant farmer.
2. **braceros** (bruh SAIR ohs) *n.* migrant Mexican farm laborers who harvest crops.

READ TO UNLOCK MEANING
1. First read the text for comprehension and enjoyment. Use the **Reading Strategy** and **Comprehension Check** questions to support your first read.
2. With your group, apply the vocabulary strategy to unlock word meanings.
3. Find other details in the text you find interesting. Ask your own questions and draw your own conclusions.

The Circuit 553

2   As the last days of August disappeared, so did the number of braceros. Sunday, only one—the best picker—came to work. I liked him. Sometimes we talked during our half-hour lunch break. That is how I found out he was from Jalisco, the same state in Mexico my family was from. That Sunday was the last time I saw him.

3   When the sun had tired and sunk behind the mountains, Ito signaled us that it was time to go home. "*Ya esora*,"[3] he yelled in his broken Spanish. Those were the words I waited for twelve hours a day, every day, seven days a week, week after week. And the thought of not hearing them again saddened me.

4   As we drove home Papá did not say a word. With both hands on the wheel, he stared at the dirt road. My older brother, Roberto, was also silent. He leaned his head back and closed his eyes. Once in a while he cleared from his throat the dust that blew in from outside.

5   Yes, it was that time of year. When I opened the front door to the shack, I stopped. Everything we owned was neatly packed in cardboard boxes. Suddenly I felt even more the weight of hours, days, weeks, and months of work. I sat down on a box. The thought of having to move to Fresno[4] and knowing what was in store for me there brought tears to my eyes.

6   That night I could not sleep. I lay in bed thinking about how much I hated this move.

7   A little before five o'clock in the morning, Papá woke everyone up. A few minutes later, the yelling and screaming of my little brothers and sisters, for whom the move was a great adventure, broke the silence of dawn. Shortly, the barking of the dogs accompanied them.

8   While we packed the breakfast dishes, Papá went outside to start the "Carcanchita."[5] That was the name Papá gave his old black Plymouth. He bought it in a used-car lot in Santa Rosa in the Winter of 1949. Papá was very proud of his little jalopy. He had a right to be proud of it. He spent a lot of time looking at other cars before buying this one. When he finally chose the Carcanchita, he checked it thoroughly before driving it out of the car lot. He examined every inch of the car. He listened to the motor, tilting his head from side to side like a parrot, trying to detect any noises that spelled car trouble. After being satisfied with the looks and sounds of the car, Papá then insisted on knowing who the original owner was. He never did find out from the car salesman, but he bought the car anyway. Papá figured the original owner must

MAKE PREDICTIONS
Make a prediction about what will happen to Panchito in Fresno based on the details in paragraph 5.

---

3. **Ya esora** (yah ehs AW rah) Spanish for "It's time." *(Ya es hora).*
4. **Fresno** (FREHZ noh) *n.* city in central California.
5. **"Carcanchita"** (kahr kahn CHEE tah) affectionate name for the car.

have been an important man because behind the rear seat of the car he found a blue necktie.

9   Papá parked the car out in front and left the motor running. "*Listo*,"[6] he yelled. Without saying a word Roberto and I began to carry the boxes out to the car. Roberto carried the two big boxes and I carried the two smaller ones. Papá then threw the mattress on top of the car roof and tied it with ropes to the front and rear bumpers.

10 Everything was packed except Mamá's pot. It was an old large galvanized[7] pot she had picked up at an army surplus store in Santa Maria. The pot had many dents and nicks, and the more dents and nicks it acquired the more Mamá liked it. "*Mi olla*,"[8] she used to say proudly.

11 I held the front door open as Mamá carefully carried out her pot by both handles, making sure not to spill the cooked beans. When she got to the car, Papá reached out to help her with it. Roberto opened the rear car door and Papá gently placed it on the floor behind the front seat. All of us then climbed in. Papá sighed, wiped the sweat from his forehead with his sleeve, and said wearily: "*Es todo*."[9]

12 As we drove away, I felt a lump in my throat. I turned around and looked at our little shack for the last time.

13 At sunset we drove into a labor camp near Fresno. Since Papá did not speak English, Mamá asked the camp foreman if he needed any more workers. "We don't need no more," said the foreman, scratching his head. "Check with Sullivan down the road. Can't miss him. He lives in a big white house with a fence around it."

14 When we got there, Mamá walked up to the house. She went through a white gate, past a row of rose bushes, up the stairs to the front door. She rang the doorbell. The porch light went on and a tall husky man came out. They exchanged a few words. After the man went in, Mamá clasped her hands and hurried back to the car. "We have work! Mr. Sullivan said we can stay there the whole season," she said, gasping and pointing to an old garage near the stables.

15 The garage was worn out by the years. It had no windows. The walls, eaten by termites, strained to support the roof full of holes. The dirt floor, populated by earth worms, looked like a gray road map.

COMPREHENSION CHECK

Why is the family moving?

---

6. ***Listo*** (LEES toh) Spanish for "Ready."
7. **galvanized** (GAL vuh nyzd) *adj.* coated with zinc to prevent rusting.
8. ***Mi olla*** (mee OH yah) Spanish for "My pot."
9. ***Es todo*** (ehs TOH thoh) Spanish for "That's everything."

The Circuit   555

16   That night, by the light of a kerosene lamp, we unpacked and cleaned our new home. Roberto swept away the loose dirt, leaving the hard ground. Papá plugged the holes in the walls with old newspapers and tin can tops. Mamá fed my little brothers and sisters. Papá and Roberto then brought in the mattress and placed it on the far corner of the garage. "Mamá, you and the little ones sleep on the mattress. Roberto, Panchito, and I will sleep outside under the trees," Papá said.

17   Early next morning Mr. Sullivan showed us where his crop was, and after breakfast, Papá, Roberto, and I headed for the vineyard to pick.

18   Around nine o'clock the temperature had risen to almost one hundred degrees. I was completely soaked in sweat and my mouth felt as if I had been chewing on a handkerchief. I walked over to the end of the row, picked up the jug of water we had brought, and began drinking. "Don't drink too much; you'll get sick," Roberto shouted. No sooner had he said that than I felt sick to my stomach. I dropped to my knees and let the jug roll off my hands. I remained motionless with my eyes glued on the hot sandy ground. All I could hear was the drone of insects. Slowly I began to recover. I poured water over my face and neck and watched the dirty water run down my arms to the ground.

19   I still felt dizzy when we took a break to eat lunch. It was past two o'clock and we sat underneath a large walnut tree that was on the side of the road. While we ate, Papá jotted down the number of boxes we had picked. Roberto drew designs on the ground with a stick. Suddenly I noticed Papá's face turn pale as he looked down the road. "Here comes the school bus," he whispered loudly in alarm. **Instinctively**, Roberto and I ran and hid in the vineyards. We did not want to get in trouble for not going to school. The neatly dressed boys about my age got off. They carried books under their arms. After they crossed the street, the bus drove away. Roberto and I came out from hiding and joined Papá. "*Tienen que tener cuidado,*"[10] he warned us.

20   After lunch we went back to work. The sun kept beating down. The buzzing insects, the wet sweat, and the hot dry dust made the afternoon seem to last forever. Finally the mountains around the valley reached out and swallowed the sun. Within an hour it was too dark to continue picking. The vines blanketed the grapes, making it difficult to see the bunches. "*Vámonos,*"[11] said Papá, signaling to us that it was time to quit work. Papá then took out a

---

Mark base words or indicate another strategy that helped you determine meaning.

instinctively (ihn STIHNGK tihv lee) *adv.*

MEANING:

---

10. ***Tienen que tener cuidado*** (tee EHN ehn kay tehn EHR kwee THAH thoh) Spanish for "You have to be careful."
11. ***Vámonos*** (BAH moh nohs) Spanish for "Let's go."

pencil and began to figure out how much we had earned our first day. He wrote down numbers, crossed some out, wrote down some more. "*Quince*,"[12] he murmured.

21 When we arrived home, we took a cold shower underneath a water hose. We then sat down to eat dinner around some wooden crates that served as a table. Mamá had cooked a special meal for us. We had rice and tortillas with "*carne con chile*,"[13] my favorite dish.

22 The next morning I could hardly move. My body ached all over. I felt little control over my arms and legs. This feeling went on every morning for days until my muscles finally got used to the work.

23 It was Monday, the first week of November. The grape season was over and I could now go to school. I woke up early that morning and lay in bed, looking at the stars and savoring the thought of not going to work and of starting sixth grade for the first time that year. Since I could not sleep, I decided to get up and join Papá and Roberto at breakfast. I sat at the table across from Roberto, but I kept my head down. I did not want to look up and face him. I knew he was sad. He was not going to school today. He was not going tomorrow, or next week, or next month. He would not go until the cotton season was over, and that was sometime in February. I rubbed my hands together and watched the dry, acid stained skin fall to the floor in little rolls.

> "Finally, after struggling for English words, I managed to tell her that I wanted to enroll in the sixth grade."

24 When Papá and Roberto left for work, I felt relief. I walked to the top of a small grade next to the shack and watched the Carcanchita disappear in the distance in a cloud of dust. Two hours later, around eight o'clock, I stood by the side of the road waiting for school bus number twenty. When it arrived I climbed in. Everyone was busy either talking or yelling. I sat in an empty seat in the back.

25 When the bus stopped in front of the school, I felt very nervous. I looked out the bus window and saw boys and girls carrying books under their arms. I put my hands in my pant pockets and walked to the principal's office. When I entered I heard a woman's voice say: "May I help you?" I was startled. I had not heard

COMPREHENSION CHECK

How do Panchito and Roberto feel at breakfast?

---

12. **Quince** (KEEN say) Spanish for "Fifteen."
13. **"carne con chile"** (KAHR nay kuhn CHIHL ay) dish of ground meat, hot peppers, beans, and tomatoes.

English for months. For a few seconds I remained speechless. I looked at the lady who waited for an answer. My first instinct was to answer her in Spanish, but I held back. Finally, after struggling for English words, I managed to tell her that I wanted to enroll in the sixth grade. After answering many questions, I was led to the classroom.

26   Mr. Lema, the sixth grade teacher, greeted me and assigned me a desk. He then introduced me to the class. I was so nervous and scared at that moment when everyone's eyes were on me that I wished I were with Papá and Roberto picking cotton. After taking

roll, Mr. Lema gave the class the assignment for the first hour. "The first thing we have to do this morning is finish reading the story we began yesterday," he said **enthusiastically**. He walked up to me, handed me an English book, and asked me to read. "We are on page 125," he said politely. When I heard this, I felt my blood rush to my head; I felt dizzy. "Would you like to read?" he asked **hesitantly**. I opened the book to page 125. My mouth was dry. My eyes began to water. I could not begin. "You can read later," Mr. Lema said understandingly.

Mark base words or indicate another strategy that helped you determine meaning.

enthusiastically (ehn thoo zee AS tihk lee) *adv.*

MEANING:

hesitantly (HEHZ uh tuhnt lee) *adv.*

MEANING:

27   For the rest of the reading period I kept getting angrier and angrier at myself. I should have read, I thought to myself.

28   During recess I went into the rest room and opened my English book to page 125. I began to read in a low voice, pretending I was in class. There were many words I did not know. I closed the book and headed back to the classroom.

29   Mr. Lema was sitting at his desk correcting papers. When I entered he looked up at me and smiled. I felt better. I walked up to him and asked if he could help me with the new words. "Gladly," he said.

30   The rest of the month I spent my lunch hours working on English with Mr. Lema, my best friend at school.

31   One Friday during lunch hour Mr. Lema asked me to take a walk with him to the music room. "Do you like music?" he asked me as we entered the building. "Yes, I like *corridos*,"[14] I answered. He then picked up a trumpet, blew on it, and handed it to me. The sound gave me goose bumps. I knew that sound. I had heard it in many corridos. "How would you like to learn how to play it?" he asked. He must have read my face because before I could answer, he added: "I'll teach you how to play it during our lunch hours."

32   That day I could hardly wait to tell Papá and Mamá the great news. As I got off the bus, my little brothers and sisters ran up to meet me. They were yelling and screaming. I thought they were happy to see me, but when I opened the door to our shack, I saw that everything we owned was neatly packed in cardboard boxes.

COMPREHENSION CHECK

How does Panchito spend his time at school?

---

14. *corridos* (koh REE thohs) *n.* ballads.

The Circuit   **559**

BUILD INSIGHT

THE CIRCUIT

First Thoughts

Choose one of the following items to discuss.

- Did the story's ending surprise you? Why, or why not?
- Some people give the advice, "Accept the things you can't change." How do you think Panchito would respond to this statement? What do you think of it?

Summary

Write a brief summary of the story that includes only its main ideas. Do not express your opinions.

Analysis and Discussion

1. **(a) Draw Conclusions** Why does Panchito call Mr. Lema his "best friend at school"? **(b) Analyze** Based on the information in the story, how would you describe Panchito's personality?

2. **(a) Analyze** What is Panchito's main goal in the story? **(b) Make Inferences** What seems to be Papa's main goal? **(c) Analyze** How does the contrast in their points of view create conflict for Panchito?

3. **(a)** What plan do Panchito and his teacher make for upcoming lunch periods? **(b) Make Inferences** What does Panchito realize when he gets home from school that day?

4. **(a) Interpret** What theme, or insight about life, does the story convey? **(b) Evaluate** Does the story's title help to convey its theme? Why, or why not?

5. **Get Ready for Close Reading** Choose a passage from the text that you find especially interesting or important. You'll discuss the passage with your group during Close-Read activities.

Exploring the Essential Question

How do we overcome life's challenges?

6. What personality traits could help someone like Panchito deal with frequent challenges? Record your ideas in your Evidence Log.

WORKING AS A GROUP

Discuss your responses to the Analysis and Discussion questions with your group.

- As your peers share, think carefully about their ideas and the details they use to support them.
- Clarify your peers' responses by asking questions.

If necessary, modify your initial responses to reflect new information you learn during the discussion.

STANDARDS

Reading Literature
- Cite several pieces of textual evidence to support analysis of what the text says explicitly as well as inferences drawn from the text.
- Provide an objective summary of the text.
- Analyze how an author develops and contrasts the points of view of different characters or narrators in a text.

Language
Spell correctly.

ANALYZE AND INTERPRET

Close Read

PRACTICE Use text evidence to complete the following activities.

1. **Present and Discuss** With your group, share the passages from the story that you found especially interesting. For example, you might focus on the following passages:

   - **Paragraphs 3–4:** Discuss ways in which the author creates a specific mood through his word choice.

   - **Paragraph 8:** Discuss the character of Papá and how the author brings him to life.

2. **Reflect on Your Learning** What new ideas or insights did you uncover during your second reading of the text?

STUDY LANGUAGE AND CRAFT

Concept Vocabulary

Why These Words? The vocabulary words are related.

| instinctively | enthusiastically | hesitantly |

1. With your group, discuss what the words have in common.
2. Add another word that fits the category. _____
3. Use each word in a paragraph that describes a person, real or imagined. Include context clues that hint at each word's meaning. Share your sentences with your group.

> **WORD WALL**
>
> Note words in the text that are related to the idea of facing adversity. Add them to your Word Wall.

Word Study

Spelling: -ly and -ally Endings When you add the suffix -ly to an adjective, you create an adverb. Follow these spelling rules to add the suffix correctly:

- If the word ends in a consonant, simply add -ly: *hesitantly*.
- If the word ends in a silent e, keep the silent e and add -ly: *instinctively*.
- If the word ends in -ic, the suffix changes, becoming -ally: *enthusiastically*. Note that there are exceptions to this rule. For example, you should add -ly, not -ally, to the word *public* to form *publicly*.

PRACTICE Correctly add the suffix -ly or -ally to the following words: *heroic, formal, mythic, brave*. Use a dictionary to check your spelling. Then, write a sentence that uses each word. Finally, share your sentences with your group.

The Circuit **561**

ANALYZE AND INTERPRET

THE CIRCUIT

Influence of Setting

A story's **setting** can shape characters' personalities, attitudes, and actions. The way characters think and behave is often influenced by the world in which they live. In some stories, the setting itself fuels conflict as characters battle elements such as snow, wind, floods, or earthquakes. As you read, analyze how elements of a story interact. In particular, note how characters and plot events are influenced by these aspects of the setting:

- **time,** such as the historical period, month, season, or even time of day
- **place,** including elements of both nature (type of terrain, type of weather) and civilization (specific city, type of building)
- **cultural values,** including a society's beliefs, attitudes, and customs

EXAMPLES: Influence of Setting

STORY SETTING	EFFECTS ON CHARACTERS / PLOT
In 1850, a family going to California breaks a wagon wheel in the Rocky Mountains. They must use natural resources to survive as night falls and the temperature drops to dangerous levels.	The setting will drive the plot of the story. Characters must race to find food and shelter before night falls.

PRACTICE Work with a partner to analyze how the setting affects the characters and develops the plot in "The Circuit." The first entry has been done for you. Add three more examples. Then, discuss your responses with the rest of your group.

SETTING DETAIL	EFFECT ON CHARACTERS / PLOT
It was that time of year again. Ito, the strawberry sharecropper, did not smile. . . . The peak of the strawberry season was over.	The characters' livelihood depends on having crops to pick. They must now move on to where other crops are in season.

STANDARDS

Reading Literature
Analyze how particular elements of a story or drama interact.

Language
- Demonstrate command of the conventions of standard English capitalization, punctuation, and spelling when writing.
- Use knowledge of language and its conventions when writing, speaking, reading, or listening.

562 UNIT 5 • FACING ADVERSITY

STUDY LANGUAGE AND CRAFT

Commas

Commas (,) are essential tools for writers. They signal brief pauses and enable readers to absorb information in meaningful, accurate chunks.

USING COMMAS	EXAMPLES FROM "THE CIRCUIT"
Use a comma before a conjunction that joins independent clauses. (A clause contains a subject and a verb.)	The pot had many dents and nicks, and the more dents and nicks it acquired the more Mamá liked it.
Use a comma after an introductory word, phrase, or clause.	**Introductory Word:** Yes, it was that time of year. **Introductory Phrase:** A little before five o'clock in the morning, Papá woke everyone up. **Introductory Clause:** When she got to the car, Papá reached out to help her with it.
Use commas to separate three or more words, phrases, or clauses in a series.	**Words in a Series:** Suddenly I felt even more the weight of hours, days, weeks, and months of work. **Phrases in a Series:** He wrote down numbers, crossed some out, and wrote down some more.

READ Reread these sentences from "The Circuit." Identify the function—why the commas are needed—in each sentence.

SENTENCE	FUNCTION
1. As the last days of August disappeared, so did the number of braceros.	
2. The buzzing insects, the wet sweat, and the hot dry dust made the afternoon seem to last forever.	
3. I sat at the table across from Roberto, but I kept my head down.	
4. After the man went in, Mamá clasped her hands and hurried back to the car.	

WRITE / EDIT Edit the following passage to show correct use of commas. Then, discuss your edits with your group.

The weirdest thing happened today. In the garden I looked at our flowers and I paused to admire our vegetables. I saw rows of herbs stalks of corn and several tomato bushes. Guess what I saw next? Quick as a wink a beanstalk vanished under the soil! If you had been there you would have laughed. Evidently there's a gopher in our garden!

The Circuit 563

PREPARE TO READ

THE CIRCUIT

HOW THIS SON OF MIGRANT FARM WORKERS BECAME AN ASTRONAUT

COMPARE: FICTION and NONFICTION
Like the short story **The Circuit**, the **interview** you are about to read features the son of migrant farm workers. As you read, notice similarities and differences between the two texts.

About the Interviewer

Octavio Blanco is a multimedia content creator, based in New York City. For 18 years, Blanco was a reporter and editor for CNN. He is an active member of the National Association of Hispanic Journalists.

Concept Vocabulary

As you read the interview, you will encounter these words. After reading, work with your group to identify what the words have in common.

| perseverance | attain | conducive |

Context Clues Using context clues, including those that relate to cause and effect, can help you figure out what some words mean.

EXAMPLE

Unfamiliar Word in Context If you practice piano <u>every day</u> for an hour, <u>even when you don't feel like it</u>, your *persistence* will pay off—you will become a better musician.

Conclusion The sentence talks about practicing repeatedly despite obstacles in order to achieve something. *Persistence* must mean "the act of repeating something to achieve a goal."

PRACTICE ▶ As you read, use cause-and-effect context clues to clarify the meanings of unfamiliar words. Mark your observations in the open space next to the text.

Reading Strategy: Paraphrase

When you **paraphrase** a section of text, you restate it in your own words so that it's easier to understand. Even though your paraphrase will be simpler than the original text, it should still contain all the ideas the writer wanted to convey. Follow these steps to paraphrase:

- Pause after any difficult or confusing sections.
- Note what the text says explicitly and ask yourself what it means.
- Restate the text using your own words, but be sure to keep the writer's main ideas.

PRACTICE ▶ As you read, paraphrase sections of the text that may be unclear after a first reading.

STANDARDS
Reading Informational Text
Cite several pieces of textual evidence to support analysis of what the text says explicitly.
Language
Use context as a clue to the meaning of a word or phrase.

INTERVIEW

How This Son of Migrant Farm Workers Became an Astronaut

José Hernández and Octavio Blanco

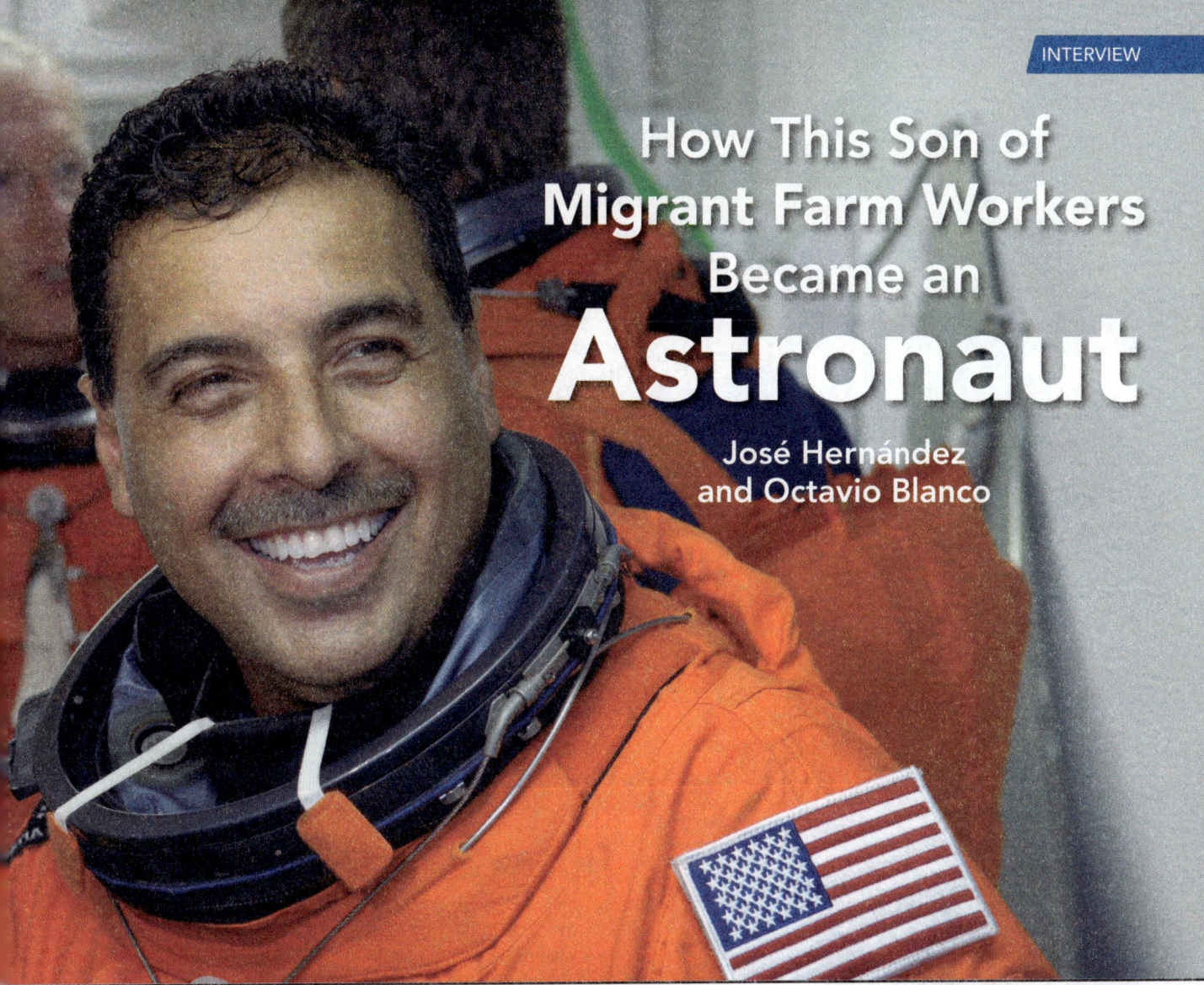

BACKGROUND

José Hernández was hard at work, hoeing a row of sugar beets in a field, when he heard the news: The first Hispanic American had been chosen to travel into space. Hernández, who was a teenager at the time, had been fascinated by science since childhood. In this interview, he talks with reporter Octavio Blanco about how he went from working on "the California circuit" to working on the International Space Station.

1 Millions of kids dream of going into space. But José Hernández made that dream a reality—and he did so against incredible odds.

2 As the son of Mexican migrant farm workers, his education was constantly interrupted as his family followed the changing crops. Often, they would spend December through February in Mexico.

3 Hernández and his siblings would home school themselves with assignments from their American teachers during those months. But with all of the constant interruptions, Hernández didn't become fluent in English until he was 12.

READ TO UNLOCK MEANING

1. First read the text for comprehension and enjoyment. Use the **Reading Strategy** and **Comprehension Check** questions to support your first read.
2. With your group, apply the vocabulary strategy to unlock word meanings.
3. Find other details in the text you find interesting. Ask your own questions and draw your own conclusions.

How This Son of Migrant Farm Workers Became an Astronaut 565

Use context clues or indicate another strategy you used that helped you determine meaning.

perseverance
(puhr suh VEER uhns) *n.*
MEANING:

attain (uh TAYN) *v.*
MEANING:

4 But through **perseverance**, Hernández managed to earn a Master's degree in electrical and computer engineering from the University of California, Santa Barbara, and **attain** his goal of becoming an astronaut. Not only has he traveled into space as the mission specialist to the International Space Station, but he now runs his own foundation, Reaching for the Stars.

5 The group aims to get youth in central California interested in STEM (science, technology, engineering and math) fields and provides first-generation[1] high school seniors with scholarships.

6 Here's Hernández's American success story:

What was life like growing up?

7 My childhood was typical of a migrant farm working family, a family that spends nine months out of the year picking fruits and vegetables from Southern California to Northern California. While others looked forward to summer vacation, I hated it. Summer vacation meant working seven days a week in the fields.

8 I had it easier than the rest of my brothers and sisters. I had three older siblings to help me with my schoolwork.

---

1. **first-generation** born in the United States to immigrant parents.

566 UNIT 5 • FACING ADVERSITY

9   My mom would sit us down at the kitchen table and we wouldn't be allowed to leave until we finished our homework. She motivated all of us by having confidence and high expectations. It wasn't *if* we went to college, it was *when*.

10 Life was rough, but we didn't know it. It was just what we were used to.

11 But then as a teenager I was embarrassed because we lived in the barrio.[2] We lived in areas that were run down because those were the areas where we could afford to live.

12 My bi-cultural upbringing made me feel out of place—not American enough, but not Mexican enough, either.

13 My parents' love, support and high expectations helped me to find my path to success. It could have been a different story. I used to hang out with four guys in the neighborhood. I last saw one of them just a little while ago; he was out on the streets.

When did things begin to change for you?

14 I remember one day, after picking cucumbers, me and my siblings were tired, hot, sweaty, dusty and stinking.

15 My dad told us, 'You're living your future now. I'm not going to force you to go to school or to get good grades. But if you don't study, this is your future.'

16 No matter how hard we studied, however, our life moving from place to place wasn't **conducive** to a good education.

17 My second-grade teacher, frustrated by the constant interruptions, made a special home visit to convince my parents that this lifestyle was hurting us kids.

18 The next year, things changed. We all moved to Stockton, California, year round, visiting Mexico only during Christmas vacations.

19 This stability really helped me. I started speaking English better and was able to focus on learning.

When did your interest in space begin?

20 I began dreaming of going into space after watching the Apollo 17 moon landing when I was 10.

21 That was the last mission to the moon. I'm so glad I saw it!

22 I'd go outside and look at the moon and come back in to see them walking on the surface of it on TV.

---

2. **barrio** (BAHR ee oh) *n.* neighborhood in a city or town where many residents speak Spanish.

Use context clues or indicate another strategy you used that helped you determine meaning.

conducive (kuhn DOO sihv) *adj.*

MEANING:

COMPREHENSION CHECK

As a child, how did Hernández initially get his education?

▲ Hernández and crew heading to a mission on the International Space Station

PARAPHRASE

Paraphrase paragraph 23 by restating it in your own words while maintaining the writer's ideas.

23 That night I shared my dream with my dad. Instead of bursting my bubble, he gave me a recipe for success: Decide what you want to do in life. Recognize how far you are from your goal. Draw a road map from where you are to where you want to go. Get your education and make an effort.

24 "Always do more than people expect, m'hijo,"[3] he said.

Is there anything else that contributed to your success?

25 My wife played a huge part in helping me to persevere. I was rejected from NASA's[4] astronaut program eleven times. People get rejected twice, on average, before they're picked.

26 The sixth year that NASA rejected me, I crumpled up the rejection letter and threw it on the bedroom floor. I was going to quit trying, but she talked me out of it.

27 "Let NASA be the one to disqualify you, don't disqualify yourself," she told me.

---

3. **m'hijo** (mee EE hoh) Spanish for "my son."
4. **NASA** National Aeronautics and Space Administration, a U.S. government agency.

568 UNIT 5 • FACING ADVERSITY

28 I was rejected eleven times. It wasn't until the twelfth time that I was selected. I was 41 when I became an astronaut. The average age of new astronauts is 34.

What was going through your mind in the moments before you blasted off into space?

29 In 2009, I was part of a 14-day mission to finish construction of the International Space Station.

30 Before launch, astronauts have hours aboard the shuttle for checks and reflection. I was looking at the American flag on my shoulder remembering that I was picking fruits in the field as a kid and now I'm about to blast off into space in the most complex piece of equipment we have representing America.

How have role models influenced you?

31 As a senior in high school I first heard about Franklin Chang Díaz, the first Hispanic astronaut. It was then that my childhood dream started to come into focus. Seeing someone who looked and sounded like me succeed pushed me to reach my goal.

32 He [Díaz] spoke with an accent, had brown skin and came from humble beginnings like me. I spoke broken English until I was 12 years old. Now I want to inspire the next generation through my foundation in central California. We invite companies like Google to help spark the interests of 5th graders. There's a science academy for 7th through 12th graders to help expose kids to math and tutor them. We also give scholarships to first-generation seniors.

From CNN.com. © 2016 CNN.com. All rights reserved. Used under license.

COMPREHENSION CHECK
What effect did Franklin Chang Díaz have on Hernández?

BUILD INSIGHT

HOW THIS SON OF MIGRANT FARM WORKERS BECAME AN ASTRONAUT

First Thoughts

What part of Hernandez's story do you find most inspiring? Why?

Summary

Confirm your comprehension by writing a brief summary of the text. Include only the central ideas, and keep your summary objective.

Analysis and Discussion

> **WORKING AS A GROUP**
>
> Discuss your responses to the Analysis and Discussion questions with your group.
>
> - Speak with the goal of making your ideas clear. Use complete sentences, and choose precise words.
> - Listen what others have to say, and build on those ideas.

1. **(a)** Why did Hernández's family move to Stockton, California?
   (b) Analyze In what ways was the move significant?

2. **Speculate** Reread Hernández's comments on being bicultural, applying to NASA, and learning about Franklin Chang Díaz. If you had been interviewing him, which of these topics would you want to explore in more depth, and why? What questions would you ask?

3. **Interpret** What insight about life is conveyed by this text? Which details support your response?

4. **Get Ready for Close Reading** Choose a passage from the text that you find especially interesting or important. You'll discuss the passage with your group during Close-Read activities.

Exploring the Essential Question

How do we overcome life's challenges?

5. What personal qualities do you think may have led to Hernández's success? Does everyone have the ability to overcome life's challenges as he did? Explain your reasoning in your Evidence Log.

STANDARDS
Reading Informational Text
Provide an objective summary of the text.
Language
- Use knowledge of language and its conventions when writing, speaking, reading, or listening.
- Use the relationship between particular words to better understand each of the words.

570 UNIT 5 • FACING ADVERSITY

ANALYZE AND INTERPRET

Close Read

PRACTICE Use text evidence to complete the following activities.

1. **Present and Discuss** With your group, share the passages from the interview that you found especially interesting. For example, you might focus on the following passages:

   - **Paragraphs 1–6:** What overall idea about Hernández is conveyed by the writer's word choice?
   - **Paragraphs 25–28:** Discuss the idea of perseverance and how that quality shaped Hernández's life choices.

2. **Reflect on Your Learning** What new ideas or insights did you uncover during your second reading of the text?

STUDY LANGUAGE AND CRAFT

Concept Vocabulary

Why These Words? The vocabulary words are related.

| perseverance | attain | conducive |

1. With your group, write what the words have in common.

2. Add another word that fits the category. _____

3. Use all three vocabulary words in a help-wanted ad. Include context clues that hint at each word's meaning.

WORD WALL

Note words in the text that are related to the idea of facing adversity. Add them to your Word Wall.

Word Study

Analogies An **analogy** is a pair of words that share a relationship. For example, the words might be synonyms or antonyms, or they might show a part-to-whole or cause-and-effect relationship. In the analogy *success is to failure as advantage is to obstacle*, each pair of words is made up of antonyms.

PRACTICE Use a vocabulary word to complete each analogy. Then, discuss your answers with your group.

1. *Scold* is to *criticize* as _____ is to *achieve*.
2. *Stretch* is to *extend* as *determination* is to _____.
3. *Whisper* is to *scream* as *unhelpful* is to _____.

How This Son of Migrant Farm Workers Became an Astronaut **571**

ANALYZE AND INTERPRET

HOW THIS SON OF MIGRANT FARM WORKERS BECAME AN ASTRONAUT

TIP: To determine the influence of setting, notice the connections Hernández makes between his circumstances and his life choices.

Influence of Setting

In autobiographical writing, biographical writing, and interviews, writers often explore ways in which settings, people, and events shape the ideas, beliefs, and actions of their subjects.

As you reflect on "How This Son of Migrant Farm Workers Became an Astronaut," notice the aspects of setting that shaped Hernández's childhood. In particular, consider how these factors influenced him:

- geographic locations and seasons
- economic aspects of his family's life
- cultural elements, including society's attitudes and the values his parents taught him

PRACTICE Analyze each passage, and describe ways in which setting influenced Hernández's early life. Share your completed chart with your group.

PASSAGE FROM THE TEXT	EFFECT ON HERNÁNDEZ
My childhood was typical of a migrant farm working family, a family that spends nine months out of the year picking fruits and vegetables from Southern California to Northern California. While others looked forward to summer vacation, I hated it. Summer vacation meant working seven days a week in the fields. (paragraph 7)	
But then as a teenager I was embarrassed because we lived in the barrio. We lived in areas that were run down because those were the areas where we could afford to live. My bi-cultural upbringing made me feel out of place—not American enough, but not Mexican enough, either. (paragraphs 11–12)	

STANDARDS
Reading Informational Text
• Analyze the interactions between individuals, events, and ideas in a text.
• Analyze the structure an author uses to organize a text, including how the major sections contribute to the whole and to the development of the ideas.

572 UNIT 5 • FACING ADVERSITY

STUDY LANGUAGE AND CRAFT

Organizational Patterns

Before sitting down with their subject, an interviewer prepares a list of questions to ask the person. They organize the questions by topic, a structure that ensures that the interview progresses smoothly and the questions follow logically. For example, the interviewer may:

- present questions chronologically so that readers learn about the life of the interview subject in time order
- present questions according to a broad category, such as early influences or failures the subject experienced
- present follow-up questions about information the subject shared to explore the response further

Transcripts of interviews, such as the one you just read, often include introductory information about the subject being interviewed. The interview itself appears in question-and-answer format.

PRACTICE Work on your own to answer the questions. Then, share your responses with your group.

1. **Analyze** Where in the text does the interviewer provide background information about Hernández? Mark the text and cite two details the background information reveals.

2. **Analyze** Review the interview questions. What basic structural pattern does the interviewer use to arrange the questions? Within that larger pattern, what subtopics are explored?

3. **Evaluate** How effective is the interview structure in showing connections among different parts of Hernández's life? Provide details from the text to support your response.

4. **Interpret** What central idea do the different parts of the interview help to develop?

TEST PRACTICE

SHORT STORY

THE CIRCUIT

INTERVIEW

HOW THIS SON OF MIGRANT FARM WORKERS BECAME AN ASTRONAUT

COMPARE: FICTION and NONFICTION

Multiple Choice

These questions are based on the short story, "The Circuit," and the interview, "How This Son of Migrant Farm Workers Became an Astronaut." Choose the best answer to each question.

1. Consider the ending of "The Circuit." Which answer choice best states how Panchito's probable future compares to the life José Hernández achieved?

   A Like Hernández, Panchito will probably stop moving from farm to farm.

   B Like Hernández, Panchito will probably get an education and achieve his dreams.

   C Unlike Hernández, Panchito will probably not leave home to pursue his dreams.

   D Like Hernández, Panchito will become an astronaut.

2. Read the passages from the short story and the interview. Which answer choice best states challenges that both Panchito and young Hernández face?

   The Circuit

   The garage was worn out by the years. It had no windows. The walls, eaten by termites, strained to support the roof full of holes. The dirt floor, populated by earth worms, looked like a gray road map. (paragraph 15)

   How This Son of Migrant Farm Workers Became an Astronaut

   But then as a teenager I was embarrassed because we lived in the barrio. We lived in areas that were run down because those were the areas where we could afford to live. (paragraph 11)

   A loneliness and lack of friendship

   B lack of nice clothing

   C poverty and poor housing

   D hunger and lack of basic necessities

3. What important insight do both the short story and the interview share?

   A People do not have to overcome challenges in order to be happy.

   B Anyone can overcome challenges with determination.

   C Hard work is all that is needed to overcome challenges.

   D Stability and education are essential to overcoming challenges.

STANDARDS

Reading Literature
Compare and contrast a fictional portrayal of a time, place, or character and a historical account of the same period as a means of understanding how authors of fiction use or alter history.

Reading Informational Text
Analyze how two or more authors writing about the same topic shape their presentations of key information by emphasizing different evidence or advancing different interpretations of facts.

Essential Question: How do we overcome life's challenges?

Short Response

1. **(a) Compare and Contrast** How is Panchito's experience of attending school different from Hernández's experience? **(b) Analyze** Who faces tougher challenges in getting an education, Panchito or Hernández? Support your response.

2. **(a) Compare and Contrast** How are Panchito's and Hernández's childhoods alike and different? Consider the challenges they face. **(b) Make Inferences** What do Panchito's and Hernández's reactions to the challenges they face reveal about the kind of people they are?

3. **Evaluate** Which format, the story or the interview, had a greater impact on you? Support your response with details from the texts.

Timed Writing

A **comparison-and-contrast essay** is a piece of writing in which you analyze the similarities and differences among two or more topics.

> ### Assignment
>
> Both "The Circuit" and "How This Son of Migrant Farm Workers Became an Astronaut" explore the challenges that children of migrant workers often face. Write a **comparison-and-contrast essay** in which you discuss similarities and differences in the insights the two texts express.

5-Minute Planner

1. Read the assignment carefully and completely.
2. Decide the most important thing you want to say—your central idea.
3. Identify which details and examples you'll use from the two texts.
4. Organize your ideas, focusing on the insights, or main messages, the authors express.
   - Explain similarities: What key ideas do both texts convey? What shared messages do the authors express?
   - Explain differences: What is the outcome for the subject of each selection? How do the authors' approaches to the topic differ? What unique insight does each selection share that the other does not?

EVIDENCE LOG

Before moving on to a new selection, go to your Evidence Log and record any additional thoughts or observations you may have about "The Circuit" and "How This Son of Migrant Farm Workers Became an Astronaut."

Test Practice **575**

LEARN ABOUT GENRE: NONFICTION

A WORK IN PROGRESS

The selection you are about to read is an oral history, taken from a speech the author gave.

Reading Oral Histories

An **oral history** is a living person's testimony about their own experiences. It is typically delivered as a speech or in storytelling form.

Author's Purpose
- to capture personal experiences that are significant in some way

Characteristics
- a first-person account (the speaker tells their own story)
- a distinctive personality, or voice, of the speaker
- often transcribed, or written down, from a spoken account
- a conversational, "think out loud" quality
- may not follow grammatical rules
- often expresses insights about life

Structure
- usually follows a time-order sequence to tell a true story

Take a Minute!

DISCUSS With a partner, discuss this question: *Would you rather read someone's story or hear the person tell it out loud?* Jot down your preference and explain your thinking.

STANDARDS
Reading Informational Text
Analyze the impact of a specific word choice on meaning and tone.

576 UNIT 5 • FACING ADVERSITY

Essential Question: How do we overcome life's challenges?

Language and Voice

One way in which a speaker shares an oral history effectively is by showing the audience their personality. An author's **voice** is the distinct personality of the speaker or writer. Voice emerges from the unique ways in which a writer or speaker uses language, including the following elements:

- **Diction:** writer's or speaker's choice of words and phrases
- **Syntax:** ways in which the writer or speaker organizes phrases, clauses, and sentences; for example, sentences can be short and punchy, long and flowing, or a mix of the two
- **Tone:** writer's or speaker's attitude toward the subject and audience; tone can be described with words we often use to name emotions, such as *cold, warm, playful, joyous,* or *harsh*

TIP: When someone refers to an author's or speaker's unique "sound," they are talking about voice.

The language a writer or speaker chooses to discuss a subject impacts the meaning and tone they convey and reveals their personality, or voice. For example, if a writer makes a joke about an embarrassing personal experience, it suggests that they are playful and have a good sense of humor.

PRACTICE With your group, read and discuss the passages. Analyze how the diction, syntax, tone, and meaning of each one reveals the writer's voice. Then, mark the set of words that best describes the voice in each passage.

SAMPLE PASSAGE	DESCRIPTION OF VOICE
I recently went to the TV studio to film an interview about the holiday food drive. To my surprise, there was great confusion when I arrived. Apparently, the staff expected not me, but a famous singer who shares my name. Since I cannot sing a note, we had to make the best of a deeply embarrassing situation.	○ Serious and Formal ○ Casual and Amused ○ Cautious and Restrained
So, I go to the TV studio to talk about the holiday food drive, but—of course—there's a mix-up. Apparently, they think I'm "The Famous Singer"… disappointment and embarrassment all around, since my "vocals" are about as sweet as car horns in a traffic jam.	○ Serious and Formal ○ Casual and Amused ○ Cautious and Restrained

Learn About Genre **577**

PREPARE TO READ

A Work in Progress

About the Author

Aimee Mullins (b. 1976) is an athlete, model, and actor. At the age of one, she needed to have both of her legs amputated below the knee. Mullins learned how to walk and run with prosthetics, enabling her to participate in the 1996 Paralympic Games, where she set three world records in running and jumping events.

STANDARDS
Reading Informational Text
By the end of the year, read and comprehend literary nonfiction.
Language
Use context as a clue to the meaning of a word or phrase.

Concept Vocabulary

As you read "A Work in Progress," you will encounter these words. After reading, work with your group to identify what the words have in common.

| accomplishments | extraordinary | celebrate |

Context Clues The **context** of a word is the other words and phrases that appear near it in a text. Clues in the context can help you figure out the meanings of unfamiliar words. Here are some examples:

Synonyms: His *aberrant* behavior was unexpected. It is strange for him to be impolite.

Restatement of an idea: Because of a rare disease, her bones are *delicate* and more likely to break.

Contrast of ideas and topics: James will not eat foods made with *artificial* ingredients; he shops only at organic food stores.

PRACTICE As you read "A Work in Progress," study the context to determine the meanings of unfamiliar words. Mark your observations in the open space next to the text.

Reading Strategy: Ask Questions

To deepen your understanding and gain more information from a text, **ask questions** about it before, during, and after reading.

- Before you read, preview the text, including the title, genre, and any additional features, such as the Background section or information about the author. Write questions the text might answer.
- As you read, notice details that raise questions for you. Jot down these questions and read on.
- After you read, reflect on the questions you asked before and during reading. Then, consider whether these questions have been answered. Write any additional questions that you have.

PRACTICE Ask questions before, during, and after you read the text. Jot them down in the open space next to the text.

578 UNIT 5 • FACING ADVERSITY

ORAL HISTORY

A Work in Progress

Aimee Mullins

BACKGROUND

A *prosthesis* is an artificial substitute for a missing body part. Over the past few decades, prosthetic technology has advanced greatly. Because of the development of more sophisticated technologies, prostheses can often perform or even out-perform the function of damaged or missing limbs.

1   So two weeks ago I was a bridesmaid, and the reception was actually here at the New York Public Library, and I will never forget this wedding. Yes, it was very beautiful. But more importantly, I survived the slick marble floors that are all over this building. Tile and marble floors are public enemy number one to a stiletto-loving girl like me. And I had five-inch heels on that night.

READ TO UNLOCK MEANING

1. First read the text for comprehension and enjoyment. Use the **Reading Strategy** and **Comprehension Check** questions to support your first read.
2. With your group, apply the vocabulary strategy to unlock word meanings.
3. Find other details in the text you find interesting. Ask your own questions and draw your own conclusions.

2   Most people learn to walk in very high heels. They bend their ankle so that the ball of the foot touches the ground first; you have more stability.

3   I don't have ankles, so I hit each step on the stiletto, which makes the possibility of the banana peel wipeout very likely. But given the choice between practicality and theatricality, I say, "Go big or go home, man. Go down in flames if you're gonna go."

4   I guess I'm a bit of a daredevil. I think that the nurses at DuPont Institute would agree. I spent a lot of time there as a child. Doctors amputated[1] both of my legs below the knee when I was an infant, and then when I was five, I had a major surgery to correct the wonky direction in which my tibia was growing. So I had two metal pins to hold that—full plaster casts on both legs. I had to use a wheelchair because I couldn't wear prosthetics.

5   One of the best things about getting out of the hospital is the anticipation of the day you return to school—I had missed so much class, I just couldn't wait to get back and see all my friends. But my teacher had a different idea about that. She tried to prevent me from returning to class, because she said that in the condition I was in, I was "inappropriate," and that I would be a distraction to the other students (which of course I was, but not because of the casts and the wheelchair).

6   Clearly she needed to make my difference invisible because she wanted to control her environment and make it fit into her idea of what "normal" looked like.

7   And it would've been a lot easier for me to fit into what "normal" looked like. I know I wanted that back then. But instead I had these wooden legs with a rubber foot that the toes broke off of, and they were held on with a big bolt that rusted out because I swam in the wooden legs.

8   You're not supposed to swim in the wooden legs, because, you know, the wood rots out.

9   So there I was in second grade music class, doing the twist, and mid-twist I hear this [*makes loud cracking sound*]. And I'm on the floor, and the lower half of my left leg is in splinters across the room. The teacher faints on the piano, and the kids are screaming. And all I'm thinking is, *My parents are gonna kill me. I broke my leg!*

10   It's a mess.

11   But then a few years later, my prosthetist[2] tells me, "Aimee, we got waterproof legs for you. No more rusty bolts!"

---

1. **amputated** (AM pyoo tayt ihd) *v.* removed surgically.
2. **prosthetist** (PROS thuh tihst) *n.* professional who fits and designs prosthetic limbs.

580 UNIT 5 • FACING ADVERSITY

12   This is a revelation, right? This is gonna change my life. I was so excited to get these legs... until I saw them.

13   They were made of polypropylene, which is that white plastic "milk jug" material. And when I say "white," I'm not talking about skin color; I'm talking about *the color white*. The "skin color" was the rubber foam foot painted "Caucasian," which is the nastiest shade of nuclear peach that you've ever seen in your life. It has nothing to do with any human skin tone on the planet. And these legs were so good at being waterproof that they were *buoyant*. So when I'd go off the high dive, I'd go down and come straight back up feet first. They were the bane of my existence.

14   But then we're at the Jersey Shore one summer. By the time we get there, there's three hundred yards of towels between me and the sea. And I know this is where I first honed my ability to run really fast. I was the white flash. I didn't wanna feel hundreds of pairs of eyes staring at me. And so I'd get myself into the ocean, and I was a good swimmer, but no amount of swimming technique can control buoyant legs.

15   So at some point I get caught in a rip current, and I'm migrating from my vantage point of where I could see my parents' towel. And I'm taking in water, and I'm fighting, fighting, fighting. And all I could think to do was pop off these legs and put one under each armpit, with the peach feet sticking up, and just bob, thinking, *Someone's gotta find me*.

16   And a lifeguard did. And I'm sure he will collect for therapy bills. You know? Like, they don't show that on *Baywatch*.[3]

17   But they saved my life, those legs.

18   And then when I was fourteen it was Easter Sunday, and I was gonna be wearing a dress that I had purchased with my own money—the first thing I ever bought that wasn't on sale.

19   Momentous event; you never forget it. I'd had a paper route since I was twelve, and I went to The Limited, and I bought this dress that I thought was the height of sophistication—sleeveless safari dress, belted, hits at the knee.

20   Coming downstairs into the living room, I see my father waiting to take us to church. He takes one look at me, and he says, "That doesn't look right. Go upstairs and change."

21   I was like, "What? My super-classy dress? What are you talking about? It's the best thing I own."

22   He said, "No, you can see the knee joint when you walk. It doesn't look right. It's inappropriate to go out like that. Go change."

ASK QUESTIONS
What questions can you ask about paragraphs 13–15 to help you understand Mullins's experience with her waterproof legs?

COMPREHENSION CHECK
When Mullins first returns to school, how does her teacher react?

---
3. **Baywatch** popular television show from the late 1990s about the lives of fictional lifeguards.

23 And I think something snapped in me. I refused to change. And it was the first time I defied my father. I refused to hide something about myself that was true, and I refused to be embarrassed about something so that other people could feel more comfortable.

24 I was grounded for that defiance.

25 So after church the extended family convenes at my grandmother's house, and everybody's complimenting me on how nice I look in this dress, and I'm like, "Really? You think I look nice? Because my parents think I look inappropriate."

26 I outed them (kinda mean, really).

27 But I think the public utterance of this idea that I should somehow hide myself was so shocking to hear that it changed their mind about why they were doing it.

28 And I had always managed to get through life with somewhat of a positive attitude, but I think this was the start of me being able to accept myself. You know, okay, I'm not normal. I have strengths. I've got weaknesses. It is what it is.

29 And I had always been athletic, but it wasn't until college that I started this adventure in Track and Field. I had gone through a lifetime of being given legs that just barely got me by. And I thought, *Well, maybe I'm just having the wrong conversations with the wrong people. Maybe I need to go find people who say, "Yes, we can create anything for you in the space between where your leg ends and the ground."*

30 And so I started working with engineers, fashion designers, sculptors, Hollywood prosthetic makeup artists, wax museum designers to build legs for me.

31 I decided I wanted to be the fastest woman in the world on artificial legs, and I was lucky enough to arrive in track at just the right time to be the first person to get these radical sprinting legs modeled after the hind leg of a cheetah, the fastest thing that runs—woven carbon fiber.[4] I was able to set three world records with those legs. And they made no attempt at approximating humanness.

32 Then I get these incredibly lifelike silicon legs—hand-painted, capillaries, veins. And, hey, I can be as tall as I wanna be, so I get different legs for different heights. I don't have to shave. I can wear open-toed shoes in the winter. And most importantly, I can opt out of the cankles[5] I most certainly would've inherited genetically.

33 And then I get these legs made for me by the late, great Alexander McQueen, and they were hand-carved of solid ash with grapevines and magnolias all over them and a six-inch heel. And I was able to walk the runways of the world with

---

4. **carbon fiber** (KAHR buhn FY buhr) *n.* very strong, lightweight material.
5. **cankles** (KANG kuhlz) *n.* informal term for thick ankles.

supermodels. I was suddenly in this whirlwind of adventure and excitement. I was being invited to go around the world and speak about these adventures, and how I had legs that looked like glass, legs covered in feathers, porcelain legs, jellyfish legs—all wearable sculpture.

34   And I get this call from a guy who had seen me speak years ago, when I was at the beginning of my track career, and he says, "We loved it. We want you to come back." And it was clear to me he didn't know all these amazing things that had happened to me since my sports career.

35   So as I'm telling him, he says, "Whoa, whoa, whoa. Hold on, Aimee. The reason everybody liked you all those years ago was because you were this sweet, vulnerable, naïve girl, and if you walk onstage today, and you are this polished young woman with too many **accomplishments**, I'm afraid they won't like you."

36   For real, he said that. Wow.

37   He apparently didn't think I was vulnerable enough now. He was asking me to be *less than*, a little more downtrodden. He was asking me to disable myself for him and his audience.

38   And what was so shocking to me about that was that I realized I had moved past mere acceptance of my difference. I was having *fun* with my difference. Thank *God* I'm not normal. I get to be **extraordinary**. And I'll decide what is a weakness and what is a strength.

39   And so I refused his request.

40   And a few days later, I'm walking in downtown Manhattan at a street fair, and I get this tug on my shirt, and I look down. It's this little girl I met a year earlier when she was at a pivotal moment in her life. She had been born with a brittle bone disease that resulted in her left leg being seven centimeters shorter than her right. She wore a brace and orthopedic[6] shoes and they got her by, but she wanted to do more.

41   And like all Internet-savvy kindergarteners, she gets on the computer and Googles "new leg," and she comes up with dozens of images of prosthetics, many of them mine. And she prints them out, goes to school, does show-and-tell on it, comes home, and makes a startling pronouncement to her parents:

42   "I wanna get rid of my bad leg," she says. "When can I get a new leg?"

43   And ultimately that was the decision her parents and doctors made for her. So here she was, six months after the amputation, and right there in the middle of the street fair she hikes up her

---

6. **orthopedic** (awr thuh PEE dihk) *adj.* designed to treat a muscular or skeletal problem.

Mark context clues or indicate another strategy you used that helped you determine meaning.

accomplishments (uh KOM plihsh muhnts) *n.*

MEANING:

extraordinary (ehk STRAWR duh nehr ee) *adj.*

MEANING:

COMPREHENSION CHECK

What does Mullins do to improve the quality of her prosthetic legs?

jeans leg to show me her cool new leg. And it's pink, and it's tattooed with the characters of *High School Musical 3*, replete with red, sequined Mary Janes on her feet.

44   And she was proud of it. She was proud of herself. And the marvelous thing was that this six-year-old understood something that it took me twenty-something years to get, but that we both did discover—that when we can **celebrate** and truly own what it is that makes us different, we're able to find the source of our greatest creative power.

Mark context clues or indicate another strategy you used that helped you determine meaning.

celebrate (SEHL uh brayt) *v.*
MEANING:

BUILD INSIGHT

First Thoughts

Choose one of the following items to discuss.
- Mullins criticizes normalcy throughout this piece. Is being "normal" really a bad thing? Is it necessary or important to be "exceptional"? Explain.
- Given what you read about Mullins's experiences, why do you think she chose the title "A Work in Progress"? Could this title apply to aspects of your own life? Explain.

Summary

Write a short summary of the text to confirm your comprehension. Be sure to include only the central ideas and to keep your summary objective.

Analysis and Discussion

1. **Make Inferences** Reread paragraphs 7–10. What does the incident in Mullins's music class suggest about her attitude toward her difference, even as a young child?

2. **Interpret** Reread paragraph 28. What does Mullins suggest is the difference between her "positive attitude" and "being able to accept myself"? Explain, citing text evidence to support your ideas.

3. (a) **Summarize** What realization does Mullins have in paragraph 29?
   (b) **Analyze Cause and Effect** How does this realization influence Mullins's life and attitude? Explain, citing specific details from the text.

4. **Get Ready for Close Reading** Choose a passage from the text that you find especially interesting or important. You'll discuss the passage with your group during Close-Read activities.

> **WORKING AS A GROUP**
>
> Discuss your responses to the Analysis and Discussion questions with your group.
> - Note agreements and disagreements.
> - Ask questions that encourage your peers to elaborate on their responses.
>
> If necessary, revise your original answers to reflect what you learn from your discussion.

Exploring the Essential Question

How do we overcome life's challenges?

5. What has this text revealed about the use of humor when facing adversity in life? Record you ideas in your Evidence Log.

STANDARDS
Reading Informational Text
- Cite several pieces of textual evidence to support analysis of what the text says explicitly as well as inferences drawn from the text.
- Provide an objective summary of the text.

A Work in Progress **585**

ANALYZE AND INTERPRET

A WORK IN PROGRESS

Close Read

PRACTICE Complete the following activities. Use text evidence to support your responses.

1. **Present and Discuss** With your group, share the passages from the text that you found especially interesting. Discuss what you notice, the questions you have, and the conclusions you reach. For example, you might focus on the following passages:

   • **Paragraphs 3–4:** Discuss ways in which Mullins's word choice helps to convey her personality.

   • **Paragraph 23:** Discuss the effect of the repetition of the word *refused*.

   • **Paragraphs 40–44:** Discuss why Mullins included the account of meeting the six-year-old girl.

2. **Reflect on Your Learning** What new ideas or insights did you uncover during your second reading of the text?

WORD WALL

Note words in the text that are related to the idea of facing adversity. Add them to your Word Wall.

STUDY LANGUAGE AND CRAFT

Concept Vocabulary

Why These Words? The vocabulary words are related.

| accomplishments | extraordinary | celebrate |

1. With your group, determine what the words have in common. Write your ideas.

2. Add another word that fits the category: _____

3. Write an introduction for someone who's winning an award. Use all three vocabulary words in your introduction. Share your work with your group.

Word Study

Latin Prefix: *extra*- The Latin prefix *extra*- means "beyond the scope of" or "in addition to what is usual or expected." At the end of the selection, the author realizes that what makes her different also makes her *extraordinary*, or beyond what is ordinary or expected.

PRACTICE With your group, identify two other words you know with the Latin prefix *extra*- and write down their meanings. Then, verify or correct your definitions by checking in a dictionary.

STANDARDS

Reading Informational Text
Analyze the impact of a specific word choice on meaning and tone.

Language
Use common, grade-appropriate Greek or Latin affixes and roots as clues to the meaning of a word.

586 UNIT 5 • FACING ADVERSITY

Essential Question: How do we overcome life's challenges?

Language and Voice

Every writer has a characteristic personality, a distinctive sound or way of "speaking" on the page. That quality is called **voice**. The subject matter, occasion and purpose of the writing, and use of language all contribute to a writer's voice.

LANGUAGE DEVICE	EXAMPLES FROM THE TEXT	ANALYSIS
Diction: the words an author chooses to use	• So two weeks ago • banana-peel wipeout • choice between practicality and theatricality	• starts sentences with conjunctions • mixes casual words, slang, and sophisticated words
Syntax: the way an author arranges words and sentences	• So two weeks ago… and I will never forget this wedding. Yes, it was very beautiful. • I broke my leg! • This is a revelation, right?	• combines longer, rambling sentences with short sentences • exclamations • conversational questions
Tone: the author's attitude toward the subject or audience	• banana-peel wipeout • the nastiest shade of nuclear peach • I don't have ankles	• hyperbole, or exaggeration for humorous effect • direct statements

PRACTICE Work on your own to answer the questions. Then, share your responses with your group.

1. **Analyze** Reread paragraph 9. How does Mullins's diction and syntax impact the meaning and tone of this paragraph?

2. **Speculate** How do you think the listening audience probably reacted to paragraph 16? Why? Describe qualities in the text that develop Mullins's voice and support your thinking.

3. **Interpret** Choose the three adjectives from this list that you think best describe Mullins's tone. Explain your choices.

direct	charming	conceited	humble
boastful	secretive	funny	insincere

A Work in Progress 587

STUDY LANGUAGE AND CRAFT

A WORK IN PROGRESS

TIP: Speech writers like Aimee Mullins may use a formal or informal style, depending on the situation and audience.

- **Informal style** is usually used to tell a story, to share an experience, or for humorous effect.
- **Formal style** is usually used to make arguments, to give information, or to present research.

Informal Grammar

"A Work in Progress" is transcribed, or copied, from a speech. While speaking, Mullins produced a certain effect by choosing **informal grammar,** or casual language, that includes the following elements:

- **Colloquial contractions:** words such as *gonna* (going to), *wanna* (want to) and *kinda* (kind of)
- **Informal transitions:** casual words and phrases such as *man, I'm like,* and *you know*
- **Introductory conjunctions:** sentences that begin with *And, But,* and *So*
- **Sentence fragments:** deliberate use of incomplete thoughts or statements

READ Work on your own to rewrite each example of informal grammar to follow standard English grammar rules. Then, discuss with your group how these changes impact the meaning and tone of the text.

INFORMAL GRAMMAR FROM TEXT	STANDARD GRAMMAR
And all I'm thinking is, My parents are *gonna* kill me. (paragraph 9)	
This is a revelation, right? This is *gonna* change my life. (paragraph 12)	
For real, he said that. Wow. (paragraph 36)	

WRITE / EDIT Complete the activity.

Write a paragraph that uses informal language to tell about a funny incident that happened to you or someone you know. Write as if you are speaking directly to an audience. Use colloquial contractions, sentence fragments, and other informal elements.

Next, take turns reading your paragraphs to the group. Speak as though you are giving a speech rather than reading a text. As others read aloud, listen carefully for their use of informal grammar.

Finally, exchange paragraphs with a member of your group. Rewrite each other's paragraph in standard English. Discuss how the changes to word choice impact the voice, tone, and meaning of your paragraphs.

STANDARDS

Reading Informational Text
Analyze the impact of a specific word choice on meaning and tone.

Speaking and Listening
Pose questions that elicit elaboration and respond to others' questions and comments with relevant observations and ideas.

Language
- Demonstrate command of the conventions of standard English grammar and usage when writing or speaking.
- Use knowledge of language and its conventions when writing, speaking, reading, or listening.

SHARE IDEAS

Speaking and Listening

A **discussion** is a conversation among two or more people about a specific topic.

Assignment

With your group, conduct a **discussion** in which you analyze one of the following quotations from the selection. Read the full quotation in the text before deciding which one to focus on.

○ "And I had always been athletic, ... your leg ends and the ground.'" (paragraph 29)

○ "And she was proud of it ... the source of our greatest creative power." (paragraph 44)

Use Questions to Guide Your Discussion As you share ideas, use the chart to take notes. Add questions of your own, and draw on evidence from the text as you jot down your responses.

DISCUSSION QUESTIONS	RESPONSES
What does the quotation mean?	
What happens that causes Mullins to express these ideas?	
Do you think Mullins's observations are inspirational? Why, or why not?	

Listen Actively You can deepen your understanding of a discussion topic by clarifying the ideas of other speakers. Here are sentence starters that you might use to politely ask questions or make comments that build on other group members' ideas:

- I wasn't sure what you meant when you said _____. Could you provide an example?
- I thought your idea about _____ was interesting. Could you elaborate on it?

EVIDENCE LOG

Before moving on to a new selection, go to your Evidence Log and record any additional thoughts or observations you may have about "A Work in Progress."

A Work in Progress **589**

LEARN ABOUT GENRE: POETRY AND PROSE

Reading Poetry and Prose

SIMILE: WILLOW AND GINGKO • FOUR SKINNY TREES

A **lyric poem** expresses the thoughts and feelings of a single speaker and captures the emotions of a moment. A **vignette** (vihn YEHT) is a short piece of prose that expresses the thoughts and feelings of a narrator and captuers a moment in time.

LYRIC POETRY

Author's Purpose
- to capture the feelings or insights related to a moment in time

Characteristics
- has a speaker, or voice, that "tells" the poem
- uses imagery, figurative language, and sensory details to paint pictures in readers' minds
- expresses an insight, or a new understanding, about life
- often conveys multiple layers of meaning
- word choice creates a song-like quality
- may break some of the rules of standard English

Structure
- poetic lines may be formed into stanzas or flow freely
- may contain patterns of rhyme or repetition

VIGNETTE

Author's Purpose
- to capture the feelings or insights related to a moment in time

Characteristics
- has a narrator that "speaks" to readers
- is short; does not have a plot
- uses sensory details and figurative language to create imagery
- may not follow the rules of standard English

Structure
- structured in paragraphs or may be free-flowing
- may have internal rhyme and/or repetition

590 UNIT 5 • FACING ADVERSITY

Essential Question: How do we overcome life's challenges?

Imagery: Sensory Details and Figurative Language

Imagery is language that appeals to the five senses of sight, hearing, taste, touch, and smell. Authors of both lyric poetry and vignettes may use imagery to create vivid and memorable descriptions for readers. In addition to **sensory details**, authors may create imagery by using **figurative language.** Common figures of speech are shown in the chart.

FIGURE OF SPEECH	DESCRIPTION	EXAMPLE
simile	uses *like* or *as* to compare things that are seemingly unalike	She studied so hard her head felt <u>like</u> an overstuffed library.
personification	describes something nonhuman as if it had human traits or abilities	The maple trees <u>nodded</u>, then <u>gestured wildly</u> as the wind grew stronger.
metaphor	describes two seemingly unalike things as if one thing were the other	The soft rain <u>was a lullaby</u>, soothing him to sleep.

PRACTICE Complete the activities.

1. Complete the chart on your own. Identify the type of figurative language used in each passage and underline the words that helped you identify it. Then, describe the imagery each example creates.

PASSAGE	MEANING / EFFECT
Kneeling on the grass, rows of parched lilies Prayed for rain	
Hail hit the tin roof like notes from a broken piano—tuneless and forceful.	
Storm clouds, stampeding herds of buffalo, cover the sky	

2. Working individually, write 4–5 lines of poetry in which you create imagery, using at least two types of figurative language. Then, share your writing with your group and discuss ways in which the use of imagery creates meaning.

STANDARDS
Reading Literature
Determine the meaning of words and phrases as they are used in a text, including figurative and connotative meanings.

PREPARE TO READ

SIMILE: WILLOW AND GINKGO • FOUR SKINNY TREES

Simile: Willow and Ginkgo • Four Skinny Trees

Concept Vocabulary

As you read the selections, you will encounter these words. When you finish reading, work with your group to identify what the words have in common.

| crude | rough | raggedy |

Reference Materials An entry in a print or online **dictionary** identifies the part of speech of an unfamiliar word. Knowing a word's part of speech can help you understand its role in a phrase or sentence. This is especially true for words with multiple meanings.

Sometimes a single word can function as different parts of speech. Read this excerpt from a dictionary entry for the word *concrete*. Notice its different definitions and parts of speech.

EXAMPLE

concrete (kon KREET) *adj.* real; able to be touched or mentally perceived; (KON kreet) *n.* building material composed of crushed rocks and minerals, which, when combined with water, forms a strong bond

PRACTICE ▸ As you read, mark unfamiliar and multiple-meaning words in the selections. Look them up in a print or digital dictionary to determine their precise meanings and parts of speech.

Reading Strategy: Make Connections

As you read, **make connections** between the texts and your personal experiences. Ask yourself questions like these:

- What are my feelings about these particular details?
- Do the situations in these texts remind me of things I've experienced or learned about? In what way?
- Do these texts confirm or challenge my views about the ideas they present?

PRACTICE ▸ As you read, use the open space next to the selections to jot down connections you make to your personal experiences or prior knowledge.

STANDARDS
Reading Literature
By the end of the year, read and comprehend literature, including stories, dramas, and poems.
Language
• Determine or clarify the meaning of unknown and multiple-meaning words and phrases based on grade 7 reading and content.
• Consult general and specialized reference materials, both print and digital, to find the pronunciation of a word or determine or clarify its precise meaning or its part of speech.

592 UNIT 5 • FACING ADVERSITY

Essential Question: How do we overcome life's challenges?

About the Texts

Simile: Willow and Ginkgo

BACKGROUND
This poem focuses on two trees, each with its own character. The willow has thin, graceful branches that are often long enough to touch the ground. The ginkgo is known for its toughness and ability to survive—ginkgos were already flourishing when dinosaurs lived. The poem's speaker observes and compares these two trees, taking an approach that is imaginative rather than scientific.

Eve Merriam (1916–1992) was fascinated with language from an early age and began writing poetry as a young girl. When she was twenty, her first book, *Family Circle*, won the Yale Series of Younger Poets award, and she later received further honors. Merriam wrote a wide range of poetry for children and also published picture books, plays, and works for adults.

Four Skinny Trees

BACKGROUND
Sandra Cisneros's novel *The House on Mango Street* is narrated through vignettes, or short scenes and reflections. Some, like this one, are much like poetry, with memorable imagery and ideas. The narrator—the voice saying the words—is Esperanza, a girl growing up in a Hispanic neighborhood in Chicago. Nenny is her younger sister. This vignette focuses on the trees outside Esperanza's house.

Sandra Cisneros (b. 1954) grew up in Chicago, Illinois, in a large family of Mexican heritage. In 1984, she published *The House on Mango Street*, which sold more than six million copies and has been translated into many languages. A poet, novelist, essayist, and children's author, Cisneros has won several literary awards, including the Poetry Foundation's Ruth Lilly Prize.

Simile: Willow and Ginkgo • Four Skinny Trees **593**

LYRIC POETRY

Simile: Willow and Ginkgo
Eve Merriam

READ TO UNLOCK MEANING

1. First read the texts for comprehension and enjoyment. Use the **Reading Strategy** question to support your first read.
2. With your group, apply the vocabulary strategy to unlock word meanings.
3. Find other details in the texts that you find interesting. Ask your own questions and draw your own conclusions.

Use a dictionary or indicate another strategy you used that helped you determine meaning.

crude (KROOD) *adj.*
MEANING:

rough (RUF) *adj.*
MEANING:

The willow is like an etching,[1]
Fine-lined against the sky.
Then ginkgo is like a **crude** sketch,
Hardly worthy to be signed.

5   The willow's music is like a soprano,
Delicate and thin.
The ginkgo's tune is like a chorus
With everyone joining in.

The willow is sleek as a velvet-nosed calf,
10 The ginkgo is leathery as an old bull.
The willow's branches are like silken thread;
The ginkgo's like stubby **rough** wool.

The willow is like a nymph[2] with streaming hair;
Wherever it grows, there is green and gold and fair.
15 The willow dips to the water,
Protected and precious, like the king's favorite daughter.

The ginkgo forces its way through gray concrete;
Like a city child, it grows up in the street.
Thrust against the metal sky,
20 Somehow it survives and even thrives.

*My eyes feast upon the willow,
But my heart goes to the ginkgo.*

"Simile: Willow and Ginkgo" copyright © 1986 by Eve Merriam. Appears in A Sky Full of Poems. Originally published by Yearling. Used by permission of Curtis Brown, Ltd.

1. **etching** (EH chihng) *n.* print of a drawing made on metal, glass, or wood.
2. **nymph** (NIHMF) *n.* goddess of nature, thought of as a beautiful young woman.

VIGNETTE

Four Skinny Trees

from The House on Mango Street

Sandra Cisneros

1   They are the only ones who understand me. I am the only one who understands them. Four skinny trees with skinny necks and pointy elbows like mine. Four who do not belong here but are here. Four raggedy excuses planted by the city. From our room we can hear them, but Nenny just sleeps and doesn't appreciate these things.

2   Their strength is secret. They send ferocious roots beneath the ground. They grow up and they grow down and grab the earth between their hairy toes and bite the sky with violent teeth and never quit their anger. This is how they keep.

3   Let one forget his reason for being, they'd all droop like tulips in a glass, each with their arms around the other. Keep, keep, keep, trees say when I sleep. They teach.

4   When I am too sad and too skinny to keep keeping, when I am a tiny thing against so many bricks, then it is I look at trees. When there is nothing left to look at on this street. Four who grew despite concrete. Four who reach and do not forget to reach. Four whose only reason is to be and be.

Use a dictionary or indicate another strategy you used that helped you determine meaning.

raggedy (RA geh dee) *adj.*

MEANING:

MAKE CONNECTIONS
Which stanza or paragraph in these texts were you able to make an emotional connection to? Explain.

BUILD INSIGHT

SIMILE: WILLOW AND GINKGO • FOUR SKINNY TREES

First Thoughts

Which of the many images in these texts is your favorite? Explain why.

Comprehension

1. **Comprehension Check (a)** In "Simile: Willow and Ginkgo," what types of things does the poet compare the trees to? **(b)** In "Four Skinny Trees," in what ways does the narrator say she and the trees are alike?

2. **Strategy: Make Connections (a)** Which selection did you make stronger connections to? Why? **(b)** In what ways did these connections add to your reading experience?

Analysis and Discussion

3. Lines 13–20 of "Simile: Willow and Ginkgo" make extended comparisons of the trees. **(a) Analyze** What single main quality do these lines express about each tree? **(b) Interpret** What insight does the poem suggest about the concepts of ease and effort?

4. **Make Inferences** Why do you think the poet uses italic type for the last two lines of "Simile: Willow and Ginkgo"?

5. **Analyze** In the first four sentences of "Four Skinny Trees," the narrator shares her thoughts about the trees. Why does she feel a close bond with them?

6. **Interpret** Reread paragraphs 3–4 of "Four Skinny Trees." What does the repeated word "keep" mean in these sentences?

7. **Get Ready for Close Reading** Choose a passage from one of the texts that you find especially interesting or important. You'll discuss the passage with your group during Close Read activities.

> **WORKING AS A GROUP**
>
> Discuss your responses to the Analysis and Discussion questions with your group.
>
> • Support your responses with text details.
> • Clarify comments of peers by restating or summarizing them.
>
> If needed, modify your responses to reflect new information you learn during the discussion.

Exploring the Essential Question

How do we overcome life's challenges?

8. Both selections include the image of concrete. Describe how this image connects to the idea of overcoming challenges.

STANDARDS
Language
Determine or clarify the meaning of unknown and multiple-meaning words and phrases based on grade 7 reading and content, choosing flexibly from a range of strategies.

596 UNIT 5 • FACING ADVERSITY

ANALYZE AND INTERPRET

Close Read

PRACTICE Use text evidence to complete the following activities.

1. **Present and Discuss** With your group, share passages from the texts that you found especially interesting. For example, you might focus on the following:

   - **"Simile: Willow and Ginkgo," lines 9–12:** Discuss the comparisons in these lines. Is it surprising that the poet chose these images to describe trees?
   - **"Four Skinny Trees," paragraph 2:** Discuss the images you feel are most powerful.

2. **Reflect on Your Learning** What new ideas or insights did you uncover during your second reading of the selections?

STUDY LANGUAGE AND CRAFT

Concept Vocabulary

Why These Words? The vocabulary words are related.

| crude | rough | raggedy |

1. With your group, discuss what the words have in common.

2. Add another word that fits the category. _____

3. With a partner, write a paragraph describing a place with trees that you know or imagine. Include all three vocabulary words.

WORD WALL

Note words in the texts that are related to the concept of facing adversity. Add them to your Word Wall.

Word Study

Multiple-Meaning Words Some words have more than one definition, and some can function as different parts of speech. For example, Eve Merriam's poem refers to "a crude sketch"; the adjective *crude* describes the sketch. *Crude* can also be a noun, as in "The oil refinery processes crude into useful products." Here, *crude* refers to unprocessed oil.

PRACTICE Look up *star* in a print or digital dictionary. Notice that it is a multiple-meaning word that can be used as three different parts of speech. Write three sentences, each using *star* as a different part of speech. Label the part of speech in each sentence. Share your sentences with your group.

Simile: Willow and Ginkgo • Four Skinny Trees **597**

ANALYZE AND INTERPRET

SIMILE: WILLOW AND GINKGO • FOUR SKINNY TREES

Imagery: Sensory Details and Figurative Language

Authors of lyric poetry and vignettes want to create vivid pictures in their readers' minds. One way they may do so is by using **imagery**, descriptive language that appeals to the five senses. To create imagery, writers use **sensory details**, or words and phrases that help readers experience details of sight, hearing, taste, touch, and smell.

SENSE OF SOUND	SENSE OF SIGHT
The ginkgo's tune is like a chorus ("Simile: Willow and Ginkgo," line 7)	[Trees] grab the earth between their hairy toes ("Four Skinny Trees," paragraph 2)

The use of **figurative language** can also create imagery. In these texts, the authors use imaginative comparisons to create memorable images that give readers a fresh look at something familiar.

A **simile** compares two seemingly unlike things using the word *like* or *as*.

> The willow's music is like a soprano
> ("Simile: Willow and Ginkgo," line 5)

Personification lends human traits to something that is not human.

> trees with skinny necks and pointy elbows
> ("Four Skinny Trees," paragraph 1)

PRACTICE Complete the activities.

1. On your own, identify the imagery in each example as *simile, personification,* or *sensory details*. Then, explain the overall effect of the imagery. Discuss your responses with your group.

EXAMPLE	IMAGERY	EFFECT
Keep, keep, keep, trees say when I sleep		
Wherever [the willow] grows, there is green and gold and fair.		
Like a city child, [the ginkgo] grows up in the street		

2. **Interpret** On your own, reread lines 9–12 in "Simile: Willow and Ginkgo." Explain how the use of imagery creates meaning.

3. With your group, write a paragraph about a tree that you are familiar with. Use both figurative and sensory language.

STANDARDS

Reading Literature
Determine the meaning of words and phrases as they are used in a text, including figurative and connotative meanings; analyze the impact of rhymes and other repetitions of sounds on a specific verse or stanza of a poem or section of a story or drama.

Language
Demonstrate understanding of figurative language, word relationships, and nuances in word meanings.

STUDY LANGUAGE AND CRAFT

Rhyme Scheme and Repetition

Patterns of sound create musical effects. **Repetition** is one type of sound pattern, and it comes in different forms. Read the beginning sentences of "Four Skinny Trees":

> They are <u>the only ones who understand</u> me. I am <u>the only one who understands</u> them.

Notice how the sentences are structured to mirror each other. They include several repeated words, in some cases different forms of the same word. This repetition emphasizes an idea: how closely the narrator identifies with the trees outside her house.

Rhyme, the repeating of words' end sounds, is another type of repetition. A poem's stanzas, or groups of lines, may have a pattern known as a **rhyme scheme** that contributes to its meaning by emphasizing certain words. Read this stanza from "Simile: Willow and Ginkgo":

> The willow is sleek as a velvet-nosed calf,
> The ginkgo is leathery as an old <u>bull</u>.
> The willow's branches are like silken thread;
> The ginkgo's like stubby rough <u>wool</u>.

The second and fourth lines end with rhyming words. The first and the third lines do not. This rhyme scheme can be shown with letters of the alphabet: *abcb*. The *b*'s stand for the lines that rhyme. If the other two lines had ended with rhyming words, the rhyme scheme would have been *abab*.

> **TIP:** **Slant rhyme** is a type of rhyming where words sound similar but do not rhyme exactly. *Sky* and *signed* in lines 2 and 4 of Eve Merriam's poem create slant rhyme.

PRACTICE Complete the first two activities on your own. Work with your group to complete the third.

1. **Analyze** Reread lines 13–16 of "Simile: Willow and Ginkgo." Mark the lines in the text, using letters to show its rhyme scheme.

2. **(a)** Read this passage from "Four Skinny Trees" and underline the repeated words.

   > Four who grew despite concrete. Four who reach and do not forget to reach.

   (b) Make Inferences Why do you think the author chose to repeat these words? What effect is created?

3. With your group, find two more examples of rhyme or repetition in the two texts. Discuss how each example creates sound and meaning.

Simile: Willow and Ginkgo • Four Skinny Trees   **599**

SHARE IDEAS

SIMILE: WILLOW AND GINKGO • FOUR SKINNY TREES

Writing

A **lyric poem** expresses a speaker's thoughts and feelings in writing that is focused, imaginative, and musical.

Assignment

Work on your own to write a **lyric poem** that compares two specific things. It might focus on what makes each thing distinct and different, as in "Simile: Willow and Ginkgo," or it may focus on shared qualities, as in "Four Skinny Trees."

Plan Your Poem Choose what to compare—for example, it could be two places, two animals, or two experiences. Gather vibrant, precise details that appeal to readers' senses. You might also choose to create vivid figures of speech, such as similes and personification, which suggest unexpected connections between ideas.

Develop Your Draft As you write, explore your two subjects from various angles. Think deeply about what makes them similar or different. Pay attention to the following elements of poetry as you work:

- **Focus:** Poetry is condensed. Use precise words and phrases to express your ideas clearly. Convey meaning through sensory details and figurative language rather than lengthy explanations.

- **Structure:** Experiment with different line lengths and consider whether or not to create stanza breaks. Give your poem whatever shape on the page you'd like so that it flows the way you want it to.

- **Rhyme and Repetition:** Consider using rhyme to create a pattern of sounds. If you'd like to emphasize certain ideas, try repeating a word or phrase.

Publish Your Work A chapbook is a small collection of poetry. Work with your group to publish a **digital chapbook** of the poems you wrote independently. Follow these steps:

1. Type your poem using a font that goes with, or enhances, your ideas.
2. Add an image to your poem to help emphasize your main point or insight.
3. Gather the poems everyone has written into a single slideshow or document.
4. Create a table of contents that includes each poem's title, its author, and the slide number or page number on which it appears.
5. Give the collection a title and choose an image that enhances the title.
6. Share your group's digital chapbook with others by posting it on your class, school, or library website.

STANDARDS

Writing
- Write narratives to develop real or imagined experiences or events using effective technique, relevant descriptive details.
- Use precise words and phrases, relevant descriptive details, and sensory language to capture the action and convey experiences and events.
- Draw evidence from literary or informational texts to support analysis, reflection, and research.

Speaking and Listening
Include multimedia components and visual displays in presentations to clarify claims and findings and emphasize salient points.

Essential Question: How do we overcome life's challenges?

Speaking and Listening

An **illustrated version** of a text includes its original words along with pictures created by one or more artists. These visual elements may portray people, places, or images found in the poem. They also show an artist's imaginative response to the text.

> ### Assignment
>
> Work with your group to create an **illustrated version** of either "Simile: Willow and Ginkgo," or "Four Skinny Trees" for an audience of young readers. Choose one of these formats:
>
> ○ a picture book, either print or digital
>
> ○ a graphic novel
>
> The illustrations should capture the ideas, feelings, and insights of your chosen text in a way that children will enjoy.

Discuss and Plan As a group, discuss the text you will illustrate and the effect you want to achieve. Consider these questions:

- Which aspects of the text will you emphasize?
- How will you divide the text across a number of pages?
- What types of art will you create in order to engage children?

Use the chart to organize your plans.

TEXT TO ILLUSTRATE	CONTENT OF ILLUSTRATION

TIP: For inspiration, look at some children's picture books. Notice the styles of art and how the visuals and text fit together.

Create the Illustrations You may draw, paint, or use art software to create your images. You might include photos as well. Illustrations created on paper can be photographed or scanned to create a digital text.

Produce a Final Version Work with your group to confirm the layout of each slide or page—where the text goes and where the art goes. If you are producing the pages digitally, choose a font that goes with the text you are illustrating. If you are handwriting the pages, use a stylish script or calligraphy. Be sure to number your pages or slides for easy reference.

Present Your Illustrated Version Tell the class which text your group chose and explain your approach to creating your illustrated version. Then, present your work, allowing time for classmates to view the images. Ask for feedback and respond to questions and comments.

EVIDENCE LOG

Before moving on, go to your Evidence Log and record any additional thoughts or observations you may have about the the texts.

Simile: Willow and Ginkgo • Four Skinny Trees **601**

PERFORMANCE TASK

SOURCES

- The Circuit
- How This Son of Migrant Farm Workers Became an Astronaut
- A Work in Progress

Present an Informational Text

Assignment

Some of the individuals presented in this unit were able to overcome great challenges. Deepen your understanding of these people and their achievements by writing and presenting three brief **biographical profiles.** Use the texts to address this question:

How do people overcome enormous obstacles?

Plan With Your Group

Analyze the Texts With your group, analyze how each selection contributes to your understanding of the obstacles that people face and the ways they overcome them. Use the chart to organize your ideas as you draw evidence from the texts.

SELECTION	PROFILE SUBJECT	OBSTACLES OVERCOME
The Circuit	Francisco Jiménez, author	
How This Son of Migrant Farm Workers Became an Astronaut	José Hernández, interview subject	
A Work in Progress	Aimee Mullins, author and speaker	

TIP: As you gather relevant evidence for your profiles, be sure to consider information presented not only in written form but also as multimedia, including audio recordings and visual displays.

Gather Evidence As a group, decide how you will collect important information about each subject. Make sure every group member has a role to play in researching and developing the profiles.

Brainstorm for resources that will provide relevant evidence. Use both print and digital sources, such as biographies, magazines, websites, and online interviews. Use effective search terms, such as the name of each subject, and assess the credibility and accuracy of each source you find before using it. Be sure to record your sources' citation information and hyperlinks to access them again later.

602 UNIT 5 • FACING ADVERSITY

Essential Question: How do we overcome life's challenges?

Organize and Draft Organize the details you have gathered and draft your profiles. Introduce each subject clearly. Develop the body of your presentation using relevant facts, details, quotations, and media from your research. Conclude in a way that leaves listeners with a memorable thought. As you write, use precise words and topic-specific terms to express your ideas clearly and concisely. Avoid being vague, repetitive, or wordy. Also, be sure to maintain a formal style and a serious tone and to follow the conventions of standard English grammar and usage.

Rehearse, Revise, and Present

Rehearse With Your Group As your group practices delivering the presentation, use this checklist to evaluate the effectiveness of your rehearsal.

CONTENT	SOURCES	PRESENTATION TECHNIQUES
◯ The presentation addresses the prompt.	◯ The presentation contains information from both print and digital sources.	◯ Speakers use an appropriately formal style and vocabulary.
◯ The presentation shares relevant information about all three subjects.	◯ All sources are credible and accurate.	◯ Speakers use appropriate volume and clear pronunciation.
◯ The presentation provides an insightful conclusion.	◯ Media or visuals enhance and clarify the ideas and information presented.	◯ Speakers make periodic eye contact with audience members.

Revise and Present As a group, use your evaluation to guide revisions to your profiles. Strengthen the presentation by revising, editing, and rewriting as needed. In addition, apply the feedback you received during rehearsal to improve your delivery. When it is your turn, adapt your speech for a formal presentation: speak confidently, use standard English, and refer to your multimedia or visual aids at appropriate times.

Discuss

Discuss the Presentations Hold a question-and-answer session after each group's presentation.

For Presenters: Listen closely to questions and comments from your audience and respond with clear explanations.

For Listeners: Ask thoughtful questions to learn more about the information presented. Provide feedback about the clarity of the profiles and the use of media. Speak respectfully and offer suggestions that are genuinely helpful.

STANDARDS

Writing
• Develop the topic with relevant facts, definitions, concrete details, quotations, or other information and examples.

• Gather relevant information from multiple print and digital sources, using search terms effectively; assess the credibility and accuracy of each source.

Speaking and Listening
• Present claims and findings, emphasizing salient points in a focused, coherent manner with pertinent descriptions, facts, details, and examples.

• Include multimedia components and visual displays in presentations to clarify claims and findings and emphasize salient points.

INDEPENDENT LEARNING

Essential Question

How do we overcome life's challenges?

Some people face extreme, even life-threatening, challenges. The ways in which they overcome those challenges can inspire and teach all of us. In this section, you will choose a selection to read independently. Get the most from this section by establishing a purpose for reading. Ask yourself, "What do I hope to gain from my independent reading?" Here are just a few purposes you might consider:

Read to Learn Think about the selections you have already read. What questions do you still have about the unit topic?

Read to Enjoy Read the descriptions of the texts. Which one seems most interesting and appealing to you?

Read to Form a Position Consider your thoughts and feelings about the Essential Question. Are you still undecided about some aspect of the topic?

Independent Learning Strategies

Throughout your life, in school, in your community, and in your career, you will need to rely on yourself to learn and work on your own. Use these strategies to keep your focus as you read independently for sustained periods of time. Add ideas of your own for each category.

STRATEGY	MY ACTION PLAN
Create a schedule	• Be aware of your deadlines and track progress toward your goals. • Make a list of all your assignments when planning out your time. •
Read with purpose	• Consider the different ways in which the text adds to your knowledge. • Notice how you respond to the text. What do you like? What don't you like? Why? •
Take notes	• Keep in mind that the act of jotting down notes can help you remember key ideas and information. • Use a note-taking strategy that works for you, such as using highlighters or sticky notes. •

Contents

Choose one selection. Selections are available online only.

PERSONAL NARRATIVE

The Girl Who Fell From the Sky
Juliane Koepcke

Can a teenage girl survive in the rainforest all by herself?

PERSUASIVE SPEECH

Malala Yousafzai: Speech to United Nations Security Council
Malala Yousafzai

One young woman changes the way millions of people see the world.

AUTOBIOGRAPHY

from The Story of My Life
Helen Keller

Just one little word can make all the difference in someone's life.

SHORT STORY

Rikki-tikki-tavi
Rudyard Kipling

Can a little mongoose protect the people and animals around him from two deadly cobras?

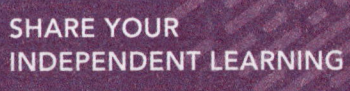

SHARE YOUR INDEPENDENT LEARNING

SHARE • LEARN • REFLECT

Reflect on and evaluate the information you gained from your Independent Reading selection. Then, share what you learned with others.

Independent Learning **605**

INDEPENDENT LEARNING

Close-Read Guide

Establish your purpose for reading. Then, read the selection through at least once. Use this page to record your close-read ideas.

> A Close-Read Guide and Annotation Model are available online.

Selection Title: _____

Purpose for Reading: _____ Minutes Read: _____

Close Read the Text

Zoom in on sections you found interesting. **Annotate** what you notice. Ask yourself **questions** about the text. What can you **conclude**?

_____
_____
_____
_____
_____
_____
_____
_____
_____

Analyze the Text

Think about the author's choices of literary elements, techniques, and structures. Select one and record your thoughts.

_____
_____
_____
_____
_____
_____
_____
_____
_____

QuickWrite

Choose a paragraph from the text that grabbed your interest. Explain the power of this passage.

_____
_____
_____
_____
_____
_____
_____
_____

Essential Question: How do we overcome life's challenges?

Share Your Independent Learning

Essential Question

How do we overcome life's challenges?

When you read something independently, your understanding continues to grow as you share what you have learned with others.

Prepare to Share

WRITE One of the most important ways to respond to a text is to notice and describe your personal reactions. Think about the text you explored independently and the ways in which it connects to your own experiences.

- What similarities and differences do you see between the text and your own life? Describe your observations.
- How do you think this text connects to the Essential Question? Describe your ideas.

Learn From Your Classmates

DISCUSS Come to the discussion prepared, having read your chosen Independent Learning selection. Share your ideas about the text. As you talk with others, take notes about new information that seems important, and consider whether it changes your views about particular ideas.

Reflect

EXPLAIN Review your notes, and mark the most important insight you gained from these writing and discussion activities. Explain how this idea adds to your understanding of facing adversity.

STANDARDS
Speaking and Listening • Come to discussions prepared, having read or researched material under study; explicitly draw on that preparation by referring to evidence on the topic, text, or issue to probe and reflect on ideas under discussion. • Acknowledge new information expressed by others and, when warranted, modify their own views.

UNIT 5 REFLECT AND RESPOND

In this unit, you encountered many different perspectives on facing adversity. Now, take some time to reflect on the texts you explored and to express your own ideas.

Reflect on Your Unit Goals

Review your Unit Goals chart from the beginning of the unit. Then, complete the activity and answer the question.

1. In the Unit Goals chart, rate how well you meet each goal now.
2. In which goals were you most and least successful?

Reflect on the Texts

Conversation If you could sit down and have a conversation with one person from this unit, who would it be? Use the chart to list the people from each text, whether author or character, real or fictional. Then, mark your top choice for someone to have a personal conversation with. Briefly explain the reason for your choice and jot down a few topics you'd like to discuss with that person.

TITLE	AUTHOR/CHARACTER	REASON AND TOPICS
Black Sunday: The Storm That Gave Us the Dust Bowl		
from Survival in the Storm: The Dust Bowl Diary of Grace Edwards		
A More Accessible World		
The Circuit		
How This Son of Migrant Farm Workers Became an Astronaut		
A Work in Progress		
Simile: Willow and Ginkgo		
Four Skinny Trees from The House on Mango Street		
Independent Learning Selection:		

608 UNIT 5 • FACING ADVERSITY

Essential Question: How do we overcome life's challenges?

Develop Your Perspective: Unit Projects

Choose one of the following Unit Project ideas.

SONG

Write a song about facing adversity. Use information you have learned from the unit selections as well as your own experiences in dealing with life's challenges. Include at least two concept vocabulary words from the unit. Then, choose a way to share your song with others, such as performing it for your class, reading aloud the lyrics, or posting it to your school website.

ILLUSTRATION

Create an illustration that depicts a scene from one of the unit texts. Your illustration should be an original artwork, but you may use any medium you choose to create it. Write a paragraph that describes the scene you have depicted and include at least two concept vocabulary words from the unit.

SPEECH

Deliver a speech detailing something you learned from the unit selections that you will always remember. Briefly describe what you learned and what makes it meaningful and important to you. Use two academic vocabulary words from the unit. Practice your delivery several times before presenting your speech to the class.

USE NEW WORDS
Academic Vocabulary
Use the academic vocabulary from the unit as you plan, draft, and discuss your project:

- deviate
- persevere
- determination
- diversity
- observation

Concept Vocabulary
Review your Word Wall and write down any words you want to use in your project:

STANDARDS
Writing
- Produce clear and coherent writing in which the development, organization, and style are appropriate to task, purpose, and audience.
- Draw evidence from literary or informational texts to support analysis, reflection, and research.

Unit 5 Reflect and Respond 609

PERFORMANCE-BASED ASSESSMENT

SOURCES

- Whole-Class Selections
- Peer-Group Selections
- Independent Learning Selections
- Your own experiences and observations

Informational Essay

Assignment

In this unit, you read different perspectives on facing adversity. You also practiced writing informational essays and biographical profiles. Now, apply what you have learned.

Write an **informational essay** in which you develop and support a thesis in response to the Essential Question.

Essential Question

How do we overcome life's challenges?

Review and Evaluate Evidence

Review your Evidence Log and your QuickWrite from the beginning of the unit. Have your ideas changed?

◯ Yes	◯ No
Identify at least three pieces of evidence that made you think differently about the topic.	Identify at least three pieces of evidence that reinforced your initial ideas about the topic.
1.	1.
2.	2.
3.	3.

State your ideas now:

What other evidence might you need to support a thesis on the topic?

Essential Question: How do we overcome life's challenges?

Share Your Perspective

The **Informational Essay Checklist** will help you stay on track.

PLAN Before you write, read the checklist and make sure you understand all the items.

DRAFT As you write, pause occasionally to make sure you're meeting the checklist requirements.

Use New Words Refer to your Word Wall to vary your word choice. Also, consider using one or more of the academic vocabulary terms you learned at the beginning of the unit: *deviate, persevere, determination, diversity, observation.*

REVIEW AND EDIT After you have written a first draft, evaluate it against the checklist. Make any changes needed to strengthen your thesis, structure, transitions, and language. Then, reread your essay and fix any errors you find.

EVIDENCE LOG

Make sure you have pulled in details from your Evidence Log to support your ideas.

INFORMATIONAL ESSAY CHECKLIST

My informational essay clearly contains . . .

- [ ] a strong thesis, or central idea that clearly addresses the topic.
- [ ] varied types of relevant supporting evidence, including facts, definitions, quotations, and examples.
- [ ] an organizational structure that contains an engaging introduction that includes your thesis statement, logical connections between body paragraphs, and a conclusion that revisits my thesis.
- [ ] conjunctive adverbs and other transitions that clarify the relationships among ideas and create cohesion.
- [ ] precise word choices that describe the topic.
- [ ] correct use of standard English grammar, usage, and conventions.
- [ ] no punctuation, capitalization, or spelling errors.
- [ ] a formal style.

STANDARDS
Writing
- Write informative/explanatory texts to examine a topic and convey ideas, concepts, and information through the selection, organization, and analysis of relevant content.
- Use appropriate transitions to create cohesion and clarify the relationships among ideas and concepts.
- Use precise language and domain-specific vocabulary to inform about or explain the topic.

RESOURCES

IN THIS BOOK...

English and Spanish Glossaries
Unit Vocabulary
- Academic Vocabulary
- Concept Vocabulary
- Media Vocabulary

Indexes
- Skills
- Authors and Titles

Acknowledgments and Credits

ONLINE RESOURCE CENTERS...

A bank of resources is available for you, if needed, while using myPerspectives. You will find writing models that you can refer to as you complete writing tasks, rubrics for guidance while writing, and interactive lessons to help you with grammar and other skills.

Grammar Center
- Interactive Minilessons
- Grammar Tutorials
- Practice Pages

Writing and Research Center
- Skills Videos
- Interactive Minilessons
- Writing Models
- Writing Rubrics
- Research Overview
- Research Models

Vocabulary Center
- Practice Pages

Digital Library
- Build background knowledge or read independently
- Short Nonfiction Texts
- Novels and Classic Texts

Collaboration Center
- Modeling Videos

Speaking & Listening Center
- Interactive Lessons

ENGLISH GLOSSARY

Pronunciation Key

Symbol	Sample Words	Symbol	Sample Words
a	at, catapult, Alabama	oo	boot, soup, crucial
ah	heart, charms, argue	ow	now, stout, flounder
air	care, various, hair	oy	boy, toil, oyster
aw	law, maraud, caution	s	say, nice, press
awr	pour, organism, forewarn	sh	she, abolition, motion
ay	ape, sails, implication	u	full, put, book
ee	even, teeth, really	uh	ago, focus, contemplation
eh	ten, repel, elephant	ur	bird, urgent, perforate
ehr	merry, verify, terribly	y	by, delight, identify
ih	it, pin, hymn	yoo	music, confuse, few
o	shot, hopscotch, condo	zh	pleasure, treasure, vision
oh	own, parole, rowboat		

Orange = Academic Vocabulary　　Blue = Concept Vocabulary　　Purple = Media Vocabulary

Unit 1 Crossing Generations

catapulted (KA tuh puhl tihd) *v.* hurled or launched with great force
charitable (CHAYR ih tuh buhl) *adj.* capable of showing affection or good will to others
composition (kom puh ZIH shuhn) *n.* arrangement of elements in a work of visual art
consequence (KON suh kwehns) *n.* effect or result
contradict (kon truh DIHKT) *v.* state the contrary or opposite; deny
dialogue (DY uh log) *n.* conversation
doubt (DOWT) *n.* uncertainty
fluently (FLOO uhnt lee) *adv.* easily and smoothly
instinct (IHN stihngkt) *n.* inborn ability; natural impulse
intense (ihn TENS) *adj.* highly focused; showing extreme concentration
interview subject (IHN tur vyoo suhb jehkt) *n.* person being interviewed
lecture (LEHK chuhr) *v.* talk in a critical way that seems unfair
light and shadow (LYT) (SHA doh) *n.* elements that define and enhance parts of an image

linguists (LIHN gwihsts) *n.* people who study how languages work
lurched (LURCHT) *v.* moved jerkily
notable (NOH tuh buhl) *adj.* outstanding; remarkable
paralysis (puh RAL uh sihs) *n.* loss of the ability to move
perspective (puhr SPEHK tihv) *n.* particular way of looking at something; point of view
philanthropist (fih LAN thruh pihst) *n.* someone who does good work or donates money to help other people
pronouncing (pruh NOWN sihng) *v.* speaking words correctly
proportion (pruh POR shuhn) *n.* sizes of objects in relation to each other or to the background
recording (rih KAWR dihng) *v.* storing sounds in a form, such as a digital file, so that they can be heard again in the future
set (SET) *n.* location where a movie, play, or other production takes place
stunned (STUHND) *adj.* astonished; completely surprised
supervision (soo pehr VIH zhun) *n.* act of overseeing something or watching over someone
term (TUHRM) *n.* word or expression that has a specific meaning

Academic / Concept / Media Vocabulary **R1**

tone (TOHN) *n.* emotional quality of the conversation between the interviewer and the subject
transported (trans PAWR tihd) *v.* carried across to another place
unexplainable (uhn ihk SPLAY nuh buhl) *adj.* impossible to make clear or describe

Unit 2 Living Among the Stars

actors' delivery (AK tuhrs dih LIHV uh ree) *n.* ways in which actors speak their lines
anxious (ANGK shuhs) *adj.* excited or nervous
assumption (uh SUHMP shuhn) *n.* something that is accepted as true, without proof or evidence
atmosphere (AT muh sfeer) *n.* gas surrounding a planet; air
background music (BAK grownd MYOO zihk) *n.* music that is not the focus of the performance
calamitous (kuh LA muh tuhs) *adj.* disastrous or devastating
canals (kuh NALZ) *n.* artificial waterways for transportation or watering land
capsules (CAP suhlz) *n.* closed containers
certainty (SUR tuhn tee) *n.* state of being free from doubt
digital art (DIH jih tuhl AHRT) *n.* art that is created or enhanced by using computers, software, or other digital tools
discredit (dihs KREHD iht) *v.* debunk; destroy the believability of
dissent (dih SEHNT) *n.* difference of opinion; disagreement
forlorn (fawr LAWRN) *adj.* abandoned or deserted
gravity (GRA vuh tee) *n.* invisible force that draws objects toward each other
habitation (ha bih TAY shuhn) *n.* act of living; residency
immense (ih MEHNS) *adj.* very large
improve (ihm PROOV) *v.* make or become better
justify (JUHS tuh fy) *v.* give a reason for something
medium (MEE dee uhm) *n.* material or technology an artist uses to create their work
mosaic (moh ZAY ihk) *adj.* made of many small pieces of colored glass or stone
ominously ((O muh nuhs lee) *adv.* in a way that suggests something bad is going to happen
persist (puhr SIHST) *v.* stubbornly continue; keep doing something
realism (REE uh lih zuhm) *n.* style of art that emphasizes natural-looking people, objects, and places
sound effects (SOWND ih FEHCTS) *n.* sounds produced artificially for a radio production
striving (STRY vihng) *v.* making a great effort to achieve or obtain something

submerged (suhb MURJD) *adj.* completely covered with a liquid

Unit 3 Transformations

altered (AWL tuhrd) *adj.* changed
contact (KON takt) *n.* connection
covetous (KUHV uh tuhs) *adj.* greedy and jealous
discards (DIHS cahrdz) *n.* things that are not wanted
dispelled (dihs PEHLD) *v.* driven away; scattered
distorting (dih STAWRT ihng) *v.* twisting out of shape or original form
dreaded (DREHD uhd) *v.* felt great fear or extreme reluctance
earnest (UR nihst) *n.* serious mental state
envision (ehn VIH zhuhn) *v.* picture to oneself
grief (GREEF) *n.* deep sadness
illusion (ih LOO zhuhn) *n.* something that produces a false or misleading impression of reality
impossible (ihm POS uh buhl) *adj.* disagreeable; unreasonable
infinitely (IHN fuh niht lee) *adv.* enormously; remarkably
ingenious (ihn JEEN yuhs) *adj.* marked by originality, resourcefulness, and cleverness
inspiration (ihn spuh RAY shuhn) *n.* something or someone that generates ideas for another action
intricate (IHN trih cuht) *adj.* complex or elaborate
lucid (LOO sihd) *adj.* clearly understandable; having full use of one's faculties
malcontent (MAL kuhn tehnt) *n.* person who is always unhappy
miser (MY zuhr) *n.* greedy person who keeps and refuses to spend money, even at the expense of their own comfort
morose (muh ROHS) *adj.* gloomy; ill-tempered
omniscient (om NIH shuhnt) *adj.* all-knowing
parallel (PAR uh lehl) *adj.* having the same direction or nature; similar
penitence (PEHN ih tuhns) *n.* sorrow for one's sins or faults
permit (puhr MIHT) *v.* allow
plaintive (PLAYN tihv) *adj.* sounding sad and mournful
rebuke (ree BYOOK) *n.* severe or stern criticism; scolding
relay (ree LAY) *v.* pass along or communicate
release (rih LEES) *v.* let go of
resolute (REHZ uh loot) *adj.* determined
sensation (sehn SAY shuhn) *n.* state of excited interest; indefinite bodily feeling
shrinking (SHRINK ihng) *v.* becoming smaller and smaller
signals (SIHG nuhlz) *n.* messages used to send information or instructions

strive (STRYV) *v.* make a great effort; try very hard
transmit (TRANZ miht) *v.* send a signal from one point to another
trembling (TREHM blihng) *v.* shaking uncontrollably

Unit 4 Learning from Nature

advocating (AD vuh kay tihng) *v.* standing up for something one believes in
affinity (uh FIHN ih tee) *n.* liking of or sympathy with something; similarity of characteristics suggesting a relationship
benefit (BEH nuh fiht) *v.* get good or helpful results; gain
biomimicry (by oh MIH mih kree) *n.* act of developing systems by imitating actual living processes
biomorphism (by oh MAWR fih zuhm) *n.* act of using the forms, shapes, or patterns of living things
biophilia (by oh FIH lee uh) *n.* appreciation for life and the living world
blight (BLYT) *n.* something that spoils, prevents growth, or destroys
chosen (CHOH zuhn) *v.* selected; decided on
close-up (KLOHS uhp) *n.* type of camera shot done at close range
colonies (KAH luh neez) *n.* groups of individuals settled together in one place
consequences (KON suh kwehns ihz) *n.* results
cut (KUHT) *n.* editing of a video that produces an abrupt shift
deserted (dih ZUR tihd) *adj.* abandoned; empty
disposal (dihs POH zuhl) *n.* act of throwing something away
elucidate (ih LOO suh dayt) *v.* make clear, especially by explanation, demonstration, or analysis
evident (EH vih duhnt) *adj.* clear to vision or understanding
extinction (ehk STINGK shuhn) *n.* act of permanently dying out
fault (FAWLT) *n.* responsibility for a bad result
generate (JEHN uhr ayt) *v.* bring into existence; cause
herbicides (UHR buh sydz) *n.* chemicals used to kill unwanted plants
honored (AH nuhrd) *v.* given special recognition
implores (ihm PLAWRZ) *v.* begs
incorporate (ihn COHR puh rayt) *v.* blend or include
incidental music (ihnt suh DEHN tuhl MYOO sihk) *n.* background music that enhances a video
logical (LOJ ih kuhl) *adj.* supported by reason or evidence
maladies (MAL uh deez) *n.* illnesses or diseases
melded (MEL dihd) *v.* melted into or merged with
mischief (MIS chuhf) *n.* trouble; naughtiness

parasites (PAR uh syts) *n.* creatures that survive by living on or in a host creature
pestering (PEH stur ihng) *n.* constant bothering
pesticides (PEHS tuh sydz) *n.* chemicals used to kill animals, especially insects
philosophy (fih LOS uh fee) *n.* pursuit of wisdom; system of beliefs and attitudes
pollinators (PAH lih nay tuhrz) *n.* creatures who spread pollen, a fine powder produced by flowers
puzzled (PUHZ uhld) *adj.* confused and unable to understand something
resolved (rih ZOLVD) *v.* settled or dealt with successfully
stillness (STIHL nihs) *n.* absence of noise or motion
stricken (STRIHK uhn) *adj.* very badly affected by trouble or illness
uncompromising (un KOM pruh my zihng) *adj.* unwilling to make a deal

Unit 5 Facing Adversity

accessible (ihk SEHS suh buhl) *adj.* easy to use
accomplishments (uh KOM plihsh muhnts) *n.* goals reached, achievements, or tasks done successfully.
attain (uh TAYN) *v.* reach or achieve
audibly (AW duh blee) *adv.* in a way that can be heard
celebrate (SEHL uh brayt) *v.* mark a happy occasion by engaging in something pleasurable
conducive (kuhn DOO sihv) *adj.* tending to promote or assist
crude (KROOD) *adj.* unfinished, unrefined; of low grade or quality
demoralized (dih MAWR uh lyzd) *adj.* discouraged; defeated
determination (dih tur muh NAY shuhn) *n.* conclusion; firm decision
deviate (DEE vee ayt) *v.* depart from an established plan
diversity (dy VUR suh tee) *n.* variety; differences within a group
embossed (ehm BAWST) *v.* marked with a raised pattern
enthusiastically (ehn thoo zee AS tihk lee) *adv.* with eager interest
exhaustion (egh ZAWS chuhn) *n.* extreme tiredness or fatigue
extraordinary (ehk STRAWR duh nehr ee) *adj.* better than ordinary; exceptional
frantically (FRAN tihk lee) *adv.* in a hurried, wild, or desperate way
hesitantly (HEHZ uh tuhnt lee) *adv.* in an unsure or cautious way

Academic / Concept / Media Vocabulary **R3**

impoverished (ihm POV uhr ihsht) *adj.* extremely poor; miserable and exhausted
instinctively (ihn STIHNGK tihv lee) *adv.* automatically, without thinking
navigate (NA vuh gayt) *v.* find a way through
observation (ob zuhr VAY shuhn) *n.* act of watching or noticing; something observed
perseverance (puhr suh VEER uhns) *n.* continued, patient effort
persevere (puhr suh VIHR) *v.* continue despite difficulty
plight (PLYT) *n.* serious or harmful condition or situation

raggedy (RA geh dee) *adj.* worn out or unkempt
ravaged (RAV ihjd) *v.* destroyed or damaged badly
rough (RUF) *adj.* coarse or bumpy
sensors (SEHN suhrz) *n.* devices that respond to a physical event such as heat or pressure
shuddered (SHUH duhrd) *v.* trembled or quivered
stammering (STA muh rihng) *v.* speaking hesitantly with starts and stops
tactile (TAK tuhl) *adj.* relating to the sense of touch
unending (uhn EHN dihng) *adj.* never stopping; constant
widespread (WYD sprehd) *adj.* occurring in many places

SPANISH GLOSSARY / GLOSARIO

Naranja = Vocabulario Académico Azul = Vocabulario de Conceptos Morado = Vocabulario de Medios

Unidad 1 Las generaciones que se cruzan

catapulted / catapultaste *v.* te arrojaste o lanzaste con gran fuerza rce

charitable / caritativo *adj.* capaz de mostrar afecto o buena voluntad a los demás

composition / composición *s.* disposición de los elementos en una obra de arte visual

consequence / consecuencia *s.* efecto o resultado

contradict / contradecir *v.* declarar lo contrario u opuesto; negar

dialogue / diálogo *s.* conversación

doubt / duda *s.* incertidumbre

fluently / con fluidez *adj.* de manera fácil y sin problemas

instinct / instinto *s.* capacidad innata; impulso natural

intense / intenso *adj.* muy enfocado; con una concentración extrema

interview subject / sujeto de la entrevista *s.* persona entrevistada

lecture / sermonear *v.* hablar de una manera crítica que parece injusta

light and shadow / luces y sombra *s.* elementos que definen y realzan partes de una imagen

linguists / lingüistas *s.* personas que estudian el funcionamiento de las lenguas e idiomas

lurched / tambaleé *v.* me moví bruscamente

notable / notable *adj.* extraordinario; destacado

paralysis / parálisis *s.* pérdida de la capacidad para moverse

perspective / perpectiva *s.* manera particular de ver las cosas; punto de vista

philanthropist / filántropo *s.* alguien que hace buenas obras o dona dinero para ayudar a otras personas

pronouncing / pronunciando *v.* diciendo correctamente las palabras

proportion / proporción *s.* tamaño de los objetos relacionados entre sí o con el fondo

recording / grabando *v.* almacenando sonidos en un formato, como un archivo digital, para que puedan volver a escucharse en el futuro

set / lugar de grabación *s.* donde tiene lugar una película, obra de teatro u otra producción

stunned / atónito *adj.* asombrado; completamente sorprendido

supervision / supervisión *s.* acto de monitorear algo o vigilar a alguien

term / término *s.* palabra o expresión que tiene un significado específico

tone / tono *s.* calidad emocional de una conversación

transported / transportaron *v.* llevaron a alguien a otro lugar o lo transformaron de manera emocional

unexplainable / inexplicable *adj.* imposible de aclarar o describir

Unidad 2 Vivir entre las estrellas

actors' delivery / interpretación del actor *s.* forma en que los actores pronuncian sus líneas

anxious / ansioso *adj.* agitado o nervioso

assumption / supuesto *s.* algo que se da por hecho, sin prueba o evidencia

atmosphere / atmósfera *s.* el gas que rodea la tierra; el aire

background music / música de fondo *s.* música que no es el centro de una presentación

calamitous / calamitoso *adj.* desastroso o devastador

canals / canales *s.* vías navegables artificiales para el transporte o el riego de tierras

capsules / cápsulas *s.* contenedores cerrados

certainty / certeza *s.* conocimiento de que algo es cierto, estando libre de toda duda

digital art / arte digital *s.* arte creado o mejorado mediante el uso de computadoras, programas informáticos u otras herramientas digitales

discredit / desacreditar *v.* desmentir; destruir la credibilidad de algo o alguien

dissent / disentimiento *s.* diferencia de opinión; desacuerdo

forlorn / desolado *adj.* abandonado o desierto

gravity / gravedad *s.* fuerza invisible que atrae los objetos unos hacia otros

habitation / asentamiento *s.* acto de vivir o habitar un lugar; residencia

immense / inmenso *adj.* muy grande

improve / mejorar *v.* hacer que algo pase a un estado de mejor calidad

justify / justificar *v.* dar razones suficientes para un acto

medium / medio *s.* material o tecnología que un artista utiliza para crear su obra
mosaic / mosaico *adj.* hecho de muchas piezas pequeñas de vidrio o piedra de colores
ominously / fatídicamente *adv.* de un modo que sugiere que algo malo va a ocurrir
persist / persisten *v.* continúan obstinadamente; siguen haciendo algo
realism / realismo *s.* estilo de arte que enfatiza el aspecto natural de las personas, los objetos y los lugares
sound effects / efectos sonoros *s.* sonidos producidos artificialmente para un programa de radio
striving / esforzarse *v.* hacer un gran esfuerzo para lograr u obtener algo
submerged / sumergido *adj.* completamente cubierto con un líquido

Unidad 3 Transformaciones

altered / alterado *adj.* cambiado
contact / contacto *s.* conexión
covetous / codicioso *adj.* ávaro; que siente un deseo excesivo de riquezas
discards / descartes *s.* cosas que no se quieren
dispelled / disipado *v.* desvanecido; evaporado
distorting / distorsionando *v.* causando una deformación de la forma original
dreaded / sintió pavor *v.* tuvo un gran miedo o extremo temor
earnest / honestidad *s.* comportamiento o estado mental de seriedad
envision / visualizar *v.* hacerse la imagen de algo
grief / pesar *s.* profunda tristeza
illusion / ilusión *s.* algo que produce una impresión falsa o engañosa de la realidad
impossible / insoportable *adj.* desagradable; difícil de tratar
infinitely / infinitamente *adv.* enormemente; notablemente
ingenious / ingenioso *adj.* caracterizado por su originalidad, maña y astucia
inspiration / inspiración *s.* algo o alguien que genera ideas para otra acción
intricate / intrincado *adj.* complejo o elaborado
lucid / lúcido *adj.* claro y comprensible; en pleno uso de sus facultades
malcontent / insatisfecho *s.* persona que es siempre infeliz
miser / ávaro *s.* persona que actúa con codicia, que guarda y se niega a gastar dinero, incluso a costa de su propia comodidad

morose / sombrío *adj.* malhumorado; de mal genio
omniscient / omnisciente *adj.* que todo lo sabe
parallel / paralelo *adj.* que tiene la misma dirección o naturaleza; similar
penitence / penitencia *s.* arrepentimiento por los propios pecados o faltas
permit / permitir *v.* dar consentimiento
plaintive / quejoso *adj.* que suena triste y lúgubre
rebuke / reprimenda *s.* crítica dura o severa; regañina
relay / comunican *v.* transfieren o transmiten
release / liberó *v.* dejó ir
resolute / rotundo *adj.* que actúa con decisión
sensation / sensación *s.* estado de interés agitado; impresión corporal indefinida
shrinking / encogiéndose *v.* haciéndose cada vez más
signals / señales *s.* mensajes utilizados para enviar información o instrucciones
strive / luchar *v.* hacer un gran esfuerzo; intentar con todas sus fuerzas
transmit / transmitir *v.* enviar una señal de un punto a otro
trembling / temblando *v.* agitándose con sacudidas

Unidad 4 Aprendiendo de la naturaleza

advocating / abogando *v.* defendiendo algo en lo que se cree
affinity / afinidad *s.* afición o simpatía por algo; similitud de características que sugieren una relación
benefit / beneficiarse *v.* obtener resultados buenos o útiles; ganar
biomimicry / biomímesis *s.* acto de desarrollar sistemas aplicando soluciones procedentes de la naturaleza a los problemas humanos
biomorphism / biomorfismo *s.* acto de utilizar las formas, figuras o patrones de los seres vivos
biophilia / biofilia *s.* aprecio por la vida y el mundo vivo
blight / plaga *s.* algo que arruina, impide el crecimiento o destruye
chosen / elegido *v.* seleccionado, escogido
close-up / primer plano *s.* tipo de toma de imágenes realizada a corta distancia
colonies / colonias *s.* grupos de individuos asentados juntos en un lugar
consequences / consecuencias *s.* resultados
cut / corte *s.* edición de un video que produce un cambio brusco
deserted / desierto *adj.* abandonado; vacío
disposal / eliminación *s.* acto de tirar un residuo
elucidate / esclarecer *v.* dejar en claro, especialmente por medio de la explicación, la demostración o el análisis

evident / evidente *adj.* claro para la visión o el entendimiento
extinction / extinción *s.* situación a partir de la cual una especie muere y desaparece definitivamente
fault / culpa *s.* responsabilidad por un mal resultado
generate / generar *v.* crear, causar la existencia de algo
herbicides / herbicidas *s.* productos químicos utilizados para matar plantas no deseadas
honored / celebrado *v.* obtuvo un reconocimiento especial
implores / implora *v.* ruega
incorporate / incorporan *v.* combinan o incluyen
incidental music / música de escena *s.* música de fondo que realza un video
logical / lógico *adj.* fundado en la razón o en la evidencia
maladies / males *s.* enfermedades o dolencias
melded / fusionaba *v.* se fundía con el entorno
mischief / travesura *s.* acción mala e ingeniosa de poca importancia; picardía
parasites / parásitos *s.* criaturas que sobreviven viviendo sobre o dentro de una criatura que actúa como huésped
pestering / fastidio *s.* molestias constantes
pesticides / pesticidas *s.* productos químicos utilizados para matar animales, especialmente insectos
philosophy / filosofía *s.* búsqueda de sabiduría; sistema de creencias y actitudes
pollinators / polinizadores *s.* criaturas que esparcen el polen, un polvo fino producido por las flores
puzzled / perplejo *adj.* confundido e incapaz de entender algo
resolved / resueltos *v.* solucionados o tratados con éxito
stillness / quietud *s.* ausencia de ruido o movimiento
stricken / asolado *adj.* muy afectado por problemas o enfermedades
uncompromising / inflexible *adj.* poco dispuesto a llegar a un acuerdo

Unidad 5 Enfrentar la adversidad

accessible / accesible *adj.* fácil de usar
accomplishments / logros *s.* objetivos alcanzados o tareas realizadas con éxito
attain / alcanzar *v.* lograr o cumplir
audibly / de forma audible *adv.* de forma que se pueda escuchar
celebrate / celebrar *v.* festejar una ocasión feliz haciendo algo placentero
conducive / propicio *adj.* que tiende a promover o ayudar
crude / inacabado *adj.* incompleto, sin refinar; de bajo grado o calidad
demoralized / desmoralizado *adj.* desanimado; derrotado
determination / determinación *s.* conclusión; decisión firme
deviate / desviarse *v.* alejarse de un plan establecido
diversity / diversidad *s.* variedad; diferencias dentro de un grupo
embossed / grabado *v.* marcado con un dibujo en relieve
enthusiastically / con entusiasmo *adv.* con gran interés
exhaustion / agotamiento *s.* cansancio o fatiga extremos
extraordinary / extraordinario *adj.* mejor que lo ordinario; excepcional
frantically / frenéticamente *adv.* de forma apresurada, desmedida o desesperada
hesitantly / de forma vacilante *adv.* de forma insegura o cautelosa
impoverished / empobrecido *adj.* extremadamente pobre; sin recursos
instinctively / instintivamente *adv.* automáticamente, sin pensar
navigate / trasladan *v.* van de un lugar a otro
observation / observación *s.* acción de contemplar; algo que se observa
perseverance / perseverancia *s.* esfuerzo continuado y paciente
persevere / perseverar *v.* seguir pese a las dificultades
plight / aprieto *s.* condición o situación grave o perjudicial
raggedy / andrajoso *adj.* desgastado o descuidado
ravaged / devastada *v.* destruida o dañada gravemente
rough / áspero *adj.* que es desagradable al tacto porque le falta suavidad
sensors / sensores *s.* dispositivos que responden a una acción física como el calor o la presión
shuddered / estremecí *v.* temblé o me sacudí
stammering / balbuceando *v.* hablando de forma vacilante y dificultosa
tactile / táctil *adj.* que se usa a través del sentido del tacto
unending / interminable *adj.* que nunca para; constante
widespread / generalizado *adj.* que sucede en muchos lugares

INDEX OF SKILLS

Text Analysis

Acknowledgments, 465
Alliteration, 447
Analogy, 334
Analyze, 19, 21, 35, 37, 39, 64, 66, 70, 91, 93, 94, 121, 141, 143, 151, 171, 173, 182, 191, 195, 247, 249, 277, 279, 281, 291, 319, 331, 333, 334, 343, 345, 346, 356, 387, 389, 391, 399, 401, 403, 415, 421, 444, 446, 463, 465, 475, 477, 478, 505, 509, 515, 519, 521, 531, 560, 570, 573, 575, 587, 596, 599
Analyze cause and effect, 35, 141, 189, 277, 289, 343, 354, 505, 529, 585
Anecdotes, 27
Argument, 109, 110, 176, 179, 186, 187, 194
Articles
    feature, 26, 29, 381, 387
    informational, 522, 525
Assess, 189, 387, 529
Author's craft
    alliteration, 447
    author's point of view, 403
    author's purpose, 39
        diction, 39
        syntax, 39
        text sections/features, 39
    central idea, 356
    diction, 192, 391
    figurative language, 94, 519
        idiom, 519
        metaphor, 94, 519
        simile, 519
    irony, 478
        situational, 478
    logical fallacy, 334
        sweeping generalization, 334
    meaning, 192, 391
    multiple themes, 281
    objective point of view, 249
    organizational patterns, 573
    poetic structures
        line, 346
        stanzas, 346
    point of view, 249, 509
        author's, 403
        objective, 249, 509
        subjective, 249, 509
    question-and-answer format, 573
    repetition, 447, 599
    rhetorical devices, 334
        analogy, 334
        direct address, 334

rhyme, 447
rhyme scheme, 599
subjective point of view, 249
theme, 478
    in lyric poetry, 446
tone, 192, 391
Author's point of view, 403
    objective, 403
    subjective, 403
Author's purpose, 39, 173
    argument, 176
    descriptive essay, 394
    diction, 39
    drama, 218
    feature articles, 26, 378
    free-verse poetry, 82
    general and specific purposes, 167
    historical fiction, 500
    historical nonfiction, 500
    human interest stories, 348
    informational articles, 522
    interview, 550
    lyric poetry, 438, 590
    magical realism, 468
    memoir, 56
    oral histories, 576
    poetry, 336
    radio-play adaptation, 124
    realistic short story, 12, 310
    science feature, 166, 454
    science fiction, 124
    science journalism, 322
    short story, 550
    syntax, 39
    television interview, 56
    text sections/features, 39
    vignette, 590
Capitalization, 93
Captions, 523
Central idea, 27, 349, 356, 379, 389, 501, 507
    multiple, 37
Character, 13, 21, 281, 469
Character development, 219, 517
    dialogue, 219, 247
    stage directions, 219, 279
Characteristics
    argument, 176
    creation story, 406
    descriptive essay, 394
    drama, 218
    feature articles, 26, 378
    free-verse poetry, 82
    historical fiction, 500

historical nonfiction, 500
human interest stories, 348
informational articles, 522
interview, 550
lyric poetry, 438, 590
magical realism, 468
memoir, 56
oral histories, 576
poetry, 336
radio-play adaptation, 124
realistic short story, 12, 310
science feature, 166, 454
science fiction, 124
science journalism, 322
short story, 550
spoken-word poetry, 438
television interview, 56
vignette, 590
Claim, 177, 184, 191
    counterclaims, 177, 184
Classify, 507
Climax, 311
Close read, 18, 28, 31, 65, 92, 127, 129, 130, 132, 134, 137, 139, 172, 183, 190, 222, 224, 227, 233, 235, 237, 241, 243, 253, 256, 258, 263, 265, 267, 272, 274, 286, 288, 318, 332, 344, 355, 385, 397, 411, 445, 464, 476, 504, 513, 528, 561, 571, 586, 597
    annotate, 20, 36, 142, 246, 278, 290, 388, 400, 416, 506, 516, 530
    close-read guide, 100, 200, 362, 484, 606
    conclude, 20, 36, 142, 246, 278, 290, 388, 400, 416, 506, 516, 530
    question, 20, 36, 142, 246, 278, 290, 388, 400, 416, 506, 516, 530
Close review
    conclusion, 71, 80, 122, 149, 451
    question, 71, 80, 122, 149, 451
Compare, 151, 387, 421
Compare and contrast, 64, 93, 121, 148, 295, 331, 356, 415, 450, 463, 515, 575
Comparing texts
    arguments, 176, 179, 186, 187, 194
    creation stories, 406, 408, 420
    drama and novella, 218, 284, 294
    fiction
        creation stories, 406, 408, 420
        and drama, 124, 126, 146, 150, 218, 284, 294
        historical nonfiction and historical fiction, 500, 502, 510, 520
        short story and interview, 550, 552, 564, 574

R8 INDEX

historical nonfiction and historical fiction, 500, 502, 510, 520
memoir and television interview, 56, 58, 68, 72
nonfiction
  arguments, 176, 179, 186, 187, 194
  historical nonfiction and historical fiction, 500, 502, 510, 520
  and media, 56, 58, 68, 72
poetry and media, 438, 440, 448, 452
science fiction and radio-play adaptation, 124, 126, 146
short story and interview, 550, 552, 564, 574
short story and radio play, 150

Concrete details, 401
Conflict, 13, 21, 281, 311
  external, 319
  internal, 319
Connect, 35, 66, 73, 79, 94, 173, 195, 245, 249, 289, 319, 331, 354, 415, 450, 453, 477, 478, 507, 517, 519, 521, 531, 575
Connotations, 395, 401
Contrast, 79, 141, 151, 289, 291, 295, 343, 399
Counterclaims, 177, 184
Creation story, 406, 408, 410, 412, 420
Cultural context, 551
Cultural values, 562
Deduce, 289
Describe, 73, 151, 560
Description, 57, 66
Descriptive essay, 394, 397
Dialogue, 57, 66, 219, 247
Diction, 39, 192, 391, 577, 587
Direct address, 334
Direct quotations, 349
Distinguish, 66, 70, 93, 143, 247, 279, 333, 507, 517, 521
Drama, 218, 221, 284, 294
  radio play, 150
  radio-play adaptation, 124, 126, 146, 147
Draw conclusions, 21, 35, 39, 91, 141, 171, 281, 317, 387, 399, 421, 475, 478, 505, 560
Essay
  descriptive, 394, 397
  informational, 494
  research-based, 371, 372
Essential Question, 10, 19, 35, 52, 64, 70, 79, 91, 98, 101, 114, 121, 141, 148, 162, 171, 182, 189, 198, 201,

216, 245, 277, 289, 306, 317, 331, 343, 354, 360, 376, 387, 399, 415, 434, 444, 450, 463, 475, 482, 498, 505, 515, 529, 546, 560, 570, 585, 596, 604

Evaluate, 19, 121, 148, 151, 182, 184, 191, 249, 334, 356, 415, 465, 478, 505, 515, 560, 573
Evidence, 27, 191
  anecdotes, 27
  examples, 27, 184
  facts, 27, 184
  personal observations, 184
  relevant, 191
  statistics, 27, 184
  sufficient, 191
  supporting evidence, 27, 37, 177, 507
Evidence log, 9, 25, 41, 67, 73, 81, 95, 105, 113, 151, 175, 195, 205, 215, 249, 283, 295, 321, 335, 347, 357, 367, 375, 393, 405, 421, 453, 467, 479, 489, 497, 509, 521, 535, 575, 589, 601, 611
Examples, 27, 184
Explain, 346
Exposition, 66, 311
Extend, 331
External conflict, 319
Facts, 27, 184
Falling action, 311
Feature articles, 26, 29, 378, 381
Feature film, 288
Fiction, 209
  creation story, 406, 408, 410, 412, 420
  historical fiction, 500, 502, 510, 511, 520
  magical realism, 468
  novella, 284, 294
  realistic, 310
  short stories, 12
  short story, 15, 150, 210, 310, 550, 552, 553, 564, 574
  realistic, 12
Figurative language, 94, 125, 143, 395, 401, 591
  extended metaphor, 94
  idiom, 519
  imagery, 591, 598
  metaphor, 94, 125, 143, 519, 591
  personification, 125, 143, 591, 598
  simile, 125, 143, 519, 591, 598
Figures of speech, 591
Foreshadowing, 311, 319
Free-verse poetry, 82, 86, 88, 89, 342

Generalize, 189, 444
General purpose, 167
Genre/Text Elements
  acknowledgments, 465
  arguments, 176, 179, 186, 187, 194
  articles
    feature, 26, 29
  author's purpose, 167, 173
    argument, 176
    descriptive essay, 394
    drama, 218
    feature articles, 26, 378
    free-verse poetry, 82
    general and specific purposes, 167
    historical fiction, 500
    historical nonfiction, 500
    human interest stories, 348
    informational articles, 522
    interview, 550
    lyric poetry, 438, 590
    magical realism, 468
    memoir, 56
    oral histories, 576
    poetry, 336
    radio-play adaptation, 124
    realistic short story, 12, 310
    science feature, 166, 454
    science fiction, 124
    science journalism, 322
    short story, 550
    television interview, 56
    vignette, 590
  central idea, 27, 349, 501, 507
    multiple, 37
  character, 469
  character development, 219
    dialogue, 219, 247
    stage directions, 219, 279
  characteristics
    argument, 176
    author's purpose, 124
    creation story, 406
    descriptive essay, 394
    drama, 218
    feature articles, 26, 378
    free-verse poetry, 82
    historical fiction, 500
    historical nonfiction, 500
    human interest stories, 348
    informational articles, 522
    interview, 550
    lyric poetry, 438, 590
    magical realism, 468
    memoir, 56

Index of Skills **R9**

INDEX OF SKILLS

oral histories, 576
poetry, 336
radio-play adaptation, 124
realistic short story, 12, 310
science feature, 166, 454
science journalism, 322
short story, 550
spoken-word poetry, 438
television interview, 56
vignette, 590
claim, 177, 184, 191
   counterclaims, 177, 184
conflict
   external, 319
   internal, 319
connotations, 395, 401
creation story, 406, 408, 410, 412, 420
description, 57, 66
descriptive essay, 394, 397
dialogue, 57, 66
direct quotations, 349
drama, 218, 221, 284, 294
   radio play, 150
   radio-play adaptation, 124, 126, 146, 147
essay
   descriptive, 394, 397
evidence, 184, 191
   examples, 184
   facts, 184
   personal observations, 184
   relevant evidence, 191
   statistics, 184
   sufficient evidence, 191
   supporting evidence, 27, 37, 177, 507
exposition, 66
feature articles, 26, 29, 378, 381
fiction
   creation story, 406, 408, 410, 412, 420
   historical, 500, 502, 510, 511, 520
   magical realism, 468
   novella, 284, 294
   realistic, 12, 310
   science fiction, 124, 126, 146
   short story, 12, 15, 150, 310, 313, 550, 552, 553, 564, 574
figurative language, 125, 395, 401, 591, 598
   imagery, 591, 598
   metaphor, 591
   personification, 591, 598
   simile, 591, 598
figures of speech, 591
free-verse poetry, 82, 86, 88, 89
graphic features, 323, 333
historical fiction, 500, 502, 510, 511, 520

historical nonfiction, 500, 502, 503, 510, 520
human interest stories, 348, 351
image gallery, 75, 117
imagery, 395, 401
images, 349
informational articles, 522, 525
informational text features, 379, 389, 455, 465
   acknowledgments, 465
   bulleted list, 455
   caption, 455
   central idea, 379, 389
   glossary, 455
   heading, 379, 389, 455
   paragraph, 379
   reference, 455, 465
   sidebar, 389, 455
   special features, 379, 455
   topic sentence, 379
interview, 550, 552, 564, 565, 574
language, 577, 587
lyric poetry, 438, 439, 441, 446, 590, 594
magical realism, 468
memoir, 56, 58, 59, 68, 72
mood, 395, 401
narrative point of view, 291
nonfiction
   arguments, 176, 179, 186, 187, 194
   descriptive essay, 394, 397
   historical, 500, 502, 503, 510, 520
   human interest stories, 348, 351
   interview, 565
   memoir, 56, 58, 59, 68, 72
   oral histories, 576, 579
   science features, 166, 169, 454, 457
   science journalism, 322
novella, 284, 294
omniscient narrator, 291
oral histories, 576, 579
organizational structure, 523, 531
plot, 311, 319, 469, 477
   climax, 311
   conflicts, 311, 319
   exposition, 311
   falling action, 311
   foreshadowing, 311, 319
   resolution, 311
   rising action, 311
   suspense, 311
poetry, 336
   free-verse poetry, 82, 86, 88, 89, 342
   lyric poetry, 340, 439, 441, 446, 590, 594

narrative poetry, 341
   spoken-word poetry, 449
   visual elements, 83, 93
print features, 323, 333
purpose
   creation story, 406
   spoken-word poetry, 438
radio-play adaptation, 124, 126, 146, 147
realistic fiction
   short story, 12, 310
reasoning, 177, 184, 191
references, 455, 465
relevant evidence, 191
science features, 166, 169, 454, 457
science fiction, 124, 126, 146
science journalism, 322
sensory language, 395, 591
setting, 469, 477, 517
   cultural context/setting, 517, 551
   cultural values, 562
   figurative language, 125
   historical context/setting, 517, 551
   influence of, 551, 562, 572
   physical setting, 517
   place, 562
   time, 562
short story, 15, 313, 550, 552, 553, 564, 574
   realistic, 12, 310
spoken-word poetry, 438, 449
structure
   argument, 176
   creation story, 406
   descriptive essay, 394
   drama, 218
   feature articles, 26, 378
   free-verse poetry, 82
   historical fiction, 500
   historical nonfiction, 500
   human interest stories, 348
   informational articles, 522
   interview, 550
   lyric poetry, 438, 590
   magical realism, 468
   memoir, 56
   oral histories, 576
   organizational, 523, 531
   poetry, 336
   radio-play adaptation, 124
   realistic short story, 12, 310
   science feature, 166, 454
   science fiction, 124
   science journalism, 322
   short story, 550
   spoken-word poetry, 438
   television interview, 56

sufficient evidence, 191
supporting evidence, 27, 37, 177, 507
    anecdotes, 27
    examples, 27
    facts, 27
    statistics, 27
television interview, 68, 69, 72
theme(s), 13, 21, 337, 345, 417, 501
    character development, 517
    characters, 13, 21
    conflict, 13, 21
    explicit, 407, 417
    imagery, 337, 345
    implicit, 407, 417
    in lyric poetry, 439
    multiple, 407, 517
    outcome, 13, 21
    setting, 517
    topics, 407
    universal, 407, 417
vignette, 590
voice, 577, 587
    diction, 577, 587
    syntax, 577, 587
    tone, 577, 587
Get ready for close reading, 64, 91, 171, 182, 189, 317, 331, 343, 354, 444, 450, 463, 475, 560, 570, 585, 596
Graphic features, 323, 333
Headings, 379, 389, 455, 523, 531
Historical context, 551
Historical fiction, 500, 502, 510, 511, 520
Historical nonfiction, 500, 502, 503, 510, 520
Human interest stories, 348, 351
Hypothesize, 529
Idiom, 519
Image gallery, 75, 117
Imagery, 337, 345, 395, 401, 591, 598
Images, 349, 523, 531
Independent learning
    close-read guide, 100, 200, 362, 484, 606
    share learning, 101, 201, 363, 485, 607
    strategies
        create a schedule, 98, 198, 360, 482, 604
        read with purpose, 98, 198, 360, 482, 604
        take notes, 98, 198, 360, 482, 604
Informational articles, 522, 525
Informational essay, 494
Informational text, 493
Informational text features
    acknowledgments, 465

bulleted list, 455
caption, 455
central idea, 379, 389
glossary, 455
heading, 379, 389, 455
paragraph, 379
reference, 455, 465
sidebar, 389, 455
special features, 379, 455
topic sentence, 379
Internal conflict, 319
Interpret, 19, 37, 64, 66, 79, 93, 94, 141, 143, 148, 151, 189, 192, 245, 279, 281, 289, 291, 317, 343, 391, 399, 415, 417, 421, 444, 446, 453, 475, 477, 478, 505, 507, 560, 570, 573, 585, 587, 596
Interview, 550, 552, 564, 565, 574
Irony, 478
    situational, 478
Label, 346
Language, 577, 587
    figurative language, 94, 125, 143, 395, 401, 519, 591, 598
        extended metaphor, 94
        idiom, 519
        imagery, 591, 598
        metaphor, 94, 125, 143, 519, 591
        personification, 125, 143, 591, 598
        simile, 125, 143, 519, 591, 598
    sensory language, 395, 591
Line, 83, 346
Line length, 93
Logical fallacy, 334
    sweeping generalization, 334
Lyric poetry, 340, 438, 439, 441, 446, 590, 594
Magical realism, 468
Make a judgment, 184, 295, 453, 465
Make inferences, 70, 91, 94, 182, 195, 245, 277, 281, 317, 345, 354, 415, 417, 465, 515, 521, 560, 575, 585, 596, 599
Meaning, 192, 391
Media
    image gallery, 75, 117
    spoken-word poetry, 438
    television interview, 56, 58, 68, 69, 72
    video, 353
Media Connection
    feature-film, 288
    video, 514
Memoir, 56, 58, 59, 68, 72
Metaphor, 94, 125, 143, 519, 591
    extended, 94
Modify, 79, 403, 509
Mood, 395, 401

Narrative, personal, 5, 6
Narrative poetry, 341
Narrative point of view
    omniscient narrator, 291
    third-person omniscient, 291
Narrator, omniscient, 291
Nonfiction
    arguments, 176, 179, 186, 187, 194
    descriptive essay, 394, 397
    feature article, 378, 381
    historical nonfiction, 500, 502, 503, 510, 520
    human interest stories, 348, 351
    informational articles, 522, 525
    interview, 565
    memoir, 56, 58, 59
    oral histories, 576, 579
    science features, 166, 169, 454, 457
    science journalism, 322
Novella, 284, 294
Nuanced words, 401
Objective point of view, 249, 403, 509
Observations, personal, 184
Omniscient narrator, 291
Oral histories, 576, 579
Organizational patterns, 573
Organizational structure, 523, 531
Outcome, 13, 21
Paraphrase, 182
Personal narrative, 5, 6
Personal observations, 184
Personification, 125, 143, 591, 598
Place, 562
Plot, 311, 469, 477
    climax, 311
    conflicts, 311, 319
    exposition, 311
    falling action, 311
    foreshadowing, 311, 319
    resolution, 311
    rising action, 311
    suspense, 311
Poetry, 336
    free-verse poetry, 82, 86, 88, 89, 342
    lyric poetry, 340, 438, 439, 441, 446, 590, 594
    narrative poetry, 341
    spoken-word poetry, 438, 449
    structure, 346
    visual elements, 93
        capitalization, 93
        line length, 93
        lines, 83
        punctuation, 93
        stanzas, 83
        white space, 93

Point of view, 509
   author's, 403
   objective, 249, 403, 509
   subjective, 249, 403, 509
Primary sources, 507
Print features, 323, 333
Pull-quotes, 523
Punctuation, 93
Purpose
   creation story, 406
   spoken-word poetry, 438
Question-and-answer format, 573
Radio play, 150
Radio-play adaptation, 124, 126, 146, 147
Realistic fiction
   short story, 12, 310
Reasoning, 177, 191
References, 455, 465
Relevant evidence, 191
Repetition, 447, 599
Research, 371, 372
Resolution, 311
Rhetorical devices, 334
   analogy, 334
   direct address, 334
Rhyme, 447
Rhyme scheme, 599
Rising action, 311
Science features, 166, 169, 454, 457
Science fiction, 124, 126, 146
Science journalism, 322
Secondary sources, 507
Section headings, 379
Sensory language, 395, 591
Setting, 125, 281, 469, 477, 517
   cultural context/setting, 517, 551
   cultural values, 562
   figurative language, 125, 143
      metaphor, 125, 143
      personification, 125, 143
      simile, 125, 143
   historical context/setting, 517, 551
   influence of, 551, 562, 572
   physical setting, 517
   place, 562
   time, 562
Short story, 15, 150, 210, 550, 552, 553, 564, 574
   realistic, 12, 310
Sidebar, 389, 523, 531
Simile, 125, 143, 519, 591, 598
Situational irony, 478
Slant rhyme, 599
Sources
   primary, 507

   secondary, 507
Specific purposes, 167
Speculate, 73, 171, 182, 317, 399, 415, 450, 515, 570, 587
Spoken-word poetry, 438, 449
Stage directions, 219, 279
Stanza, 83, 346
Statistics, 27, 184
Structure
   argument, 176
   creation story, 406
   descriptive essay, 394
   drama, 218
   feature articles, 26, 378
   free-verse poetry, 82
   historical fiction, 500
   historical nonfiction, 500
   human interest stories, 348
   informational articles, 522
   interview, 550
   lyric poetry, 438, 590
   magical realism, 468
   memoir, 56
   oral histories, 576
   organizational structure, 523, 531
   poetry, 336
   radio-play adaptation, 124
   realistic short story, 12, 310
   science feature, 166, 454
   science fiction, 124
   science journalism, 322
   short story, 550
   spoken-word poetry, 438
   television interview, 56
   vignette, 590
Subjective point of view, 249, 403, 509
Sufficient evidence, 191
Summarize, 66, 399, 463, 529, 585
Support, 21, 35, 37, 171, 192, 391, 478, 505, 515
Supporting evidence, 177, 507
Suspense, 311
Sweeping generalization, 334
Syntax, 39, 577, 587
Synthesize, 73, 141, 389, 521
Take a position, 79, 277
Television interview, 56, 58, 68, 69, 72
Text features, 39, 523, 531
   captions, 523
   headings, 523, 531
   illustrations, 523
   images, 523, 531
   pull-quotes, 523
   sidebars, 523, 531
Text sections, 39
Theme(s), 13, 21, 337, 345, 417, 478, 501

   character development, 517
   characters, 13, 21, 281
   conflicts, 13, 21, 281
   explicit, 407, 417, 446
   imagery, 337, 345
   implicit, 407, 417, 446
   in lyric poetry, 439, 446
   multiple, 407, 517
   outcome, 13, 21
   setting, 281, 517
   topics, 407
   universal, 407, 417
Third-person omniscient point of view, 291
Time, 562
Tone, 192, 391, 577, 587
Topics, 407
Universal themes, 407, 417
Video, 353
Vignette, 590
Voice
   diction, 577, 587
   syntax, 577, 587
   tone, 577, 587
White space, 93

Composition

Adjectives, 305
Adverbs, conjunctive, 541, 545
Agreement
   in number, 47
   pronoun-antecedent agreement, 47, 50
Alternative endings, 479
Antecedents, 47
Argument, 204, 404
   Argument Checklist, 205
   editorial, 152
   review and evaluate evidence, 204
Argumentative essay, 195
Audience, 43, 537, 540
Biographical profiles, 602
   discuss, 603
   plan with your group, 602
   rehearse, revise, and present, 603
Capitalization, 51
   titles, 433
Cause-and-effect structure, 539
Chapbook, 600
Characters, 46, 299
Citations
   direct quotation, 429
   paraphrase, 429
   summary, 429
   Works Cited list, 433
Claim, 155, 156
Clarity, 49, 158, 303, 431, 543

Clauses
    dependent, 157, 161
    independent, 157
Coherence, 47, 301, 541
    complex sentences, 157
    dependent clause, 157
    independent clause, 157
    subordinating conjunctions, 157
    transitions, 541
        conjunctive adverbs, 541
        transitional words and phrases, 541
Comic strip, 487
Commas
    with adjectives, 305
Comma splices, 301, 544
Comparison-and-contrast essay, 73, 151, 421, 453, 521, 575
Complete sentences, 301
Complexity, 425
Complex sentences, 157, 160, 304, 544
Conflict, 46, 299
Conjunctions, subordinating, 157, 544
Conjunctive adverbs, 541, 545
Critical review, 295
Definitions, 537
Dependent clause, 157, 161
Details, sensory, 300
Development, 46, 49, 156, 158, 303, 431, 540, 543
Dialogue, 24, 51, 300
Direct quotations, 537
Drafting
    audience, 540
    characters, 46
    citations, 429
    claim, 156
    coherence, 47, 157, 301, 541
    conflict, 46
    development, 46, 156, 540
    dialogue, 300
    evidence, 429
    precise language, 300
    pronoun-antecedent agreement, 47
    sensory details, 300
    setting, 46
    style, 156
    thesis, 428
    tone, 540
Editing
    citations
        Works Cited list, 433
    sentences
        comma splices, 544
        complex sentences, 160, 304, 544
        pronoun-antecedent agreement, 50

run-on sentences, 544
        subject-verb agreement, 304, 432
Editorial, 152
    drafting, 156
    editing, 160
    elements, 152
    planning and prewriting, 154
    publishing and presenting, 161
    revising, 158
Email, persuasive, 534
Essay
    argumentative, 195
    comparison-and-contrast, 73, 151, 421, 453, 521, 575
    informational, 536, 610
    research-based, 488
Evidence
    accurate sources, 153
    citation, 429
    credible sources, 153
    definitions, 537
    direct quotations, 537
    examples, 537
    facts, 537
    relevant, 537
Examples, 537
Facts, 537
First-person point of view, 297
Formal letter, 392
Free-verse poem, 95
Freewrite, 44, 154, 298, 538
Friendly letter, 282
Genre, 297
Home design, 203
Homophones, 161
Illustration, 609
Independent clause, 157
Informational essay, 536, 610
    drafting, 540
    editing, 544
    elements, 536
    Informational Essay Checklist, 611
    planning and prewriting, 538
    publishing and presenting, 545
    review and evaluate evidence, 610
    revising, 542
Informational text, 602
Journal entry, 321
Language, precise, 300
Letter
    formal letter, 392
    friendly letter, 282
Lyric poem, 600
Message, 45
Narrative point of view, 297

Nestorian order, 155
Nouns, proper, 51
Order of importance, 155
Organization, 49, 158, 303, 431, 543
Pacing, 299
Packing list, 203
Personal narrative, 42, 104
    drafting, 46
    editing, 50
    elements, 42
    Personal Narrative Checklist, 105
    planning and prewriting, 44
    publishing and presenting, 51
    review and evaluate evidence, 104
    revising, 48
Personal pronouns, 47
Persuasive email, 534
Planning and prewriting
    freewrite, 44, 154, 298, 538
    identify sources, 426
    research questions, 424
        complexity, 425
        scope, 425
        significance, 425
Poem, 365
    chapbook, 600
    free-verse, 95
    lyric, 600
Point of view
    first-person, 297
    narrative, 297
    third-person limited, 297
    third-person omniscient, 297
Precise language, 300
Prepositional phrases, 432
Pronoun-antecedent agreement, 47, 50
Pronouns, 47
Pronouns, personal, 47
Proper nouns, 51
Publishing and presenting
    integrate media, 51, 161, 305, 432, 545
Punctuation
    author's names, 433
    commas, with adjectives, 305
    comma splices, 544
    conjunctive adverbs, 545
    dependent clauses, 161
    dialogue, 51
    transitions, 541
Purpose, 43
    general, 153
    specific, 43, 153
    vague, 43
QuickWrite, 9, 100, 113, 200, 215, 362, 375, 484, 497, 606

Index of Skills **R13**

Quotations, direct, 537
Reflect on your writing, 24, 40, 123, 282, 392, 404, 534
Relevant evidence, 537
Research-based essay, 488
   Research-Based Essay Checklist, 489
   review and evaluate evidence, 488
Research paper, 422
   drafting, 428
   editing, 432
   elements, 422
   planning and prewriting, 424
   publishing and presenting, 432
   revising, 430
Research report, 405, 467
Revising
   clarity, 49, 158, 303, 431, 543
   development, 49, 158, 303, 431, 543
   organization, 49, 158, 303, 431, 543
   style, 49, 158, 543
   style and tone, 303, 431
Run-on sentences, 301, 544
Scope, 425
Sensory details, 300
Sentence fragments, 301
Sentences
   comma splices, 301, 544
   complete sentences, 301
   complex sentences, 157, 160, 304, 544
   pronoun-antecedent agreement, 50
   run-on sentences, 301, 544
   sentence fragments, 301
   sentence variety, 541
   subject-verb agreement, 304
      prepositional phrases, 432
Sentence variety, 541
Sequence of events, 45
Setting, 46, 299
Short story, 296, 366
   drafting, 300
   editing, 304
   elements, 296
   planning and prewriting, 298
   publishing and presenting, 305
   review and evaluate evidence, 366
   revising, 302
   Short Story Checklist, 366
Significance, 425
Social media post, 365
Song, 103, 609
Sources, 422, 426
   accurate, 153
   credible, 153
   direct quotation, 429
   online, 426
   paraphrase, 429

   primary, 422, 426
   secondary, 422, 426
   summary, 429
Spelling
   adding suffixes, 545
   dge or *ge* for ending *j* sound, 305
   homophones, 161
Story synopsis, 123
Structure, 299, 539
   cause-and-effect, 539
   character, 299
   claim, 155
   conflict, 299
   Nestorian order, 155
   order of importance, 155
   pacing, 299
   sequence of events, 45
   setting, 299
   subtopic, 539
Style, 49, 156, 158, 303, 431, 543
Subject-verb agreement, 304, 432
Subordinating conjunctions, 157, 544
Subtopic, 539
Summary, 8, 19, 35, 70, 112, 141, 171, 182, 189, 214, 245, 277, 289, 317, 331, 354, 374, 387, 399, 415, 444, 463, 475, 496, 505, 515, 529, 560, 570, 585, 596
Thesis, 428
Thesis statement, 539
Third-person limited point of view, 297
Third-person omniscient point of view, 297
Timed Writing, 73, 151, 195, 295, 421, 453, 521, 575
Title
   capitalization of, 433
   formatting, 433
Tone, 303, 431, 540
Transitional words, phrases, and clauses, 301
Transitional words and phrases, 541
Transitions, 429, 541
   conjunctive adverbs, 541
   transitional words and phrases, 541
Travel guide entry, 40
T-shirt design, 487
Word choice, 24, 40, 123, 282, 392, 404, 534
Works Cited list, 433

Comprehension Skills

Reading check, 79, 91, 343
Strategy
   adjust fluency, 408
   annotate, 250, 440
   ask questions, 578
   background knowledge, 510

   create mental images, 84, 91, 146, 338, 343
   determine central ideas, 58
   establish a purpose, 312, 502
   listen actively, 350, 448
   make connections, 68, 186, 284, 324, 396, 470, 592
   make inferences, 14, 116, 121, 126, 168
   make predictions, 28, 178, 380, 456, 552
   paraphrase, 220, 564
   preview and predict, 524
   synthesize information, 74, 79
Viewing check, 121

Conventions

Adjectives, 533
   coordinate, 533
   cumulative, 533
Clauses
   dependent, 67, 145, 185
   independent, 67, 145, 185
   subordinate, 67
Colloquial contractions, 588
Commas, 563
Common nouns, 23
Complex sentence, 145
Compound-complex sentence, 145
Compound sentence, 145
Conjunctions, 293
   coordinating, 293
   correlative, 293
   introductory, 588
   subordinating, 293
Contractions, colloquial, 588
Coordinate adjectives, 533
Coordinating conjunctions, 293
Correlative conjunctions, 293
Cumulative adjectives, 533
Dangling modifiers, 419
Dependent clause, 67, 145, 185
Future perfect tense, 466
Future tense, 466
Gerund phrases, 174
Independent clause, 67, 145, 185
Infinitive phrases, 174
Informal grammar, 588
   colloquial contractions, 588
   informal transitions, 588
   introductory conjunctions, 588
   sentence fragments, 588
Informal transitions, 588
Introductory conjunctions, 588
Misplaced modifiers, 419
Modifiers, 419
   dangling, 419

misplaced, 419
Nouns
  common, 23
  possessive, 23
  proper, 23
Past perfect tense, 466
Past tense, 466
Personal pronouns, 23
Phrases
  gerund, 174
  infinitive, 174
Possessive nouns, 23
Possessive pronouns, 23
Prepositional phrases, 320
Prepositions, 320
Present perfect tense, 466
Present tense, 466
Pronouns
  personal, 23
  possessive, 23
Proper nouns, 23
Punctuation
  commas, 563
Sentence fragments, 588
Sentences
  complex, 145
  compound, 145
  compound-complex, 145
  dependent clause, 145
  independent clause, 145
  sentence fragments, 588
  simple, 145
Simple sentences, 145
Subordinate clause, 67
Subordinating conjunctions, 293
Transitions, informal, 588
Verb tenses, 466
  future, 466
  future perfect, 466
  past, 466
  past perfect, 466
  present, 466
  present perfect, 466

Inquiry and Research
Research and extend, 20, 36, 142, 149, 246, 278, 290, 388, 400, 416, 506, 516, 530
Research paper, 422
Research report, 335, 405, 467

Response Skills
First Thoughts, 19, 35, 64, 70, 79, 91, 121, 141, 148, 171, 182, 189, 245, 277, 289, 317, 331, 343, 354, 387, 399, 415, 444, 450, 463, 475, 505, 515, 529, 560, 570, 585, 596

Speaking and Listening
Autobiographical anecdote, 96
  listen and discuss, 97
  prepare and plan, 96
  rehearse and present, 97
Class discussion, 8
Commercial, 203
Costume plans, 283
Debate, 193, 196
  Debate Checklist, 196
  discuss and evaluate, 196
  four-corner, 112, 214, 496
  hold the debate, 196
  informal, 365
  prepare for the debate, 196
  rehearse, 196
Discussion, 589
  class discussion, 8
  group discussion, 103
Dramatic adaptation, 347, 358
  deliver your adaptation, 359
  discuss and evaluate, 359
  plan with your group, 358
  write and rehearse, 358
Dramatic reading, 25
Four-corner debate, 112, 214, 496
Group discussion, 103
Illustrated version of a text, 601
Informal debate, 365
Instructions, 480
  follow, 481
  give, 481
  plan, 480
Let the people decide, 374
Multimedia presentation, 81, 357, 393
Multimedia research presentation, 535
Oral presentation, 41
Peer-group learning
  analyzing explicit and implicit meanings, 437
  building your vocabulary, 308
  giving and receiving constructive feedback, 549
  making a schedule, 55, 165, 308, 437, 549
  reflect on and modify your views, 165
  strategies
    clarify, 52, 162, 306, 434, 546
    participate fully, 52, 162, 306, 434, 546
    prepare, 52, 162, 306, 434, 546
    support others, 52, 162, 306, 434, 546
  using textual evidence, 55
  working as a group
    apply the rules, 54, 164, 308, 436
    create a communication plan, 54, 164, 308, 436, 548
    discuss the topic, 54, 308
    list your rules, 54, 164, 308, 436
    name your group, 308, 436, 548
    take a position, 164, 436, 548
    use text evidence, 548
Personal narrative, 96
Poster, 103
Presentations
  biographical profiles, 602
  commercial, 203
  informational texts, 602
  multimedia, 81, 357, 393
  multimedia research, 535
  personal narrative, 96
  poster, 103
  speech, 609
Radio ad, 487
Song, 609
Speech, 609
Summary of research findings, 175
Whole-class learning strategies
  demonstrate respect, 10, 114, 216, 376, 498
  describe personal connections, 376, 498
  interact and share ideas, 10, 216
  listen actively, 10, 114, 216, 376, 498
  make personal connections, 114
  show interest, 10, 216

Vocabulary
Academic vocabulary
  assumption, 109
  certainty, 109
  consequence, 5
  contradict, 5
  determination, 493
  deviate, 493
  dialogue, 5
  discredit, 109
  dissent, 109
  diversity, 493
  elucidate, 371
  envision, 209
  evident, 371
  generate, 371
  ingenious, 209
  justify, 109
  logical, 371
  lucid, 209
  notable, 5
  observation, 493
  omniscient, 209
  persevere, 493

perspective, 5
philosophy, 371
sensation, 209
Concept vocabulary
　accessible, 524, 525, 532
　accomplishments, 578, 583, 586
　advocating, 440, 442, 445
　affinity, 456, 459, 464
　altered, 250, 270, 280
　anxious, 186, 188, 190
　atmosphere, 126, 136, 144
　attain, 564, 566, 571
　audibly, 524, 526, 532
　benefit, 408, 411, 418
　blight, 396, 398, 402
　calamitous, 186, 188, 190
　canals, 126, 135, 144
　catapulted, 84, 89, 92
　celebrate, 578, 584, 586
　charitable, 58, 61, 65
　chosen, 408, 411, 418
　colonies, 380, 384, 390
　conducive, 564, 567, 571
　consequences, 470, 474, 476
　contact, 312, 314, 318
　covetous, 220, 222, 248
　crude, 592, 594, 597
　demoralized, 502, 504, 508
　deserted, 396, 398, 402
　discards, 338, 342, 344
　dispelled, 250, 271, 280
　disposal, 470, 473, 476
　distorting, 338, 341, 344
　doubt, 14, 16, 22
　dreaded, 284, 286, 292
　earnest, 250, 272, 280
　embossed, 524, 528, 532
　enthusiastically, 552, 559, 561
　exhaustion, 510, 513, 518
　extinction, 380, 385, 390
　extraordinary, 578, 583, 586
　fault, 408, 414, 418
　fluently, 28, 29, 38
　forlorn, 126, 134, 144
　frantically, 510, 512, 518
　grief, 284, 286, 292
　herbicides, 380, 382, 390
　hesitantly, 552, 559, 561
　honored, 408, 411, 418
　illusion, 350, 352, 355
　immense, 126, 135, 144
　implores, 440, 443, 445
　impossible, 220, 226, 248
　impoverished, 502, 504, 508
　improve, 178, 179, 183
　incorporate, 456, 458, 464
　infinitely, 250, 276, 280

inspiration, 350, 352, 355
instinct, 14, 17, 22
instinctively, 552, 556, 561
intense, 14, 18, 22
intricate, 350, 352, 355
lecture, 28, 32, 38
linguists, 28, 30, 38
lurched, 84, 89, 92
maladies, 396, 398, 402
malcontent, 220, 230, 248
melded, 456, 458, 464
mischief, 408, 414, 418
miser, 220, 230, 248
morose, 220, 224, 248
mosaic, 126, 137, 144
navigate, 524, 528, 532
ominously, 186, 188, 190
parallel, 250, 267, 280
paralysis, 14, 16, 22
parasites, 380, 385, 390
penitence, 284, 286, 292
permit, 312, 314, 318
perseverance, 564, 566, 571
persist, 178, 181, 183
pestering, 408, 413, 418
pesticides, 380, 382, 390
philanthropist, 58, 61, 65
plaintive, 284, 288, 292
plight, 502, 503, 508
pollinators, 380, 384, 390
pronouncing, 28, 33, 38
puzzled, 396, 398, 402
raggedy, 592, 595, 597
ravaged, 502, 503, 508
rebuke, 284, 286, 292
recording, 28, 33, 38
release, 312, 314, 318
resolute, 220, 225, 248
resolved, 470, 474, 476
rough, 592, 594, 597
sensors, 524, 526, 532
shrinking, 338, 340, 344
shuddered, 510, 512, 518
stammering, 510, 512, 518
stillness, 396, 398, 402
stricken, 396, 398, 402
strive, 250, 270, 280
striving, 178, 181, 183
stunned, 14, 15, 22
submerged, 126, 128, 144
supervision, 58, 59, 65
tactile, 524, 526, 532
term, 28, 32, 38
transported, 84, 87, 92
trembling, 284, 286, 292
uncompromising, 440, 443, 445
unending, 502, 503, 508

unexplainable, 14, 16, 22
widespread, 502, 503, 508
Media vocabulary
　actors' delivery, 146, 149
　background music, 146, 149
　close-up, 448, 451
　composition, 74, 80
　cut, 448, 451
　digital art, 116, 122
　incidental music, 448, 451
　interview subject, 68, 71
　light and shadow, 74, 80
　medium, 116, 122
　proportion, 74, 80
　realism, 116, 122
　set, 68, 71
　sound effects, 146, 149
　tone, 68, 71
Technical vocabulary
　capsules, 168, 170, 172
　gravity, 168, 169, 172
　habitation, 168, 169, 172
　relay, 324, 329, 332
　signals, 324, 327, 332
　transmit, 324, 328, 332
Word study skills
　analogies, 476, 571
　antonyms, 92, 355, 532
　base words, 58, 552
　connotation, 518
　connotation and denotation, 190, 418, 508
　context clues, 84, 178, 312, 470, 564, 578
　　cause-and-effect clues, 312
　dictionary, 324, 350, 440, 592
　Greek prefix
　　para-, 280
　Greek root
　　-log-, 371
　　-logue-, 5
　　-phil-, 65
　　-philo-, 371
　　-soph-, 371
　Latin prefix
　　extra-, 586
　　in-, 532
　　mal-, 248
　Latin root
　　-cert-, 109
　　-cred-, 109
　　-dict-, 5
　　-fin-, 464
　　-gen-, 209, 371
　　-grav-, 172
　　-jus-, 109
　　-luc-, 209, 371

R16 INDEX

-not-, 5
-omni-, 209
-sens-, 209
-sent-, 109
-sequ-, 5
-serv-, 493
-sever-, 493
-sign-, 332
-spec-, 5
-sum-, 109
-term-, 493
-tort-, 344
-ver-, 493
-via-, 493
-vid-, 371
-vis-, 209
-voc-, 445
Latin root word
   lingua, 38
Latin suffix
   -able, 22
multiple-meaning words, 318, 597
nuance, 144, 292
prefix
   extra-, 586
   in-, 532
   mal-, 248
   para-, 280
root
   -cert-, 109

-cred-, 109
-dict-, 5
-fin-, 464
-gen-, 209, 371
-grav-, 172
-jus-, 109
-log-, 371
-logue-, 5
-luc-, 209, 371
-not-, 5
-omni-, 209
-phil-, 65
-philo-, 371
-sens-, 209
-sent-, 109
-sequ-, 5
-serv-, 493
-sever-, 493
-sign-, 332
-soph-, 371
-spec-, 5
-sum-, 109
-term-, 493
-tort-, 344
-ver-, 493
-via-, 493
-vid-, 371
-vis-, 209
-voc-, 445
root word

   lingua, 38
spelling patterns
   long *i*, 402
   -ly and *-ally* endings, 561
   -tion, *-sion*, 390
suffix
   -able, 22
synonyms, 92, 144, 183, 292, 355, 518
thesaurus, 186, 338, 456
word choice, 22, 38, 65, 92, 144, 172, 183, 190, 248, 280, 292, 318, 332, 344, 355, 390, 402, 418, 445, 464, 476, 508, 518, 532, 561, 571, 586, 597
Word Wall, 7, 111, 213, 373, 495

Assessment

Argument, 204
Informational essay, 610
Personal narrative, 104
Research-based essay, 488
Short response, 73, 151, 195, 295, 421, 453, 521, 575
Short story, 366
Test practice, 72, 150, 194, 294, 420, 452, 520, 574
Timed Writing, 73, 151, 195, 295, 421, 453, 521, 575
Unit Projects, 103, 203, 365, 487, 609

Index of Skills **R17**

INDEX OF AUTHORS AND TITLES

Purple = Independent Learning

A

Against the Odds, 494
Alarcón, Francisco X.
Andre-Clark, Alice, 28, 29
Angelou, Maya, 58, 59, 69
Atwood, Margaret

B

Bee Highway, The: Making a Place for Bees in the City, 381
Beyawned Earth: Pillownauts and the Downside of Space Travel
Black Sunday: The Storm That Gave Us the Dustbowl, 503
Blakemore, Erin, 502, 503
Blanco, Octavio, 564, 565
Bradbury, Ray, 126, 127
Bruchac, Joseph, 409, 410
Buckner, Sheri, 178, 179

C

Caduto, Michael J., 409, 410
Calise, Gabrielle
Carson, Rachel, 396, 397
Case of the Disappearing Words, The: Saving the World's Endangered Languages, 29
Chang, Lan Samantha
Chikhoune, Ryma, 350, 351
Christensen, Lisa, 524, 525
Christmas Carol, A, from, 285
Christmas Carol, A: Scrooge and Marley, Act I, 221
Christmas Carol, A: Scrooge and Marley, Act II, 251
Circuit, The, 553
Cisneros, Sandra, 593, 595
Climate Reality Project, 448
Cofer, Judith Ortiz
Colón, Jesús
Cox, Mary Beth, 456, 457
Coyote Steals the Sun and Moon, 412
Creature Comforts: Three Biology-Based Tips for Builders, 457

D

Danger! This Mission to Mars Could Bore You to Death!
Dark They Were, and Golden-Eyed, 127
Dark They Were, and Golden-Eyed (Radio Play), 147
de la Peña, Matt, 14, 15
Dickens, Charles, 220, 221, 251, 284, 285
Do not trust the eraser, 342
Don't Just Sit There Like a Punk, 15
Dorminey, Bruce, 186, 187
Dunbar, Paul Laurence

E

Earthrise, 449
Erdoes, Richard, 409, 412

F

Family
Four Skinny Trees, 595

G

Garcia, Ariana
George, Jean Craighead
Girl Who Fell From the Sky, The
Golden Windows, The, 210
González, Ángel, 339, 341
Gorman, Amanda, 440, 441, 449
"Gotcha Day" Isn't a Cause for Celebration
Grandfather's Garden, 6
Grimm, Jacob and Wilhelm

H

Hendricks, Mica Angela, 74, 75
Hendricks, Myla, 75
Henry, O.
Hernández, José, 565
He—y, Come on Ou—t!, 471
Hogan, Linda
Horne, Frank, 85, 89
Hoshi, Shinichi, 470, 471
Hour With Abuelo, An
How Grandmother Spider Stole the Sun, 410
How the Teens of St. Pete Youth Farm Fight Food Insecurity, One Harvest at a Time
How This Son of Migrant Farm Workers Became an Astronaut, 565
Humans Are Not Meant to Live in Space, 110
Hughes, Langston, 85, 88, 312, 313
Hulick, Kathryn, 380, 381

I

I Myself, 341

J

Jaguar
Janke, Katelan, 510, 511
Japan to Start Research on the Moon and Mars for Humans, 169
Jiménez, Francisco, 552, 553
Johnson, Sophie

K

Keller, Helen
King, Rosamond S., 339, 342
Kipling, Rudyard
Koepcke, Juliane
Koerth, Maggie

R18 INDEX

L

Learning Rewires the Brain, 325
Learning to Love My Mother, 69
Lineage
Little Things Are Big

M

Maher, Michael, 68, 69
Makeup Artist Mimi Choi's Mesmerizing Art-Inspired Beauty Looks, 351
Malala Yousafzai: Speech to United Nations Security Council
Mason, Jennifer
McCall, Guadalupe García, 85, 86
McDonough, Michael, 146, 147
Merriam, Eve, 593, 594
Mimi Choi Brings Fear to Life With Her Makeup Artistry, 353
Mom & Me & Mom, from, 59
Montalban, Eloise
More Accessible World, A, 525
Mother-Daughter Drawings, 75
Mother to Son, 88
Mullins, Aimee, 578, 579
My Side of the Mountain, from

N

National Space Society, The, 116, 117
Nye, Naomi Shihab, 339, 340

O

Ode to My Papi, 86
Old Man and His Grandson, The
Ortiz, Alfonso, 409, 412
Our Purpose in Poetry: Or, Earthrise, 441

P

Paley, Grace

R

Retreived Reformation, A
Rice University Researchers Are Turning Dead Spiders Into "Necrobots"
Richards, Laura E., 210
Rikki-tikki-tavi

S

Silent Spring, from, 397
Simile: Willow and Ginkgo, 594
Space Comics
Space Settlement Art, 117
Sparrow, The
Stevens, Alison Pearce, 324, 325
Story of My Life, The, from
Story of Victor d'Aveyron, the Wild Child, The
Survival in the Storm: The Dust Bowl Diary of Grace Edwards, from, 511
Suzuki, Tomoyuki, 169

T

Thank You, M'am, 313
Time Capsule Found on the Dead Planet
To James, 89
True Calling Media, 353
Trying to Name What Doesn't Change, 340
Turtle Watchers

W

Walker, Margaret
Water Names
Wildlife Rehabbers Are Here to Help, 372
Why We Should Continue to Explore Space, 179
Why We Should Save Earth Before Colonizing Mars, 187
Work in Progress, A, 579

Y

Yousafzai, Malala

ACKNOWLEDGMENTS AND CREDITS

Text Acknowledgments

Unit 1

15-18 DON'T JUST SIT THERE LIKE A PUNK. Text copyright © 2017 by Matt de la Peña. Reprinted by permission of Writers House LLC acting as agent for the author; 29-34 The Case of the Disappearing Words Save the World's Endangered Languages by Alice Andre-Clark, from Muse, copyright © 2017 by Alice Andre-Clark. Used with permission from Cricket Media. All rights reserved; 59-64 Chapter 3 and Chapter 4 from MOM & ME & MOM by Maya Angelou, copyright ©2013 by Maya Angelou. Used by permission of Random House, an imprint and division of Penguin Random House LLC. All rights reserved and Reproduced with permission of the Little, Brown Book Group Limited through PLSclear; 75-78 "Mother-Daughter Drawings" by Mica and Myla Hendricks. Used by permission of the author; 86-87 "Ode to My Papi" from LIVING BEYOND BORDERS GROWING UP MEXICAN IN AMERICA edited by Margarita Longoria, compilation copyright © 2021 by Margarita Longoria. Used by permission of Viking Children's Books, an imprint of Penguin Young Readers Group, a division of Penguin Random House LLC. All rights reserved; 88 Hughes, Langston, Mother to Son, The Crisis, 1922; 89-90 ©NYPL; 103 Stein, G. (1926). Composition as explanation (pp. 511-23). L. & V. Woolf at the Hogarth Press.

Unit 2

118-120 © Ray Cassel; 126-140 Reprinted by permission of Don Congdon Associates, Inc. Copyright © 1949 by Standard Magazines, renewed 1976 by Ray Bradbury; 169-170 Suzuki, Tomoyuki. Japan to start research on places on moon, Mars for humans. The Asahi Shimbun, July 6, 2022. Reproduction without permission from The Asahi Shimbun is prohibited. Approval number 3-0084; 187-188 From Forbes. © 2018 Forbes. All rights reserved. Used under license.

Unit 3

211-213 "Golden Windows" by Laura E. Richard, Leopold Classic Library, June 24, 2016; 222-244 A Christmas Carol Scrooge and Marley, Act I and Act II, a drama adapted by Israel Horowitz, based on the novel by Charles Dickens. Copyright © 1979. Used by permission of Fountain Pen, Inc; 251-276 A Christmas Carol Scrooge and Marley, Act I and Act II, a drama adapted by Israel Horowitz, based on the novel by Charles Dickens. Copyright © 1979. Used by permission of Fountain Pen, Inc; 285-288 Dickens, Charles, A Christmas Carol A Story, Chapman & Hall, 1843; 313-316 "Thank You, M'am" from SHORT STORIES by Langston Hughes. Copyright © 1996 by Ramona Bass and Arnold Rampersad. Reprinted by permission of Hill and Wang, a division of Farrar, Straus and Giroux. All Rights Reserved. And reprinted by permission of Harold Ober Associates. Copyright © 1997 by Farrar, Straus and Giroux; 325-330 Stevens, Alison Pearce. Science News Explores. Learning Rewires the Brain. September 2, 2014; 340 By permission of the author, Naomi Shihab, Nye, 2022; 341 Used with permission of Princeton University Press, from "Harsh World" and Other Poems, Ángel González, 1977; permission conveyed through Copyright Clearance Center, Inc; 342 "Do not trust the eraser" © 2021 Rosamond S. King, used with permission; 351-352 Written by Ryma Chikhoune for WWD/Courtesy of Fairchild Archive. Copyright © 2022 by Fairchild Publishing, LLC. All Rights Reserved. Used by Permission.

Unit 4

381-386 The Bee Highway Making a Place for Bees in the City by Kathryn Hulick, Muse, April 2021. Reprinted by permission of Cricket Media. All rights reserved; 397-398 "A Fable for Tomorrow" from Silent Spring by Rachel Carson. Copyright ©1962 by Rachel L. Carson. Copyright © renewed 1990 by Roger Christie. Used by permission of HarperCollins Publishers. Also, reprinted by permission of Frances Collin, Trustee. All copying, including electronic, or re-distribution of this text, is expressly forbidden; 410-411 How Grandmother Spider Stole the Sun from Keepers of the Earth by Michael J. Caduto and Joseph Bruchac, copyright © 1988 by Michael J. Caduto and Joseph Bruchac. Used with permission from Fulcrum Publishing. All rights reserved; 412-414 "Coyote Steals the Sun and Moon" from AMERICAN INDIAN MYTHS AND LEGENDS by Richard Erdoes and Alfonso Ortiz, copyright © 1984 by Richard Erdoes and Alfonso Ortiz. Used by permission of Pantheon Books, an imprint of the Knopf Doubleday Publishing Group, a division of Penguin Random House LLC. All rights reserved. Also, published by Ebury. Reprinted by permission of The Random House Group Limited; 441-443 "Earthrise" Copyright © 2018 by Amanda Gorman. Used by permission of the author; 457 Creature Comforts Three Biology-Based Tips for Builders by Mary Beth Cost, Odyssey, May 2014. Reprinted by Permission of Cricket Media. All rights reserved; 471-474 "He-y, Come On Ou-t!" from The Best Japanese Science Fiction Stories by Shinichi Hoshi, translated by Stanleigh Jones. Reprinted by permission of the translator.

Unit 5

503-504 Erin Blakemore; 511-514 From SURVIVAL IN THE STORM The Dust Bowl Diary of Grace Edwards by Katelan Janke. Copyright © 2002 by Katelan Janke. Reprinted by permission of Scholastic Inc.; 525-528 Christensen, Lisa. A More Accessible World. Muse Science Magazine, January 2022; 553-559 From The Circuit Stories From the Life of A Migrant Child by Francisco Jiménez. Copyright © 1997 University of New Mexico Press, 1997; 565-569 From CNN.com. © 2016 Cable News Network. A Warner Bros. Discovery Company. All rights reserved. Used under license; 579-584 From The Moth by The Moth, copyright © 2013. Reprinted by permission of Hachette Books an imprint of Hachette Book Group, Inc., and Burns, Catherine, The Moth. The Moth, 2013. Also, Profile Books, 2014; 594 "Simile Willow and Ginkgo" copyright © 1986 by Eve Merriam Appears in A Sky Full of Poems Originally published by Yearling. Used by permission of Curtis Brown, Ltd.; 595 From THE HOUSE ON MANGO STREET. Copyright © 1984 by Sandra Cisneros. Published by Vintage Books, a division of Penguin Random House, and in hardcover by Alfred A. Knopf in 1994. By permission of Susan Bergholz Literary Services, Lamy, NM. All rights reserved. And Bloomsbury Publishing Plc.

Photography Credits

Cover

Hcreate/Shutterstock; Trend Creatives/Shutterstock; Aleshyn_Andrei/Shutterstock; Prettycolors/Shutterstock; Ardea-studio/Shutterstock; Vectorpouch/Shutterstock; Ron and Joe/Shutterstock; Vit-Mar/Shutterstock; R. Rizvanov/Shutterstock; Rose Rodionova/Shutterstock; Andrey_Kuzmin/Shutterstock; Clusterx/Shutterstock; Miloje/Shutterstock; Artplay/Shutterstock; Dotted Yeti/Shutterstock; Artmari/Shutterstock; Vik Y/Shutterstock; Macrovector/Shutterstock; Oniks Astarit/Shutterstock.

Front Matter

vii "3 Generations" mural by Joel Bergner, designed and painted in collaboration with dozens of community participants at the Boulevard Houses in Brooklyn, New York in 2020. Partners Artolution, Center of Court Innovation and the Mayor's Action Plan; viii-ix Dima Zel/

Shutterstock; x-xi Andrey_I/Shutterstock; xii (TL) Francois Roux/Shutterstock; xiv-xv Liudmila Habrus/Alamy Stock Photo.

Unit 1

2 "3 Generations" mural by Joel Bergner, designed and painted in collaboration with dozens of community participants at the Boulevard Houses in Brooklyn, New York in 2020. Partners Artolution, Center of Court Innovation and the Mayor's Action Plan; 6 Botany Vision/Alamy Stock Photo; 14 Larry D. Moore, CC BY 4.0, via Wikimedia Commons; 15 South_Agency/E+/Getty Images; 17 Brocreative/Shutterstock; 29 Lucky Team Studio/Shutterstock; 30 Photographs by Yuri Marder; 32 Photographs by Yuri Marder; 33 Photographs by Yuri Marder; 34 Photographs by Yuri Marder; 58 Ken Charnock/Getty Images; 59 Everett Collection Historical/Alamy Stock Photo; 62 Acme News Photo/Agence Quebec Presse/Newscom; 74-78 © Mica Hendricks; 85 (T) CSU Archives/Everett Collection Inc/Alamy Stock Photo; (B) Schomburg Center for Research in Black Culture; 86 Nuttapong punna/Alamy Stock Photo; 88 Aditya Gujaran/EyeEm/Getty Images; 89 Corbis/VCG/Getty Images; 99 (TL) Everett Collection Inc/Alamy Stock Photo; (TC) © Alyson Aliano; (TR) Dean Conger/The Image Bank/Getty Images; (BL) Ronnie Kaufman/Larry/Blend Images/Age Fotostock.

Unit 2

106 Dima Zel/Shutterstock; 110 Supamotionstock/Shutterstock; 117 "Imitating the Earth" © by Javier Arizabalo. All rights reserved; 118 © Ray Cassel; 119 Art by Alfred Twu; 120 "Closest Approach" © by Jonathan Chapin. All rights reserved; 126 (B) Everett Collection Inc/Alamy Stock Photo; 127 Lovattpics/iStock/Getty Images; 131 Lonia/Shutterstock; 135 Altanaka/Shutterstock; 146 Michael McDonough; 147 Patrick Koslo/Stockbyte/Getty Images; 169 Artificial gravity habitat Lunar Glass, Provided by Kajima Corp.; 170 Artificial gravity habitat Mars Glass, Provided by Kajima Corp.; 179 Blue Planet Studio/Shutterstock; 186 Photo by Bruce Dorminey; 187 Vadim Sadovski/Shutterstock; 199 (TL) Ekaterina Minaeva/Alamy Stock Photo; (TC) Michael Lewis/Corbis/Getty Images; (TR) Kelly vandellen/Shutterstock; (BL) Six Chix © 2014 Rina Piccolo, Distributed by King Features Syndicate, Inc.

Unit 3

206 Andrey_I/Shutterstock; 210 Konradlew/iStockbyte/Getty Images; 212 Olivier Le Queinec/Shutterstock; 221, 229 C.M.Pennington-Richards/Everett Collection; 232 Hulton Archive/Moviepix/Getty Images; 239, 251, 257 C.M.Pennington-Richards/Everett Collection; 262 John Springer Collection/Corbis Historical/Getty Images; 270 Hulton Archive/Moviepix/Getty Images; 273 John Springer Collection/Corbis Historical/Getty Images; 285 Entertainment Pictures/Alamy Stock Photo; 287 A Christmas Carol by Charles Dickens (gouache on paper), Nicolle, Pat (Patrick) (1907-95)/Private Collection/©Look and Learn/The Bridgeman Art Library; 312 Fred Stein Archive/Archive Photos/Getty Images; 313 Akg-Images/Newscom; 325 Ktsdesign/Shutterstock; 326 Ronak Patel, R. Nathan Spreng, Gary R. Turner, Functional Brain Changes Following Cognitive and Motor Skills Training A Quantitative Meta-analysis, copyright © 2013 by SAGE Publications Reprinted by Permission of SAGE Publications; 327 Sciepro/Shutterstock; 330 Blueringmedia/Shutterstock; 339 (T) Handout/KRT/Newscom; (C) Sofia Moro/Cover/Getty Images; (B) Rosamond S. King; 340 Incamerastock/Alamy Stock Photo; 341 Matthias Clamer/Getty Images; 342 Andrey_Popov/Shutterstock; 350 Stefanie Keenan/Getty Images; 351-352 (All) ©Mimi Choi Makeup Artistry Inc.; 361 (TL) Chad McDermott/Fotolia; (TC) Lmpc/Getty Images; (TR) Vladimir Salman/123RF; (B) Rizky Panuntun/Moment/Getty Images.

Unit 4

368 Francois Roux/Shutterstock; 372 Jay Ondreicka/Shutterstock; 380 Kathryn Hulick Gargolinski; 381 Dies-Irae/Shutterstock; 383 Kosolovskyy/Shutterstock; 384 Botany vision/Alamy Stock Photo; 396 Globe Photos/Zuma Press, Inc./Alamy Stock Photo; 397 Christopher Meder/Shutterstock; 409 (T) Greg Nesbig Photography; (CT) Photo by Eric Jenks; (CB) Ulf Andersen/Hulton Archive/Getty Images; (B) Alfonso Ortiz Center for Intercultural Studies; 410 Budimir Jevtic/Shutterstock; 412 Outdoorsman/Shutterstock; 440 David Livingston/Getty Images; 441 Mopic/Shutterstock; 443 Ledyx/Shutterstock; 457 Anton Grassl; 458 (L) Sue Stokes/Shutterstock; (R) Ifong/Shutterstock; 459 (L) F11photo/Shutterstock; (R) Miles Away Photography/Shutterstock; 460 WDG Photo/Shutterstock; 461 (L) Enrico Della Pietra/Shutterstock; (R) Thomas Cockrem/Alamy Stock Photo; 470 Kyodo News Stills/Getty Images; 471 Loree Johnson/Shutterstock; 483 (TL) Happetr/Shutterstock; (TC) © Tampa Bay Times via ZUMA Press Wire; (TR) Martina_L/Shutterstock; (B) Idreamphoto/Shutterstock.

Unit 5

490 Liudmila Habrus/Alamy Stock Photo; 494 Bebeto Matthews/Associated Press; 502 (B) Erin Blakemore/Juli Dimos; 503 Photo Researchers/Science History Images/Alamy Stock Photo; 511 Picturelux/The Hollywood Archive/Alamy Stock Photo; 513 Photo Researchers/Science History Images/Alamy Stock Photo; 525 Thomsond/Shutterstock; 527 Fotografixx/E+/Getty Images; 552 Francisco Jimenez; 553 Library of Congress; 558 Michael Rougier/The LIFE Picture Collection/Getty Images; 564 (B) Octavio Blanco; 565 Jim Grossmann/NASA; 566 NASA; 568 JSC/NASA; 578 Andy Kropa/Invision/Associated Press; 579 Lynn Johnson/Sports Illustrated Classic/Getty Images; 593 (T) David Cooper/Toronto Star/Getty Images; (B) David Livingston/Getty Images; 594 (T) Jamesbrey/E+/Getty Images; (B) Barbara Fischer, Australia/Moment/Getty Images; 595 Triff/Shutterstock; 605 (TL) Johan Swanepoel/Shutterstock; (TC) European Pressphoto Agency b.v./Alamy Stock Photo; (TR) AKG-Images; (B) Oleg Senkov/Shutterstock.